CRITICAL SURVEY
OF
SHORT FICTION

CRITICAL SURVEY

OF

SHORT FICTION

Second Revised Edition

Volume 6
Isaac Bashevis Singer - Mikhail Zoshchenko

Editor, Second Revised Edition
Charles E. May
California State University, Long Beach

Editor, First Edition
Frank N. Magill

SALEM PRESS, INC.
Pasadena, California   Hackensack, New Jersey

Managing Editor: Christina J. Moose
Research Supervisor: Jeffry Jensen
Acquisitions Editor: Mark Rehn
Photograph Editor: Philip Bader
Manuscript Editors: Lauren M. Mitchell
Melanie Watkins
Research Assistant: Jeff Stephens
Production Editor: Cynthia Beres
Layout: Ross Castellano

Library of Congress Cataloging-in-Publication Data

Critical survey of short fiction / editor, Charles E. May.—2nd rev. ed.

    7 v. ; cm.

First edition edited by Frank Northen Magill.

Includes bibliographical references and index.

    ISBN 0-89356-006-5 (set : alk. paper) — ISBN 0-89356-007-3 (v. 1 : alk. paper) — ISBN 0-89356-008-1 (v. 2 : alk. paper) — ISBN 0-89356-009-X (v. 3 : alk. paper) — ISBN 0-89356-010-3 (v. 4 : alk. paper) — ISBN 0-89356-011-1 (v. 5 : alk. paper) — ISBN 0-89356-012-X (v. 6 : alk. paper) — ISBN 0-89356-013-8 (v. 7 : alk. paper)

    1. Short story. 2. Short story—History and criticism. 3. Short story—Bio-bibliography. I. May, Charles E. (Charles Edward) 1941 -   . II. Magill, Frank Northen, 1907-1997.

PN3321 .C7 2001
809.3′1—dc21

00-046384

Fourth Printing

CONTENTS

COMPLETE LIST OF AUTHORS

Volume I

Volume II

Volume III

Volume IV

Volume V

Volume VI

CRITICAL SURVEY

OF

SHORT FICTION

SINGER, ISAAC BASHEVIS

Born: Leoncin, Poland; July 14 or November 21, 1904
Died: Surfside, Florida; July 24, 1991

PRINCIPAL SHORT FICTION

Gimpel the Fool and Other Stories, 1957
The Spinoza of Market Street, 1961
Short Friday and Other Stories, 1964
The Séance and Other Stories, 1968
A Friend of Kafka and Other Stories, 1970
A Crown of Feathers and Other Stories, 1973
Passions and Other Stories, 1975
Old Love, 1979
The Collected Stories, 1982
The Image and Other Stories, 1985
The Death of Methuselah and Other Stories, 1988

OTHER LITERARY FORMS

Among Isaac Bashevis Singer's prodigious output are several translations; numerous novels, including *Der Sotn in Gorey* (1935; *Satan in Goray*, 1955), *Der Knekht* (1961; *The Slave*, 1962), and *Sonim, de Geshichte fun a Liebe* (1966; *Enemies: A Love Story*, 1972); several volumes of memoirs and autobiographical stories; more than a dozen collections of children's stories; and a variety of adaptations of his stories or novels for other media, including opera, stage, and film.

ACHIEVEMENTS

Isaac Bashevis Singer, more than any other writer in the twentieth century, kept alive the rich traditions of a vanishing language and culture. Born into Eastern European Orthodox Judaism, Singer witnessed both the gradual assimilation of his generation into gentile culture and the tragic Nazi Holocaust that decimated Eastern Europe's Jewish populations.

Yiddish, a language written in Hebrew characters and derived from German, with borrowings from Polish, Lithuanian, and other languages, was spoken by millions of Jews. Inextricably connected to it are centuries of traditional beliefs and customs, as well as fascinating folklore, demonology, and mysticism that evolved from religious teaching. Writing exclusively in Yiddish (though translating much of his work into English himself) and mining both the language and the culture, Singer nourished a population stricken with tragedy and dispersed by exile.

His greatest achievement, however, lay in expressing the universality of that very particular milieu. Never did Singer cater to audiences unfamiliar with Yiddish culture, yet, by finding the truly human aspects of the people and conflicts in his stories, he earned impressive popularity among a wide and varied audience. It is no doubt the profound universality of his vision that earned for Singer election to the National Institute of Arts and Letters in 1964, as the only member writing in a language other than English, and the Nobel Prize in Literature in 1978.

BIOGRAPHY

Isaac Bashevis Singer was born in Leoncin, Poland, on either July 14 or November 21, 1904. His grandfathers had been rabbis, and his father was a Hasidic scholar, whom Singer's mother chose over other suitors for his scholarly excellence. The Singers moved to Warsaw in 1908, and the young Bashevis (a name adapted from his mother's name Bathsheba) grew up with his sister and two brothers in a ghetto tenement at 10 Krochmalna Street, which was his father's rabbinical court.

Rabbi Pinchos-Mendel Singer was a warm, mystical, and deeply spiritual man who was loved and revered by the entire community. Bathsheba Singer was a cool, sharp, practical, and rational woman who in many ways held the family together. The young Singer grew up among parental balances and contrasts that inform much of his writing. Singer read widely, including Fyodor Dostoevski's *Prestupleniye i nakazaniye* (1866; *Crime and Punishment*, 1886) in Yiddish at age nine, and studied languages. In addition, his older brother Israel Joshua, eleven years his senior, was an intelligent and rebellious spirit who very early began to influence Singer's intellectual development.

In 1917, Singer accompanied his mother to her native Bilgoray, where they lived for four years. There, he taught Hebrew—considered an affront to tradition, as the language of the Scriptures was not to be used for mundane purposes. In 1921, Singer's father took a rabbinical post in a small town in Galicia; Singer, then seventeen, refused to follow, and instead stayed in Warsaw to study at the Tachkemoni Rabbinical Seminary. He later characterized his stay in Warsaw as the worst year of his life: Undernourished and ill fit to follow in his forefathers' footsteps, Singer left the seminary after a year to rejoin his family, only to return to Warsaw in 1923. He would never see his parents and younger brother Moishe again.

His father wrote religious tracts, and Israel Joshua wrote secular pieces: It was inevitable that Singer too would write. During his year at the seminary, he had translated Knut Hamsun's novel *Sult* (1890; *Hunger*, 1899). In 1923 he became a proofreader for six dollars a week at the *Literarische Bletter*, a Yiddish literary magazine. He translated popular novels into Yiddish for newspaper serialization and experimented with writing in both Hebrew and Yiddish. In the late 1920's, the *Literarische Bletter* and *Warshaver Shriften* began accepting his Yiddish stories, such as "Women," "Grandchildren," and "The Village Gravedigger" for publication; meanwhile, his brother Israel Joshua's first novel, *Blood Harvest*, appeared in 1927.

Singer became involved with a young Communist woman, Runia; they lived in common-law marriage, and in 1929 they had a son, Israel. They became estranged, however, and Runia and the child left for Russia, then Turkey and Palestine. Singer would not meet his son again for decades.

During the 1930's, the Singer brothers' lives and careers became interwoven. In 1932, Isaac Bashevis became the editor of *Globus*, another literary magazine, and Israel Joshua published *Yoshe Kalb*, the popularity of which led to serial publication in the *Jewish Daily Forward* in New York. Isaac Bashevis's first novel, *Satan in Goray*, was serialized in *Globus* in 1933; in 1934, the older brother left for New York

Isaac Bashevis Singer, Nobel Laureate for Literature in 1978 (©The Nobel Foundation)

to escape the rise of European Nazism and to find success in the thriving Yiddish American community; and in 1935 the younger brother followed.

Singer moved into the Williamsburgh section of Brooklyn. The poverty and hunger that he met there were not new to him, but exile brought on an unprecedented spiritual collapse. He felt isolated from his family in Poland, his wife and child in Palestine, and his beloved culture devastated by war and genocide across Europe. He could not write, virtually forgot Yiddish, despaired for the future of Yiddish literature, and even at times became suicidal.

In 1937, Singer met Alma, a married German Jew with a son and daughter, who captured his mind and heart. She was divorced from her husband in 1939, and the following year they married. He was freelancing for the *Forward*, which continually encouraged him to resume his writing, in Yiddish. In 1943, he became an American citizen, and in 1944, with World War II raging, Singer was struck by a personal tragedy: His brother Israel Joshua, to whom he was devoted personally and artistically, died suddenly at the age of fifty-one.

The following year, the war ended and Singer began work on a novel, *Di Familye Muskat* (1950; *The Family Moskat*, 1950), which was serialized in the *Forward* over the next three years, broadcast on a Jewish radio station, chosen by publisher Alfred A. Knopf for translation into English, and awarded the Louis Lamed Prize in 1950. He began to write steadily, and in the early 1950's, nearing the age of fifty himself, Singer came to the attention of the American literary community. Editor Cecil Hemley and his wife Elaine Gottlieb helped Singer in several ways: They translated his stories, got them placed in major periodicals such as *Commentary* and *Partisan Review*, and published his novels through their Noonday Press, which in 1960 became part of Farrar, Straus & Giroux.

In the 1960's and 1970's, Singer produced a steady stream of stories and novels. His stories were published in numerous magazines as well as collections; some collections included reissues of much older pieces; translations appeared under his own hand or those of his nephew Joseph, Hemley, Gottlieb, writer Saul Bellow, or others. In the late 1960's, well past his sixtieth birthday, Singer took the suggestion of a friend and began writing stories for children as well. He also taught widely, serving as writer-in-residence at such institutions as Oberlin College and the University of Wisconsin.

Ironically, though well known in Yiddish and literary circles, Singer did not enjoy mass popularity and recognition until the 1983 release of the film *Yentl*, featuring Barbra Streisand, based on Singer's 1952 story "Yentl der Yeshive Bucher" ("Yentl the Yeshiva Boy"). A similar success was enjoyed by the 1989 film *Enemies: A Love Story*, based on Singer's 1972 novel.

For much of his later life, Singer lived with his wife Alma on West Eighty-sixth Street in New York; he later divided his time between New York and Miami Beach, where he ultimately retired. He died of a stroke on July 24, 1991, ten days after his eighty-seventh birthday.

ANALYSIS

Isaac Bashevis Singer relished the short story; he believed that it offered, much more than the novel, the possibility of perfection. His stories, however, seldom reveal signs of a painstaking artisan conscious of form; rather, they flow naturally, even mindlessly, without any sense of manipulation. Indeed, Singer's art grows out of a thriving tradition of oral storytelling that had been fermenting through Eastern Europe for centuries.

Like many authors, Singer writes about the places and lives he knows. He sets most of his stories in pre-World War II Poland, in the small villages (Shtetlach) or the urban ghettoes of his childhood and youth. In his stories, these places are the Polish cities of Warsaw and Kraków, or semifictional towns such as Goray and Frampol; they appear over and over again with recurring motifs and character types, until most of Singer's tales seem to happen in the same prototypical settings.

Given the specificity of Singer's cultural milieu, the individual's relationship to his or her community becomes important, whether that relationship focuses on the collective attitude toward unusual characters and behavior or the individual's dislocation from family, community, and nation. Singer spent most of his life with such dislocation; it is not surprising that many of his characters are in some sort of exile. That exile can involve a new country, a new language, a new culture, or a new identity. Later in his career, Singer set stories among the expatriate Yiddish communities of New York or Israel and dealt explicitly with issues faced by an aging writer in exile.

As de facto chronicler of twentieth century Jewish experience, Singer chooses to leave untouched its central event: the Holocaust and the slaughter of six million European Jews under Adolf Hitler's Third Reich. Believing that a simple storyteller could never tell such an incomprehensible and horrific story, he rather evokes it through the richness with which he portrays the culture that it eradicated and the scattered pathos that it left in its wake. Like the Jewish people as a whole, Singer's characters struggle with identity in a changing world, they confront incomprehensible horrors and either surrender or survive. The individual in his community and his world is ultimately the individual in his universe, often alone with the supernatural powers that govern it.

Singer borrows from and embellishes on the wide array of Jewish mysticism and demonology to personify such powers and their involvement in the human condition. Sometimes the result is explicitly mythological; sometimes it explores the depths of possibility in very real circumstances. Whatever the form, Singer never hesitates to explore life and death, sin and redemption, good and evil, and heaven and hell in broad, literal terms. For him, imagination is paramount, and there are never any limits to what is possible. Much of the charm in his stories comes from the striking juxtaposition of the astoundingly cosmic with the laughably trivial, the apocalyptic with the quotidian, the macabre with the sentimental.

Nowhere is this approach more successful than in Singer's treatment of human sexuality. He never takes for granted the difficulties that sex engenders or the social rules and taboos that it confronts; at the same time, however, he consistently attributes to it its role as a driving force, and a truly beautiful one, in human affairs. His characters—be they rabbis, devils, simpletons, maidens, or whores—are all of flesh and blood, and they act accordingly. Singer portrays violence, rape, and hatred as unflinchingly as he portrays the deepest romantic love or most spiritual piety, never with judgment or disapproval, always striving to plumb the depths of the human heart.

"Two Corpses Go Dancing"

One of Singer's early stories shows the playfulness with which he treats death, demons, and infidelity. "Two Corpses Go Dancing," first published in *The Jewish Daily Forward* in 1943, is told from the point of view of the so-called Evil One, a device Singer also employs in such stories as "The Destruction of Kreshev" and "The Unseen." In "Two Corpses Go Dancing," the Evil One amuses himself by reinvigorating the corpse of a forgotten pauper named Itche-Godl, who "had been a corpse even when alive." Itche-Godl returns to his home, only to find his widow remarried to a more substantial man. His two appearances at her door inspire terror, but, be-

lieving himself to be alive, Itche-Godl cannot understand her behavior.

He soon encounters Finkle Rappaport, a widow who had gone to Vienna with a serious illness a year before and had long been believed dead but had recently reappeared in Warsaw. Finkle and Itche-Godl soon become betrothed; the couple's mysterious romance and macabre appearance astonish those around them. After the wedding, they retire to their wedding chamber only to find themselves transformed into corpses again and to realize that their return to life was only an illusion.

In "Two Corpses Go Dancing," Singer avoids all pretense of realism and rather depicts a surreal universe where no assumptions are valid. The physical and spiritual worlds are interwoven: Corpses are visible to the outside world but lack self-knowledge; they possess desire but are ultimately incapable of consummating it; they have superhuman powers but are essentially powerless.

"Taibele and Her Demon"

A story that similarly plays on the border between the real and spiritual realms but does not in the end sacrifice literal plausibility is "Taibele and Her Demon." Taibele is an abandoned wife in the shtetl of Frampol. Forbidden to remarry until her husband is proven dead, she is sentenced to a life of solitude. The village prankster Alchonon one day overhears Taibele's fascination with a story of a woman seduced by a demon, and he devises a scheme to take advantage of her credulity. One night he appears naked in her bedroom claiming to be the demon Hurmizah. He testifies that her husband is dead, charms her with tales of the demon world, and is welcomed into her bed. Though at first fearful and ashamed, Taibele gradually becomes dependent on Hurmizah's biweekly visits.

Winter comes, however, and with it the inescapable truth of Alchonon's humanity. His naked body cannot tolerate the cold during his nocturnal visits; he is taken ill and stops coming to see Taibele. She despairs at Hurmizah's absence and takes it as a pronouncement on her. Then one day, she sees a modest funeral procession on the snowy village street. When she realizes that it is the idler Alchonon, whom she often mocked at the well, she feels a deep sympathy and accompanies him to the grave. She lives the rest of her life alone and carries her secret to the grave.

The power of this story lies in the irony of Taibele's passion for the demon Hurmizah. Here, the surreal world exists only in the minds of the characters: So long as people believe in demons, their existence is real enough. Singer is suggesting the unseen and unknown connections that can be forged between individuals when the imagination is free. At the same time, the love that results is not without its price. For Alchonon, that price is untimely death; for Taibele, it is the burden of sin, mystery, and desertion.

"GIMPEL THE FOOL"

One of Singer's most celebrated stories, "Gimpel the Fool," also locates the individual's happiness in his or her power to believe. This, however, is a light-hearted tale where the willingness to let go of belief, to distrust one's senses and logic, defines the shape of the story. Gimpel the baker is known throughout Frampol for his gullibility. He recounts the nicknames that people have given him and the tricks that they have played on him but does not regret his simpleness, for he feels that he must always be open to all possibilities.

As such, he allows himself to be prodded into marrying an unprincipled woman named Elka. He accepts her bastard son as her little brother and believes her explanation of a premature birth when she bears another son seventeen weeks after their wedding night. She is repeatedly unfaithful to him; he accuses and even catches her but always eventually accepts her explanations and returns to his natural state of contentment. They live in this way for twenty years. Finally, on her deathbed, Elka confesses that she has lived sinfully and deceived him constantly. Soon after her death, Gimpel is tempted by the Evil Angel to have revenge on the scornful townsfolk by baking urine into their bread, but a vision of Elka returns and stops him. With his innocence restored, he leaves Frampol and travels the world, witnessing falsehood and truth in people. At the story's end, he is old, wise, accepting, prepared for death, free of regret, and full of love.

Throughout the story, Gimpel knows that the true factuality of events is less important than their effect on people's minds and hearts. He knows that he is incapable of skepticism but that his innocence and belief are his strength. Though Singer makes it clear that Gimpel is indeed a gullible fool, the simple joy with which he approaches life ultimately reveals itself to be a subversive wisdom. "Whatever doesn't really happen is dreamed at night," he says. "It happens to one if it doesn't happen to another, tomorrow if not today, or a century hence if not next year. What difference can it make?" Gimpel's doctrine is essentially Singer's affirmation of the power and validity of creating and telling stories.

"THE SPINOZA OF MARKET STREET"

"The Spinoza of Market Street" is another of Singer's most popular and most often reprinted tales. It is the story of Dr. Nahum Fischelson, a librarian, teacher, and revered philosopher who has devoted his life to studying the ideas of the seventeenth century Dutch Jewish philosopher Baruch Spinoza. Spinoza's *Ethics* dictates a rigid rational philosophy that Fischelson strives to embody. He contemplates the heavens and the mysteries of astronomy and contrasts them with the world below, in which the mindless rabble represents the antithesis of reason.

Then, as World War I descends on Warsaw, Fischelson's bitterness and stomach problems worsen, and he takes to a sickbed, where he has a stunning apocalyptic dream that he immediately dismisses as irrational. He seems to be on the verge of death, but a grotesque old spinster neighbor named Black Dobbe comes to take care of him. She nurses him back to health with simple attention and conversation, and soon Fischelson's study of Spinoza begins to seem less relevant. Before long, Black Dobbe announces to the rabbi that she and Fischelson will wed, and the story ends with their wedding night. When Black Dobbe comes to the so-called Spinoza of Market Street, he drops the *Ethics* to which he has devoted his life, and in his new wife's arms miraculously regains his health, his youth, and his passion for living.

"ZEITL AND RICKEL"

In "Zeitl and Rickel," Singer again focuses on an unpredictable relationship and the depth of human love and obsession, this time setting it more firmly in a context of social attitudes. The narrator says that the incredible tale she is about to relate demonstrates that anything is possible. She tells of two women, Zeitl and Rickel, one the daughter of a follower of the false Messiah, and the other an abandoned wife and the daughter of the town's ritual slaughterer. Rickel comes to attend on Zeitl's dying father, and the two women become absorbed in each other. Their relationship becomes steady and secretive, as seen from outside by the women of the community. They are overheard one day in a seeming catechism regarding hell and their shared future and eventually commit suicide in succession by throwing themselves into the well.

On one level, this is a story about an obsessive love shared by two women (with the suggestion, though never explicit, of lesbianism) and the mystical and eventually self-destructive form it assumes. On another level, it is about community perception: As told by one of Rickel's former students, the tale is an accumulation of gossip ennobled into spiritual mystery. Implicit in the story is a view of the place of women as daughters and wives in shtetl society, and the unorthodoxy of two women forging a spiritual connection and devoting their lives to each other. While Singer has never been accused of feminism, he is sometimes keenly aware, and even in awe, of the shape and power of the female psyche.

"GRANDFATHER AND GRANDSON"

"Grandfather and Grandson" powerfully reflects the tension between the old insularity of Yiddish culture and the new worldliness that comes with greater exposure and assimilation. Reb Mordecai Meir is a widowed Hasid who devotes his life to his study of Judaism. He abhors everything worldly, including newspapers, theater, atheism, religious reform, and even the integration of the sexes. Having disowned his liberal-minded daughter, he is surprised when his long-forgotten grandson Fulie shows up on his Warsaw doorstep. Fulie, dressed like a Gentile, is a Communist sought by the authorities for political subversion. Though his presence and beliefs threaten Reb Mordecai Meir, blood flows deep and the grandfather welcomes the fugitive into his home. Their shared life is precarious: Each wants to convert the other,

each has guarded distrust, and ultimately they find a silent and respectful balance.

When Fulie announces that he must leave, possibly never to return, and asks his grandfather to keep an envelope to be passed on to a contact from the movement, Reb Mordecai Meir is put to a test of faith and conscience. He begrudgingly complies, and even when he later sees his grandson's revolver, accepts with silence the world's intrusion into his life. Finally, Fulie's dead body is returned to his bewildered grandfather, who utters prayers over the slain youth as best he can, finding reaffirmation of his faith and identity in their tragic blood connection.

"Grandfather and Grandson" reflects a larger awareness of the political events that shook European Jewry through the twentieth century. Though still set in prewar Poland, it is a story that reaches beyond to a universal experience of the painful changes that mark the passage of generations.

"THE MANUSCRIPT"

"The Manuscript" also reflects larger historical realities and creates a sense of political urgency. Set at the outbreak of World War II, it is a story, retold much later in a café in Tel Aviv, of a woman's sacrifice for the man she loves and her response to his betrayal.

Shibtah is an actress married to a writer and womanizer named Menasha. When war comes to Warsaw, they flee to Białystok, leaving behind all Menasha's writing except a promising novel called *Rungs*. When a Białystok publisher expresses interest in the piece, they discover that they have someone else's manuscript; *Rungs* was left in Warsaw. Seeing no other option, and against Menasha's wishes, Shibtah undertakes a perilous ten-day journey back to Warsaw to retrieve it. On her return to Białystok, however, she finds Menasha in bed with another woman. She impulsively tosses the manuscript in the stove and leaves Białystok alone the following day.

Shibtah was never obsessively jealous; it is the particular infidelity, set against her journey and the backdrop of war, that constitutes a deception she cannot tolerate. Singer is not telling a simple story of broken vows; rather, he portrays the response of the human heart to a unique and complex set of circumstances, where love, sex, art, politics, and history find dramatic junction in a particular moment of time. As in much of his later work, the world of all possibility becomes a world where the individual can depend on nobody and nothing but his or her own heart and will to act.

"SCHLOIMELE"

Many of Singer's stories are loosely biographical, drawn from specific people and events from his own experience. "Schloimele," written during the period that the adaptation was being done for the film *Yentl,* is about a virtually unknown Yiddish writer in New York and a fast-talking aspiring stage producer whose perennial promise of a lucrative deal for the narrator dissolves into a humorous and pathetic refrain. In a series of vignettes tracing the two men's encounters over the course of several years, the pretentious Schloimele becomes a symbol first for the artifice of "showbiz" and ultimately for the narrator's own idleness, professional failure, mediocre love life, and general discontent. At the story's end, the two men escape the city on a bus to bucolic Monticello, but their departure is more like a funeral than a vacation.

"Schloimele" no doubt draws on both the despair that Singer felt at times in his career and the type of ambitious businessman that he knew well. While free of the tortures of demons or melodrama of lost worlds, straightforward, unsensational narratives such as "Schloimele" evoke, in their understated realism, an amazingly strong and personal sense of tragedy and longing.

"THE SMUGGLER"

There are certainly links from Taibele to Rickel to Shibtah, from Dr. Fischelson to Reb Mordecai Meir, or from Alchonon to Gimpel to Schloimele, and while no story can be said to sum up Singer's vision, some come strikingly close to a clear articulation of deep existential belief. An example is "The Smuggler," published three years before the author's death. It is a simple tale, most certainly based in truth (if only loosely), about a stranger's visit to the narrator (an author himself, living in a small New York apartment), seeking autographs for a cartload of his books. The man is a gentle old bum who met the narrator years before at a speech in Philadelphia; he does not

want to intrude, only to get his books signed and leave.

During his short visit, however, he offers samples of the wisdom by which he has lived. Born to a family of Polish Jews, he learned to smuggle for a living, until he eventually realized that he survived by smuggling himself. He has come to recognize the intrinsic corruptibility of human beings, that power breeds wickedness, and that victims who overcome tyrants become tyrants themselves. He knows that evil and good are not mutually exclusive opposites, that there is nothing strange or inhuman about a Nazi leaving a concentration camp, where humans are systematically killed, and returning home to write heartfelt poetry. Finding security in this knowledge, the smuggler is at peace.

While the message is harsh, it is for Singer, as for the smuggler of the story, only a starting point. Beyond it is a world of possibilities—for goodness and evil, love and violence, sex and piety—in which the human heart and mind rule. In his clever and paradoxical way, Singer affirms, "We must believe in free will. We have no choice."

OTHER MAJOR WORKS

LONG FICTION: *Der Sotn in Gorey,* 1935 (*Satan in Goray,* 1955); *Di Familye Mushkat,* 1950 (*The Family Moskat,* 1950); *Der Hoyf,* 1953-1955 (*The Manor,* 1967, and *The Estate,* 1969); *Shotns baym Hodson,* 1957-1958 (*Shadows on the Hudson,* 1998); *Der Kuntsnmakher fun Lublin,* 1958-1959 (*The Magician of Lublin,* 1960); *Der Knekht,* 1961 (*The Slave,* 1962); *Sonim, de Geshichte fun a Liebe,* 1966 (*Enemies: A Love Story,* 1972); *Neshome Ekspeditsyes,* 1974 (*Shosha,* 1978); *Der Bal-Tshuve,* 1974 (*The Penitent,* 1983); *Reaches of Heaven: A Story of the Baal Shem Tov,* 1980; *Der Kenig vun di Felder,* 1988 (*The King of the Fields,* 1988); *Scum,* 1991; *The Certificate,* 1992; *Meshugah,* 1994.

PLAYS: *The Mirror,* pr. 1973; *Yentl, the Yeshiva Boy,* pr. 1974 (with Leah Napolin); *Shlemiel the First,* pr. 1974; *Teibele and Her Demon,* pr. 1978.

NONFICTION: *Mayn Tatn's Bes-din Shtub,* 1956 (*In My Father's Court,* 1966); *The Hasidim,* 1973 (with Ira Moskowitz); *A Little Boy in Search of God:*

Mysticism in a Personal Light, 1976; *A Young Man in Search of Love*, 1978; *Isaac Bashevis Singer on Literature and Life*, 1979 (with Paul Rosenblatt and Gene Koppel); *Lost in America*, 1980; *Love and Exile*, 1984; *Conversations with Isaac Bashevis Singer*, 1985 (with Richard Burgin).

CHILDREN'S LITERATURE: *Zlateh the Goat and Other Stories*, 1966; *The Fearsome Inn*, 1967; *Mazel and Shlimazel: Or, The Milk of a Lioness*, 1967; *When Shlemiel Went to Warsaw and Other Stories*, 1968; *A Day of Pleasure: Stories of a Boy Growing Up in Warsaw*, 1969; *Elijah the Slave*, 1970; *Joseph and Koza: Or, The Sacrifice to the Vistula*, 1970; *Alone in the Wild Forest*, 1971; *The Topsy-Turvy Emperor of China*, 1971; *The Wicked City*, 1972; *The Fools of Chelm and Their History*, 1973; *Why Noah Chose the Dove*, 1974; *A Tale of Three Wishes*, 1975; *Naftali the Storyteller and His Horse, Sus, and Other Stories*, 1976; *The Power of Light: Eight Stories*, 1980; *The Golem*, 1982; *Stories for Children*, 1984.

TRANSLATIONS: *Romain Rolland*, 1927 (by Stefan Zweig); *Die Vogler*, 1928 (by Knut Hamsun); *Victoria*, 1929 (by Knut Hamsun); *All Quiet on the Western Front*, 1930 (by Erich Remarque); *Pan*, 1931 (by Knut Hamsun); *The Way Back*, 1931 (by Erich Remarque); *The Magic Mountain*, 1932 (by Thomas Mann); *From Moscow to Jerusalem*, 1938 (with Leon Glaser).

BIBLIOGRAPHY

Alexander, Edward. *Isaac Bashevis Singer: A Study of the Short Fiction*. Boston: Twayne, 1990. An introduction to Singer's stories in terms of their themes, types, and motifs, for example: moral tales, holocaust stories, supernatural tales, tales of apocalypse and politics, stories of faith and doubt. Focuses on Singer's universal appeal rather than his Jewish appeal. Includes a section of quotations from Singer about his work, as well as essays on Singer by Irving Howe and two other critics.

Allentuck, Marcia, ed. *The Achievement of Isaac Bashevis Singer*. Carbondale: Southern Illinois University Press, 1969. A collection of eleven essays devoted to various aspects of Singer's work. While most articles focus on themes in individual novels, the collection does include pieces on Singer's memoirs and children's stories, and examinations of "The Spinoza of Market Street" and "Gimpel the Fool." Though inevitably uneven, the volume is generally straightforward and easy to read.

Buchen, Irving H. *Isaac Bashevis Singer and the Eternal Past*. New York: New York University Press, 1968. Buchen provides an interesting though not painstakingly detailed look at Singer's early career. While his efforts to relate the author to other contemporary writers and the overall tradition of English and American literature are excessive, he explores and understands the balances of Singer's writing. Includes a chapter on selected early stories and a good bibliography.

Farrell, Grace, ed. *Critical Essays on Isaac Bashevis Singer*. New York: G. K. Hall, 1996. An extensive introduction on Singer's critical reception and the issues that have preoccupied him and his critics. Collects both contemporary reviews and a wide range of essays, including Leslie Fiedler's "I. B. Singer: Or, The American-ness of the American Jewish Writer."

_____, ed. *Isaac Bashevis Singer: Conversations*. Jackson: University Press of Mississippi, 1992. A collection of interviews with Singer that reveal the connections among his philosophy of life, his perspective on literature, and his mode of living.

Guzlowski, John. "Isaac Bashevis Singer's Satan in Goray and Bakhtin's Vision of the Carnivalesque." *Critique* 39 (Winter, 1998): 167-175. Argues that Bakhtin's notion of the grotesque illuminates Singer's and that Wolfgang Kayser's theories of the grotesque oversimplify his message; concludes, however, that Singer departs from Bakhtin is in his less hopeful belief about society's ability to build a new order out of carnival.

Hadda, Janet. "Isaac Bashevis Singer in New York." *Judaism* 46 (Summer, 1997): 346-363. Discusses the transformation of Singer from Bashevis, the sharp-witted, conflicted, occasionally harsh, literary genius, to Isaac Bashevis Singer—and even Isaac Singer—the quaint, pigeon-feeding vegetarian, the serene and gentle embodiment of the timeless values of Eastern European Jews.

_____. *Isaac Bashevis Singer: A Life.* New York: Oxford University Press, 1997. Focusing on both the forces of family and that social environment that influenced Singer, Hadda uncovers the public persona to reveal a more complex man than heretofore understood.

Kresh, Paul. *Isaac Bashevis Singer: The Magician of West Eighty-sixth Street.* New York: Dial Press, 1979. A lively account of Singer's first seventy-five years, told in an often seemingly day-by-day account that creates a delightful sense of intimacy for the reader. Kresh incorporates refreshing quotes and anecdotes and includes thirty-two photographs. His careful attention to facts clarifies the often ambiguous details of Singer's works in terms of creation, translation, publication, and reissue. More than four hundred pages, with a good index and a bibliography.

Mulbauer, Asher Z. *Transcending Exile.* Miami: Florida International University Press, 1985. A thoughtful contemplation of exile in the works of three writers: Joseph Conrad, Vladimir Nabokov,

and Singer. The fifty-page chapter on Singer focuses on three novels–*Shosha, The Slave*, and *Enemies: A Love Story*—but is mindful of thematic parallels to the short stories.

Sinclair, Clive. *The Brothers Singer.* London: Allison & Busby, 1983. A fascinating examination of Singer and his work in the context of one of the most important personal and literary relationships of the author's life. Sinclair effectively interweaves biography and literary analysis, conveying a deep understanding of the lives and works of Isaac and Joshua Singer.

Spilka, Mark. "Empathy with the Devil: Isaac Bashevis Singer and the Deadly Pleasures of Misogyny." *Novel* 31 (Summer, 1998): 430-444. Discusses Singer's preoccupation with demonology and sexuality, focusing on his struggles with misogyny; claims the admonitory sequences of Singer's fiction exemplify the risks and hazards of his own personal and fictional struggle to make sense of the pre- and post-Holocaust world he inherited from his parents.

Barry Mann

ANDREI SINYAVSKY

Born: Moscow, U.S.S.R.; October 8, 1925
Died: Fontenay-aux-Roses, France; February 25, 1997

PRINCIPAL SHORT FICTION

Fantasticheskie povesti, 1961 (*Fantastic Stories*, 1963; also as *The Icicle, and Other Stories*, 1963)

Kroshka Tsores, 1980 (novella; *Little Jinx*, 1992)

OTHER LITERARY FORMS

Before his arrest in 1965 for smuggling "anti-Soviet propaganda," Andrei Sinyavsky was a senior research associate at the Gorky Institute of World Lit-

erature in Moscow and had become a well-known literary critic, focusing primarily on modern Russian literature. After emigrating to Paris in 1973, he published more criticism as well as book-length literary essays. The works that led to his arrest, however, were, except for the literary essay *Chto takoe sotsialisticheskii realizm* (1959; *On Socialist Realism*, 1960), fiction: two novels and some half-dozen stories. All appeared in the West under the pseudonym Abram Tertz. He also wrote a book of aphorisms, *Mysli vrasplokh* (1966; *Unguarded Thoughts*, 1972), and the nonfiction works *Soviet Civilization: A Cultural History* (1990) and *The Russian Intelligentsia* (1997).

ACHIEVEMENTS

Andrei Sinyavsky's literary efforts served as a daring challenge to the tenets of Socialist Realism, the doctrine that was supposed to guide Soviet authors in their choice of subject matter as well as in their treatment of it. His essay *On Socialist Realism*, written in 1956, at the height of the post-Stalinist thaw, contained an attack on the very conjunction of the words "socialist" and "realism," as well as a historical analysis of the manner in which the doctrine had harmed Soviet literature. His own underground fiction was both antisocialist, in his effort to include a religious dimension antithetical to Marxism, and antirealistic with a strong inclination toward the fantastic and the grotesque. The consequences of writing in isolation as well as of determinedly breaking with the dominant tradition sometimes show—he occasionally seems to be trying too hard for effect or to make a point—but Sinyavsky nevertheless stands as a writer who helped undermine the influence of Socialist Realism.

Along with his fellow writer Yuli Daniel he also helped popularize the very notions of *samizdat* (self-publishing) and *tamizdat* (publishing "there," or abroad). Despite the government's persecution of these two authors, many others throughout the 1960's and 1970's came to write outside the permissible norms—sometimes circulating their work privately, sometimes attempting to publish outside the Soviet Union, and sometimes simply writing "for the drawer." His example did much to help a clandestine Soviet literature flourish during a trying period. In 1978, Sinyavsky received the Bennett Award from the Grolier Club.

BIOGRAPHY

By the time he was in his early forties, Andrei Donatovich Sinyavsky had achieved a large measure of success within Soviet society. Born and reared in Moscow, he attended Moscow University, from which he received the Soviet equivalent of a doctorate in 1952. His thesis was on Maxim Gorky, often considered the "father" of Socialist Realism. He then received a position at the Gorky Institute of World Literature, a branch of the Soviet Academy of Sciences; during the next dozen years, he published several

Andrei Sinyavsky, center, during his trial in Moscow in 1966. He and another writer, Yuli Daniel at far left, were accused of writing anti-Soviet propaganda. (AP/Wide World Photos)

studies on Gorky and also wrote about twentieth century poetry. At the end of the 1950's, he began to publish reviews in the prestigious literary journal *Novy mir*, aligning himself with those struggling for greater artistic freedom through his attacks on some of the more conservative writers. Still, his name was not widely known until he published the introductory essay to a major 1965 collection of Boris Pasternak's poetry (translated in *For Freedom of Imagination*, 1971).

Later that same year, much to the surprise of nearly everyone, he and a close friend, Yuli Daniel, were arrested; employing the pseudonyms Abram Tertz (the rogue hero of a thieves' song once popular in Odessa) and Nikolai Arzhak, respectively, each had smuggled out stories to the West that were seen by the authorities as examples of "anti-Soviet propaganda." Their trial, in February of 1966, was significant in that it was the first time that Soviet writers were actually convicted of a crime on the basis of their literary works. It also marked the end of the fitful liberalizing tendencies that had characterized the years since the death of Joseph Stalin in 1953 and the imposition of a harsher regime that was to force many writers into exile.

As it turned out, Sinyavsky's life prior to his arrest was more complex than it might have appeared on the surface. Although he grew up as a believer in the ideals of the revolution that brought the Communists to power in the Soviet Union, his faith was shaken by the arrest of his father in 1951 for political activities that predated the Revolution of 1917 and by efforts of the secret police, beginning in 1948, to involve him in a plot that would somehow compromise a friend, Hélène Peltier-Zamoyska, daughter of the French naval attaché in Moscow. He managed to resist, but the machinations continued for several years; later, she served as the courier for bringing the manuscripts of "Abram Tertz" out of the Soviet Union. In 1955, Sinyavsky wrote the first of his underground works, the story "V tsirke" ("At the Circus"). Then in 1956, the year that is generally regarded as marking the height of the post-Stalinist "thaw," he composed both his essay *On Socialist Realism* and his first novel, *Sud idyot* (1960; *The Trial Begins*, 1960), which can be seen as a literary illustration of the writing that Sinyavsky advocates in the essay. Over the next several years, he continued to compose the works that made Abram Tertz a well-known figure in the West and a wanted man in the Soviet Union.

Sinyavsky eventually served five and one-half years of a seven-year term (and Daniel four of the five years to which he had been sentenced). While in prison, Sinyavsky continued to write, sending out his works in letters to his wife: *Golos iz khora* (1973; *A Voice from the Chorus*, 1976), *Progulki s Pushkinym* (1975; *Strolls with Pushkin*, 1993), and *V teni Gogolya* (1975; In Gogol's shadow). He was allowed to emigrate in 1973 and became a professor of Russian literature at the Sorbonne. Remaining active in the literary world, Sinyavsky began his own journal (*Sintaksis*) and wrote the autobiographical novel *Spokoynoy nochi* (1984; *Goodnight!*, 1989). His works remained sufficiently controversial in the Soviet Union that he could be published there only well into the period of *glasnost*; in 1989, he was allowed to visit the country to pay respects upon the death of Yuli Daniel. His Russian citizenship was restored in 1990. He died of cancer in France in 1997.

ANALYSIS

Andrei Sinyavsky's short fiction resembles his longer work in both its themes and its manner. While for the most part less overt in their political message

than the novels, the stories contain heroes who are equally alienated—from society, from themselves, or from both—and who seem trapped in an existence from which they would like to escape. Elements of fantasy abound; in some cases the stories verge on science fiction, while in others the emphasis is more on extreme psychological states. The plots, to the extent that they can be discerned at all, are usually fairly straightforward. Interpretation, however, can be difficult; sometimes a given scene may be viewed as fantastic, as reflecting a character's mental aberration, or as purposefully ambiguous. The first-person narrators are often not helpful in this regard, and situations may appear to be allegorical or metaphorical representations of themes that are not mentioned directly within the works. In short, Sinyavsky is demanding of his readers.

"AT THE CIRCUS"

"At the Circus" stands out from the other stories: It predates them by several years and is also the most conventional in form. The narrator has a distinctive voice, but for once he is not a chief figure within the story itself. Still, the tale offers an early glimpse into some of Sinyavsky's concerns. The hero, Kostia, is a ne'er-do-well who dreams of achieving the skill of those he admires at the circus. During a botched burglary, he kills the very magician he has admired, is sentenced to twenty years of hard labor, and then is himself killed during an attempt to escape. Kostia is the first of Sinyavsky's many outsiders, those who feel in some way oppressed and want to escape into new lives; indeed, dreams of, or efforts at, getting away from ordinary life lie behind all the major events. Despite the third-person narration, Sinyavsky often limits the perspective to that of Kostia; the narrow focus and the frequent absence of conventional transitions pull the reader deep into the protagonist's psyche, so that his distorted outlook becomes the norm for the world of the story. The narrative, as well as the settings and the subject matter, thus emphasizes the sense of oppression and enclosure; nearly all Sinyavsky's stories seem, in this way, to be claustrophobic.

"TENANTS"

"Kvartiranty" ("Tenants"), composed in 1959, is

perhaps among his most obscure stories. The setting of "Tenants," a Russian communal apartment, is sufficiently realistic, but the narrator turns out to be a house sprite. His addressee—not interlocutor, since he does not say a word—is Sergei Sergeevich, a drunkard and writer who now lives within the apartment. The story is open to a variety of interpretations: It can be seen as a genuine fantasy or, less likely, as the drunken hallucinations of Sergei Sergeevich. The tales related by the house sprite are themselves fantastic, filled with references to literature or writers, and at first seem to be of little purpose. Eventually, though, certain themes emerge. The house sprite points to the prevalence of evil; not only do the names often contain hidden references to the devil or various spirits but also relatively mundane occurrences, such as a spat in the communal kitchen, lead to dire consequences. Many of the figures in the story have been driven out of one existence into another; even water nymphs and wood sprites have been forced from the country to the city. Ultimately, though, "Tenants" concerns the writer: the threats to his well-being, his position as an outsider, his (perhaps unfulfilled) obligation to deal with the evil around him.

"YOU AND I"

"Ty i ya" ("You and I") is arguably even more resistant to any single interpretation. Much of the work employs a second-person narrative, with the "You" of the title addressed directly. This individual is named Nikolai Vasilyevich (the first name and patronymic of Nikolai Gogol, who, along with Fyodor Dostoevski, clearly influenced this and other works by Sinyavsky) and apparently suffers from a persecution mania. After an opening scene at a party, he hides out in his apartment, refusing to have contact with others until he eventually slashes his throat. The true mystery of the story, though, is the identity of "I," who plays a direct role in the fate of "You." Some critics have seen "You and I" as describing a single individual who suffers from schizophrenia as well as paranoia; others believe that the relationship is more that between the author and his character or between a godlike figure and the individual (there is sufficient evidence to support all these views).

Despite the purposeful complexity of the narrative—which includes disjointed descriptions of wildly different events taking place simultaneously throughout the city—it is possible to discern several of Sinyavsky's major concerns in "You and I." Part of Nikolai Vasilyevich's paranoia is based on a fear of women; the erotic scenes that are sprinkled throughout the stories, beginning with "At the Circus," not only serve to violate one of the restrictions of Socialist Realism but also portray sex in a less than flattering manner. The perception of the outside world recalls that of the house sprite in "Tenants": Evil forces threaten "You" and promise to drive him out of his refuge. Most crucially, though, Sinyavsky again raises the question of the responsibility of the creator, the "I," and of his relationship to the world around him.

"THE ICICLE"

"Gololeditsa" ("The Icicle"), written in 1961, is both the longest of Sinyavsky's early stories and one of the richest. The narrator abruptly achieves the power to see into the future and the past. He finds out that the woman he loves, Natasha, will be killed by a falling icicle in a specific place in Moscow at a certain time. He attempts to flee the city with her, but on the way he is arrested by the authorities and questioned about his magical powers. Natasha returns to Moscow and is killed by the icicle, at which point the narrator loses his special gift.

The topic allows Sinyavsky to display fully his talents as a writer and to probe his most deeply felt ideas. The narrative is fast-paced and almost jaunty; while some old-fashioned suspense makes the work gripping, Sinyavsky imparts a special air by interspersing the sad and at times tragic events with comic interludes. Particularly effective is his portrayal of Colonel Tarasov, the interrogator, whose naïve efforts to obtain politically useful predictions allow Sinyavsky to satirize the mentality of those in power under Stalin (the story is subtly but clearly dated at the very end of Stalin's reign). Most striking, though, are the meditations that arise from considering the effects of being able to see endlessly into the past and the future; besides the more obvious question of how a knowledge of the future would affect an individual's actions in the present, Sinyavksy considers the meaning of death, experiments with converting time into space (so that the present self represents a simultaneous amalgam of past and future selves), and suggests that an individual with special knowledge or powers has some degree of moral responsibility for others.

"PKHENTZ"

"Pkhentz" appeared in the West later than the other "fantastic stories," in 1966, and has been widely seen as an allegory for the situation of the writer in Soviet Russia. Only little by little does it become clear that the narrator of the story is an alien creature, stranded on earth, who has wrapped his body and put on a disguise to hide his true identity. In some ways, his dilemma resembles that of Sinyavsky before his arrest: the creature's pseudonym resembles Sinyavsky's real name, and he too has a fear of discovery. More broadly, though, "Pkhentz" is concerned with the threat of persecution and mockery directed by society toward the one who is different and also with the alienation of the outsider—which here is presented through the revulsion that the alien feels toward such basic human activities as sex and eating. It is one of Sinyavsky's simplest, most direct, and yet most powerful stories.

LITTLE JINX

Little Jinx was written after Sinyavsky's emigration and is generally referred to as a novella, though it is no longer than "The Icicle." The story is dedicated to E. T. A. Hoffmann and inspired by his *Klein Zaches, genannt Zinnober* (1819; *Little Zaches, Surnamed Zinnober*, 1971). Sinyavsky replaces Hoffmann's good fairy with a pediatrician, Dora Alexandrovna, who cures the stuttering that afflicts the narrator Tsores (Yiddish for grief; he is also sometimes called Sinyavsky). Tsores achieves a gift with words, but he also unintentionally causes the deaths of each of his five half-brothers. Here, it becomes possible to discern a clear direction in Sinyavsky's short fiction; even more clearly than in "Pkhentz," he is writing simultaneously about himself (this story was originally intended to serve as an episode in his autobiographical *Goodnight!*) and more broadly about the condition of the writer, particularly in a to-

talitarian society. Thus, the story is both about isolation on the one hand and about moral responsibility and guilt on the other; like so many of the earlier heroes, Tsores/Sinyavsky finds that the role of creator becomes an obligation and incurs inescapable burdens—such is the dilemma with which Tertz/Sinyavsky has had to cope as well.

OTHER MAJOR WORKS

LONG FICTION: *Sad idzie*, 1959 (in Polish; *Sud idyot*, 1960, as Abram Tertz; *The Trial Begins*, 1960); *Lubimow*, 1963 (in Polish; *Lyubimov*, 1964, as Abram Tertz; *The Makepeace Experiment*, 1965); *Spokoynoy nochi*, 1984 (*Goodnight!*, 1989).

NONFICTION: *Istoriya russkoy sovetsky literatury*, 1958, 1961; *Chto takoe sotsialisticheskii realizm*, 1959 (as Abram Tertz; *On Socialist Realism*, 1960); *Pikasso*, 1960 (with I. N. Golomshtok); *Poeziya pervykh let revolyutsii, 1971-1920*, 1964 (with A. Menshutin); *Mysli vrasplokh*, 1966 (as Abram Tertz; *Unguarded Thoughts*, 1972); *For Freedom of Imagination*, 1971 (essays); *Golos iz khora*, 1973 (*A Voice from the Chorus*, 1976); *Progulki s Pushkinym*, 1975 (*Strolls with Pushkin*, 1993); *V teni Gogolya*, 1975; *"Opavshie list' ya" V. V. Rozanova*, 1982; *Soviet Civilization: A Cultural History*, 1990; *The Russian Intelligentsia*, 1997.

BIBLIOGRAPHY

Carrington, Ildiko de Papp. "Demons, Doubles, and Dinosaurs: Life Before Man, the Origins of Consciousness, and 'The Icicle'." *Essays on Canadian Writing* 33 (1986) 68-88. A useful study of Sinyavsky's story.

Dalton, Margaret. *Andrei Siniavskii and Julii Daniel: Two Soviet "Heretical" Writers*. Würzburg: Jalverlag, 1973. Along with a discussion of the other works that Sinyavsky wrote prior to his arrest, this study contains a detailed story-by-story analysis of the six stories from that period. Throughout, Dalton pays special attention to the unusual literary devices that often make the works difficult to interpret. Contains notes and a bibliography.

Durkin, Andrew R. "Narrator, Metaphor, and Theme in Sinjavskij's *Fantastic Tales*." *Slavic and East*

European Journal 24 (1980); 133-144. Durkin divides the six early stories into three pairs for the purposes of analysis, but his goal is to discern the thematic concerns and formal devices that link all the stories. He emphasizes the role of art and of the artist, as well as the theme of escape, or liberation.

Fenander, Sara. "Author and Autocrat: Tertz's Stalin and the Ruse of Charisma." *The Russian Review* 58 (April, 1999): 286-297. Discusses Sinyavsky in his role as both cultural critic and provocateur, Abram Tertz; claims that by turning the discredited Joseph Stalin into a double for himself, Sinyavsky/Tertz reveals both the artistry of Stalinism and the mythical privileged place of the writer in Russian culture.

Frank, Joseph. "The Triumph of Abram Tertz." *The New York Review of Books* 38 (June 27, 1991): 35-43. A brief biographical and critical discussion of the events of Sinyavsky's life and the nature of his fiction. Notes the importance of his trial for having his works published out of the Soviet Union.

Haber, Erika. "In Search of the Fantastic in Tertz's Fantastic Realism." *Slavic and East European Journal* 42 (Summer, 1998): 254-267. Shows how the presence of an eccentric narrator who often plays a double role as both character and narrator, creating a highly self-conscious text is a basic feature of Tertz's fantastic realism; claims that his narrators at times contradict and even oppose the characters and events they describe, thereby creating a tension between the content of the stories and the manner of their presentation.

Kolonosky, Walter. "Andrei Sinyavsky: Puzzle Maker." *Slavic and East European Journal* 42 (Fall, 1998): 385-388. Compares Sinyavsky's works to puzzles; his pieces are not simply read, but contain historical references, allegorical links, language peculiarities, grotesque allusions, and autobiographical asides that require interpretation.

_____. "Inherent and Ulterior Design in Sinyavsky's 'Pxenc.'" *Slavic and East European Journal* 26 (1982): 329-337. Accepting the notion that "Pkhentz" is, on one level, a work of scientific fiction, Kolonosky claims that it is primarily an alle-

gory about faith, and he traces examples of Christian symbolism within the story.

Lourie, Richard. *Letters to the Future: An Approach to Sinyavsky-Tertz*. Ithaca, N.Y.: Cornell University Press, 1975. Lourie devotes a separate chapter to the *Fantastic Stories*; his analyses are distinctive both for his critiques of certain stories (he believes that only "The Icicle" and "Pkhentz" are totally successful) and for his efforts to show their relationship to other works in Russian literature. Includes notes, bibliography, and an index.

Morsberger, Grace Anne. "'The Icicle' as Allegory." *Odyssey* 42 (1981): 15-18. A short but interesting study of the story.

Nepomnyashchy, Catharine Theimer. "Andrei Donatovich Sinyavsky (1925-1997)." *Slavic and East European Journal* 42 (Fall, 1998): 367-371. Claims that Sinyavsky's works have been misunderstood; challenges the characterization of him as a political dissident and argues for a view of his texts as works that engage fantasy and encourage the fanciful.

Peterson, Ronald E. "The Writer as Alien in Sinjavskij's 'Pkhens'." *Wiener Slavistischer Almanach* 12 (1982): 47-53. Examines the autobiographical element in this stort story.

Pevear, Richard. "Sinyavsky in Two Worlds: Two Brothers Named Chénier." *The Hudson Review* 25 (1972): 375-402. Pevear contrasts Sinyavsky and Yevgeny Yevtushenko in an effort to elucidate Sinyavsky's views about the tasks of the writer. Contains a thoughtful analysis of "The Icicle."

Theimer Nepomnyashchy, Catherine. "Andrei Sinyavsky's 'You and I': A Modern Day Fantastic Tale." *Ulbandus Review* 2, no. 2 (1982): 209-230. Notes Sinyavsky's flaunting of his literary antecedents (Hoffmann, Gogol, Dostoevski). Prefers to view the story not so much as a study in mental disorder as "a realized metaphor—a literal working out of the vision of the artist as God" and thus as a tale combining both the biblical and the fantastic.

_____. "Sinyavsky/Tertz: The Evolution of the Writer in Exile." *Humanities in Society* 7, no. 314 (1984): 123-142. After providing a brief overview of Sinyavsky's career during his first decade in the West, the author goes on to detail Sinyavsky's concerns with the role of the writer in relationship to reality and society at large. Concludes with a discussion of *Kroshka Tsores*.

Barry Scherr, updated by Vasa D. Mihailovich

JULIA SLAVIN

Born: not listed

PRINCIPAL SHORT FICTION

The Woman Who Cut Off Her Leg at the Maidstone Club, 1999

OTHER LITERARY FORMS

Julia Slavin began work on a novel shortly after the publication of *The Woman Who Cut Off Her Leg at the Maidstone Club*, her first book.

ACHIEVEMENTS

Julia Slavin has published short stories in a number of well-respected literary journals. She won a Pushcart Prize and the Frederick Exley Fiction Award, both in 1999.

BIOGRAPHY

Julia Slavin grew up in Bethesda, Maryland, among four older brothers. In a *Washington Post* interview, she said that she was "a complete washout at school. I had one of those diseases with initials that when I was growing up just meant screwing up." Her parents influenced her writing career in different ways. Her father, a psychologist, taught about the unconscious mind and the role of dreams, while her mother gave her a love of language.

She graduated from college with a degree in art history, although her career goal was to go to New York and be a playwright. A few days in New York demonstrated to her how difficult it would be to make a living in this way. She took a job at American Broadcasting Company (ABC) television, where she finally became the producer of *Prime Time Live*. After ten years in New York, she decided to return to writing. She, her husband, and her two daughters moved to Chevy Chase, Maryland, in 1992. She met with success almost immediately, placing several stories in respected literary journals. The appearance of *The Woman Who Cut Off Her Leg at the Maidstone Club* marked her first book-length publication.

ANALYSIS

Julia Slavin's stories are quirky and hip, revealing a quick wit and close attention to the language. Often, Slavin seems to select an image, metaphor, or slang phrase and follow it to its logical (or illogical) conclusion. In so doing, her writing at times resembles Donald Barthelme's surreal flights of fancy. Slavin's language is generally straightforward and uncomplicated, in keeping with her suburban settings. This down-to-earth language, however, contrasts with the sometimes absurd, sometimes fantastic situations in which she places her characters. Thematically, Slavin's stories run more deeply than the humorous and quirky situations might suggest. Indeed, these little stories often embody complex psychological issues and fears. Using figurative language as a starting place, Slavin constructs stories that behave in ways similar to dreams by revealing the inner workings of the human psyche.

With their ironic twists, smooth exteriors, and multilayered interiors, these stories fit comfortably into the postmodern project, revealing and concealing simultaneously. The title story in particular seems to poke fun at itself and at a whole social class, maintaining ironic distance from its subject, a common tactic in many postmodern works. At yet other moments, Slavin seems to be aligning herself with the Magical Realists of the late twentieth century; certainly the story "Blight" brings the writer Laura Esquival to mind. Other reviewers compare Slavin's

Julia Slavin (©Miriam Berkley)

work to that of John Updike or John DeLillo. In the final analysis, the stories generally work well, leading the reader through the sometimes amusing, sometimes surreal, sometimes horrendous landscapes of the twentieth century. What Slavin's stories share is a concern with the big issues in life: How can we ever understand each other? How can we protect each other from harm? How can we not be alone in a world that is frequently cruel?

"SWALLOWED WHOLE"

The opening story in the collection *The Woman Who Cut Off Her Leg at the Maidstone Club*, "Swallowed Whole" takes a common off-color expression and expands it to an absurd degree. The humor in the story depends on the double meaning of "swallowing a man." Slavin commented in an article in *The Washington Post* that the story had its roots in her own fantasy concerning her lawn boy. However, under the humor is a darker subtext concerning fear of pregnancy and miscarriage. In the story, a thirtyish suburban housewife named Sally engages in what starts out as a flirtation with her lawn boy, Chris. Before the story travels more than a few paragraphs, Sally and Chris have engaged in a "deep" kiss, a kiss so deep that

Sally ends up swallowing Chris whole. Chris resides in Sally's abdomen for weeks, the two of them carrying on a bizarre internal affair. At the end of the story, Sally awakens to bloody sheets and the sound of Chris's lawn mower outside. The ending forces the reader back into the story to reread the clues that Slavin strews along the way. The feelings of movement in Sally's abdomen, her ongoing problems with vomiting, and the odd fantasies in which she engages all suggest that what Sally is experiencing is not some fantastic encounter with her lawn boy. Rather, these all point to a pregnancy. Sally's concern that her "affair" with Chris is distracting her from her husband also highlights another common fear during pregnancy, that the new baby will interfere with the normal functioning of the couple, particularly the couple's sex life. When Sally says that she drinks a household cleanser to rid herself of Chris, it is difficult to determine if this is the common pregnancy fantasy of wishing to rid oneself of the fetus or if Sally truly does ingest large amounts of cleanser. In any event, when she rouses herself, she finds that her sheets are bloody and that Chris has left her body, clearly a signal that what she has really experienced is a miscarriage. Again, Slavin's images are so dreamlike that is difficult to separate the fantasies within fantasies. It is possible that Sally dreams the bloody sheets, just as she has dreamed having Chris in her belly; such blood-filled dreams are also common during pregnancy. In any event, Slavin has craftily woven these common pregnancy images and fantasies with the controlling metaphor, swallowing a man.

"BABYPROOFING"

In the story "Babyproofing," Slavin once again uses a common expression and carries it to the extreme. At the same time, she also uncovers one of the deepest fears young parents can have, that something will happen to their child as the result of their own carelessness. As the story opens, a young couple has put themselves into the hands of Mitzy Baker, the owner of a company that will come into a home and render it completely harmless to a child. By the time Mitzy is finished with the house, however, all the couples belongings have disappeared, to be replaced with thick foam padding. Even the trees in the yard have been removed. Perhaps the most disturbing removal of all, however, is the removal of the husband as a safety hazard. By the end of the story, the husband forces his way back into his transformed house to find his wife and child sitting on the floor. Surprisingly, the family is not unhappy with the results of the babyproofing. Walter says,

> The three of us sit on the cushy floor, covered with Mitzy Baker's foam padding. . . . Caroline can drag herself up on her toys and fall and not feel a thing. . . . Tomorrow we can wake up and relax, finally. Tonight we can sleep without dreaming.

Slavin identifies a number of common fears and fantasies in this story. Certainly, most new parents consider extreme and extravagant ways of keeping their child safe. Further, what father has not felt slightly superfluous in the flurry of activity that overtakes a new family when the baby comes home? Slavin's ending also points to the sacrifice young parents are willing to make; while they may be willing to take risks with their own lives, they will sacrifice their own freedoms and individuality for the sake of protecting their child. In so doing, she demonstrates that the instinctual protection of the young still overrides postmodern individuality.

"DENTOPHILIA"

A beautiful woman named Helen, much beloved by her husband, begins to sprout teeth all over her body. This is the unlikely situation in the short story "Dentophilia." In this case, Slavin takes the mythological motif of the "vagina dentata" and gives it a contemporary twist. Psychologists claim that the motif of the vagina filled with teeth surfaces so frequently across cultures because it reveals deep, subconscious fears of castration and the dangers of sexual intercourse. The symbolic element of the story seems most clear after Helen's deciduous teeth all fall out and permanent teeth take their place, a process that roughly coincides with puberty in young women. Further, Helen tells the narrator that her "wisdom teeth" have erupted "down there." Clearly, the juxtaposition of the words "wisdom" and "teeth" along with the indication that they have erupted in Helen's

vagina point to the notion of biblical wisdom, that of "knowing" one's spouse. After all, it was partaking of the fruit of the tree of knowledge that led to the expulsion from Eden. Thus, Slavin seems to be suggesting that sexual intercourse, which is a kind of wisdom, is not without dangers. For the couple in the story, Helen's dentition leads to her death, and the narrator is bereft, alone on a beach that resembles in its own way the lost paradise.

"LIVES OF THE INVERTEBRATES"

An eight-pound lobster named Max, yet another creature with a bony exoskeleton, stars in another of Slavin's odd little stories. The narrator of the story soon renames Max "Gina," after discovering that he is really a she. The relationship between the narrator and Gina is nothing if not obsessive. Gina attacks a young zookeeper responsible for the invertebrates when she exhibits sexual interest in the narrator. In an odd twist, it seems that the narrator is not only obsessed with Gina but also identifies with her. He notes that they are about the same age. The narrator is metaphorically a "horny" creature, given his constant thoughts of sexual encounters; Gina is literally horny. Thus, although Gina is identified as female, she continues to behave like a male. Indeed, even the imagery that Slavin uses to describe Gina suggests something horrifically phallic about the creature. She is an invertebrate, yet she is hard and stiff, just as the human penis, a soft "invertebrate" most of the time, becomes hard and stiff when preparing for sex. Even the attack on the invertebrate keeper resonates with sexual violence: "Gina, who'd been slack in my hands suddenly arched the front section of her body back . . . she lunged toward Katherine, scissoring through her upper lip with her cutter claw." Consequently, in spite of the sex change of the creature, in spite of the unlikeliness of the situation, Slavin is able to turn a flight of fantasy into a study of psychological fixation and obsession.

BIBLIOGRAPHY

Lewis, Nicole. "Outer Suburbia: Julia Slavin's Stories Chart Some Very Unfamiliar Territory." *The Washington Post,* September 15, 1999, p. C01. A feature article on Slavin and her book. Provides some useful background information on the writer as well as comments from Slavin on the writing of the book.

Pakenham, Michael. "Debut Stories by Julia Slavin: Deliciously Insane." Review of *The Woman Who Cut Off Her Leg at the Maidstone Club*, by Julia Slavin. *The Baltimore Sun*, July 25, 1999, p. 10F. Another reviewer noting the fantastic, surreal, and dreamlike quality of the stories. Calls the book "wonderfully strong, delightfully readable stuff."

Reynolds, Susan Salter. "Voyage to the Future of Fiction." Review of *The Woman Who Cut Off Her Leg at the Maidstone Club*, by Julia Slavin. *Newsday*, July 18, 1999, p. B12. Reviews *The Woman Who Cut Off Her Leg at the Maidstone Club* in the context of contemporary fiction. Argues that the stories exhibit "a quietly desperate, normalized insanity that has a brave tradition in literature."

Rosenfeld, Lucinda. "Down and Dirty." *Harper's Bazaar* (July, 1999): 144. Rosenfeld traces male-female relationships in several works of contemporary fiction, including *The Woman Who Cut Off Her Leg at the Maidstone Club*. Suggests that Slavin's characters "find their internal malaise mirrored in the external world."

Taylor, Charles. "Nightmares on Elm Street." *The New York Times Book Review* (August 15, 1999): 7. Taylor comments on Slavin's notion of the grotesque and points out that Slavin's subject is the fear and anxiety of contemporary life.

Wittman, Juliet. "Storied Presents: Two Collections." Reviews *The Woman Who Cut Off Her Leg at the Maidstone Club*, by Julia Slavin. *The Washington Post*, September 9, 1999, p. C2. A review of *The Woman Who Cut Off Her Leg at the Maidstone Club* that calls Slavin "a major discovery." Notes the surreal, fantastic qualities of the stories and suggests that Slavin could be compared to Franz Kafka.

Diane Andrews Henningfeld

JANE SMILEY

Born: Los Angeles, California; September 26, 1949

PRINCIPAL SHORT FICTION

The Age of Grief: A Novella and Stories, 1987
"Ordinary Love" and "Good Will": Two Novellas, 1989

OTHER LITERARY FORMS

Jane Smiley has published several novels as well as collections of short fiction. In addition to studies of family life, she has experimented with several novelistic subgenres, including a murder thriller (*Duplicate Keys*, 1984) and a historical epic (*The Greenlanders*, 1988). With the publication of her academic satire *Moo* in 1995 and the 1998 picaresque fiction *The All-True Travels and Adventures of Lidie Newton* (an exploration of the intersections of racism and violence in American history inspired in part by the 1993 Oklahoma City Bombing), Smiley completed a self-imposed task of writing fiction in the four major literary modes: epic (*The Greenlanders*), tragedy (*A Thousand Acres*), comedy (*Moo*), and romance (*The All-True Travels and Adventures of Lidie Newton*). In 1996 Smiley found herself unwittingly at the center of an editorial firestorm when she published an essay in *Harper's* that challenged the canonized status of Mark Twain's *Adventures of Huckleberry Finn* (1884) by criticizing its moral dishonesty and aesthetic flaws, touting instead Harriet Beecher Stowe's *Uncle Tom's Cabin: Or, Life Among the Lowly* (1852) as an underappreciated realist and morally serious masterpiece.

ACHIEVEMENTS

Jane Smiley's short fiction, for which she received a Pushcart Prize in 1977 and O. Henry Awards in 1982, 1985, and 1988, has drawn consistent praise for its linguistic economy and incisive detail in the service of the complex mysteries of American family life. *The Age of Grief*, which signaled a new gathering of creative force in Smiley's writing, was nominated for the National Book Critics Circle Award. With *A Thousand Acres* (1991), a novel retelling the family drama of William Shakespeare's *King Lear* (pr. c. 1605-1606) in terms of an Iowa farm family, Smiley attained new levels of national and even international recognition, winning the Pulitzer Prize (1992) and the National Book Critics Circle Award for fiction (1991), in addition to a number of regional awards.

BIOGRAPHY

Born to James LaVerne Smiley and Frances Graves Nuelle on September 26, 1949, during her father's military tour of duty in California, Jane Graves Smiley was transplanted at a young age to the Midwest and grew up in a suburb of St. Louis, Missouri. The daughter of a writer-mother, she attended Vassar College and received her B.A. in English in 1971; in composing her first novel as her senior thesis, she discovered that "this was for me, this creation of worlds." Smiley completed a master's of fine arts at the University of Iowa in 1976, and received an M.A. (1975) and a Ph.D. (1978) in medieval literature from the same institution. Toward completion of that work, a Fulbright Fellowship in 1976-1977 allowed her to spend time in Iceland, where her study of Norse sagas laid the groundwork for her 1988 epic novel *The Greenlanders*.

In 1981 Smiley began teaching literature and creative writing as a member of the faculty of Iowa State University, where she became a full professor in 1989. In 1981 and 1987 she also served as visiting professor at the University of Iowa. Though awarded the title of distinguished professor in 1992, she left Iowa State in 1996 to become a full-time writer at a horse-breeding ranch she bought in Northern California with the substantial earnings provided her

Jane Smiley (Stephan Mortensen)

from the book sales of and film rights to *A Thousand Acres*.

Smiley has commented that a childhood shadowed by the existence of the atomic bomb and an adolescence marked by the invention of "the Pill" have given her two major subjects: "sex and apocalypse." Her personal history indicates a familiarity with the challenges of family life. A first marriage to John Whiston in 1970, while she was still at Vassar, lasted until 1975. Her second marriage, to editor William Silag in 1978, produced daughters Phoebe and Lucy. A third marriage in 1987 to screenwriter Stephen Mark Mortensen led to the birth of son Axel James when Smiley was forty-three years old; the couple later divorced. Among her avocations Smiley lists cooking, swimming, playing piano, quilting, and raising horses on her California ranch.

ANALYSIS

David Leavitt has called Jane Smiley "the contemporary American master of the novella form," and she herself regards the novella's "more meditative" thematic concentration and streamlined plotting as particularly congenial to her artistic ends. Having begun her career as what she calls a "devoted modernist" preoccupied with the nihilistic anomie dramatized in the great literature of the early twentieth century, Smiley found herself losing that alienated edge when she first became pregnant. In trying to resolve the ensuing creative challenge that plagued her—"Can mothers think and write?"—she discovered her true subject: the continually shifting dynamics of familial relationship. Her best work captures the intricate dance of need, love, retribution, and loss that entwines competing subjectivities within every family. Smiley has proven especially adept at writing the maternal experience into literature, challenging the familiar cultural idealizations and caricatures of "mother love" produced by writers invariably engaging their subject from the position of the child; she regards her version of parenting as "a critique and correction" of both the child's and the father's stories. Yet Smiley's investigations are not limited to female protagonists; she regularly assumes male personas and argues that doing so is a less arduous imaginative feat for her than writing as a mother, since few viable models exist for the latter. Smiley's versatile experiments in character, voice, and plot line are well suited to short-fictional forms. The psychological immediacy she achieves bespeaks a compassionate interest in decent people caught at dramatic crossroads, where they must assess the compromises and delusions that have shaped their lives.

Although an extremely eclectic writer in terms of the range of projects she has completed, in her short fiction Smiley offers perhaps the purest distillation of her long-standing fascination with the domestic spaces individuals construct as assumed havens from the otherwise chaotic assaults of daily living—spaces inevitably disrupted, despite the best intentions of their decently bourgeois inhabitants, by their own convulsive desires. Smiley discovered early in her career that the critical contempt regularly directed toward such "feminine" domestic themes willfully ignored a rich dramatic venue into which she quickly moved and made her own (propelled not a little by her newly married status and plans to raise a family

of her own). She explains that her writerly endeavors show a sustained interest

> in how people relate to the groups that they're in (whether those groups are families or communities), in how power is negotiated among people, in character idiosyncrasies, and in the relationship of power to love.

She not only demonstrates her attunement to the mundane rhythms and speech of family life but also deftly captures the hunger for connection and empathy that the nuclear family promises to satisfy—doing so only to reveal its heartbreakingly predictable insufficiency. Loyalties abruptly give way to shattering betrayals, and love fails repeatedly to transcend the imperatives of sexual longing or personal doubt. Family members and childhood friends face the challenge of finding ways to survive their tortured devotions, a pattern critic Vivian Gornick in *The End of the Novel of Love* (1997) laments as evidence of the diminished belief in romantic love's transformative potential that has characterized fiction since the 1960's. Gornick fails, however, to recognize that Smiley's emotional realism is as firmly grounded in her medievalist training as her contemporary worldview, both of which posit a tragic and incomprehensible universe in which the steady turn of the wheel of fortune insistently exposes the transitoriness of all earthly pursuits, pleasure as well as profit. Within that context the misery that fallible human beings inflict upon themselves and others—violence, sexual betrayal, greed, and envy—continually upends the most strenuous efforts to create social harmony, be it in the family or the community at large, and even love proves as likely to destroy as to create. In such a world, Smiley's most admirable characters are those who, despite their limitations and failures, stumble toward a personal vision of moral responsibility and communal obligation that both enables their survival and dignifies their self-awareness.

THE AGE OF GRIEF

The Age of Grief, nominated for a National Book Critics Circle Award, is a loosely constructed volume. Consisting of five short stories and a novella, it presents an array of characters who range from active aggressors to passive victims in the contemporary battles for and against emotional commitment raging among adults not yet willing to see themselves in their parents' shoes. The stories evoke a cultural ambiance of fragmentation and insubstantiality through which the longed-for idyll of family life demolished in the volume's closing novella achieves its tragic incandescence.

Thus *The Age of Grief* breaks essentially into two parts: The short-story section examines family life through a series of characters on the periphery of domesticity. In "Lily" and "The Pleasure of Her Company," the female protagonists are admiring outsiders to the marriages they observe, and both find themselves unprepared for the destruction of their illusions. Their limited notions about the potential for sudden psychological violence within seemingly conventional contexts result in part from the absence of such entanglements in their own lives. Lily's emotional "virginity" permits the freedom she needs for her work as a poet but also leads her to meddle unwittingly in the heart of marital darkness, whose capacity for long-borne compromise and truce she disastrously misreads. Florence in "The Pleasure of Her Company" (one of Smiley's O. Henry Award winners) is allowed a more graceful if ironically inflected exit. Faced with the dissolution of a marriage that she once regarded as ideal, she rejects the cynic's conclusion that all love is delusion and instead pursues her own blossoming relationship, believing that "it's worth finding out for yourself." Florence, unlike Lily, risks emotional involvement because the experience it will provide will be its own reward, despite clear evidence of its price.

Within this collection Smiley is most harshly disposed toward those who orchestrate their emotional destinies with the same professional calculation they apply to their stock portfolios, as does the female letter-writer of "Jeffrey, Believe Me." Smiley caricatures the narcissistic self-gratification of upwardly mobile urbanites by making this protagonist so intent on satisfying her biological clock that she seduces a gay male friend to achieve pregnancy and then willfully resists personal responsibility for the other human beings she exploits. Her opposite in the volume is the male protagonist of "Long Distance," whose odyssey to join his brothers for the Christmas holidays prompts a reassessment of his callousness toward a Japanese woman with whom he has had an affair. Never having acknowledged the continual negotiations at the heart of family life, he now sees the moral bankruptcy in his self-serving flight from attachments.

Emotional stock-taking of this kind is central to Smiley's most deeply felt writing, and hence her narratives are often most effective when they enter the unmediated psychological terrain of the first person. Her characteristic tone, a laconic meditative stillness, emerges for the first time in *The Age of Grief* in "Dynamite," a piece in which the outsiders of the earlier stories give way to the hybrid insider/outsider Sandy, a woman in early middle age caught between lifelong conflicting impulses to connect and to disrupt. Oscillating between past and present, as well as between the discrete identities into which her life has split as a result of the radical politics that sent her underground for twenty years, she juggles a desire for the mother she feels she has never known with a restless urge "to do the most unthought-of thing, the itch to destroy what is made—the firm shape of my life, whether unhappy, as it was, or happy, as it is now." Memory and fantasy weave an elaborate web of old and new longings that explain her wild behavior swings and puncture the bourgeois stability that she seems, superficially, to covet. Sandy's paradoxes defy taming and make her representative of the struggle against self that is typical of Smiley's characters.

With *The Age of Grief*, Smiley moves full force into that theme, shifting the angle of vision from the aggressor to the victim of another family in crisis. By so doing she exposes the insufficiency of such categories to explain the emotional upheavals that beset "normality" from within its own preserve. The novella centers on dentist David Hurst, whose wife and professional partner in a busy dentistry practice suddenly falls in love with another man. At the center of the drama is David's struggle with his knowledge of Dana's affair and his choice to remain silent about it. Smiley is familiar not only with the routines of parenting small children but also with the social changes that have necessitated fathers becoming full participants in all the nuances of that routine. David is intimately involved in the daily lives—and illnesses—of his young daughters, ages seven, five, and two. The emotional tyranny of Leah, a toddler who insistently demands all her father's attention, mimics the jealous ownership of a lover and stands in bittersweet counterpoint to the waning love between her parents. Neither spouse can speak to the other of their estrangement, and in his anguish David concludes:

> I am thirty-five years old, and it seems to me that I have arrived at the age of grief. . . . It is not only that we know that love ends, children are stolen, parents die feeling that their lives have been meaningless. . . . It is more that the barriers between the circumstances of oneself and of the rest of the world have broken down, after all—after all that schooling, all that care . . . it is the same cup of pain that every mortal drinks from.

The family moves to the end of dissolution as Dana's obsession finally upends her carefully maintained schedule altogether and for the first time keeps her away from home for twenty-four hours. When she inexplicably reappears, the couple agree not to discuss what has led her to return. With a generosity of spirit—or failure of will—steeped in sadness, David offers by way of explanation his dearly bought insight that "marriage is a small container after all. . . . Two inner lives . . . burst out of it and out of it, cracking it, deforming it." Thus Smiley reveals the impossible burden placed on the emotional bonds of family and marriage and quietly ponders the challenge of learning to live with diminished faith in the future.

ORDINARY LOVE

Each of the novellas constituting *"Ordinary Love" and "Good Will"* offers another sustained examination into the disruption of a once-idyllic household. While strikingly dissimilar in story line, atmospherics, and point of view, the two works together provide variations on a common theme: the loss of parental illusions about one's protective power and authority within the family circle and the compensatory wisdom of discovering the mysterious otherness and humanity of one's children.

The first-person narrator of *Ordinary Love*, a fifty-two-year-old divorced Iowan mother of five adult children, typifies Smiley's clear-eyed rejection of sentimental pieties about the heartland matriarch. Rachel Kinsella does indeed tend to the baking of cakes and spoiling of grandchildren as she awaits the homecoming of a long-absent son. Her story, however, matter-of-factly told in a voice both accepting and unrepentant, includes the jarring paradox of her having, years earlier, proudly borne five babies in five years with a doting, ambitious doctor husband, then inexplicably initiating an adulterous affair that ruptured the family idyll so completely that even her identical twin sons were separated in the ensuing custody battles. Rachel's history, an arc of emotional devastation and recovery, leads her in middle age to a maturity brought into being out of wildness, grief, and tenacity.

Rachel's perspective, however, is not self-serving. She admits the contradictions driving her emotional life: the allure of creating a timeless domestic haven free from the typical ravages of family life; her relief upon being freed from the marriage that lay as the cornerstone to that haven; her "terror" upon entering the void left when her family collapsed and her children disappeared for a time from her life. Smiley plots Rachel's history as an arc of emotional loss and recovery, and in late middle age she is self-possessed and steady, a mature woman who, because she has consciously made herself anew out of wildness, grief, and perseverance, now possesses the strength to confront the ongoing costs of the past within the present.

The novella's present-tense drama, while inseparable from the rupture of twenty years earlier, involves Rachel's effort to manage the return of her son Michael from a two-year stint as a teacher in poverty-stricken India. In a family where each separation reprises the primal severance of mother from child and sibling from sibling, Michael's transformation overseas exposes once again the instability afflicting even the most fundamental human ties. Within this charged atmosphere, a series of confidences delivers a powerful lesson about the tantalizing impenetrability of each family member's private reality. Rachel tells her children for the first time of the love affair that upended their young lives; her elder daughter, Ellen, retaliates with a description of their neglect by a vengeful father who transplanted them to London; Michael reveals his destructive relationship with a married woman, which resulted in an abortion and the loss of the woman he really loved. The shock created by each of these "secrets" is multiple, and Rachel registers them all. Unlike her former husband, she struggles to subordinate the possessive assumptions of a parent and instead tries "to accept the mystery of my children, of the inexplicable ways they diverge from parental expectations, of how, however much you know or remember of them, they don't quite add up." She muses on the disruptive irrationality of human desire and realizes that Michael's new maturity reflects his own discovery of that fact. The real fruit of knowledge, she concedes, lies not simply in one's own suffering but in learning one's potential to inflict suffering on others, especially those one holds most dear. With a fatalism balanced against faith in the human capacity for renewal, Rachel squarely confronts the fact that she cannot spare her children life's bitterest lesson—the perverse and unrelenting hunger of the heart for what it cannot have and that given the destructive pressure of the inner life, a parent may unforgivably offer her children "the experience of perfect family happiness, and the certain knowledge that it could not last."

GOOD WILL

Good Will places its stark dramatic enactment of another adult's acquiring wisdom too late within a matrix of suspense about what is coming rather than through a melancholy retrospective about what has been. In placing a mother's story beside a father's, Smiley describes the first piece in this volume as "more feminine . . . things are hidden and revealed," while the second is "more masculine" and "linear." *Good Will* also shows Smiley's talent for exposing the tensions generated by the endless daily struggles for psychological control underlying even the smoothest family surfaces. Here the first-person narrator is Bob Miller, a Vietnam veteran who has systematically created a world for his nuclear family of three which exists parallel to, not within, mainstream American society. The novella opens eighteen years

into his countercultural experiment, when the rearing of the child he and his wife Liz thought would complete their idyll begins instead to erode their illusory self-sufficiency.

Bob's considerable talents as a craftsman correspond to his principled determination to live by a moral code purged of the empty materialism of his time. Slowly, however, he reveals the contours of a personality whose virtues slip over into dogmatism and whose ingenuity is actually trained on keeping his loved ones within the range of his authority. The evidence of discord within Bob's self-willed paradise comes from the very people he believes to be his allies. Liz becomes a member of a fundamental religious community whose pull on her suggests the spiritual hunger she cannot satisfy through her marriage. More sinister and ultimately more devastating is the racist hostility conceived seemingly in a vacuum by their seven-year-old son for the African American newcomer whose affluent home life focuses the boy's rage at his own marginality. Tommy's innocence of the world offers him no defense against the corrosive envy he conceives for Annabelle's possessions, and in coolly destroying them he forces his parents to confront their arrogance in assuming they have the right, much less the power, to direct Tommy's responses to the world.

Finally even Bob finds that he has not renounced the world as completely as he has assumed: Lydia Harris, Annabelle's mother and a professor of mathematics, whose specialty is the suggestive realm of probability, offers her own fascination for him. To compensate for Tommy's vandalism he does various odd jobs for her and becomes preoccupied with her home, her personality, her assessment of his life. To the degree that he feels drawn to the mother, he finds himself growing perversely angrier toward the daughter on whom she lavishes much affectionate concern. Like Tom, Bob struggles with the shock of seeing the limitations of his own meager existence so baldly exposed.

Bob's stubborn refusal to accept his family's dissatisfaction with their lives contributes to a steadily escalating tension, which climaxes in a catastrophe that unfolds with the surreal pacing of a dream. The drowning of Tom's beloved pony, Sparkle, is closely followed by an arson fire that destroys the Harris home, and Tom's complicity becomes increasingly undeniable. His real target is the father who has isolated him from the world of his peers and who has refused him his own choices in that world.

The spotlight Tommy casts on his parents puts in motion a grim social-services machinery that has all the inexorability of a Dreiserian tragedy. Demands for reparations by the insurance company force the sale of the Millers' homestead and the conversion of both parents to wage earners struggling simply to keep up with the expenses of apartment living. All three family members enter therapy and face the threat of further legal action for the "recklessness" that led them to live without the amenities that could have enabled interception of, and intervention in, the unfolding crisis. Bob's anguish takes the form of a metaphysical stoicism that his wife regards as more stubborn unwillingness to yield to processes beyond his control, but his thoughts reveal that he has conceded to the incoherence of modern life that his farm was an attempt to keep at bay:

> Let us have fragments, I say. . . . if no wholes are made, then it seems to me that I can live in town well enough . . . and remember the vast, inhuman peace of the stars pouring across the night sky above the valley.

He rejects efforts to buffer the grinding truth of Eden's evanescence or of his own role as a worm at the very heart of that dream.

In her fictional preoccupation with the family, then, Smiley has decidedly not abandoned her early artistic attraction to the condition of modernist anomie that inspired her to become a writer. Rather, she has concentrated upon the innumerable ways in which the family, that bulwark against meaninglessness of middle-class American faith, dramatizes the unbridgeable chasm between an individual's simultaneous capacity for selflessness and self-love and the terrible grief to be had in experiencing that gap.

OTHER MAJOR WORKS

LONG FICTION: *Barn Blind*, 1980; *At Paradise Gate*, 1981; *Duplicate Keys*, 1984; *The Green-*landers, 1988; *A Thousand Acres*, 1991; *Moo*, 1995; *The All-True Travels and Adventures of Lidie Newton*, 1998; *Horse Heaven*, 2000.

NONFICTION: *Catskill Crafts: Artisans of the Catskill Mountains*, 1988.

BIBLIOGRAPHY

Bernays, Anne. "Toward More Perfect Unions." Review of *The Age of Grief*, by Jane Smiley. *The New York Times Book Review* (September 6, 1987): 12. Bernays praises Smiley's powerful use of short-fictional forms to examine the contours of troubled personal relationships. Most of the commentary is devoted to the "splendid" title novella, which offers "a poignant and rich meditation on the nature of love and change."

Carlson, Ron. "King Lear in Zebulon County." Review of *A Thousand Acres*, by Jane Smiley. *The New York Times Book Review* (November 3, 1991): 12. Carlson examines the ways in which Smiley adopts the terrain of *King Lear* to explore contemporary family dynamics in rural Iowa. He praises the novel's skill in conveying the interplay of factors—nature, business, community—that shape the farmer's life. He also cites the powerful impact of telling the tale through the eyes of the eldest daughter of the tyrant-father at the center of the tale.

Humphreys, Josephine. "Perfect Family Self-Destructs." Review of *"Ordinary Love" and "Good Will,"* by Jane Smiley. *The New York Times Book Review* (November 5, 1989): 1, 45. Calling the novella a fictional form "most closely resembling a troubled dream," Humphreys discusses Smiley's artistry in *"Ordinary Love" and "Good Will"* and praises her provocative investigations into the role of power, imagination, and desire in family life. The first piece in the collection explores the consequences of desire, while the second involves "imagination as an act of power," the two together elaborating "the myth of the family, told by two principals: an Eve and an Adam," both of whom achieve a "realized ignorance" as "one ancient form of wisdom."

Kakutani, Michiko. Review of *The Age of Grief*, by

Jane Smiley. *The New York Times*, August 26, 1987, p. C21. This strong review examines each of the pieces in the collection and pays particular attention to the novella *The Age of Grief*, wherein Smiley proves her "talent for delineating the subtle ebb and flow of familial emotions" and her attunement for the multiple levels on which everyday communication operates in such close quarters—so much so that "we are left with a sense of having participated in her characters' lives."

Klinkenborg, Verlyn. "News from the Norse." Review of *The Greenlanders*, by Jane Smiley. *The New Republic* 198 (May 16, 1988): 36-39. Cites Smiley's ability to bring to life the experience of a culture remote both in time and worldview. Noting Smiley's debt to the Old Norse sagas on which the novel is based, Klinkenborg notes the complex narrative structuring of the text, its skillful narrative voice, and its powerful fusion of grim story line and philosophical "grace" in the midst of inevitable disaster.

Leavitt, David. "Of Harm's Way and Farm Ways." *Mother Jones* 14 (December, 1989): 44-45. Leavitt praises the probing power of *"Ordinary Love" and "Good Will,"* calling Smiley "one of our wisest writers" for her insight into the tragic center of her characters' most admirable dreams. He also cites her knowledgeable evocation of the real-world activities that fill their lives and her sensitivity to the physical landscape through which they move.

Smiley, Jane. "The Adventures of Jane Smiley." Interview by Katie Bacon. *Atlantic Unbound* (May 28, 1998). In this interview about the influences shaping *The All-True Travels and Adventures of Lidie Newton*, Smiley discusses her controversial 1996 *Harper's* essay comparing Twain's *Huckleberry Finn* unfavorably to Stowe's *Uncle Tom's Cabin*, her interest in the unresolved question of race in American life, her belief that all of her writing is on some level historical fiction, and her continually evolving perspective on the family drama as literary subject.

_____. "Cheltenham Festival: Talking About a Revolution: Feminism, Horses, Sex, and Slavery—Jane Smiley's Novels Are a Potent Mixture of All of Them." Interview by James Urquhart. *The Independent*, October 16, 1998. Even though it is plagued with factual errors, this 1998 interview with Smiley provides illuminating commentary on the ways feminism informs her perspective on family as a "political system," "what it means to be a daughter," and her anti-romantic sensibility.

_____. "A Conversation with Jane Smiley." Interview by Lewis Burke Frumkes. *The Writer* 112 (May, 1999): 20-22. Smiley discusses her work, her favorite contemporary writers, and her own writing habits.

_____. Interview by Marcelle Thiebaux. *Publishers Weekly* 233 (April 1, 1988): 65-66. Notes that in all her books, Smiley focuses on the theme of family life. Smiley discusses the research that goes into her writing.

Barbara Kitt Seidman

LEE SMITH

Born: Grundy, Virginia; November 1, 1944

PRINCIPAL SHORT FICTION

Cakewalk, 1981

Me and My Baby View the Eclipse: Stories by Lee Smith, 1990

The Christmas Letters: A Novella, 1996

News of the Spirit, 1997

OTHER LITERARY FORMS

Lee Smith's first published work was a novel, *The Last Day the Dogbushes Bloomed*. It was followed by the novels *Something in the Wind* and *Fancy Strut* (1973). After a seven-year hiatus, Smith brought out what has been called the first work of her second career, *Black Mountain Breakdown* (1980), which was followed by additional novels, including *Saving Grace* (1995) and *The Christmas Letters* (1996).

ACHIEVEMENTS

Lee Smith received a Book-of-the-Month Club fellowship in 1967, O. Henry Awards in 1979 and 1981, a Sir Walter Raleigh Award in 1984, a North Carolina Award for Literature in 1985, a Lila Wallace-*Reader's Digest* Award in 1995 and an Award in Literature from the American Academy of Arts and Letters in 1999.

BIOGRAPHY

Lee Smith was born on November 1, 1944, in Grundy, Virginia, a mining town in the southwestern part of the state. Her father, Ernest Lee Smith, was in business, running the local Ben Franklin store; her mother, Virginia Marshall Smith, was a teacher. An only child who was born to her parents late in their lives, Lee had a watchful and observant childhood, spending much of her time reading and writing.

Smith was educated at St. Catherine's School in Richmond, Virginia, and then studied in the well-known writing program at Hollins College. Her first novel, *The Last Day the Dogbushes Bloomed*, developed out of a senior writing project. It was published and earned her a Book-of-the-Month Club fellowship. In 1967, Smith was graduated from Hollins College and married the poet James E. Seay, the father of her two children. The marriage later ended in divorce.

From 1968 to 1969, Smith was in Tuscaloosa, Alabama, working as a writer for the *Tuscaloosa News* and gathering the material that would appear in her third novel, *Fancy Strut*. In 1971, the year her second novel appeared, she began teaching seventh grade in Nashville, Tennessee; in 1974, after the publication of *Fancy Strut*, she moved to Durham, North Carolina, to teach language arts and continue writing.

By 1977, Smith was teaching creative writing at the University of North Carolina at Chapel Hill. After three of her books lost money for her publishers, however, her fourth novel was rejected, and other publishers followed suit. As years went by, Smith began to believe that her career as a writer was ending. She credits a new agent and a new editor, one who wished to work actively with her, for enabling her to begin writing again. The critics were impressed with *Black Mountain Breakdown* (1980), the first book from Smith's second period.

In 1981, Smith joined the faculty of North Carolina State University at Raleigh. In 1985, she married Hal Crowther. Smith's growing importance can be seen in the increasing number of interviews with her, the articles about her work published each year, the full-length studies on her, and her major awards.

ANALYSIS

With the publication of *Black Mountain Breakdown*, Lee Smith was recognized as one of the outstanding southern writers of her generation; the novels and short stories that appeared after *Black Mountain Breakdown* have only strengthened this estimation. Like earlier southern writers, Smith has an eye for interesting characters and an ear for colorful speech, as well as both a sense of place and a sense of humor. Except when she reaches back into history, Smith's settings are the New South, and her characters are ordinary people, most of them trying to come to terms with their ordinary lives. Perhaps the quality for which Smith is most admired is her compassion; although she dramatizes her characters' limitations and often satirizes their pretensions, she respects them as human beings, who cope as best they can with the human condition, and admires their individuality and singularity.

Smith's short stories are set primarily in the contemporary South of shopping malls and convenience stores, where dreams and hopes are defined not by tradition or faith but by the images on the television screen. Her protagonists are apparently ordinary people, who are not quite satisfied with their ordinary lives but have small chance of changing them because they have neither the opportunity nor the initiative that would enable them to move up in the world. Furthermore, because most of Smith's protagonists are women, many of whom have been betrayed and abandoned by men, they are especially vulnerable, both emotionally and socially. It is clear that Smith is realistic about the future of such characters, and perhaps, by extension, about life in general. One cannot, however, simply define her tone as pessimistic. There is too much comedy and gentle satire in Smith's works for that kind of assessment; furthermore, she emphasizes the courage of her characters, who despite defeat and disappointment refuse to give up on life.

CAKEWALK

It is interesting that of the fourteen stories in *Cakewalk*, thirteen are told through the eyes of women. This focus is typical of Smith's fiction. The point of view varies; frequently the writer uses first person, sometimes third person with limited omniscience, which concentrates on the thoughts and activities of a single character and thus has much the same effect as first person. No matter which technique she chooses, Smith does not interfere with or comment on her characters but lets them reveal themselves in the words and rhythms of everyday speech.

For example, Mrs. Jolene B. Newhouse, the first-person narrator in "Between the Lines," seems to be speaking to the reader rather than writing her own story. She begins by explaining why her gossip column is called "Between the Lines," but it is soon

clear that what Jolene really wants to do is to point out how superior both she and her newspaper column are. There are dozens of lines in the story that enable Smith to satirize Jolene's character—for example, all the smug self-evaluations: She has a sunny nature, she is naturally good, she is highly intelligent, she has always been a remarkable writer. There is also comedy of situation, such as the real story of Alma Goodnight, who has been hospitalized because her husband hit her with a rake and who now is getting her revenge, lying in luxury in a hospital bed while he suffers the torments of guilt. Clearly, Jolene is not so self-centered that she cannot see a situation as it really is. Her admirable grasp of reality is later illustrated when she describes her youngest daughter as an indecisive whiner. The realist Jolene, however, has a surprising depth to her character. She responds to the beauties of nature, which she describes in her column. Furthermore, she cherishes the memory of an almost mystical sexual encounter in the woods with a visiting evangelist. Perhaps because of her own experience, she has accepted her husband's frailty, along with all the mysterious human actions that are written "between the lines" of her column.

Another of Smith's first-person stories in *Cakewalk*, "Dear Phil Donahue," is told by a woman who, like Jolene, has broken the rules, but who, unlike Jolene, has not been able to control her own situation. Having married her high school sweetheart, twenty-eight-year-old Martha Rasnick is living the life she always expected to live. However, isolated with her babies, uncertain who she is and uncertain who her husband really is, she has a mental breakdown. When a mentally disturbed boy hides in her garage, she feeds him as if he were a stray cat and even comforts him. As a result, she is abandoned by both her husband and their supposed friends, and she has to tell her story to her only human contact, a television personality.

Many of Smith's characters are as isolated as Martha, but, because of what might be interpreted either as an unwillingness to face reality or as a triumph of the human spirit, they refuse to give up hope. For example, the protagonist in "All the Days of Our Lives" is a mother of three who has been divorced by her husband because she ran off to Daytona Beach with an insurance claims adjuster, long since departed, and who now alternates between disappearing into the world of television and imagining her lost husband to be some ideal creature, instead of the perfectionist who actually drove her away. At the end of the story, however, she snaps out of her depression and makes some decisions, including a resolution to take another look at the neighbor, who obviously adores her and who might give her a new love or at least a new interest. Similarly, in "Gulfport," a young girl who has been used, betrayed, and abandoned by a lover, who she had convinced herself was going to marry her, clings to some possibilities for the future. Her lover might come back to her, she thinks, or she might go for a walk with the young Mormon missionary, or she might take a job in a lounge. As long as there is life, there are possibilities; as long as there are possibilities, there is hope.

Like "All the Days of Our Lives" and "Gulfport," the title story of the collection, "Cakewalk," is told in the third person. The character whose thoughts are related, however, Stella Lambeth, is not really the protagonist. When she emphasizes her own superiority in the community and her elegance at the department store cosmetic counter and points out the deficiencies of her disorganized, cake-baking sister, it becomes clear which of the two is more capable of loving and of being loved. At the end of the story, a brief excursion into the thoughts of Stella's husband suggests that Stella's own world is not as secure as she believes it to be. Again, Smith ends with possibilities, leaving the future up to her characters.

Indeed, one of the major themes in Lee Smith's stories is the fragility not only of life itself but also of a seemingly fixed pattern. Actually, it takes very little to change a life: a chance encounter, an impulse, a vivid memory, a sudden glimpse of happiness. The protagonist of "Heat Lightning," Geneva, comments on this fact, when, in the midst of cooking and mothering, she senses that a change is coming. In the past, this feeling foretold a major event in her life—the death of her father, the first glimpse of the man she was to marry, and the death of a baby she was carrying. As it turns out, the fourth prediction is as insig-nificant as heat lightning. Geneva takes the children to a carnival, grins at a carnival worker, and returns cheerfully to her husband.

An event so slight, however, might have had tragic results. In "Saint Paul," it is unclear whether Paul Honeycutt was destroyed by the fact that in his childhood he could not bring himself to declare his love for his young playmate or by the fact that she shattered his image of himself and of her by offering herself to him many years later. At any rate, at the end of the story, although the narrator has proceeded with her life, she realizes that Paul has become almost as important to her as she has always been to him. This suggestion that the world is ruled not by Providence but by chance is basic to Smith's clear-eyed realism. It is consistent with the fact that her characters do not ordinarily make significant choices. They do not act in accordance with some larger plan; instead, they look at the limited possibilities for their lives and then drift in one direction or another, directed by impulse, whim, or instinct.

ME AND MY BABY VIEW THE ECLIPSE

The first story in Smith's second collection of short stories, *Me and My Baby View the Eclipse*, illustrates this kind of aimlessness. Again, the central character in this story, which is entitled "Bob, A Dog," is a wife deserted by her husband, who at thirty-nine has decided that he needs to make his life simpler and has left his family for a singles apartment complex and a young woman. His wife, Cheryl, a good-natured woman who has spent her life being agreeable to everyone, especially to men, cannot even bring herself to be angry with him. Meanwhile, she drifts. She sleeps with one man, then drops him; she refuses to sleep with another. The central problem in the story illustrates both Cheryl's kindness and her purposelessness. She has adopted a dog, who, not unlike her husband, is determined to run free. Despite all the trouble that Bob, the dog, causes her, Cheryl continues to love him and to forgive him. At the end of the story, she considers the possibility that her husband will return to her; ironically, just at that point, Bob runs away.

Sometimes a Smith story will move not merely toward possibilities but toward love. "Life on the

Moon" is the story of two cousins, the narrator, June, who stayed at home, lived by the rules, took care of her family, and has just been abandoned for a younger woman, and Lucie, who went away to college and made her own decisions. Even though June has not approved of Lucie, it is Lucie who persuades her to load the children in the car for a trip to Washington, and it is Lucie who enables June to see her marriage and her husband as they really were. The story ends with a scene of reconciliation between the cousins. Similarly, at the end of the title story, "Me and My Baby View the Eclipse," even though Sharon Shaw knows that she cannot continue her affair with her imaginative lover, Raymond Stewart, she also knows that she will never forget the magic he has brought into her life. Although they will part and she will once again be faithful to her dull husband, Sharon will always be grateful to Raymond, and, in her way, she will always love him.

Because in each of her stories Smith concentrates on a single point of view and because she so expertly imitates the rhythms of speech, reading her work is like listening to various individuals discussing their lives. Although Smith's comedy is delightful and her satire effective, her most memorable stories are those such as "Between the Lines," "Cakewalk," "Life on the Moon," and "Me and My Baby View the Eclipse," which prove that ordinary people can sometimes break free of life's prisons through the power of emotional energy. Even if life is ruled by chance and people are ruled by impulse, Smith suggests that there can be relationships that make life worthwhile, that there can be memories that cast their spell over the years that follow. That is probably the most that human beings can expect out of life, but in Smith's stories, it can be enough.

NEWS OF THE SPIRIT

Smith's third collection, *News of the Spirit*, continues to explore the themes which she has introduced in her earlier work, while widening the range of experience of her characters and extending the segments of their lives that are covered. "This collection is all about storytelling," she has commented, "time, memories, and women trying to lead authentic lives," but she has also observed that at this point in her writing life, "It has become harder for me to stick to the classic short story format because I am really interested in the long haul." Two of the stories, "Blue Wedding" and "The Southern Cross," maintain what Smith calls "the classic form . . . a story that covers a very short period in a character's life . . . emblematic of an entire life" while the others, particularly "Live Bottomless" and the title story, "are more like collapsed novels."

The initial selection, "The Bubba Stories," is a kind of recapitulation of Smith's earlier concerns and an extension beyond the boundaries of region and experience which have often contained her characters. The narrator, a writer in mid-career recalling her youth in a small southern town and her emergence into experience at college in the turbulence of the 1960's, a demonstration of how background shapes character and then how character transcends (without discarding) background. Smith calls the story "very autobiographical" while also pointing out how many key elements are drawn from her imagination, illustrating the vital function that the imaginative capacity occupies in "the struggle to find an authentic voice." As the narrator tells her friends about her mythical brother, the thwarted fantasies of her own life are actualized in fiction as the character she has created takes over and takes off on an unplanned, unanticipated tangent of delight.

A mode of recollection also operates in "Live Bottomless," at just over one hundred pages the longest of the stories. She recalls, beginning in 1958, her beloved father's family-shattering affair, which anticipates her own growth toward sexual awakening. The unexpected and exciting turns her life takes as she moves through adolescence, culminating in her idealistically romantic, almost desperate, attempt to bring her parents back together, leads to a conclusion that mixes Hollywood fantasy with the seemingly mundane to suggest the deeper dimensions of almost everything in the characters' lives.

"Southern Cross" and "Happy Memories Club" are both extrapolations from incidents that Smith noticed almost obliquely, providing her with situations in which "ordinary people" are carried beyond familiar geographical and psychic regions. The narrator of

"Southern Cross" has refashioned herself from a small-town girl (*Mayruth*) into an international adventurer (*Chanel Keen*), able and ready to use every trick of style and beauty to hold her own with rapacious men on a Caribbean cruise. The narrator of the ironically titled "Happy Memories Club" is a retired English teacher, aging but still very lucid, fusing the past and present in a vivid tableau of memory and immediacy. Like the title story—an extended exposition of a character overcoming uncertainty by learning to treasure the things of her life that are valuable and energizing—they bring the "news of the spirit" which Smith defines as "what storytelling means to me," a way "we find our authentic selves over the course of our lives."

OTHER MAJOR WORKS

LONG FICTION: *The Last Day the Dogbushes Bloomed*, 1968; *Something in the Wind*, 1971; *Fancy Strut*, 1973; *Black Mountain Breakdown*, 1980; *Oral History*, 1983; *Family Linen*, 1985; *Fair and Tender Ladies*, 1988; *The Devil's Dream*, 1992; *Saving Grace*, 1995.

BIBLIOGRAPHY

Buchanan, Harriette C. "Lee Smith: The Storyteller's Voice." In *Southern Women Writers: The New Generation*, edited by Tonette Bond Inge. Tuscaloosa: University of Alabama Press, 1990. An introduction to Smith's life and art, focusing primarily on her novels. Claims that the irony that shows the difference between Smith's humanism and the narrow, judgmental views of her characters can best be seen in her short stories.

Canin, Ethan. "The Courage of Their Foolishness." Review of *Me and My Baby View the Eclipse*, by Lee Smith. *The New York Times Book Review* (February 11, 1990): 11. A brief but perceptive summary of Smith's themes, her strengths, and her weaknesses. Although it deals specifically with the short-story collection cited, this essay is an excellent introduction to Smith's fiction as a whole.

Guralnick, Peter. "The Storyteller's Tale." *Los Angeles Times Magazine* (May 21, 1995): 15. Biographical sketch of Smith's childhood in West Virginia and her college career at Hollins College; includes quotations from Smith about the influences on her literary career, what motivates her writing, and what most fascinates her about the South.

Hill, Dorothy Combs. *Lee Smith*. New York: Twayne, 1992. A critical study which includes a bibliography and an index.

Jones, Anne Goodwyn. "The World of Lee Smith." In *Women Writers of the Contemporary South*, edited by Peggy Whitman Prenshaw. Jackson: University Press of Mississippi, 1984. An incisive exploration of the relation between the spoken and written word in Smith's fiction, which makes classification of her work according to the tenets of contemporary criticism extremely difficult, while richly rewarding her readers. The stories in *Cakewalk* are analyzed separately and in relation to the novels.

MacKethan, Lucinda H. "Artists and Beauticians: Balance in Lee Smith's Fiction." *The Southern Literary Journal* 15 (Fall, 1982): 3-14. This important article discusses the problem of attaining a balance in life, which is involved in every choice Smith's characters make. Also looks at Smith's own attempts to achieve artistic balance, primarily through alterations in tone and variations in point of view.

Ostwalt, Conrad. "Witches and Jesus: Lee Smith's Appalachian Religion." *The Southern Literary Journal* 31 (Fall, 1998): 98-118. Discusses the dual religious consciousness in Smith's fiction: traditional religions that try to go beyond the Appalachian landscape and an elemental, supernatural force bound up with nature.

Parrish, Nancy C. *Lee Smith, Annie Dillard, and the Hollins Group: A Genesis of Writers*. Baton Rouge: Louisiana State University Press, 1998. Describes the importance of Smith's literary development at Hollins College during the 1960's. Discusses a number of Smith's early short stories, such as "The Wading House," "The Red Parts," and "Fatback Season," and how they experiment with themes and techniques that she develops in her novels.

Smith, Virginia A. "Luminous Halos and Lawn Chairs: Lee Smith's *Me and My Baby View the Eclipse.*" *The Southern Review* 27 (Spring, 1991): 479-485. Argues that the stories in this collection have a repeated pattern, which takes the characters from darkness to moments of illumination, occurring primarily through the power of love. Stresses Smith's sensitivity to the experiences of women.

Teem, William M., IV. "Let Us Now Praise the Other: Women in Lee Smith's Short Fiction." *Studies in Literary Imagination* 28 (Fall, 1994): 63-73. Discusses the means by which Smith's female characters in her short stories deal with the conflicts that result from clashes between rural culture and urban values.

Walsh, William J. "Lee Smith." In *Speak So I Shall Know Thee: Interviews with Southern Writers.* Jefferson, N.C.: McFarland, 1990. In this interview, conducted in November, 1987, Smith comments on her development as a writer, her experience with editors and publishers, her methods of research, and her evaluation of her own work, as well as on various opinions and personal details.

Wesley, Debbie. "A New Way of Looking at an Old Story: Lee Smith's Portrait of Female Creativity." *The Southern Literary Journal* 30 (Fall, 1997): 88-101. Discusses Smith's female characters, who refuse to conform to traditional stereotypes and bring meaning and order to their communities; argues that what makes her protagonists artists is the fellowship they create and the rituals they maintain.

Rosemary M. Canfield Reisman,
updated by Leon Lewis

ALEKSANDR SOLZHENITSYN

Born: Kislovodsk, U.S.S.R.; December 11, 1918

PRINCIPAL SHORT FICTION

Dlya pol'zy dela, 1963 (*For the Good of the Cause*, 1964)

Dva rasskaza: Sluchay na stantsii Krechetovka i Matryonin dvor, 1963 (*We Never Make Mistakes*, 1963)

Krokhotnye rasskazy, 1970

Rasskazy, 1990

OTHER LITERARY FORMS

Although Aleksandr Solzhenitsyn is best known for his novels and his multivolume historical-artistic investigation of the Soviet prison system, *Arkhipelag GULag, 1918-1956: Opyt khudozhestvennogo issledovaniya*, 1973-1975 (*The Gulag Archipelago, 1918-1956: An Experiment in Literary Investigation*, 1974-1978), in which inset tales figure notably, he has also written independent short fiction, prose poems, narrative poetry, a film scenario, essays, biography and autobiography, and drama. His short novel *Odin den' Ivana Denisovicha* (1962; *One Day in the Life of Ivan Denisovich*, 1963) was adapted for American television. Solzhenitsyn was awarded the Nobel Prize in Literature in 1970, but Soviet authorities blocked a reception ceremony. His *Nobelevskaya lektsiya po literature 1970 goda* (the Nobel lecture) was published in 1972.

ACHIEVEMENTS

Seldom has a writer emerged from total obscurity and risen so meteorically in such a short time as has Aleksandr Solzhenitsyn, achieving in little more than a decade world fame and winning the Nobel Prize. He has accomplished all this by adhering to the nineteenth century realistic tradition and also by bringing new elements into Russian literature. His greatest successes lie in the field of the novel, but he has been as forceful in his nonfiction writings, especially in his *Gulag Archipelago* trilogy. Even his prose poems or miniature stories are comparable to the best in their genre. Through his artistic achievements, resistance to tyranny, and personal courage, he has become the conscience not only of Russian people but also of all humankind and one of the greatest writers in Russian literature.

BIOGRAPHY

Aleksandr Isayevich Solzhenitsyn grew up fatherless and poor in Rostov-on-Don, where he took his university degree in mathematics in 1941, having also studied literature by correspondence from Moscow University. After four years of unbroken service as a frontline artillery officer, he was sentenced in 1945 to eight years of hard labor in *gulag*, the Soviet prison system, for criticizing Joseph Stalin in a private letter. Inexplicably exiled to Kazakhstan from 1953 to 1956, Solzhenitsyn recovered from a near-fatal cancer, taught mathematics and physics in a high school, and began to set his prison experiences down as fiction. Rehabilitated in 1956, he moved to Ryazan, near Moscow, where he continued to write. The publication of his camp novel *One Day in the Life of Ivan Denisovich* marked a brief thaw in Soviet literary restrictions under Nikita S. Khrushchev in 1962. Upon the retightening of censorship, Solzhenitsyn's work was banned from publication in the Soviet Union. After being expelled from the Soviet Writers' Union in 1969 and barred from formal acceptance of the Nobel Prize in Literature he had won in 1970, Solzhenitsyn was ejected from the Soviet Union in 1973. He settled in Vermont with his second wife and children. In his later years, Solzhenitsyn has experienced some misgivings in the West on account of his uncompromising stand against the regime in his country and "conservative" views on the future of Russia. He has retired from public life, spending all his time writing the *Red Wheel* novels.

ANALYSIS

Aleksandr Solzhenitsyn initially responded to his prison and labor camp experiences in easy-to-memorize poetry and later in tiny self-contained prose poems, written down in the 1950's and assembled as a rough set around 1962, although not published at that time in the Soviet Union. Shortly after

Aleksandr Solzhenitsyn, Nobel Laureate for Literature in 1970
(©The Nobel Foundation)

his initial success in the journal *Novy Mir* with the short novel *One Day in the Life of Ivan Denisovich*, Solzhenitsyn also published there his short stories "Incident at Krechetovka Station," "Matryona's House," and "For the Good of the Cause" in 1963. Like "The Easter Procession," "The Right Hand" never appeared in the Soviet Union until the end of *glasnost* in the late 1980's, although "Zakhar the Pouch" was published in *Novy Mir* in 1966 and was the last of Solzhenitsyn's works printed publicly in the Soviet Union. Each of these short pieces contains the germ of a larger work to come, just as each of the individuals or groups named in the titles of the stories reflects one facet of Solzhenitsyn's overriding theme of his country's agony under Communism.

The essence of Solzhenitsyn's message lies in his peculiarly Russian view of shared suffering as vital, even necessary, to human spiritual survival. To this end, he announced in his Nobel lecture that only art, only literature, can bridge the immense gulfs of time and space between human beings, bringing experiences of those faraway others close enough so that their lessons may help overcome evil. Although Solzhenitsyn has not completed large-scale treatments of all the themes presented in his short fiction, the individualization of experience he began with Ivan Denisovich, the lowly camp inmate whose shining humanity enables him to survive, clearly emerges from the prose poems and the short stories, its successive stages mirroring Solzhenitsyn's own existence in Stalin's prison system.

"INCIDENT AT KRECHETOVKA STATION"

"Incident at Krechetovka Station" draws heavily upon Solzhenitsyn's wartime experience. Set in the critical autumn of 1941, this story defies all the conventions of Soviet war literature, in which the cliché of patriotic self-sacrifice predominates. Its protagonist, Lieutenant Zotov, an assistant transit officer, is sympathetically portrayed in sharp contrast to the self-serving functionaries around him, who collectively form the story's antagonist, the "system" to blame for categorically condemning both the guilty and the innocent.

"Incident at Krechetovka Station" opens in cold pouring rain with one of Solzhenitsyn's typically abrupt laconic dialogues which achieve a forceful immediacy. Zotov, a youngish man isolated by the war from his family, has gentle features that toughen as he self-consciously straightens his glasses. He observes the misery of the wretched civilians who clutter the station, but he submerges his sympathy for them in his devotion to Marxism. Soon Zotov is miserable himself, however, distressed by a growing suspicion that the war is not proceeding in tune with Party propaganda.

For more than half of the story, Solzhenitsyn shuttles between the chilly "present" and events in Zotov's past, gradually hinting at the shattering perception Solzhenitsyn himself had grasped as a youth: the vast gap between communism's promises and reality. Zotov haltingly approaches the truth through chance encounters with other actors in the drama,

first in a few poems from line officers critical of their leadership, then in the hunger and cold of the old people and the children in the town. Solzhenitsyn characteristically allows Zotov to linger over the predicament of starving Russian soldiers being repatriated, like Ivan Denisovich, to Stalin's labor camps, their only crime being their surrender to the German army. Lonely and often despairing, Zotov tries to take refuge in his cheap volume of *Das Kapital*, but somehow he cannot finish it. Distracted by the pain of the war's victims, which his heart sees, and by his revulsion at those who prey on them, which his Communist glasses cannot quite shut out, Zotov is disturbed time and again, finally by an "incident" in the bedraggled person of Tveritinov, a former actor trying to find the military detachment from which he had somehow become separated.

Tveritinov strikes up an acquaintance with Zotov, and, as they reminisce about prewar times, the actor's rich voice and winning manner create a mood that for the first time warms the dreary little station with the ceaseless rain beating down on its roof. Solzhenitsyn characteristically insinuates a darker undercurrent when they speak of 1937. Zotov associates that year only with the Soviet involvement in the Spanish Civil War, but Tveritinov, older, recalls an entirely different side to it, the height of Stalin's terrifying purges; his moment of silence, eyes downcast, reveals far more than any speech.

The rapport is suddenly shattered when Tveritinov mistakenly uses the pre-Communist name for Stalingrad. Zotov, struck by the horrifying possibility that he may be harboring an enemy of the state, deceitfully leads the actor into the arms of the security police. Not long after, when Zotov inquires about Tveritinov, he is ominously warned not to look into the matter further. This "incident" at apparently insignificant Krechetovka Station is Solzhenitsyn's metaphor for his country's wartime tragedy. So caught up in Communist zeal that they are able to see the world as Zotov at first did, only through a point of view that obliterates their vital connection to the rest of humanity, Solzhenitsyn's countrymen were being forced to share a perverted brotherhood of opportunism and betrayal, brutality, and inhumanity. As a measure of Solzhenitsyn's burningly ironic message in this story, the "incident" at Krechetovka Station remains Zotov's torment forever.

"THE RIGHT HAND"

In "The Right Hand," a miniature forerunner of *Rakovy korpus* (1968; *Cancer Ward*, 1968), Solzhenitsyn ruthlessly depicts what Zotov might have become if he had not experienced that cruel enlightenment. The story not only excoriates a state-run hospital system that dehumanizes the very patients it purports to serve but also unveils the devastating fate of those whose Party blinders are not removed until it is too late. Having served Communism faithfully, a new patient, clearly terminal, is hypocritically refused admittance to a cancer clinic on a technicality, and this denial of every Party ideal he has slavishly followed snaps his last thread-thin hold on life.

"MATRYONA'S HOUSE"

Like the narrator of "The Right Hand," himself a sufferer, the man who tells the story of "Matryona's House" recently emerged from the crucible of the prison system. All he wants at the outset is to lose himself in the heart of Russia, yearning for the peace of its countryside to restore his soul. Like Solzhenitsyn himself, he takes a position as a mathematics teacher in a shabby ancient village, living in a large old ramshackle house with a sick and aged peasant woman named Matryona. Matryona owns few things, and what she does have is as decrepit as her cockroach-ridden kitchen: a lame cat, a marginal garden, a dirty white goat, and some stunted house plants. Although she had worked on the collective farm for twenty-five years, bureaucratic entanglements have choked off her dead husband's pension—she herself is entitled to nothing—and she is almost destitute. Meager as her life is, however, Matryona's goodness sustains both herself and her lodger, who comes to prize her smile even more than the bit of daily bread they share.

In a strange though altogether convincing way, Matryona's very generosity is responsible for her death. She had loved one of the villagers deeply and waited three years for him to return from World War I. Thinking him dead then, she married his brother, and when the first man returned, he cursed them both.

After Matryona's six children died in infancy, she reared one of the daughters of her former sweetheart as her own, and now, feeling she has not long to live, Matryona allows the girl and her friends to dismantle the top part of her house for its lumber. In struggling to help pull the heavy timber sledge over a railroad crossing, Matryona is killed by a speeding train.

For Solzhenitsyn, generosity, purity of heart, goodness, and love, the best qualities of the Russian folk, are as endangered under Communism as they had been under the czars. Now it may even be worse; Matryona's village has become wretchedly poor, with women instead of horses plowing the kitchen gardens, and the system that promised so much offers only corruption, lackadaisical confusion, and mistrust, racing carelessly over people like Matryona on its way to some future too obscure to believe. And yet (one of the hallmarks of Solzhenitsyn's fiction is the simple "and yet" that illuminates an otherwise hopeless life), he says, Matryona, poor in all but spirit, is the one righteous person without whom not a village or a city or the world can stand. Matryona is the personification of the mystical regeneration held inviolate in the Russian people that Solzhenitsyn instinctively sought upon his release and found intuitively in her. Like the old caretaker of a tatterdemalion monument to a forgotten battle in "Zakhar the Pouch," Matryona's stubborn, patient self-sacrifice restored Solzhenitsyn's faith in humanity at a time when he had learned its opposite all too well.

"FOR THE GOOD OF THE CAUSE"

In his political polemic of the early 1960's, "For the Good of the Cause," Solzhenitsyn again pits genuine human affection against villainous bureaucracy. Students of a provincial technical college have helped build themselves a badly needed building, but Party officials usurp it, with the resulting disillusionment wrenching the consciences of director and teachers and breaking the will of many of the students. Their helpless, bitter frustration at official hypocrisy underlies the actions of the vicious hoodlums, inhuman products of a system Solzhenitsyn feels they eventually will indiscriminately trample down, who aimlessly harass "The Easter Procession" in Solzhenitsyn's last short story.

Solzhenitsyn's short fiction resembles an Easter procession of his own, advancing from the Good Friday of the repatriated Soviet prisoner of war through loving recognition of the healing goodness in the peasants Matryona and Zakhar and a clear-eyed estimate of perversion of an honest teacher's responsibility to his students, finally arriving at the realization that the Soviet system and its creatures contain the seeds of universal destruction. The only hope Solzhenitsyn can see lies in the willing acknowledgment of the bond between human beings that springs from the Christian consciousness that all people share their fellows' suffering. In Solzhenitsyn's short fiction, his overture to a powerful literary and spiritual mission, we recognize that, however separated we are in time and space, his is the voice of our brother.

OTHER MAJOR WORKS

LONG FICTION: *Odin den' Ivana Denisovicha*, 1962 (novella; *One Day in the Life of Ivan Denisovich*, 1963); *Rakovy korpus*, 1968 (*Cancer Ward*, 1968); *V kruge pervom*, 1968 (*The First Circle*, 1968); *Avgust chetyrnadtsatogo*, 1971 (*August 1914*, 1972); *Lenin v Tsyurikhe*, 1975 (*Lenin in Zurich*, 1976); *Krasnoe kolesco* (includes *Avgust chetyrnadtsatogo*, expanded version, 1983 [*The Red Wheel*, 1989]; *Oktiabr' shestnadtsatogo*, 1984 [*October 1916*, 1999]; *Mart semnadtsatogo*, 1986-1988; *Aprel' semnadtsatogo*, 1991); *Oktiabr' shestnadtsatogo*, 1984 (*October 1916*, 1999); *Mart semnadtsatogo*, 1986-1988; *Aprel' semnadtsatogo*, 1991).

PLAYS: *Olen'i shalashovka*, pb. 1968 (*The Love Girl and the Innocent*, 1969; also known as *Respublika truda*); *Svecha na vetru*, pb. 1968 (*Candle in the Wind*, 1973); *Dramaticheskaya trilogiya-1945: Pir pobediteley*, pb. 1981 (*Victory Celebrations*, 1983); *Plenniki*, pb. 1981 (*Prisoners*, 1983).

SCREENPLAYS: *Znayut istinu tanki*, 1981; *Tuneyadets*, 1981.

POETRY: *Etyudy i krokhotnye rasskazy*, 1964 (trans. in *Stories and Prose Poems by Alexander Solzhenitsyn*, 1971); *Prusskie nochi*, 1974 (*Prussian Nights*, 1977).

NONFICTION: *Les Droits de l'écrivain*, 1969; *Nobelevskaya lektsiya po literature 1970 goda*, 1972 (*The Nobel Lecture*, 1973); *A Lenten Letter to Pimen, Patriarch of All Russia*, 1972; *Solzhenitsyn: A Pictorial Autobiography*, 1972; *Arkhipelag GULag, 1918-1956: Opyt khudozhestvennogo issledovaniya*, 1973-1975 (*The Gulag Archipelago, 1918-1956: An Experiment in Literary Investigation*, 1974-1978); *Iz-pod glyb*, 1974 (*From Under the Rubble*, 1975); *Pis'mo vozhdyam Sovetskogo Soyuza*, 1974 (*Letter to Soviet Leaders*, 1974); *Bodalsya telyonok s dubom*, 1975 (*The Oak and the Calf*, 1980); *Amerikanskiye rechi*, 1975; *Warning to the West*, 1976; *East and West*, 1980; *The Mortal Danger: How Misconceptions About Russia Imperil America*, 1980; *Kak nam obustroit' Rossiiu?: Posil'nye soobrazheniia*, 1990 (*Rebuilding Russia: Reflections and Tentative Proposals*, 1991); *Russkii vopros*, 1994 (*The Russian Question: At the End of the Twentieth Century*, 1994); *Invisible Allies*, 1995.

MISCELLANEOUS: *Sochineniya*, 1966; *Stories and Prose Poems by Alexander Solzhenitsyn*, 1971; *Six Etudes by Aleksandr Solzhenitsyn*, 1971; *Mir i nasiliye*, 1974; *Sobranie sochinenii*, 1978-1983 (10 volumes); *Izbrannoe*, 1991.

BIBLIOGRAPHY

Emerson, Caryl. "The Word of Aleksandr Solzhenitsyn." *The Georgia Review* 49 (Spring, 1995): 64-74. A critical overview of Solzhenitsyn's achievement; discusses why the Russian literary word has been so inescapably political for most of Russian history—and thus why Solzhenitsyn understands that to be a Russian writer is to be more powerful than a holder of a political post.

Ericson, Edward E., Jr. *Solzhenitsyn and the Modern World*. Washington, D.C.: Regnery Gateway, 1993. An examination of the reputation of Solzhenitsyn in the West that tries to clear up previous misunderstandings. Argues that Solzhenitsyn has never been antidemocratic and that his criticisms of the West have been made in the spirit of love, not animosity.

_____. *Solzhenitsyn: The Moral Vision*. Grand Rapids, Mich.: William B. Eerdman's, 1980. An analysis of Solzhenitsyn's work from the point of view of his Christian vision. After a discussion of

Solzhenitsyn's theory of art as enunciated in his Nobel Prize lecture, Ericson provides chapters on the major novels as well as the short stories and prose poems.

Feuer, Kathryn, ed. *Solzhenitsyn*. Englewood Cliffs, N.J.: Prentice-Hall, 1976. A collection of thirteen essays. The articles illuminate Solzhenitsyn as a writer, which, in turn, inform readers' understanding of his works, including short fiction. In this connection, Robert Louis Jackson's "'Matryona's Home': The Making of a Russian Icon" offers some keen interpretations of the story.

Kobets, Svitlana. "The Subtext of Christian Asceticism in Aleksandr Solzhenitsyn's *One Day in the Life of Ivan Denisovich*." *Slavic and East European Journal* 42 (Winter, 1998): 661-676. Discusses Christian asceticism in the novella. Notes visual images, linguistic formulas, and conventional symbols in the text that give the book a religious dimension.

Lottridge, Stephen S. "Solzhenitsyn and Leskov." *Russian Literature Triquarterly* 6 (1973): 478-489. In this comparative essay, Lottridge examines Solzhenitsyn's debt to Russia's greatest storyteller, Nikolai Leskov. He sees the connection in Solzhenitsyn's creation of "Christian" and righteous characters, especially in "Matryona's Home" and in the use of *skaz* technique.

Ragsdale, Hugh. "The Solzhenitsyn That Nobody Knows." *The Virginia Quarterly Review* 71 (Autumn, 1995): 634-641. Discusses the story "Matryona's Home" as an account of the author's return from his first exile in the Gulag; shows how the story is also a statement of the code of values of the Slavophile creed and an allegorical history of Russia in fictional form.

Scammel, Michael. *Solzhenitsyn*. New York: W. W. Norton, 1989. This exhaustive but lively biography deals with practically all important aspects of Solzhenitsyn's life. Unfortunately, his works, especially the short fiction, are not discussed at great length.

_____, ed. *The Solzhenitsyn Files*. Chicago: Edition q, 1995. A carefully edited documentation of Solzhenitsyn's struggles with Soviet literary and political authorities.

Thomas, D. M. *Alexander Solzhenitsyn: A Century in His Life*. New York: St. Martin's Press, 1998. An imaginative, well-documented, and at times combative biography of Solzhenitsyn. It includes discussion of his return to Russia in 1994.

Zekulin, Gleb. "Solzhenitsyn's Four Stories." *Soviet Studies* 16, no. 1 (1964): 45-62. In this compact and authoritative essay, Zekulin discusses "Matryona's House," "Incident at Krechetovka Station," "We Never Make Mistakes," and "One Day in the Life of Ivan Denisovich," which Zekulin treats as a short story rather than as a novel.

Mitzi M. Brunsdale, updated by
Vasa D. Mihailovich

SUSAN SONTAG

Born: New York, New York; January 16, 1933

PRINCIPAL SHORT FICTION

I, Etcetera, 1978

OTHER LITERARY FORMS

Susan Sontag has published a number of novels, including *The Benefactor* (1963), *Death Kit* (1967), *The Volcano Lover* (1992), *In America* (2000), and several collections of essays, including *Against Interpretation* (1966), *Styles of Radical Will* (1969), *On Photography* (1977), *Illness as Metaphor* (1978), *Under the Sign of Saturn* (1980), and *AIDS and Its Metaphors* (1989). She has published a play, *Alice in Bed* (1993), and the screenplays *Duet for Cannibals* (1969) and *Brother Carl* (1972).

ACHIEVEMENTS

Susan Sontag has been the recipient of many awards and honorary degrees, including the Arts and Letters Award of the American Academy of Arts and Letters and a National Book Critics Circle Award for *Illness as Metaphor*. In 1990, she received a John D. and Catherine T. MacArthur Foundation Fellowship, and in 1993 Harvard University awarded her an honorary degree.

BIOGRAPHY

Born Susan Rosenblatt in New York City on January 16, 1933, Sontag, her younger sister, and their mother moved to Tucson, Arizona, in 1939, shortly after her father died. Sontag attended local schools in Tucson. Her mother remarried in 1945. The family moved to Southern California, where Sontag took her stepfather's last name and attended North Hollywood High School.

A precocious student, Sontag graduated from high school at the age of fifteen. After spending a semester at the University of California at Berkeley, she transferred to the University of Chicago, earning a B.A. degree in two years and marrying Philip Rieff, a sociology professor. The couple moved to Cambridge,

Massachusetts, where Sontag began work on a graduate degree at Harvard and Rieff taught at Brandeis University. After a year of study abroad at Oxford University and the Sorbonne, Sontag returned to the United States in 1959, divorcing Rieff and taking custody of their son, born in 1952.

In New York City, Sontag taught at Columbia University and other schools while writing her first novel. It was the publication of her essays, however, that brought her recognition as a new young critic with provocative ideas. She quickly established herself as a cultural commentator and independent intellectual. She quit teaching in 1964 and has made her living as a writer, lecturer, and filmmaker.

ANALYSIS

Susan Sontag's fiction has often been linked with that of the French New Novel, advocated and practiced by Alain Robbe-Grillet and Natalie Sarraute. These novelists rejected the conventions of realistic fiction; they did not create lifelike characters and compelling plots. Rather, they wanted to promulgate a view of literature as a contrivance, a calculated construction of an independent world. Literature did not imitate reality; literature created its own reality, its own reason for being.

Sontag found the New Novelists compelling because the American fiction of her period (the 1950's) seemed stale. Novelists seemed to have nothing new to say about their environment or about the form of fiction itself. A good example of Sontag's effort to create a new kind of fiction is her story "American Spirits," collected in *I, Etcetera*. Essentially the story is a satire about the boredom of American middle-class life. Instead of documenting the life of realistic characters, Sontag turns her fiction into an allegory, naming her main character "Miss Flatface," a name that suggests a person with no dimension, a person who lacks a rounded, enriching life. Miss Flatface forsakes her family and embarks on a flamboyant life with Mr. Obscenity.

By making her characters types or symbols of

Susan Sontag in 1967 (Library of Congress)

"American Spirits" Sontag attempts to broaden the focus of American fiction, making it less concerned with the minute particulars of individual lives and more perceptive about the broad patterns of cultural behavior. Miss Flatface, for example, is looking for thrills, entertainment, and a sense of destiny that is continuously alluded to in the story as Sontag mentions such classic American strivers as Benjamin Franklin, Abraham Lincoln, and John F. Kennedy.

Sontag's fiction is often about the narrator's or writer's dilemma: How to be creative, how to find the proper structure for a story, a story which is often an account of the writer's own perceptions. Thus Sontag's stories tend to be autobiographical. "Project for a Trip to China," for example, reads like a diary of her feelings about her father and mother, and "Baby," she has admitted in interviews, is partly a reminiscence of how she and her husband responded as parents of their son David.

"PROJECT FOR A TRIP TO CHINA"

The lead story in *I, Etcetera* deals with the narrator's anticipation of a journey that will take her, for the first time, to the land where her father died. Rather than presenting a narrative of her feelings about her father, the narrator jots down her earliest memories involved with hearing about China from her mother, who brought back souvenirs from her stays in the country with her husband. The narrator tries to re-create her sense of China, of her father, of her family, from these tokens of the past. Ultimately she concludes that the real "trip" is the one she has taken in her imagination, for as she says at the end of her story, "Perhaps I will write the book about my trip to China before I go."

This final sentence provides the clue that what Sontag is most interested in as a writer is how she can transform the raw materials of life into a story. "Project for a Trip to China" is unique in her collection because it reads like the listing of the raw materials themselves, the fragments that she tries to fuse into fiction.

"DEBRIEFING"

The second story in *I, Etcetera* reads more like a continuous narrative. The narrator mourns the loss of her best friend, Julia, an intense thinker who troubles herself about the meaning of existence. Is life coherent? If not, then all is chaos and meaninglessness. However, if everything in life that happens is meant to happen, then everything is determined, and there is not much reason to assert oneself—and not much reason, in Julia's case, to go on living. The narrator, also a serious thinker, nevertheless tries to humor Julia out of the black moods that isolate her from the world. The narrator points out that some questions just cannot be answered and do not bear thinking about.

Once a question is asked, however, it is difficult not to want an answer. This is as true for the narrator as it is for Julia. Thus the narrator weaves into her reminiscence the stories of several women named Doris. Each Doris leads a separate life, yet elements of their stories suggest that they may be linked in ways the narrator cannot understand. The narrator's inability to understand is, in fact, linked to the fact that Julia (as the end of the story reveals) commits suicide. The narrator is as powerless to prevent Julia's death as she is to understand how the stories of the different Dorises are linked.

The term "debriefing," which refers to questioning or interrogating someone to extract information, serves as an ironic title for the story. The narrator tries to explore what the story of Julia, of the different Dorises means, but the interrogation does not result in knowledge; rather, the knowledge obtained is about the heartbreaking ambiguity of life and the difficulty of warding off despair.

"THE DUMMY"

The fourth story in *I, Etcetera*, coming after "American Spirits," "The Dummy" is another version of Sontag's playing with the idea of shifting identities. The narrator, who does not name himself, is like Miss Flatface in "American Spirits," bored with his middle-class family life. To relieve himself of his responsibilities at home and at work, he employs a dummy who is an exact copy of himself and who is able to do everything the narrator does. The trouble is that the dummy falls in love with a woman at the narrator's office and demands precisely the sort of freedom that the narrator coveted for himself in employing the dummy in the first place. The narrator's solution is to employ yet a second dummy who seems better suited to the job.

Given the story's title, it seems appropriate to ask who is the "dummy." Obviously it is the replacement self the narrator employs, but is it also the narrator? Is he as happy with his solution, as he suggests at the end of the story? Or is he rationalizing? In other words, the form of the story expresses the narrator's seeming complacency about using a dummy, yet the form also leaves open the possibility that perhaps the narrator is a dummy for fooling himself into thinking he has found a happy solution to his problems. Certainly the narrator's final words seem too pat, too self-satisfied, to be believed without qualification, for he congratulates himself for "having solved in so equitable and responsible a manner the problems of this one poor short life that was allotted me." Yet his vaunted freedom seems to consist in not much more than allowing himself to lead an indolent life and to affect a "shabby appearance." What exactly has he accomplished?

"BABY"

The sixth story in *I, Etcetera*, concerns an unnamed couple's worries about their precocious son. They are bringing him up to be a genius, but they are concerned about his willful nature. They want him to be independent, yet they want him under their control. These parents are, in short, befuddled by their contradictions, and they have come to a psychiatrist for help in sorting out how they should bring up their baby.

The entire story is told through the words of the two frustrated parents. The psychiatrist's advice is alluded to in their responses. Like their child, they behave in contradictory fashion. That is, they come seeking advice but they reject it almost as soon as the psychiatrist offers it. Just as they try to shape their son's responses, they try to manipulate the psychiatrist.

"Baby" is about the tyranny of family life and about the power relationships that infest the parent-child relationship. It is also, on a simpler level, an account of anxious parents who mean well and yet do devastating things to their child. Like the other stories in *I, Etcetera*, "Baby" is not realistic. It does not give characters names or spend much time describing settings. However, the story deals with real issues in the same way that a dream or a fantasy does. Thus when the parents tell the psychiatrist that they have begun cutting off their son's limbs, they are expressing the desire to hobble a child, to keep him a "baby," that parents can sometimes express in less extreme forms.

OTHER MAJOR WORKS

LONG FICTION: *The Benefactor*, 1963; *Death Kit*, 1967; *The Volcano Lover*, 1992; *In America*, 2000.

NONFICTION: *Against Interpretation and Other Essays*, 1966; *Trip to Hanoi*, 1968 (journalism); *Styles of Radical Will*, 1969; *On Photography*, 1977; *Illness as Metaphor*, 1978; *Under the Sign of Saturn*, 1980; *AIDS and Its Metaphors*, 1989.

PLAY: *Alice in Bed: A Play in Eight Scenes*, pb. 1993.

SCREENPLAYS: *Duet for Cannibals*, 1969; *Brother Carl*, 1972; *Promised Lands*, 1974; *Unguided Tour*, 1983.

EDITED TEXTS: *Selected Writings*, 1976 (by Antonin Artaud); *A Barthes Reader*, 1982.

MISCELLANEOUS: *A Susan Sontag Reader*, 1982.

BIBLIOGRAPHY

Bruss, Elizabeth W. *Beautiful Theories: The Spectacle of Discourse in Contemporary Criticism*. Baltimore, Md.: The Johns Hopkins University Press, 1982. A thorough exploration of Sontag's essays and screenplays, with discussions of her theory of literature that contribute greatly to an understanding of the aims of her short fiction.

Kennedy, Liam. *Susan Sontag: Mind as Passion*. Manchester: Manchester University Press, 1995. A detailed study of Sontag's career. Kennedy is especially insightful about the intellectual influences on Sontag's writing. His book includes discussions of individual stories.

Poague, Leland, ed. *Conversations with Susan Sontag*. Jackson: University Press of Mississippi, 1995. An indispensable guide to Sontag's writing. Not only do her interviews contain many illuminating remarks about her short fiction, but also Poague's introduction and chronology provide the best introduction to Sontag's work as a whole.

Sayres, Sohnya. *Susan Sontag: The Elegiac Modernist*. New York: Routledge, 1990. Sayres's introduction and biographical chapter provide significant insight into the background of Sontag's short fiction. Sayres also discusses individual stories, but her jargon will prove difficult to the beginning student of Sontag's work.

Vidal, Gore. *United States Essays 1952-1992*. New York: Random House, 1993. Contains essays on the French New Novel and on Sontag's second novel, *Death Kit*. Although Vidal does not discuss Sontag's short fiction, his lucid explanation of the New Novel and of Sontag's theory of fiction provide an excellent framework for studying the stories in *I, Etcetera*.

Carl Rollyson

MURIEL SPARK

Born: Edinburgh, Scotland; February 1, 1918

PRINCIPAL SHORT FICTION

The Go-Away Bird and Other Stories, 1958
Voices at Play, 1961
Collected Stories I, 1967
Bang-Bang You're Dead and Other Stories, 1983
The Stories of Muriel Spark, 1985
Open to the Public: New and Collected Stories, 1997

OTHER LITERARY FORMS

Muriel Spark is known primarily for her novels and short fiction, but her body of work also includes works of nonfiction, children's literature, poetry, film adaptations, and radio plays. She began her career writing news articles as a press agent. Later she expanded her range to include works of poetry and literary criticism, contributing poems, articles, and reviews to magazines and newspapers, occasionally using the pseudonym Evelyn Cavallo. Spark published her first short story in 1951. In 1954, she began writing novels, her best known being *The Prime of Miss Jean Brodie*.

ACHIEVEMENTS

Muriel Spark's honors and awards include the Prix Italia (1962) for her radio play adaptation of *The Ballad of Peckham Rye* (1960); the Yorkshire Post Book of the Year Award (1965) and the James Tait Black Memorial Prize (1966), both for *The Mandelbaum Gate* (1965); Commander, Order of the British Empire (1967); the Booker McConnell Prize nomination (1981) for *Loitering with Intent* (1981); the Scottish Book of the Year Award (1987) for The Stories of Muriel Spark; Officier de l'Ordre des Arts et des Lettres (1988); the Ingersoll T. S. Elliot Award (1992); Dame, Order of the British Empire (1993); and the

Muriel Spark (©Jerry Bauer)

David Cohen British Literature Prize for Lifetime Achievement (1997).

BIOGRAPHY

Muriel Sarah Spark, née Camberg, was born and educated in Edinburgh, Scotland. In 1937, she went to Rhodesia. During her stay in Africa, she married S. O. Spark but was divorced a short time later. She has one child, her son Robin. Spark's parents, Bernard and Sarah Elizabeth Camberg, held diverse religious faiths; her father was Jewish, while her mother was Presbyterian. Spark practiced the Anglican faith until her interest in the writings of John Henry Newman, a nineteenth century Catholic theologian, convinced her to convert to Catholicism in 1954. Her personal search for spiritual belief is reflected in many of the themes of her fiction. Consequently her works often express some moral or spiritual truth.

Spark spent several years living in British colonies in Central Africa. In 1944, she returned to England. During the war years, she wrote news articles for the political intelligence department of the British government. After the war, she held various posts in the publishing field, including a position as founder of the short-lived literary magazine *The Forum*. In the early 1950's, Spark began to produce serious work in literary criticism and poetry. Hand and Flower Press published her first volume of poetry in 1952. At the same time, she was involved in editing and researching critical and biographical work on several nineteenth century literary figures, including William Wordsworth, Mary Wollstonecraft Shelley, and Emily Brontë.

Spark's initial attempt at fiction writing received considerable attention when her short story "The Seraph and the Zambesi" won top honors in a writing contest in 1951. She was encouraged to expand the scope of her fiction in 1954, when Macmillan, Spark's publisher, persuaded her to write a full-length novel. At the same time that Spark began to develop a technique for composing a novel, she was also struggling with her religious beliefs and her decision to convert to Catholicism. Consequently, her first novel, *The Comforters*, completed in 1957, examines theological issues, reflecting Spark's own private search for a belief that was consistent with her personal need for an adequate faith during the time that she was writing the novel. The link between her conception of the world, both physically and spiritually, and the subjects of her fiction is evident in her later novels as well.

Spark presents facts about her life and the beginnings of her writing career in her autobiography, *Curriculum Vitae* (1992).

ANALYSIS

Muriel Spark is an adept storyteller with a narrative voice that is often distant or aloof. Her tales are psychologically interesting because Spark is reluctant to reveal all that her characters think and feel; in consequence, readers are forced to evaluate the stories, think about issues from a different perspective, and try to fill in the gaps. Critics regard Spark's novels as her strongest genre, but her short stories are also well constructed and intriguing. Her volumes of short stories, published over four decades contain many of the same stories reprinted, with new stories added to each new edition.

Spark's tales are often set in England, British colonies in Africa, or European locations. Her works reflect a sense of moral truth, which some critics view as the influence of her conversion to Catholicism in 1954. Her narrative is rarely wordy. The story line relies on the impressions and dialogue of the characters or narrator to convey the plot. She makes frequent use of first-person narrative, but none of her voices "tells all." One of the distinguishing elements in Spark's style is her penchant for leaving gaps that her readers must fill for themselves.

"THE SERAPH AND THE ZAMBESI"

Spark's first short story, "The Seraph and the Zambesi," won an award in a Christmas contest sponsored by *The Observer* in 1951. In characteristic Spark style, this story does not mince words but focuses on action and sparse dialogue. Set in Africa at Christmastime, the story portrays the events surrounding preparations for a Christmas pageant. Besides sweltering temperatures, curious natives, and preoccupied performers, the presentation is "hindered" by the presence of a heavenly Seraph, complete with six wings and a heat-producing glow. The writer of the nativity play is incensed when a real angel appears. He expresses rage rather than awe and destroys the stage in his attempts to banish the Seraph. Though Spark refuses to offer a moral at the close of "The Seraph and the Zambesi," the story resembles a parable, illustrating the egocentrism of human beings, especially "artists." The narrative also serves as a metaphor for the definition of genuine "art."

A related story dealing with art and creativity is entitled "The Playhouse Called Remarkable." This story, published several years after "The Seraph and the Zambesi," features a character named Moon Biglow. Moon confesses to the narrator that he is really a native of the moon who migrated to Earth on the "Downfall of [the] Uprise" some time in the distant past. His primary mission was to save earth's residents from suffocating aesthetic boredom. It seems human beings had no form of recreation other than that of gathering in groups to chant "Tum tum ya" each evening. The moon migrants organize the "play-

house called Remarkable" to offer alternative entertainment and also to give earthlings a creative outlet for their imaginations.

"THE PAWNBROKER'S WIFE"

Often Spark's short fiction depicts varied types of female personalities. These stories, narrated in first person and set in Africa, tell little about the narrators themselves but focus on the manipulative power of the central female characters. In "The Pawnbroker's Wife," the narrator tells the story of Mrs. Jan Cloote, who is never identified by her first name. Her pawnbroker husband has disappeared, and Mrs. Cloote carries on the business herself but denies the slightly sordid reputation of her vocation by claiming that she is only the pawnbroker's wife. Thus, in her name and her speech, she tries the separate her actions from her image. Such "distancing" allows Mrs. Cloote freedom in refusing to accept responsibility for her conduct, no matter how cruel or petty, as she performs the duties of a pawnbroker (and ironically she is far more successful in business than her husband had been.) She uses a show of politeness to remain corrupt without having to admit fault or make concessions. She breaks her promises to customers and sells the pawned items of her friends at the first opportunity. Mrs. Cloote's poor taste, grasping manipulation, and innocent pretense give her character an insidious cast. Yet the narrator who reveals these facts refuses to pass judgment regarding Mrs. Cloote's morality. That matter is left to the reader.

"A CURTAIN BLOWN BY THE BREEZE"

In a similar story, Sonia Van der Merwe, the female protagonist in "The Curtain Blown by the Breeze," gains power over her domain in the absence of her husband. Mr. Van der Merwe, who lives in the remote territory of Fort Beit, is imprisoned for fatally shooting a young native boy who was a Peeping Tom. While her husband's conviction and imprisonment might have prompted a feeling of tragedy, the opposite occurs. Sonia finds that she has considerable financial resources at her disposal with her husband gone. Like Mrs. Cloote, Sonia takes charge, encouraged on by the British medical women serving in the colony. She soon learns to use her feminine wiles to access power and control in Fort Beit. The male British medical workers seek her attention, captivated by her "eccentric grandeur." Much to the chagrin of the British women who helped to create the "new Sonia," Sonia gains influence even over government officials. Just as the English nurse, however, who narrates the story can never truly decide what she wants, the same applies to Sonia. At the close of the story, Mr. Van der Merwe returns from prison unexpectedly. When he discovers his wife Sonia in the company of another man, he shoots them both. Thus, Sonia and her image are quickly eliminated. In her stories, Spark explores the roles of greedily ambitious females, the irony of their plight, and their cloaks of politeness.

Often Spark deals with themes of childhood or adolescent memories in her short fiction. She may contrast the innocent but terrifyingly real fears of children with the more serious cruelty of adults or reverse the irony and explore the cruelty of "devilish" children, who are shielded by a guise of adult politeness. For example, "The Twins" is a story about two seemingly polite children who exercise some invisible but insidious control over their parents and other adults who enter their household.

"THE PORTOBELLO ROAD" AND "BANG-BANG YOU'RE DEAD"

"The Portobello Road" and "Bang-Bang You're Dead" juxtapose the childhood memories of two young girls with their lives as "grown-ups." These stories explore the serious ramifications of situations in which childish conceptions or antagonisms are transferred into adulthood. Both stories are examples of Muriel Spark's ability to create unique narrative forms. "The Portobello Road" is narrated by Needle, a young girl whose childhood nickname was given to her because she found a needle in a haystack. When the story opens, Needle is dead and her ghostly voice chronicles the events that led to her murder—when she becomes the "Needle" who is murdered and buried in a haystack by a childhood friend.

"Bang-Bang You're Dead" connects the present and the past in a complex narrative using a series of flashbacks. In the present, represented in the story's opening scene, a group of Sybil's friends gather to view four reels of eighteen-year-old films from Sybil's past years spent in Africa. As the group views

the "silent movies," the third-person narrative reveals Sybil's memories—not those seen by the spectators of the film but as Sybil remembers them. As each reel ends, Sybil's mental narrative is interrupted by the surface chatter of her friends, who are impressed by the appearance of the people and exotic scenes revealed in the film. When the final reel ends, the reader finds, through Sybil's mental recollections, that two murders were committed shortly after the scenes were recorded on film. As the acquaintances agree to view the last reel again because it is their "favorite," Sybil remains stoically unmoved by the memories of the tragedy. Her indifference and objectivity regarding the memories of her deceased friends reveal a chilling aspect of her personality. Coldly intellectual and detached, Sybil remains indifferent and unmoved by the recorded memories even though she was largely responsible for the murders.

"THE GO-AWAY BIRD" AND "THE FIRST YEAR OF MY LIFE"

"The Go-Away Bird" is one of the longest of Spark's stories. It is also about a woman and murder. Daphne, the central female figure, is reared in a British colony in Africa. Caught between two cultures, that of the Dutch Afrikaners and the English colonists, Daphne searches for her identity—for a world in which she can not only belong but also find safety. Set in Africa and England during World War II, "The Go-Away Bird" presents characters who reflect diverse backgrounds, personalities, motivations, and societies. Daphne's struggles and her relationship with the African Go-Away Bird illustrate an individual's difficulty in trying to fulfill one's need for love and identity within diverse cultural and social structures.

At the opposite end of the spectrum, "The First Year of My Life" does not struggle with maturing in society but presents the first-person commentary of an infant, born during World War I. The adults who care for the baby treat the child as an "innocent infant," unaware of the newborn's ability to grasp the tragedy of war. Such diversity in narrative voice, subject, and style is a trademark of Muriel Spark. As a writer, she avoids classification and is unafraid of experimentation.

OPEN TO THE PUBLIC: NEW AND COLLECTED STORIES

Spark's collection *Open to the Public* contains ten stories not included in the previous volume, *The Stories of Muriel Spark* (1985). The title story "Open to the Public" is a sequel to "The Fathers' Daughters." "The Fathers' Daughters" centers on a thirty-year-old intellectual, Ben, who pursues the daughters of famous writers in order to meet the authors themselves. When the young, beautiful Carmelita is unable to gain an audience for Ben with her father, a successful novelist, Ben abandons her to marry Dora, the forty-six-year-old daughter of an aged author whose popularity has faded. Spark creates an ironic situation in which the characters use one another for their own purposes. Ben wants to write essays based on another author's work; Dora's father craves an audience for his forgotten books; and Dora needs someone to provide income for their impoverished household.

The sequel "Open to the Public" presents Ben and Dora five years later. Dora's father dies, but Ben's promotion of his works restores the family's fortune. However, the dead man's memory is not enough to sustain the relationship; the couple separate. Their plans to open the writer's house and personal documents to the public are abandoned when both Ben and Dora realize that museums "have no heart." In a humorous turn, they burn the father's archives instead. The story demonstrates the hopelessness of trying to maintain perpetual fame, and the futility of attempting to build one's future on another's achievements.

In a story with similar elements "The Executor," the protagonist Susan, who is a middle-aged spinster like Dora, must dispose of her uncle's literary estate. She sells his papers to a university foundation but retains an unfinished manuscript which she hopes to complete and publish as her own. However, her plans are thwarted when her uncle's ghost returns to write warning messages to her. Thus Susan, like the women in "The Father's Daughters," must abandon her schemes to find success vicariously and learn to build her own future.

The remaining additions in the *Open to the Public* collection are stylized and brief. Some plots turn on a single ironic twist as in "The Girl I Left Behind Me" when the narrator finds her own body "lying strangled on the floor." Other stories feature the troubling imposition of the supernatural into the natural world. For example, in "The Pearly Shadow" a shady specter haunts the staff and patients in a medical clinic. The specter finally disappears when doctors begin dispensing sedatives to his "stressed-out" victims. "Going Up and Coming Down" is a poetic vignette about a man and woman who ride to work in the same elevator every day. Once the couple actually meet, their speculations about each other disappear in the face of "plain real facts."

The stories included in *Open to the Public* demonstrate Spark's mastery of the short-story form. Her plots expose human foibles with an ironic, mysterious, or sarcastic tone. She is adept at illustrating the slightly macabre or deceitful nature of human actions. Her characters may be subtly malevolent or sinisterly civilized, but evil is punished and hypocrisy exposed in Spark's comic tales.

OTHER MAJOR WORKS

LONG FICTION: *The Comforters*, 1957; *Robinson*, 1958; *Memento Mori*, 1959; *The Ballad of Peckham Rye*, 1960; *The Bachelors*, 1960; *The Prime of Miss Jean Brodie*, 1961; *A Muriel Spark Trio*, 1962 (contains *The Comforters, Memento Mori*, and *The Ballad of Peckham Rye*); *The Girls of Slender Means*, 1963; *The Mandelbaum Gate*, 1965; *The Public Image*, 1968; *The Driver's Seat*, 1970; *Not to Disturb*, 1971; *The Hothouse by the East River*, 1973; *The Abbess of Crewe: A Modern Morality Tale*, 1974; *The Takeover*, 1976; *Territorial Rights*, 1979; *Loitering with Intent*, 1981; *The Only Problem*, 1984; *A Far Cry from Kensington*, 1988; *Symposium*, 1990; *The Novels of Muriel Spark*, 1995; *Reality and Dreams*, 1996.

PLAY: *Doctors of Philosophy*, pr. 1962.

POETRY: *The Fanfarlo and Other Verse*, 1952; *Collected Poems I*, 1967 (published as *Going Up to Sotheby's and Other Poems*, 1982).

NONFICTION: *Child of Light: A Reassessment of Mary Wollstonecraft Shelley*, 1951 (rev. as *Mary Shelley*, 1987); *Emily Brontë: Her Life and Work*,

1953 (with Derek Stanford); *John Masefield*, 1953; *Curriculum Vitae*, 1992 (autobiography); *The Essence of the Brontës: A Compilation with Essays*, 1993.

CHILDREN'S LITERATURE: *The Very Fine Clock*, 1968; *The Small Telephone*, 1993.

EDITED TEXT: *Tribute to Wordsworth*, 1950 (with Derek Standord); *My Best Mary: The Letters of Mary Shelley*, 1953 (with Derek Stanford); *The Letters of the Brontës: A Selection*, 1954 (pb. in England as *The Brönte Letters*, 1954); *Letters of John Henry Newman*, 1957 (with Derek Stanford).

BIBLIOGRAPHY

Bold, Alan. *Muriel Spark*. London: Methuen, 1986. Bold is concerned with the relationship between Spark's personal background and the development of her characters, particularly links between Spark's religious experience and the religious facets of her fiction. He includes biographical information, then discusses Spark's works in chronological order, specifically the novels. An extensive bibliography is included, listing criticism, articles, essays, interviews, and books related to Spark and her work.

_____, ed. *Muriel Spark: An Odd Capacity for Vision*. Totowa, N.J.: Barnes & Noble Books, 1984. Bold has compiled a collection of nine essays from different contributors, regarding various aspects of Spark's fiction. The volume is organized into two sections. The first four essays explore Spark's background and the content of her work. The remaining chapters contain critical articles centered on the diverse forms of Spark's writings, including discussions of her use of satire, her poetry, and an essay by Tom Hubbard that deals exclusively with her short stories.

Edgecombe, Rodney Stenning. *Vocation and Identity in the Fiction of Muriel Spark*. Columbia, Mo.: University of Missouri Press, 1990. A critical and historical study of the psychological in Scottish literature. Includes a bibliography and index.

Hynes, Joseph, ed. *Critical Essays on Muriel Spark*. New York: G. K. Hall, 1992. A comprehensive collection of reviews, essays, and excerpts from books on Spark's fiction, by both her detractors and her admirers. Includes autobiographical essays and a survey and critique of past criticism.

Little, Judy. "Muriel Spark's Grammars of Assent." In *The British and Irish Novel Since 1960*, edited by James Acheson. New York: St. Martin's Press, 1991. Argues that in Spark's fiction, characters often reject the steadying control of a notional assent and allow their personal obsessions to turn their lives to the freely imaginative. Asserts that most of her narrators distrust the presumption of realism and that her post-1960's fiction focuses more on text than on realistic character portrayal.

Randisi, Jennifer Lynn. *On Her Way Rejoicing: The Fiction of Muriel Spark*. Washington, D.C.: Catholic University of America Press, 1991. Argues that Spark's vision is metaphysical, combining piety and satire, deception and anagogical truth. Discusses the tension between mysticism and satire in Spark's novels and stories.

Richmond, Velma B. *Muriel Spark*. New York: Frederick Ungar, 1984. Richmond explores Spark's writing in terms of content and emphasis. Spark's novels, poetry, and short stories are discussed in relation to their themes rather than their chronology. The closing chapter includes a discussion of Spark's "comic vision." Richmond includes biographical material along with a detailed chronology, a bibliography, and an extensive index.

Spark, Muriel. *Curriculum vitae: Autobiography*. Boston: Houghton Mifflin, 1993. Spark examines her life and literary career.

Sproxton, Judy. *The Women of Muriel Spark*. New York: St. Martin's Press, 1992. Looks at the female characters in Sparks's fiction. Includes an index.

Stubbs, Patricia. *Muriel Spark*. Essex: Longman, 1973. Stubbs's essay deals with theme in Spark's novels, from *The Comforters* through *Not to Disturb*. She traces the chronological development of Spark's work, range, and attempts at experimentation. She criticizes Spark's sense of distance and failure to solve problems but praises her efforts to force readers to view the world in a new way.

Whittaker, Ruth. *The Faith and Fiction of Muriel Spark*. New York: St. Martin's Press, 1982. Whittaker's work elaborates on the diversity of Spark's themes, meanings, and purpose. The chapter divisions are organized according to topics—religion, style, structure, and form. The book is limited primarily to a discussion of Spark's novels. Whittaker includes a biographical section as well as an extensive bibliography, notes, and an index.

Paula M. Miller

ELIZABETH SPENCER

Born: Carrollton, Mississippi; July 19, 1921

PRINCIPAL SHORT FICTION

Ship Island and Other Stories, 1968
Marilee: Three Stories, 1981
The Stories of Elizabeth Spencer, 1981
Jack of Diamonds and Other Stories, 1988
On the Gulf, 1991

OTHER LITERARY FORMS

In addition to numerous short stories published in periodicals as well as in book-length collections, Elizabeth Spencer has produced several novels and novellas, including her best-known work, *The Light in the Piazza* (1960), which was made into a film. She has also written the novels *The Salt Line* (1984) and *The Night Travellers* (1991) and a memoir, *Landscapes of the Heart: A Memoir* (1998).

ACHIEVEMENTS

Elizabeth Spencer's artistic achievement has garnered her many awards during her lifetime, including a Women's Democratic Committee Award in 1949, a recognition award from the National Institute of Arts and Letters in 1952, the Richard and Hinda Rosenthal Foundation Award from the American Academy of Arts and Letters in 1957, a John Simon Guggenheim Memorial Foundation Fellowship in 1953, a McGraw-Hill fiction award in 1960, the Henry H. Bellamann Foundation Award for creative writing in 1968; an Award of Merit Medal for the short story from the American Academy of Arts and Letters in 1983, the Salem Award for Literature in 1992, the John Dos Passos Award for fiction in 1992, the North Carolina Governor's Award for Literature in 1994, the Corrington Award for Literature in 1997, and the Richard Wright Award for Literature in 1997. She was also a Kenyon College Fellow in Fiction in 1957, a Bryn Mawr College Donnelly Fellow in 1962, and a National Endowment for Arts grantee in literature in 1983 as well as a Senior Arts Award grantee by the National Endowment for Arts in 1988.

BIOGRAPHY

Elizabeth Spencer was born on July 19, 1921, in Carrollton, Mississippi, the daughter of Mary J. McCain Spencer and James L. Spencer, a businessman. Both her mother's and her father's families had lived in northern Mississippi for almost a century. Spencer's childhood was almost ideal for a writer. Her mother and her mother's family gave her a passion for books, and her father gave her a love of nature. During long summer visits to the McCain plantation, she developed an appreciation of the land. Meanwhile, like the character in her short stories who she says most resembles her, the intensely curious Marilee Summerall, Spencer was storing local legends and gossip. She would never lack material for her fiction, and even as a child, she had begun to write.

After graduating from her local high school, Spencer attended Belhaven College, a Presbyterian girls' school in Jackson, Mississippi. There, she edited a newspaper, won awards for fiction and poetry, and became a friend of Eudora Welty, who lived across the street from the college. Welty comments in her foreword to *The Stories of Elizabeth Spencer* that there was a seriousness and determination about Spencer that convinced Welty that she would indeed become a writer. After receiving her B.A., Spencer went to Vanderbilt University in Nashville, carrying with her a partially completed novel. While there, she encountered the scholar and writer Donald Davidson, who later helped her to get a book contract for the novel at the publishing firm Dodd, Mead. In 1948, the book was published under the title *Fire in the Morning*. After receiving her M.A. from Vanderbilt University in 1943, Spencer taught English at Northwest Mississippi Junior College in Senatobia and at Ward-Belmont College in Nashville, Tennessee. She also worked for a year as a reporter for the Nashville *Tennessean*. In 1948, she went to the University of Mississippi to teach creative writing while she worked on *This Crooked Way* (1952). After this second novel was published, Spencer was given an award by the National Institute of Arts and Letters, which enabled her to spend a summer in New York. In 1953, she went to Italy on a John Simon Guggenheim Memorial Foundation Fellowship. There, Spencer met and married an Englishman from Cornwall, John Arthur Blackwood Rusher, a language school director.

After five years in Italy, Spencer and Rusher moved to Montreal, Canada, where he had been offered a position. That city was to be their home for twenty-eight years. For most of that time, Spencer worked full time at her writing, publishing novels, novellas, and short stories at regular intervals. In 1976, however, she began to teach creative writing courses and conduct workshops at Concordia University in Montreal. In 1986, Spencer and her husband moved to Chapel Hill, North Carolina. There, she continued to write, while also teaching courses in creative writing at the University of North Carolina.

ANALYSIS

Elizabeth Spencer established herself as one of the major fiction writers of the Southern Renaissance, a writer whose subjects and preoccupations have kept pace with the times through which she has lived, while her style has remained unique. Throughout her career, Spencer has been particularly interested in the influence of memory, the sense of place, and the power of tradition in the life of the individual. Although in theme and complexity she reminds critics of fellow Mississippian William Faulkner and in subtlety of Henry James, no comparisons do justice to Spencer's art, for, as her readers inevitably realize, the voice in Spencer's fiction is unmistakably her own.

In terms of tone, Spencer's fiction might be described as a combination of disciplined detachment from her subject matter and passionate attachment to her southern roots, to lush, semitropical natural settings, to the rich language of born storytellers, and to the conviction that the past dwells in the present. Spencer is much admired for her craftsmanship, which enables her to handle complexities of time, memory, and imagination so deftly that the shifts of focus are almost imperceptible. It is this combination of intellectual power and disciplined skill that en-

Elizabeth Spencer (©Miriam Berkley)

sures Spencer permanent recognition as one of the important writers of her generation.

For the subject matter of her novels and novellas, Spencer often chooses issues tied to a particular place and time; for example, *The Voice at the Back Door* (1956) deals with changing attitudes toward race after World War II; *The Salt Line* (1984) describes the transformation of the Mississippi Gulf Coast after Hurricane Camille; and *The Night Travellers* (1991) examines the ongoing plight of Vietnam War activists. In most of Spencer's short stories, however, the narrative is less clearly dependent on a particular time in history. Instead, Spencer concentrates on a brief period in an individual's life, when that person comes to recognize some need or some truth.

The themes of Spencer's short stories remain constant from her earliest works to her later ones. One of these themes pits the demands for social conformity, often expressed in the family, against an individual's need for freedom; similarly, the conflict may be internalized, with the individual torn between two desires, one for security, the other for independence. A related theme is the search for identity, particularly by women, whose enslavement to conformity has been especially evident in the conservative South. In addition, there is always a moral element in a Spencer story; to her, evil is very real, and her characters make difficult choices between good and evil. Spencer also recognizes, however, the fact that fate, or chance, can restrict those choices. Finally, as a writer, she is conscious of the importance of imagination and memory as a part of life; these human faculties can torment or liberate her characters.

"The Little Brown Girl"

The imagination dominates the earliest story in *The Stories of Elizabeth Spencer*, "The Little Brown Girl." The story is told in the third person, but the point of view is limited to that of the seven-year-old white girl, Maybeth, who is charmed by a black man, Jim Williams, who works for her father. Maybeth loves Jim's stories, some of which she knows he invented. She chooses, however, to believe that he has a little girl who is going to come and play with her. Even though her parents tell her that Jim is not telling the truth, and even though she half knows it, Maybeth

lets herself think about the little girl and even gives Jim her own birthday money, supposedly to buy the little girl a dress. Prompted by Jim, she even sees a glimpse of her playmate in the yellow dress. At this point, frightened, Maybeth runs home to her mother's arms. What Spencer leaves unstated is the source of Maybeth's fear. Is it the fact that she can be so deceived by a friend, or is it that her imagination can be prompted to see the unseen? Obviously, Maybeth is too young to analyze her own reactions. Even with adult protagonists, Spencer frequently ends her short stories with this kind of uncertainty, which leaves room for the reader's interpretation.

"First Dark"

"First Dark" and "A Southern Landscape" illustrate the conflict between conformity and independence, the security to be found in family and home and the freedom to be experienced when one escapes. In "First Dark," Frances Harvey is surprised to find her elderly mother urging her marriage to Tommy Beavers, whose family background is distinctly inferior to that of the Harveys. In fact, Mrs. Harvey evidently commits suicide to make sure that she will not stand in the way of the marriage. What both Frances and Tommy know, however, is that the house in which Mrs. Harvey expected them to live would possess them and stifle them. At the end of the story, Tommy insists that Frances leave with him, and she chooses to do so.

"A Southern Landscape"

In "A Southern Landscape," however, the earliest of the Marilee Summerall stories, Spencer reveals her very real appreciation of those things that never change, symbolized by Windsor, an antebellum mansion in ruins, and by Foster Hamilton, whom Marilee is dating. Like the mansion, Foster has grace. He so admires Marilee's mother, his ideal of southern womanhood, that simply the suggestion of her presence can shock him into instant sobriety. Foster, too, is already in ruins, joyfully addicted to drink. Years later, when she tells the story, Marilee rejoices that some things have not changed, among them, the mansion Windsor, the heavenward-pointing hand on a Presbyterian church, and Foster's addiction. Obviously, Spencer is not arguing for alcoholism; her point, instead, has to do with permanence: "I feel the need of a land, of a sure terrain, of a sort of permanent landscape of the heart." Spencer does realize that this sense of a sure terrain may be one of the fringe benefits that comes with an assured place in society, such as that which is given at birth to a Harvey or a Summerall. Tommy Beavers knows that if he stays in the Harvey house, it will possess and govern him; he will become less than nothing.

"SHIP ISLAND"

Similarly, in "Ship Island: The Story of a Mermaid," one of the stories to which Spencer frequently refers, Nancy Lewis is painfully aware that she is, and always will be, an outsider in Mississippi Gulf Coast society. Her family has no money, no background, and no taste. Nancy is accepted by the young aristocrats only because one of them has chosen to sponsor her, and, even then, she must watch every word she says, every move she makes. As the story progresses, Nancy rebels against her own denial of her self. The subtitle, "The Story of a Mermaid," suggests that Nancy will die if she attempts to live outside her own natural element, where she can be free. To save herself, she runs off to New Orleans with a couple of men she has met. The action is heroic and potentially tragic; certainly it could have caused Nancy's death. When she returns home, however, she knows that she can never become a part of Gulf Coast society. Therefore she need not worry about being tempted to do something that she knows is wrong: to deny her own self in order to become socially and financially secure.

"KNIGHTS AND DRAGONS"

In an essay on Spencer, Elsa Nettels points out that, after the mid-1950's, the theme of women's search for their identity took on major importance in Spencer's fiction. The long short story "Knights and Dragons," which was expanded into a novella and published separately in 1965, is concerned with this issue. The title is significant: Trained from childhood to look for knights to rescue them from dragons, women often mistake selfish, destructive men for good, protective ones. Martha Ingram knows that the husband she divorced is determined to play psychological games with her, but she cannot resist reacting

when he decides to pull her strings, either with a letter from his lawyer or with carefully chosen clippings sent in the mail. Gordon Ingram is her dragon. When two other men help Martha to break free from Ingram's tyranny, she sees them as her chivalric knights, providentially appearing to protect their lady. Martha comes to understand, however, that life is not so simple. In their own benevolent way, these knights are as oppressive as her dragon husband. Like him, they demand the surrender of her identity; each has invented a role that she must play. That is the price of a knight's protection. At the end of the story, Martha realizes that she has freed herself from all roles. In a kind of death of the old self, she has become truly free.

"THE BUFORDS"

Although Spencer never resorts to simplistic delineations of good and evil, it is obvious that she believes in those opposing forces. Even though Gordon Ingram's friends find him delightful, he is clearly motivated by malice in his attempt to destroy Martha. There is a difference, however, between malice such as his and simple nonconformity, which seeks to harm no one. "The Bufords," for example, is the story of an unequal battle between a young schoolteacher and a large family of people who seem to live life simply for the joy of it. The teacher is determined to discipline the Buford children. Unable to make headway at school, she goes to see their parents. There, she discovers that the behavior that she has found outrageous is a source of pride to the rest of the family. The adults all find it wonderful that their offspring are the most irrepressible in school. The fact that there is no ill-will in the Buford temperament, however, is shown by the warm hospitality that they offer the teacher. Although they do not understand her, they forgive her for lashing out at their children. Actually, they consider her, and her way of thinking, simply a bit exotic, as if she were a member of another species or of another society. At the end of the story, the well-meaning teacher realizes not only that she has been defeated by the family at whose table she has just been entertained but also that she has been adopted by them, as an interesting if peculiar pet, like their possum in a cage.

"Jean-Pierre"

The sense of family, which is treated so comically in "The Bufords," is at the center of a very different narrative, set not in the Deep South but in Montreal. "Jean-Pierre" is a love story, in which a Protestant, English-speaking woman and a Catholic, French-speaking man marry and then begin to understand each other. After the couple have been married almost a year, Jean-Pierre Courtois disappears without any explanation to his young wife. Courageously, she gets a job, endures her loneliness, and waits until he returns. In the meantime, she picks up bits and pieces of knowledge about him and his people, enough to know that, for some reason, he had to go to his home. When Jean-Pierre returns, his wife is waiting. Despite being tempted to leave him, she has remained faithful. At that point, then, he is ready to change his emotional address and to establish a new home with her.

On the Gulf

Four of the short stories from *On the Gulf*, including "Ship Island," were reprinted from *The Stories of Elizabeth Spencer*, and a fifth was first published elsewhere. These stories are brought together with a previously unpublished story ("A Fugitive's Wife") and an evocative introduction by Spencer. Illustrated by a series of pen-and-ink drawings made in the 1940's by Gulf Coast artist Walter Anderson, the collection exhibits Spencer's love for the Gulf Coast as well as her love-hate relationship with the southern family. Although the title story is humorous, it links the collection thematically in its depiction of the desire of families to dictate the very thoughts of their children. In this brief tale, the family prepares for the annual visit of acquaintances from New Orleans, whom no one really likes. When young Mary Dee voices the opinion of all by wishing the Meades were gone before they have arrived, her mother rebukes her, "What are you trying to grow up to be? . . . Stop listening to us! Stop hearing anything we say!"

In "The Legacy," by contrast, Dottie Almond attempts to escape the tyranny of her aunts by taking an inheritance and going to Miami, where she meets an exciting young man. For a while, she blends into his social group, but on discovering that he has a dark secret, she decides to return to the confining society she had momentarily escaped. Mary's separation from her husband in the delicate "A Fugitive's Wife" is forced, and, though she attempts to reassure her husband that she and the baby are well, pain and loneliness pervade her being. In "Mr. McMillan" Aline and the late Mr. McMillan fulfill and resist the expectations their families place on them. Aline

> believed in self-knowledge, even though trying to find it in the bosom of a Mississippi family was like trying to find some object lost in a gigantic attic, when you really didn't know what you were looking for.

Like her, Mr. McMillan has come to New Orleans to lead life on his own terms. Upon his death he allows his family to bury him and then discover in his will that he wanted to be cremated and have one of his friends cast his ashes into the waters off Hawaii, where he had served during the war. As Aline relates the story of Mr. McMillan to her friend from Chicago, he senses her bitterness, which she attributes to her failure (whether to fulfill Mr. McMillan's wishes or her own is ambiguous).

The penultimate story, "Go South in the Winter" recounts the tale of an older wife vacationing alone and feeling a welcome detachment from life, when dreams of her son as a child intrude on her consciousness along with a radio announcement of a traffic accident that killed a man with her son's same last name. Overcome by emotion, she cannot make the young couple who have befriended her understand that her son was not killed. When she is able to clear the situation up with them she feels ready to engage herself in society again.

Most of Spencer's short stories are essentially optimistic. Her characters have proven their courage by being willing to seek understanding, both of themselves and of their relationship to their families and their societies. Spencer's protagonists, armed with understanding and courage, are ready to seek their destinies.

Other major works

LONG FICTION: *Fire in the Morning*, 1948; *This Crooked Way*, 1952; *The Voice at the Back Door*,

1956; *The Light in the Piazza*, 1960; *Knights and Dragons*, 1965; *No Place for an Angel*, 1967; *The Snare*, 1972; *The Salt Line*, 1984; *The Night Travellers*, 1991.

NONFICTION: *Landscapes of the Heart: A Memoir*, 1998.

BIBLIOGRAPHY

Entzminger, Betina. "Emotional Distance as Narrative Strategy in Elizabeth Spencer's Fiction." *The Mississippi Quarterly* 49 (Winter, 1995/1996): 73-87. Discusses emotional detachment in Spencer's fiction; argues that Spencer's female characters become separate and autonomous by repressing the emotion that traditionally binds them to their confining domestic roles; claims that Spencer involves the reader with the emotions that her characters hide from themselves.

Greene, Sally. "Mending Webs: The Challenge of Childhood in Elizabeth Spencer's Short Fiction." *Mississippi Quarterly* 49 (Winter, 1995/1996): 89-98. Argues that, as human relationships become more fragile in her fiction, Spencer repeatedly turns to the imaginative perspective of a child to mend and protect these relationships. However, because of social fragmentation, Spencer's children face increasingly difficult challenges in holding their world together.

Nettels, Elsa. "Elizabeth Spencer." In *Southern Women Writers: The New Generation*, edited by Tonette Bond Inge. Tuscaloosa: University of Alabama Press, 1990. This insightful essay draws on biographical details, as well as on comments in a number of published interviews with Spencer, in order to trace the development of her art and thought. The extensive annotations and the list of interviews in the bibliography are particularly helpful.

Phillips, Robert. "The Art of Fiction CX: Elizabeth Spencer." *The Paris Review* 31 (Summer, 1989): 184-213. A lengthy series of questions and answers assembled from Phillips's three interviews with Spencer, as well as from some questions submitted in written form. Focuses on her theories about writing and her personal approach to the practice of her craft. The essay contains some interesting comments about literary influences on her work. A one-page typed draft, with handwritten corrections, is printed opposite the initial page of the article.

Prenshaw, Peggy Whitman. *Elizabeth Spencer*. Boston: Twayne, 1985. An authoritative book-length study based on numerous interviews with the author and checked by her for factual accuracy. The novella *Knights and Dragons* and "Ship Island" are treated together; other short stories are discussed in another chapter. Contains a chronology and a helpful selected bibliography.

Roberts, Terry. "Mermaids, Angels, and Free Women: The Heroines of Elizabeth Spencer's Fiction." In *Women Writers of the Contemporary South*, edited by Peggy Whitman Prenshaw. Jackson: University Press of Mississippi, 1984. Argues that, in Spencer's later fiction, strong female heroines characteristically move from confusion through pain and dislocation to assertion of the self, courageously accepting the alienation that that implies.

_____. *Self and Community in the Fiction of Elizabeth Spencer*. Baton Rouge: Louisiana State University Press, 1994. Discusses a wide range of themes appearing in Spencer's fiction. Includes a bibliography and an index.

Spencer, Elizabeth. *Conversations with Elizabeth Spencer*. Edited by Peggy Whitman Prenshaw. Jackson: University Press of Mississippi, 1991. Interviews with Spencer about her writing and the representation of Mississippi in her work. Includes an index.

_____. "Elizabeth Spencer: The Southern Writer Optimistically Explores the Almost Impenetrable Mysteries of the Human Heart." Interview by Amanda Smith. *Publishers Weekly* 234 (September 9, 1988): 111-112. This interview took place after Spencer's return to the South, where she established a permanent residence. Focuses on Spencer's assessment of her own relationship with the South. Includes perceptive comments by the author about the stories in the collection *Jack of Diamonds and Other Stories*.

_____. "An Interview with Elizabeth Spencer." Interview by Betina Entzminger. *The Mississippi Quarterly* 47 (Fall, 1994): 599-618. Comments on the quality of detachment in *The Stories of Elizabeth Spencer* and on whether constantly writing in a hard, masculine style contributes to that detachment; discusses her handling of women protagonists, her feelings of empathy with her characters, and individual characters in her fiction.

Welty, Eudora. Foreword to *The Stories of Elizabeth Spencer*. Garden City, N.Y.: Doubleday, 1981. Welty offers a brief but significant description of her first meeting with Spencer and the friendship that developed between the two writers. Welty's succinct evaluation of Spencer as a writer who is both part of the southern tradition and uniquely herself is essential reading for students.

Winchell, Mark Royden. "A Golden Ball of Thread: The Achievement of Elizabeth Spencer." *The Sewanee Review* 97 (Fall, 1989): 581-586. In this overview of Spencer's fiction, Winchell argues that its excellence can be explained, at least in part, by two facts: that moral issues and moral decisions are inherently complex and that real independence can be attained only by someone who recognizes and accepts every human being's need for a memory of home.

Rosemary M. Canfield Reisman, updated by
Jaquelyn W. Walsh

JEAN STAFFORD

Born: Covina, California; July 1, 1915
Died: White Plains, New York; March 26, 1979

PRINCIPAL SHORT FICTION

Children Are Bored on Sunday, 1953
Bad Characters, 1964
The Collected Stories of Jean Stafford, 1969

OTHER LITERARY FORMS

Jean Stafford's first three books were novels, *Boston Adventure* (1944), *The Mountain Lion* (1947), and *The Catherine Wheel* (1952). She also published juvenile fiction and a short, book-length interview with the mother of Lee Harvey Oswald, *A Mother in History* (1966).

ACHIEVEMENTS

Although critics suggest that her insightful, carefully crafted fiction deserves more attention, Stafford is generally considered to be a minor writer. Best known for her more than forty short stories, which—like her novels—are largely autobiographical, Jean Stafford investigates the complexities of human nature and explores the powerlessness of women in society as a major theme. Her treatment of women has generally been viewed as a metaphor for universal human alienation in modern society.

Stafford's reputation as a fiction writer was established with the publication of *Boston Adventure* in 1944, the same year she was awarded a prize by *Mademoiselle*. Over the years, she received numerous other awards, including grants from the National Institute of Arts and Letters, the Guggenheim and Rockefeller foundations, and the National Press Club. She also received an O. Henry Memorial Award for her story "In the Zoo" in 1955 and the Pulitzer Prize for *The Collected Stories of Jean Stafford* in 1970.

BIOGRAPHY

Although born in California, where she spent part of her childhood, Jean Stafford grew up in Colorado, attended the University of Colorado (A.M., 1936), and did postgraduate work at the University of Heidelberg. Her father, at one time a reporter, had written a number of Western stories. After a year teaching at Stephens College in Missouri and then briefly at the

Writer's Workshop in Iowa, Stafford decided to focus on her own writing and moved to Boston. There she married poet Robert Lowell in 1940; they were divorced in 1948. After a short marriage to Oliver Jensen in 1950, Stafford married again in 1959—to A. J. Liebling, critic and columnist for *The New Yorker*. After Liebling's death in 1963, Stafford withdrew from the New York literary world and made her home in Springs, Long Island. There she lived, becoming more and more reclusive, until her death in 1979.

ANALYSIS

It is clear from a brief preface she wrote for *The Collected Stories of Jean Stafford* that Jean Stafford did not wish to be considered a regional writer. Her father and her mother's cousin had both written books about the West, but she had read neither before she began writing. Moreover, as soon as she could, she "hotfooted it across the Rocky Mountains and across the Atlantic Ocean" and came back to the West only for short periods. Her roots might therefore remain in Colorado, but the rest of her abided "in the South or the Midwest or New England or New York." The short stories in this collection, which span twenty-five years of her productive life, she grouped under headings that both insisted on the national and international character of her art and echoed universally known writers with whom she clearly wished to associate herself: Henry James, Mark Twain, Thomas Mann.

It is true, as one discovers from the stories themselves, Stafford's fiction is not limited geographically but is set in such widely separated places as Colorado, Heidelberg, France, New York, and Boston; if, therefore, one thinks of these stories as the result of social observation they do indeed have the broad national and international scope their author claimed for them. Her stories, however—and this may have been as apparent to Stafford as it has been to some of her critics—are not so much the result of observation and intellectual response as they are expressions of Stafford's personal view of life, a reflection of her own feeling of having been betrayed by family and friends. Her protagonists are often girls or young

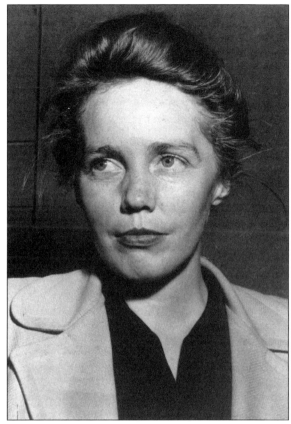

Jean Stafford in 1945 (AP/Wide World Photos)

women, pitted against persons who feel themselves superior but are revealed to be morally, emotionally, or even physically corrupt. Although Stafford's fiction was all but forgotten at the time of her death, it has been rediscovered by a new generation of readers, mainly through the work of feminist scholars. This is ironic because Stafford herself did not embrace feminist views and, in fact, spoke harshly about aspects of the feminist movement.

The thirty stories in Stafford's *The Collected Stories of Jean Stafford* are unified by one pervasive theme, illness—physical, mental, and emotional—and the snobbery which she finds an accompaniment, the snobbery of aberrant behavior. Fascinated, repelled, and at times outraged by the way illness can be used to purchase power over vulnerable individuals, Stafford describes the various forms of this currency, the number of places where it can be spent, and the way it can be used by those of any age or sex willing to employ it. The emotional and physical invalids in these stories clearly think themselves superior to ordinary folk, and the tensions built up in these stories are often the result of conflicts between a protagonist (who usually appears to speak for the author) and neurotic individuals who think themselves justified in exploiting others. Sometimes there is an actual physical sickness—disease, old age—but the illness or psychological aberration frequently becomes a metaphor for moral corruption.

"MAGGIE MERIWETHER'S RICH EXPERIENCE"

In "Maggie Meriwether's Rich Experience" the protagonist is a naïve young American woman from Tennessee visiting in France, where she has been invited to spend the weekend at a fashionable country house. There she discovers a crowd of titled Europeans, rich, overdressed, and eccentric, who look down their collective nose at the simple girl from the American South. The reader, who looks through the eyes of the young American, sees how stupid and arrogant these aristocrats are and understands Maggie's relief at escaping to Paris where she telephones the older brother of her roommate at Sweet Briar and spends the evening delighting in the wholesome provincialism of her southern American friends, regaling them with stories about her recent experience.

"THE ECHO AND THE NEMESIS"

In "The Echo and the Nemesis" the combination of neurosis and snobbery becomes more convincingly sinister. The story is also set in Europe, in Heidelberg, but the two main characters are Americans. The protagonist, Sue, appears to be a rather unexceptional young woman from a family of ordinary means; the "invalid," Ramona, is an enormously fat girl from a very rich family (so she says), living permanently in Italy. Sue is at first impressed by Ramona's learning and by the stories she tells of her family's wealth, and the two girls become constant companions. At first the relationship, with frequent meetings in cafés, becomes routine, like another philosophy lecture or seminar in Schiller, but then Ramona begins a series of revelations about herself and her family that embarrass, mystify, and then entrance Sue. Ramona reveals that she had a twin sister who died at an early age, a beautiful girl of whom there are many draw-

ings and paintings, and whose room had been turned into a shrine. Ramona next reveals that she has come to Heidelberg not to study but to lose weight, and she enlists Sue's aid. Captivated by Ramona's stories about her loose-living family, Sue readily accepts an invitation to visit Ramona's brothers at a ski resort in Switzerland.

Thereafter Ramona begins to change. She misses lunches, fails to show up for appointments, and wildly indulges herself in food. When Sue makes inquiries about the coming trip and questions her about her doctor, Ramona snaps at her and, once, even slaps her face. Ramona tells Sue that she (Sue) resembles her dead sister Martha and implies that the trip to Switzerland must therefore be called off, since Ramona's family would be too upset by the resemblance. Ramona's mysterious behavior is partially explained by Sue's discovery in Ramona's room of a photograph of a younger, thinner, and beautiful Ramona. In a final scene prior to Ramona's departure from Heidelberg, the revelation about her is made complete: Sue promises to remain her friend, and Ramona replies "'Oh, no, no, there would be nothing in it for you. Thank you just the same. I am exceptionally ill.' She spoke with pride, as if she were really saying, 'I am exceptionally talented' or 'I am exceptionally attractive.'" When Sue responds, "I'm sorry," Ramona snaps back, "I'm not sorry. It is for yourself that you should be sorry. You have such a trivial little life, poor girl. It's not your fault. Most people do."

"THE BLEEDING HEART"

The neurotics in Stafford's stories are not always so aggressive and unappealing. In "The Bleeding Heart" an elderly dandy who is browbeaten by his invalid mother attempts to establish a "fatherly" relationship with a young Mexican girl who has come East and works as a secretary in a "discreet girl's boarding school." The girl is at first impressed with the old gentleman's aristocratic bearing and imagines she would like him for a stepfather, but when she visits his mother with a plant, a gift from the school, she is appalled by the odors, the repellent condition of the mother, and the disgusting behavior of a parrot. When the old man attempts to force his attentions on her, she turns on him and tells him to leave her alone. "Rose," he tells her, "All I am asking is a little pity."

"THE LIBERATOR"

A briefer summary of several other stories will show how pervasive is this theme in Stafford's stories, both in the way characters are conceived and relationships established, and in the way the main action is resolved. The point of the story "The Liberation" has to do with the way an old couple, pathetic in their loneliness, try to prevent their young niece from marrying. At her announcement of her forthcoming marriage in Boston to a teacher at Harvard (the story takes place in Colorado), the aunt (who "suffers" from chronic asthma) wrings her hands and her uncle glares at her and both are outraged at the idea of her marrying and going off to live somewhere else. The story takes a curious turn as word comes that the girl's fiancé has died of a heart attack. The girl is at first stunned and about to resign herself to remaining in Colorado, but her uncle and aunt try to "appropriate" her grief and bind her even faster to themselves. In a panic, without luggage, the girl flees for Boston and her emotional freedom from the "niggling hypochondriacs she had left behind."

"THE HEALTHIEST GIRL IN TOWN"

"The Healthiest Girl in Town" also takes place in Colorado, where a girl, whose mother is a practical nurse in a town inhabited mainly by tuberculous patients and their families, is forced to become friends with two sisters because her mother nurses the girls' grandmother. At first the girl is impressed with the sisters (they also have illnesses) and their Eastern pretentiousness and ashamed of her own good health, but then, after a quarrel with them, she proudly declares herself to be the healthiest girl in town.

ABNORMALITIES AND NEUROSES

Two other Easterners also proud of their abnormalities are a Boston spinster in "The Hope Chest" who delights in humiliating her maid and in tricking a boy who comes to her door selling Christmas wreaths into kissing her, and an elderly woman in "Life Is No Abyss" from a rich and socially prominent Boston family whom she punishes by going to the poorhouse and allowing them to come and observe her in her impoverishment. "A Country Love Story" also deals with an invalid, in this instance a writer who neglects his wife and then accuses her of being unfaithful to him and so drives her to the brink of insanity. Other characters include a woman (in "The End of a Career") who devotes her life to looking beautiful and dies when her hands betray her age and a woman ("Beatrice Trublood's Story") who marries three times and each time selects the same brutal kind of husband.

"Bad Characters," which is perhaps Stafford's most amusing story, treats her usual theme comically. Here the neurotic invalid is cast as a vagabond girl with an appealing swagger, a female Huck Finn but without Huck's decency. She charms the daughter of a respectable family into shoplifting and, when the two are caught, feigns deaf-and-dumbness and allows the respectable girl (the protagonist) to bear the responsibility alone.

F. Scott Fitzgerald said that a writer has but one story to tell. Stafford tells hers in many different places, about people from rather different social levels, ages, education, and backgrounds: There is almost always an innocent charmed or somehow trapped by neurotic individuals from whom she finally escapes. Sometimes Stafford gives the stage to this neurotic individual and gradually peels away the mystery that always shrouds those who think themselves superior to others. The story holds up well in the retelling, for it is a universal and timeless theme.

OTHER MAJOR WORKS

LONG FICTION: *Boston Adventure*, 1944; *The Mountain Lion*, 1947; *The Catherine Wheel*, 1952; *A Winter's Tale*, 1954.

NONFICTION: *A Mother in History*, 1966.

CHILDREN'S LITERATURE: *Arabian Nights: The Lion and the Carpenter and Other Tales from the Arabian Nights, Retold*, 1959; *Elephi: The Cat with the High I.Q.*, 1962.

BIBLIOGRAPHY

Avila, Wanda. *Jean Stafford: A Comprehensive Bibliography*. New York: Garland, 1983. This reference contains short summaries of 220 publications by Stafford (books, stories, articles, essays, book and movie reviews) and 428 critical works about her.

Goodman, Charlotte. *Jean Stafford: The Savage Heart*. Austin: University of Texas Press, 1990. This 390-page literary biography emphasizes the connections between Stafford's life and art, with their often contradictory demands. Drawing heavily from Jean Stafford's letters, it is well researched and makes interesting reading.

Hulbert, Ann. *The Interior Castle: The Art and Life of Jean Stafford*. New York: A. A. Knopf, 1992. An excellent guide to the works and life of the author.

Oates, Joyce Carol. "The Interior Castle: The Art of Jean Stafford's Short Fiction." *Shenandoah* 30 (Spring, 1979): 61-64. Part of a memorial issue for Jean Stafford, this article looks closely at characters in some of Stafford's short stories. The issue also includes Stafford's last story, "Woden's Day," which was extracted from her unfinished novel *The Parliament of Women*; parts of Stafford's letters to friends; and essays and reminiscences by Peter Taylor, Nancy Flagg, Howard Moss, Dorothea Straus, and Wilfrid Sheed.

Roberts, David. *Jean Stafford: A Biography*. Boston: Little, Brown, 1988. This comprehensive, 494-page biography includes photographs and a select bibliography of primary and secondary sources.

Rochette-Crawley, Susan. "'Enjoying the Conceit of Suddenness': An Analysis of Brevity, Context, and Textual 'Identity' in Jean Stafford's 'Caveat Emptor.'" *Short Story*, n.s. 2 (Spring, 1994): 69-78. A theoretical discussion of how brevity is a narrative strategy that decenters the reader's generic expectations, using Jean Stafford's story "Caveat Emptor" as an example of the short story's method of displacement.

Ryan, Maureen. *Innocence and Estrangement in the Fiction of Jean Stafford*. Baton Rouge: Louisiana State University Press, 1987. This detailed study of Stafford's themes and technique includes two chapters that focus on the feminine situations Stafford creates in her short fiction. Supplemented by a bibliography.

Walsh, Mary Ellen Williams. *Jean Stafford*. Boston: Twayne, 1985. This extended critique examines Stafford's fiction from the perspective of the stages in women's lives: childhood, adolescence, young womanhood, maturity, and old age. It gives considerable attention to her stories, both collected and uncollected, and includes a chronology and select bibliography.

Wilson, Mary Ann. *Jean Stafford: A Study of the Short Fiction*. New York: Twayne, 1996. Discusses a representative sample of Stafford's stories under Stafford's own regional headings. Includes several critical comments about fiction writing by Stafford and brief critical comments on her fiction by a number of critics, including Joyce Carol Oates and Peter Taylor. Discusses such stories as "A Country Love Story" and "The Interior Castle," as well as many lesser-known stories.

W. J. Stuckey, updated by
Jean C. Fulton

RICHARD STEELE

Born: Dublin, Ireland; March, 1672
Died: Carmarthen, Wales; September 1, 1729

PRINCIPAL SHORT FICTION

The Tatler, 1709-1711 (with Joseph Addison; periodical essays)
The Spectator, 1711-1712, 1714 (with Addison; periodical essays)
The Englishman, 1713-1714, 1715 (periodical essays)
The Guardian, 1713 (with Addison; periodical essays)
The Lover, 1714 (periodical essays)

OTHER LITERARY FORMS

Sir Richard Steele is well known for his four plays, his prose work, *The Christian Hero* (1701), and his later periodicals. His plays are strongly didactic in purpose and tone, and this intention carries over to his short fiction in his periodicals. Perceived as a reformer of the stage, Steele was named Governor of the Drury Lane Theatre in order to improve the moral tone of the playhouse. His last play, *The Conscious Lovers* (1722), is often identified as "sentimental" drama whose influence changed the course of the English theater.

ACHIEVEMENTS

Richard Steele enjoyed a well-rounded and successful writing career. He was well known as "Mr. Spectator" and enjoyed a tremendous success with his daily. Nearly all fashionable London knew about *The Spectator*, and its influence on the taste, fashion, and opinions of the well-to-do is hard to discount. Steele was also widely influential when he began his dramatic career. His play *The Conscious Lovers* was touted as a new genre, the domestic comedy. It was controversial because it broke the dramatic rules of the day, but the controversy merely improved its popularity. Steele increased his influence on Londoners yet again when he became stage manager of Drury Lane, one of the leading theaters. He became respon-sible for deciding the very plays they would see in an era when the theater was the major source of entertainment. In 1714, Steele was knighted, having served the government's cause through his writing.

BIOGRAPHY

Educated at the Charterhouse and the University of Oxford, Richard Steele lived in England and made his living first as a soldier and later as a writer and a politician. Although his plays and periodicals earned him some money, he always seemed to be in debt. He married Margaret Ford Stretch in 1705, but, unfortunately, she died the following year. In 1707, he married Mary Scurlock, owner of a small estate in Wales where he ultimately retired. He became the major propagandist for the Whigs from 1710 to 1714, when they were the opposition, and, after the Whigs regained power under King George I in 1714, he was knighted as a reward for his industriousness in the Whig cause. His later life was filled with financial difficulties, family problems, and political discouragement; after a stroke, he retired to Wales in 1724, where he died in 1729.

ANALYSIS

Sir Richard Steele's short fiction appears in *The Tatler*, *The Spectator*, and *The Guardian*, as well as in some shorter periodicals. There is a double level of fiction in all three of these periodicals: The first is the fictional creation of the narrator and his family or club, with all the telling details that make Steele's narrators interesting; the second is the storytelling of the narrator himself. The narrator of *The Tatler* is Isaac Bickerstaff, a name made popular by Jonathan Swift in his attack on the astrologer John Partridge. Bickerstaff is an elderly, benevolent astrologer who enjoys relating humorous stories about his family and friends while good-naturedly poking fun at himself. In contrast, *The Spectator* has as its narrator Mr. Spectator, the most taciturn member of The Spectator Club and the undisputed master observer of human nature and human foibles. Because of his careful ob-

Richard Steele (Library of Congress)

servation of those around him, Mr. Spectator is an excellent storyteller as well. Finally, the narrator of *The Guardian* is Nestor Ironside, the feisty protector of the Lizard family and adviser to the British nation. To a large degree, *The Tatler* and *The Spectator* are the mutual creation of Steele and his friend and schoolfellow Joseph Addison, although Steele alone signed his name to the final issue of both periodicals; in contrast, *The Guardian* is largely Steele's and is generally recognized as inferior to the two earlier works. Steele's contribution to these works is a lively imagination and a facile wit; he promotes benevolence as the proper response to the sorrows and sufferings of one's fellow humans, and he satirizes slavish adherence to fashion. Plain-dealing honesty and kindly benevolence are Steele's major moral themes in both *The Tatler* and *The Spectator*; Steele's didactic purpose is always foremost, in both his fiction and his plays.

THE TATLER

In *The Tatler*, Isaac Bickerstaff enjoys teaching the correct way to treat one's spouse by describing his sister's marital problems. Poor Jenny Distaff has more than her share of difficulties to overcome with her spouse, Tranquillus; Isaac's bachelor wisdom helps them both to achieve happiness. The essential problem is Jenny's desire for domination over her husband, and Isaac teaches her to accept her husband's superior position in marriage. At first glance, it appears that Steele is preaching a very reactionary attitude toward marriage; however, this is not quite the case. Steele believes that women are people, not objects, and that they must be treated as thinking human beings by their husbands. Such an attitude was not universally held by men in the early eighteenth century, and, although Steele's attitude may seem conservative by modern standards, he deserves to be credited with some advancement of women's situations in his own century. For example, he decries the double standard of sexual morality and the marriage contract based solely on financial considerations. Women were losers in both situations, and Steele saw and spoke against what he considered serious social evils. In *The Tatler*, Steele is master of the dramatic scene, nowhere better exemplified than in the reconciliation between Jenny and Tranquillus through the efforts of Isaac Bickerstaff.

THE SPECTATOR

It is reasonable to assert that Steele was fascinated by all the various pleasures and problems in domestic relationships. Primary are courtship, marriage, and married life, but the parent-child relationship was also very important to Steele. Mr. Spectator enjoys almost nothing more than a didactic story about the improvement of marital relations, parent-child relations, or a study of the potential for happiness in an impending marriage. *The Spectator* proves the ideal vehicle for these short, succinct stories, providing a different story daily and a need for constant reinforcement of central themes. One of Steele's often reinforced themes is the difficulty caused by parents who insist on choosing a spouse for their child. In *The Spectator* 533, in a letter appealing to Mr. Spectator's sense of justice, a male correspondent describes his unhappy situation as his elderly family insist that they choose their son's wife. This twenty-two-year-old is pleading for assistance: "You have often given us very excellent Discourses against that unnatural Custom of Parents, in forcing their Children to marry contrary to their Inclinations." The same theme in a different setting appears in *The Spectator* 220, in a letter from a twenty-one-year-old woman to an elderly suitor who is appealing to her father and not to her. She complains stridently of the injustice foisted upon her by a father and a suitor who believe that she must accept the suitor because her father does. Steele lets the letter communicate its message without additional comment, but it is clear that he wholly supports the unjustly treated young woman.

Steele enjoyed using the letter device as a mode of developing his short fictions; he used letters, for example, much more often than did Addison. Letters helped him to develop various perspectives, which are more effectively presented through various points of view than through Steele's voice alone. A parallel example might be the epistolary format in Samuel Richardson's *Clarissa* (1747-1748), where four perspectives are well developed through letters. Steele is interested in brevity as well as perspective, and yet his need as an author to create perspectives other than his own is similar to Richardson's. Steele presents another of his favorite themes in a letter to Mr. Spectator from an admirer in *The Spectator* 268, wherein the correspondent laments the tragedy of so many people marrying for the wrong reasons. What are these wrong reasons? They are: money, position, power. What then are proposed as the right reasons to marry? They are: virtue, wisdom, a person's good qualities, good humor, similar manners and attitudes. In this letter—and throughout Steele's writings— marriage is spoken of reverently, as the state which may "give us the compleatest Happiness this Life is capable of." For this to happen, however, Steele warns repeatedly through precept and example, men and women must be free to choose their spouses on the basis of lasting and endearing qualities.

One of the most famous stories in *The Spectator*, "Inkle and Yarico," depicts the suffering and misery of a less than circumspect love. In *The Spectator* 11, Steele describes the selfish and mean treatment by Mr. Thomas Inkle of a Native American maiden who trusted him completely. Inkle, having landed with a group of Englishmen in America, was attacked by Native Americans and retreated into the woods, where he was found and protected by Yarico, the Native American maid. They fell in love, he made great promises of wealth and comfort, and, when the ship came, Yarico left her people to go with Inkle. Shortly thereafter and safe once again with his own people, Inkle sold Yarico to a Barbadian merchant as a slave. The story is a warning to both sexes, but especially to women, to be circumspect in choosing a mate. Although the potential for great happiness does exist in marriage, numerous traps for the unwary, Steele warns, may make marriage a source of great unhappiness as well.

On another narrative level, two members of Mr. Spectator's club, Sir Roger de Coverley and Sir Andrew Freeport, provide a continuing story line and numerous little anecdotes. Sir Roger is an old-fashioned country squire, while Sir Andrew is a vigorous, intelligent merchant. Whereas loveable Sir Roger's ideas are as out of date as his clothing, Sir Andrew's clear concepts on the role of trade in England's future are of the utmost importance. Usually these two club members get along well, but, when an argument develops on the relative value of merchants to the British nation, Sir Andrew proves his superiority. Many of these little stories subtly identify the Tories with Sir Roger and the Whigs with Sir Andrew. Both Steele and Addison were wholeheartedly committed Whigs, and, despite their assurances that *The Spectator* was nonpolitical, their political beliefs inevitably surfaced. Their propaganda is delightfully subtle, as it slowly proves Sir Roger's ineffectiveness and Sir Andrew's undeniable capability.

THE GUARDIAN

As one might suppose, Steele remained consistent in his attitudes on marriage, parent child relationships, and politics as he discontinued writing for *The Spectator* in order to begin *The Guardian*. Although in some places the tone does become more stern and foreboding, there are still delightful stories in *The Guardian* that promote the values of charity, benevolence, and love rather than authority, and unselfishness rather than self-centeredness. For example, Nestor Ironside himself, although he would like to appear stern and crusty, exemplifies in his own story an overriding concern with the joys and sufferings of those about him. Nestor accepts the responsibility of guiding the Lizard family upon the death of his good friend, Sir Marmaduke Lizard. The lessons he inculcates in the family are based on love of neighbor rather than of self; he leads the daughters away from vanity and pride, while he admonishes the eldest son against keeping a mistress.

Steele's approach to moral issues remained essentially fixed from 1701, the date of his lengthy explication of moral values in his prose tract, *The Christian Hero*. Steele argued there that reason is incapable of guiding the passions to virtue, that only religion is capable of aiding reason sufficiently to guide the passions effectively, and that once so directed the passions may become an additional impetus to virtue. Steele posits in *The Christian Hero* a fundamentally irrational view of human nature. For this reason, perhaps, he teaches morality in his periodicals not by precept and argument but by example and story.

The influence of *The Tatler* and *The Spectator*, and to a lesser degree *The Guardian*, was extraordinary. When one realizes that each periodical lasted less than two years, the fact of such widespread influence is all the more remarkable. In both England and America, *The Spectator* was revered in many families as a repository of moral teaching as well as an entertaining book, and one may imagine that there were many, such as Benjamin Franklin, who developed a polished writing style through imitation of *The Spectator*. Although some topics contemporary to the eighteenth century may appear of little interest to the modern reader, many of the stories still prove enjoyable.

OTHER MAJOR WORKS

PLAYS: *The Funeral: Or, Grief à-la-mode*, pr. 1701; *The Lying Lover: Or, The Lady's Friendship*, pr. 1703 (based on Pierre Corneille's play *Le Menteur)*; *The Tender Husband: Or, The Accomplished Fools*, pr., pb. 1705 (based on Molière's play *Le Sicilien*); *The Conscious Lovers*, pr., pb. 1722 (based on Terence's play *Andria*); *The Plays of Richard Steele*, pb. 1971 (Shirley Strum Kenny, editor).

POETRY: *The Procession*, 1695; *Prologue to the University of Oxford*, 1706; *Epilogue to the Town*, 1721; *The Occasional Verse of Richard Steele*, 1952 (Rae Blanchard, editor).

NONFICTION: *The Christian Hero*, 1701; *The Importance of Dunkirk Considered*, 1713; *The Theatre*, 1720 (later published as *Richard Steele's "The Theatre,"* 1920, 1962; John Loftis, editor); *Tracts and Pamphlets by Richard Steele*, 1944 (Blanchard, editor); *The Correspondence of Richard Steele*, 1968 (Blanchard, editor).

BIBLIOGRAPHY

Calhoun, Wineton. *Captain Steele: The Early Career*. Baltimore: The Johns Hopkins University Press, 1964. Primarily a biographical study, this book discusses *The Tatler* and *The Spectator* but focuses mostly on the circumstances surrounding them rather than on actual analysis.

Connely, Willard. *Sir Richard Steele*. New York: Charles Scribner's Sons, 1934. This volume is the standard biography on Steele. While it is old, it is relatively useful. The chapters on *The Tatler* and *The Spectator* are helpful, including information on the business aspects of producing the two papers.

Dammers, Richard H. *Richard Steele*. Boston: Twayne, 1982. A good overview of Steele's work. This study discusses Steele's essays, dramas, and includes two excellent chapters on his short fiction in *The Tatler* and *The Spectator*. Contains a chronology and a select bibliography.

Ketcham, Michael G. *Transparent Designs: Reading, Performance, and Form in the Spectator Papers*. Athens: University of Georgia Press, 1985. This study takes apart *The Spectator* by examining its readers, its treatment of time, family, and language, and the social and historical context. A good, closely detailed examination of *The Spectator*.

Knight, Charles A. *Joseph Addison and Richard Steele: A Reference Guide, 1730-1991*. New York: G. K. Hall, 1994. A useful tool for students of Steele.

_____. "The Spectator's Moral Economy." *Modern*

Philology 91 (November, 1993): 161-179. Examines principles of moral economy presented by Joseph Addison and Steele in *The Spectator* to control dreams of endless gains. Argues that Addison and Steele found in the economic order a secular basis for moral behavior that emphasized the common good over individual gain. Suggests that they connected commercial values to values of politeness and restraint.

Loftis, John. *Steele at Drury Lane*. Berkeley: University of California Press, 1952. The book details Steele's theatrical career and provides a good understanding of the eighteenth century stage and business management. Includes a useful appendix.

McCrea, Brian. *Addison and Steele Are Dead: The English Department, Its Canon, and the Professionalization of Literary Criticism*. Newark: University of Delaware Press, 1990. Examines the legacy of Steele and Joseph Addison.

Richard H. Dammers, updated by
Kimberley L. Jacobs

WILBUR DANIEL STEELE

Born: Greensboro, North Carolina; March 17, 1886
Died: Essex, Connecticut; May 26, 1970

PRINCIPAL SHORT FICTION
Land's End and Other Stories, 1918
The Shame Dance and Other Stories, 1923
Urkey Island, 1926
The Man Who Saw Through Heaven and Other Stories, 1927
Tower of Sand and Other Stories, 1929
The Best Stories of Wilbur Daniel Steele, 1946
Full Cargo: More Stories, 1951

OTHER LITERARY FORMS
Between 1914 and 1955, Wilbur Daniel Steele published ten novels, none of which achieved any critical success or extended life. Despite his early association with the Provincetown Players, his several attempts at writing plays came to nothing. Much of the popular success of Steele's short stories derived from his manipulation of the O. Henry ending, a knack that does not transport to other genres.

ACHIEVEMENTS
Of Wilbur Daniel Steele's nearly two hundred published short stories, nine were included in the annual collection *The Best American Short Stories*, and eleven won various O. Henry story awards. One story, "How Beautiful with Shoes," was not only chosen for *The Best American Short Stories 1933* but also produced as a Broadway play in 1935.

BIOGRAPHY
Wilbur Daniel Steele was born on March 17, 1886, in Greensboro, North Carolina. His father, the Reverend Wilbur Fletcher Steele, taught the Bible at the University of Denver from 1892 until 1923, and the young Wilbur received a bachelor's degree from that university before enrolling at the Boston Museum School of Fine Arts in 1907 and spending the next two years painting and etching in Paris and Italy. In 1913 Steele married the painter Margaret Thurston and moved from Greenwich Village to Provincetown, Massachusetts, where he apprenticed with such writers as Susan Glaspell and Eugene O'Neill, and where their two sons, Thurston and Peter, were born. Margaret died in 1931, and in 1932 Steele married the actress Norma Mitchell and moved to Hamburg, Connecticut.

Wilbur Daniel Steele's first story, "On the Ebb Tide," was published in *Success Magazine* in 1910, and for the next two decades he published prolifically and traveled to many of the locales that appear in his fiction, including Bermuda, North Africa, the Caribbean, and the South Carolina coast. In 1932 he was awarded an honorary doctorate from the University of Denver. *The Best Stories of Wilbur Daniel Steele*, published in 1946, included most of the stories for which Steele would want to be remembered, and it was supplemented by *Full Cargo* in 1951.

Steele moved to Old Lyme, Connecticut, in 1956, spent 1964 at Essex Rest Home in Connecticut, and in 1965 entered Highland Hall Convalescent Home in Essex, where he died in 1970.

ANALYSIS

Wilbur Daniel Steele enjoyed a long and highly successful career writing for *Harper's Magazine* and other popular periodicals. In stories that typically ran about twenty carefully plotted pages, he presented smooth, flowing narratives blessed with convincing dialogue that sometimes featured regional dialects. Commonly, Steele's tales work up endings that recall the plot switches of O. Henry, who shared Steele's birthplace of Greensboro, North Carolina. The great variety of settings compensates somewhat for the reader's eventual sense that a Steele story will lead to a contrived and often predictable ending. Of the twenty-four tales in *The Best Stories of Wilbur Daniel Steele*, four are set along the Massachusetts coast and feature Portuguese immigrants, one is set in the Caribbean, one in the South Pacific, three in North Africa, and two in the South Carolina coastal islands. The others take place in American locales that have no significant plot function.

Steele has had only negligible impact on literary history. He did not chronicle a period, as did F. Scott Fitzgerald, nor did he create a vivid microcosm to compare with William Faulkner's Yoknapatawpha, but he was an accomplished storyteller for middle-class audiences looking for the kind of short reading experience praised by Edgar Allen Poe. Steele's best stories create characters for whom the reader genuinely cares (for example, the wife and mother in "When Hell Froze" and the girl who is "How Beautiful with Shoes"), but he seldom achieves the kind of convincing moral and psychological complexity of Nathaniel Hawthorne in "The Birthmark," Herman Melville in "Bartleby," or, much later, John Cheever.

Steele was a graceful stylist, but he frequently lapsed into the kind of ethnic stereotyping and demeaning epithets that later generations would find offensive. In this respect, as in his sense of the taste of his audience, Steele was thoroughly a writer of his time.

"THE SHAME DANCE"

"The Shame Dance," included in *The Best American Short Stories 1921*, is set on a tiny island in the South Pacific and reads a little like one of Joseph Conrad's stories set in the same region. The narrator, Cole, captains a trading schooner, and when he puts in at Taai he finds himself trapped in conversation with Signet, an American vagabond on board as a passenger. The man is a blatherer, borrowing cigarettes and chattering about making a lot of money in Manhattan. When Cole goes ashore, he is entertained by the de facto ruler of Taai known only as "the Dutchman." They watch that evening an entertainment staged by three touring "Kanaka" men and a woman who is described as their common "wife." The husbands play a beguiling melody on primitive instruments while the wife performs the so-called Shame Dance, an extraordinarily erotic arabesque, which hypnotizes the Dutchman, the vagabond, and the narrator. Later, the Dutchman implants in the vagabond's mind the idea of killing the husbands, and then he imprisons the hapless murderer and appropriates the woman. Cole returns thirteen days later to find the Dutchman apparently dead and Signet briefly ruling Taai before disappearing with the dancer. Sitting in a bar in Honolulu sometime later, Cole hears a startling tune, which he recalls from the Shame Dance, and learns that it is an old melody called "Paragon Park" and the original music of the "Shimmie" dance. Moreover, his bar companion, a telegraph operator from Colorado, tells of being visited in his station one night by a woman in a horse blanket and a nearly insane man, who becomes distressed when he hears "Paragon Park" on the juke box. The distraught visitor exclaims, "Seas o' blood!" and he and the woman disappear. Later, Cole returns to the Marquesas to find Signet "quite nude save for a loincloth," established with his dancer, and still fantasizing schemes to overwhelm Manhattan. "At last, despite the malignant thrusts and obstacles of destiny, this guttersnipe of Gotham had come to a certain estate."

"WHEN HELL FROZE"

A farm wife, Addie Joslin, has devoted her eighteen years of married life to being a faithful helpmeet to her husband John and a loving mother to her sons Ray, sixteen, and Frankie, four. Awaiting John and Ray's return from a business trip to New York one day, Addie chats innocently with a wandering tinker who plays some familiar harmonica tunes, and as he recites some trite lyrics about *"Kiss me, kiss me, again . . . ,"* Frankie misinterprets the conversation, thinking that Addie has been kissing the stranger. The menfolk return that evening, and the next day Frankie tells Ray that Addie had kissed the vagrant with the harmonica. The upset Ray then confides to others in town. From this moment, everyone is against the innocent Addie: John and Ray reject her delicious meals, and John presents her with a can of lye water in which to wash her hands. Addie's responds, "You can leave it there till hell freezes over." When three local farmers confront Addie in the pasture, warning her against "unholy, un-Christian goings on," she rushes home to find the local minister preparing an orgy of prayer in which Addie is supposed to confess after John and Ray wash their hands in the lye water. After the defiant Addie has exiled herself in town for five months, everyone is emotionally exhausted, and Ray is ready to fight John to get Addie back. At this point Addie walks in, looking splendid in new clothes and bringing a harmonica for Frankie. When John asks if hell has frozen over, Addie replies, "Oh yes. Oh, long ago," and dips her hands in the lye can. The ending is happy, with buckwheat cakes all around and Addie dreaming of the green rye growing in the spring.

"THE MAN WHO SAW THROUGH HEAVEN"

"The Man Who Saw Through Heaven" tells the story of the Reverend Hubert Diana whose contemplation of the immensities of space leads him to a more profound faith. On the night before the Reverend Diana is to embark from Boston for missionary work in East Africa, his whole vision of God changes during a visit to an observatory, where he is shocked by the immensities of space, especially when his as-

tronomer-guide speculates that the opal ring on the Reverend's finger may contain universes that in the scale of the whole creation may be as our universe to the boundlessness of space. Because of his shocking public nakedness en route to East Africa, Diana has to be put ashore in Algiers, from which he escapes and wanders to East Africa, where the narrator and Mrs. Diana track him down months later. It seems that he has recapitulated the evolution of man in his own way. Following him from village to village, they find a trail of sculpted mud blobs that progress from low life forms through lizards to bulls, all executed "to give the Beast of the Infinite a name and a shape." The natives at his final village had named him "Father Witch" Diana's mud figure had become a recognizable man distinguished by a carefully molded finger bearing an opal ring. The ending is triumphant. When Mrs. Diana expresses her shock that the Reverend had "sunk to idolatry," the narrator explains: "'To the bottom, yes. And come up its whole history again. And from here he walked out into the sunshine to kneel and talk with "Our Father Witch—." ' "

"HOW BEAUTIFUL WITH SHOES"

Amarantha Doggett, a "broad-fleshed, slow-minded" farm girl called simply Mare, allows the attentions of her tobacco chewing yokel of a beau, not knowing anything more romantic until Humble Jewett, a deluded escapee from the nearby asylum, takes her hostage and quotes poetry to her. Jewett quotes Richard Lovelace: "Amarantha sweet and fair—/ Ah, braid no more that golden hair," the Middle English lyric that ends "Christ, that my love were in my arms/ And I in my bed again," and "How beautiful are thy feet with shoes, O prince's daughter" from the Song of Solomon. Amarantha remains unharmed and is kept under duress only for a night before Humble Jewett dies from shotgun blasts, but despite her fright she has been moved in ways she does not understand by the only poetry and tenderness she will ever know in life. When her loutish lover later importunes her for a kiss, "She pushe[s] him to the door and through it with all her strength, and close[s] it in his face, and st[ands] with her weight against it, crying, 'Go 'way! Go 'way! Lea' me be!'" "How Beautiful with Shoes" anticipates Flannery O'Connor in some ways and is a story that many better-known authors would be glad to claim.

OTHER MAJOR WORKS

LONG FICTION: *Storm*, 1914; *Isles of the Blest*, 1924; *Taboo*, 1925; *Meat*, 1928; *Undertow*, 1930; *Sound of Rowlocks*, 1938; *That Girl from Memphis*, 1945; *Diamond Wedding*, 1950; *Their Town*, 1952; *The Way to the Gold*, 1955.

PLAYS: *The Giant's Stair*, pb. 1924; *The Terrible Woman and Other One-Act Plays*, pb. 1925; *Post Road*, pr. 1934 (with Norma Mitchell).

BIBLIOGRAPHY

Bucco, Martin. *Wilbur Daniel Steele*. New York: Twayne, 1972. This volume in the Twayne series provides an introduction, conclusion, and indispensable bibliography. Seven chapters of summary and commentary discuss the seven collections of stories in chronological order.

Elser, Frank B. "Oh, Yes . . . Wilbur Daniel Steele." *The Bookman* 62 (February, 1926): 691-694. An interview that gives a good picture of Steele as a person and insight into his writing practices.

Gelb, Arthur, and Barbara Gelb. *O'Neill*. New York: Harper and Brothers, 1960. This biography of Eugene O'Neill describes the circumstances of life at Provincetown when Steele was there and alludes to Steele's friendship with O'Neill.

Mirrielees, Edith R. "The Best of Steele." A review of *The Best Stories of Wilbur Daniel Steele*, by Wilbur Daniel Steele. *New York Times* (July 14, 1946), pp. 5, 20. This review provides an overall assessment of his work.

Peterson, Theodore. *Magazines in the Twentieth Century*. Urbana: University of Illinois Press, 1964. Does not treat Steele directly but explains the editorial policies of his publishers.

Williams, Blanche Colton. *Our Short Story Writers*. New York: Dodd, Mead and Company, 1926. One chapter appraises Steele's work.

Frank Day

WALLACE STEGNER

Born: Lake Mills, Iowa; February 18, 1909
Died: Santa Fe, New Mexico; April 13, 1993

PRINCIPAL SHORT FICTION

The Women on the Wall, 1950
The City of the Living and Other Stories, 1956
Collected Stories of Wallace Stegner, 1990

OTHER LITERARY FORMS

Primarily a novelist and historian, Wallace Stegner is the author of many novels, from *Remembering Laughter* (1937) to *The Spectator Bird* (1976); his best-known and perhaps his best novel, *The Big Rock Candy Mountain*, was published in 1943, and *Angle of Repose* (1971) was awarded the Pulitzer Prize. *Mormon Country*, his first book of nonfiction, was published in 1942; it was followed by approximately a dozen others, including *Beyond the Hundredth Meridian: John Wesley Powell and the Second Opening of the West* (1954), *The Sound of Mountain Water* (essays, 1969), and *The Uneasy Chair: A Biography of Bernard DeVoto* (1974). In addition, he edited many books, including *Great American Short Stories* (with Mary Stegner, 1957), numerous annual volumes of *Stanford Short Stories* (with Richard Scowcroft), and *The Letters of Bernard DeVoto* (1975).

In 1987, Stegner published the novel *Crossing to Safety*, which he said is "a sort of memoir . . . for Mary [his wife] and myself." A gentle and affectionate portrait of two very different academic couples,

Crossing to Safety met with great critical and popular acclaim. In an offshoot to his long teaching career, Stegner published *On the Teaching of Creative Writing: Responses to a Series of Questions* in 1988.

ACHIEVEMENTS

Wallace Stegner's talent lay in his evocation of the West, which otherwise has been poorly documented in so-called Westerns, whether they be films or novels. As writer Richard Etulain has noted, what gives Stegner's work "its essential character is a deep familiarity with American historical, cultural, and political terrain." Stegner's work reveals the many aspects that make up American culture, or Americana. In addition, it provides a basis for understanding modern life in the United States. His literary efforts in this pursuit to portray fast-disappearing cultural and geographic sections of the United States were recognized with the Western History Association Prize in 1990.

Stegner received many awards and honors, including a Guggenheim Fellowship, a Rockefeller Fellowship, the Pulitzer Prize, a National Endowment for the Humanities Senior Fellowship, and an American Academy in Rome fellowship. In the spring of 1990, Stegner was given a lifetime achievement award by PEN USA Center West. In September of the same year, he was awarded a senior fellowship by the National Endowment for the Arts.

BIOGRAPHY

Born in Iowa on his grandfather's farm, Wallace Earle Stegner moved with his family to East End, Saskatchewan at the age of five. He was educated in Utah, where he received an A.B. from the University of Utah, in 1930; and in his native state, where he earned an M.A., in 1932, and a Ph.D., in 1935, from the University of Iowa. Although he was briefly enrolled at the University of California at Los Angeles, he never actually attended any classes—he did not like California and returned to Utah as soon as he could.

Stegner once commented that his subjects and themes, both in fiction and in nonfiction, "are mainly out of the American West, in which I grew up." He

Wallace Stegner (Library of Congress)

taught at various colleges and universities, primarily at Stanford University, where he was director of its creative writing program. Stegner coauthored books with both his wife, Mary, and his son, Page, but he stopped publishing short stories after 1960. He said that everything he wanted to write "somehow wanted to be long." His attention continued to remain focused on the environment, a concern that began after World War II but that probably dated back to his childhood, when, as he said, he was "imprinted by the prairies."

ANALYSIS

Of the eighteen stories in *The Women on the Wall*, almost half are concerned with incidents in the life of Brucie, a young boy growing up in Saskatchewan in the later years of the second decade of the twentieth century. In these semirelated stories, strongly rooted in time and place, Wallace Stegner is in complete control of his material and writes with insight and understanding which never lapse into sentimentality. The Brucie stories revolve around relatively commonplace subjects: the trapping of a gopher, the slaughtering of a sow, a family picnic.

"TWO RIVERS"

"Two Rivers," an O. Henry second-prize winner in 1942, is characteristic. The action is simple. Following an unhappy Fourth of July (the failure of the family's dilapidated Ford and the subsequent missed ball game in Chinook, the missed parade and fireworks, climaxed by the cuff on the ear from his father), the family set off for a picnic. Very little actually happens in this effective account of family relations, but at the story's end the reader shares Brucie's quiet pleasure:

> The boy looked up at his father, his laughter bubbling up, everything wonderful, the day a swell day, his mother clapping hands in time to his father's fool singing (an impromptu song about "a kid and his name was Brucie").
>
> "Aw, for gosh sakes," he said, and ducked when his father pretended he was going to swat him one.

"BEYOND THE GLASS MOUNTAIN"

In his stories about adults, Stegner's vision is considerably darker. Life was essentially good for a boy in 1917, he suggests; for an adult in the 1940's, it is likely to be just the opposite. "Beyond the Glass Mountain" (like "Two Rivers," the recipient of an O. Henry Award, second-prize, 1948) is characteristic. The narrative is structurally simple, uncluttered, and admirably economical: an account of a few moments during the reunion of two men who had been close friends during their college days. The narrator, "prepared . . . for nostalgia," finds his friend to be a pathetic alcoholic, irreparably damaged by the passing of time and a destructive marriage. (For the "love of God," he thinks, "Get rid of her. . . . She'll cheat on you. . . . She'll suck you dry like an old orange skin)."

"Beyond the Glass Mountain," "The View from the Balcony," "The Women on the Wall," and others similarly depict the encroachment of the always present scourges of humanity on lives that might or should be "ordinary" or "happy": the itch for domination, the dark shadow of emotional instability or insanity, the tyranny of sex, and the insecurity of the unloved.

THE CITY OF THE LIVING AND OTHER STORIES

The seven stories and one novella of *The City of the Living and Other Stories* share in common with *The Women on the Wall* Stegner's thoroughly disciplined narrative skill and his unblinking understanding of his characters. These later stories are more varied than their predecessors, ranging as they do from a flea bag of a California pool hall during the American Depression ("The Blue-Winged Teal," the O. Henry Memorial Award first-prize winner in 1950); to Egypt ("The City of the Living"); to Salt Lake City ("Maiden in a Tower"); to the French Riviera ("Impasse"); to an unspecified snowswept rural landscape-with-figures piece ("The Traveler"); to life among the wealthy and not-so-beautiful people in Southern California ("Field Guide to the Western Birds").

Stegner is again at his best in his shorter, less complicated, pieces. "Maiden in a Tower," for example, is virtually without incident: The drama of the story is the evocation of the past. The narrator has driven from San Francisco to a funeral home in Salt Lake City where his aunt lies awaiting burial. By coincidence, the funeral home was, a quarter of a century ago, the setting of the narrator's first love, and evokes in him memories of life in the Jazz Age and his infatuation with the girl who epitomized all the glamour, the folly, the joy of youth and love and aspiration of the past, a past as dead as the narrator's aunt and the corpse of another woman whom he contemplates in her coffin in what had been the enchanted tower of his youth. Thoroughly controlled, moving, and full of emotion which never degenerates into sentimentality, "Maiden in a Tower" is a masterly piece. So too is the title story "The City of the Living," a glimpse of a father and son during a few hours of almost unbearable crisis (the son is desperately ill in a hotel in Egypt); here Stegner presents a brilliant picture of father-son relations; and the setting, with its contrast of luxury and poverty, sickness and health, is unforgettable. Stegner is equally effective in his other stories of parent-child relations which furnish subject and theme for "The Blue-Winged Teal," "Impasse," and "The Volunteer."

The novella, "Field Guide to the Western Birds," however, in spite of some memorable moments, seems rather too long for what it accomplishes, too predictable in its denouement. As social history, however, Stegner's creation of well-heeled intellectuals and pseudo-intellectuals, frauds, hangers-on and circuit riders of the "good and opulent life," narrated by a self-congratulatory retired literary agent, has about it the ring of permanence. As John Galsworthy said of his Forsytes, here are characters miraculously preserved, pickled in their own juices.

OTHER MAJOR WORKS

LONG FICTION: *Remembering Laughter*, 1937; *The Potter's House*, 1938; *On a Darkling Plain*, 1940; *Fire and Ice*, 1941; *The Big Rock Candy Mountain*, 1943; *Second Growth*, 1947; *The Preacher and the Slave*, 1950; *A Shooting Star*, 1961; *All the Little Live Things*, 1967; *Angle of Repose*, 1971; *The Spectator Bird*, 1976; *Recapitulation*, 1979; *Joe Hill*, 1980; *Crossing to Safety*, 1987.

NONFICTION: *Mormon Country*, 1942; *One Nation*, 1945 (with the editors of *Look*); *Look at America: The Central Northwest*, 1947; *The Writer in America*, 1951; *Beyond the Hundredth Meridian: John Wesley Powell and the Second Opening of the West*, 1954; *Wolf Willow: A History, a Story, and a Memory of the Last Plains Frontier*, 1962; *The Gathering of Zion: The Story of the Mormon Trail*, 1964; *The Sound of Mountain Water*, 1969; *The Uneasy Chair: A Biography of Bernard DeVoto*, 1974; *Ansel Adams: Images 1923-1974*, 1974; *One Way to Spell Man*, 1982; *American Places*, 1983; *Conversations with Wallace Stegner on Western History and Literature*, 1983; *The American West as Living Space*, 1987; *On the Teaching of Creative Writing: Responses to a Series of Questions*, 1988 (edited by Edward Connery Lathem); *Where the Bluebird Sings to the Lemonade Springs: Living and Writing in the West*, 1992.

EDITED TEXTS: *An Exposition Workshop*, 1939 (edited); *Readings for Citizens at War*, 1941 (edited); *Stanford Short Stories, 1946*, 1947 (with Richard Scowcroft); *The Writer's Art: A Collection of Short Stories*, 1950 (with Scowcroft and Boris Ilyin); *This Is Dinosaur: The Echo Park and Its Magic Rivers*, 1955 (edited); *The Exploration of the Colorado River of the West*, 1957 (edited); *Great American Short Stories*, 1957 (with Mary Stegner); *Selected American Prose: The Realistic Movement*, 1958; *Report on the Lands of the Arid Region of the United States*, 1962 (edited); *Modern Composition*, 1964 (edited, 4 volumes); *The American Novel: From Cooper to Faulkner*, 1965 (edited); *Twenty Years of Stanford Short Stories*, 1966. *The Letters of Bernard DeVoto*, 1975 (edited);

BIBLIOGRAPHY

Arthur, Anthony, ed. *Critical Essays on Wallace Stegner*. Boston: G. K. Hall, 1982. Although not an exhaustive discussion of Stegner's works, these essays cover much of his most important writing, including his short fiction. Notes for further reference are included, as are primary and secondary bibliographical information and an index.

Benson, Jackson J. *Wallace Stegner: His Life and Work*. New York: Viking Press, 1996. A biography that argues against pigeonholing Stegner as a Western writer. Focuses largely on the people and events that most influenced Stegner's art, including Robert Frost and Bernard DeVoto; covers Stegner's teaching career and his influence on such writers as Ken Kesey, Edward Abbey, Wendell Berry, and Larry McMurty.

Burrows, Russell. "Wallace Stegner's Version of Pastoral: The Topic of Ecology in His Work." *Western American Literature* 25 (May, 1990): 15-25. Stegner's environmentalist stance has had a definite effect on his work, and this article discusses Stegner's use of the pastoral setting in much of his fiction, both long and short. Includes bibliographical information and notes for further reference on points within the article.

Colberg, Nancy. *Wallace Stegner: A Descriptive Bibliography*. Lewiston, Idaho: Confluence Press, 1990. This text contains detailed descriptions of Stegner's works, from his very early writing to *The American West as Living Space*. Colberg also provides sections for other Stegner material, such as contributions to books and edited works. A short appendix that also serves as a secondary bibliography is a good resource for the original publication information for Stegner's individual short stories.

Cook-Lynn, Elizabeth. *Why I Can't Read Wallace*

Stegner and Other Essays. Madison: University of Wisconsin Press, 1996. In the title essay of this collection, Cook-Lynn, a Native American, argues with Stegner's view of Native American culture. She particularly takes issue with Stegner's claim that Western history ended in 1890, the year of the massacre at Wounded Knee, and his unchallenged statement that the Plains Indians are done forever.

Meine, Curt, ed. *Wallace Stegner and the Continental Vision: Essays on Literature, History, and Landscape.* Washington, D.C.: Island Press, 1997. A collection of papers presented at a 1996 symposium in Madison, Wisconsin. Includes essays on Stegner and the shaping of the modern west, the art of storytelling, history, environmentalism, politics, and bioregionalism.

Nelson, Nancy Owne. "Land Lessons in an 'Unhistoried' West: Wallace Stegner's California." In *San Francisco in Fiction: Essays in a Regional Literature,* edited by David Fine and Paul Skenazy. Albuquerque: University of New Mexico Press, 1995. Argues that Stegner's California experience from the 1940's to the 1970's helped to shape the environmental philosophy of his work. Discusses Stegner's preservationist position in several fictional and nonfictional works.

Rankin, Charles E., ed. *Wallace Stegner: Man and Writer.* Albuquerque: University of New Mexico Press, 1996. A collection of essays by various critics on Stegner's life and art. Most helpful for understanding Stegner's short fiction are the essays by Elliott West on "Storytelling and Western Identity," Jackson J. Benson's "The Story of Wallace Stegner's Fiction," and William Bevis's "The Civic Style."

Robinson, Forrest G. *Wallace Stegner.* Boston: Twayne, 1977. This text is a combination of biographical information on Stegner and interpretation and literary criticism of his work up to the mid-1970's. Robinson provides a chronology of Stegner's life and writings as well as detailed bibliographical information, both primary and secondary. Supplemented by notes and an index.

Stegner, Wallace. "The Art of Fiction: An Interview with Wallace Stegner." Interview by James R. Hepworth. *The Paris Review* 115 (Summer, 1990): 58-90. In this interview, Stegner talks about how he became a writer, as well as about writing in general. Although no references are included, this article is useful for the first-hand information it provides about Stegner through the interview process.

Stegner, Wallace, and Richard Etulain. *Conversations with Wallace Stegner.* Rev. ed. Salt Lake City: University of Utah Press, 1990. This edition is an expanded version of a book that first came out in 1983—a later interview section has been added to the first part of the book. In it, Stegner talks about all of his work up to *Crossing to Safety.* Includes biographical information in the form of answers to interview questions and also covers Stegner's view of the American literary West as well as the West—such as Western history and the wilderness areas of the West—in general. References to individual short stories (as well as to the collections) can be found in the index.

Willrich, Patricia Rowe. "A Perspective on Wallace Stegner." *The Virginia Quarterly Review* 67 (Spring, 1991): 240-258. This article covers the high points of Stegner's long career as a writer and scholar, giving both biographical details and information about his work. Good for an overview of, as well as for specifics on, Stegner's literary output.

Zahlan, Anne Ricketson. "Cities of the Living: Disease and the Traveller in the *Collected Stories* of Wallace Stegner." *Studies in Short Fiction* 29 (Fall, 1992): 509-515. Discusses a number of thematically complementary stories in which characters travel into or away from exile, attempt to recover the past, or explore new avenues to discover the self.

William Peden,
updated by Jo-Ellen Lipman Boon

GERTRUDE STEIN

Born: Allegheny, Pennsylvania; February 3, 1874
Died: Neuilly-sur-Seine, France; July 27, 1946

PRINCIPAL SHORT FICTION

Three Lives, 1909 (three linked novellas)
Tender Buttons: Objects, Food, Rooms, 1914 (often
    considered a form of prose poetry)
*Mrs. Reynolds and Five Earlier Novelettes, 1931-
    1942*, 1952
As Fine as Melanctha, 1954
Painted Lace and Other Pieces, 1914-1937, 1955
Alphabets and Birthdays, 1957

OTHER LITERARY FORMS

It is difficult to classify Gertrude Stein's writings, because she radically upset the conventions of literary genres and because she worked in many different forms. Traditional generic labels simply do not describe individual works. Even when Stein names the genre in a work's title (*Ida, a Novel*, 1941, for example), the conventional form marks only how far Stein has digressed from the norm. Works such as *Ida, a Novel* and *Mrs. Reynolds and Five Earlier Novelettes* are Stein's version of the novel, while *The Autobiography of Alice B. Toklas* (1933) and *Operas and Plays* (1932), among other works, encourage comparison with other genres. Stein became famous in the United States with *The Autobiography of Alice B. Toklas*, and her success encouraged her to experiment further with the genre (*Everybody's Autobiography*, 1937). Even when writing "autobiography," however, Stein did not adhere to conventional restrictions, using multiple viewpoints in the composite work. Similarly, although Stein wrote many plays, some of which have been performed, they do not follow dramatic conventions, for frequently they lack plot and character. Stein also wrote meditations and other quasi-philosophical and theoretical musings, and in numerous essays she attempted to explain her theories of composition and her notions of art. In addition, she experimented in verse and developed a special genre which she called portraits. Regardless of the form,

however, the style is unmistakably Stein's and serves as a signature to all her works.

ACHIEVEMENTS

Gertrude Stein's greatest achievement was her wily and strong independence, which revealed itself as much in her lifestyle as in her work. She was a creative person with a strong personality, a gift for conversation, and a good ear, and her home became a center for the avant-garde circle of artists in Paris during the early 1900's. Perhaps this salon would not be so famous were it not for the fact that those associated with it were later accepted as the outstanding figures of the modern art world. In time, artists as different as Ernest Hemingway, Sherwood Anderson, Virgil Thomson, Guillaume Apollinaire, Henri Matisse, and Pablo Picasso became associated with Stein and were drawn into the discussions and activities that took place in her home. Among contemporaries she was recognized as a fascinating individual, a woman of strong opinions and definite views, a lively intelligence and vibrant mind; among the cultural historians who came later, she was acknowledged to be a person of enormous creative influence and empowering force.

Stein's achievements were not limited to her role as a cultural catalyst, however, for she was a pioneering writer in her own right. Working from a sense that the present moment of consciousness is supreme, Stein increasingly radicalized her writing to focus on the here and now, on the mystery of consciousness, and ultimately on the enigma of language and words. This drive led Stein increasingly away from the conventions of language as commonly understood and practiced through the structures and preoccupations of genre, through the patterns and assumptions of syntax, and finally even through the basic referential quality of words. Repetition—of sounds and words themselves—became the hallmark of Stein's writing. Some temporaries thought her experimental language to be foolish and childlike, but others hailed her efforts as truly pioneering literary breakthroughs. Most of the key terms in the criticism of modern literature have been applied to Stein at one time or another—abstractionist, cubist, minimalist, and so on. Indeed, most historians of the period agree that her work and her personality must be acknowledged before any serious discussion of any of these movements can proceed. However her work is defined, regardless of whether one likes or dislikes it, it has made a significant impact on the development of modern literature.

In addition to its variety and inventiveness, the sheer bulk of Stein's canon should not be overlooked as an accomplishment. Richard Bridgman's *Gertrude Stein in Pieces* (1970) lists nearly six hundred titles in the Stein bibliography, some very short pieces but others significantly longer. She was prolific, flexible, and varied—at her best in the unclassifiable writings that mingle verse, prose, and drama into a unique species of art that bears the imprint of Gertrude Stein alone.

Stein had the misfortune of living through two world wars. During the first she obtained a Ford van, which she drove for the American Fund for French Wounded. In 1922, she was awarded the Médaille de la Reconnaissance Française for wartime activities.

Gertrude Stein in 1935 (AP/Wide World Photos)

BIOGRAPHY

When Daniel Stein and Amelia Keyser were married in 1864, the seeds of Gertrude Stein's future independence were sown, for the couple had some unusual ideas about child rearing and family life. Perhaps most psychologically damaging to the children was the parents' firm decision to have five children—no more and no fewer. Consequently, Gertrude's beloved older brother Leo and she were conceived only after the deaths of two other Stein children. In *Everybody's Autobiography* Stein says that the situation made her and her brother feel "funny." Knowing that one's very existence depends on the deaths of others surely would have some psychological effect, and some biographers attribute Stein's lifelong interest in identity to her knowledge of her parents' decision about family size.

Daniel Stein was apparently as quarrelsome and independent as his daughter was to become. Having operated a successful cloth and clothing business in Baltimore with his brothers, Daniel and another brother broke up the partnership by moving out to Pittsburgh to open a new business. When Daniel had earned enough money, he moved the family across the Ohio to Allegheny, and it was there that Gertrude Stein was born in 1874. She was the last child the Steins were to have, completing the unit of five children. Michael Stein was the oldest child (born in 1865); Simon was next (1867); then came Bertha (1870) and Leo (1872). When Allegheny was hit with fire and flood, Daniel once again moved the family, this time to Austria, having decided that the older children needed the benefits of a European education.

The family went first to Gemünden and then to Vienna. Although not wealthy, they lived well and were able to afford a nurse, a tutor, a governess, and a full domestic staff. The children were exposed to music and dancing lessons, and they enjoyed all the sights and activities of the upper middle class in Europe at the time. In his concern for the education of his children, Daniel resembled Henry James, whose educational theories also featured the advantages of the European experience to a developing mind. During this period, letters from Amelia and her sister Rachel

Keyser, who accompanied the Steins, reveal that the baby was speaking German and experiencing an apparently contented, pampered, and protected infancy.

The roaming continued. In 1878, the family moved to Paris, and Stein got her first view of the city she would later make her home. When the Steins returned to the United States in 1879, they lived at first with the Keyser family in Baltimore, but Daniel was set on living in California. By 1880, the family had relocated to Oakland, where they stayed for some time (until 1891), long enough for the artist to develop an attachment to the place. It was Oakland that Stein always thought of as home.

The unsettled life of the Steins continued with the death of Amelia when the artist was fourteen. Three years later (in 1891), Daniel died, leaving Michael head of the family. He moved the family to San Francisco that year, but by the following year the family was dispersed—Michael and Simon remaining in San Francisco, Gertrude and her sister Bertha going back to Baltimore to live with their mother's sister, and Leo transferring from the University of California at Berkeley to Harvard. In the fall of 1893, Gertrude Stein herself entered Harvard Annex (later renamed Radcliffe College), thus rejoining the brother to whom she had grown so attached. Their strong bond was to survive into adulthood, being broken only by Gertrude's lifelong commitment to Alice B. Toklas and her ascendancy in Parisian art circles.

Stein was at Harvard during a wonderful period in that institution's history. She had the good fortune to study under William James, whose theories of psychology intrigued the young woman and initiated a lifelong interest in questions of personality, identity, and consciousness. Stein's later attempts to present in her writing awareness of a continuing flux in the present, the immediacy of present existence, and the inclusiveness and randomness of consciousness can be traced in part to James's influence. Stein's first publication came out during this Harvard period. "Normal Motor Automatism," co-authored with Leon M. Solomons, was published in *Psychological Review* in September, 1896. Although this essay was primarily Solomons's, Stein published her own work on the subject in the *Psychological Review* of May,

1898—"Cultivated Motor Automatism: A Study of Character in Its Relation to Attention." Stein's early interest in automatic writing has led some readers to believe that the method directed her own subsequent writing, but that claim has been generally discredited. Harvard did more to focus her attention on the consciousness behind the work than on the techniques and strategies of the writing process.

The Harvard experience was not, however, completely successful. In the spring of 1897, Stein failed the Radcliffe Latin entrance examination and consequently was not awarded her bachelor's degree. Undaunted, in the fall of 1897 she entered The Johns Hopkins School of Medicine, and she received the Harvard degree in 1898, having been privately tutored in Latin so that she could pass the examination. It was William James who encouraged her to take the Harvard degree and to continue her education; Johns Hopkins seemed a likely choice both because it was funded to accept women into the program on a basis equal to men and because her brother Leo was studying there. The first two years of medical study went well, but after that, Stein complained of boredom and began to dislike her classes. In the end, she did not pass her final examinations and never took the degree. She had learned what she wanted to learn and had no interest in practicing medicine.

For some time, Stein had been spending her summers in Europe with Leo, so it seemed natural that they would settle in London in September, 1902. In February of the following year, Stein sailed back to the United States, this time staying in New York until rejoining Leo once again for summer travel. In the fall of 1903, they occupied the house at 27 rue de Fleurus, the address which was to become famous as an artistic mecca. *Quod Erat Demonstrandum* (1950; also known as *Things as They Are*) was written there, although Stein then overlooked the work for some thirty years.

In 1904, Gertrude and Leo began purchasing paintings by men destined to become the leading figures of modern art. Having studied the great masters throughout the museums of Europe, the Steins were not automatically impressed with the world of modern art, yet something about Paul Cézanne's work struck Leo, and he took his sister to a gallery of his works. After the purchase of their first Cézanne, they were soon given freer rein to look among the canvases of the Paris art dealers. They purchased works by Honoré Daumier, Édouard Manet, Pierre-Auguste Renoir, Henri Toulouse-Lautrec, Paul Gauguin, and others. Thus Leo and Gertrude Stein laid out a new direction in their own cultural life and established a new model for American art collectors. People began to go to the rue de Fleurus address to see the paintings and then to talk about art and to socialize. The cultural center of modern art was born.

During this time, Stein was also writing. *The Making of Americans* (1925) and *Three Lives* date to this period, *Three Lives* being published in 1909 as Stein's first book. Another important event of the period was Stein's meeting Alice Toklas in September, 1907; Toklas moved into the Stein household on rue de Fleurus early in 1909. Her presence hastened the deterioration of the relationship between Stein and her brother (he finally left in 1913) and facilitated Stein's writing, because Toklas learned to type and transcribed Stein's work. She was Stein's companion for the remainder of the artist's life.

In June, 1914, *Tender Buttons* was published. The work marks a significant movement on Stein's part toward abstractionism, as she focuses more on things than on people and blurs the distinction between poetry and prose. When war broke out, Stein and Toklas were house guests of the Alfred North Whiteheads in Lockridge, and they did not return to Paris until October of that year. In 1915, they left Paris for Spain, returning in 1916. In 1917, Stein obtained a Ford van from the United States, which she drove for the American Fund for French Wounded as a supply truck, and Stein's preoccupation with automobiles, especially Fords, began. She contributed to the war effort in France in various ways and in various areas of France, not returning to Paris "permanently" until May of 1919.

After the war, writing and socializing could once again begin in earnest. In 1922, she met Hemingway and became godmother to his son born the following year. Stein continued to write and began also to lecture during this period; she continued also to cultivate her interest in cars (she was now on her third) and in pet dogs. In 1930, *Lucy Church Amiably* was published, and in 1932, *The Autobiography of Alice B. Toklas* was written at Bilignin. It became a literary sensation in 1933, and it continues to be the most widely read and appreciated of all Stein's writings. Early in 1934, the first public performance of *Four Saints in Three Acts* (1932) took place in Hartford, Connecticut. Performances in other cities soon followed, and Stein began a lecture tour in the United States that established her reputation.

When Paris was occupied in 1940, Stein was advised to leave, which she did, not returning until December of 1944. In the following year, she toured United States Army bases in occupied Germany and lectured in Belgium and elsewhere. In July of 1946, en route to a friend's summer house, Stein fell ill and was admitted to the American hospital at Neuilly-sur-Seine. On July 27, she died following an operation for cancer. Her brother Leo died a year later, almost to the day, and Toklas, Gertrude Stein's dearest companion, survived another twenty-two years. A chapter in the history of modern art had come to an end.

ANALYSIS

Gertrude Stein's work has never been easily accessible to the reader. During her lifetime, her work was both ridiculed and celebrated, and indeed these two attitudes continue to prevail among Stein's readers. Historical distance has provided a supportive context for Stein's work, however, and now that readers can see Stein in a milieu of highly creative artists devoted to wrenching art from the restrictions of realism and verisimilitude, her work is more easily appreciated for the inroads it makes against conventions, although perhaps not more easily understood. Stein was a powerful initiator, a ruthless experimenter, and a bold and forthright manipulator of words.

TENDER BUTTONS

Having already written *Things as They Are*, *Three Lives*, and *The Making of Americans*, Stein was in full command when she made the surprising innovations of *Tender Buttons*. The author herself always rated the work highly, considering it to be one of her most significant writings despite the ridicule and scorn it received from those who did not agree that it added a new dimension to literature. Prior to *Tender Buttons*, Stein had grown increasingly abstract in her writing. *Tender Buttons* marks something of a culmination in this progressing abstractionism, for here she produces a set of "still lifes," each of which sustains abstraction. The subject matter, too, has changed from earlier writing. In *Tender Buttons*, Stein moves from people to things. The book is divided into three sections: "Objects," "Food," and "Rooms." While the divisions classify, the effect is still that of eclecticism, for no perceptible principles of order determine either the arrangement within each section or the sequencing of the sections themselves.

The title of *Tender Buttons* indicates some of the ironies of the collection. A button is something hard, concrete, and functional, while the word "tender" as an adjective suggests the opposite—something soft. "Tender" can also be a verb, and, in this sense, the collection is Stein's offering of discrete bits of prose. "Tender" may suggest an emotional state, but, if so, the emotion must emanate from the reader, for the hard little buttons of prose in *Tender Buttons* do not themselves develop an emotional state. In the title, as in the name of each passage within the work, Stein seems to be offering the reader something tangible, something realistic, but she does so only to challenge the reader's notions of reality and to tease the mind.

The verbal fragments in *Tender Buttons* reveal a variety of strategies, and it is the flexibility of language and idea that keeps one reading. Each entry is titled; "A Red Stamp," "A Plate," "Roastbeef," "Sugar," and "Oranges" are typical examples. Entries range in length from a single short line to the approximately twelve pages of the undivided section "Rooms." In some of the entries, the title shapes the suggestions and hints, while in others, the title seems to bear little or no relationship to what follows. Stein's prose does not describe the objects realistically, but rather, opens the mind to the flow of thoughts that the title evokes. In these verbal fragments there is no logic, no sequence; sometimes an entry shows accretion, but no line of thought is developed. Indeed, even the logic of syntax is refused in favor of phrases and, ultimately, in favor of single words.

The work is abstract not only because it collects seemingly discrete verbal fragments but also because it seems to follow one of Stein's axioms about abstract painting: that a painting has its own existence, its own life. Aesthetic value does not derive from a work's referential quality but rather from itself. In modern painting, the focus is on the colors of the paint, the shapes, the textures, the forms. In *Tender Buttons*, the focus is on the words themselves, their sounds, juxtapositions, and the life that emanates from their unconventional arrangement. Stein recognized that words bring with them a whole series of associations that are different for each reader and uncontrollable by the artist, so she deliberately aimed to remove words from their usual contexts to reduce their associational qualities and to cause new associations to arise from novel juxtapositions. A reader of Stein's work must surrender selfhood to the text and accept the linguistic experience offered.

"As Fine as Melanctha"

In naming volume 4 of the Yale edition of Stein's writings *As Fine as Melanctha*, the editors draw attention to one of Stein's short pieces of prose that takes the appearance of a short story but turns out to defy the conventions of that genre, just as Stein defies other literary conventions. "As Fine as Melanctha" was Stein's answer when requested to write something "as fine as 'Melanctha,'" one of the three pieces that constitute *Three Lives*; yet "As Fine as Melanctha" is radically different from the earlier work. The 1922 piece has no characters, no setting, no plot, and no chronology. The opening line announces that it is "a history of a moment," but a moment has no history. "As Fine as Melanctha" is a moment out of time, or rather many moments out of time, moments so common as to be timeless and timely simultaneously.

"As Fine as Melanctha" is a good example of Stein's perfected verbal strategies throughout the decade of the 1920's as she attempted to make immediate and alive the verbal moment. She ignores, for example, the rules of syntax, mingling phrases and clauses and sentences indiscriminately. The only punctuation mark in the piece is the period, and it closes sentence fragments and sentences alike. Even questions end in a period rather than the expected question mark. The effect is that syntax no longer aids communication; consequently, readers must release their fierce hold on sentence structure as a way to capture meaning. Where, however, can they turn in their drive to understand? The logical next step is the word itself. yet the reader is so accustomed to thinking of words as they relate to one another that when Stein violates expected word order as well as the rules of syntax, the reader confronts the stunning reality that words themselves are empty. Since everything one knows is understood through context, the removal of context both in the larger areas of character development and plot and in the smaller areas of language renders the reading of "As Fine as Melanctha" something of an existential experience.

Reading Stein's work puts the reader in tension with the text—that is, when the sparks fly for those willing to accept the challenge. Repeatedly, and in a variety of ways, Stein makes language meaningless. One of the hallmarks of Stein's work is repetition. Yet repetition does not contribute to communication by stressing meaning; instead, it reduces meaning. The following sentence from "As Fine as Melanctha" uses internal repetition: "I mean that it has been noticed again and again that abundance that in abundance that the need of abundance that there is therein a need of abundance and in this need it is a necessity that there is stock taking." A reader is grateful to emerge from the tangled web in the inner core of the sentence—repetition of "abundance," "need," and "need of abundance." The sentence seems to accumulate words that lose meaning in the process of being accumulated. Even the apparent meaning at the end vanishes in the light of "abundance." The repetition so confuses the reader that the end of the sentence seems to have meaning because it apparently follows normal English syntax, yet even that meaning reduces itself to the redundancy of "stock taking" and "abundance." The reader is left with a single, uncontextualized word, systematically emptied of meaning and association.

There are other kinds of repetition in "As Fine as

Melanctha." Repetitions of sounds as well as words prevail in a passage such as the following: "How dearly clearly merely is she me, how dearly clearly merely am I she. How dearly is she me how dearly is she me how dearly how very dearly am I she." The words "dearly," "clearly," "merely," "she," and "me" are repeated in varied arrangements that challenge syntax. The sounds of the words tend to flatten them, to make them anonymous. Repetition of the sound "erely" eventually is reduced to repetition of the "e" sound, as in "me." The sentence shows Stein's progressive reductionism: The meanings of different words are reduced to sounds; the repetition of multiple sounds is reduced to a single sound. Not only do the words become meaningless when repeated in such close proximity, but also characters become such close approximations of one another that identity is destroyed. Language here is subversive and destructive.

In another example, repetition is used to change syntax: "The difference between humming to-day yesterday and to-morrow is this, it always means more. The difference between humming to-day yesterday and to-morrow is this. It always means more." The reader yearns to believe that this variation of syntax is meaningful, because that is the way readers have been taught to read. Yet once again, the repetition is used to destroy meaning. When Stein's reader puts mind against text, the mind returns as a wet noodle, aware only of its own limpness. Such awareness, however, is knowledge of one's fleeting consciousness, and Stein's objective is achieved.

"BRIM BEAUVAIS"

"Brim Beauvais" represents Stein's work during the decade of the 1930's, when she became increasingly minimalist. In this work, her paragraphs are shorter, most being only a single line, and formal sections come from division into chapters, although such divisions are useless. Many chapters have the same identifying label: For example, three sections are identified as "Chapter X"; two are "Chapter Ten." Furthermore, the numbers are not always sequential. More confusion in the structure occurs through embedding. Several pages into "Brim Beauvais" appears the heading "Beauvais and His Wife: A Novel."

There are labeled episodes within sections, although neither the chapter headings nor other labels contribute to communication. The work has a "Part II," but no Part I. All these devices are merely added to the verbal disruptions seen in earlier work. Even the opening of "Brim Beauvais" suggests how much further Stein has gone in her developing abstractionism. The work begins with the single word "once." It functions elliptically to suggest the "once upon a time" opening of fairy tales. Yet the second line truncates that suggestion. "Always excited to say twice" forces readers to understand "once" in a numerical framework and thus to count something they do not know; similarly, the adjective "excited" describes a person not yet introduced. Stein is a master at invoking emptiness. Like the cubists, she presented a part without feeling it necessary to fill in or even suggest the surrounding whole. She believed that the mind partakes of the world through fragments, not through complete systems, and that her writing was an open window on this process.

ALPHABETS AND BIRTHDAYS

By the winter of 1940, another war had begun in Europe, and Stein was finding it difficult to carry on any sustained writing project. "To Do: A Book of Alphabets and Birthdays" (published in 1957 as *Alphabets and Birthdays*) provided a structure while allowing for the intermittent composition that met Stein's needs during this period. The structure was provided by the alphabet, which Stein marched progressively through, assigning four names to each letter and creating episodes, events, and nonsense rhymes around each. The work has the fantastic actions and situations that children love, and Stein had children in mind when she wrote it. However, some publishers have insisted that the work is really more appropriate for adults than for children. If so, it must be adults who are young at heart, for the work has a delightful lightness, a happy flippancy, and a joy of language that emerges from repetition of sounds and words. The alphabet book shows Stein's skill at duplicating the rhythms and sounds of conversation and thoughts as people silently talk to themselves. Stein's ear for speech has often been noted, and here the speech of conversation conveys a swiftness and easy familiarity

that make the work especially pleasant to read. At the same time, it remains true to the developing minimalism throughout Stein's career, for the letter is a reduction of the word.

Stein adhered to her principles throughout her life, always finding new ways to bring the meaning of her craft to the reader's awareness—even if this meant shocking the reader out of the lethargy of language. When she began to attract more people than her brother, Leo's support deteriorated and he claimed to find her work silly. His evaluation is shared by many. Stein is not a writer for all readers. Indeed, she tends to attract only coterie groups. Because her work is amenable to literary critics practicing deconstruction, however, and because the feminist movement has brought lesbian relationships into the open and searches out the quiet subversions such a lifestyle encouraged, both the work of Gertrude Stein and the artist herself have been looked at anew. The new reader and the returning reader alike will find Stein's work ever fresh, ever varying, ever innovative, and ever shocking, and for that reason alone it will always have enthusiastic readers somewhere, someplace.

OTHER MAJOR WORKS

LONG FICTION: *The Making of Americans*, 1925; *Lucy Church Amiably*, 1930; *A Long Gay Book*, 1932; *Ida, a Novel*, 1941; *Brewsie and Willie*, 1946; *Blood on the Dining-Room Floor*, 1948; *Things as They Are*, 1950 (later as *Quod Erat Demonstrandum*); *A Novel of Thank You*, 1958.

PLAYS: *Geography and Plays*, pb. 1922; *Operas and Plays*, pb. 1932; *Four Saints in Three Acts*, pr., pb. 1934; *In Savoy: Or, Yes Is for a Very Young Man (A Play of the Resistance in France)*, pr., pb. 1946; *The Mother of Us All*, pr. 1947; *Last Operas and Plays*, pb. 1949; *In a Garden: An Opera in One Act*, pb. 1951; *Lucretia Borgia*, pb. 1968; *Selected Operas and Plays*, pb. 1970.

POETRY: *Two (Hitherto Unpublished) Poems*, 1948; *Bee Time Vine and Other Pieces: 1913-1927*, 1953; *Stanzas in Meditation and Other Poems: 1929-1933*, 1956.

NONFICTION: *The Autobiography of Alice B. Toklas*, 1933; *Matisse, Picasso, and Gertrude Stein*, *with Two Shorter Stories*, 1933; *Portraits and Prayers*, 1934; *Lectures in America*, 1935; *Narration: Four Lectures*, 1935; *The Geographical History of America*, 1936; *Everybody's Autobiography*, 1937; *Picasso*, 1938; *What Are Masterpieces?*, 1940; *Wars I Have Seen*, 1945; *Reflections on the Atomic Bomb*, 1973; *How Writing Is Written*, 1974.

CHILDREN'S LITERATURE: *The World Is Round*, 1939.

MISCELLANEOUS: *The Gertrude Stein First Reader and Three Plays*, 1946; *The Yale Edition of the Unpublished Writings of Gertrude Stein*, 1951-1958 (eight volumes, edited by Carl Van Vechten); *Selected Writings of Gertrude Stein*, 1962; *The Yale Gertrude Stein*, 1980.

BIBLIOGRAPHY

Bowers, Jane Palatini. *Gertrude Stein*. New York: St. Martin's Press, 1993. A succinct, feminist-oriented introduction to Stein, with separate chapters on the short fiction, novels, and plays. Includes notes and bibliography.

Bridgman, Richard. *Gertrude Stein in Pieces*. New York: Oxford University Press, 1970. The first detailed, chronological study of all Stein's work. Bridgman's approach is primarily psychobiological; he locates Stein's experimentalism in pathology rather than intention, seeing guilty evasiveness about lesbian sexuality as the crucial impetus for her avant-garde writing.

Brinnin, John Malcom. *The Third Rose: Gertrude Stein and Her World*. Boston: Little, Brown, 1959. Aside from its significant biographical value, this study contains provocative comments on Stein's writing, twentieth century painting, and modern intellectual and artistic movements. Includes a useful bibliography.

DeKoven, Marianne. *A Different Language: Gertrude Stein's Experimental Writing*. Madison: University of Wisconsin Press, 1983. DeKoven's feminist study focuses on Stein's experimental work published after *Three Lives* and before *The Autobiography of Alice B. Toklas*. She argues that this period of Stein's writing is important not so much because of its influence on other writers but because of its attempt to redefine patriarchal language and provide alternatives to conventional modes of signification.

Hoffman, Michael J. *Critical Essays on Gertrude Stein*. Boston: G. K. Hall, 1986. A collection of reviews and essays, most of which appeared during and immediately after Stein's long career in letters. Diverse literary criticisms, such as new criticism, structuralism, feminism, and deconstruction are represented. Among the contributors are Lisa Ruddick, Marianne DeKoven, Wendy Steiner, Catharine R. Stimpson, Donald Sutherland, and Allegra Stewart. Also included are Sherwood Anderson, Marianne Moore, William Carlos Williams, B. F. Skinner, Katherine Anne Porter, Edmund Wilson, and W. H. Auden.

_____. *The Development of Abstractionism in the Writings of Gertrude Stein*. Philadelphia: University of Pennsylvania Press, 1965. Hoffman traces the progressive development of abstractionism in Stein's early writing (1903-1913), focusing on the varieties of abstractionism manifesting themselves in each work. In his subsequent study, published more than a decade later, Hoffman again focuses on the abstract, refining his earlier definition of Stein's abstractionism as a "leaving-out" of stylistic and thematic elements normally appearing in the major works of American and European literature. This second study, covering the period from 1902-1946, stresses the ways in which Stein progressively abstracted from her writing most of the traditional elements of fictional prose narrative.

Knapp, Bettina. *Gertrude Stein*. New York: Continuum, 1990. A general introduction to Stein's life and art. Discusses her stylistic breakthrough in the stories in *Three Lives*, focusing on repetition and the use of the continuous present. Devotes a long chapter to *Tender Buttons* as one of Stein's most innovative and esoteric works; discusses the nonreferential nature of language in the fragments.

Murphy, Margueritte S. *A Tradition of Subversion: The Prose Poem in English from Wilde to Ashbery*. Amherst: University of Massachusetts Press, 1992. Devotes a chapter to *Tender Buttons*; argues that Stein borrowed her genre from painting; discusses the experimental nature of Stein's prose poems in the collections.

Neuman, Shirley, and Ira B. Nadel, eds. *Gertrude Stein and the Making of Literature*. Boston: Northeastern University Press, 1988. A collection of essays on Stein from a variety of theoretical perspectives that attempt to "reread" her work in the 1970's and 1980's. Includes essays on Stein and the modernist canon, her relationship to American art and to Henry James, and her experimental collection of prose fragments, *Tender Buttons*.

Ruddick, Lisa. *Reading Gertrude Stein: Body, Text, Gnosis*. Ithaca, N.Y.: Cornell University Press, 1990. Examines the cultural and psychosocial contexts of "Melanctha," *The Making of Americans, G.M.P.* (Stein's abbreviated title for the work she also called *Matisse, Picasso, and Ger-*

trude Stein), and *Tender Buttons*—works that Ruddick argues have a creative momentum rarely achieved in Stein's later experimental works because all four are serial acts of self-definition. Ruddick's study combines poststructuralism with a humanist understanding of the artistic process; she sees *Tender Buttons* as Stein's work of genius because it orients the reader ethically rather than disorienting the reader in the play of language.

Sutherland, Donald. *Gertrude Stein: A Biography of Her Work*. Westport, Conn.: Greenwood Press, 1951. The first substantial critical book on Stein's writing, this work treats Stein's radical writings as an illustration of her own modernist philosophy and aesthetics. The book also justifies the modern movement in writing and painting. Includes a useful appendix, which catalogs Stein's writing according to stylistic periods.

Paula Kopacz, updated by Cassandra Kircher

JOHN STEINBECK

Born: Salinas, California; February 27, 1902
Died: New York, New York; December 20, 1968

PRINCIPAL SHORT FICTION
The Pastures of Heaven, 1932
Saint Katy the Virgin, 1936
The Long Valley, 1938

OTHER LITERARY FORMS

Besides two volumes of short fiction, John Steinbeck produced numerous novels, among which is his masterpiece, *The Grapes of Wrath* (1939). He also authored several screenplays and three dramas, two of which were based on his novels, *Of Mice and Men* (1937) and *The Moon Is Down* (1942). Among his nonfiction are several travel books and a collection of war sketches. His last work was a translation of Sir Thomas Malory's Arthurian stories. A volume of letters was published posthumously.

ACHIEVEMENT

John Steinbeck assumes an important place in American literature chiefly for his powerful and deft portrayal of the common people—the migrant worker, the ranch hand, and the laborer—whose capacity for survival surpassed the attempts of economic and corporate forces to defeat them. His novels, especially, render the human condition with sensitivity and lyrical grace. His work often shows a versatility unrivaled among his contemporaries. The comic, the tragic, the whimsical, and the naturalistic all merge in such a way as to make Steinbeck one of the United States' most popular writers, one whose art form is particularly suited to the cinema. Many of his books have been turned into successful films. Though much of Steinbeck's best work was written in the 1930's, he is not only a propagandist of the Great Depression era but also a writer who is deeply concerned with the dignity of human beings. A human being as an individual may pass away, but the human being as a group, humankind as a species, is immortal. As Ma Joad remarked in the final pages of The Grapes of Wrath: "We're the people. We go on."

BIOGRAPHY

The Salinas Valley, where John Steinbeck was born, lies about a hundred miles south of San Francisco. It is a fertile, temperate trough between two mountain ranges and encompasses some of central California's most picturesque areas, notably Pacific Grove and the serenity of Monterey Bay. Such a landscape was at the heart of Steinbeck's boyhood experience and forms a crucial link with the characteristics of the writer's work. The son of a mill owner and a schoolteacher, Steinbeck grew up in the small railroad town just entering the twentieth century, a town not quite pastoral yet not quite industrial, whose people were farmers and ranchers and shopkeepers but whose location and natural resources were quickly making it an agricultural and mercantile hub. This unique duality of the Salinas Valley—the long valley of Steinbeck's fiction—became a formative agent in the quality of Steinbeck's work, stories at once gently romantic and mythic as they were also realistic and proletarian. His early reading was evidence of his growing dualism. The realistic novels of Gustave Flaubert and Thomas Hardy were supplemented by his readings in Greek and Roman mythology, the Bible, and especially Sir Thomas Malory's *Le Morte d'Arthur* (c. 1469, printed 1485), the first book given to him as a child and the last to serve as a source for his fiction. (A retelling of the King Arthur stories was published posthumously in 1976).

By the time Steinbeck entered Salinas High School in 1915, he was a widely read young man, tall, with rugged good looks and a desire to write. At seventeen, he entered Stanford University, already convinced that he was going to be a writer. Like many creative artists before and since, Steinbeck found the discipline of the college curriculum too irksome. Though he enjoyed reading contemporary European and American writers such as Theodore Dreiser and Sinclair Lewis, he was uninterested in much else and

John Steinbeck, Nobel Laureate for Literature in 1962
(AP/World Wide Photos)

took a leave of absence after two years. For the next few years, he worked in the San Francisco area as a clerk and a field hand on a ranch, gaining the invaluable experience of ranch life and ranch hands that was to figure in such works as *Of Mice and Men* and *The Long Valley*.

He returned to Stanford University briefly as an English major but finally left in 1925 without a degree. He had written two stories for the *Stanford Spectator*, one a satire on college life and the other a bizarre tale about a strangely inarticulate woman and her marriage to a migrant worker who kept horses' heads in a rain barrel. The story is insignificant but interesting for its odd mixture of the real and the whimsical, a characteristic typical of much of Steinbeck's mature work.

Steinbeck was in New York during the late 1920's, working as a construction worker on the original Madison Square Garden by day and writing stories by night. Unsuccessful, he returned to California, married, and settled in his family's cottage in Pacific

Grove. He wrote constantly, and in 1929, his first novel, *Cup of Gold*, was published. This thinly fictionalized account of the pirate Henry Morgan was both an artistic and a financial failure. *The Pastures of Heaven* (1932), Steinbeck's second book, was a collection of short stories about the people of an almost mythically beautiful valley. Influenced by Sherwood Anderson's *Winesburg, Ohio* (1919), published a decade earlier, neither it nor his next novel, *To a God Unknown* (1933), brought Steinbeck much critical or popular success.

His apprenticeship, however, was over. Beginning in 1935 with the publication of *Tortilla Flat*, Steinbeck was to produce half a dozen books over the next ten years, works that were to establish his reputation as a writer of power and versatility. *Tortilla Flat* was followed by *In Dubious Battle* (1936), regarded by some as one of the best strike novels ever written. *Of Mice and Men* was followed by *The Long Valley*, containing his best short stories. His masterpiece, on which he had been working for three years, was published as *The Grapes of Wrath* in 1939.

During World War II, Steinbeck wrote propaganda scripts for the U.S. Army and published *The Moon Is Down*, a short novel set in Nazi-occupied Norway. His postwar work showed a marked decline. Aside from the massive *East of Eden* (1952), the works of this period are marked by a bland whimsy. *Cannery Row* (1945) is generally recognized as the novel that signaled the beginning of Steinbeck's decline. Throughout the 1950's and 1960's, Steinbeck, then a national celebrity, continued to produce a variety of fiction, novels such as *Sweet Thursday* (1954), *The Short Reign of Pippen IV* (1957), and *The Winter of Our Discontent* (1961). They are works of minor importance and show little of the narrative strength that won for Steinbeck the Nobel Prize in Literature in 1962.

His last years were spent quietly in New York City and on Long Island. By then he had become an honored American writer. In 1963, he was selected as honorary consultant in American literature for the Library of Congress. He was elected to the National Arts Council in 1966. Steinbeck died peacefully in his sleep on December 20, 1968.

ANALYSIS

The qualities that most characterize the work of John Steinbeck are a supple narrative style, a versatility of subject matter, and an almost mystical sympathy for the common human being. His fiction is peopled with men and women somehow shoaled from society's mainstream yet possessed of a vision that is itself a source of strength. His characteristic narrative method is to portray these people with an unerring mixture of realism and romance.

Though the Great Depression is the central social focus of his best work, his characters respond to those social forces not only in terms of realistic confrontation but also in the form of a romantic, intuitive escape. His characters become not so much victims of social or economic failure but celebrants of a life-force beyond society and economics. The best of Steinbeck's work maintains this tension—developed by a narrative tone—between the world of harsh reality and the world of animal-like freedom. Even in a late novel such as *East of Eden*, his best books behind him, Steinbeck symbolically construed this duality in the reference to the two mountain ranges that defined the territory of his narrator's childhood, the "sunny" flowered slopes of the Gabilans to the east and the dark, brooding peaks of the Santa Lucias to the west.

THE PASTURES OF HEAVEN

Nowhere is this duality—the tension between realism and romance—more evident than in Steinbeck's earliest short stories, those forming his first major work, *The Pastures of Heaven*. Structurally the book shows the influence of Anderson's *Winesburg, Ohio*, a series of short stories, each independent but each connected by the locale and the theme of psychic isolation.

Using the frame narrative of *Winesburg* as a model, *The Pastures of Heaven* deals with the lives of a number of characters living in the peaceful, idyllic valley in the hills beyond Monterey. Secluded like some medieval bower or enchanted castle, the place evokes images of romance and peace. Yet for all the outward tranquillity, the valley cannot remain isolated from the real world of economic hardship and violence.

The Munroe farm, for example, is cursed, and the curse executes itself on all the characters who come into contact with the Munroes. The theme of this collection of short stories is the conflict inherent in the tension between the characters' desire to live in the peaceful valley and their own human weaknesses, which prevent them from fulfilling their desires. Put in another way, the stories form a latter-day Garden of Eden myth. The land is beautiful, fruitful, prosperous; but the people of the land are thwarted by the serpent of human frailty.

Though some of the characters are spiritual kin to the "grotesques of Anderson's famous collection," they are markedly different in their attempts to reconcile their romantic intuition with the reality of social convention. Tularecito, for example, is all instinct. Though an idiot, he possesses great strength and an intuitive ability to draw. The title of the story, "The Legend of Tularecito," suggests that, like a legend, Tularecito is a child of romance. In his contradictory nature, he is the archetype of all the characters in the collection. Foreshadowing the half-witted giant, Lenny, in *Of Mice and Men*, Tularecito brings destruction on himself when he attacks Bert Munroe and is sent to a state asylum outside the valley. His punishment is not physical death, as in Lenny's case, but banishment from the valley, from Eden. Tularecito has come into contact with the reality of social convention and is defeated. Intuition is thwarted in the interest of social stability.

The conflict between an idyllic life, communing with nature, and the demands of middle-class respectability is the focus of another story, "Junius Maltby." Like prelapsarian man, Junius lives innocently off the land. Reminiscent of the *paisanos*, such as Danny and Mac in later novels such as *Tortilla Flat* and *Cannery Row*, Junius is shiftless and, by society's standards, an irresponsible dreamer. Like Tularecito, Junius is intuitive, instinctual, indifferent to the economic imperatives of being a farmer, and casually indecorous in his personal appearance. To Mrs. Munroe, Junius's life of the imagination is a threat. Junius is forced to abandon his farm and to leave the valley. There is no place for the poor and the romantic in Eden.

"THE CHRYSANTHEMUMS"

The garden as instinct, as the life of the spirit, is a prominent image in two stories in a later collection. Published in 1938, *The Long Valley* contains some of Steinbeck's most brilliant work in the genre of short fiction. In "The Chrysanthemums," Steinbeck presents the figure of Eliza Allen, a woman whose romantic gentleness conflicts with the brusque matter-of-factness of her husband and the deceitful cunning of a tinker. The story reveals a skillful meshing of character and setting, of symbol and theme. The garden is at once the chief setting and abiding symbol that define Eliza's character and her predicament as a woman.

Dressed in a man's clothing, Eliza is working in her garden when the story opens. Already the contrast is clear between Eliza's sensitive nature and the man-like indifference of her dress, her husband and life on the ranch, bathed in "the cold greyflannel fog of winter." Eliza's only emotional outlet, her only contact with a deeper life-pulse, is her growing of chrysanthemums, symbolic of both her sexual need and her recognition of the dominance in her nature of the life of the instinct. Like the virgin queen Elizabeth, Eliza has no children and her mannish ways merely disguise her sensitivity, a sensitivity that her husband Henry does not understand.

When a tinker stops his wagon at the ranch, looking for pots to repair, Eliza at first has no work for him, but when he praises her chrysanthemums, implying an understanding of her nature, Eliza gives him the flowers in a pot. That night, on their way to town for dinner and—the husband teases—to the prizefights, Eliza sees the discarded flowers on the road and realizes that the tinker had deceived her. Like her husband, the tinker did not really understand her; he had merely used her to his own advantage. At the end of the story, Eliza cries quietly, "like an old woman."

"THE WHITE QUAIL"

Still another story in the collection presents the image of the garden as both physical and psychic landscape. The garden that Mary Tiller tends in "The White Quail," however, is symbolic not of a healthy life of the spirit but of self-love and egotism. Mary's happiness with her garden, complete when she sees a white quail in it one night, is at the expense of her love for her husband. Harry is shut out of her love, often forced to sleep alone, though he virtually idolizes her. Mary's garden is her dream of an ordered, nonthreatening and nonsexual existence. In a sense, Mary "quails" before a life of passion or the body. When a cat one day wanders into the garden, Mary is fearful of its potential as a predator and demands that Harry shoot it. Inexplicably, he shoots the quail; in destroying Mary's dream, he has brought his wife back to the real world, to a sexuality that she had refused to admit.

"FLIGHT"

A story of maturity and death is the much-praised "Flight." Opening amid the rocky crags of the Torres farm, the story centers on Pepe, the oldest son of the widow Torres. A tall, lazy youth, Pepe has inherited his father's knife and yearns for the day when he will become, like his father, a man. Sent into Monterey on an errand, Pepe is insulted by a townsman and kills the man with his knife. Returning, he bids his mother good-bye and, armed with his father's rifle and horse, leaves his home to flee into the mountains. Gradually, he loses his rifle, then his horse. Now alone, he faces the threat of natural forces and the human pursuers. In the end, he is shot by one of the unseen "dark watchers."

Significantly, Pepe relies more on his own strength and courage as he flees deeper into the wild mountain passes; as he leaves his childhood behind, however, he also approaches his own death. Pepe's journey has become not only a physical escape from society's retribution but also a symbolic pilgrimage toward manhood and a redemptive death.

OTHER MAJOR WORKS

LONG FICTION: *Cup of Gold*, 1929; *To a God Unknown*, 1933; *Tortilla Flat*, 1935; *In Dubious Battle*, 1936; *Of Mice and Men*, 1937; *The Red Pony*, 1937, 1945; *The Grapes of Wrath*, 1939; *The Moon Is Down*, 1942; *Cannery Row*, 1945; *The Pearl*, 1945 (serial), 1947 (book); *The Wayward Bus*, 1947; *Burning Bright*, 1950; *East of Eden*, 1952; *Sweet Thursday*, 1954; *The Short Reign of Pippen IV*, 1957;

The Winter of Our Discontent, 1961.

PLAYS: *Of Mice and Men*, pr., pb. 1937; *The Moon Is Down: A Play in Two Parts*, pr. 1942; *Burning Bright*, pb. 1951.

SCREENPLAYS: *The Forgotten Village*, 1941; *Lifeboat*, 1944; *A Medal for Benny*, 1945; *The Pearl*, 1945; *The Red Pony*, 1949; *Viva Zapata!*, 1952.

NONFICTION: *Their Blood Is Strong*, 1938; *The Forgotten Village*, 1941; *Sea of Cortez*, 1941 (with Edward F. Ricketts); *Bombs Away*, 1942; *A Russian Journal*, 1948 (with Robert Capa); *Once There Was a War*, 1958; *Travels with Charley: In Search of America*, 1962; *Letters to Alicia*, 1965; *America and Americans*, 1966; *Journal of a Novel*, 1969; *Steinbeck: A Life in Letters*, 1975 (Elaine Steinbeck and Robert Wallsten, editors).

TRANSLATION: *The Acts of King Arthur and His Noble Knights*, 1976.

BIBLIOGRAPHY

Astro, Richard, and Tetsumaro Hayashi, eds. *Steinbeck: The Man and His Work*. Corvallis: Oregon State University Press, 1971. One of the first full-length works published after Steinbeck's death, this superb collection of essays presents opinions which regard Steinbeck as everything from a mere proletarian novelist to an artist with a deep vision of humans' essential dignity.

Benson, Jackson D. *The True Adventures of John Steinbeck, Writer*. New York: Viking Press, 1984. This biography emphasizes Steinbeck's rebellion against critical conventions and his attempts to keep his private life separate from his role as public figure. Benson sees Steinbeck as a critical anomaly, embarrassed and frustrated by his growing critical and popular success.

Fontenrose, Joseph. *John Steinbeck: An Introduction and Interpretation*. New York: Holt, Rinehart and Winston, 1963. A good introduction, this book discusses some of the symbolism inherent in much of Steinbeck's fiction and contains some insightful observations on Steinbeck's concept of the "group-man"—that is, the individual as a unit in the larger sociobiological organism.

French, Warren. *John Steinbeck's Fiction Revisited*.

New York: Twayne, 1994. The chapter on *The Long Valley* in this revision of French's earlier Twayne book on Steinbeck provides brief discussions of the major stories, including "Flight" and "Chrysanthemums."

Hayashi, Tetsumaro, ed. *Steinbeck's Short Stories in "The Long Valley": Essays in Criticism.* Muncie, Ind.: Steinbeck Research Institution, 1991. A collection of new critical essays on the stories in *The Long Valley* (excluding *The Red Pony*), from a variety of critical perspectives.

Hughes, R. S. *John Steinbeck: A Study of the Short Fiction.* New York: Twayne, 1989. A general introduction to Steinbeck's short fiction, focusing primarily on critical reception to the stories. Also includes some autobiographical statements on short-story writing, as well as four essays on Steinbeck's stories by other critics.

Johnson, Claudia Durst, ed. *Understanding "Of Mice and Men," "The Red Pony," and "The Pearl": A Student Casebook to Issues, Sources, and Historical Documents.* Westport, Conn.: Greenwood Press, 1997. This casebook contains historical, social, and political materials as a context for Steinbeck's three novellas. Contexts included are California and the West, land ownership, the male worker, homelessness, and oppression of the poor in Mexico.

McCarthy, Paul. *John Steinbeck.* New York: Frederick Ungar, 1980. Though much of this study is a recapitulation of earlier critical views, the book has the virtues of clarity and brevity and contains a fairly thorough bibliography.

Noble, Donald R. *The Steinbeck Question: New Essays in Criticism.* Troy, N.Y.: Whitston Publishing, 1993. A collection of essays on most of Steinbeck's work; most important for a study of the short story is the essay by Robert S. Hughes, Jr., on "The Art of Story Writing," Charlotte Hadella's "Steinbeck's Cloistered Women," and Michael J. Meyer's "The Snake."

Parini, Jay. *John Steinbeck: A Biography.* New York: Henry Holt, 1995. This biography suggests psychological interpretations of the effect of Steinbeck's childhood and sociological interpretations of his fiction. Criticizes Steinbeck for his politically incorrect gender and social views; also takes Steinbeck to task to what he calls his blindness to the political reality of the Vietnam War.

Steinbeck, Elaine, and Robert Wallsten. *Steinbeck: A Life in Letters.* New York: Viking Press, 1975. An indispensable source for the Steinbeck scholar, this collection of letters written by Steinbeck between 1929 and his death forty years later shows a writer both well read and well disciplined. Those letters to his friend and publisher, Pascal Covici, shed light on the writer's working methods and are particularly revealing.

Timmerman, John H. *The Dramatic Landscape of Steinbeck's Short Stories.* Norman: University of Oklahoma Press, 1990. A formalist interpretation of Steinbeck's stories, focusing on style, tone, imagery, and character. Provides close readings of such frequently anthologized stories as "The Chrysanthemums" and "Flight," as well as such stories as "Johnny Bear" and "The Short-Short Story of Mankind."

Edward Fiorelli

RICHARD G. STERN

Born: New York, New York; February 25, 1928

PRINCIPAL SHORT FICTION

Teeth, Dying, and Other Matters, 1964
1968: A Short Novel, an Urban Idyll, Five Stories, and Two Trade Notes, 1970
Packages, 1980
Noble Rot: Stories, 1949-1988, 1989
Shares and Other Fictions, 1992

OTHER LITERARY FORMS

Richard Stern is best known as a novelist. He has written literary criticism, both of his work and of that of others. He has also written autobiographical sketches and several poems.

ACHIEVEMENTS

Richard Stern has written numerous volumes of prose. His novels have received wide critical acclaim from reviewers, including Saul Bellow, Joan Didion, and Bernard Malamud, yet none has been widely read, and few have received attention from professional literary critics. His first novel, *Golk* (1960), was hailed as one of the best fictive accounts of the early days of television and the ways in which it intrudes into the lives of people who work in the medium and those who watch it. He has received numerous awards for his work, including a Longwood Award (1960), a Friends of Literature Award (1963), a Rockefeller Foundation grant (1965), an American Academy and Institute of Arts and Letters grant (1968), a National Endowment for the Arts grant (1969), a John Simon Guggenheim Memorial Foundation Fellowship (1973-1974), a Carl Sandburg Award from the Friends of the Chicago Public Library (1979), an American Academy and Institute of Arts and Letters Award of Merit Medal (1985), and a Heartland Award for best work of nonfiction (1995). In 1965, his novel *Stitch* was selected as an American Library Association book of the year, and in 1989 his *Noble Rot* was named the *Chicago Sun-Times* book of the year.

BIOGRAPHY

Richard Gustave Stern was born in New York City on February 25, 1928, the son of German-Jewish immigrants. He married Gay Clark in 1950 and was divorced in 1972. He married Alane Rollings in 1985. He has four children. Stern received his B.A. degree from the University of North Carolina at Chapel Hill in 1947, where he became a member of Phi Beta Kappa. After graduating, he worked in a department store in Indiana, in a Florida radio station, and at Paramount International Films in New York. He earned his M.A. degree from Harvard University in 1949, writing the Bowdoin Prize essay on the poet John Crowe Ransom. He was a lecturer at Collège Jules Ferry in Versailles, France, from 1949 to 1950; a lecturer at the University of Heidelberg in Germany from 1950 to 1951; and an educational adviser for the U.S. Army from 1951 to 1952. While teaching at the University of Heidelberg, he worked nights as a cable clerk with the American occupation army. He received his Ph.D. from the University of Iowa in 1954. From 1954 to 1955, he was an instructor at Connecticut College in New London, Connecticut.

In 1956, Stern became an assistant professor of English at the University of Chicago, where he continued to teach. He became an associate professor in 1962 and a full professor in 1965. In 1991, he was named Helen A. Regenstein Professor of English. He has been a visiting lecturer at the University of Venice (1962-1963); the University of California, Santa Barbara (1964, 1968); the State University of New York at Buffalo (1966); Harvard University (1969); the University of Nice (1970); and the University of Urbino (1977).

In one of his autobiographical sketches, he describes his elation at having his first important story accepted in 1952 for *The Kenyon Review* by Ransom, who was the subject of Stern's prizewinning essay. This acceptance occurred in the same year that he went to Iowa to begin work on his Ph.D. Following this first publication, he contributed numerous stories and essays to literary magazines, including *The*

Richard G. Stern

Kenyon Review, The Antioch Review, Commentary, The Atlantic, Harper's, The Hudson Review, Partisan Review, The Paris Review, Encounter, Transatlantic Review, TriQuarterly, and *Western Review*.

In 1957, he met Saul Bellow, a former colleague at the University of Chicago, who became his friend and who greatly influenced his ideas about writing and about the writer's life. Bellow, Stern has said, showed him that one could be a Jew and still be a great American novelist. Stern continued to live in the Chicago area, to write, and to teach at the University of Chicago.

Analysis

Bellow has been known to wonder aloud why Richard Stern's work is not more popular. Like many other discerning reviewers, Bellow notes the excellence of Stern's novels and short stories and their lack of readers. The answer to Bellow's question probably lies in the kinds of demands that Stern makes on his readers. According to Stern, his early writing was done under the influence of *Understanding Fiction* (1945), a highly influential textbook-anthology edited by Robert Penn Warren and Cleanth Brooks. Under the influence of Brooks and Warren, Stern tried to achieve what he calls a polished style, to integrate the materials in his stories, and "to suspend the meaning of the story in action as 'naturally' as orange bits in jello." Between 1952 and 1954, he said, he wrote about ten stories following these principles, but he became dissatisfied with what he was producing and, in 1957, stopped working on short stories, interrupted work on what became his second published novel, *Europe: Or, Up and Down with Schreiber and Baggish* (1961), and started working on what became his first published novel, *Golk*.

Like Bellow's writing, Stern's tends to be highly erudite and allusive. In fact, it tends to be even more erudite and allusive than Bellow's. To understand Stern's stories fully, readers must be familiar with a large body of Western literature. They must also be at least slightly familiar with several languages, including French, German, and Italian. In some stories, he demands that his readers be familiar with such topics as Eastern and Western European history, anatomy, and the history of philosophy. Stern is at his best as a humorist. He is sometimes classified as a black humorist and even a satirist, but his works tend to reflect more love for humankind than those of most black humorists and satirists. Stern's short stories provide a mirror of the absurdity of the human situation at the same time that they display not only a tolerance of human foibles but also a love for humankind. A consummate craftsman, he admits to polishing his works by revising them again and again. The resulting stories are worth the time and effort he puts into them, and they are certainly worth the time and effort the reader must expend to appreciate them.

"Good Morrow, Swine"

Even in many of his short works of humorous fiction, Stern makes inordinate demands on his readers. Most of his best short works are collected in *Noble Rot*, a book that can serve as an excellent introduction to Stern's techniques as a story writer. His extremely short story "Good Morrow, Swine," for example, is included in the collection. This early work is hilarious, yet to comprehend the jokes in it one must recognize the allusions in the title and be able to understand at least a bit of French, since most of the jokes within the story depend on recognizing French mistranslations of English phrases. In the story, Mr. Perkins constantly misinforms his young male students about the meanings of English words, quotations, and everyday expressions.

"VENI, VIDI . . . WENDT"

Similarly, in "Veni, Vidi . . . Wendt," a long short story that Stern calls a short novel, which was collected in *1968*, he writes a comic study of Jeffrey Charles Wendt, a composer of operas to which no one listens and who desires to have his operas listened to by no one. This story, not collected in *Noble Rot*, is set in the same year as the assassinations of Martin Luther King, Jr., and Robert F. Kennedy and the Democratic Convention in Chicago that nominated Hubert H. Humphrey while young people rioted in the streets. Yet Wendt, who has been called a modern Nero, although aware of these events, largely ignores them, concentrating instead on writing an opera based on the life of Horace Walpole and trying to satisfy his own sexual lust and desire in order to show his superiority to his colleagues. Wendt and his wife and children are spending the summer in Santa Barbara, California. In the course of the story, he rediscovers his love for his wife and children.

Still, to understand the humor in "Veni, Vidi . . . Wendt," the reader must bring something to the story. The title itself alludes to Julius Caesar's famous words "Veni, Vidi, Vici" ("I came, I saw, I conquered"), which he used to report to the Roman Senate about his Pontic victory. Wendt, however, does not conquer. He came, he saw, and through a terrible pun, he left (Wendt-went). Even the Latin pronunciation of the letter "v" as "w" and the German pronunciation of the letter "w" as "v" seem part of the joke involved in the story's title.

The irony of comparing Wendt to Caesar becomes greater when one compares Caesar's amorous conquests to Wendt's. In his Egyptian conquest, achieved shortly before his Pontic one, Caesar also won Cleopatra. Comparing Caesar's conquest to Wendt's one amorous conquest in "Veni, Vidi . . . Wendt" produces more humor. Unlike Caesar, Wendt finds that he can ultimately take no pride in his dalliance, even though the woman with whom he has an affair is Patricia Davidov, the beautiful wife of a musicologist whom Wendt abhors. In the course of his first assignation with Patricia, he wonders whether there is no mouthwash in the Davidov household. Shortly thereafter, he finds himself exhausted by his extramarital affair and extremely anxious for it to end. No Caesar, Wendt runs from the affair back to his home in Chicago, feeling only relief that he has escaped from the demanding Patricia. The writing throughout the story is similarly allusive and erudite.

For a reader able or willing to make a way through Stern's short stories, the rewards are great. At his best, he is wildly comic, illustrating the absurdity of the human situation in humorous scene after humorous scene in stories such as "Good Morrow, Swine," "Veni, Vidi . . . Wendt," "Packages," "Milius and Melanie," and "A Recital for the Pope."

"ARRANGEMENTS AT THE GULF"

In fact, Stern is often classified as a writer of the absurd. He can write good, slightly sentimental fiction in works such as "Arrangements at the Gulf." In it, Mr. Lomax, an old man, wants to die away from his family in Lake Forest, Illinois but with his bachelor friend Granville, whom he sees every other summer on the Florida Gulf Coast. On the summers in between, Granville goes to California. The arrangements of the title involve seeing to it that Granville will go to the Gulf Coast every summer so that he can be present when Mr. Lomax dies.

"DOUBLE CHARLEY" AND "A COUNTERFACTUAL PROPOSAL"

Many of Stern's stories involve the kinds of reversals found in "Arrangements at the Gulf." In one, "Double Charley," Charley Rangel discovers that his girlfriend, Agnes, slept with his partner in songwriting, Charley Schmitter, when he asks Olive, Schmitter's wife, to allow Agnes to visit Schmitter's grave. In another, "A Counterfactual Proposal" (collected only in *Teeth, Dying, and Other Matters*), after years of longing for a beautiful woman, Patchell finally is able to get Twyla K. Diggs into bed with him. Diggs is a student at the college where Patchell teaches. Shortly after they go to bed, they are discovered by Diggs's roommate and landlady. Immediately after the discovery, Patchell confronts the college president, Miss Emory, and succeeds in persuading her to grant him a year's research grant, which he will use to go to France to study at the Bibliothéque Nationale. He also enlists Miss Emory's aid in getting Diggs's father to agree to send her to the Sorbonne for the year.

"Wissler Remembers"

In "Wissler Remembers," a fairly sentimental story, an aging teacher recalls the students he has taught over the years and the love that he has felt for all of them. In this work, too, Stern shows the absurdity of the human situation. "Wissler Remembers" also has its humorous moments, especially when Wissler recalls that, while teaching at the Collége Jules Ferry in Versailles, France, where Stern himself taught, Wissler assigned his students the task of translating back into English a poem for which he supplied the French translation. Anyone who could come within twelve words of the original would, Wissler announced, get a present. The poem itself is a French version of Robert Frost's "Stopping by Woods on a Snowy Evening," and the student translation that Wissler recalls is hilarious. Yet the reader must understand enough French to recognize the original poem in order to see how hilarious the student version is.

"A Recital for the Pope"

Critics have recognized in Stern's novels a unique mixture of what they call the language of the street and of the library. This same mixture of colloquialisms and book language pervades his tales. Story after story in *Noble Rot* and in *Shares and Other Fictions* exemplifies this mixture. At the same time, the actions in the stories often echo this mixture by placing grotesque characters in extremely formal situations. "A Recital for the Pope," for example, begins like a history textbook, describing magnificent old buildings in Rome, but quickly places in that setting a violinist, Yerva Grbisz, who tortures horrible tunes

out of the violin and refuses to use deodorant or practice other elements of hygiene. Yerva has a brief audience with the pope, after which she and others pose for a picture with the pope. As they pose, she tells the pope that she wants to play her violin for him. He says that he would love for her to do so. She then plays execrable music, which he claims to enjoy very much.

"La Pourriture Noble"

Similarly, "La Pourriture Noble" (meaning "noble rot," from which the collection gets its title) shows Dennis Sellinbon climbing up some very expensive curtains in a very elegant apartment at which he is attending a party. Readers never discover any reasonable explanation for Dennis's actions but cannot help laughing when they hear the excuse that Dennis makes up to get himself released from the mental ward to which he has had himself committed.

"Dying"

Another story in the collection that deserves special attention is "Dying," in which F. Dorfman Dreben, through repeated entreaties, gets Professor Bly, a plant physiologist who has published a volume of poetry, to write a poem to be entered into a competition, the winner of which will receive $250, with the winning poem to be inscribed on Dreben's mother's tombstone. Dreben's persistence leads Bly to understand that his poem will be the only one in the contest. At first, Bly is uninterested. Then, however, he decides to use the money for a trip, so he quickly conceives of, writes, and sends what he considers a good poem to Dreben, requesting that Dreben send the prize by return mail. After not hearing from Dreben, Bly, while in bed with his girlfriend, calls Dreben to find out why he has not received his check. As it turns out, there were two other contestants, a yearbook editor and a friend of Dreben's sister. The yearbook editor won first prize, the sister's friend won second, and Bly, Dreben says, won honorable mention.

"Aurelia Frequenzia Reveals the Heart and Mind of the Man of Destiny"

In one of his uncollected tales, "Aurelia Frequenzia Reveals the Heart and Mind of the Man of Destiny" (*The Paris Review*, 1976), Frequenzia writes the transcript of several interviews presented as though they are one interview with Tao Thinh, once ruler of Annam, which the reader quickly recognizes as a thinly disguised version of Vietnam. In the story, Stern shows the basic similarity between Frequenzia and Thinh, even though she claims to hate him and all for which he stands. She especially hates his having worked beside colonial powers—the French and Americans—while claiming to be a patriot, and his having enriched himself at the expense of his country. Yet the reader quickly discovers that Frequenzia and Thinh lust for each other. Actually, the transcript reveals far more about Frequenzia than it does about either the heart or mind of Thinh.

SHARES AND OTHER FICTIONS

"Veni, Vidi . . . Wendt" is collected also in *Shares and Other Fictions* and fits nicely into the stories there, for at the center of the stories lies the family with all of its problems. In "The Degradation of Tenderness" Stern treats the family of a psychotherapist named Charlie who used his children as case studies. In two articles, "The Father as Clinical Observer I, II," he "dismantled his children," but he could not understand the anger with which his children reacted to the articles. The children saw them as an indication of lack of real tenderness or love; they saw them as a degradation of tenderness. In turn, Anna, the narrator, is a childless psychotherapist who apparently was Charlie's mistress and claims to feel affection for the children; she explains the father-child interactions in psychoanalytic terms, ironically converting the whole family into a case study. Thus, she indicates her own lack of or unwillingness to deal with real emotion and her similarity to Charlie. Anna's psychoanalytic jargon becomes a means of dehumanizing the children, Charlie, and Anna herself.

The title story, "Shares: A Novel in Ten Pieces," as its subtitle indicates, is a series of stories or "pieces." In it Stern explores the Share family, focusing on George and Robert, two brothers. George remains unmarried and childless. A successful shoe salesman who eventually owns his own stores, he founds the Share Museum, which gives a grant each year for a woman to travel to Europe with George, but she has to be his mistress. Robert becomes a lawyer, a Deputy Secretary of State, marries, and has two

children, a boy, Reg, and a girl, Obie. Robert's ability to compromise works well in his job, and he is a faithful husband and tries to be a good father. His children do not, however, respect his work and see his compromises as doing more harm than good. Obie writes him letters in which she tells him how he should be running the nation's affairs, and Reg tends to fail at all he tries, blaming his father for his problems. Using money his father gives him, Reg travels to Venice, meets and begins a relationship with his uncle's current lover, and starts a business taking people on balloon flights over Venice. At first, the business is extremely successful, but a tragedy occurs, and Reg is again a failure.

The final story in the collection, "In a Word, Trowbridge," treats the problems involved in having "a famous name." Charlotte, daughter of a well-known artist, dwells on the verbal abuse she suffered as a child, especially from her mother. She does not begin really to live until she is mugged. Then, she and her mother are reunited, she sees that her mother really cares about her, and she is able to recognize that having a famous parent is not such a burden after all.

OTHER MAJOR WORKS

LONG FICTION: *Golk*, 1960; *Europe: Or, Up and Down with Schreiber and Baggish*, 1961; *In Any Case*, 1962 (reissued as *The Chaleur Network*, 1981); *Stitch*, 1965; *Other Men's Daughters*, 1973; *Natural Shocks*, 1978; *A Father's Words*, 1986.

PLAY: *The Gamesman's Island*, pb. 1964.

NONFICTION: *One Person and Another: On Writers and Writing*, 1993; *A Sistermony*, 1995.

EDITED TEXTS: *Honey and Wax: The Powers and Pleasures of Narrative*, 1966; *American Poetry of the Fifties*, 1967.

MISCELLANEOUS: *The Books in Fred Hampton's Apartment*, 1973; *The Invention of the Real*, 1982; *The Position of the Body*, 1986.

BIBLIOGRAPHY

Cavell, Marsha. "Visions of Battlements." *Partisan Review* 38, no. 1 (1971): 117-121. Cavell reviews four books in this article, including *1968*, by

Stern. She discusses "Veni, Vidi . . . Wendt" and "East, West . . . Midwest" from Stern's collection, seeing him as a satirist whose writing is "at once gentle and biting."

Harris, Mark. *Saul Bellow: Drumlin Woodchuck.* Athens: University of Georgia Press, 1980. This book is primarily a study of Stern's friend, Saul Bellow. It is dedicated to Stern and repeatedly treats him, especially in connection with his friendships with Harris and Bellow. Also discusses his friendship with Philip Roth and recognizes the difficulty most readers have with Stern's work. Although Harris treats Stern throughout the book, the treatment is especially intensive in chapters 2 and 3.

Rogers, Bernard. Foreword to *Golk.* Chicago: University of Chicago Press, 1987. This introduction to the Phoenix reprint of Stern's first novel treats his fiction in general, especially his novels. It traces through Stern's novels four of his major themes: adapting to change, handling moral responsibility, dealing with problems of fatherhood and domestic life, and handling power. It also discusses his distinctive narrative voice.

Rosenberg, Milton, and Elliot Anderson. "A Conversation with Richard Stern." *Chicago Review* 31 (Winter, 1980): 98-108. Stern talks about the nature of the novel, the purpose of a serious novel, his intentions in some of his own fiction, his opinion of other contemporary fiction writers, and the protagonists of his fiction.

Schiffler, James. *Richard Stern.* New York: Twayne, 1993. The first book-length critical study of Stern; includes a brief overview of his life, a survey of his novels and short stories, and discussions of his style and themes; chapter 5 is primarily on the theme of the "comedy of failure" in his short stories.

Stern, Richard G. "Conversation with Richard Stern." Interview by Milton Rosenberg and Elliot Anderson. *Chicago Review* 31 (Winter, 1980): 98-108. This article is an edited transcript of an interview that took place on WGN radio. In it, Stern traces what he calls the change in his writing from creating stories drawn from the external world to creating ones drawn from inside himself. He also briefly discusses the works of several other contemporary American writers, including John Barth, Donald Barthelme, John Gardner, Truman Capote, and Irving Wallace.

_____. Interview by Molly McQuade. *Publishers Weekly* 235 (January 20, 1989): 126-128. This interview appeared after the publication of Stern's collection of short stories *Noble Rot.* It briefly traces his life, literary career, and career as a university professor. Includes a photograph of Stern.

Richard Tuerk

ROBERT LOUIS STEVENSON

Born: Edinburgh, Scotland; November 13, 1850
Died: Vailima, near Apia, Samoa; December 3, 1894

PRINCIPAL SHORT FICTION

The New Arabian Nights, 1882
More New Arabian Nights, 1885
The Merry Men and Other Tales and Fables, 1887
Island Nights' Entertainments, 1893

OTHER LITERARY FORMS

Despite poor health, Robert Louis Stevenson was a prolific writer, not only of juvenile fiction but also of poetry, plays, and essays. He is best known for adventure romances such as *Treasure Island* (1881-1882, serial; 1883, book), *Kidnapped* (1886), and the horror-suspense novel *The Strange Case of Dr. Jekyll and Mr. Hyde* (1886), works that appeal principally to youthful readers. A habitual voyager, Stevenson also wrote travelogues and sketches recounting his personal experiences. His children's poems, published in *A Child's Garden of Verses* (1885), remain perennial favorites, as do several of his beautiful family prayers.

ACHIEVEMENTS

For clarity and suspense, Robert Louis Stevenson is a rarely equaled raconteur. He reveals his mastery of narrative in his economical presentation of incident and atmosphere. Yet, despite his sparse, concise style, many of his tales are notable for dealing with complex moral ambiguities and their diagnoses. Although influenced by a host of romantic writers, including Charles Lamb, William Hazlitt, William Wordsworth, and Nathaniel Hawthorne, Stevenson's theories of prose fiction were most directly provoked by Henry James's *The Art of Fiction* (1884). Stevenson placed himself in literary opposition to James and the "statics of character," favoring instead an action-fiction whose clear antecedents are allegory, fable, and romance. His tales of adventure and intrigue, outdoor life and old-time romance, avidly read by children and young adults, have had a continuous and in-calculable influence since their first publication in the 1880's.

BIOGRAPHY

The only child of a prosperous civil engineer and his wife, Robert Louis Stevenson was a sickly youth, causing his formal education to be haphazard. He reacted early against his parents' orthodox Presbyterianism, donning the mask of a liberated Bohemian who abhorred the hypocrisies of bourgeois respectability. As a compromise with his father, Stevenson did study law at Edinburgh University in lieu of the traditional family vocation of lighthouse engineer. In 1873, however, he suffered a severe respiratory illness, and, although he completed his studies and was admitted to the Scottish bar in July, 1875, he never practiced. In May, 1880, Stevenson married Fanny Van de Grift Osbourne, a divorcée from San Francisco and ten years his senior. The new couple spent most of the next decade in health resorts for Stevenson's tuberculosis: Davos in the Swiss Alps, Hyéres on the French Riviera, and Bournemouth in England. After his father's death, Stevenson felt able to go farther from Scotland and so went to Saranac Lake in the Adirondack Mountains of New York, where treatment arrested his disease. In June, 1888, Stevenson, his wife, mother, and stepson sailed for the South Seas. During the next eighteen months they saw the Marquesas, Tahiti, Australia, the Gilberts, Hawaii, and Samoa. In late 1889, Stevenson decided to settle and bought "Vailima," three miles from the town of Apia, Upolu, Samoa, and his home until his death. His vigorous crusading there against the white exploitation of native Samoans almost led to expulsion by both German and English authorities. Stevenson's tuberculosis remained quiescent, but he suddenly died of a cerebral hemorrhage on December 3, 1894, while working on the novel *Weir of Hermiston* (1896), a fragment which many modern readers think to be his best writing. Known to the natives as "Tusitala," the Storyteller, Stevenson was buried on the summit of Mount Vaea.

ANALYSIS

Robert Louis Stevenson has long been relegated to either the nursery or the juvenile section in most libraries, and his mixture of romance, horror, and allegory seems jejune. In a century where narrative and well-ordered structure have become the facile tools of Harlequin paperbacks and irrelevant to high-quality "literature," Stevenson's achievement goes quietly unnoticed. To confine this technique of "Tusitala" solely to nursery and supermarket, however, is to confuse Stevenson's talents with his present audience.

Stevenson's crucial problem is the basic one of joining form to idea, made more difficult because he was not only an excellent romancer but also a persuasive essayist. In Stevenson, however, these two talents seem to be of different roots, and their combination was for him a lifelong work. The aim of his narratives becomes not only to tell a good story, constructing something of interest, but also to ensure that all the materials of that story (such as structure, atmosphere, and character motivation) contribute to a clear thematic concern. Often Stevenson's fictional talents alone cannot accomplish this for him, and this accounts—depending in each instance on whether he drops his theme or attempts to push it through—for both the "pulp" feel of some stories and the "directed" feel of others.

"A LODGING FOR THE NIGHT"

Appearing in the *Cornhill Magazine* for May, 1874, an essay on Victor Hugo was Stevenson's very first publication. The short stories he began writing soon after demonstrate a strong tendency to lapse into the more familiar expository techniques either as a solution to fictional problems or merely to bolster a sagging theme. A blatant example of this stylistic ambiguity is the early story "A Lodging for the Night."

The atmosphere of the first part of the story is deftly handled. It is winter, and its buffets upon the poor are reemphasized in every descriptive detail. Paris is "sheeted up" like a body ready for burial. The only light is from a tiny shack "backed up against the cemetery wall." Inside, "dark, little, and lean, with hollow cheeks and thin black locks," the medieval poet François Villon composes "The Ballade of Roast

Robert Louis Stevenson (Library of Congress)

Fish" while Guy Tabard, one of his cronies, sputters admiringly over his shoulder. Straddling before the fire is a portly, purple-veined Picardy monk, Dom Nicolas. Also in the small room are two more villains, Montigny and Thevenin Pensete, playing "a game of chance." Villon cracks a few pleasantries, quite literally gallows humor, and begins to read aloud his new poem. Suddenly, between the two gamesters:

> The round was complete, and Thevenin was just opening his mouth to claim another victory, when Montigny leaped up, swift as an adder, and stabbed him to the heart. The blow took effect before he had time to utter a cry, before he had time to move. A tremor or two convulsed his frame; his hands opened and shut, his heels rattled on the floor; then his head rolled backward over one shoulder with the eyes wide open; and Thevenin Pensete's spirit had returned to Him who made it.

Tabard begins praying in Latin, Villon breaks into hysterics, Montigny recovers "his composure first" and picks the dead man's pockets. Naturally, they must all leave the scene of the murder to escape implication, and Villon departs first.

Outside, in the bitter cold, two things preoccupy the poet as he walks: the gallows and "the look of the dead man with his bald head and garland of red curls," as neat a symbol as could be for the fiery pit of hell where Villon eventually expects to find himself. Theme has been handled well, Stevenson's fiction giving us the feeling of a single man thrown by existence into infernal and unfavorable circumstances, being pursued by elements beyond his control, the gallows and Death, survival itself weaving a noose for him with his own trail in the snow, irrevocably connecting him to "the house by the cemetery of St. John." The plot is clear and the situation has our interest. On this cold and windy night, after many rebuffs, Villon finally finds food and shelter with a "refined," "muscular and spare," "resonant, courteous," "honorable rather than intelligent, strong, simple, and righteous" old knight.

Here, the structure of "A Lodging for the Night" abruptly breaks down from fiction, from atmospheric detail, plot development, and character enlargement, to debate. What Stevenson implied in the first part of his story, he reasserts here in expository dialogue, apparently losing faith in his fictional abilities as he resorts back to the directness of the essay.

Villon takes the side of duty to one's own survival; he is the first modern skeptic, the prophet of expediency. In contrast, the knight stands for honor, *bonne noblesse*, with allegiance always to something greater than himself. The moral code of the criminal is pitted against the hypocrisy of the bourgeoisie. One's chances in life are determined by birth and social standing, says Villon. There is always the chance for change, implores the knight. In comparison to Stevenson's carefully built atmosphere and plot, this expository "solution" to his story is extremely crude.

"MARKHEIM"

"Markheim," a ghost story that deals with a disturbing problem of conscience, also contains a dialogue in its latter half. This dialogue, however, is a just continuation of the previous action. Different from "crawlers" such as "The Body-Snatcher," "Markheim" reinforces horror with moral investiga-

tion. Initial atmospherics contribute directly to Stevenson's pursuit of his thematic concern, and the later debate with the "visitant" becomes an entirely fitting expression for Markheim's own madness.

An allegory of the awakening conscience, "Markheim" also has the limits of allegory, one of which is meaning. For readers to understand, or find meaning in, an allegory, characters (or actors) must be clearly identified. In "Markheim" this presents major difficulties. Not only is an exact identity (or role) for the visitant finally in doubt, but also the identity of the dealer is unclear. It can be said that he usually buys from Markheim, not sells to him, but exactly what the dealer buys or sells is a good question. Whatever, on this particular occasion (Christmas Day), Markheim will have to pay the dealer extra "for a kind of manner that I remark in you today very strongly."

Amid the "ticking of many clocks among the curious lumber" of the dealer's shop, a strange pantomime ensues. Markheim says he needs a present for a lady and the dealer shows him a hand mirror. Markheim grows angry:

> "A glass," he said hoarsely, and then paused, and repeated it more clearly. "A glass? For Christmas? Surely not!"
> "And why not?" cried the dealer. "Why not a glass?"
> Markheim was looking upon him with an indefinable expression. "You ask me why not?" he said. "Why, look here—look at it—look at yourself! Do you like to see it? No! nor I—nor any man."

After damning the mirror as the "reminder of years, and sins, and follies—this hand-conscience," Markheim asks the dealer to tell something of himself, his secret life. The dealer puts Markheim off with a chuckle, but as he turns around for something more to show, Markheim lunges at him, stabbing him with a "long, skewerlike dagger." The dealer struggles "like a hen" and then dies. The murder seems completely gratuitous until Markheim remembers that he had come to rob the shop: "To have done the deed and yet not to reap the profit would be too abhorrent a failure."

Time, "which had closed for the victim," now becomes "instant and momenteous for the slayer." Like

Villon, Markheim feels pursued by Death, haunted by "the dock, the prison, the gallows, and the black coffin." The blood at his feet begins "to find eloquent voices." The dead dealer extracts his extra payment, becoming the enemy who would "lift up a cry that would ring over England, and fill the world with the echoes of pursuit." Talking to himself, Markheim denies that this evil murder indicates an equally evil nature, but his guilt troubles him. Not only pursued by Death, Markheim is pursued by Life as well. He sees his own face "repeated and repeated, as it were an army of spies"; his own eyes meet and detect him. Although alone, he feels the inexplicable consciousness of another presence:

> Ay, surely; to every room and corner of the house his imagination followed it; and now it was a faceless thing, and yet had eyes to see with; and again it was a shadow of himself; and yet again beheld the image of the dead dealer, reinspired with cunning and hatred.

Eventually, Markheim must project an imaginary double, a *Doppelgänger* or exteriorized voice with which to debate his troubles. Here, action passes from the stylized antique shop of the murdered to the frenzied mind of the murderer. The visitant, or double, is a product of this mind. Mad and guilty as Markheim appears to be, his double emerges as a calm sounding sanity who will reason with him to commit further evil. Thus, the mysterious personification of drives buried deep within Markheim's psyche exteriorizes evil as an alter ego and allows Markheim the chance to act against it, against the evil in his own nature. Stevenson's sane, expository technique of debate erects a perfect foil for Markheim's true madness.

In the end, although Markheim thinks himself victorious over what seems the devil, it is actually this exteriorized aspect of Markheim's unknown self that conquers, tricking him into willing surrender and then revealing itself as a kind of redemptive angel:

> The feature of the visitor began to undergo a wonderful and lovely change; they brightened and softened with a tender triumph; and, even as they brightened, faded and dislimned. But Markheim did not pause to watch or understand the transformation.

Material and intention are artistically intertwined in "Markheim," but the moral ambiguities of Stevenson's theme remain complex, prompting various questions: is Markheim's martyrdom a victory over evil or merely a personal cessation from action? Set on Christmas Day, with its obvious reversal of that setting's usual significance, is "Markheim" a portrayal of Christian resignation as a purely negative force, a justification for suicide, or as the only modern solution against evil? What is the true nature and identity of the visitant? Finally, can the visitant have an identity apart from Markheim's own? Even answers to these questions, like Markheim's final surrender, offer only partial consolation to the reader of this strange and complex story of psychological sickness.

"THE BEACH OF FALESÁ"

With Stevenson's improved health and his move to the South Seas, a new type of story began to emerge, a kind of exotic realism to which the author brought his mature talents. "The Bottle Imp," for example, juxtaposes the occult of an old German fairy tale (interestingly enough, acquired by Stevenson through Sir Percy Shelley, the poet's son) with factual details about San Francisco, Honolulu, and Papeete. These settings, however, seem used more for convenience than out of necessity.

The long story "The Beach of Falesá" fulfills Stevenson's promise and gives evidence of his whole talents as a writer of short fiction. Similar to Joseph Conrad's *Heart of Darkness* (1902), Stevenson's story deals with a person's ability or inability to remain decent and law-abiding when the external restraints of civilization have been removed. Action follows simply and naturally a line laid down by atmosphere. Stevenson himself called it "the first realistic South Sea story," while Henry James wrote in a letter the year before Stevenson's death, "The art of 'The Beach of Falesá' seems to me an art brought to a perfection and I delight in the observed truth, the modesty of nature, of the narrator."

In this adventure of wills between two traders on a tiny island, Stevenson is able to unify fitting exposition with restrained description through the voice of first-person narrator John Wiltshire. Three decades later, using Stevenson as one of his models, W. Somerset Maugham would further perfect this technique using the same exotic South Sea setting.

Stevenson's "The Beach of Falesá," along with the incomplete *Weir of Hermiston* and perhaps the first part of *The Master of Ballantrae* (1888), rests as his best work, the final integration of the divergent roots of his talents. If he had lived longer than forty-four years, "Tusitala" might have become one of the great English prose writers. As history stands, however, Stevenson's small achievement of clear narrative, his victory of joining form to idea, remains of unforgettable importance to students and practitioners of the short-story genre.

OTHER MAJOR WORKS

LONG FICTION: *Treasure Island*, 1881-1882 (serial), 1883 (book); *Prince Otto*, 1885; *The Strange Case of Dr. Jekyll and Mr. Hyde*, 1886; *Kidnapped*, 1886; *The Black Arrow*, 1888; *The Master of Ballantrae*, 1889; *The Wrong Box*, 1889; *The Wrecker*, 1892 (with Lloyd Osbourne); *Catriona*, 1893; *The Ebb-Tide*, 1894 (with Lloyd Osbourne); *Weir of Hermiston*, 1896 (unfinished); *St. Ives*, 1897 (completed by Arthur Quiller-Couch).

PLAYS: *Deacon Brodie*, pb. 1880 (with William Ernest Henley); *Admiral Guinea*, pb. 1884; *Beau Austin*, pb. 1884; *Macaire*, pb. 1885 (with William Ernest Henley); *The Hanging Judge*, pb. 1914 (with Fanny Van de Grift Stevenson).

POETRY: *Moral Emblems*, 1882; *A Child's Garden of Verses*, 1885; *Underwoods*, 1887; *Ballads*, 1890; *Songs of Travel and Other Verses*, 1896.

NONFICTION: *An Inland Voyage*, 1878; *Edinburgh: Picturesque Notes*, 1879; *Travels with a Donkey in the Cévennes*, 1879; *Virginibus Puerisque*, 1881; *Familiar Studies of Men and Books*, 1882; *The Silverado Squatters, Sketches from a Californian Mountain*, 1883; *Memories and Portraits*, 1887; *Across the Plains*, 1892; *A Footnote to History*, 1892; *Amateur Emigrant*, 1895; *Vailima Letters*, 1895; *In the South Seas*, 1896; *The Letters of Robert Louis Stevenson to His Family and Friends*, 1899 (2 volumes), 1911 (4 volumes); *The Lantern-Bearers and Other Essays*, 1988.

BIBLIOGRAPHY

Arata, Stephen D. "The Sedulous Ape: Atavism, Professionalism, and Stevenson's *Jekyll and Hyde*." *Criticism* 37 (Spring, 1995): 233-259. Discusses the story as a self-conscious exploration of the relation between professional interpretation and the construction of criminal deviance; argues that it is also a displaced meditation on what Stevenson considered the decline of authorship into "professionalism."

Bell, Ian. *Dreams of Exile: Robert Louis Stevenson: A Biography.* New York: Henry Holt, 1992. Bell, a journalist rather than an academic, writes evocatively of Stevenson the dreamer and exile. This brief study of Stevenson's brief but dramatic life does a fine job of evoking the man and the places he inhabited. It is less accomplished in its approach to the work.

Bevan, Bryan. "The Versatility of Robert Louis Stevenson." *Contemporary Review* 264 (June, 1994): 316-319. A general discussion of Stevenson's work, focusing on his versatility in a number of genres; discusses early influences on his writing, and comments on his essays and his fiction.

Calder, Jenni. *Robert Louis Stevenson: A Life Study.* New York: Oxford University Press, 1980. This excellent study, by the daughter of literary historian David Daiches, is richly documented with Stevenson's letters. Less a biography than a study of the writer's mind, it focuses on the personal values and attitudes informing Stevenson's work.

Chesterton, G. K. *Robert Louis Stevenson.* London: Hodder & Stoughton, 1927. An older but distinguished critical study of Stevenson that is still highly regarded for its insights as well as for its wit and lucidity.

Daiches, David. *Robert Louis Stevenson.* Norwalk, Conn.: New Directions, 1947. Along with J. C. Furnas, Daiches is credited with pioneering a positive reappraisal of Stevenson. His study is urbane and penetrating in the tradition of G. K. Chesterton.

Furnas, J. C. *Voyage to Windward.* New York: William Sloane, 1951. Furnas, who briefly lived in Stevenson's home in Samoa, traced the author's steps backward to his native Scotland. The work is a popular and sympathetic biography documented with unpublished letters. It contains an elaborate works-consulted bibliography.

McLaughlin, Kevin. "The Financial Imp: Ethics and Finance in Nineteenth-Century Fiction." *Novel* 29 (Winter, 1996): 165-183. Examines the key issue of finance that can be found at the center of some works of British fiction during this time, focusing particularly on Stevenson's treatment of these issues in his short story "The Bottle Imp."

McLynn, Frank. *Robert Louis Stevenson: A Biography*. New York: Random House, 1995. A biography that argues that Stevenson's wife was a negative influence on his life and work. Discusses Stevenson's struggle with agnosticism and his conflicted attitude toward women. Tries to counter the critical view of Stevenson as an unimportant writer of boys' literature by discussing the moral seriousness of his work.

Saposnik, Irving S. *Robert Louis Stevenson*. New York: Twayne, 1974. A useful critical survey of Stevenson's major works. Saposnik's volume is the best starting point for serious study of Stevenson's fiction. Supplemented by a helpful annotated bibliography.

Wright, Daniel L. "'The Prisonhouse of My Disposition': A Study of the Psychology of Addiction in *Dr. Jekyll and Mr. Hyde*." *Studies in the Novel* 26 (Fall, 1994): 254-267. Argues that the story is a portrait of a subject whose aggregate pre-addictive personality disorders reveal a substantial number of risk factors associated with high receptivity to addictive behavior; claims that the story is not just a quaint experiment in gothic terror but Victorian literature's premiere revelation, intended or not, of the etiology, character, and effects of chronic chemical addiction.

Kenneth Funsten, updated by
John W. Fiero

FRANK R. STOCKTON

Born: Philadelphia, Pennsylvania; April 5, 1834
Died: Washington, D.C.; April 20, 1902

PRINCIPAL SHORT FICTION

The Floating Prince and Other Fairy Tales, 1881
Ting-a-Ling Tales, 1882
The Lady or the Tiger?, and Other Stories, 1884
A Christmas Wreck and Other Stories, 1886
Amos Kilbright: His Adscititious Experiences, with Other Stories, 1888
The Stories of the Three Burglars, 1889
The Rudder Grangers Abroad and Other Stories, 1891
The Clock of Rondaine and Other Stories, 1892
The Watchmaker's Wife and Other Stories, 1893
Fanciful Tales, 1894
A Chosen Few, 1895

New Jersey: From the Discovery of the Scheyichbi to Recent Times, 1896
Stories of New Jersey, 1896 (also known as *New Jersey*)
A Story-Teller's Pack, 1897
Afield and Afloat, 1900
John Gayther's Garden and the Stories Told Therein, 1902
The Magic Egg and Other Stories, 1907
Stories of the Spanish Main, 1913
Best Short Stories, 1957

OTHER LITERARY FORMS

Frank R. Stockton wrote many articles for periodicals and was on the staffs of *Hearth and Home, The Century Illustrated Monthly Magazine*, and assistant editor of *St. Nicholas* from the time he was thirty-nine until he was forty-seven. He began as a juvenile writer, and some of his children's stories are still popular, particularly "The Bee Man of Orn," illustrated by Maurice Sendak. Of his many adult novels, the best loved was *Rudder Grange* (1879), for which the public demanded two sequels, *The Rudder Grangers Abroad and Other Stories* and *Pomona's Travels* (1894).

ACHIEVEMENTS

A prolific writer, Frank R. Stockton is to be classed with Mark Twain and Joel Chandler Harris as one of the finest humorists of the last quarter of the nineteenth century. He was widely admired during his lifetime, especially for his short stories, and was perhaps the first American science-fiction novelist. Yet Stockton's name is all but unknown to the modern reader. The choice presented in his most popular story "The Lady or the Tiger?" may be familiar to some today, but the story itself—which has been cited as a predecessor of modern recreative fiction—has been essentially forgotten.

It has been suggested that Stockton led the way for other more well-known authors. His novel *What Might Have Been Expected* (1874) was a forerunner of Twain's *The Adventures of Tom Sawyer* (1876) and *The Adventures of Huckleberry Finn* (1884); his portrayal of ordinary middle-class life in the 1880's preceded James Thurber's stories of the 1940's. Stockton's experiments with narrative technique inspired Gertrude Stein's approach in her *The Autobiography of Alice B. Toklas* (1933), and his political satire "The Governor-General" (1898) is remarkably similar to Leonard Patrick O'Connor Wibberley's 1950's bestseller *The Mouse That Roared* (1955).

BIOGRAPHY

Frank R. (Francis Richard) Stockton was a descendant of American pioneers, one of whom, Richard Stockton, had been one of the signers of the Declaration of Independence. The third son of nine children, he was expected to become a doctor. Instead, upon graduating from high school he studied wood engraving, at which he was proficient enough to support himself until he was thirty-two, when he

Frank R. Stockton (Library of Congress)

decided to become a journalist. Until 1880 he specialized in children's stories; then he began writing for adults, although the tone and the situations were not much different from his earlier works. He completed more than a dozen novels, comedies, satires, scientific speculations, and whimsies.

ANALYSIS

Because the masses read Stockton mainly for escape, it was easy for them to miss the underlying thought and sophistication in much of his work. Simply because he was so popular with the general public, Stockton has tended to be ignored by scholars and critics.

"THE MAGIC EGG"

In "The Magic Egg," Frank R. Stockton successfully employed a narrative device as old as *The Arabian Nights' Entertainments:* the frame story. The enclosed tale is about a magic show put on by Herbert Loring for a few carefully invited friends. The first part of the exhibition is a slide show projected on the screen of what Loring calls "fireworks," a kind of kaleidoscope arrangement of pieces of colored glass which form, by means of mirrors and lights, into fascinating patterns. After half an hour of this, the host brings out a table upon which he places a box containing an egg. When he touches the egg with a wand, it hatches into a downy chick that continues to grow until it is an enormous cock. Flapping his wings, the cock ascends to a chair placed upon the table for that purpose, his weight nearly tipping it over. The audience stands, cheers, and becomes extremely excited. Then the magician reverses the growth process and the bird grows smaller and smaller until it enters the egg again, is put back into the box, and the host leaves the stage.

The frame narrative tells how the audience assembled at the Unicorn Club by invitation at three o'clock on a January afternoon has to wait fifteen minutes, because Loring sees that two reserved seats in the front row have not yet been filled. Because the audience is becoming restless, Loring decides to begin even though someone important has not yet arrived. A few minutes after the fireworks part of the show, Edith Starr, who had been betrothed to Herbert Loring a month before, enters unobtrusively; not wishing to disturb the proceedings to find her front-row reserved seat, she sits in the back behind two large gentlemen who completely conceal her person. Her mother had had a headache so she stayed with her until she fell asleep and then came alone to "see what she could."

At this point the narration changes from omniscient to first person, as the magician describes what is happening in a long monologue of six and a half pages which concludes the frame story. Elated with his success, Loring uses a metaphor in which he becomes the rooster that he produced. He feels as if he "could fly to the top of that steeple, and flap and crow until all the world heard me." Since the crowing cock who lords it over the hen yard is soon to be deflated, the emblem of masculine power is thus used as ironic foreshadowing, as well as summing up what preceded.

Herbert and Edith meet in her library. He has been in the habit of calling on her every night, so this is part of the acknowledged routine of the engaged

lover. The remainder of the action is unfolded in dialogue. She says that she saw the audience wild with excitement. She, however, saw no chick, nor any full-grown fowl, no box, no wand, and no embroidered cloth. Nothing was what he said it was. "Everything was a sham and a delusion; every word you spoke was untrue. And yet everybody in the theatre, excepting you and me, saw all the things that you said were on the stage." Loring explains that he had hypnotized the audience with the revolving pieces of colored glass by which he had forced them to strain their eyes upward for half an hour in order to induce hypnotic sleep. He had been careful to invite only "impressionable subjects." When he was absolutely sure that they were under his influence, he proceeded to test his hypnotic powers with the illusion which they believed they saw.

"Did you intend that I should also be put under that spell?" she asks, indignant that he would have considered taking away her reason and judgment and making her "a mere tool of his will." She now understands that "nothing was real, not even the little pine table—not even the man!" She says a final good-bye to him, never to see him again, because she wants nothing further to do with a man who would cloud her perceptions, subject her intellect to his own, and force her to believe a lie. As the rejected suitor leaves, he says "And this is what came out of the magic egg!"

This is an inverted fairy tale. The normal formulaic plot would have ended in a marriage whose happy ending was achieved by the use of magical objects. Instead, the magic object here leads to the dissolution of the happy ending because the "princess" has a mind of her own; she is a strong-willed woman who refuses to submit to male domination. The second important aspect of the story is that it is a metaphor for the art of storytelling. The speaker, with his words alone, hypnotizes his audience into suspending their disbelief. His power over them is very like that of a magician, and Stockton, whose enthusiastic public followed his legerdemain through more than a dozen novels, must have at times confronted the ambiguities of his position. The blank page must have seemed the white shell of a magic egg which he alone could "crack" to release wonders that lasted only as long as he was relating them and then, when the cover was closed, went back to being only an object.

"HIS WIFE'S DECEASED SISTER"

"His Wife's Deceased Sister" is a charming tale built on the interrelations between life and literature and on the paradox that failure results from too-great success. A newly married author in the elation of his honeymoon writes a moving story. He has supported himself quite adequately up to that time with his fictions, but this story is a masterpiece. The problem is that everything he writes afterward is rejected because it would disappoint the public for not being on the same level which they have come to expect from him. The author then meets a pauper who earlier had the same paradoxical experience of having been ruined by the success of one story. Depressed by his visit to the pauper's room, where the pauper sleeps on newspapers and lives by grinding heads on pins, the author consults his editor, saying he faces similar ruin. They hit on the device of an assumed name.

Once more the author is making a good, steady income when a son is born. In his first joy of fatherhood, he composes a story which is even superior to "His Wife's Deceased Sister." He buries it in a tin box with the edges soldered together, which he hides in the attic with instructions to throw away the key to the solid lock he has purchased for it. The underlying assumption is that great fiction is inspired by happy events in life, which contradicts the Freudian notion that art sublimates suffering. The problem with the plot is that readers may think they have a better solution to the author's problem. Why not publish the story under his real name? The spark for "His Wife's Deceased Sister" is clearly Stockton's own experience with "The Lady or the Tiger?"—which made him a cult figure—and subsequent publication problems that ensued. Although Stockton's work generally expressed admiration for the middle class, with all its weaknesses, he could also be satirical and interpreted on many levels. In this story, the main character chooses to relegate his masterpiece to oblivion rather than again subject himself to the upheaval of public adulation.

OTHER MAJOR WORKS

LONG FICTION: *What Might Have Been Expected*, 1874; *Rudder Grange*, 1879; *A Jolly Fellowship*, 1880; *The Story of Viteau*, 1884; *The Transferred Ghost*, 1884; *The Late Mrs. Null*, 1886; *The Casting Away of Mrs. Lecks and Mrs. Aleshine*, 1886; *The Hundredth Man*, 1887; *The Dusantes: A Sequel to "The Casting Away of Mrs. Lecks and Mrs. Aleshine,"* 1888; *The Great War Syndicate*, 1889; *Personally Conducted*, 1889; *Ardis Claverden*, 1890; *The Squirrel Inn*, 1891; *The House of Martha*, 1891; *Pomona's Travels*, 1894; *The Adventures of Captain Horn*, 1895; *Mrs. Cliff's Yacht*, 1896; *Captain Chap: Or, The Rolling Stones*, 1896; *The Great Stone of Sardis: A Novel*, 1898; *The Girl at Cobhurst*, 1898; *The Buccaneers and Pirates of Our Coasts*, 1898; *The Associate Hermits*, 1899; *The Vizier of the Two-Horned Alexander*, 1899; *The Young Master of Hyson Hall*, 1899; *A Bicycle of Cathay: A Novel*, 1900; *Kate Bonnet: The Romance of a Pirate's Daughter*, 1902; *The Captain's Toll-Gate*, 1903; *The Lost Dryad*, 1912; *The Poor Count's Christmas*, 1927.

NONFICTION: *A Northern Voice Calling for the Dissolution of the Union of the United States of America*, 1860; *The Home: Where It Should Be and What to Put In It*, 1872.

CHILDREN'S LITERATURE: *Ting-a-Ling*, 1870; *Roundabout Rambles in Lands of Fact and Fancy*, 1872; *Tales Out of School*, 1875; *The Bee-Man of Orn and Other Fanciful Tales*, 1887; *The Queen's Museum*, 1887.

MISCELLANEOUS: *The Novels and Stories of Frank R. Stockton*, 1899-1904 (23 volumes).

BIBLIOGRAPHY

Golemba, Henry L. *Frank R. Stockton*. Boston: Twayne, 1981. Part of Twayne's United States Authors series, this extended examination of Stockton and his art includes an introductory bibliography and chronological investigation of Stockton's works. Golemba also suggests reasons for Stockton's neglect, in relation not only to the works themselves but also to the history of publishing and literary criticism over the last hundred years. The 182-page volume contains a select bibliography of primary and secondary sources.

Griffin, Martin I. J. *Frank R. Stockton*. Philadelphia: University of Pennsylvania Press, 1939. This biography gathers together details of Stockton's life—many taken from original sources—and shows the relationship between his life and his works. In the discussion of Stockton's work, however, plot summary dominates over critical interpretation. Includes a bibliography.

Howells, William Dean. "Stockton's Stories." *The Atlantic Monthly* 59 (January, 1887): 130-132. Citing particular Stockton stories, Howells discusses Stockton's influence on the short-story form, analyzing characteristics of both the author and the form that make them such a good match. This article, along with three others Howells wrote during Stockton's lifetime, provides some of the best criticism of Stockton's art.

Johnson, Robert U. *Remembered Yesterdays*. Boston: Little, Brown, 1923. This memoir by a former editor in chief of *The Century Illustrated Monthly Magazine* includes information about many men and women memorable in the fields of letters and publishing. His short chapter on Stockton, entitled "A Joyful Humorist," gives a feeling for the man through personal recollections and anecdotes.

May, Charles. *The Short Story: The Reality of Artifice*. New York: Twayne, 1995. Brief comment on Stockton's best-known story, "The Lady or the Tiger?" as a so-called trick-ending story; suggests the story is not as open-ended as it is often claimed to be.

Vedder, Henry C. *American Writers of Today*. Boston: Silver Burdett, 1894. This analysis of American writers includes a twelve-page chapter on Stockton and his work. Although obviously dated and considering works only to the early 1890's, the chapter offers interesting insights and a flavor of the times in which Stockton wrote. Vedder gives considerable attention to Stockton's originality and droll humor.

Ruth Rosenberg, updated by
Jean C. Fulton

ROBERT STONE

Born: Brooklyn, New York; August 21, 1937

PRINCIPAL SHORT FICTION

Bear and His Daughter: Stories, 1997

OTHER LITERARY FORMS

Robert Stone is best known as an award-winning novelist, but he also wrote the screenplay adaptations of his first two novels, *A Hall of Mirrors* (1967) and *Dog Soldiers* (1974), entitled *WUSA* (1970) and *Who'll Stop the Rain* (1978), respectively. He has also written the novel *Damascus Gate* (1998) and contributed dozens of literary and social essays, travel pieces, and political commentaries to leading journals, and he edited (with Katrina Kenison) *The Best American Short Stories 1992*.

ACHIEVEMENTS

Robert Stone was awarded the William Faulkner Foundation First Novel Award in 1967 and won a John Simon Guggenheim Memorial Foundation Fellowship in 1971. *Dog Soldiers* won the National Book Award in 1975; *A Flag for Sunrise* (1981) was a finalist for that award and for the Pulitzer Prize in Letters in 1982. He has been the recipient of numerous later awards, including a National Endowment for the Humanities Fellowship in 1982 and the Mildred and Harold Strauss Living Award in 1987.

BIOGRAPHY

Robert Stone's life has mirrored the colorful life so frequently portrayed in his stories and novels. After Catholic school and a stint in the U.S. Navy (1955 to 1958), Stone and his wife (they married in 1959) traveled and supported themselves through various odd jobs. (Their daughter Deirdre was born in a charity hospital in New Orleans.) In New York, Stone supported his growing family—a son Ian was born in 1964—as an advertising copywriter, worked on his first novel, and soon won a Wallace Stegner writing fellowship at Stanford. Since his first novel, he has been able to support himself with his writing, supplemented by fellowships and teaching positions. (He has taught at Princeton and Harvard Universities, among other schools.) For someone who is largely self-educated (he spent less than a year at New York University), Stone has commented extensively on a wide range of political topics and has engaged in a number of public literary controversies.

ANALYSIS

Robert Stone has published a number of short stories and the short-story collection *Bear and His Daughter*. Many of his stories have been reprinted in other collections, however, and in the annual publica-

Robert Stone (©Jerry Bauer)

tion *The Best American Short Stories*. Stone's fictional world does not initially look appealing. His stories deal with violent and troubling events: abortion, drug dealing, alcoholism, the effects of war. Yet there is a moral vein running beneath the surface of these stories—even when the world they reflect seems without moral structure—and many of his characters are desperately seeking freedom from their demons. One of Stone's themes seems to be the consequences of early actions and the need for mercy and forgiveness—of self as well as of others. Stone's characters are sometimes mad, often brutal—the surface of his stories has constant tension—but they are often seeking spiritual transcendence. His writing is spare, he renders dialogue beautifully, and it is easy for readers to identify with his characters, in spite of their troubled lives.

BEAR AND HIS DAUGHTER

Robert Stone has published more than a dozen short stories over the course of his career, and his collection *Bear and His Daughter* brings together six stories written over some thirty years with the previously unpublished title novella. The collection includes "Helping," which was also reprinted in *The Best American Stories 1988*, and "Under the Pitons," which appeared in *The Best American Stories 1997*. The remaining five stories are equally strong and represent Stone's fictional style at its best. Stone is a realist who captures contemporary American life in its starkest, often most brutal moments. In his minimalist style Stone often reads like Raymond Carver, but in his deeper ethnical concerns he resembles no one more than British novelists like Joseph Conrad and Graham Greene.

"MISERERE"

"Miserere" leads off the *Bear and His Daughter* collection, and it is a powerful story of contemporary American life and a ready example of Stone's fictional style. Mary Urquhart, a librarian in a decaying northern New Jersey city, receives a call from her friend Camille Innaurato as she finishes work one night. She drives to Camille's house, as she has done on earlier occasions. Camille's brother is a policeman who recovers fetuses disposed of by abortion clinics and brings them to Camille, who then enlists Mary and Mary's priest friend, Father Hooke, to inter the fetuses in a Catholic rite. On this cold night, when they arrive at Father Hooke's rectory, however, they learn that he has changed his mind and will not perform the service. "'I think women have a right,'" he announces. There is an ugly scene in which Mary reduces Father Hooke to tears, and he accuses the women of violence and cruelty. They drive to a second priest, Monsignor Danilo, who performs the ceremony, but it is an unsatisfactory experience for Mary. The title of the story comes from the Latin prayer "Agnus Dei, qui tollis peccate mundi,/ Miserere nobis" ("Lamb of God, who takest away the sins of the world,/ Have mercy on us"). In the argument with Father Hooke, readers learn that thirteen years earlier Mary lost her husband and three children in a skating accident when the ice on a frozen lake gave way, and the four fetuses before the alter remind readers of that tragedy. After recovering from alcoholism and then converting to Catholicism, Mary became a rabid antiabortionist, but her rage at life simmers just beneath the taut surface of this story. The prayer that closes the short story, "Have mercy on us," applies to all the flawed characters here.

"ABSENCE OF MERCY"

"Absence of Mercy" is another story of violence—and mercy. Mackay is a young man in his late twenties working to support his wife and baby. The greatest impact on his life, it is clear, came from his brief stay in an orphanage where he was placed in the 1940's, when his mother was institutionalized. He survived the violence and "absence of mercy" at St. Michael's, and his years in the U.S. Navy, and he is working his way up to middle-class respectability when he reads that a friend from the orphanage, also a young married man, has been killed in a New York City subway trying to be a good Samaritan. The murder haunts Mackay, for somehow the violence of his childhood has reached out to touch him again. A year later on a nearby subway platform, Mackay tries to intervene when a crazed man attacks an old woman. The woman escapes, but Mackay and the man fall into a struggle on the platform. Mackay finally gets away, but the attacker yells for help, and the crowd sees Mackay as the criminal. Mackay will survive,

Stone implies, but "he wondered just how far he would run and where it was that he thought to go." His childhood violence and "absence of mercy" have followed him, in the upside-down moral order that seems to describe this world. There are no easy ethical answers here.

"HELPING"

"Helping" is one of Stone's best-known stories and has been anthologized several times and included in *The Best American Stories 1988*. Elliot—and all Stone's male protagonists seem to be known by their last names—has been sober for some eighteen months, until his client Blankenship comes into the office at the state hospital where Elliot is a counselor. Blankenship has not been to Vietnam, while Elliot has, but Blankenship appropriates Elliot's experience, even his dreams of that awful war. Elliot's anger soon gives way to anxiety, and he ends up drinking and driving home with a bottle. When Elliot's wife Grace returns from her own nightmarish day to discover the drunken Elliot, she announces she is not going to stay with him this time. Grace works for a service that helps battered children and has lost a battered child to parents in a court case, so both partners have been unable to help others. When the child's father, Vopotik, calls to abuse her verbally, Elliot invites him over and gets out his shotgun. He awakens the next morning in the chair by the window, where he has been waiting for Vopotik, and goes outside with the gun. Standing in a snow-covered field, he sees his wife in their bedroom window and hopes for some sign of forgiveness from her. The story ends on this ambiguous note. Will Elliot recover? Will his wife stay and help him? In the universe of Stone's stories, anxiety, desperation, and rage dominate, and mercy can never be taken for granted.

"UNDER THE PITONS"

"Under the Pitons" was included in *The Best American Stories 1997* and is a tale of adventure that could have been written by Ernest Hemingway. The story covers several days as a motley crew of one-time drug dealers sail from St. Vincent to Martinique in the Caribbean. Blessington is aboard to pilot the *Sans Regret*, but it is his French partner Freyincet who has set up the dope deal. Along for the ride are the women Marie and Gillian. The four picked up the dope in St. Vincent some days ago and must deliver it to Martinique. When Marie becomes sick, Freyincet insists they anchor off the southwest coast of St. Lucia, under the shadow of the Pitons, twin peaks whose name means "stakes." The stakes here are high, and all four will lose. Two pirates come out to the boat, and Freyincet scares them off with a shotgun. The four smugglers go swimming in the clear Caribbean water, suddenly realize they have forgotten to put down the ladder, and, when they discover that the pirates have cut their ropes, are unable to keep up with the drifting boat. Blessington tries to save Gillian, but she is too stoned to help herself and eventually drowns. Blessington makes it to shore and sees what may be one of the other two near the stranded boat, but he heads off into the jungle and to the imagined comfort of an Irish bar in the island town of Soufriere. Gillian goes down singing "Praise God, from whom all blessings flow," but there is little to praise in this tale of drugs and mistakes. All the characters believed they could make easy money and escape without consequences—"without regret," as the boat's name declares—but that is impossible in the world Robert Stone creates.

"Bear and His Daughter"

The title story of Robert Stone's collection of short fiction is a grim and gripping tale. "Bear" is William Small, a famous poet who is doing a western tour of readings, when he stops to visit his daughter Rowan, a ranger at a national park in Nevada. His last tour ended in disaster, and this one seems headed the same way. On the night that readers are introduced to him, Small is kicked out of a casino after getting drunk. When he finds his daughter, she has been taking crystal methedrine all day, and the two of them drink wine and talk about their failed and fragmented lives. Both are haunted by their sexual relations in the past, and Rowan is filled with a rage that the drugs and alcohol only fuel. Small has been trying all day to remember a poem about returning salmon he wrote

for her years earlier. After she shoots her father and then kills herself—in a natural cavern where she claims Indian sacrifices were once made—her boyfriend finds the poem. The story is completed, like the troubled lives of these two, but there is little else to salvage.

Other major works

LONG FICTION: *A Hall of Mirrors*, 1967; *Dog Soldiers*, 1974; *A Flag for Sunrise*, 1981; *Children of Light*, 1986; *Outerbridge Reach*, 1989; *Damascus Gate*, 1998.

SCREENPLAYS: *WUSA*, 1970; *Who'll Stop the Rain*, 1978 (with Judith Roscoe).

Bibliography

Bonetti, Kay, et al., eds. *Conversations with American Novelists*. Columbia: Missouri, 1997. Stone talks about his early stories in this far-ranging 1982 interview.

Finn, James. "The Moral Vision of Robert Stone: Transcendent in the Muck of History." *Commonweal* 119 (November 5, 1993): 9-14. Although focused on the novels, this article in a *Commonweal* series on contemporary Catholic writers of fiction identifies the peculiarly moral strain of Stone's writing.

Parks, John G. "Unfit Survivors: The Failed and Lost Pilgrims in the Fiction of Robert Stone." *CEA Critic* 53 (Fall, 1990): 52-57. Examines the characters of Stone's fiction.

Solotaroff, Robert. *Robert Stone*. New York: Twayne, 1994. In this first full-length study of Stone's fiction, Solotaroff's final chapter, "The Stories and the Nonfiction," is a trenchant treatment of Stone's work with analyses of "Helping" and "Absence of Mercy," as well as two other stories from *Bear and His Daughter*, "Porque No Tiene, Porque Le Falta," and "Aquarius Obscured."

David Peck

JESSE STUART

Born: W-Hollow, Riverton, Kentucky; August 8, 1907
Died: Ironton, Ohio; February 17, 1984

PRINCIPAL SHORT FICTION
Head o' W-Hollow, 1936
Men of the Mountains, 1941
Tales from the Plum Grove Hills, 1946
Clearing in the Sky and Other Stories, 1950
Plowshare in Heaven: Tales True and Tall from the Kentucky Hills, 1958
Save Every Lamb, 1964
My Land Has a Voice, 1966
Come Gentle Spring, 1969
Come Back to the Farm, 1971
Votes Before Breakfast, 1974
The Best-Loved Short Stories of Jesse Stuart, 1982

OTHER LITERARY FORMS

Although Jesse Stuart probably found the best outlet for his artistic expression in the short story, he published more than two thousand poems, a number of autobiographical works, nine novels—the latter including the best-selling *Taps for Private Tussie* (1943), and six children's books.

ACHIEVEMENTS

Through the vivid pictures that he presents in his stories of life in the Kentucky hill country, Jesse Stuart opened up significant veins of material for other writers who follow him. While not adding new dimensions to the short story, he did nevertheless produce many excellent examples in that genre.

Virtually all Stuart's stories deal with the hill country of eastern Kentucky, where generations ago people dropped off from the movement West to settle in the hills and hollows of what has come to be a part of Appalachia. The life depicted in these stories is hard, and the people who live it are fundamentally religious and close to the earth. A natural storyteller, Stuart captured not only the idiom of his characters but also the very essence of their relationship to one another and to the natural world around them. He does not take solely the realist's approach but blends in a strain of romantic optimism.

Although cast in what appears to be a realist mode, Stuart's stories often blend a romantic optimism with an exuberance for life that is sometimes expressed in comic juxtapositions that verge on the grotesque. A popular as well as prolific author, Stuart was named poet laureate of Kentucky in 1954, won an award for *Taps For Private Tussie* in 1943, and was nominated for a Pulitzer Prize in 1975 for *The World of Jesse Stuart: Selected Poems* (1975).

BIOGRAPHY

A native of Kentucky, Jesse Hilton Stuart was educated at Lincoln Memorial University. Following his graduation, he began a career as a writer and teacher, starting what was, for him, a lifetime concern for educational reform and a lifelong struggle with the educational establishment. During his long career, he served as both teacher and administrator, and, after retiring from teaching to turn to full-time farming, writing, and lecturing, he never lost his passionate belief in the power of knowledge.

In 1939, after a courtship of seventeen years, Stuart married Naomi Deane Norris. They had one child, a daughter, Jessica Jane, born in 1942. During World War II, he served in the U.S. Navy, accepting disability in 1945. During subsequent years, though he traveled extensively, Stuart continued to live on the working farm in W-Hollow, the area where he was born and that he made famous through his poems, novels, and stories, many of which were published in *Esquire*.

He suffered the first of several heart attacks in 1954 but was able to return to normal activity. After a second stroke in 1982, however, he was unable to recover and remained more or less bedridden until his death two years later.

ANALYSIS

America's southern highlands have long been

Jesse Stuart (Library of Congress)

viewed as an area removed from the influences of the "civilized" world; indeed, for more than a century they were. Rich in folklore and tradition, these highlands have provided stimulus to a vast number of writers as far back as William Gilmore Simms. The majority produced mostly second-rate novels and stories that relied on melodrama, sentimentality, and effusive description of natural setting to carry their plots. A few writers, however, have risen above that level to present the southern highlanders and their land in a more graphic and realistic light. Jesse Stuart was one such writer.

Once commenting that as a child he "read the landscape, the streams, the air, and the skies," Stuart had "plenty of time to grow up in a world that I loved more and more as I grew older." With his abiding love and respect for the people and the land of this picturesque region, Stuart, in a fashion matched by few American regional writers, brought the southern

highlands into sharp focus for his readers. His short stories—the fictional form in which he was at his best—are a journey of exploration into the many aspects of life in the region. Using his home place of W-Hollow as a vantage point and springboard, Stuart treated various themes and motifs in his stories: religion, death, politics, folklore, sense of place, nature, and the code of the hills. While these themes are treated from a realistic stance, through all of them runs the romantic idea of the ever-renewing power of the earth, and through many of them an exuberant sense of humor, where the comic juxtaposition is the primary structural pattern.

"DAWN OF REMEMBERED SPRING"

A story that clearly illustrates a blending of realism and Romanticism is "Dawn of Remembered Spring." Like so many of Stuart's stories, this one has an autobiographical ring to it. The main character is Shan, a young boy who appears in a number of Stuart's stories. In this particular instance, Shan is being cautioned by his mother not to wade the creek because of the danger of water moccasins. Just a few days prior, Roy Deer, another youngster, was bitten by a water moccasin and is now near death. To Shan's comment that all water moccasins ought to be killed, his mother agrees but adds, "They're in all these creeks around here. There's so many of them we can't kill 'em all." As idyllic as one side of life in W-Hollow may be, there is the ever-present factor of death, in this case symbolized by water moccasins.

Shan, however, is not to be deterred by his mother's warning, and, armed with a wild-plum club, he sets out wading the creek to kill as many water moccasins as he can. It is a suspenseful journey as Shan, frightened but determined, kills snake after snake. "This is what I like to do," he thinks. "I love to kill snakes." He wades up the creek all day, and when he steps out on the bank at four o'clock, he has killed fifty-three water moccasins. As he leaves the creek, he is afraid of the snakes he has killed and grips his club until his hands hurt, but he feels good that he has paid the snakes back for biting Roy Deer—"who wasn't bothering the water moccasins that bit him. He was just crossing the creek at the foot-log and it jumped from the grass and bit him."

As he goes near home, Shan sees two copperhead snakes in a patch of sunlight. "Snakes," he cries, "snakes a-fightin' and they're not water moccasins! They're copperheads!" The snakes are wrapped around each other, looking into each other's eyes and touching each other's lips. Shan's Uncle Alf comes upon the scene and tells Shan that the snakes are not fighting but making love. A group of onlookers soon gathers, including Shan's mother who asks him where he has been. "Killin' snakes," is his reply. To her statement that Roy Deer is dead, Shan says that he has paid the snakes back by killing fifty-three of them. At this point his mother, along with the rest who have gathered at the scene, is spellbound by the loving copperheads. She sends Shan to the house to get his father. As the boy goes, he notices that the snakes have done something to the people watching: "The wrinkled faces were as bright as the spring sunlight on the bluff; their eyes were shiny as the creek was in the noonday sunlight."

In "Dawn of Remembered Spring" Stuart has juxtaposed images of death and life; Shan has killed fifty-three snakes, and Roy Deer has died from his snake bite. The two copperheads making love remind the reader and the people watching that, cruel though nature may be at times, there is always the urge for life. The hate that demands revenge is somehow redeemed in the laughter that Shan hears from the group—a laughter "louder than the wild honeybees I had heard swarming over the shoemake, alderberry, and wild flox blossoms along the creek."

"SYLVANIA IS DEAD"

In "Sylvania Is Dead" Stuart uses the death motif to bring out the prevalent stoicism of the highlanders as well as their ability to see humor in a grotesque situation. The story opens as Bert Pratt and Lonnie Pennix are on their way to the funeral of the story's namesake. It is September, and nature is presented through images of death: "The backbone of the mountain was gray and hard as the bleached bone of a carcass. The buzzards floated in high circles and craned their necks." When the men reach Sylvania's cabin at the top of the mountain, they see a large crowd already gathered and buzzards circling low overhead. Lonnie pulls his pistol and shoots into the

buzzards, scaring them away. When Skinny, Sylvania's husband, runs from the cabin scolding them for firing guns at such a sorrowful time, they respond that they were only trying to shoo away buzzards. Skinny says it is all right, for buzzards are a "perfect nuisance in a time like this."

The black humor in the story derives from Sylvania's size and her occupation. She weighs six hundred and fifty pounds; her husband, only about one hundred. Her occupation has been selling moonshine, and as one of the men digging her grave says, "I say we'll never miss Sylvania until she's gone. She's been a mother to all of us." Sylvania is so big that when she was caught "red handed" by the revenuers on one occasion, she simply laughed and said that even "if they could get her out of the house, they couldn't get her down the mountain."

Getting Sylvania out of the house is the big problem now. Building a coffin that takes six men to carry, they finally get Sylvania in it, but it will not go through the door. The only answer is to tear down the chimney. Before carrying the coffin out, however, the men stop for a drink from Sylvania's last barrel. "I patronized Sylvania in life and I'll patronize her in death," Bert says. The drinks from Sylvania's last barrel, combined with the sorrow at her death, make the crowd noisy. As the coffin is carried to the grave, there is laughing, talking, and crying, accompanied by another pistol shot at circling buzzards. Finally Sylvania is lowered to her rest, and, as Skinny is led back to his cabin, there are "words of condolence in the lazy wind's molesting the dry flaming leaves on the mountain."

The human drama played out at this mountaintop funeral is marked not predominantly by sorrow but by acceptance and humor. Sylvania was mother to them all in life, and it is only fitting that her "children" should see her to her grave. The humor in the story is not strained or out of place; on the contrary, the comedy underlines the grotesque element of human behavior as juxtaposed with the natural order. Humor is part of the hard life lived close to nature that is common to the people of Stuart's fictional world—as much a part as are Sylvania's moonshine and the buzzards circling overhead.

"SUNDAY AFTERNOON HANGING"

In "Sunday Afternoon Hanging," Stuart again blends the comedy with grim realism, as an old man describes to his grandson what old-time hangings in Blakesburg, Kentucky, were like. Viewing the electric chair as a poor substitute for a hanging, he points out that at a hanging "everybody got to see it and laugh and faint, cuss or cry." Indeed, they would come from as far as forty miles for such an opportunity. As the old man relates one particular incident to his grandson, the reader is made aware of a combination of characteristics in the people Stuart writes about—violence, vengeance, fatalism, and a desire to escape the tedium of their daily lives.

The Sunday afternoon hanging that the old man describes is the result of the brutal murder of an elderly couple by five men—Tim and Jake Sixeymore, Freed Winslow, Dudley Toms, and Work Grubb. They are all sentenced to be hanged on the same day, and hundreds of people congregate to witness the affair. In contrast to the grisly vengeance to be exacted, the day is bright, with a June wind blowing and roses in bloom. Providing music for the event is a seven-piece band dressed in gaudy yellow pants with red sashes and green jackets. "It was the biggest thing we'd had in many a day," recalls the old man. "Horses broke loose without riders on them and took out through the crowd among the barking dogs, running over them and the children. People didn't pay any attention to that. It was a hanging and people wanted to see every bit of it."

The procedure for the hanging is to have each man brought to the hanging standing on his coffin in a horse-drawn wagon. After a rousing number by the band and a confession from the condemned, the wagon is pulled away, leaving him "struggling for breath and glomming at the wind with his hands." When he is pronounced dead, the procedure begins for the next man. As each man is hanged, the gruesome scene becomes even more grotesque. The last to be hanged is Tim Sixeymore, and he is so large that he breaks six ropes before the execution is finally carried out. His confession, reminiscent of the ballad "Sam Hall," begins, "Gentlemen bastards and sonofabitches. Women wenches and hussies and

goddam you all." As the hanging is completed and the parents of the Sixeymores carry off their dead sons, the band plays softer music. The crowd breaks up, "getting acquainted and talking about the hanging, talking about their crops and the cattle and the doings of the Lord to the wicked people for their sins"; and so life goes on. The blending of the comic and the tragic in "Sunday Afternoon Hanging" is so subtle that one is not sure whether to be horrified at the terrible vengeance exacted amid frivolity and hatred or to laugh at the black humor apparent in the contradiction.

"THE MOONSHINE WAR"

Whatever his feelings of admiration for the people about whom he wrote, Stuart was not blind to the aspect of their character that encourages a kind of macho violence. A number of his stories, for example, deal with feuding and selling moonshine, which, although they are usually thought of now in a more or less humorous vein, were in reality serious and often deadly activities. Fiercely proud, Stuart's characters consider such activities their own business and go about them in their own way, as shown in the story "The Moonshine War."

Combining moonshine and feuding, this story is narrated by Chris Candell, whose father in earlier days was one of four moonshine sellers in Greenwood County, Kentucky. With the help of his three sons, Charlie, Zeke, and Chris, he sold moonshine for twenty years before his wife prevailed upon him to lay his sins on the mourner's bench in the Methodist Church and give up "the business." Shortly after, the federal agents close in on the other three families that are still moonshining—the Whaleys, the Fortners, and the Luttrells—sending members from each to prison for varying terms.

When Willie Fortner is released because of his youth, he returns to Greenwood County, vowing revenge on the other families because he thinks that they helped the federal agents to discover his father's still. Two weeks later Jarwin Whaley is found stabbed to death. In quick succession, two more deaths by stabbing occur, of Lucretia Luttrell and Charlie Candell, Chris's brother. There is no real evidence to connect these crimes to Willie Fortner, and, although he is arrested, he is acquitted, moving Zeke Candell to say, "Damn this circumstantial evidence stuff! We've got to take the law into our own hands." Before the Candells can do anything, however, Willie Fortner is killed in an auto wreck, the only one of five in the car who dies in the crash. Chris's father, obviously attributing Willie's death to the Lord, says that "we'll have peace. The knife killings are over."

Stuart does not condemn any of the actions in "The Moonshine War," but, as in all his stories, he accepts the characteristics of his highland ancestors. Indeed, in another story, "My Father Is an Educated Man," he says of the fiercely independent men of his family now sleeping in the Virginia, West Virginia, and Kentucky mountains, "Though I belong to them, they would not claim me since I have had my chance and unlike them I have not killed one of my enemies." The code of conduct that arises from such a life view may be a combination of savagery, civility, and moral contradiction, but it attests to the belief of the highlander that he is master of his own destiny.

SAVE EVERY LAMB

For those wishing to see another side of Stuart's writing, there is the volume of stories entitled *Save Every Lamb*. Virtually all the stories in this volume are autobiographical in background and have nature themes. In them Stuart harks back to another era—a time "when everybody in the country lived by digging his livelihood from the ground." It was a time when humans were in tune with the natural world about them and were better for it. "My once wonderful world has changed into a world that gives me great unhappiness," Stuart says in the introduction to *Save Every Lamb*. For the moment, at least, Stuart in these stories takes the reader back with him to that wonderful world of his youth.

In all his stories Stuart writes with an easy, almost folksy, style. Avoiding experimentation and deep symbolism, he holds his readers by paying close attention to detail and by painting starkly graphic scenes as he brings to life the characters and settings of W-Hollow. As a regionalist, Stuart draws constantly on his background in his stories, with the result that his style is underlined by an autobiographical bias, which contributes strongly to the sense of immediacy that marks all his work. Just as William Faulkner has his microcosm of the universe in Yoknapatawpha County, so too does Stuart in W-Hollow, and the American literary chronicle is the richer for it.

OTHER MAJOR WORKS

LONG FICTION: *Trees of Heaven*, 1940; *Taps for Private Tussie*, 1943; *Foretaste of Glory*, 1946; *Hie to the Hunters*, 1950; *The Good Spirit of Laurel Ridge*, 1953; *Daughter of the Legend*, 1965; *Mr. Gallion's School*, 1967; *The Land Beyond the River*, 1973; *Cradle of the Copperheads*, 1988.

POETRY: *Harvest of Youth*, 1930; *Man with a Bull-Tongue Plow*, 1934; *Album of Destiny*, 1944; *Kentucky Is My Land*, 1952; *Hold April*, 1962; *The World of Jesse Stuart: Selected Poems*, 1975.

NONFICTION: *Beyond Dark Hills*, 1938; *The Thread That Runs So True*, 1949; *The Year of My Rebirth*, 1956; *God's Oddling*, 1960; *To Teach, to Love*, 1970; *My World*, 1975; *The Kingdom Within: A Spiritual Autobiography*, 1979; *Lost Sandstones and Lonely Skies and Other Essays*, 1979; *If I Were Seventeen Again and Other Essays*, 1980.

CHILDREN'S LITERATURE: *Mongrel Mettle: The Autobiography of a Dog*, 1944; *The Beatinest Boy*, 1953; *A Penny's Worth of Character*, 1954; *Red Mule*, 1955; *The Rightful Owner*, 1960; *Andy Finds a Way*, 1961.

BIBLIOGRAPHY

Blair, Everetta Love. *Jesse Stuart: His Life and Works*. Columbia: University of South Carolina Press, 1967. Blair opens with a brief account of Stuart's life and background. Subsequent chapters survey his poetry, short stories, novels, and other accomplishments. General discussions provide insight into particular works and overall trends.

Foster, Ruel E. *Jesse Stuart*. New York: Twayne, 1968. One of the earliest, and with a few exceptions, one of the best of the critical studies. Contains biographical information as well as extensive critiques on Stuart's work up to the date of publication.

Le Master, J. R. ed. *Jesse Stuart: Selected Criticism.*

St. Petersburg, Fla.: Valkyrie Press, 1978. A good start to Stuart criticism, this volume includes previously published articles by different scholars. Excellent introduction to Stuart's work.

Le Master, J. R. and Mary Washington Clark, eds. *Jesse Stuart: Essays on His Work*. Lexington: University Press of Kentucky, 1977. These essays (written specifically for this volume) provide critical perspectives on different facets and forms of Stuart's work, including poetry, short fiction, and novels, as well as his humor and use of folklore. The editors indicate that a primary purpose here is to bring into sharper focus Stuart's use of multiple perspectives.

Lowe, Jimmy. *Jesse Stuart: The Boy from the Dark Hills*. Edited by Jerry A. Herndon, James M. Gifford, and Chuck D. Charles. Ashland, Ky.: Jesse Stuart Foundation, 1990. A good, updated biography of Stuart.

Pennington, Lee. *The Dark Hills of Jesse Stuart*. Cincinnati: Harvest Press, 1967. Pennington discusses Stuart's system of symbolism as it emerges in his early poetry and later through his novels. Argues that Stuart is far more than a regionalist; rather, he is an important creative writer and spokesman not only for a region but for all humankind.

Richardson, H. Edward. *Jesse: The Biography of an American Writer—Jesse Hilton Stuart*. New York: McGraw-Hill, 1984. This inclusive study, printed in the year of Stuart's death, contains some photographs. Sensitively written, it offers invaluable reading for anyone with more than a passing interest in Stuart's life and work.

Thompson, Edgar H. "A Cure for the Malaise of the Dislocated Southerner: The Writing of Jesse Stuart." *Journal of the Appalachian Studies Association* 3 (1991): 146-151. A good survey of Stuart emphasizing his regional heritage.

Towles, Donald B. "Twenty Stories from Jesse Stuart." *The Courier-Journal*, September 20, 1998, p. O51. A review of *Tales from the Plum Grove Hills*; surveys the themes and subjects of the stories and comments on their use of Eastern Kentucky dialect.

Ward, William S. *A Literary History of Kentucky*. Knoxville: University of Tennessee Press, 1988. Includes a biographical-critical discussion of Stuart's work, pointing out that Stuart deals with people as individuals rather than in sociological terms; claims that a principle source of his success with the short story was the zest with which he carried a story through in a flood of detail.

Wilton Eckley, updated by
Mary Rohrberger

THEODORE STURGEON
Edward Hamilton Waldo

Born: Staten Island, New York; February 26, 1918
Died: Eugene, Oregon; May 8, 1985

PRINCIPAL SHORT FICTION

Without Sorcery, 1948
E Pluribus Unicorn, 1953
Caviar, 1955
A Way Home, 1955
A Touch of Strange, 1958
Aliens 4, 1959
Beyond, 1960
Sturgeon in Orbit, 1964
. . . And My Fear Is Great/Baby Is Three, 1965
The Joyous Invasions, 1965
Starshine, 1966
Strugeon Is Alive and Well, 1971
The Worlds of Theodore Strugeon, 1972
To Here and the Easel, 1973
Sturgeon's West, 1973 (with Don Ward)
Case and the Dreamer, 1974
Visions and Venturers, 1978
The Stars Are the Styx, 1979
The Golden Helix, 1980

OTHER LITERARY FORMS

It seems as though no literary form was wrong for Theodore Sturgeon. He wrote newspaper stories in the late 1930's, book and film reviews in the 1950's, and for twenty years after that, radio and television scripts, and a wide variety of fiction. He also published a coauthored Western novel, a (pseudonymous) historical romance, a psychological vampire novel, a film novelization, and five highly acclaimed science-fiction novels.

ACHIEVEMENTS

Theodore Sturgeon's name is one of those most cited in lists of the writers of science-fiction's golden age. Many consider him the best golden age author, mainly because he concentrated less on scientific hardware and more on character interaction than did his contemporaries. A moralistic and romantic writer, his major themes are tolerance for otherness of all kinds and concern for the environment before these became fashionable opinions. He was among the first American science-fiction writers to write plausibly about sex, homosexuality, race, and religion. He has sometimes been accused of writing pornography by those who prefer their science fiction in the standard starched-collar puritan mode. In reality, Sturgeon is among the first to turn American science fiction into a fiction for mature, thinking adults, as his influence on writers such as Ray Bradbury and Samuel R. Delany attests. He received several awards nominations and won three awards: the International Fantasy Award in 1954, for *More Than Human* (1953), and the science-fiction Hugo and Nebula awards in 1970, for "Slow Sculpture." The University of Kansas offers an annual science-fiction short-story award in his name.

BIOGRAPHY

Born Edward Hamilton Waldo, Theodore Sturgeon led one of those archetypal writer's lives, roaming the world and holding many different kinds of jobs. In 1929, his name was officially changed to Theodore Sturgeon. As a child, he wanted to be a circus performer, even gaining an athletic scholarship to Temple University, but his career in gymnastics was stopped by rheumatic fever. As an adult, he sold newspapers; collected garbage; sailed the seas as an engine-room wiper; worked as a musician, a ghostwriter, and a literary agent; operated a bulldozer and a gas station; and held several door-to-door sales positions. During World War II, he worked building airstrips and later writing technical manuals. Married five times, usually to younger women, he fathered six children. Sturgeon died in Eugene, Oregon, on May 8, 1985.

ANALYSIS

In a commercial literature devoted to galaxy-spanning concepts of paper-thin consistency, mechanical characters of whatever origin (human, alien, metal, or chemical), and wooden verbal expression, Theodore Sturgeon was an anomaly as early as 1939, when his stories began appearing in science-fiction magazines. A writer more of fantasy than of science fiction, whose predilection for words over machines was immediately apparent, Sturgeon was concerned with specific fantasies less for themselves than as means to the end of writing about human beings and human problems. Unlike those of so many of his colleagues, his tales usually take place in small, circumscribed locations, where love and healing can overshadow lesser, more conventional marvels and wonders.

Although style has always been somewhat suspect in science fiction, Sturgeon (along with Alfred Bester and Ray Bradbury) fought a rear-guard action throughout his career. His example speaks louder than theory about the importance of words, especially in terms of the planned resonance of images and the conscious manipulation of symbols to invite emotional responses to his romantic, even utopian view of the relationship between human beings and their technologies. Viewing "science" as "wisdom," he wrote of the search for wholeness, often without the aid of conventional means of attaining knowledge. He was antimachine in a way but more opposed to people's self-enslavement to mechanical procedures, be they metal or mental. Illustration of these themes calls forth as often as not a kind of fantasy that bears a close relationship to magic, events being caused by words and gestures. His is not a "science" that tediously accumulates and interprets observations of the world as it can be measured with instruments fashioned by and limited to the rational capacities of human beings.

There is no typical Sturgeon story, so varied is his surface subject matter, which includes many traditional science-fiction "inventions" and "discoveries," space travel, planetary exploration, matter transmission, cloning, alien contact, and paranormal powers among them. Sturgeon's stories usually speculate on love and sex in terms often considered radical for their market. Like D. H. Lawrence, he showed concern for the roots of human behavior in publicly repressed areas of behavior and thought; like Law-

rence, too, he may have exaggerated the usefulness for everyone of his own particular cures. More sentimental than Lawrence, he was also more experimental, obviously with respect to subject matter but also in terms of literary forms, playing with chronology, point of view, and other elements of storytelling in a way highly unusual for science fiction prior to the mid-1960's.

Sturgeon sold some remarkable "horror" stories in his early years of writing, such as "It," told from the point of view of a putrescent monster as dead as it is alive, and "Bianca's Hands," about a man in love with, and eventually strangled by, the hands of a girl who has the mind of an idiot. In "Killdozer," he created a masterpiece of contemporary terror in which two members of an eight-man construction crew on a deserted Pacific island barely withstand and defeat a malevolent alien consciousness which has taken possession of one of their bulldozers. The television motion picture made from this story did not do it justice.

"MICROCOSMIC GOD"

The most anthologized of Strugeon's early pieces, however, is "Microcosmic God," whose popularity he resented because its relatively clumsy handling and apparently ruthless attitude toward certain life-forms are uncharacteristic of his best work and his own self-image.

Primarily narrative, what dialogue there is being rather stiff and self-conscious, "Microcosmic God" is somewhat of a self-parody, with its protagonist a "Mister Kidder" and his antagonist a stereotyped grasping banker named Conant who would exploit Kidder's discoveries to take over the world. Almost lost in the reader's obvious antipathy to Conant's manipulation of human beings is its direct parallel to Kidder's even more ruthless manipulation of the tiny conscious beings whose evolution he has accelerated purely to satisfy his own curiosity.

Explicitly science fictional, the story is not rooted in practical experience with the details of construction machinery which makes "Killdozer" so dramatically convincing. Kidder's literal creation of an entire race for experimental purposes is couched, rather, in more theoretical and conceptual detail. The story's headlong pace races past problems in verisimilitude, in keeping with the simplistic morality of good (Kidder) versus evil (Conant), but intrusive commentary by the narrator reminds the reader sporadically that this is a fable, even if it does not specifically single out Kidder for censure.

Characterizing Kidder only minimally—both men are comic-book figures—the story shows his impatience with other people, with orthodox science (he claims no academic degrees), and with practical applications for his findings. In Conant, his alter ego, the reader sees explicitly the potential for abuse in his work, which reflects back on Kidder's own amorality. A god to his creatures, Kidder is a stand-in, not for the "mad scientist" whose image Sturgeon specifically disavows, but for the shortsighted tinkerer, representing all those who endeavor by mechanical means to improve the lot of human beings. The danger within the story is that, when Kidder dies, the creatures will conquer the world; the real danger to which the story points is that the misapplication of science to means or ends in the real world will do the same.

IRRESPONSIBILITY VS. HEROISM

Irresponsibility is also the theme of "Mewhu's Jet," in which an alien visitor with fabulous technological powers turns out to be a young child; of "The Sky Was Full of Ships," in which a naïve meddler unwittingly calls to Earth a menacing alien fleet; and of "Maturity," in which that quality is disavowed as the ripeness immediately preceding death. Sturgeon, however, was also concerned with the other side of the coin. In "Thunder and Roses," the beautiful Starr Anthim tries, in a nuclear-devastated America, to prevent late retaliation that might wipe out all human civilization. In "Saucer of Loneliness," another girl preserves the message given her by a miniature flying saucer, which assuages her despair with the knowledge that loneliness is shared. In "The Skills of Xanadu," an entire planet's people have overcome dependence on ugly machine technology and achieved a utopian state which is both dynamic and transferable.

Communication is central to these stories, as it is to "Bulkhead," in which the "partner" assigned to a space pilot with whom he has an intense love-hate relationship turns out to be another part of himself, part

of a schizophrenic condition deliberately induced by his employers for his own good. In the classic novella, "Baby Is Three," centerpiece of the award-winning novel *More than Human*, a "gestalt" being, composed of adolescent parapsychological misfits, fights to define its identity, which the last section of the novel will provide with maturity, responsibility, even community. Although this is arguably Sturgeon's best story, the novel to which it is converted is too well known to require analysis here of one of its parts.

The many ways that love and sex connect fascinated Sturgeon as early as "Bianca's Hands," but several provocative variations on this theme occupied him in the 1950's. *Venus Plus X* (1960) hypothesized physiological bisexuality in a "utopian" community on Earth. *Some of Your Blood* (1961) is a psychological case study of physiological vampirism. In "Affair with a Green Monkey," a psychologist obsessed with adjustment confuses gentleness with homosexuality, completely misjudging a humanoid alien whose sexual equipment would put to shame the best-endowed pornographic film star.

"THE WORLD WELL LOST"

Sturgeon's best treatment of "aberrant" sexuality is probably "The World Well Lost." Again attacking the obsession with normality of America in the 1950's, Sturgeon describes a future world enchanted by the love for each other and for things earthly of a couple of unexpected alien visitors, before their home world requests the return of the "loverbirds." Having once sent an ambassador to Earth and found it wanting, the planet Dirbanu has stonewalled further contact attempts until this time, when humans' intolerance at being kept out prompts them to sacrifice the fugitives in quest of anticipated interplanetary relations. The "prison ship," however, is crewed by two men whose perfect record results from a complementariness unrecognized by Rootes and unspoken by Grunty. Discovery of the aliens' telepathic powers threatens the tongue-tied Grunty, whose threat to kill them is countered by two things: the fact that Dirbanu wants them dead, and the reason why.

Dirbanu females are so different in appearance from males that all human beings look to them to be of the same sex and just as repulsive as the two fugitive "lover-birds." Acknowledging their homosexuality, the alien prisoners recognize the same propensity in their captors. Rootes's tales of heterosexual exploits are repetitive and hollow-sounding, while Grunty suffers consciously from an involuntary attraction to his partner which he can never voice, for all the poetry that swirls within his mind. Grunty lets the prisoners escape in a lifeboat which will isolate them for years before, if ever, they reach planet-fall. Although Rootes berates Grunty, Dirbanu is grateful for the presumed deaths; they still will have nothing to do with Earth, however, and their bigotry strikes a sympathetic chord in Rootes, as presumably it would back home. For all the "space opera" trappings, the tenuous coincidences, and the dated attitude toward homosexuality—even contextually, it seems inconsistent with an Earth that pursues, the reader is told, many other euphoric and aphrodisiac thrills—the story evokes with minimal sentimentality a love that literally "cannot speak its name" and the pathetic intolerance that will not let it.

"THE MAN WHO LOST THE SEA"

In contrast to such a plot-laden construct, "The Man Who Lost the Sea" is as near to stream-of-consciousness style as market considerations would allow. Exploring the senses, hallucinatory experiences, and memories of the first astronaut to reach Mars alive, the story weaves past and present, childhood and adulthood, mechanical and psychological drives into a haunting impression of a time which might prove as traumatic and epoch-making as the emergence of the first air-breathers out of the sea of life's origin on Earth. As shifting point of view and chronology represent the man's dazed mental and emotional state, Sturgeon only gradually reveals the nature of the man's predicament (his ship has crashed and there is no way back), until the emotional shock of simultaneous gain and loss has prepared the way for the triumphant irony of the protagonist's dying exultation: "We made it!"

"SLOW SCULPTURE"

Sturgeon's rather few stories of the 1960's and 1970's continued to deal with love and responsibility, especially healing, but often in a talky mode. His greatest success in that period is "Slow Sculpture," named best of the year by science-fiction fans and readers alike. This novella is a loving exploration of how an unnamed "man" and a "girl" come tentatively to know each other, although the specific means are entwined with science-fiction and fantasy motifs as the two people are with each other and with the fifteen-foot bonsai tree that grows in this garden. Like other Sturgeon protagonists, the man is a polymath, credentialed in law and in two kinds of engineering, who in this instance practices medicine without a license.

That his cure for her cancer works the reader is asked to take on faith as she does, since establishment means and methods are deliberately eschewed, and the "technology" that he uses is more obscured than revealed by the metaphorical language with which he describes it. There are some appropriate "special effects," suggesting the interrelatedness of house and garden, house and mountain, man and tree, matter and energy, mind and body. The medium and the message, however, are primarily communication, in conversation which may be more expressive than it is true to life, but which is far from stilted. The speeches, moreover, are contextually true, since the man, whatever his healing powers for others, fends off the girl's involvement with him, her own halting attempts to connect with the anger, fear, and frustration in him at the world's resistance to all he has offered to better it.

Throughout the story, the dominant symbol is the bonsai, which resists "instruction" because it knows how it should grow and achieves its form by compromising between its essential nature and the manipulation to which it is subjected, not by its "owner" but by its "companion." As in many of Sturgeon's works, but never more appropriately than here, the prose itself is "sculptured," reminding the reader that the magic of fantasy resides less in the act than in the telling of it.

Sturgeon's stories are in some ways "hopelessly romantic," conjuring impossible cures and utopian solutions, even when they are not projected long ahead and far away. Like the best science fiction, they lead the reader back to the present, not to external realities, but rather to emotional confrontations with human problems, situations, characters. Although readers may detach themselves from the ostensible subjects, removed from the here and now, the situation of the writer, often as a stand-in for the reader-as-dreamer, is frequently apparent, sometimes intensely personal. For all their variety, Sturgeon's stories betray an almost obsessive concern for wholeness and healing, for communication and tolerance of the misfit, and often for "September-June" relationships between "men" and "girls." That his work maintained, even increased its popularity as he wrote less and less suggests that he mined a vein of ore rich in its appeal, to women as well as men, to the adolescent in everyone. Almost despite their paraphernalia of science fiction and fantasy, Sturgeon's modern-day fairy tales communicate what his characters continually try to communicate: the truth of emotion and the magic of words.

OTHER MAJOR WORKS

LONG FICTION: *The Dreaming Jewels*, 1950 (also known as *The Synthetic Man*, 1957); *More Than Human*, 1953; *I, Libertine*, 1956 (as Frederick R. Ewing, with Jean Shepherd); *The Cosmic Rape*, 1958; *Venus Plus X*, 1960; *Some of Your Blood*, 1961; *Voyage to the Bottom of the Sea*, 1961; *Alien Cargo*, 1984; *Godbody*, 1986.

BIBLIOGRAPHY

Delany, Samuel. "Sturgeon." In *Starboard Wine: More Notes on the Language of Science Fiction*. Pleasantville, N.Y.: Dragon Press, 1984. Delany is not only one of science fiction's best authors, but also he is one of its best critics, particularly in analysis of style. Here Delany explores some of the nuances of Sturgeon's language and the "realism" of Sturgeon's stories.

Diskin, Lahna. *Theodore Sturgeon*. Mercer Island, Wash.: Starmont House, 1981. The first book-length study of Sturgeon's fiction, this volume focuses primarily on his most famous science fiction.

Malzberg, Barry N. "Grandson of the True and the Terrible." In *The Engines of the Night*. Garden City, N.Y.: Doubleday, 1982. A brief but poignant evaluation of Sturgeon's importance in the history of science fiction.

Moskowitz, Sam. "Theodore Sturgeon." In *Seekers of Tomorrow: Masters of Modern Science Fiction*. Westport, Conn.: Hyperion Press, 1966. This essay is a good general introduction to Sturgeon in terms of his place in science-fiction history and in what makes him "unique."

Sackmary, Regina. "An Ideal of Three: The Art of Theodore Sturgeon." In *Critical Encounters*, edited by Dick Riley. New York: Frederick Ungar, 1978. Sackmary discusses the motif of threes in Sturgeon's fiction as his symbol for unity.

Stephensen-Payne, Phil, and Gordon Benson, Jr. *Theodore Sturgeon, Sculptor of Love and Hate: A Working Bibliography*. San Bernardino, Calif.: Borgo Press, 1992. Part of the Galactic Central Bibliographies for the Avid Reader series, this is a helpful tool for students of Sturgeon.

Streitfield, David. "Science Fiction and Fantasy." *The Washington Post*, March 7, 1999, p. XO8. Discusses the renaissance of interest in Sturgeon, with the reissue of his *More than Human* and *To Marry Medusa* in paperback, as well as his collected short stories; discusses briefly the story "Scars" and the unfinished "Quietly."

Westfall, Gary. "Sturgeon's Fallacy." *Extrapolation* 38 (Winter, 1997): 255-277. Takes issue with so-called Sturgeon's Law—that ninety percent of everything, especially science fiction, is worthless. Analyzes the output of science fiction in the twentieth century and argues that science fiction is a worthwhile form of writing.

David N. Samuelson, updated by
David Layton

ITALO SVEVO
Ettore Schmitz

Born: Trieste, Austria (now Italy); December 19, 1861

Died: Motta di Livenza, Italy; September 13, 1928

PRINCIPAL SHORT FICTION

Una burla riuseita, 1929 (*The Hoax*, 1929)

La novella del buon vecchio e della bella fanciulla, 1930 (*The Nice Old Man and the Pretty Girl and Other Stories*, 1930)

Corto viaggio sentimentale e altri racconti inediti, 1949 (*Short Sentimental Journey and Other Stories*, 1966)

Further Confessions of Zeno, 1969

OTHER LITERARY FORMS

As a young man Italo Svevo wrote two novels: *Una vita* (1892; *A Life*, 1963) and Senilità (1898; *As a Man Grows Older*, 1932). Both books were ignored by readers and critics, and Svevo confined himself to writing essays and stories until his novel *La coscienza di Zeno* (1923; *Confessions of Zeno*, 1930) won great acclaim and awakened interest in his earlier work.

ACHIEVEMENTS

Although Italo Svevo received little attention until the end of his life, he came to be seen as one of the major modernists of the twentieth century, ranked with such writers as James Joyce, Marcel Proust, Robert Musil, and Franz Kafka.

BIOGRAPHY

Aron Hector "Ettore" Schmitz, who took the pen name Italo Svevo, lived in and wrote about Trieste. He grew up in a patriarchal Jewish family but in 1896 reluctantly converted to Catholicism when he married his cousin, Livia Veneziani. Even as a young boy Svevo was obsessed with writing, but his domineering father, Francesco Schmitz, decided his son had to prepare for a business career. Svevo first attended a Jewish elementary school and then completed his ed- ucation in business schools. In 1890 he went to work for a bank and later joined his wife's family business. Throughout his adult life, Svevo led a dual existence, spending his days engaged in business and devoting his free time to his real love, literature.

After Italian literary circles ignored his first two novels, Svevo, considering himself a failure, dropped his plans for further novels. "I can't fathom this in- comprehension," he wrote: "It shows that people just do not understand. It's useless for me to write and publish." He did continue to publish but confined himself to essays and short stories. In 1905 he met James Joyce, who praised his novels and encouraged him to continue his work. In 1923 Svevo published *Confessions of Zeno* and sent a copy to Joyce, who introduced it to leading figures in the literary world. Prominent European critics took notice, and starting in 1926 Svevo finally began to be honored as a major writer. By that time his health was failing, and on September 13, 1928, after being injured in an auto- mobile accident, he died.

ANALYSIS

Italo Svevo's writings possessed the happy quality of becoming fresher and ever more relevant as the de- cades passed following his death. He was attuned to the intellectual currents that shaped twentieth century thought, mastering the work of such figures as Charles Darwin, Arthur Schopenhauer, Karl Marx, and Sigmund Freud. He used them to enrich his por- trait of people living in urban, industrial society, characterized by huge institutions that order everyday life and overwhelm the individual.

His stories always deal with a similar set of char- acters facing the same set of problems. He invented the antihero, before that figure became central to modern literature. Svevo's central characters are ordinary people trying to cope with modern life, so self-absorbed and self-analytical that they become paralyzed and impotent. While they are often inept bunglers, they are endearing figures, who learn to accept the buffeting of existence with humor and resignation, bringing to mind Charlie Chaplin's little clown character. Svevo offers naturalistic descriptions of modern social and economic life, but when he begins his masterful character development, he becomes subjective and psychological, sketching a Kafkaesque world of anxiety, angst, and ambiguity. Alienation is his theme, as it is with most modernist writers. His generation's destiny, Svevo wrote, "will be that of studying life without understanding it because we shall not have known how to live it."

Svevo experienced personally the ambiguity that paralyzes his characters. He was a divided personality: a businessman and writer, a socialist in belief and a capitalist in practice, an atheist who converted to Catholicism, a Jew whose conversion to Catholicism never felt right, a gentle and humorous man who never for a moment lost sight of life's tragedy.

THE HOAX

In *The Hoax*, a novella written in 1929, Svevo explores the themes that concerned him throughout his career: writing, the business world, the maladjusted antihero, often elderly, trying to make sense of a life which seems endlessly challenging and puzzling, often enticing even old and supposedly wise individuals into self-deception.

Mario Samigli is a sixty-year-old businessman, who published a novel forty years before the time of the story. Although he still fantasizes about achieving literary fame, his novel was greeted with silence at the time of its publication and sank into oblivion, although as a published author he still has a literary reputation among his friends.

One of these, Enrico Gaia, a failed poet, jealous of the literary aura that clings to Mario, stages an elaborate practical joke. He tells Mario that a representative of a major publishing firm is in Trieste and wants to republish Mario's novel, promising him a huge sum of money and, more important, the literary fame that has eluded him. When Mario, a gentle and happy man, finds he has been the victim of a public and embarrassing hoax, he beats Enrico. Mario soon recovers his equilibrium, regarding the humiliation as another of life's many setbacks, and continues to write for his own amusement. Mario's life and personality reflect that of Svevo, and this story can be read as the author gently poking fun at his alter ego, businessman Ettore Schmitz.

THE NICE OLD MAN AND THE PRETTY GIRL AND OTHER STORIES

This early collection of Svevo's short fiction contains four stories, including the appropriately titled "The Old, Old Man." It also includes an introductory note by Eugenio Montale, Italy's foremost poet, who encouraged his countrymen to recognize that Svevo was the greatest Italian fiction writer of his time. The stories display Svevo's brilliance at characterization, his acute psychological insight, and his understanding of the inner displacement experienced by many modern individuals, thrust into a life that no longer feels natural to them. Svevo confronts his aging antiheroes with the confusing present that contains an array of challenges and tragedies. Age does not seem to bring them wisdom, but it often does bring the serenity that comes through resigned acceptance of life's surprises.

In the title story, an elderly businessman meets a beautiful young tram driver, and, when she solicits him for a better job, he invites her to his house and begins planning her seduction. He is torn by his ambivalent feelings, since this is his first romantic adventure following his wife's death: An "old man is a lover out of gear," he thinks; the "lovemaking machine within him is at least one little wheel short." He is not troubled by considerations of morality, as he would have been in youth; he feels rejuvenated and youthfully vigorous. As usual with Svevo characters, second guessing gets in the way of action, and he thinks that perhaps instead of seducing the young girl he should act as a philanthropist and help her get a good start in life. He finally does make her his mistress, giving her money after each visit, but he tries to maintain the fiction that their relationship is based on love. After the old man suffers a physical collapse, he is convinced that sin ruined his health. He decides to atone by writing a book for the moral edification of the young girl. He dies with his pen in his mouth. The theme is at the center of Svevo's chosen terrain: an elderly man separated from a past that exists only in his failing memory and too old to have a future, leaving him stranded in the bewildering present.

SHORT SENTIMENTAL JOURNEY AND OTHER STORIES

This collection contains eight stories, three published during Svevo's lifetime. It includes "The Hoax," along with one of Svevo's most beautifully written stories, "Generous Wine." The title story traces the journey of an elderly businessman, Signor Aghios, on a train trip from Milan to Trieste. The story quickly draws the reader into Signor Aghios's fantasies about the lives of his fellow travelers and into his relentless psychological self-examination. He feels old and rusty and enjoys the feeling of youth that floods him when he sees a beautiful young woman. He feels put upon by the demands of his family and friends. He is torn between his generous responses to those around him and his selfish feeling that everyone is out to use him. He responds generously to a young man on the train who is in obvious despair, but while Signor Aghios falls asleep, the young man robs him. The manuscript, unfinished at Svevo's death, breaks off in midword, but it is a wonderful example of his mastery of the modern psyche.

FURTHER CONFESSIONS OF ZENO

Confessions of Zeno is a novel in the form of an autobiography that the character Zeno writes at the suggestion of his psychiatrist. Zeno is a gentle man who bumbled through the confusing turns of life, usually finding some way to turn defeat into victory. The novel brought Svevo his long-delayed recognition, and he died before he completed *Further Confessions of Zeno*.

Further Confessions of Zeno contains five stories and a long play, which together show Svevo's conception of the unfinished novel. Zeno is now seventy, and after having feared old age all of his life, he finds that his fears were well founded; old age does not bring a period of peaceful golden years. Life, however, is simpler in some ways: "I continue to struggle between the present and past; but at least hope—anxious hope for the future—does not come crowding in between."

Zeno faces death with the hard-won serenity that comes from the one gift that aging has given him: the ability to accept life with its unending array of often unpleasant surprises, which calls forth resignation as an appropriate substitute for wisdom.

OTHER MAJOR WORKS

LONG FICTION: *Una vita*, 1892 (*A Life*, 1963); *Senilità*, 1898; (*As a Man Grows Older*, 1923); *La coscienza di Zeno*, 1923 (*Confessions of Zeno*, 1930).

NONFICTION: *James Joyce*, 1950 (lecture given in 1927); *Corrispondenza*, 1953; *Saggi e pagini sparse*, 1954 (essays).

MISCELLANEOUS: *Opera omnia*, 1966-1969.

BIBLIOGRAPHY

Furbank, P. N. *Italo Svevo: The Man and the Writer*. Berkeley, Ca.: University of California Press, 1966. In one of the first major works on Svevo in English, Furbank considers Svevo to be the creator of modern Italian fiction. The book consists of a biography of Svevo, followed by literary analyses of his works, including a chapter largely devoted to his short fiction.

Gatt-Rutter, John. *Italo Svevo: A Double Life*. Oxford, England: Clarendon Press, 1988. Gatt-Rutter stresses the duality of Svevo's life: a writer and businessman, an atheist who converted from Judaism to Catholicism, a socialist who was a successful capitalist. While it is short on literary criticism, this is the best work available on the details of Svevo's life and is based on letters and other primary sources.

Lebowitz, Naomi. *Italo Svevo*. New Brunswick, N.J.: Rutgers University Press, 1978. In an excellent study that focuses on Svevo's writing rather than on his life, Lebowitz regards him as the father of modern Italian literature and as one of the great modernists, ranked with James Joyce, Franz Kafka, and William Faulkner.

Moloney, Brian. *Italo Svevo: A Critical Introduction*. Edinburgh, Scotland: Edinburgh University Press, 1974. An excellent short critical introduction to Svevo's work, which includes chapters on his short fiction.

Svevo, Livia Veneziani. *Memoir of Italo Svevo*. Marlboro, Vt.: Marlboro Press, 1990. A loving memoir by Svevo's widow which captures his humor and his gentle nature. It includes many of his letters and an appendix that includes a 1927 lecture by Svevo on James Joyce.

Weiss, Beno. *Italo Svevo*. Boston: Twayne, 1987. Weiss considers Svevo to be one of the seminal figures in modern European literature. Weiss stresses the divided nature of Svevo's life and the importance of Judaism to his life and literature. It follows the usual Twayne format, with a brief biographical overview, followed by chapters on Svevo's major works, including one on his short stories.

William E. Pemberton

GRAHAM SWIFT

Born: London, England; May 4, 1949

PRINCIPAL SHORT FICTION

Learning to Swim and Other Stories, 1982

OTHER LITERARY FORMS

Graham Swift is best known for his novels, *The Sweet Shop Owner* (1980), *Shuttlecock* (1981), *Waterland* (1983), *Out of This World* (1988), *Ever After* (1992), and *Last Orders* (1996).

ACHIEVEMENTS

Graham Swift's best-known novel, *Waterland*, was a finalist for England's Booker McConnell Prize and was named best English novel of 1983 by the newspaper *The Guardian*. His novel *Last Orders* won the Booker McConnell Prize in 1996 as well as the James Tait Black Memorial Prize.

BIOGRAPHY

Graham Colin Swift was born in London, England, on May 4, 1949. His mother's family, prosperous Jewish tailors, immigrated from Poland around the beginning of the nineteenth century; his father was a civil servant in the National Debt Office. He attended Dulwich College in London, after which he graduated from Cambridge University with a B.A. in 1970 and an M.A. in 1975. He taught for one year in Greece and was a part-time English instructor in London until the success of his third novel *Waterland* in 1983.

ANALYSIS

Because of his largely experimental novels, which examine the relationship between history and fiction, Graham Swift is often cited as one of the most important British postmodernists. Although he published only a small number of short stories—the eleven included in his collection *Learning to Swim and Other Stories*—both his importance in contemporary British fiction and the fact that the British short story is often ignored make them deserving of attention.

Whereas Swift deals with the large social and cultural issues of history in his novels, his short fiction focuses more sharply on the nature of story, which, in an interview, he argued is always a "magical, marvelous, mysterious, wonderful thing." Because of Swift's belief that telling stories is a therapeutic means of coming to terms with the past, his stories, in which characters must try to come to terms with their personal pasts, form the core of his novels, in which the personal past becomes cultural history.

"LEARNING TO SWIM"

The focus of "Learning to Swim" begins with Mrs. Singleton, lying on a beach in Cornwall, watching her husband try to teach their six-year-old son Paul how to swim; however, most of the story takes place in her memory as she recalls having thought about leaving her husband three times in the past primarily because of his lack of passion. The story then shifts to the two times Mr. Singleton has thought of leaving his wife—once when he considered jumping into the water and swimming away.

Indeed, swimming is a central metaphor in the story, for Mr. Singleton had been an excellent swimmer in school, winning titles and breaking records; in the Spartan purity of swimming he feels superior to others who will "go under" in life, unable to "cleave the water" as he did. Mr. Singleton dreams of swimming; even when he makes love to his wife, he feels her body gets in the way, and he wants to swim through her.

The undercurrent of marital conflict between Mr. and Mrs. Singleton comes to a head at the end of the story. Mrs. Singleton is indifferent to her husband and wants the kind of close relationship with her son typical of women who have rejected their husbands; she thinks that when he is grown he will become a sculptor and she will pose naked for him. At the same time, Mr. Singleton thinks that if Paul could swim he would be able to leave his wife. The story shifts finally to the boy, who fears that his mother will swallow him up and that he will not win the love of his father if he fails to swim; even though he is terrified of the water, he knows if he swims his mother will be forsaken. The story ends with Paul swimming away both from his father and his mother, finding himself in a strange new element that seems all his own.

"HOFFMEIER'S ANTELOPE"

The title refers to a rare, almost extinct, pygmy antelope discovered by a German zoologist named Hoffmeier. However, the focus of the story is the relationship of the narrator to his uncle, an animal keeper at a London zoo, after the uncle's wife dies. The story centers on the fact that the two surviving antelopes are placed together in the zoo under the uncle's care. The narrator, who teaches philosophy part-time in London, argues with his uncle that, if an unknown species exists, it is the same as if it did not exist at all; therefore, if something known to exist ceases to exist, it is the same as something that exists but is not known to exist. The idea that there may be animals existing in the wilds still unknown to humans is exciting to the protagonist; he notes that, even given the variety of known species, humans still like to dream up such mythical creatures as griffins, dragons, and unicorns.

The nature of reality is a central issue in the story; the narrator even begins to doubt the reality of Hoffmeier, for his actual life seems as elusive as that of the antelope he rescued from anonymity. The story comes to a climax when the male antelope dies and the uncle feels more closely bound to the surviving female, suffering from the illusion, common among children, that mere loving brings babies into the world and that she could conceive by the strong affection he has for her. When the antelope disappears from the zoo, the uncle disappears also.

"THE TUNNEL"

Typical of Barnes's stories, "The Tunnel" begins broadly and narrows its focus near the end. The story centers on a young male narrator and his girlfriend Clancy during a spring and summer, when they live together in an old tenement after having run away from the girl's parents. Underlying their idyllic, albeit shabby, retreat is the girl's confidence that her

Graham Swift (Bernard Gotfryd/Archive Photos)

seventy-three-year-old crippled uncle, who has a soft spot for her, will leave her everything when he dies.

A motif that runs throughout the story is the life of the painter Paul Gauguin, which fascinates the boy and causes the girl to buy him paints and brushes and urge him to paint the walls of their tenement apartment. Their romantic escape turns sour when, just as the boy felt he was transforming their little hole into a miniature Tahiti, they begin to become aware of the filth surrounding them. As they both get laboring jobs, the tenement area where they live begins to be demolished, and they start to see the paintings and the place as worthless, sentimental trash.

The crisis in their lives becomes more acute when the boy severely burns his hands in a kitchen accident and is confined to the apartment alone to think, particularly about the crippled uncle, with whom he now identifies; he begins to wonder if the uncle is a fiction Clancy invented. The title metaphor of the tunnel is evoked near the end of the story when below his window five boys begin to dig a tunnel out of a fenced-in playground into which they have climbed. He thinks that in their minds the boys have transformed the playground into a prison camp and are trying to escape from a place they had entered and could leave at their own free will. He wants them to succeed because he sees their situation as that of his own. The story ends when the boys break through and when Clancy arrives to say that her uncle has died and left her everything. What the couple will do with this windfall, however, is left unresolved.

"THE WATCH"

Because "The Watch" is based on a thematic premise, it is fabulistic rather than realistic. The premise is announced in the first sentence, with the narrator musing that nothing is more magical and sinister, yet more consoling and expressive of the constancy of fate than a clock. The narrator has descended from a family of clock makers who once had the primitive faith that clocks not only recorded time but also caused it, that without clocks the world would vanish into oblivion.

The central metaphor governing the story is a magical watch, invented in 1809 by the narrator's great-grandfather, which not only could function per-

petually without winding but also had a magnetic charge that infected its wearer with its longevity. Thus, his great-grandfather lived to be 133 years old and his grandfather lived to be 161. Although his father died young in the war, the narrator, Adam Krepski, is now the owner of the watch.

The final event in the story occurs one week before the time of the telling, when Krepski hears a female cry in the room below him and discovers a woman in childbirth. He recognizes that the cries come from a region ungoverned by time and thus are as poisonous to him as fresh air to a fish. When the baby is born close to death, he understands that time is not something that exists outside human beings but rather that all people are the distillation of all time; that each human being is the sum of all the time before him. He dangles the watch near the baby, and when the child grasps it, it is brought back to life and simultaneously the watch stops. The narrator stumbles out into the street and is struck by an internal blow, which he says topples family trees. The story ends with doctors bending over him to lift his wrist to check his pulse against their own ordinary watches, and he knows that his breaths are numbered.

OTHER MAJOR WORKS

LONG FICTION: *The Sweet Shop Owner*, 1980; *Shuttlecock*, 1981; *Waterland*, 1983; *Out of This World*, 1988; *Ever After*, 1992; *Last Orders*, 1996.

BIBLIOGRAPHY

Broich, Ulrich. "Muted Postmodernism: The Contemporary British Short Story." *Zeitschrift für Anglistik und Amerikanistik* 41 (1993): 31-39. Discusses the market conditions of the contemporary British short story, surveys three major types of British short fiction: the feminist story, the cultural conflict story, and the experimental, postmodernist story. Discusses Swift's story "Seraglio" as a story in which postmodernist narrative strategies are used in a muted way.

Frumkes, Lewis Burke. "A Conversation with Graham Swift." *The Writer* 111 (February, 1998): 19-21. Swift discusses the plot of his highly praised novel *Last Orders*, talks about the symbolic value of water in his fiction, comments on how he evolved as a writer, and gives some advice to young, beginning authors.

Higdon, David Leon. "Double Closures in Postmodern British Fiction: The Example of Graham Swift." *Critical Survey* 3 (1991): 88-95. A theoretical discussion of the lack of closure in British postmodern fiction, using Swift as an example of a writer who successfully combines the postmodern sense of lack of certainty with the aesthetic demands of some type of boundary; argues that Swift has created a kind of double closure, maintaining the ambiguity of postmodern narratology while at the same time providing a firm, clear response.

_____. "'Unconfessed Confessions': The Narrators of Graham Swift and Julian Barnes." In *The British and Irish Novel Since 1960*, edited by James Acheson. New York: St. Martin's Press, 1991. 174-191. Argues that the fiction of Swift and Barnes defines what is meant by British postmodernism; claims they share themes of estrangement, obsession, and the power of the past; examines their creation of what Higdon calls "the reluctant narrator," who, although quite perceptive, has experienced something so traumatic he must tell it through indirections, masks, and substitutions.

Swift, Graham. "An Interview with Graham Swift." Interview by Catherine Bernard. *Contemporary Literature* 38 (Summer, 1997): 217-231. In this in-terview, Swift discusses the importance of voice in his fiction, his use of repetition for thematic and aesthetic effect, his relationship to the tradition of nineteenth century English fiction, his rejection of formalism that is mere artifice and cleverness, his literary theory that writers are either defensive or vulnerable, and his respect for the magic and mystery of storytelling.

_____. Interview by Amanda Smith. *Publishers Weekly* 239 (February 17, 1992): 43-44. Swift discusses his background, his entrance into publishing, his experiences with American publishers, novel writing, and his most recent fiction. Swift says he sees the structure of his fiction in terms of rhythm, movement, pace, and tension; it is a musical thing, rather than an intellectual thing, he says. Notes that he is very concerned about the ambiguities of knowledge.

Widdowson, Peter. "Newstories: Fiction, History, and the Modern World." *Critical Survey* 7 (1995): 3-17. A theoretical discussion of the relationship between history and story in postmodernist fiction, using Swift as the most self-conscious and sophisticated British writer concerned with the interface between history and story. Although the essay focuses primarily on Swift's *Out of This World*, which Widdowson calls a "historiographic metafiction," the focus is on a thematic/narrative tactic, which Swift uses in other fiction as well.

Charles E. May

T

ELIZABETH TALLENT

Born: Washington, D.C.; August 8, 1954

PRINCIPAL SHORT FICTION
In Constant Flight, 1983
Time with Children, 1987
Honey, 1993

OTHER LITERARY FORMS

Elizabeth Tallent is the author of the novel *Museum Pieces* (1985) and a collection of criticism, *Married Men and Magic Tricks: John Updike's Erotic Heroes* (1982).

ACHIEVEMENTS

Elizabeth Tallent's first story, "Ice," was selected for *The Best American Short Stories 1981*; "The Evolution of Birds of Paradise" was included in 1984's *Prize Stories: The O. Henry Awards*; "Prowler" was selected for *The Best American Short Stories 1990*. Tallent received a National Endowment for the Arts Fellowship in 1993.

BIOGRAPHY

Elizabeth Ann Tallent was born on August 8, 1954, in Washington, D.C., where her father worked for the government as an expert on agriculture. She grew up mostly in various areas of the Midwest, receiving a B.A. degree in anthropology at Illinois State University at Normal in 1975. Although accepted for graduate school in anthropology at the University of New Mexico at Taos, Tallent and her husband settled in Santa Fe, New Mexico, instead.

Her first story, "Ice," published in *The New Yorker* in 1980, received enough attention that Leonard Michaels invited her to a writers' workshop in Berkeley, California. She gave readings with the important fiction trio, Raymond Carver, Richard Ford, and Tobias Wolff throughout England in 1985. The next year she taught writing at the University of California at Irvine and then the following year at the University of Nevada at Reno. In 1989, she was invited to teach in the prestigious University of Iowa Writers' Workshop. She accepted a full-time teaching position at the University of California at Davis in 1990.

ANALYSIS

Elizabeth Tallent's stories have been praised by many of her reviewers for the same reasons that they have been criticized by others: her precise detail, her metaphoric plots, her highly polished structure, and her elegant style—all characteristics that have changed little over the course of her writing career. Frequently, Tallent's critics charge, her stories are simply too geometrically structured and predictable, and her language is too mannered and forced. However, all Tallent's critics seem to agree that her understanding of the complexities that arise from broken marriages and reconstituted families is artistically acute.

Like her most obvious literary inspiration, John Updike, about whom she has written a critical book, Tallent creates stories that at first seem straightforwardly realistic and transparent, like chapters out of a domestic novel, but which, on closer reading, are recognized as tightly structured, symbolic stories in which no matter how loosely related and tangential events seem to be, they all inevitably come together by the end.

"PROWLER"

The story's conflict begins when Dennis's former wife Christie returns from Europe after breaking up with her most recent boyfriend, and Dennis decides not to let their thirteen-year-old son Andy spend the summer with her because she has ignored the boy for the past year. The first event that contributes to changing Dennis's mind is Andy's getting a tattoo of a skeleton on a motorcycle, telling his father, "It's my body"—a realization which astonishes Dennis.

However, the most important event that changes Dennis's mind occurs when he enters Christie's apartment while she is not home. Dennis knows he is an intruder and feels an "amazed apprehension of his own wrongdoing" but is fascinated by this glimpse into the life of a woman no longer his wife. He is even more enthralled when he lies down in a bedroom meant for Andy, for he knows there are things in it that Andy would like. Dennis dreams a dream he feels was meant for Andy about the boy and his mother cutting animals from construction paper when he was young, and "what he's seen won't let go easily." As a result of his "prowler" experience, Dennis takes Andy to his mother a few days later, although he can give her only a wave that means "I can't explain it."

"Prowler" is fairly typical of many of Tallent's stories. Dennis's refusing his former wife visitation rights for the summer is only a conventional motivation to make possible Dennis's dual realization. The tattoo then makes possible Dennis's realization that Andy is a separate entity, since it allows Andy to say that his body is his own and since it is a permanent change that cannot be undone. The more extended epiphany occurs when Dennis lies down on the bed in the room his former wife has prepared for Andy and sees that his son would like how she has prepared it, realizing that his former wife knows her son well and loves him. His knowledge that his son does not "belong" to him and that the boy has both a mother and a father makes him change his mind about the visitation.

"ICE"

Although the "ice" of the title of this story derives from the fact that the central figure is a young woman who skates in a traveling ice show with a man dressed as a bear, this is counterpointed by her memory of her grandmother, who slipped on icy stairs and died while trying to avoid being confined because of her delusions. A second counterpoint to the young woman's story is the family Abyssinian cat who spontaneously aborts her kittens and then eats her mother's prize roses.

There is no plot conflict in the story except the mother's distress that her daughter works at a carnival-like job and the girl's desire for more "artistic" skating. The girl's lover, Ben, a photographer, has left the show for Los Angeles but writes to the man who skates as the dancing bear to say that he is sorry he left. Images of the girl skating on the ice with the dancing bear dominate the story. She understands that the appeal of the bear is that he seems like a "clumsy, blotchy human being" who courts her with elegance while she skates in carefully circumscribed arcs, the light shining in her blond hair. The story ends with the girl crying while skating in the circle of the bear's shaggy arms.

Thematically, the story brings together several images of female fantasy and fear. The predominant image is the Goldilocks fantasy of the blond girl skating with the bear—an objectification of a childlike female wish fulfillment, which brings young girls to her performances. However, this is juxtaposed against images of the cat refusing to have offspring, the mother for whom roses are her entire life, and the grandmother who dies trying to avoid the final humiliation of being shut up in a room because of delusions. At the end, when the bear whispers in the young woman's ear—"You know, don't you, that you are not yourself"—the girl, in fact, does not know who she is.

"NO ONE'S A MYSTERY"

Although this is one of Tallent's shortest stories—less than four pages—it is a favorite anthology piece because of its tight compression and its focus on a single, highly suggestive scene. The central character is a young woman who is having an affair with Jack, a married man, who has just given her a five-year diary for her eighteenth birthday. The story centers on their driving around in his pickup when he sees his wife's Cadillac coming toward them and pushes her down on the floorboards. After the wife's car passes, Jack tells the girl that, although tonight she will write in the diary that she cannot imagine loving anyone more than she does him, in a year she will wonder what she ever saw in him.

She responds, however, that in one year she will write that Jack will be home any minute and that she does not know if she can wait until after their fancy dinner to make love to him; in two years, she will write that he will be home soon and little Jack is hungry for supper; and in three years she will write that her breasts are sore from nursing their little girl whose breath smells like vanilla. This brief story, which consists mostly of dialogue, ends when Jack says he likes her story better but believes his; he tells her that in her heart of hearts she believes his story also and, reflecting the bittersweetness of the relationship, that the little girl's breath would have a bittersweet smell. In its one brief encounter, the story quite poignantly captures the girl's unrealistic fantasies and the dead-end nature of the affair.

"HONEY"

In the title story of Tallent's most recent collection, she returns to characters introduced in her earlier book, *Time with Children:* Hart, a math teacher in New Mexico; Hannah, his first wife; Kevin, his son; Cao, his second wife; and Mercedes, his mother-in-law. The story begins with Mercedes flying into Albuquerque from her apartment in Brooklyn to be with Cao for the birth of her first child.

The story centers on old wounds that refuse to heal. Kevin, whose girlfriend committed suicide in "Black Dress," another story in the collection, is sullen because of his loss and his anxiety that the new baby will force him out. Mercedes fears that her daughter's marriage is not strong and harbors old rancor about her dead husband's infidelities. Hart continues to feel guiltily aligned with his first wife, Hannah, and emotionally unfaithful to Cao because he does not want the new baby.

Tallent heals all these old hurts by the end of the story in symbolically significant ways. When Mercedes tends to Kevin's mosquito bites and urges him to give up his own thoughts of suicide, she makes peace with her own demons by assuring Kevin that time will heal and everyone eventually stops feeling his or her hurt. At the same time in another room, Cao assures Hart that her mother likes him, simultaneously reminding herself not to become the isolated mystery that her mother always was. The story ends with Hart and Cao making love in an effort to start the contractions for their overdue baby.

OTHER MAJOR WORKS

LONG FICTION: *Museum Pieces*, 1985.

NONFICTION: *Married Men and Magic Tricks: John Updike's Erotic Heroes*, 1982.

BIBLIOGRAPHY

Broyard, Anatole. "In Constant Flight." Review of *In Constant Flight*, by Elizabeth Tallent. *The New York Times*, April 29, 1983, p. C29. In this review of Tallent's first collection, Broyard is concerned that she tries too hard to divorce her characters from the ordinary. He says her characters often seem to be on the brink of an epiphany, but when they have one their emotions are unidentifiable.

Elder, Richard. "Extraordinary Tales from Ordinary Lives." *Los Angeles Times*, November 11, 1993, p. E6. Discusses Tallent's basic themes and typical characters. Comments on her subjects of broken marriages, family ties, shuffled children, and blind and aggressive men. Discusses the story "Prowlers" as a compendium of her most typical elements.

Gilbert, Matthew. "Tallent Lights Up a Troubled Terrain." *The Boston Globe*, January 21, 1994, p. 73. Argues that Tallent is able to make everything her characters do mirror their emotional states. Says her plots are metaphorical and her style is graceful and incisive, but that occasionally the elegance of her stories gets in the way. Suggests that the stories in *Honey*, a kind of sequel to *Time with Children*, show thematic strides, for more is at stake in them.

Kakutani, Michiko. "Families Bound by Ties That Stifle." *The New York Times*, December 10, 1993, p. C29. Discusses how the stories in *Honey* continue the sagas of characters created in her earlier collection, *Time with Children*. Argues that although in terms of technique the stories are beautifully assembled and meticulously controlled, their emotional dilemmas reflect a stultifying sameness.

Milton, Edith. "What Changes and What Doesn't." *The New York Times Book Review*, August 14, 1983, p. 12. Praises the control and technical perfection of Tallent's stories in *In Constant Flight*, but criticizes Tallent for constantly reaching for surprise. The eleven stories seem like variations on a single theme, each one filled with paradox and the unexpected.

Parini, Jay. "Torn Between Two Exes." Review of *Honey*, by Elizabeth Tallent. *The New York Times*, November 7, 1993, p. 11. A review of *Honey* which argues that language rather than plot is what interests Tallent most. Compares her work to that of John Updike; says she can summon up the sensations of everyday life concretely but that she sometimes seems to strain for effect.

Yagoda, Ben. "No Tense Like the Present." *The New York Times Book Review* 91: 1. Discusses the use of present tense by Tallent and other contemporary fiction writers; argues that the present tense can remind us that the story is an artifice or emphasize the narrator's alienation from the events described. Claims that in much contemporary fiction, the present tense suggests that, in a meaningless age, expounding on meaning is not appropriate.

Charles E. May

AMY TAN

Born: Oakland, California; February 19, 1952

PRINCIPAL SHORT FICTION
The Joy Luck Club, 1989

OTHER LITERARY FORMS

Also considered a novel, Amy Tan's *The Joy Luck Club* has been translated into twenty languages. Her second novel *The Kitchen God's Wife* was a *Booklist* editor's choice. Her third novel is *The Hundred Secret Senses* (1995). She wrote two children's books, *The Moon Lady* (1992) and *The Chinese Siamese Cat* (1994). Her essays include "The Language of Discretion" and "Mother Tongue."

ACHIEVEMENTS

The Joy Luck Club was a finalist for the National Book Award and the National Book Critics Circle Award. Amy Tan cowrote (with Ronald Bass) the screenplay for a film based on the novel, released in 1993. Her essay "Mother Tongue" was included in *Best American Essays of 1991*, edited by Joyce Carol Oates. She received an honorary doctorate (Litterarum Humaniorum Doctor) from Dominican College in 1991.

BIOGRAPHY

Amy Ruth Tan was born in Oakland, California, on February 19, 1952, the middle child (and only daughter) of John Yuehhan and Daisy Tu Ching Tan, who had emigrated from China. Her father was an electrical engineer in China, but he became a minister in the United States. The family moved frequently, finally settling in Santa Clara, California. After the death of her husband and older son when Amy was fifteen years old, Daisy took the family to Switzerland and enrolled her children in schools there, but she returned to California in 1969.

Tan's parents hoped she would become a physician and concert pianist. She began a premedical course of study but switched to English and linguistics, much to her mother's dismay. She received her B.A. in 1973 and her M.A. in 1974 from San Jose State University. She attended the University of California, Berkeley, from 1974 to 1976, beginning studies toward a doctorate. In 1974, she married Louis M. DeMattei, a tax attorney; they settled in San Francisco.

Tan was a language consultant, a reporter, a managing editor, and a freelance technical writer before she turned to fiction writing. She joined a writing

Amy Tan (Lee/Archive Photos)

workshop in 1985 and submitted a story about a Chinese American chess prodigy. The revised version was first published in a small literary magazine and reprinted in *Seventeen* magazine as "Rules of the Game." When Tan learned that the story had appeared in Italy and had been translated without her knowledge, she obtained an agent, Sandra Dijkstra, to help handle publication. Although Tan had written only three stories at that time, Dijkstra encouraged her to write a book. At her suggestion, Tan submitted an outline for a book of stories and then went on a trip to China with her mother. On her return, she learned that her proposal had been accepted by G. P. Putnam's Sons.

ANALYSIS

Amy Tan's voice is an important one among a group of "hyphenated Americans" (such as African Americans and Asian Americans) who describe the experiences of members of ethnic minority groups.

Her short fiction is grounded in a Chinese tradition of "talk story" (*gong gu tsai*) a folk art form by which characters pass on values and teach important lessons through narrative. Other writers, such as Maxine Hong Kingston, employ a similar narrative strategy.

A central theme of Tan's stories is the conflict faced by Chinese Americans who find themselves alienated both from their American milieu and from their Chinese parents and heritage. Other themes include storytelling, memory, and the complex relationships between mother and daughter, husband and wife, and sisters. By using narrators from two generations, Tan explores the relationships between past and present. Her stories juxtapose the points of view of characters (husband and wife, mother and daughter, sisters) who struggle with each other, misunderstand each other, and grow distant from each other. Like Tan, other ethnic writers such as Louise Erdrich use multiple voices to retell stories describing the evolution of a cultural history.

Tan's stories derive from her own experience as a Chinese American and from stories of Chinese life her mother told her. They reflect her early conflicts with her strongly opinionated mother and her growing understanding and appreciation of her mother's past and her strength in adapting to her new country. Daisy's early life, about which Tan gradually learned, was difficult and dramatic. Daisy's mother, Jing-mei (Amy Tan's maternal grandmother), was forced to become the concubine of a wealthy man after her husband's death. Spurned by her family and treated cruelly by the man's wives, she committed suicide. Her tragic life became the basis of Tan's story "Magpies," retold by An-mei Hsu in *The Joy Luck Club.* Daisy was raised by relatives and married to a brutal man. After her father's death, Tan learned that her mother had been married in China and left behind three daughters. This story became part of *The Joy Luck Club* and *The Kitchen God's Wife.*

Tan insists that, like all writers, she writes from her own experience and is not representative of any ethnic group. She acknowledges her rich Chinese background and combines it with typically American themes of love, marriage, and freedom of choice. Her first-person style is also an American feature.

THE JOY LUCK CLUB

Although critics call it a novel, Tan wrote *The Joy Luck Club* as a collection of sixteen short stories told by the club members and their daughters. Each chapter is a complete unit, and five of them have been published separately in short-story anthologies. Other writers, such as the American authors Sherwood Anderson (*Winesburg, Ohio*) and Gloria Naylor (*The Women of Brewster Place*), and the Canadian Margaret Laurence (*A Bird in the House*), have built linked story collections around themes or groups of characters.

The framework for *The Joy Luck Club* is formed by members of a mah-jongg club, immigrants from China, who tell stories of their lives in China and their families in the United States. The first and fourth sections are the mothers' stories; the second and third are the daughters' stories. Through this device of multiple narrators, the conflicts and struggles of the two generations are presented through the contrasting stories. The mothers wish their daughters to succeed in American terms (to have professional careers, wealth, and status), but they expect them to retain Chinese values (filial piety, cooking skills, family loyalty) as well. When the daughters become Americanized, they are embarrassed by their mothers' old-fashioned ways, and their mothers are disappointed at the daughters' dismissal of tradition. Chasms of misunderstanding deepen between them.

Jing-mei (June) Woo forms a bridge between the generations; she tells her own stories in the daughters' sections and attempts to take her mother's part in the mothers' sections. Additionally, her trip to China forms a bridge between her family's past and present, and between China and America.

"THE JOY LUCK CLUB"

The first story, "The Joy Luck Club," describes the founding of the club by Suyuan Woo to find comfort during the privations suffered in China during World War II. When the Japanese invaders approached, she fled, abandoning her twin daughters when she was too exhausted to travel any farther. She continued the Joy Luck Club in her new life in San Francisco, forming close friendships with three other women. After Suyuan's death, her daughter Jing-mei "June" is in-

vited to take her place. June's uncertainty of how to behave there and her sketchy knowledge of her family history exemplify the tensions experienced by an American daughter of Chinese parents. The other women surprise June by revealing that news has finally arrived from the twin daughters Suyuan left in China. They present June with two plane tickets so that she and her father can visit her half-sisters and tell them her mother's story. She is unsure of what to say, believing now that she really did not know her mother. The others are aghast, because in her they see the reflection of their daughters who are also ignorant of their mothers' stories, their past histories, their hopes and fears. They hasten to tell June what to praise about their mother: her kindness, intelligence, mindfulness of family, "the excellent dishes she cooked." In the book's concluding chapter, June recounts her trip to China.

"RULES OF THE GAME"

One of the daughters' stories, "Rules of the Game," describes the ambivalent relationship of Lindo Jong and her six-year-old daughter. Waverly Place Jong (named after the street on which the family lives), learns from her mother's "rules," or codes of behavior, to succeed as a competitive chess player. Her mother teaches her to "bite back your tongue" and to learn to bend with the wind. These techniques help her persuade her mother to let her play in chess tournaments and then help her to win games and advance in rank. However, her proud mother embarrasses Waverly by showing her off to the local shopkeepers. The tensions between mother and daughter are like another kind of chess game, a give and take, where the two struggle for power. The two are playing by different rules, Lindo by Chinese rules of behavior and filial obedience, Waverly by American rules of self-expression and independence.

"TWO KINDS"

Another daughter's story, "Two Kinds," is June's story of her mother's great expectations for her. Suyuan was certain that June could be anything she wanted to be; it was only a matter of discovering what it was. She decided that June would be a prodigy piano player, and outdo Waverly Jong, but June rebelled against her mother and never paid attention to her lessons. After a disastrous recital, she stops playing the piano, which becomes a sore point between mother and daughter. On her thirtieth birthday, the piano becomes a symbol of her reconciliation with her mother, when Suyuan offers it to her.

"BEST QUALITY"

"Best Quality" is June's story of a dinner party her mother gives. The old rivalries between June and Waverly continue, and Waverly's daughter and American fiancé behave in ways that are impolite in Chinese eyes. After the dinner Suyuan gives her daughter a jade necklace she has worn in hopes that it will guide her to find her "life's importance."

"A PAIR OF TICKETS"

This is the concluding story of *The Joy Luck Club.* It recounts Jing-mei (June) Woo's trip to China to meet her half-sisters, thus fulfilling the wish of her mother and the Joy Luck mothers and bringing the story cycle to a close, completing the themes of the first story. June learns from her father how Suyuan's twin daughters were found by an old school friend. He explains that her mother's name means "long-cherished wish" and that her own name Jing-mei means "something pure, essential, the best quality." When at last they meet the sisters, she acknowledges her Chinese lineage: "I also see what part of me is Chinese. It is so obvious. It is my family. It is in our blood."

OTHER MAJOR WORKS

LONG FICTION: *The Kitchen God's Wife,* 1991; *The Hundred Secret Senses,* 1995.

NONFICTION: "The Language of Discretion," 1990 (in *The State of Language,* Christopher Ricks and Leonard Michaels, editors).

CHILDREN'S LITERATURE: *The Moon Lady,* 1992; *The Chinese Siamese Cat,* 1994.

BIBLIOGRAPHY

Benanni, Ben, ed. *Paintbrush: A Journal of Poetry and Translation* 22 (Autumn, 1995). This is a special issue of the journal focusing on Tan and on *The Joy Luck Club* in particular. It includes articles on mothers and daughters, memory and forgetting.

Cooperman, Jeannette Batz. *The Broom Closet: Secret Meanings of Domesticity in Postfeminist Novels by Louise Erdrich, Mary Gordan, Toni Morrison, Marge Piercy, Jane Smiley, and Amy Tan.* New York: Peter Lang, 1999. A study of the role of traditionally feminine concerns, such as marriage and family, in the works of these postfeminist writers.

Huh, Joonok. *Interconnected Mothers and Daughters in Amy Tan's 'The Joy Luck Club.'* Tucson, Ariz.: Southwest Institute for Research on Women, 1992. Examines the mother and adult child relationship in Tan's novel. Includes a bibliography.

Huntley, E. D. *Amy Tan: A Critical Companion.* Westport, Conn.: Greenwood Press, 1998. Discusses Tan's biography and analyzes her novels in the context of Asian American literature. Analyzes major themes such as the crone figure, food, clothing, language, biculturalism, mothers and daughters. Includes useful bibliography.

Karen F. Stein

JUN'ICHIRŌ TANIZAKI

Born: Tokyo, Japan; July 24, 1886
Died: Yugawara, Japan; July 30, 1965

PRINCIPAL SHORT FICTION
"Kirin," 1910
"Shisei," 1910 ("The Tattooer," 1963)
"Shōnen," 1910
"Hōkan," 1911
"Akuma," 1912
"Kyōfu," 1913 ("Terror," 1963)
"Otsuya goroshi," 1913
"Watakushi," 1921 ("The Thief," 1963)
"Aoi Hano," 1922 ("Aguri," 1963)
"Mōmoku monogatari," 1931 ("A Blind Man's
    Tale," 1963)
"Ashikari," 1932 (English translation, 1936)
"Shunkinshō," 1933 ("A Portrait of Shunkin,"
    1936)
Hyofu, 1950
"Yume no ukihashi," 1959 ("The Bridge of
    Dreams," 1963)
Yume no ukihashi, 1960
Fūten rōjin nikki, 1961-1962 (serial), 1962 (no-
    vella; *Diary of a Mad Old Man*, 1965)
Kokumin no bungaku, 1964
Tanizaki Jun'ichirō, 1970
Seven Japanese Tales, 1981

OTHER LITERARY FORMS

For Western readers, Jun'ichirō Tanizaki is best known for his short stories and short novels. Throughout his career, however, he was a prolific writer of plays, essays, and translations as well. Many English readers favor his long novel *Sasameyuki* (1943-1948, 1949; *The Makioka Sisters*, 1957) as his best work. It is the story of a family's efforts to arrange a marriage for Yukiko, the third of four daughters in a respectable Osaka family. Tanizaki has written a number of plays, and also noteworthy are his two translations into modern Japanese of Murasaki Shikibu's *Genji monogatari* (c. 1004; first English translation, *The Tale of Genji*, 1925-1933). The ear-

lier translation was restricted by the severe censorship during the time of the war with China; the later one was in more liberal and colloquial language.

ACHIEVEMENTS

The modern Japanese writers most commonly suggested as comparable to Jun'ichirō Tanizaki for the quality of their fiction are the 1968 Nobel Prize winner Yasunari Kawabata, and Yukio Mishima. It is widely believed that Tanizaki was Kawabata's chief rival for the Nobel Prize that year. Mishima's easier fiction gains more readers but cannot match Tanizaki's more innovative complexity. From his earliest years, however, Tanizaki has had his detractors, because many found his youthful "demoniac" works offensive. Throughout his career, for that matter, his frank portrayal of unconventional, even bizarre sexual and marital relationships among his characters caused consternation. In spite of such reservations, Tanizaki was elected to the Japanese Academy of Arts in 1937. He was awarded the Mainichi Prize for Publication and Culture for *Sasameyuki*, 1943-1948, 1949 (*The Makioka Sisters*, 1957) and the Asaki Culture Prize and the Imperial Cultural Medal, both in 1949. These are the most important awards the Japanese can give a writer.

BIOGRAPHY

Jun'ichirō Tanizaki, whose father owned a printing establishment, was born in Tokyo on July 24, 1886. He attended the Tokyo Imperial University, studying classical Japanese literature, but had little interest in attending lectures and did not earn a degree. Even at the university, however, he wrote stories and plays for small magazines, some of them serialized; indeed, he continued to be productive throughout his life. In his early years, he was noted for dissolute habits, and some readers blamed him for what they believed was worship of women. His three marriages were unconventional, the experiences of which some will say are hinted at in his short fiction. The suggestion is made occasionally that Tanizaki's moving from Tokyo to the Kansai after the earthquake of 1923 contributed to changes in his writing, but changes in phrasing, characterization, or dialogue in these different years are not easy to see in English translations. As one reviews the publications of his life, one finds no time when he was unproductive. In fact, he continued writing to the time of his death, on July 30, 1965, in Yugawara.

ANALYSIS

The dominant theme in Jun'ichirō Tanizaki's best work is love, but few writers so successfully explore this universally preferred topic with such unconventional revelations. Commentators often identified his earliest writings as "demoniac"; his later work they might have characterized as "sardonic." As labels prove to be insufficient for most good writers, however, one must struggle to understand Tanizaki's probing style as he uncovers complicated motives for lovers, spouses, family members, and friends, who continually surprise one another. In addition, as one finishes reading Tanizaki's works of fiction, most characteristically, one finds oneself more than a little uncertain as to how things really work out. The dispute, the rivalries, or the resentments always seems resolved or brought to a close; most commonly, though, the reader finds himself needing to fill in indeterminate gaps using his own imagination. This challenge, in fact, contributes to much of the pleasure in reading Tanizaki's fiction.

"THE TATTOOER"

In his early sensational tale "The Tattooer," the exceptional tattooer, Seikichi, behaves much like a sadist in his attitudes toward some of his customers, as he revels in the excruciating pain they endure for the honor of having such an artist adorn their bodies. He outdoes himself in embellishing the back of a beautiful young woman with a huge black widow spider. Readers are told that "at every thrust of his needle Seikichi . . . felt as if he had stabbed his own heart." After he assures the woman that he has poured his soul into this tattoo and that now all men will be her victims, she accepts this prophecy, turns her resplendently tattooed back to him, and promptly claims the tattooer himself as her first conquest.

"TERROR"

With similar emphasis upon intimate revelation of pain, and with similarly ambivalent implications for the suffering endured, in "Terror," a young man describes his peculiar phobia for riding in a train or any other vehicle. For the occasion in the story, he must travel by train to take a physical examination for military duty. His nervous trembling almost drives him mad and certainly drives him to excessive alcoholic consumption. With the combination of neurotic fearfulness and drunkenness, he seems unlikely to pass his physical; the reader, however, hears a doctor reassuring the young man: "Oh, you'll pass all right. A fine husky fellow like you." Such openendedness in Tanizaki's short fiction seems practically his trademark.

"THE THIEF"

The probing into the psychology of nonconforming personalities reveals itself also in "The Thief." In this story, a young man shares the discomfort and embarrassment with his university dormitory roommates as one by one they admit their shame at having suspected the narrator as the perpetrator of recent thefts. Readers can hardly avoid sympathizing with the young man as he reveals his private thoughts about the unfortunate, painful admissions by others who suspect and distrust him. Then one suddenly discovers that this sensitive young man, in fact, truly is the thief. In fact, the thief boasts that, with an outward show of innocence, he can deceive not only roommates and readers but also himself.

"AGURI"

In the story "Aguri," Tanizaki goes further, with his presentation of a self-conscious narrator brooding over his fears and inadequacies. The middle-aged Okada, accompanied by his slim, shapely mistress on a shopping trip, describes in extravagant detail how he is wasting away physically while the young woman, Aguri, craves the most expensive luxuries. As in "The Thief," the narrator of this story carries the reader along with him in his imagination, momentarily at least, with a painful scene of ruinously expensive purchases for Aguri, followed by Okada's fainting embarrassingly in public from weakness. Almost before one realizes the change, however, the reader learns that these disasters were mercly an imagined vision. The man and woman end up making modest purchases and with no physical collapse.

"A BLIND MAN'S TALE"

In "A Blind Man's Tale," Tanizaki offers what might be his boldest experiment in narrative point of view. A blind masseur, while massaging a nobleman, recalls the insight he gained thirty years before into a complicated series of events in sixteenth century Japanese history. What he knows he learned largely through the experience of serving as masseur for a beautiful noblewoman. The blind man depends upon his own intuition, overheard conversations, and confidential hints. His story not only opens up multiple perspectives on historical events, interesting for their own sake, but also leaves readers pondering choices in judging these acts as honorable, cowardly, or opportunistic.

"ASHIKARI"

In "Ashikari" the author appeals to easy emotionalism by beginning with a sentimental narrator taking a walk, visiting the Shrine of Minase and then, in the evening, enjoying the moonlight on the river. His detailed observations of ancient scenes and nostalgic thoughts about the past are accompanied by recitation of favorite verses, Chinese and Japanese. He also composes verses of his own, reciting them aloud while admiring the moonlight. Soon, however, this simple sentimentalism gives way.

The brash visitor, Serizawa, who appears suddenly, dominates the scene from this point. Serizawa tells the story of his father's love for the elegant widow Oyu, a woman surrounded by symbols of refinement. This leads to the self-sacrificing of both the father and Oyu's younger sister Oshizu, who marry but remain chaste in respect for the love between Oyu and the father. The three of them remain close companions in this setting for two or three years. In retrospect, though, one is left intrigued with the mystery of what kind of satisfaction either the father or the son gained from their limited sharing in the Lady Oyu's aristocratic way of life.

"A PORTRAIT OF SHUNKIN"

"A Portrait of Shunkin" invites attention for another narrative technique favored by Tanizaki, the use of abundant circumstantial detail to lend an initial air of credence to the unusual love story that follows. At the beginning, the narrator gives precise descriptions of a pair of tombstones in a temple graveyard and then of a privately printed biography, and the only known photograph of the beautiful, blind woman Shunkin, famous for her samisen lessons. With this narrator, however, one discovers Tanizaki's characteristic ambivalence as the storyteller regularly admits uncertainty about how to interpret the evidence he has found. One suspects that Shunkin gained pleasure from tormenting Sasuka, her disciple, who may have been, in effect, her slave, but quite possibly he also was her lover. The most startling event, Sasuka's blinding of himself following the cruel, disfiguring scalding of Shunkin by an assailant, invites a great range of speculation about Sasuka's motives: to preserve the memory of her beauty, to gain a measure of acceptance from her, or to distract her from demanding so much of him because of her own handicaps.

"THE BRIDGE OF DREAMS"

Certainly one of Tanizaki's most difficult tales is "The Bridge of Dreams," the story of a boy's affectionate memories of his mother and stepmother with resulting family complications. The most striking images in Tadasu's few recollections of his mother are of her sitting by the pool soaking her pretty feet in the water and of her permitting him to suckle her breasts at night when they were in bed together. This was when he was nearly five years old. The new mother, who had been a geisha, was chosen for her striking resemblance to Tadasu's real mother. She even took the same name and adopted similar habits as a full replacement. In time, as the boy grew old enough to marry, he had difficulty distinguishing the two mothers in his memory. When the second mother has a son, too, the new baby is sent off for adoption. The narrator even relates that Tadasu sucked the milk from his stepmother's swollen breasts after she had given up the child. Following the deaths of his father and second mother, Tadasu adopted his stepbrother with a vow to protect him from loneliness. In this story, with the powerful emphasis on family protectiveness, readers can hardly avoid pondering the relative gains and losses from the characters' exceptional watchfulness over their loved ones.

DIARY OF A MAD OLD MAN

Another excellent comic representation of obsessive love reveals itself in Tanizaki's novella *Diary of a Mad Old Man*. In this story, Utsuki, a sickly old man, age seventy-seven, fits into the traditional family pattern as the unchallengeable head of the family, whose word is law. The narrative comes across mostly through the old man's notes in his diary. Tanizaki leaves indeterminate the private thoughts of Utsuki's wife and grown children, but they know of his squandering wealth and affection on his daughter-in-law, the scheming Satsuko. The family had been suspicious of her as a bride for the son, Jokichi, right from the start, because of her background as a lowly cabaret dancer. In fact, as the story begins, Jokichi has already lost interest in her anyway, and Satsuko is visited frequently by another young man, Utsuki's nephew, Haruhisa. Nevertheless, the old man's dotage reveals itself in expensive gifts for her, including a cat's-eye ring costing three million yen, the plan to enshrine her footprints on his gravestone, and niggardliness toward his own children. One's disgust for the old man grows with the combination of abundant references to Utsuki's medicines, drugs, and treatments, and Satsuko's obvious contempt for him. After Utsuki boldly kisses her on the neck one time, she tells him that she felt as if she had "been licked by a garden slug." Near the end, the narrative trails off with a long series of notes attesting the failing health of an apparently dying man. Then, in the final entry, one reads that Utsuki recovered enough to supervise excavation of the garden to construct a swimming pool for his darling Satsuko. Even in his last years, Tanizaki never lost his ability to catch his readers off guard.

OTHER MAJOR WORKS

LONG FICTION: *Chijin no ai*, 1924-1925 (serial), 1925 (book; *Naomi*, 1985); *Kōjin*, 1926; *Manji*, 1928-1930; *Yoshinokuzu*, 1931 (*Arrowroot*, 1982); *Tade kuu mushi*, 1928-1929 (serial), 1936 (book; *Some Prefer Nettles*, 1955); *Bushōkō hiwa*, 1931-1932 (serial), 1935 (book; *The Secret History of the Lord of Musashi*, 1982); *Sasameyuki*, 1943-1948 (serial), 1949 (book; *The Makioka Sisters*, 1957); *Shōshō Shigemoto no haha*, 1950 (*The Mother of Captain Shigemoto*, 1956); *Kagi*, 1956 (*The Key*, 1960).

PLAYS: *Aisureba koso*, pb. 1921; *Okumi to Gohei*, pb. 1922; *Shirogitsune no yu*, pb. 1923 (*The White Fox*, 1930); *Mumyō to Aizen*, 1924; *Shinzei*, pb. 1949.

NONFICTION: *Bunsho no dukohon*, 1934; "In'ei raisan," 1934 ("In Praise of Shadows," 1955); *Kyō no yume, Ōsaka no yume*, 1950; *Yōshō-jidai*, 1957 (*Childhood Years: A Memoir*, 1988).

TRANSLATION: *Genji monogatari*, 1936-1941, 1951-1954 (of Murasaki Shikibu's medieval *Genji monogatari*).

MISCELLANEOUS: *Tanizaki Jun'ichirō zenshu*, 1930 (12 volumes); *Tanizaki Jun'ichirō zenshu*, 1966-1970 (28 volumes).

BIBLIOGRAPHY

Chambers, Anthony Hood. *The Secret Window: Ideal Worlds in Tanizaki's Fiction.* Cambridge, Mass.: Harvard University Press, 1994. Chapters on "ideal worlds," "A Portrait of Shunkin," and "The Bridge of Dreams." Includes notes and bibliography.

Gessel, Van C. *Three Modern Novelists: Soseki, Tanizaki, Kawabata.* New York: Kodansha International, 1993. Concentrates on Tanizaki's handling of the theme of modernism. With detailed notes but no bibliography.

Golley, Gregory L. "Tanizaki Junichiro: The Art of Subversion and the Subversion of Art." *The Journal of Japanese Studies* 21 (Summer, 1995): 365-404. Examines the "return to Japan" inaugurated by Tanizaki's *Some Prefer Nettles*. Discusses themes and images in the work and suggests that Tanizaki's traditionalist fiction both championed and undermined the idea of an essential Japanese traditional culture.

Ito, Ken K. *Visions of Desire: Tanizaki's Fictional Worlds.* Stanford, Calif.: Stanford University Press, 1991. Chapters on his handling of the "Orient" and the "West," on his treatment of the past,

"The Vision of the Blind," "Fair Dreams of Hanshin," "Writing as Power," and "A Mad Old Man's World." Includes notes, bibliography, and a section on names and sources.

Lippit, Noriko Miuta. *Reality and Fiction in Modern Japanese Literature*. White Plains, N.Y.: M. E. Sharpe, 1980. Considers the struggle of several Japanese writers to define the function of art and literature both socially and personally. Sections on Tanizaki deal with his aesthetic preference for fantasy and complex structure, with a comparison to Edgar Allan Poe. Notes.

Rubin, Jay. *Injurious to Public Morals: Writers and the Meiji State*. Seattle: University of Washington Press, 1984. In this unusual approach, the author tackles censorship in Japan and analyzes the relationship between writers and the government. The sections on Tanizaki, an apolitical period writer, suggest ways censorship affected his early career. Contains interesting discussions of the bans on his short stories. Chronology, notes, a bibliography, and an index.

Suzuki, Tomi. *Narrating the Self: Fictions of Japanese Modernity*. Stanford, Calif.: Stanford University Press, 1996. See especially the epilogue, "Tanizaki's Speaking Subject and the Creation of Tradition." Includes notes and bibliography.

Thornbury, Barbara E. "Kagura, Chaban, and the Awaji Puppet Theatre: A Literary View of Japan's Performing Arts." *Theatre Survey* 35 (May, 1994): 55-64. Discusses the traditional performing works of Tanizaki Jun'ichiro and Uno Chiyo; claims that for both authors the traditional performing arts were a connection between the present and past, an important element in Japan's cultural identity—and one that could be lost.

Ueda, Makoto. "Tanizaki Jun'ichirō." In *Modern Japanese Writers and the Nature of Literature*. Stanford, Calif.: Stanford University Press, 1976. Discusses Tanizaki as one of the eight major writers who make up the bulk of modern Japanese fiction familiar to Western readers. Provides an introduction to major literary theories underlying Japanese novels and stories. Supplemented by source notes, a bibliography, and an index.

Yamanouchi, Hisaaki. *The Search for Authenticity in Modern Japanese Literature*. Cambridge, England: Cambridge University Press, 1978. Discusses twelve modern Japanese writers, analyzing the ways each dealt with the difficult personal, social, and intellectual questions in art. The sections on Tanizaki focus on the concept of eternal womanhood in his works. Includes notes, a bibliography, and an index.

David V. Harrington, updated by
Shakuntala Jayaswal

BARRY TARGAN

Born: Atlantic City, New Jersey; November 30, 1932

PRINCIPAL SHORT FICTION

Harry Belten and the Mendelssohn Violin Concerto, 1975
Surviving Adverse Seasons: Stories, 1979
Falling Free, 1989

OTHER LITERARY FORMS

Barry Targan is the author of the collections of poetry *Let the Wild Rumpus Start: Poems* (1971) and *Thoreau Stalks the Land Disguised as a Father: Poems* (1975) and several novels, including *Kingdoms: A Novel* (1980), *The Tangerine Tango Equation: Or, How I Discovered Sex, Deception, and a New Theory of Physics in Three Short Months* (1990), and *The Ark of the Marindor* (1998).

ACHIEVEMENTS

Barry Targan won the 1975 University of Iowa Short Fiction Award for *Harry Belten and the Mendelssohn Violin Concerto*, the Associated Writing Programs Award for *Kingdoms* in 1980, the Saxifrage Award for *Surviving Adverse Seasons* in 1981. He received a National Endowment for the Arts Grant in 1983. Several of his stories have appeared in *Prize Stories: The O. Henry Awards* and *The Best American Short Stories* and have won Pushcart Prizes.

BIOGRAPHY

Barry Targan was born in Atlantic City, New Jersey, on November 30, 1932, to Albert Targan, a grocer, and Blanche Simmons Targan. He received his B.A. degree with a major in English from Rutgers University in 1954 and an M.A. degree from University of Chicago in 1955. He then served in the U.S. Army for two years. He married Arleen Shanken, an artist, in 1958, with whom he had two children. Targan received a Ph.D. degree in English from Brandeis University in 1962 and started a teaching career at Syracuse University. He has taught at the State University of New York at Cortand, Skidmore

College, and, beginning in 1978, at the State University of New York at Binghamton.

ANALYSIS

There is a determined optimism at the heart of many of Barry Targan's stories, perhaps best summed up in the title of one of his collections, *Surviving Adverse Seasons*. His middle-aged male characters are possessed of a quiet integrity that makes them survivors regardless of the adversity they face. Integrity is an important element in Targan's writing; he has spoken of his awe of great authors who write with honor and authenticity, feeling that to write with such "integrity . . . was one of the finest things a human being could do with a life."

Targan's characters are often driven by a passionate engagement in a meaningful action, a deep-seated desire and commitment to give oneself wholly to a task, craft, or art. Many of his characters, without the aid of dogma or social rules, develop and abide by their own quiet codes of conduct, and they manage to succeed in spite of the odds against them. As a result, the reader is irresistibly aligned with these men, for it is clear that they are honestly engaged in doing the best they can under adverse circumstances.

"HARRY BELTEN AND THE MENDELSSOHN VIOLIN CONCERTO"

Targan's best-known story, anthologized several times, is the most representative expression of his central theme—one's passionate and honest devotion to a creative act. Harry Belten is a middle-aged man who has worked in a hardware store in a small town in southwest New York for thirty-two years. A reliable man whose "life had closed in upon him quickly," Harry has but one interest other than his family and his work—the violin, which, with modest lessons, he started learning how to play in 1941. More than two decades later, Harry has decided to take more serious professional lessons and to stage his own concert—renting a hall and paying for an orchestra—even though he and everyone else know he is not a concert-caliber violinist.

Among the pieces he plans to play at the concert is the Felix Mendelssohn *Violin Concerto*, a particularly difficult piece that Harry has been studying for the past eighteen years. Although his wife tells him they can ill afford the concert and people kid him and try to discourage him, Harry is determined. When the orchestra he has hired tries to cancel, he fights them for breach of contract and wins. When his family insists he see a psychiatrist, he agrees and successfully convinces the doctor that he should give the concert. He even manages to get his professional teacher, who has doubted him from the beginning, to fully support him.

The success of Targan's story depends on the irresistibility of Harry Belten himself, whose quiet and dignified determination, humility, and courage put the reader so much on his side that at the end of the story when he is ready to play the Mendelssohn piece, the reader waits breathlessly, fingers crossed, silently cheering him on. The tension is at its highest when one of Harry's strings loses the exact tautness needed, forcing him to try to play all the notes on that one string slightly off while playing the notes on the other three strings correctly.

Although Harry plays the worst finale to the Mendelssohn concerto ever played with a real orchestra before the a live audience, it is enough to make his teacher almost weep with pride. When Harry's family and friends cheer and shout for an "encore," Harry tunes his violin and plays one encore and then another. It is one of the most delightfully fulfilling conclusions in modern short fiction.

"DOMINION"

Highly praised and often anthologized, "Dominion" is another Targan story that focuses on the integrity and honest courage of one man. When the central character, Morton Poverman, is driven to bankruptcy by the embezzlement of his partner, he simply forgives him and begins again with what little he has left, working long hours, doing practically everything by himself. When his son Robert, a senior in high school, offers to help, Poverman generously tells the boy to stick to his school and extracurricular activities.

The son, who has been accepted into Yale University, Cornell University, and the State University of New York at Binghamton, is the most serious source of heartache for Morton when the boy says he is considering not going to college and joining a religious cult instead. Poverman quietly begins an understated effort to save his son from what he considers a mistake by going to the headquarters of the cult, a branch of a large corporate religious entity, and declaring his own interest in their message to their smooth-talking representatives.

When Poverman begins attending the discussion meetings of the group, his son, formerly an active participant, withdraws, accusing his father of not being sincere. When the cult leaders try to get Poverman to stop attending, he challenges them and asks to receive further instruction. The climax of the story occurs when Poverman stands up at a meeting and declares himself for Jesus. Although he is doubted by the leaders, the young people accept this avowal with such enthusiasm that they have no choice but to receive Poverman into their organization. However, when Poverman stands in the midst of the group and repeats their codes—that he is an infection of evil, that he has made the world foul with his pride, that he is a bad man stained with sin—his son, knowing that these things are not true, tearfully urges him to stop. The story ends with Poverman telling his son not to worry, while he advances "upon his Hosts in dubious battle. And f[ights]. Not without glory."

It is another wonderfully fulfilling Targan conclusion, for Poverman has not only defeated his foes but also done so by means of the very virtues of love, forgiveness, and honesty that they espouse—values that he naturally and unselfconsciously possesses without their rituals, codes, or dogma. It is not just that Poverman has outsmarted the slick businessmen who run the cult, although that is cause enough for the reader's pleasure, it is that Poverman is a true religious man in the most basic sense of that word, courageously willing to abase himself for his the sake of his son.

"FALLING FREE"

Although Frank Higgins, the protagonist of this story, is relatively rootless and has broken the law by organizing bullfights in Texas, he is not the morally lax, down-and-out drifter encountered in the stories of a number of other American short-story writers of the 1970's and 1980's, such as Richard Ford, Barry Hannah, Richard Bausch, and Lee K. Abbott. The defining event in Higgins's life occurred when, as a nineteen-year-old soldier engaged in an airborne experiment, he jumped out of a C-47 at twenty-five thousand feet over Texas and "was seized by a nearly unutterable intention to possess what from this height appeared to be the boundlessly offered." Seeing the world below him as a "vast continent of possibility," Higgins has spent his life in one unsuccessful get-rich scheme after another—from selling cars to panning for gold, for his experience has left him "unmoored, untethered by vicissitude, necessity, or even dreams."

Having been ordered out of the state by the Texas Rangers, Higgins and his wife Miranda, who is ill, have decided to return to Southern California to a poor carob tree orchard they own. However, their plans are altered by a burnt-out wheel bearing and the arrival of a hitchhiker who offers to help in exchange for a ride to El Paso. It is soon clear that the hitchhiker, who calls himself Joe Smith, has something to hide, although Higgins, feeling a sympathetic identification with Smith, thinks the young man lacks menace, the "hanging tangle of danger."

The story, however, does take a menacing turn when Miranda worsens; she desperately needs to get to El Paso for medication and notices that Smith has a gun. In a parallel to Higgins's own search for gold, success, and ultimate possibility after his youthful "free fall," Smith reveals that he has a million dollars worth of cocaine in his backpack smuggled out of Mexico. The situation worsens when Smith insists that they head south through rough country, endangering Miranda's life. Although Higgins knows that Smith has been broken by exactly what he has always believed—"that he was a potentate, and that any rock he held in his hand was a jewel"—he also knows that whereas at twenty-five thousand feet he had "fallen free," for Smith it is too late.

The story comes to a head when Higgins gets his rifle and Smith points his gun at him and pulls the trigger, only to have nothing happen because he did not take off the safety. At this point, Higgins fires and shoots Smith through the head. The postlude of the story has Higgins and Miranda at the carob orchard on the coast of Southern California, with Higgins thinking of the sea voyages they and Smith could have taken, out to where they were only "imagined images of places." However, Miranda holds him to earth with a squeeze of the hand.

OTHER MAJOR WORKS

LONG FICTION: *Kingdoms: A Novel*, 1980; *The Tangerine Tango Equation: Or, How I Discovered Sex, Deception, and a New Theory of Physics in Three Short Months*, 1990; *The Ark of the Marindor*, 1998.

POETRY: *Let the Wild Rumpus Start: Poems*, 1971; *Thoreau Stalks the Land Disguised as a Father: Poems*, 1975.

BIBLIOGRAPHY

"Barry Targan." In *Contemporary Authors*. New Revision Series 71, Detroit: Gale Research, 1999. A brief biographical survey of Targan's literary career. Summarizes critical reception of Targan's work and comments on his novel *The Ark of the Marindor*.

Clements, Arthur L. "Barry Targan." In *Dictionary of Literary Biography* 130. In a rare general discussion of Targan's fiction, Clements comments on some of the general themes and characters in *Harry Belten and the Mendelssohn Violin Concerto*, *Surviving Adverse Seasons*, and *Falling Free*. Argues that Targan works within the realistic tradition and often focuses on the theme of engaging in life with as much honesty, skill, love, and devotion as one can muster.

Evanier, David. "Storytellers." *The New York Times*, July 27, 1980, p. 18. A review of *Surviving Adverse Seasons;* discusses "Kingdoms," which Evanier says is the best story in the collection. Says Targan's stories embody a tug of war between his abstract turn of mind and his concrete gifts as a story writer. Says Targan needs to be less ponderous and more immediate and responsible.

Lotozo, Elis. "Life: Want to Make Something of It?" Review of *Falling Free*, by Barry Targan. *The New*

York Times, March 3, 1990, p. 24. Lotozo calls the stories passionate arguments with and love songs to a world that offers "no guarantees, only opportunities, and vicissitudes." Comments on the three stories in which aging men confront the choices they have made with their lives.

Morgan, Speer. "The Plot Thickens." *St. Louis Post-Dispatch*, September 9, 1998, p. E3. Says *The Ark of the Marindor* is reminiscent of a Joseph Conrad novel, complete with compelling incident. Argues that the real story of this "beautifully crafted novel" is the protagonist's growing understanding of the bearing of her life.

Sweeney, Aoibheann. "Bermuda Triangle." Review of *The Ark of the Marindor*, by Barry Targan. *The New York Times*, June 14, 1998, p. 14. Says Targan's work focuses on the theme of self-discovery; argues that what saves the book is the sensual descriptions of sailing rather than the dizzying pace of the plot and the page-turning Hollywood machinery of suspense.

Charles E. May

ELIZABETH TAYLOR

Born: Reading, Berkshire, England; July 3, 1912
Died: Penn, Buckinghamshire, England; November 19, 1975

PRINCIPAL SHORT FICTION

Hester Lilly and Twelve Short Stories, 1954 (pb. in England as *Hester Lilly and Other Stories*, 1954)
The Blush and Other Stories, 1958
A Dedicated Man and Other Stories, 1965
The Devastating Boys and Other Stories, 1972

OTHER LITERARY FORMS

Elizabeth Taylor is best known for her "genteel novels" of social comedy. However, because critics have viewed them as relatively lightweight entertainments, they are often more appreciated by general readers than by university scholars. Critics have noted that much of her longer fiction focuses on how people become victims of their own self-delusion. Her career as a novelist extends from the postwar *At Mrs. Lippincote's* (1945) to the posthumously published *Blaming* (1976).

ACHIEVEMENTS

Elizabeth Taylor's fiction was reissued in paperback in the 1980's, reaching a wider audience; her stories have been praised by critics, but her novels have been more popular with general readers. Her 1957 novel *Angel* was selected by the Books Marketing Council in 1984 as one of the "Best Novels of Our Time."

BIOGRAPHY

Born in Reading, England, on July 3, 1912, Elizabeth Taylor became a governess after attending the Abbey School and then a librarian at the public library at High Wycombe. In 1936, she married John William Kendell Taylor, a manufacturer, and began writing full time, publishing stories in popular journals both in England and America. After World War II, she and her husband settled in the village of Penn, in Buckinghamshire, where she wrote most of her fiction. Taylor said that she loved England and would find it painful to live any place else, commenting, "I should like to feel that the people in my books are essentially English and set down against a truly English background."

ANALYSIS

Elizabeth Taylor said that one basic difference between the short story and the novel is that, whereas the novel is conscious scheming, short stories are inspired, "breathed in a couple of breaths." For them to succeed, she argued, there must be an immediate impact resulting from suggestiveness and compression. Indeed, critics have suggested that what makes Taylor's stories so fascinating is her ability to crystallize a particular "moment of being."

Great short stories, said Taylor, are so charged with a sense of unity, they are like lyric poetry, thus giving a "lovely impression of perfection, of being lifted into another world, instead of sinking into it, as one does with longer fiction." Many of Taylor's stories are social comedies that satirize class distinctions and social expectations; however, the best of them begin as social comedies, only to become subtle evocations of characters caught in elusive psychological conflicts.

"THE FIRST DEATH OF HER LIFE"

This popular anthology piece is so short and slight that many readers may feel it is not a story at all, but rather a simple emotional reaction to, as the title suggests, the first death the central character has experienced. Although the story starts with tears, it immediately moves to writing, in this case, the protagonist's writing a letter in her mind telling her boss why she will not be in to work for the next four days.

The basic method the story uses to communicate emotion is Chekhovian, for instead of focusing on feelings, it focuses on concrete details—either in the present or in the past—that evoke emotion. The thoughts of the protagonist shift first to an image of her father riding through the streets on his bicycle and then to images of her mother, most of which recall the boredom, drabness, and denial of her life. The detail at the end of the story—when the protagonist opens the window and thinks that it is like the end of a film, but without music rising up and engulfing the viewer—suggests that the story is about one of those experiences that is such a disruption of everyday reality it seems unreal. The final image of the father propping his bicycle against the wall and running across the wet gravel completes in actuality what the protagonist earlier imagined.

"A RED-LETTER DAY"

The story opens with a gothic ominousness—leaves "dripping with deadly intensity, as if each falling drop were a drop of acid." The "malevolent" land-

scape is redolent with the horrors of family life: rotting cabbages, rakish privies, rubbish heaps, and gray napkins drooping on clotheslines. The central female character, Tory Foyle (a figure from Taylor's novel *A View of the Harbour*), is attending Visiting Day at her son's school, but without a husband. Because Tory's husband has asked for a divorce, her own life is frail and precarious; she feels she and her son are amateurs without tradition and no gift for the job. On Tory's arrival at the school, the point of view shifts to her son Edward, age eleven. When the mother and son go to the Museum at the Guildhall to see Roman remains, Tory flirts with the attendant and Edward feels unsafe with her; thoughts of the future and death disturb him, as they would not do if he were at school, "anonymous and safe." At the end of the story, when Tory leaves, her son waves at her, "radiant with relief." When she disappears around the curve of the drive, he runs "quickly up the steps to find his friends, and safety."

The relief that both mother and son feel at the end of the story when the required visit is completed suggests that this is not simply a story about a woman who is not comfortable as a mother; rather it is about the depressing fall into reality from the ideal of what society says a mother/son relationship should be. It is a story about the loss of the ideal of marriage, family, and motherhood, and one woman's halting and uncertain efforts to cope with that loss.

"A DEDICATED MAN"

In this combination social comedy and psychological drama, a stereotypical, stiff-necked British waiter, Silcox, enters into a "partnership" with a reserved waitress, Edith, pretending they are husband and wife in order to procure a more prestigious position in a fancy hotel restaurant; however, they sleep in twin beds, maintaining strict decorum. The focus of the story is on Edith, a woman who has known from childhood that she is not attractive to men and thus exaggerates her gracelessness to such an extent that she becomes sexless. Her attitude toward Silcox is that he is always a waiter and nothing else; the two are "hardly even human beings" in each other's eyes.

The story is complicated by the fact that the pretense Silcox creates includes a fictional son, complete with a photograph placed prominently in the couple's room. However, Edith begins to believe more and more in the reality of the fictional son, bragging to the other employees about his successes. Although Silcox thinks she is losing her mind, she says she has never been so happy.

The ruse crashes when Edith finds a photograph in Silcox's drawer that reveals the boy is his son by a previous marriage; because the picture also includes the boy's real mother, Edith feels she has been displaced; her hatred for Silcox's deception increases when he laughs at her disappointment. This shift from social comedy to domestic poignancy makes a final turn at the end of the story when Edith spreads rumors that her "son" has been disgraced as a thief. When she packs and leaves the hotel, Silcox is left to confront a loss of prestige in the eyes of the staff because of his son's disgrace.

"THE BLUSH"

In this short, highly compressed story, Taylor once again combines social comedy with psychological drama. The story centers on two women of the same age—Mrs. Allen and the woman who comes to do her housework every day, Mrs. Lacey. The domestic drama element of the story stems from Mrs. Allen's sadness at not being able to have children. She imagines them in fleeting scenes, like snatches of a film, even crying when she dreams of the day her eldest boy will go off to boarding school.

Ms. Allen's sadness is contrasted with Mrs. Lacey's complaints about her own children, who make demands of her and treat her disrespectfully. The life in Mrs. Lacey's house fascinates Mrs. Allen, and Mrs. Lacey's children are vivid in her imagination although she has never actually seen them. Mrs. Lacey, however, envies Mrs. Allen her pretty house and clothes, her figure, and her freedom. The central conflict of the story occurs when Mrs. Lacey misses work because of nausea, suggesting that she might be pregnant again.

The story's climactic scene centers on Mrs. Lacey's husband coming to Mrs. Allen's house, concerned about his wife working too hard. When he tells Mrs. Allen that Mrs. Lacey can no longer come to the house in the evenings to care for Mrs. Allen's

children while she and her husband go out to parties, Mrs. Allen knows that Mrs. Lacey has been lying to her husband and has been sneaking out to the pub in the evenings to drink with other men. She does not tell Mr. Lacey this, only promising not to ask his wife to baby-sit in the evenings again. When Mr. Lacey leaves, Mrs. Allen begins to blush and she goes to the mirror to study "with great interest this strange phenomenon."

OTHER MAJOR WORKS

LONG FICTION: *At Mrs. Lippincote's*, 1946; *Palladina*, 1946; *A View of the Harbor*, 1947; *A Wreath of Roses*, 1949; *A Game of Hide and Seek*, 1951; *The Sleeping Beauty*, 1953; *Angel*, 1957; *In a Summer Season*, 1961; *The Soul of Kindness*, 1964; *The Wedding Group*, 1968; *Mrs. Palfrey at the Claremont*, 1971; *Blaming*, 1976.

BIBLIOGRAPHY

Baldwin, Dean. "The English Short Story in the Fifties." In *The English Short Story 1945-1980*, edited by Dennis Vannata. New York: Twayne, 1985. 34-74. Argues that "shaming nature," which is what the Matron does at the beginning of the story, is a good description of the theme of "A Red-Letter Day," for Tory is unable to connect with her son; she is the prototype of the modern parent—alienated, awkward, divorced—unable to say where she has failed.

Gillette, Jane Brown. "'Oh, What a Something Web We Weave': The Novels of Elizabeth Taylor." *Twentieth Century Literature* 35 (Spring, 1989): 94-112. Discusses Taylor's fiction in three stages: the early period, in which she is critical of the distortion of the imagination; the middle period, in which she moderates her criticism, and the later years, when she celebrates the creative imagination. Argues that Taylor struggles with two major paradoxes: the novelist's use of fiction to depict the real and the novelist's condemnation of egotistical isolation.

Grove, Robin. "From the Island: Elizabeth Taylor's Novels." *Studies in the Literary Imagination* 9 (1978): 79-95. Discusses the critical neglect of

Taylor's work. Argues that her books claim that watching the mind's ironies and reflections on itself is a natural and nourishing activity. Says that she is the funniest and the most poignant writer of her generation. Discusses the comic nature of her work.

Hicks, Granville. "Amour on the Thames." *Saturday Review* 44 (January 21, 1961): 62. Hicks compares Taylor to Jane Austen. Brief comments about her work generally, with more extended comments on *In a Summer Season*.

Kingham, Joanna. Introduction to *A Dedicated Man and Other Stories*. London: Virago Press, 1993. An article based on an interview with Taylor in 1971, in which she talks about when and why she started to write, her writing habits, her reactions to feminism, and the things that give her pleasure. Taylor's daughter talks about her childhood and her relationship with her mother.

Leclercq, Florence. *Elizabeth Taylor*. Boston: Twayne, 1985. In this general introduction to Taylor's work, Leclercq devotes one chapter to Taylor's short stories; says that what makes her stories so fascinating is her "crystallization of one particular 'moment of being'." Argues that her craft is more clearly defined in her stories than in her novels. Discusses her stories in three categories: small psychological dramas, social comedies, and anecdotes detached from social context.

Taylor, Elizabeth. "England." *Kenyon Review*, 1969, 469-73. In her contribution to this symposium on the short story, Taylor says some stories are nearer to poetry than the novel; others are like paintings, full of suggestion and atmosphere; the unity of the short story gives an impression of perfection, of being lifted into another world, instead of sinking into it, as one does with the novel.

Charles E. May

PETER TAYLOR

Born: Trenton, Tennessee: January 8, 1917
Died: Charlottesville, Virginia; November 2, 1994

PRINCIPAL SHORT FICTION

A Long Fourth and Other Stories, 1948
The Widows of Thornton, 1954
Happy Families Are All Alike, 1959
Miss Leonora When Last Seen and Fifteen Other Stories, 1963
The Collected Stories of Peter Taylor, 1968
In the Miro District and Other Stories, 1977
The Old Forest and Other Stories, 1985
The Oracle at Stoneleigh Court, 1993

OTHER LITERARY FORMS

In addition to his short fiction, Peter Taylor published the novels *A Woman of Means* (1950), *A Summons to Memphis* (1986), and *In the Tennessee Country* (1994), as well as plays. Several of his plays were performed at Kenyon College, and three of them have

been published separately; a collection of seven dramas was also published in 1973. Taylor was one of three editors of a memorial volume, *Randall Jarrell, 1914-1965* (1967).

ACHIEVEMENTS

The publication of *The Collected Stories of Peter Taylor* brought general acknowledgment that he was one of the most skillful practitioners of the modern short story in the United States. While his reputation prior to that volume had for the most part been limited to a fairly small circle of enthusiastic readers, the list of his awards indicates the respect in which he was always held by his peers. Taylor was honored twelve different times by inclusion in the annual volume of *The Best American Short Stories* and was included six times in the *O. Henry Award Stories*.

He was awarded a John Simon Guggenheim Memorial Foundation Fellowship (1950), a National Institute of Arts and Letters grant (1952), a Fulbright

Fellowship (1955), first prize from the O. Henry Memorial Awards (1959), an Ohioana Book Award (1960), a Ford Foundation Fellowship (1961), a Rockefeller Foundation grant (1964), second prize from the *Partisan Review-Dial* and a National Institute of Arts and Letters gold medal (1979), a Ritz Paris Hemingway Award and the PEN/Faulkner Award (1986), and a Pulitzer Prize (1987).

While acknowledging his admiration for the work of Anton Chekhov, Ivan Turgenev, and Henry James, Taylor has put his own unique mark on the short story. Much of his fiction is set in the South, recalling the work of William Faulkner and Flannery O'Connor, but he is less concerned with violence and moral themes than either of those writers, concentrating instead on social relationships and the inevitability of betrayal in the interactions between men and women.

BIOGRAPHY

Peter Hillsman Taylor grew up in middle-class circumstances in border states. His family moved to Nashville when he was seven, spent several years in St. Louis, and settled in Memphis when he was fifteen. Expected to follow his father and older brother into the practice of law, Taylor chose early to try to make his career as a writer. He studied with the poet Allen Tate. After a brief enrollment at Vanderbilt University, he preferred to follow the poet, editor, and teacher John Crowe Ransom to Kenyon College in Ohio. At Kenyon College, he was befriended by the poet and critic Randall Jarrell and shared a room with the poet Robert Lowell.

After service in the United States Army during World War II, Taylor took up teaching as a profession. Between 1945 and 1963, he held faculty appointments at Indiana State University and Ohio State University, and on three different occasions he was appointed to teaching positions at the University of North Carolina at Greensboro. In 1967, he accepted a professorship at the University of Virginia, where he remained until his retirement in 1984.

Success as a short-story writer came fairly early in his career. Prestigious magazines such as *The Southern Review* and *The New Republic* published some of his stories written while he was still in college, and

Peter Taylor (©Miriam Berkley)

his first recognition in *Best American Short Stories* came in 1941, just after his graduation from Kenyon College. By 1948, his work was appearing in *The New Yorker*, which over the next three decades would publish more than two dozen of his works. Popular success, however, waited until the publication of *A Summons to Memphis* in 1986. The novel was a bestseller and won for Taylor the Pulitzer Prize for fiction. One scholar has hypothesized that Taylor saw this as a means of gaining validation for his short stories, the genre he considered more demanding of real artistry. Taylor died on November 2, 1994, in Charlottesville, Virginia.

ANALYSIS

The art of Peter Taylor is ironic and subtle. In a typical story, the narrator or point-of-view character is an observer, perhaps a member of a community who remembers someone or something in the town's past that is puzzling or strange, or a character whose understanding of his or her life falls short of reality. In tone, the stories are deceptively simple and straightforward, masking their complex ironies in seemingly ordinary actions. Taylor does not experiment with form or structure in the manner of a Jorge Luis Borges or a Robert Coover, but his stories are not always about commonplace experience; the grotesque plays a major role in such stories as "The Fancy Woman" and "Venus, Cupid, Folly, and Time."

Low-keyed and rarely involving violent action, the stories are more complex in their effect than at first appears, often revealing more about the narrator or the society than about the character being described. Their settings are often in small towns or minor cities in the upper South, Tennessee or Missouri, places such as those where Taylor lived as a boy and young man. Familial relationships, including those between husband and wife, are often central. Racial and economic matters enter into many of the stories, but such major social issues are generally depicted in the context of the social interactions of ordinary people. Nevertheless, Taylor provides considerable insight into the effects of the radical changes that affected the South in the 1960's and 1970's.

"DEAN OF MEN"

Betrayal is a recurrent theme in Taylor's short fiction, and it is no accident that the story he chose to place first in *The Collected Stories of Peter Taylor* is the relatively late "Dean of Men," a recital of the history of the men in a family. The narrator, an older man and a successful academic, tries in the story to explain to his son the background of his career and his divorce from his first wife, the son's mother. The story unfolds by an examination of the past, in which the narrator's grandfather was a successful politician, governor of his state, and then United States senator. Younger men in his party convinced him to give up his Senate seat and run for governor again to save the party from a man he despised, and he agreed. It turned out that the plan was intended to get him out of his Senate seat. As a result, he gave up politics in disgust and lived out his life as an embittered man.

The narrator's father was similarly betrayed by a man he had known all his life, who had installed the father on the board of a bank. During the Great Depression of the 1930's, the friend promised to come from New York to explain doubtful investments he had made, but he never arrived, and the father was left holding the bag. In his turn, the narrator, as a young instructor in a small college, was used by other faculty members to block an appointment they all feared, but when the move was avenged by its target, the young man was left to suffer the consequences alone. In the aftermath, he left to take another job, but his wife did not go with him; both later remarried. The story is the narrator's attempt to explain his life to the son who grew up without him. What the narrator is unaware of is the decline in the importance and stature of his family through the generations; his achievements and his place in life, of which he is unduly proud, are notably less important than those of his father, which were in turn significantly less than those of the grandfather. The entire family's history is flawed by the men's lack of initiative, their acceptance of what others do to them. This lack of self-knowledge on the part of a narrator will characterize Taylor's first-person fictions as late as "The Captain's Son."

"A SPINSTER'S TALE"

The narrator's or central figure's ignorance of her or his own attitudes is present from the beginning of Taylor's career, in his first published story, "A Spinster's Tale," a study of sexual repression. Taylor's only explicit investigation of sexual deviance would come much later, in "The Instruction of a Mistress," although "Venus, Cupid, Folly, and Time" contains strong overtones of incest. In "A Spinster's Tale," the narrator, the spinster of the title, is a woman whose youth was blighted by her fear of an old drunk who often passed the house in which she lived with her father and brother. As she tells the story, it is clear that her fear of "Mr. Speed" is a transference of her inadmissible attraction to her older brother, who also drinks, often and to excess. She is unaware that her irrational fear is really fear of any kind of departure from the most repressed kinds of behavior. In the old man, drunkenness is revolting; in her brother, she fears it only because her dead mother had told the young man that he would go to hell if he continued, but her brother's antic behavior when drunk exercises an attraction on her that she struggles to deny. In her old age, she still has revealing dreams laden with sexual implications. The betrayal in this story, of which she is only dimly aware, is the narrator's calling the police to haul away Mr. Speed when he stumbles onto their lawn during a driving rainstorm. She acknowledges late in life that she had acted "with courage, but without wisdom."

"WHAT YOU HEAR FROM 'EM?"

Betrayal of one kind or another seems to be inevitable in the relations between races, especially as those relations undergo the changes brought about by the Civil Rights movement and the push for integration. Since most of Taylor's stories are set in the South of the 1930's and 1940's, those relations are often between masters and servants, but that will change in the later tales. "What You Hear from 'Em?" is written from the point of view of an old black servant, Aunt Munsie, who lives in retirement, raising pigs and dogs and a few chickens. Her only real interest is in the lives of the two white men she reared when their mother died, and the question she addresses to people she meets in her daily rounds asks when they will return to the small town where she still lives. Their visits to her, bringing wives and children and eventually grandchildren, do not matter to Aunt Munsie; things will not be right until they again live in Thornton, a Nashville suburb. The betrayal is by the two men. Worried by her refusal to acknowledge automobiles or traffic rules as she goes through town collecting slop for her pigs, they arrange for an ordinance to be enacted that will forbid pig farming within the town limits. Aunt Munsie knows what they have done; she sells her pigs and loses her individuality, becoming a kind of parody of an old former servant.

"A WIFE OF NASHVILLE"

A different kind of betrayal and a different kind of response occur in another early story, "A Wife of Nashville." On the surface, this is a story about a marriage between John R. and Helen Ruth Lovell, in some ways a typical southern couple. He has succeeded in the insurance business, but he has spent much of his time over the years with other businessmen, hunting and traveling. Helen Ruth, as a result, has been occupied with rearing her children, and her chief companions over the years have been the black women who have cooked and cleaned for her: Jane Blackemore, when they were first married; Carrie,

during the time their two younger boys were born; Sarah, who at the age of sixty-eight left for Chicago and a new marriage; and Jess, hired during the Depression and the most durable and helpful of them all.

"A Wife of Nashville," however, is only partly about the marriage and the rearing of a family. It becomes clear as the story develops that Helen Ruth's genuine emotional life has increasingly been centered on her relationships with her servants and that they have been an integral part of the family. Jess, who does not drive a car herself, is essential to the boys' learning to drive, a symbol of their adulthood. In the end, she concocts a scene to explain her leaving the family; Helen Ruth knows that the explanation is false and that Jess and a friend are leaving Nashville for what they think is a more glamorous life in California. The husband and sons are shocked and resentful at the way they think Helen Ruth has been treated by Jess; Helen Ruth herself, however, rejects their sympathy and refuses to share their anger. It is clear that she wishes she had a means of escape, even one as improbable as that taken by Jess and her friend. On another level, it is clear also that she, unlike the men in the family, recognizes the social changes that are under way, changes that will alter the ways in which the races will survive. Other stories having to do with difficult marital relations were written throughout Taylor's career and include the early "Cookie," "Reservations," and "The Elect."

"MISS LEONORA WHEN LAST SEEN"

Perhaps the story most typical of Taylor's work, and one of the most powerful, is the one he chose to conclude *The Collected Stories of Peter Taylor*, "Miss Leonora When Last Seen." Narrated by one of the middling-successful men who populate this fiction, a small-town druggist, the story operates on several levels. It encompasses the narrator's sadness at having to carry bad news to the woman who was his teacher and who had encouraged him to aspire to greater things than he was able to achieve. At the same time, it is a story about a town's revenge on Miss Leonora's family, the wealthiest and most powerful residents of the town; over the years, they had prevented every "improvement" that might have brought business and "progress" to Thomasville, using their influence to keep out the railroad, the asylum, and other projects that would have changed the town. Most of them moved away, but they retained the home place, and they continued to exercise their influence. Now the town has decided to condemn the old manor house in which Miss Leonora lives in order to build a new high school. The irony that Miss Leonora had been a superb teacher in the old school is not lost on the narrator.

More important, "Miss Leonora When Last Seen" shows the mixed blessings and curses of the old ways and of the changes that are coming to the "New South." The old ways were autocratic and sometimes unfair, and they depended upon a servant class descended from slaves, such as the blacks who still live on Miss Leonora's place. Modernity, however, may not be much of an improvement; the new high school is being pushed as a final attempt to avoid the supposed horrors of racial integration. The narrator is caught between these times and has nothing to look to for support.

While these elements are at work, and the narrator is showing his own lack of understanding of Miss Leonora, the story is presenting a picture of an eccentric but fascinating individual who has lived in Thomasville all her life, teaching, trying to inspire the young men who were her favorites to achievement, and living close to the blacks who still reside on the family property, which she has inherited. In her retirement, she has taken to traveling by car, driving always at night in an open convertible, wearing one of two strange costumes, and stopping at "tourist homes," which were the motels of the time. Informed of the town's decision, she has taken to the road. Postcards come from surrounding states, but "She seems to be orbiting her native state of Tennessee." There is no sign that she will ever return; the old ways are indeed dead, and those who lived in the old way are anachronisms.

"THE OLD FOREST"

"The Old Forest" is a good example of Taylor's interest in the tensions between the old and new South. The story's action takes place in Memphis in 1937, although the story is told more than forty years later by Nat, the central character. Nat relates how in

the 1930's a young man in Memphis, even if he was engaged, might continue to go out with the bright young women he and his friends jokingly called *demimondaines*. These were intelligent young women who had good jobs, read good books, and attended concerts and plays. Nevertheless, they were not quite in the social class of Nat and his friends. The two groups went out for their mutual amusement without expecting long term commitments, either sexual or matrimonial. Young men like Nat intended to marry duller girls of their own class who lived by the standards of the Memphis Country Club. Nat says that the *demimondaines* were at least two generations ahead of themselves in their sexual freedom, for although they did not usually sleep with Nat and his friends, they often entered sexual relationships with men they truly loved.

Although Nat is already working for his father's cotton firm, he is also studying Latin in a lackadaisical way at the local college. His family ridicules his interest in Horace's *Odes*, but he enjoys the distinction it brings him among his friends, even though he is nearly failing the course. This particular Saturday, about a week before Nat's December wedding to Caroline Braxton, he invites Lee Ann Deehart, his "other" girl, to come out to the college with him while he studies for a test. On snow-packed roads in the primeval forest near the Mississippi, they have a car accident. Nat is slightly hurt and hardly notices that Lee Ann has climbed out of the car and disappeared in the snow and virgin forest. When she does not return to her boardinghouse that evening, Nat knows he must confess the affair to Caroline, who is surprisingly understanding and agrees that he must find her.

Lee Ann's friends know where she is, but Nat soon realizes that she is deliberately hiding from him, and he fears the scandal when the story hits the newspapers. Especially he fears that Caroline will break off their engagement. In the end, Caroline is the one who finds Lee Ann and discovers her motives for hiding, motives which ironically involve her own fear of publicity and the identification of her family.

Throughout, Nat contrasts the Memphis of 1937 with the present Memphis and the two sorts of girls represented by Lee Ann and Caroline. Typically, Taylor invites the reader to take a slightly different view from Nat's. For all her supposed dullness, Caroline uses real intelligence in finding Lee Ann and real compassion in responding to her crisis. Moreover, ten years later she supports Nat's decision to leave cotton for a career teaching college. Caroline's own analysis of what happened, however, is straight from the old forest of Memphis convention. She has not set herself free, she says, like Lee Ann, so in protecting Nat she has protected for herself "the power of a woman in a man's world," the only power she can claim.

OTHER MAJOR WORKS

LONG FICTION: *A Woman of Means*, 1950; *A Summons to Memphis*, 1986; *In the Tennessee Country*, 1994.

PLAYS: *Tennessee Day in Saint Louis: A Comedy*, pr. 1956; *A Stand in the Mountains*, pb. 1965; *Presences: Seven Dramatic Pieces*, pb. 1973.

EDITED TEXT: *Randall Jarrell, 1914-1965*, 1967 (with Robert Lowell and Robert Penn Warren).

BIBLIOGRAPHY

Baumbach, Jonathan. *Modern and Contemporaries: New Masters of the Short Story*. New York: Random House, 1968. Includes a brief analysis of Taylor's place in the development of the post-World War II short story.

Kramer, Victor A., Patricia A. Bailey, Carol G. Dana, and Carl H. Griffin. *Andrew Lytle, Walker Percy, Peter Taylor: A Reference Guide*. Boston: G. K. Hall, 1983. One of the later and most complete bibliographies of Taylor's work and the reviews and criticism.

Oates, Joyce Carol. "Realism of Distance, Realism of Immediacy." *The Southern Review* 7 (Winter, 1971): 295-313. A novelist's sensitive apprecia-tion of other writers, including Taylor.

Robinson, Clayton. "Peter Taylor." In *Literature of Tennessee*, edited by Ray Will-banks. Rome, Ga.: Mercer University Press, 1984. This article relates Taylor's fiction to his early years and explains his mother's influence on his techniques and subject matter.

Robison, James C. *Peter Taylor: A Study of the Short Fiction*. Boston: Twayne, 1987. This volume not only is the only extended study of Taylor's short stories but also contains two interviews with the author as well as essays by a number of critics. Robison's comments are occasionally wide of the mark, but he is an earnest and generally intelligent reader of Taylor's work. Essential reading.

Samarco, C. Vincent. "Taylor's 'The Old Forest.'" *The Explicator* 57 (Fall, 1998): 51-53. Argues that the car accident represents a collision between Nat Ramsey's pursuit of knowledge and the history of his upbringing within the narrow walls of privilege.

Stephens, C. Ralph, and Lynda B. Salamon, eds. *The Craft of Peter Taylor*. Tuscaloosa: The University of Alabama Press, 1995. A collection of essays on Taylor's work, including discussions of his poetics, his focus on place, his relationship to the Agrarians, his treatment of absence, his role in American pastoralism, and such stories as "The Other Times," "The Old Forest," and "The Hand of Emmagene."

Taylor, Peter. "Interview with Peter Taylor." Interview by J. H. E. Paine. *Journal of the Short Story in English* 9 (Fall, 1987): 14-35. The most extended interview with Taylor, dealing with his techniques and influences.

John M. Muste, updated by
Ann D. Garbett

WILLIAM MAKEPEACE THACKERAY

Born: Calcutta, India; July 18, 1811
Died: London, England; December 24, 1863

PRINCIPAL SHORT FICTION

The Yellowplush Papers, 1837-1838
Some Passages in the Life of Major Gahagan,
   1838-1839
Stubb's Calendar: Or, The Fatal Boots, 1839
Barber Cox and the Cutting of His Comb, 1840
The Bedford-Row Conspiracy, 1840
Comic Tales and Sketches, 1841 (2 volumes)
*The Confessions of George Fitz-Boodle, and Some
   Passages in the Life of Major Gahagan*, 1841-
   1842
Men's Wives, 1843 (as George Savage Fitz-Boodle)
A Legend of the Rhine, 1845 (as M. A. Titmarsh)
Jeame's Diary: Or, Sudden Wealth, 1846
The Snobs of England, by One of Themselves,
   1846-1847 (later as *The Book of Snobs*, 1848,
   1852)
Mrs. Perkin's Ball, 1847 (as M. A. Titmarsh)
"Our Street," 1848 (as M. A. Titmarsh)
A Little Dinner at Timmins's, 1848
Doctor Birch and His Young Friends, 1849 (as M.
   A. Titmarsh)
The Kickleburys on the Rhine, 1850 (as M. A.
   Titmarsh)
A Shabby Genteel Story and Other Tales, 1852
*The Rose and the Ring: Or, The History of Prince
   Giglio and Prince Bulbo*, 1855 (as M. A.
   Titmarsh)
*Memoirs of Mr. Charles J. Yellowplush [with] The
   Diary of C. Jeames De La Pluche, Esqr.*, 1856

OTHER LITERARY FORMS

William Makepeace Thackeray published seven novels during his lifetime, and the unfinished *Denis Duval* was printed posthumously in 1864. *Vanity Fair* (1847-1848) and *The Luck of Barry Lyndon* (1844), which was filmed, are considered his masterpieces, both of them featuring memorable protagonists who exhibit both heroic and venal qualities. Thackeray was a prolific contributor to periodicals of parodies, satires, humorous sketches, essays, reviews, and articles. He was a correspondent for many newspapers and an editor of several magazines. He also issued popular Christmas annuals for many years.

ACHIEVEMENTS

In the last decade of his life, William Makepeace Thackeray was considered one of Great Britain's most powerful novelists. His novels, taken together, form an appraisal of English social history and morals between 1690 and 1863. The lasting value of both the novels and his shorter works, however, rests in their huge cast of vivid characters, ranging from despicable, amoral scoundrels through attractive rascals to truly noble heroes, male and female, from every class. What brings these characters to energetic life is Thackeray's command of style and narrative technique and his gift for satire. Thackeray experimented with every sort of first-person narration. By manipulating his various personae, he created subtle distinctions in tone. Even when Thackeray employed an omniscient narrator, he was always a mask, distinct from the author. For his Victorian audience, this mediating voice was one of the pleasures of reading Thackeray, who built on the oral nature of storytelling. To moderns, however, the tendency to tell rather than to dramatize can seem an intrusive disruption of illusion, and thus, they sometimes do not appreciate the very commentary that made him so popular in his own time.

Almost as valuable is the impression that remains of Thackeray's personality. He was a man of good will and a loving father, financially improvident but generous and kindly. Even the difficult times in his own life he reshaped in his works into positive experiences. As a writer and talented caricaturist, he deftly skewered pretension and folly where he found them; as a man, he seemed to view human nature with charity and tolerance, above all affirming what he saw as its inherent good sense.

BIOGRAPHY

Born in India, William Makepeace Thackeray was the only son of Richmond and Ann Becher Thackeray. His grandfathers on both sides of the family had been with the Indian civil service, and after his father died in September, 1815, he was sent to school in England. He attended schools in Southampton, Chiswick, and Charterhouse; the bullying he received there was later fictionalized. One of his first pen names was Michael Angelo Titmarsh, adopted because his nose was broken by a classmate, as Michelangelo's had been three centuries earlier. He called his school "Slaughterhouse" for the brutality he endured there. His mother remarried, and he spent 1828 in Devon with her and Major-General Henry Carmichael-Smythe. From February, 1829, to July, 1830, he attended Trinity College, Cambridge. He traveled in Germany until May, 1831, and met Johann Wolfgang von Goethe in Weimar. He briefly studied law in England. In 1832, he spent four months in Paris, and from 1834 he began training as a professional artist since he had always had a talent

William Makepeace Thackeray (Library of Congress)

for drawing. On August 20, 1836, he married Isabel Shawe, whose neurotic, domineering mother became the model for all the terrible mothers-in-law in Thackeray's fiction. Their daughter Anne was born in June, 1837; she later became a novelist and the editor of her father's letters to Edward Fitzgerald, and of his complete works. She married Sir Richmond Ritchie of the India office. Jane was born in July, 1838, and died eight months later. Harriet, born in May, 1840, was to marry Sir Leslie Stephen in 1867. In 1840, Isabel became so depressed that she attempted suicide, and in 1846 she was declared incurably insane. The fortune Thackeray had inherited was dissipated by 1833, and the professional gamblers who swindled him out of his money figure in several of his stories. His stepfather invested in a paper so that Thackeray could write for it, but it failed, leaving them financially ruined. He wrote for twenty-four different periodicals between 1830 and 1844 trying to support his family, even applying to Charles Dickens for the job of illustrating the *Pickwick Papers* (1836-1837). Finally, the publication of *Vanity Fair* in 1848 made him a public figure. He began a series of public lectures which took him twice to the United States, from 1852 to 1853 and from 1855 to 1856. He died at the age of fifty-two on Christmas Eve, 1863.

ANALYSIS

William Makepeace Thackeray's "Yellowplush" was first introduced in *Fraser's* in November, 1837, and was republished in the United States and translated into German. In 1845, the footman was revived in *Punch*, having been promoted to Charles James De La Pluche, Esq., through successful speculation in railway shares.

"MISS SHUM'S HUSBAND"

On his first appearance in "Miss Shum's Husband," Yellowplush tells how he got his name. His mother, who always introduced him as her nephew, named him for the livery of a famous coachman, Yellowplush. Although he was illegitimate, he has gentlemanly tastes, and his cockney speech is spiced with affectations. His employer, Frederic Altamont, takes rooms in a crowded house in John Street. The footman reports that they breakfast from his master's tea leaves and dine on slices of meat cut from his joints, but Frederic endures this to be near his loved one Mary. In the next episode and with his next employer, Yellowplush has descended to petty thievery (which he calls his "perquisites") himself. During his courtship, Altamont refuses to reveal where he works but assures Mary that he is honest and urges her never to question him about what it would cause her misery to learn.

After their marriage, Frederic and Mary move to an elegantly furnished house in Islington, from which he mysteriously disappears each day. After their baby is born, Mrs. Shum becomes a daily visitor. This mother of twelve daughters who spent her time reading novels on the drawing room sofa, scolding, screaming, and having hysterics is the first of the terrible mothers-in-law so prominent in Thackeray's fiction, including Mrs. Gam, Mrs. Gashleigh, Mrs. Cuff, Mrs. Crum, Lady Kicklebury, and Mrs. Baynes. They are always snobbish, interfering, and domineering. Mrs. Shum undermines the mutual affection in her daughter's household by implanting suspicions. "Where does his money come from? What if he is a murderer, or a housebreaker, or a forger?" When Mary answers that he is too kind to be any of those things, Mrs. Shum suggests that he must be a bigamist. At this moment, as Mary faints, Mrs. Shum has hysterics, the baby squalls, the servants run upstairs with hot water, and Frederic returns. He expels Mrs. Shum, double-locks the door, and tries to appease his wife without exposing his secret. His in-laws set up a spy network and finally discover that he is a crossing sweeper. Frederic sells his house and starts his new life abroad. His footman renders his snobbish judgment of the whole affair:

> Of cors, I left his servis. I met him, a few years after, at Badden-Badden, where he and Mrs. A. were much respectid, and pass for pipple of propaty.

The satire depends for its effect on the dissonance between the social pretensions and the misspellings in which they are conveyed. In Victorian England, a gentleman did not work for a living, and a footman conscious of his position could not work for a laborer. He could "pass" abroad, because foreigners were unable to tell the difference between inherited and earned money. Obviously, only income from property qualified one to enter society.

"DIMOND CUT DIMOND"

"Dimond Cut Dimond" is about Yellowplush's next master, who is penniless but titled. He is the Honorable Algernon Percy Deuceace, fifth son of the Earl of Crabs. If he had been a common man, he would have been recognized as a swindler, but since he is a gentleman, with his family tree prominently displayed in his sitting room, his gambling is considered acceptable. Dawkins, just out of Oxford, moves in with his entire fortune of six thousand pounds to establish himself as a barrister. Deuceace manipulates an introduction by tripping the servant carrying Dawkins's breakfast tray. He substitutes a pastry he has purchased for this purpose with an elaborate letter, claiming it had been sent to him by an aristocratic friend. Once they are acquainted, he suggests a game of cards, which he deliberately loses as a setup.

The scheme is complicated by a second con man, Richard Blewitt, who tells Deuceace that Dawkins is his pigeon to pluck and that he means to strip this one alone since he already has him securely in his claws. Deuceace makes a deal to split the gains; after he wins, however, he coldly announces to Blewitt, who has come for his share, that he never had any intention of keeping his promise. Blewitt, "stormed, groaned, bellowed, swore" but gets nothing, and the villain escapes to Paris, telling Yellowplush that he can come too if he likes.

Thackeray, as a student, had lost large sums to such gamblers. The insolent criminality with which Deuceace robs both Dawkins and Blewitt is not condemned by his footman, who is engaged in robberies of his own. "There wasn't a bottle of wine that we didn't get a glass out of . . . we'd the best pickens out of the dinners, the livvers of the fowls, the forcemit balls out of the soup, the egs from the sallit . . . you may call this robbery—nonsince—it's only our rights—a suvvant's purquizzits." In the eyes of the footman, the cold-blooded malice of his master is superior to the blustering passion of Blewitt.

"FORING PARTS"

The next episode, "Foring Parts," tells how

Deuceace has posted a sign on his door, "Back at seven," and departed, owing the laundress. The footman learns that to gain respect in France, one must be rude. His master had abused the waiters, abused the food, and abused the wine, and the more abusive he was, the better service he got; on his example, the footman also practices insolence because people liked being insulted by a lord's footman. Deuceace writes to Lord Crabs for his allowance; but the answer comes back that, since all London knows of Deuceace's winnings, could he instead lend Lord Crabs some money. He encloses clippings from the newspapers about the transaction. Shortly afterward, a retraction appears in the paper for which Deuceace had sent a ten-pound note, with his compliments. The narrator comments that he had already sent a tenner before it came out, although he cannot think why.

"CONFESSIONS OF FITZ-BOODLE"

"Dorothea" appeared in 1843 along with "Miss Loewe" and "Ottilia" as part of "Confessions of Fitz-Boodle." Since their narrator is a leisured gentleman, these stories differ in pace and tone from the Yellowplush series; Fitz-Boodle's aristocratic birth and classical education enable him to make social commentary of a different sort. The story turns on his failure to have learned dancing at Slaughterhouse school, where he learned little that was useful. He adds ruefully, however, that such is the force of habit that he would probably send his sons there, were he to have any. In a series of semiscenes typical of Thackeray's style, Fitz-Boodle describes the many dancing lessons he has taken from various instructors in London, in Paris, and finally in Germany, from Springbock, the leader of the Kalbsbraten ballet.

The continual shifting of temporal perspectives is also typical of Thackeray. He interrupts chronology for an amiable digression which meanders back to the starting point and also digresses into the future consequences of an action, or presents retrospective memories of an even from years later. For example, the discursive soliloquy on dancing is suddenly interrupted by "The reader, perhaps, remembers the brief appearance of his Highness, the Duke." This is followed by an elaborate description of the Duke's pump, the whole point of which is that Speck, who designed it,

is Dorothea's father. He ingratiates himself into the family by sketching the pump and is consequently introduced to the beauty, whose charms inspire him to classical allusions. Then the narrative redoubles again:

> In thus introducing this lovely creature in her ball-costume, I have been somewhat premature, and had best go back to the beginning of the history of my acquaintance with her.

Next follows a history of the Speck family leading up to the narrator's first glimpse of her, and the narrative resumes.

The next semiscene, midway between summary and dramatization, is characteristic of Thackeray's refusal to disguise his fictions, to mount them dramatically. His narrators set the stage but do not retire from it; they remain to pose alternatives, suggest possibilities, speculate, and muse expatiatingly. Thackeray constructs a model which the reader must then fill in; by concealing as much as he discloses, he forces the reader's participation in completing his paradigm, using a pronoun shift to the second person which asks "you" to participate. Thackeray appeals to universality (an eighteenth century device probably derived from his study of Henry Fielding, whom he had both imitated and parodied), and the interjected "I have often said" is a strategy found throughout his work. *Vanity Fair* contains countless "Captain Rawdon often said" interspersings, a technique that allows the author to interpolate commentary and to leave the rest to the reader's imagination. The story concludes with the ball at which Fitz-Boodle has managed to sign up Dorothea for a waltz, and his subsequent fall on the dance floor.

"MR. AND MRS. FRANK BERRY"

"Mr. and Mrs. Frank Berry" is part of the story sequence called *Men's Wives* which first appeared in *Fraser's* in March, 1843. In two parts, it shows Frank as a boy bravely battling the school bully and being hero-worshiped by the narrator; then, in a later encounter, he is seen as a uxorious husband who has shaved off his mustache and grown fat and pale. Part 1 is called "The Fight at Slaughter House." After the preliminaries, as the air resounds with cries of "To it,

Berry!" there is a typical Thackerayan footnote, "As it is very probable that many fair readers may not approve of the extremely forcible language in which the combat is depicted, I beg them to skip it and pass on to the next chapter."

This chapter is entitled "The Combat at Versailles," and this time the heroic Frank is not the victor. Mrs. Berry has "a rigid and classical look" and wears a miniature of her father, Sir George Catacomb, around her thin neck. Her genteel coldness is aptly caught in her maiden name, Miss Angelica Catacomb. She spends her time making notes in the Baronetage on her pedigree, and she entertains her guest with an icy silence. After several pages about the other guests, Thackeray provides the apostrophe that, if there had been anything interesting, "I should have come out with it a couple of pages since, nor have kept the public looking for so long a time at the dishcovers and ornaments of the table. But the simple fact must now be told, that there was nothing of the slightest importance at this repast."

The narrator then tells how Angelica controlled her husband's smoking, drinking, and conversation. The narrator decides to rescue Frank from his captivity and orders claret, which, after sufficient quantity has been consumed, leads to riotous singing. He feels free enough to complain, when he is inebriated, about having to spend his evenings reading poetry or missionary tracts out loud, about having to take physics whenever she insists, about never being allowed to dine out, and about not daring even to smoke a cigar. In a moment of daring, the narrator accepts an invitation for the next night, but he is not permitted to keep the appointment, and the next time he meets Frank, the latter sheepishly crosses over to the other side of the street; he is wearing galoshes. The boy who was courageous enough to beat the school bully has turned into a henpecked husband.

OTHER MAJOR WORKS

LONG FICTION: *Catherine: A Story*, 1839-1840 (as Ikey Solomons, Jr.); *The History of Samuel Titmarsh and the Great Hoggarty Diamond*, 1841 (later as *The Great Hoggarty Diamond*, 1848); *The Luck of Barry Lyndon: A Romance of the Last Century*, 1844; *Vanity Fair: A Novel Without a Hero*, 1847-1848; *The History of Pendennis: His Fortunes and Misfortunes, His Friends and His Greatest Enemy*, 1848-1850; *Rebecca and Rowena: A Romance upon Romance*, 1850 (as M. A. Titmarsh); *The History of Henry Esmond, Esquire, a Colonel in the Service of Her Majesty Q. Anne*, 1852 (3 volumes); *The Newcomes: Memoirs of a Most Respectable Family*, 1853-1855; *The Virginians: A Tale of the Last Century*, 1857-1859; *Lovel the Widower*, 1860; *The Adventures of Philip on His Way Through the World, Shewing Who Robbed Him, Who Helped Him, and Who Passed Him By*, 1861-1862; *Denis Duval*, 1864.

PLAY: *The Rose and the Ring*, pb. 1854.

POETRY: *The Chronicle of the Drum*, 1841.

NONFICTION: *The Paris Sketch Book*, 1840 (as M. A. Titmarsh, 2 volumes); *The Irish Sketch Book*, 1843 (as M. A. Titmarsh, 2 volumes); *Notes of a Journey from Cornhill to Grand Cairo, by Way of Lisbon, Athens, Constantinople and Jerusalem, Performed in the Steamers of the Penninsular and Oriental Company*, 1846 (as M. A. Titmarsh); *The English Humourists of the Eighteenth Century*, 1853; *Sketches and Travels in London*, 1856; *The Four Georges: Sketches of Manners, Morals, Court and Town Life*, 1860.

BIBLIOGRAPHY

Bloom, Harold, ed. *William Makepeace Thackeray.* New York: Chelsea House, 1987. A collection of essays on various aspects of Thackeray's fiction, including such issues and concepts as humor, realism, characterization, point of view, and irony.

Carey, John. *Thackeray: Prodigal Genius.* London: Faber & Faber, 1977. Carey's appreciation of Thackeray's "imaginative vitality," particularly as it is expressed in his earlier, shorter, largely satirical literary and journalistic work, provides the focus for this absorbing study. Many of Thackeray's major short works are discussed and analyzed in their chronological context.

Clarke, Michael M. *Thackeray and Women.* DeKalb: Northern Illinois University Press, 1995. Examines Thackeray's treatment of female characters. Includes bibliographical references and an index.

Dodds, John Wendell. *Thackeray: A Critical Portrait.* New York: Oxford University Press, 1941. This scholarly, twelve-chapter study of Thackeray's genius and the art of his fiction includes, particularly in chapter 3, "The Early Humorist and Story-Teller: 1838-1840," an assessment of his short satirical sketches and stories. A thorough index is useful. An important book in the canon of Thackeray criticism.

Fletcher, Robert P. "'The Foolishest of Existing Mortals': Thackeray, 'Gurlyle,' and the Character(s) of Fiction." *Clio* 24 (Winter, 1995): 113-125. Discusses Thomas Carlyle's and Thackeray's different conceptions of history and fiction. Claims that a contrast between Thackeray's and Carlyle's opinions on novels and knowledge uncovers the buried anxiety in Carlyle's emphatic preference for history over fiction.

Harden, Edgar F. *Thackeray the Writer: From Journalism to "Vanity Fair."* New York: St. Martin's Press, 1998. A thorough study of Thackeray's literary career.

Mudge, Isadore Gilbert, and M. Earl Sears. *A Thackeray Dictionary: The Characters and Short Stories Alphabetically Arranged.* 1910. Reprint. New York: Humanities Press, 1962. As the title indicates, this volume is an essential reference book for students of Thackeray's works. The "Chronological List of Novels and Stories" clarifies and lists the individual and collected works titles under which many of Thackeray's short sketches and stories were published and republished; "Synopses" provides invaluable annotations on the contents of all Thackeray's works, short and long. The main "Dictionary" section is an alphabetical reference book for Thackeray's characters.

Peters, Catherine. *Thackeray's Universe: Shifting Worlds of Imagination and Reality.* New York: Oxford University Press, 1987. The purpose of this thorough, fresh, intelligent, and readable twelve-chapter study is, in the author's words, "to identify the raw materials, but to be aware that the finished work is a work of art, and not a covert autobiography." In defining what Thackeray's writings owed both to his life and to his particular genius, Peters provides invaluable insights. Short works such as *Men's Wives* and *The Yellowplush Papers* are analyzed, and individual short pieces are discussed in context. A thorough index helps readers to search out discussion of individual works.

Welsh, Alexander, ed. *Thackeray: A Collection of Critical Essays.* Englewood Cliffs, N.J.: Prentice-Hall, 1968. Thirteen essays by a selection of the foremost Thackeray scholars are a useful introduction to the student of Thackeray's works, though discussion of the short works is included only in the analyses of Thackeray's narrative techniques and style.

Wheatley, James H. *Patterns in Thackeray's Fiction.* Cambridge, Mass.: MIT Press, 1969. This volume is a lucid, readable study of the development of Thackeray's techniques and concerns as a fiction writer. Follows his literary career from chapter 1, "Early Parody," through chapter 6, "Later Fiction: The Sentiment of Reality." Two works of short fiction, *The Yellowplush Papers* and *A Shabby Genteel Story and Other Tales*, are discussed at some length in chapter 2, "Developments from Parody." The "Works Cited" guides the reader to other relevant critical sources.

Ruth Rosenberg, updated by
Jill Rollins

DYLAN THOMAS

Born: Swansea, Wales; October 27, 1914
Died: New York, New York; November 9, 1953

PRINCIPAL SHORT FICTION

Portrait of the Artist as a Young Dog, 1940
Selected Writings of Dylan Thomas, 1946
A Child's Christmas in Wales, 1954
Quite Early One Morning, 1954
Adventures in the Skin Trade and Other Stories,
   1955
A Prospect of the Sea and Other Stories, 1955
Early Prose Writings, 1971
The Followers, 1976
The Collected Stories, 1984

OTHER LITERARY FORMS

In addition to his short fiction, Dylan Thomas published several collections of poetry, including *Eighteen Poems* (1934), *Twenty-five Poems* (1936), *New Poems* (1943), and *Collected Poems: 1934-1952* (1952). *Under Milk Wood* (1954) is a verse drama that affectionately portrays a day in the life of the inhabitants of a tiny Welsh fishing village. Thomas also wrote many screenplays, most notably *The Doctor and the Devils* (1953) and a comic detective novel *The Death of the King's Canary* (1976).

ACHIEVEMENTS

The lyricism of Dylan Thomas's poetry probably constitutes his most powerful contribution to twentieth century verse and is also a notable characteristic of his prose. One source of that lyric quality is surely Thomas's Welsh origins and his awareness of the depth and richness of Welsh poetic traditions. He also paid homage to Wales in his short fiction, lovingly (if sometimes satirically) describing it in works such as *A Child's Christmas in Wales* and in the stories that make up *Portrait of the Artist as a Young Dog* and *Adventures in the Skin Trade*. In those works appear characters and events from his childhood in Swansea and his early work as a news reporter.

His poetry won the "Poet's Corner" Prize of the *Sunday Referee* in 1934, the Blumenthal Poetry Prize in 1938, the Levinson Poetry Prize in 1945, and Foyle's Poetry Prize (for *Collected Poems: 1934-1952*) in 1952. Thomas also received a grant from The Authors' Society Traveling Scholarship Fund in 1947.

BIOGRAPHY

Dylan Marlais Thomas's father, John David Thomas, was an embittered schoolmaster, emotionally remote from his son, but he possessed a fine library of contemporary fiction and poetry in which his son was free to read. His father's distance and unhappiness may have made Thomas more susceptible to the indulgences of his mother, Florence Williams Thomas. It is her family who appears in Thomas's work as the chapel-going farmers, and it is her oldest sister whose husband owned the farm near Llangain where the young Thomas often spent summer vacations. Thomas also had a sister, Nancy, nine years older than he. The family home at 5 Cwmdonkin Drive, Swansea, was across the street from the park which sometimes appears in his poems ("The Hunchback in the Park," for example). Likewise the beautiful Gower peninsula and his aunt's farm appeared in his adult work as subjects for his poetry and memoirs (most notably in "Fern Hill"). Thomas's early life in Wales furnished him with material that surfaced in his work for the rest of his life.

Thomas was a lackadaisical student at Swansea Grammar School. Talented in English, he edited the school magazine while he was there, and he began to keep the notebooks that reveal his early attempts to form his style, but he gave little attention to subjects that did not interest him. It was at school that he began his friendship with Dan Jones with whom he composed poems and played elaborate word games. In adulthood, Jones became Dr. Daniel Jones, musical composer and editor of Thomas's work.

Thomas left school in 1931 to work—not very successfully—as a reporter for the *South Wales Evening Post*, a job which gave him material for many of his stories. During the next three years, he also experienced a period of exciting poetic growth, learning about Welsh poets of the past and producing much work of his own. Late in 1934, he moved to London where he cultivated a conscious bohemianism and began to gain a reputation as drinker, brilliant conversationalist, and poet of merit. Through the rest of his life, the two parts of his personality—the serious poet who cared about his craft and the hard-drinking bohemian—were at odds in dominating his behavior.

In 1937, he married Caitlin Macnamara, a strong-willed, passionate dancer with whom he was intensely in love. They had three children—Llewelyn, Aeron, and Colm. During the war, Thomas, a conscientious objector, wrote mostly prose. Afterward, his life alternated between London and the Welsh fishing village of Laugharne, where he lived with his family and did his most profitable work. In London, when he was in need of money (as he usually was), he often worked for the British Broadcasting Corporation, but there too, his drinking began to cause him more and more troubles.

In 1950, he made the first of four tours to the United States, reading his work at colleges and universities. It was an enormous success, but it documented his reputation as an "outlaw" poet—a hard drinker and womanizer who spent the proceeds of his readings on women and whiskey while his family went without necessities. The subsequent tours intensified that legend. He died of alcohol poisoning in St. Vincent's Hospital in New York City in 1953.

ANALYSIS

Dylan Thomas's ten stories in *Portrait of the Artist as a Young Dog* are charming reminiscences of his relatives, school friends, and neighbors in the town where he grew up. Their wit and accessibility made them immediately popular, in contrast to the dark, subjective stories he had written prior to 1938, for which he had difficulty finding a publisher. In March, 1938, he wrote to Vernon Watkins that "A Visit to Grandpa's" was "the first of a series of short, straightforward stories about Swansea." Published on March 10, 1939, in the *New English Weekly*, it told of a boy's waking up on a mild summer night to the sounds of

Dylan Thomas (CORBIS/Bettmann)

"gee-up and whoa" in the next room where his grandfather, wearing his red waistcoat with its brass buttons, is reining invisible horses. On their morning walks, the grandfather has expressed his wish not to be buried in the nearby churchyard. When he is missing a few days later, the entire village is summoned to go in search of him, and they find him on Carmarthen Bridge in his Sunday trousers and dusty tall hat on his way to Llangadock to be buried. They try to persuade him to come home to tea instead.

"THE PEACHES"

In "The Peaches," first published in the October, 1938, issue of *Life and Letters Today*, the naïve narrator tells of his spring holiday on a farm in Gorsehill. His uncle Jim drives him there in a green cart late one April evening, stopping for a drink at a public house. The squeal coming from the wicker basket he takes inside with him prepares the reader for the fact that cousin Gwilym will note that one of the pigs is missing the next day. The terror of being abandoned in a dark alley is assuaged by Aunt Annie's warm welcome of him later that night at the farmhouse. He enters, small, cold, and scared, as the clock strikes midnight, and is made to feel "among the shining and striking like a prince taking off his disguise." Next morning, Gwilym takes him to see the sow, who has only four pigs left. "He sold it to go on the drink," whispers Gwilym rebukingly. The boy imagines Jim transformed into a hungry fox: "I could see uncle, tall and sly and red, holding the writhing pig in his two hairy hands, sinking his teeth in its thigh, crunching its trotters up; I could see him leaning over the wall of the sty with the pig's legs sticking out of his mouth." Gwilym, who is studying to be a minister, takes him to the barn which he pretends is his chapel and preaches a thunderous sermon at him, after which he takes up a collection.

Next, the complication begins. Gwilym and Jim are told to dress up for Jack Williams, whose rich mother will bring him in an automobile from Swansea for a fortnight's visit. A tin of peaches has been saved from Christmas; "Mother's been keeping it for a day like this." Mrs. Williams, "with a jutting bosom and thick legs, her ankles swollen over her pointed shoes," sways into the parlor like a ship. Annie precedes her, anxiously tidying her hair, "clucking, fidgeting, excusing." (The string of participles is typical of Thomas's prose style; one sentence [in "Return Journey"] contains fifteen.) The rich guest declines refreshments. "I don't mind pears or chunks, but I can't bear peaches." The boys run out to frolic, climb trees, and play Indians in the bushes. After supper, in the barn, Gwilym demands confessions from them, and Jack begins to cry that he wants to go home. That night in bed, they hear Uncle Jim come in drunk and Annie quietly relating the events of the day, at which he explodes into thunderous anger: "Aren't peaches good enough for her!" At this, Jack sobs into his pillow. The next day Mrs. Williams arrives, sends the chauffeur for Jack's luggage, and drives off with him, as the departing car scatters the hens and the narrator waves good-bye.

Two aspects of the point of view are significant. The first, its tone, is what made all the stories so immediately beloved. The genial Chaucerian stance, which perceives and accepts eccentricities, which

notes and blesses all the peculiarities of humanity, is endearing without being sentimental, because the acuteness of the observations stays in significant tension with the nonjudgmental way in which they are recorded. This combination of acuity and benevolence, of sharpness and radiance, is the special quality of Thomas's humor. The second aspect of the author's style is its expansion and contraction, which indicates the view of a visionary poet. The narrator is both a homesick, cold, tired little boy, and "a royal nephew in smart town clothes, embraced and welcomed." The uncle is both a predatory fox and an impoverished farmer, as he sits in "the broken throne of a bankrupt bard." The splendid paradise where the narrator romps is simultaneously a poor, dirty "square of mud and rubbish and bad wood and falling stone, where a bucketful of old and bedraggled hens scratched and laid small eggs." The "pulpit" where Gwilym's inspired sermon is "cried to the heavens" in his deepest voice is a dusty, broken cart in an abandoned barn overrun with mice; but this decrepit building on a mucky hill becomes "a chapel shafted with sunlight," awesome with reverence as the "preacher's" voice becomes "Welsh and singing." The alternate aggrandizement and diminution of the perceptions energize the style as the lyric impulse wars with the satiric impulse in the narrator's voice.

"Patricia, Edith and Arnold"

The naïve narrator of the third of the *Portrait of the Artist as a Young Dog* stories, entitled "Patricia, Edith and Arnold," is totally engrossed in his imaginary engine, whose brake is "a hammer in his pocket" and whose fuel is replenished by invisible engineers. As he drives it about the garden, however, he is aware of his maid, Patricia, plotting with the neighbor's servant, Edith, to confront Arnold with the identical letters he wrote to both of them. The girls take the child to the park as it begins to snow; Arnold has been meeting Edith there on Fridays, and Patricia on Wednesdays. As the girls wait for Arnold in the shelter, the boy, disowning them, pretends he is a baker, molding loaves of bread out of snow.

Arnold Matthews, his hands blue with cold, wearing a checked cap but no overcoat, appears and tries to bluff it out. Loudly he says, "Fancy you two knowing each other." The boy rolls a snowman "with a lop-sided dirty head" smoking a pencil, as the situation grows more tense. When Arnold claims that he loves them both, Edith shakes her purse at him, the letters fall out all over the snow, and the snowman collapses. As the boy searches for his pencil, the girls insist that Arnold choose between them. Patricia turns her back, indignantly. Arnold gestures and whispers to Edith behind Patricia's back and then, out loud, chooses Patricia. The boy, bending over his snowman, finds his pencil driven through its head.

Later, during a discussion of lying, the boy tells Patricia that he saw Arnold lying to both of them, and the momentary truce, during which Patricia and Arnold have been walking arm in arm, is over. She smacks and pummels him as he staggers backward and falls. The boy says he has to retrieve the cap that he left near his snowman. He finds Arnold there, re-reading the letters that Edith dropped, but does not tell Patricia this. Later, as his frozen hands tingle and his face feels on fire, she comforts him until "the hurting is gone." She acknowledges her pain and her own by saying, "Now we've all had a good cry today." The story achieves its effects through the child's detachment. Totally absorbed in his play, he registers the behavior of the adults, participating in their sorrows without fully comprehending them. In spite of his age-appropriate egocentricity and his critical remarks about her girth (her footprints as large as a horse's), he expresses deep affection for her and such concern as he is capable of, given the puzzling circumstances.

"THE FIGHT"

The narrator of "The Fight" is an exuberant adolescent. Although he is fourteen, he deliberately adds a year to his age, lying for the thrill of having to be on guard to avoid detection. The self-conscious teenager is continually inventing scenarios in which he assumes various heroic postures. The story tells of his finding an alter ego, as gifted as he, through whom he can confirm his existence, with whom he can share his anxieties, collaborate imaginatively, and play duets. The opening incident illustrates Dylan's testing himself against the adults about him. He is engaged in a staring contest with a cranky old man who lives

beside the schoolyard when a strange boy pushes him down. They fight. Dylan gives Dan a bloody nose and gets a black eye in return. Admiring each other's injuries as evidence of their own manliness, they become fast friends.

Dylan postures, first as a prizefighter, then as a pirate. When a boy ridicules him at school the next day, he has a revenge fantasy of breaking his leg, then of being a famous surgeon who sets it with "a rapid manipulation, the click of a bone," while the grateful mother, on her knees, tearfully thanks him. Assigned a vase to draw in art class, the boys sketch inaccurate versions of naked girls instead. "I drew a wild guess below the waist." This boyish sexual curiosity leads him mentally to undress even Mrs. Bevan, the minister's wife, whom he meets later at supper at Dan's house, but he gets frightened when he gets as far as the petticoats.

Dan shows Dylan the seven historical novels he wrote before he was twelve, plays the piano for him, and lets him make a cat's noise on his violin; Dylan reads Dan his poems out of his exercise book. They share feelings, such as their ambivalences toward their mothers, a love tinged with embarrassment. They decide to edit a paper. Back upstairs, after supper, they imitate the self-important Mr. Bevan and discuss the time Mrs. Bevan tried to fling herself out the window. When she joins them later, they try to induce her to repeat this by pointedly opening the window and inviting her to admire the view. When he has to leave at 9:30, Dan announces that he "must finish a string trio tonight," and Dylan counters that he is "working on a long poem about the princes of Wales." On these bravura promises, the story closes.

"A PROSPECT OF THE SEA"

Thomas called these luminous remembrances of his youth "portions of a provincial autobiography." The stories he wrote earlier, drafts of which exist in "The Red Notebook" which he kept from December, 1933, to October, 1934, were not published until later. Considered obscure, violent, and surrealistic, the stories are difficult because of the use of narrative devices borrowed from lyric poetry. In "A Prospect of the Sea," for example, the scenery seems to contract and expand. A boy lying in a cornfield on a summer day sees a country girl with berry-stained mouth, scratched legs, and dirty fingernails jump down from a tree, startling the birds. The landscape shrinks, the trees dwindle, the river is compressed into a drop, and the yellow field diminishes into a square "he could cover with his hand." As he masters his fear and sees she is only "a girl in a torn cotton frock" sitting cross-legged on the grass, things assume their proper size. As she makes erotic advances, his terror rises again, and everything becomes magnified. Each leaf becomes as large as a man, every trough in the bark of the tree seems as vast as a channel, every blade of grass looks as high as a house. This apparent contraction and expansion of the external world is dependent upon the protagonist's internal state.

Thomas uses another device commonly employed in lyric poetry, the literalized metaphor. Because a thing seems like another, it is depicted as having been transformed into that other thing. For example, the "sunburned country girl" frightens the lonely boy as if she were a witch; thus, in his eyes, she becomes one. "The stain on her lips was blood, not berries; and her nails were not broken but sharpened sideways, ten black scissorblades ready to snip off his tongue." Finally, not only space and character are subject to transformations but also time. As the narrator fantasizes union with this girl, he attains a mystical vision of history unrolling back to Eden. The story ends as it began; she disappears into the sea. He had imagined, at the beginning, as he dabbled his fingers in the water, that a drowned storybook princess would emerge from the waves. The apparent obscurities are resolved by seeing the plot of this story as simply the daydreams of a lonely boy on a summer's day.

"THE ORCHARDS"

"The Orchards" is another prose-poem about a man's attempt to record a vision in words. Marlais has a repetitive dream about blazing apple trees guarded by two female figures who change from scarecrows to women. He tries and fails to shape this into a story, and finally sets out on a quest. Striding through eleven valleys, he reaches the scene he has dreamed of, where he reenacts the kissing of the maiden as the orchard catches fire, the fruit falls as cinders, and she and her sister change to scarecrows. These smoldering trees may be related to the sacrificial fires of the Welsh druids on Midsummer Day. The woman figure might be connected with Olwedd, the Welsh Venus, associated with the wild apple. Marlais's adventure, however, is a mental journey undertaken by the creative writer through the landscape of his mind, and the temporal and spatial fluctuations are the projections of that mind, mythicized.

"THE TREE"

"The Tree" illustrates this same process. A gardener tells a boy the story of Jesus, reading the Bible in his shed by candlelight. While he is mending a rake with wire, he relates the twelve stages of the cross. The boy wants to know the secrets inside the locked tower to which the bearded gardener has the key. On Christmas Eve, the gardener unlocks the room through whose windows the boy can see the Jarvis Hills to the east. The gardener says of this "Christmas present" in a tone which seems prophetic: "It is enough that I have given you the key."

On Christmas morning, an idiot with ragged shoes wanders into the garden, "bearing the torture of the weather with a divine patience." Enduring the rain and the wind, he sits down under the elder tree. The boy, concluding that the gardener had not lied and that the secret of the tower was true, runs to get the wire to reenact the crucifixion. The old man's obsessive religiosity has been transmitted to the boy, who takes it literally: "A tree" has become "The Tree," "a key" has become "The Key," and a passive beggar stumbling from the east has become Christ inviting his martyrdom.

"THE VISITOR"

"The Visitor" is the story of a dying poet, Peter, tended lovingly by Rhiannon, who brings him warm milk, reads to him from William Blake, and at the end pulls the sheet over his face. Death is personified as Callaghan, whose visit he anticipates as his limbs grow numb and his heart slows. Callaghan blows out the candles with his gray mouth, and, lifting Peter in his arms, flies with him to the Jarvis Valley where they watch worms and death-beetles undoing "brightly and minutely" the animal tissues on the shining bones through whose sockets flowers sprout, the blood seeping through the earth to fountain forth in springs of water. "Peter, in his ghost, cried with joy." This is the same assurance found in Thomas's great elegies: Death is but the reentry of the body into the processes of nature. Matter is not extinguished, but transformed into other shapes whose joyous energies flourish forever.

OTHER MAJOR WORKS

LONG FICTION: *The Death of the King's Canary*, 1976 (with John Davenport).

PLAY: *Under Milk Wood*, pb. 1954.

SCREENPLAYS: *Three Weird Sisters*, 1948 (with Louise Birt and David Evans); *No Room at the Inn*, 1948 (with Ivan Foxwell); *The Doctor and the Devils*, 1953; *The Beach at the Falesá*, 1963; *Twenty Years A'Growing*, 1964; *Rebecca's Daughters*, 1965; *Me and My Bike*, 1965.

RADIO PLAYS: *Quite Early One Morning*, 1944; *The Londoner*, 1946; *Return Journey*, 1947; *Quite Early One Morning*, 1954 (twenty-two radio plays).

POETRY: *Eighteen Poems*, 1934; *Twenty-five Poems*, 1936; *The Map of Love*, 1939; *New Poems*, 1943; *Deaths and Entrances*, 1946; *Twenty-six Poems*, 1950; *In Country Sleep*, 1952; *Collected Poems, 1934-1952*, 1952; *The Poems of Dylan Thomas*, 1971 (Daniel Jones, editor).

NONFICTION: *Letters to Vernon Watkins*, 1957 (Vernon Watkins, editor); *Selected Letters of Dylan Thomas*, 1966 (Constantine FitzGibbon, editor); *Poet in the Making: The Notebooks of Dylan Thomas*, 1968 (Ralph Maud, editor); *Twelve More Letters by Dylan Thomas*, 1969 (Constantine FitzGibbon, editor).

MISCELLANEOUS: *"The Doctor and the Devils" and Other Scripts*, 1966 (two screenplays and one radio play).

BIBLIOGRAPHY

Ackerman, John. *Dylan Thomas: His Life and Work*. New York: St. Martin's Press, 1996. An excellent introduction to the life and works of Thomas.

Cox, C. B., ed. *Dylan Thomas: A Collection of Critical Essays*. Englewood Cliffs, N.J.: Prentice-Hall, 1966. Of the thirteen essays in this collection, only Annis Pratt's deals specifically with Thomas's prose; three others analyze *Under Milk Wood*.

Davies, James A. *A Reference Companion to Dylan Thomas*. Westport, Conn.: Greenwood Press, 1998. A useful tool for the student of Thomas. Includes bibliographical references and an index.

Emery, Clark M. *The World of Dylan Thomas*. Coral Gables, Fla.: University of Miami Press, 1962. This volume contains explications of ninety of Thomas's poems with some brief commentary on the short fiction.

FitzGibbon, Constantine. *The Life of Dylan Thomas*. London: J. M. Dent & Sons, 1965. The standard biography, this work includes a list of Thomas's screenplays, itineraries of his reading tours, and a detailed index that gives the reader access to references to individual works.

Kidder, Rushworth M. *Dylan Thomas: The Country of the Spirit*. Princeton, N.J.: Princeton University Press, 1973. This volume analyzes three types of religious imagery found in Thomas's poetry.

Korg, Jacob. *Dylan Thomas*. Boston: Twayne, 1965. Korg includes a long chapter on Thomas's prose and analyzes several stories. Supplemented by a bibliography.

Mayer, Ann Elizabeth. *Artists in Dylan Thomas's Prose Works*. Montreal: McGill-Queen's University Press, 1995. In this detailed study of the image of the artist in Thomas's prose, Mayer provides a close analysis of "Peaches" and "One Warm Saturday." Discusses the folktale basis of "Peaches" and the child-as-artist figure who places himself within the stories he tells. Argues that "Peaches" sets up many themes further explored and developed in the other stories in *Portrait of the Artist as a Young Dog*.

Peach, Linden. *The Prose Writings of Dylan Thomas*. Totowa, N.J.: Barnes & Noble Books, 1988. Shows how Thomas's prose rather than his poetry demonstrates his concern with Wales. Examines Thomas's focus on a backward, rural Wales and discusses how the early stories examine the restrictions of close-knit communities, which act as straitjackets on the emotional development of the Welsh people.

Tindall, William York. *A Reader's Guide to Dylan Thomas*. Syracuse, N.Y.: Syracuse University Press, 1996. Although primarily offering analyses of the poems, Tindall includes some biography as well as some discussion of themes and interests in the introduction.

Ruth Rosenberg, updated by
Ann Davison Garbett

JAMES THURBER

Born: Columbus, Ohio; December 8, 1894
Died: New York, New York; November 2, 1961

PRINCIPAL SHORT FICTION

Is Sex Necessary?, 1929 (with E. B. White)
The Owl in the Attic and Other Perplexities, 1931
The Seal in the Bedroom and Other Predicaments, 1932
My Life and Hard Times, 1933
The Middle-Aged Man on the Flying Trapeze, 1935
Let Your Mind Alone! And Other More or Less Inspirational Pieces, 1937
Fables for Our Time and Famous Poems Illustrated, 1940
My World—And Welcome to It!, 1942
The Great Quillow, 1944
The White Deer, 1945
The Thurber Carnival, 1945
The Beast in Me and Other Animals: A New Collection of Pieces and Drawings about Human Beings and Less Alarming Creatures, 1948
The Thirteen Clocks, 1950
Thurber Country: A New Collection of Pieces About Males and Females, Mainly of Our Own Species, 1953
Further Fables for Our Time, 1956
The Wonderful O, 1957
Alarms and Diversions, 1957
Lanterns and Lances, 1961
Credos and Curios, 1962

OTHER LITERARY FORMS

James Thurber's more than twenty published volumes include plays, stories, sketches, essays, verse, fables, fairy tales for adults, reminiscences, biography, drawings, and cartoons.

ACHIEVEMENTS

James Thurber's writings are widely known and admired in English-speaking countries and his drawings have a world following. He has been compared with James Joyce in his command of and playfulness with English, and he invites comparison with most of his contemporaries, many of whom he parodies at least once in his works. He greatly admired Henry James, referring to him often in his works and parodying him masterfully several times, for example, in "Something to Say." While Thurber is best known as a humorist (often with the implication that he need not be taken seriously as an artist), his literary reputation has grown steadily. His short story "The Secret Life of Walter Mitty" became an instant classic after it appeared in 1939 and was subsequently reprinted in *Reader's Digest*. After his death in 1961, several major studies and a volume in the Twentieth Century Views series have appeared, all arguing that Thurber should rank with the best American artists in several fields including the short story. In 1980, "The Greatest Man in the World" was chosen for dramatization in the American Short Story series of the Public Broadcasting Service. Thurber received numerous awards for his work, including honorary degrees from Kenyon College (1950), Williams College (1957), and Yale University (1953), as well as the Antoinette Perry Award for the revue, *A Thurber Carnival* (1960). His drawings were included in art shows worldwide. He was the first American after Mark Twain to be invited to *Punch*'s Wednesday Luncheon (1958).

BIOGRAPHY

On December 8, 1894, James Grover Thurber was born in Columbus, Ohio, where he spent his childhood except for a two-year stay in Washington, D.C. In Columbus, he absorbed the midwestern regional values that remained important to him all of his life: a liberal idealism, a conservative respect for the family, a belief in the agrarian virtues of industry and independence, and a healthy skepticism about the human potential for perfecting anything. He lost his left eye in a childhood accident that eventually led to almost complete blindness forty years later. He attended but did not graduate from Ohio State University, where he met Elliott Nugent, who was crucial in helping and encouraging Thurber to write. Thurber began his writing career as a journalist, earning his living primarily as a reporter in Ohio and France before he joined *The New Yorker* in 1927. There his friendship with E. B. White provided opportunities for him to perfect and publish the stories he had been working on since college. Within five years of beginning at *The New Yorker*, he became one of the best-known humorists in America. He married Althea Adams on May 20, 1922, and they had one daughter before their divorce in 1935. He married Helen Wismer on June 25, 1935. Despite impaired vision that seriously interfered with his work, beginning in the early 1940's, Thurber nevertheless continued writing, though he gave up drawing in 1951. He published more than twenty volumes in his lifetime and left many works uncollected at his death. He died of pneumonia on November 2, 1961, a month after suffering a stroke.

ANALYSIS

James Thurber is best known as the author of humorous sketches, stories, and reminiscences dealing with urban bourgeois American life. To discuss Thurber as an artist in the short-story form is difficult, however, because of the variety of things he did that might legitimately be labeled short stories. His essays frequently employ stories and are "fictional" in recognizable ways. His "memoirs" in *My Life and Hard Times* are clearly fictionalized. Many of his first-person autobiographical sketches are known to be "fact" rather than fiction only through careful bio-

graphical research. As a result, most of his writings can be treated as short fiction. Thurber seemed to prefer to work on the borderlines between conventional forms.

There is disagreement among critics as to the drift of the attitudes and themes reflected in James Thurber's work. The poles are well represented by Richard C. Tobias on the one hand and the team of Walter Blair and Hamlin Hill on the other. Tobias argues that Thurber comically celebrates the life of the mind: "Thurber's victory is a freedom within law that delights and surprises." Blair and Hill, in *America's Humor* (1978), see Thurber as a sort of black humorist laughing at his own destruction, "a humorist bedeviled by neuroses, cowed before the insignificant things in his world, and indifferent to the cosmic ones. He loses and loses and loses his combats with machines, women, and animals until defeat becomes permanent." While Tobias sees women as vital forces in Thurber's work, Hill and Blair see Thurber as essentially a misogynist bewailing the end of the ideal of male freedom best portrayed in 1950's Western film and pathetically reflected in the fantasies of Walter Mitty. In fact, it seems that critics' opinions re-

James Thurber (Library of Congress)

garding Thurber's attitudes about most subjects vary from one text to the next, but certain themes seem to remain consistent. His weak male characters do hate strong women, but the males are often weak because they accept the world in which their secret fantasies are necessary and, therefore, leave their women no choice but to try to hold things together. When a woman's strength becomes arrogance as in "The Catbird Seat" and "The Unicorn in the Garden," the man often defeats her with the active power of his imagination. Characterizing Thurber as a Romantic, Robert Morsberger lists some themes he sees pervading Thurber's writing: a perception of the oppression of technocracy and of the arrogance of popular scientism especially in their hostility to imagination; an antirational but not anti-intellectual approach to modern life; a belief in the power of the imagination to preserve human value in the face of contemporary forms of alienation; and a frequent use of fear and fantasy to overcome the dullness of his characters' (and readers') lives.

"THE SECRET LIFE OF WALTER MITTY"

"The Secret Life of Walter Mitty" is Thurber's best-known work of short fiction. Its protagonist, the milquetoast Walter Mitty, lives in a reverie consisting of situations in which he is a hero: commander of a navy hydroplane, surgeon, trial witness, bomber pilot, and condemned martyr. The dream is clearly an escape from the external life which humiliatingly interrupts it: his wife's mothering, the arrogant competence of a parking attendant and policeman, the humiliating errands of removing tire chains, buying overshoes, and asking for puppy biscuits. In his dreams, he is Lord Jim, the misunderstood hero, "inscrutable to the last"; in his daily life he is a middle-aged husband enmeshed in a web of the humdrum. Tobias sees Mitty as ultimately triumphant over dreary reality. Blair and Hill see him as gradually losing grip of the real world and slipping into psychosis. Whether liberated or defeated by his imagination, Mitty is clearly incompetent and needs the mothering his wife gives him. Often described as an immoral and malicious woman, she is actually just the wife he needs and deserves; she seems to exist as a replacement ego to keep him from catching his death of cold

as he somnambulates. The story's artfulness is readily apparent in the precise choice and arrangement of details such as sounds, objects, and images that connect fantasy and reality. The technical devices are virtually the same as those used by William Faulkner and Joyce to indicate shifts in levels of awareness in their "free-association internal monologues." Mitty has become a representative figure in modern culture like T. S. Eliot's Prufrock and Faulkner's Quentin Compson, although perhaps more widely known. While many of Thurber's stories are similar to this one in theme and form, they are astonishingly diverse in subject, situation, and range of technique.

"THE BLACK MAGIC OF BARNEY HALLER"

Another large group of Thurber stories might be characterized as fictionalized autobiography. One of the best of these sketches is "The Black Magic of Barney Haller" in *The Middle-Aged Man on the Flying Trapeze*. In this story, "Thurber" exorcises his hired man, a Teuton whom lightning and thunder always follow and who mutters imprecations such as "Bime by I go hunt grotches in de voods," and "We go to the garrick now and become warbs." The narrator becomes convinced that despite his stable and solid appearance, Barney is a necromancer who will transform reality with his incantations. At any moment, Barney will reveal his true devilish from and change "Thurber" into a warb or conjure up a grotch. It does not comfort him to learn the probable prosaic meanings of Haller's spells, even to see the crotches placed under the heavy peach tree branches. At the end of the story, he feels regret that the only man he knows who could remove the wasps from his garret has departed.

The humor of these incidents is clear, and a humorous meaning emerges from them. The narrator would rather hide in *Swann's Way*, reading of a man who makes himself in his book, but he feels threatened by the external supernatural power of another's language to re-create the world. He first attempts exorcism with Robert Frost, well-known for having successfully disposed of a hired man. He quotes "The Pasture" in an attempt to make the obscure clear, but succeeds only in throwing a fear that mirrors his own into Barney. This gives "Thurber" his clue; in the next attempt he borrows from Lewis Carroll and the American braggart tradition, asserting his own superior power as a magician of words, "Did you happen to know that the mome rath never lived that could outgrabe me?" The man with the superior control of language, the man of superior imagination, really is in control; he *can* become a playing card at will to frighten off black magicians. This story is typical of Thurber in its revelation of the fantastic in the commonplace, its flights of language play, and its concern for the relations among reality, self, imagination, and language. *My Life and Hard Times* is the best-known collection of fictional/autobiographical sketches.

"THE MOTH AND THE STAR"

Also an author of fables, Thurber published two collections of fables. "The Moth and the Star" is a typical and often anthologized example. A moth spends a long life trying to reach a star, defying his disappointed parents' wish that he aspire normally to get himself scorched on a street lamp. Having outlived his family, he gains in old age "a deep and lasting pleasure" from the illusion that he has actually reached the distant star: "Moral: Who flies afar from the sphere of our sorrow is here today and here tomorrow." The moth and the star suggest images in F. Scott Fitzgerald's *The Great Gatsby* (1925), one of Thurber's favorite books, but in partial contrast to that book, this story echoes the import of the great artist of the "Conclusion" of Henry David Thoreau's *Walden* (1854). The aspiring idealist who rejects the suicidal life of material accumulation and devotes himself to some perfect work ultimately conquers time and enriches life whether or not he produces any valuable object. Because the moth, like the artist of Kouroo, succeeds and is happy, this story seems more optimistic than *The Great Gatsby*. Many of the fables are more cynical or more whimsical, but all are rich in meaning and pleasure like "The Moth and the Star."

Critics and scholars have noted ways in which Thurber's career and writings parallel Mark Twain's. For example, both, as they grew older, grew more interested in fables and fairy tales. In the latter, Thurber was perhaps the more successful, publishing four fantasy stories for adults in the last twenty years of his

life. Completed while blindness was descending upon him, these stories are characterized by heightened poetic language, highly original variations on the fairy formulae, sparkling humor, and a common theme: in the words of Prince Jorn, hero of *The White Deer*, "Love's miracle enough." Love is the key that frees imagination by giving it strength to do, and strength of imagination makes the wasteland fertile. The fairy tales may be seen as intentional responses to Eliot's vision of the wasteland in his famous poem of 1922, perhaps from a point of view similar to that of Percy Bysshe Shelley's *A Defence of Poetry* (1840). While "The Secret Life of Walter Mitty" and *Further Fables for Our Time* may be seen as affirming the view of modern life as a wasteland, the fairy tales suggest that the ash heap of modern culture is escapable. It seems especially significant that the mode of escape is represented in tales of magic in remote settings.

THE WHITE DEER

The White Deer opens in the third period in King Clode's memory of waiting for the depleted game of his hunting grounds to replenish. The story develops in triads, the central one being the three perilous tasks set for the three sons of King Clode to determine which shall claim the hand of the fair princess who materializes when the king and his sons corner the fleet white deer in the enchanted forest. The sons complete their tasks simultaneously, but, in the meantime, King Clode determines that the nameless Princess is not a disenchanted woman but an enchanted deer. When the returned sons are told of this, Thag and Gallow refuse her. If denied love three times, she would be a deer forever, but Jorn accepts her: "What you have been, you are not, and what you are, you will forever be. I place this trophy in the hands of love. . . . You hold my heart." This acceptance transforms her into a new and lovelier princess, Rosanore of the Northland, and the April fragrance of lilacs fills the air suggesting direct opposition to the opening of Eliot's *The Waste Land*: "April is the cruellest month, breeding/Lilacs out of the dead land." As King Clode later sees the full wisdom and beauty of Rosanore, he repeats, "I blow my horn in waste land." Echoes of Eliot show up repeatedly in the fairy tales, but the greater emphasis falls on the powers of love and imagination, which in this fairy world inevitably blossom in beauty and happiness.

The cast of secondary characters and the perilous labors provide opportunities to characterize wittily the world in need of magic. There are an incompetent palace wizard as opposed to the true wizards of the forest, an astronomer-turned-clockmaker who envisions encroaching darkness ("It's darker than you think"), and a royal recorder who descends into mad legalese when the Princess's spell proves to be without precedent. Gallow's labor is especially interesting because he must make his way through a vanity fair bureaucracy in order to conquer a sham dragon, a task that tests his purse and persistence more than his love. This task allows a satire of the commercial values of modern culture. Each of the fairy tales contains similar delights as well as bizarre and beautiful flights of language: the Sphinz asks Jorn, "What is whirly?/What is curly?/Tell me, what is pearly early?" and in a trice, Jorn replies, "Gigs are whirly,/ Cues are curly/ and the dew is pearly early."

OTHER MAJOR WORKS

PLAYS: *The Male Animal*, pr., pb. 1940 (with Elliott Nugent): *Many Moons*, pb. 1943; *A Thurber Carnival*, pr. 1960 (revue).

NONFICTION: *The Thurber Album*, 1952; *The Years with Ross*, 1959; *Selected Letters of James Thurber*, 1982.

BIBLIOGRAPHY

Bernstein, Burton. *Thurber: A Biography.* New York: Dodd, Mead, 1975. This official biography, written with the cooperation of Thurber's widow, provides a thorough survey of Thurber's life and career.

Bowden, Edwin T. *James Thurber: A Bibliography.* Columbus: Ohio State University Press, 1968. This book provides a complete listing of Thurber's published writings and drawings.

Grauer, Neil A. *Remember Laughter: A Life of James Thurber.* Lincoln: University of Nebraska Press, 1994. A biography that examines the context of Thurber's work. Provides an interesting discussion of the background to the writing of "The Se-cret Life of Walter Mitty" and its reception when first published in *The New Yorker*.

Holmes, Charles S. *The Clocks of Columbus: The Literary Career of James Thurber.* New York: Atheneum, 1972. This literary biography devotes special attention to the relations between Thurber's Ohio background and his works. Supplemented by drawings, photographs, and a bibliography.

_____, ed. *Thurber: A Collection of Critical Essays.* Englewood Cliffs, N.J.: Prentice-Hall, 1974. This useful collection includes twenty-five critical and biographical essays, as well as a chronology and a brief annotated bibliography.

Kaufman, Anthony. "'Things Close In': Dissolution and Misanthropy in 'The Secret Life of Walter Mitty.'" *Studies in American Fiction* 22 (Spring, 1994): 93-104. Discusses dissolution and misanthropy in the story; argues that Mitty's withdrawal is symptomatic not of mild-mannered exasperation with a trivial world but of anger; concludes that Mitty is the misanthrope demystified and made middle-class—the suburban man who, unable to imagine or afford the drama of a retreat into the wilderness, retreats inward.

Kenney, Catherine McGehee. *Thurber's Anatomy of Confusion.* Hamden, Conn.: Archon Books, 1984. A survey of Thurber's creative world, including discussions of his most characteristic works. Discusses *Fables for Our Time* and such stories as "The Greatest Man in the World" and "The Secret Life of Walter Mitty." Argues that the latter examines the impotent world of modern urban America, embodying all of the elements of Thurber's fictional world.

Kinney, Harrison. *James Thurber: His Life and Times.* New York: Henry Holt, 1995. A biography that focuses largely on Thurber's relationship to the development of *The New Yorker* magazine. Discusses how Thurber made use of overheard conversation, wordplay, and literary allusions in his stories. Discusses Thurber's obsession with the war between the sexes in his prose and cartoons.

Long, Robert Emmet. *James Thurber.* New York:

Continuum, 1988. This biographical and critical study divides Thurber's works into drawings, fiction, autobiography, fables, fairy tales, and occasional pieces, giving each a chapter. Complemented by a bibliography.

Morsberger, Robert E. *James Thurber*. New York: Twayne, 1964. Morsberger sketches Thurber's life and then analyzes his works, looking at his contributions to various art forms and his characteristic themes. Contains a chronology of Thurber's life and a brief annotated bibliography.

Tobias, Richard Clark. *The Art of James Thurber*. Athens: Ohio University Press, 1970. Tobias studies Thurber's themes and worldview, with special attention to his methods and techniques in creating humor.

Terry Heller

CHRISTOPHER TILGHMAN

Born: Boston, Massachusetts; 1946

PRINCIPAL SHORT FICTION
In a Father's Place, 1990
The Way People Run, 1999

OTHER LITERARY FORMS

In addition to his collections of short stories, Christopher Tilghman is the author of the novel *Mason's Retreat* (1996).

ACHIEVEMENTS

Christopher Tilghman won a thirty thousand dollar Whiting Writers Award, given to "emerging writers of exceptional talent and promise," for *In a Father's Place*. He has also received a John Simon Guggenheim Memorial Foundation Fellowship and an Ingram Merrill Award.

BIOGRAPHY

Christopher Tilghman was born in Boston, Massachusetts, in 1946, the son of an executive for the publishing house Houghton Mifflin. He attended Fesenden School and St. Paul's Academy and received his B.A. from Yale University in 1968; during the summers while he was in college he worked in Montana. After graduation, Tilghman joined the U.S. Navy. Three years later he moved to New England, took on freelance corporate writing, and built a house in rural northern Vermont, all the while writing fiction. His first public recognition came with his collection of stories *In a Father's Place*, which was featured on the cover of *The New York Times Book Review* in May, 1990.

ANALYSIS

Christopher Tilghman's first book, *In a Father's Place*, filled with fictions that are like the later stories of Raymond Carver, fictions that Carver's mentor, John Gardner, champion of "moral fiction" would have endorsed wholeheartedly, marks the end of the so-called minimalism of the 1980's. Rather than challenging the foundations of Western culture as absurdist stories of the 1960's did or laying bare the basic mystery of individual human experience as minimalist stories of the 1970's did, Tilghman's stories represent straightforward storytelling, firmly grounded in the conservative values most other contemporary short stories challenge. His second collection, *The Way People Run*, focuses on some of the same characters and many of the same longings for a lost center that his first collection does.

Tilghman holds up a set of basic American values of family and commitment against the rebellion of the 1960's, the deconstruction of the 1970's, and the "me" generation of the 1980's. Whether Tilghman's stories represent a general reaction against the self-reflexive and minimalist short fiction of the 1960's,

1970's, and 1980's, or whether they simply express one writer's personal convictions about the importance of traditional values, Tilghman is clearly more interested in moral truths and values than aesthetic ones.

"ON THE RIVERSHORE"

This is not a story in which the fairly straightforward values of working-class men, landed gentry, and God-fearing women are questioned, probed, examined, or put to the test. A Chesapeake Bay fisherman kills a young man for annoying his daughter and gets help disposing of the body from friends who agree with him that the boy was basically no good. The story is told by a twelve-year-old boy who is the only witness to the killing by his own father of the troublemaker Tommie Todman. Instead of being placed in a wrenching conflict by this horror, the boy recites a litany of Tommie's offenses. As a man in the story says, Tommie has no family and no one cares what happens to him—all of which seems to justify sinking the boy's body in deep water with heavy blocks because that is what is best for the community. The story is not cold-blooded or heartless; it is simply coldly reasonable about what is of value and what is not.

"HOLE IN THE DAY"

In this story, when Lonnie, a young wife in her twenties, finds out she is pregnant a fifth time—in spite of the fact that she is aging early and has told her husband she wants no more children—she decides to take it no longer and heads out across the midwestern plains to escape. The story, however, focuses on her husband Grant, who drops off three of the kids with family and friends and departs in his old pickup with the youngest, a baby of two years, in search of her. Never does he consider the individual needs of his wife; he only wants to find her so she can return to him. When he does find her, somehow she instantly realizes that she wants nothing else but Grant and her babies, although that decision has not been motivated by anything in the story except the general value system of home, family, and commitment that underlies Tilghman's fictional universe.

"IN A FATHER'S PLACE"

One of the best stories in Tilghman's first collection is the title piece, for it is the most ambitious and potentially the most complex, even though ultimately it too asserts rather than questions the solid values of family and property on which the other stories are based. The story centers on Dan, an elderly patriarch of an old Chesapeake Bay family, who tries to come to terms with his children, Nick, who is writing a novel, and Rachel, who is planning to move to the state of Washington. Although Dan is worried about missing Rachel, his primary concern is with Nick, who has brought a strong-minded and domineering girlfriend, Patty Keith, home with him.

The primary metaphor for the conflict between the values of family and land represented by Dan and the iconoclastic vales of Patty Keith is Patty's urging Nick to write a novel influenced by her own interest in deconstructionist philosopher and literary critic Jacques Derrida. Patty is always reading Derrida during the visit (although Dan doubts she is really getting very far in the book) and tells Dan that the novel Nick is writing is intended to "deconstruct" his family. When Dan asks if she means "destroy," she condescendingly replies that "deconstruct" is a complicated literary term.

However, it is not such a complicated literary term as Tilghman uses it. The conflict here is basically and simply between the solidity of the old historical traditions and the threat to those traditions by modernist and postmodernist thought. In the end, the traditional wins out by the simple measure of the old patriarch kicking the interloper out of his house. With Patty sent away with Derrida under her arm, Dan wonders if Nick will leave also, never to return. Still, as he looks over his life, he feels a tide of joy rising over his mistakes and triumphs. Thus the story ends not only with the triumph of the traditional but also with the unquestioning celebration of that triumph.

"LOOSE REINS" AND "ROOM FOR MISTAKES"

These two stories focus on Hal, who, after being raised on a ranch in Montana, becomes a well-to-do banker in the northeast. In the first story, from *In a Father's Place*, he returns home two years after his father's death, when his mother marries one of the ranch hands. What the story is really about is Hal's having to come to terms with the realization that his father never really had time for him and that the old ranch hand, Roy, the living embodiment of the instinctive values of the "natural," is his true spiritual father.

"Room for Mistakes," from *The Way People Run*, is also a return-home-for-realization story; this time Hal is middle aged, and the occasion is the death of his mother. He nostalgically remembers the pastoral simplicity of his childhood, rhapsodizes about the hope for renewal in the heart of America, and considers following the "dream-pull back to boyhood" by staying in Montana, although his mother's will has denied him the ranch. There is some vacillating indecision at the end of both of these stories—about whether to affirm or deny the father in the first one and whether to embrace and desert the land in the second—but there is no irony about the nostalgic pull of the past or the romantic allure of place in either of them. At the end of the story, Roy affirms the hope of the title, telling Hal that there is "room for mistakes" living naturally on the land, for there are "mercies" all though it.

"THE WAY PEOPLE RUN"

In many ways the title story of Tilghman's second collection, perhaps because it is less straightforward than most of the other stories, is the purest and most thoughtful example of his use of the short-story genre. Barry, the protagonist is driving east across the country, on the way home to face his wife, his child, and numerous unpaid and unpayable bills. Stopping at a rundown western town on the plains, he becomes fascinated with the pull of permanence and place.

The center of this magnetism is a beat-up café where he has a casual conversation with the waitress, but the simple act of returning to the restaurant and having her remember what kind of beer he drinks makes him feel "utterly, extravagantly at home." Later, when she offers to rent him a spare bedroom, he puts his wife, child, and responsibilities out of his mind, and, against all reason, rents the room. Later, after he and the waitress have sex, he has become so infatuated with the idea of being "at home" in the small town that, when she talks about his leaving, he talks about finding a place and staying. Whether this is a momentary hallucinatory reaction or whether it is

a realistic possibility is the culminating ambiguity that refuses to be as simple and straightforward as many of Tilghman's fictions. The story ends with a haunting metaphor: a deserted school bus on the side of the road that makes Barry stop on his way out of town. In the final image, he stands on the vast "ownerless domain" of the prairie, wondering if this is the way such things happen, "the way people run."

OTHER MAJOR WORK

LONG FICTION: *Mason's Retreat*, 1996.

BIBLIOGRAPHY

Arana-Ward, Marie. "Christopher Tilghman." *The Washington Post*. June 16, 1996, p. X10. An interview/biographical sketch in which Tilghman talks about growing up surrounded by a sense of family and history. Tilghman also talks about his education, his stint in the navy, and his long apprenticeship trying to learn to write.

Elder, Richard. "The Flash and Fragility of Revolt." *Los Angeles Times Book Review* (April 29, 1990): 3. Elder says that Tilghman's characters in *In a Father's Place* are value-seekers who care a lot and prize their caring. He discusses several of the stories, particularly "Hole in the Day," in which Elder says that Tilghman does what only a true storyteller can do—make the impossible inevitable.

Gilbert, Matthew. "Flight from the Sad Past Toward Epiphany." *The Boston Globe*. May 23, 1999, p. D2. A review of *The Way People Run* that argues that Tilghman creates a world that is both organic and spiritual, where men are interconnected with the family members from whom they run; notes that once again Tilghman focuses on people who are facing unwanted feelings as they revisit a family home but that more than those in his first collection these stories showcase his intuitive sense of the speed at which human feeling moves.

Hulbert, Ann. "*In a Father's Place*." *The New Republic* 202 (June 4, 1990): 40. An extensive and detailed review of *In A Father's Place* that praises the stories for their transcendent impulse that returns the characters to the world in their epiphanies rather than taking them away from it; discusses the importance of place, plot, and history in the stories.

Kakutani, Michiko. "Going Home Again and Finding You Can't." *The New York Times*. April 3, 1990, p. C17. A review of *In a Father's Place* that calls Tilghman a gifted new writer and the book a radiant new collection. Discusses Tilghman's theme of a man or woman returning to a family home, tracing the hold that childhood memories and a familial past exert on them. Says that Tilghman has the ability to compress a characters's life into a couple of pages and to delineate the complexities and complications of familial love.

Lyons, Bonnie, and Bill Oliver. "Places and Visions." *Literary Review* 38 (Winter, 1995): 244-56. A detailed, extensive interview with Tilghman in which he discusses the relationship between his fiction and his own family, the importance of place in his stories, and the need for compassionate empathy to be a good writer. Tilghman says that one reason he writes is to grapple with the "holy mysteries," those things that do not make sense but seem to be always present. He affirms his preference for old-fashioned, nineteenth century storytelling with a strong plot.

Payne, Doug. "Small Stories, Big Windows." *The San Diego Union- Tribune*. May 16, 1999, p. B8. A review of *The Way People Run* that argues that Tilghman focuses on family history, individual careers, and the influence of community in the expansive way we usually associate with novels; claims that Tilghman does not so much sum up as let dramatic moments resonate with ordinary experiences over the long run.

Charles E. May

TATYANA TOLSTAYA

Born: Leningrad, U.S.S.R.; May 3, 1951

PRINCIPAL SHORT FICTION

Na zolotom kryl'tse sideli, 1987 (*On the Golden Porch*, 1989)
Sleepwalker in a Fog, 1992

OTHER LITERARY FORMS

Tatyana Tolstaya is known primarily for her short fiction.

ACHIEVEMENTS

When her first collection of short stories was published in the United States in 1989 as *On the Golden Porch*, Tatyana Tolstaya was acclaimed by critics as an original and important new voice in Soviet literature. Her second book, also a group of stories, published in 1992 as *Sleepwalker in a Fog*, was generally conceded to be a worthy successor to her well-received first collection. Among those who paid enthusiastic tribute to Tolstaya were the American poet laureate Joseph Brodsky and Helena Goscilo, a prominent Slavist known especially for her contributions on Slavic women authors.

BIOGRAPHY

Tatyana Tolstaya was born in Leningrad, in the U.S.S.R., on May 3, 1951, the daughter of Nikita Tolstoy, a professor of physics, and Natalia Lozinskaya. Her great-granduncle was the writer Leo Tolstoy, and her grandfather, also a writer, was Alexei Tolstoy. Tolstaya was graduated from Leningrad State University in 1974 with a degree in languages and literatures. She worked as a junior editor in the Oriental literature department of a publishing house in Moscow and later held various positions in American universities, including the University of Richmond, the University of Texas at Austin, Texas Tech University in Lubbock, Skidmore College, and Princeton University. In May, 1974, she married Andrei Lebedev, a professor of philology; they settled in Moscow with their two sons. In the early 1990's they moved to the

United States, where they gained permission to reside. Her short stories have been published in several Soviet journals as well as in *The New Yorker*.

ANALYSIS

The title of Tatyana Tolstaya's story "Na zolotom kryl'tse sideli" ("On the Golden Porch") comes from an old Russian counting song that names several different unrelated persons—a czar, a king, a cobbler, and so forth. This is an appropriate title for the first collection because the collection comprises stories about all sorts of people—a five-year-old girl and her nanny, a little boy in love with a beautiful neighbor, an old woman who still dreams of joining her first lover, a desperate young woman who traps a coarse and insensitive man into marriage, a shy fat man who dreams his life away—to mention only a few of the disparate and varied characters. The stories have some elements in common. Similar settings, themes, and styles give the stories more unity and connection with one another than the nursery-rhyme title might suggest. A similar kind of variety as well as unifying elements characterize the stories in *Sleepwalker in a Fog*.

The stories are all set in Moscow or Leningrad, with an only slightly less frequent setting being the dacha, or country summer home, so often found in Russian literature. More particularly, the stories repeatedly contrast the cramped, drab, and dismal environments of late twentieth century Soviet citizens with the idyllic life in rural surroundings. There are exceptions to the idyllic quality of the dacha settings, but the connotation is always consistent with relaxation, plenitude, and natural beauty.

Tolstaya seems to have particular favorites among the kinds of characters she portrays: innocent though sometimes mischievous children; hardworking and loving elderly people, especially women; and a distinctive group of weak, deluded, and disillusioned persons of less determinate age but all suffering from vulnerability, deprivation of one sort or another, and a strong tendency to mix dreams and fantasy with harsh reality.

While there is not a totally cheerful story in the two collections, there is much that is joyful, merry,

tender, and humorous. The stories are not tightly plotted. Incidents and events are used to reveal characters' interactions, situations, and conditions. Tolstaya seems to be more concerned with evoking moods and portraying unforgettable characters, whether they be a child dreaming of running away with a beautiful woman who betrays him, an old nanny who spends her life living for others, a weak and ineffectual librarian who longs for love, or a no-longer-young woman who traps a man into a loveless marriage. In fact, every principal character in her collections has a story that lifts each of them out of the ordinary, into the realms of brilliant, rich imagination.

Tolstaya has been lauded again and again as one of the most original and impressive Soviet writers of the late twentieth century. Her use of multivoiced narrators has been cited, as has her ability to combine sadness with humor, tenderness with cruelty. Her tendency to use objects in anthropomorphic ways has also been praised: Gardens wave handkerchiefs, cabbage soup talks to itself, dresses tuck up their knees inside dark trunks, and a lamp shade is young and skittish. The metaphor of dream is one of Tolstaya's most distinctive devices. It appears in almost all of her stories; some of them consist almost entirely of dreams. The overall effect is evocative, evanescent, wry, and sometimes bizarre. Her stories have a natural, conversational style, whether in the narrator's voice, in the talk among characters, or even in a character's monologue. Tolstaya's themes reveal her special concerns: the dreadful contrasts between the disappointments and failures of everyday life and the joyful life of the imagination, between reality and fantasy, and between dreams and nightmares.

For the reader delighted with Tolstaya's prose of the 1980's and early 1990's, unfortunately, there is little to add. One story from the 1990's, "Siuzhet" (1992; the story) is not considered to be of the same, high artistic quality as her earlier prose. In 1988, she began residence in the United States with tours of teaching and duties as writer-in-residence in many American universities. She applied for, and was granted, the proper documents for remaining in the United States with her husband and younger son, who joined her. Like Aleksandr Solzhenitsyn, she has found in the New World both a new audience and a new outlook on her ideas. She published articles in *The New Republic* (May 27, 1991) and the *Wilson Quarterly* (Winter, 1992) which expressed her opinion of literary life in Russia. Such a self-conscious, Western reorientation may have been an inevitable result of emigration. Still, the accomplishments already made by Tolstaya stand on their own merit, both in Russia and in the West. In a world of conservative views on gender and nationality, Tolstaya has found a useful flashpoint, literature, where she can meld together articles of faith and pure fantasy, challenging reality and collective consciousness, artistically and, thus, substantively.

ON THE GOLDEN PORCH

Three stories in Tolstaya's first collection exemplify both the similarities and contrasts in her writing. One is set in Leningrad, the other two in a dacha. All three stories are told from the point of view of a child, one of Tolstaya's favorite narrative forms. This method allows her to use a fluid, rambling conversational style, laden with images and strong feeling. In all three stories, the nature of childhood, which is not entirely innocent, is contrasted with cruel betrayals by adults, indeed, by life. The differences, however, are what make each story distinctive and memorable in its own way.

The title story of the first collection alludes to a Russian counting rhyme in its title. Beginning with a brief poetic description of childhood as a garden, it shifts to the less idyllic aspects of childhood and uses several images of blood to convey the cruel and frightening side of that period. For example, a beautiful neighbor sells strawberries, her fingers red with berry blood. The narrator recalls how the same beautiful neighbor once smiled about her red hands after she had just killed a calf, and thus the contrast is established. The child narrator's fears are expressed in fantasies about her mother crawling over broken glass to steal a strawberry runner. Uncle Pasha, the scary neighbor's elderly, meek, henpecked husband, an accountant, runs every day to catch the commuter train to Leningrad. With his black cuff protectors and his scurrying to and from his job in a smoky basement, Uncle Pasha inevitably reminds one of Nikolai

Gogol's Akaky Akakyevich. Uncle Pasha's house, however, is an Aladdin's cave of treasures, which are described in fantastic terms. With abrupt speed, the accountant grows old, and his treasure-filled room is now seen with the adult eyes of the narrator as filled with trash and rubbish, tacky, worn, cheap, fake. Uncle Pasha freezes to death on the porch. Juxtaposed against the picture of him face down in the snow are white snow daisies growing between his still fingers.

"LOVES ME, LOVES ME NOT"

"Liubish'—ne liubish'" ("Loves Me, Loves Me Not"), the first story in the collection, is also told by a child, a five-year-old who resents having to be taken to the park by Maryvanna, an old servant, whom the child hates because of her ugliness, her poverty, and her endless boring reminiscences. The old woman appears to be harmless, but the poems that she recites to the child are filled with frightening images that express night fears of monsters and other threatening creatures that never appear in the daytime. The child's occasional bouts of flu give rise to a different kind of fantasy, fever dreams of banging red drums, a round loaf of bread running along an airfield with a nasty smile, tiny planes like bugs with claws. A flea market provides another setting for fantastic people and objects. In contrast to Maryvanna, who personifies the self-absorption and silly, scary kind of adult, there is Nanny Grusha, who is too old and feeble to go out but who understands the child's anxieties and suffering and weeps compassionate tears with wordless love.

"DATE WITH A BIRD"

"Svidanie s ptitsei" ("Date with a Bird") is another story set in the country, told by a detached and omniscient narrator who observes the boyish play and infatuation with a beautiful woman named Tamila. Petya, the narrator, is completely captivated by her stories and her possessions—a ring in the form of a snake, a squashed silver toad, a black robe with a red dragon on the back. Petya vows to himself that he will marry Tamila and lock up Uncle Borya in a tower because he teases and torments the boy with ridicule and nagging. The contrast between the two male figures, the boy and the man, is sharply drawn. Between them is the seductive enchantress.

Frightened by a nightmare, Petya wakes up and goes to the room where his grandfather has lain ill for a long time; he is dead. Petya runs to Tamila's dacha and there encounters a final betrayal and disillusionment.

"PETERS"

Another group of stories illustrates the capacity to dream and apprehend fantasy on a somewhat more adult level. Among these stories, "Peters" serves as an outstanding example. Abandoned by his parents, Peters is brought up by his grandmother, is never allowed to play with other children, and imagines his scoundrel father living on a tropical island. He attends a library school and goes to work in a library after his grandmother dies. Fat and clumsy, Peters lives in fantasies about beautiful ladies and love. When Faina begins her employment in the library, Peters's dreamworld becomes connected to the real world, a trick that Tolstaya often plays on her characters. Then Peters happens to overhear Faina call him "a wimp . . . an endocrinological sissy," and he realizes that his youth is over. Nevertheless, when spring comes, he falls in love with Valentina, a young woman whom he happens to see buying postcards. He imagines that he might be able to astonish and impress her if he knew German; then, in a restaurant, he is picked up by a "flying flower" named Peri, who steals his money. Peters continues to live as in a dream, sleeping through several years of marriage to a stern, unfeeling woman who eventually abandons him. Now old, Peters feels stirring within him a renewed sense of life. Now he neither desires nor regrets but is simply grateful for life, though it is slipping past him indifferently, treacherously, mysteriously. Still, he sees it as "marvelous, marvelous, marvelous," and with these significant words, the book ends.

SLEEPWALKER IN A FOG

In the title story of *Sleepwalker in a Fog*, Tolstaya blends several of her characteristic devices and portraits. Denisov is one of her favorite types: middle-aged, pensive, fearful of dying and being forgotten. His fiancé, Lora, is thoughtless, talkative, affectionate. With her in a cramped communal apartment lives her gentle widower father, a retired zoologist who is a bit strange but harmless. In her incessant, mindless chatter, Lora provides a considerable amount of humor in the story, while Papa, laboring over scientific articles for children, is the source of an anxious kind of pathos, wandering every night in his sleep.

Denisov, tormented by doubts and despair, lives in a constant round of visions, nightmares, and dreams. Thus he too, like the old somnambulist, walks through his troubled life in confusion, his waking life a dream. The story takes a bizarre turn as Denisov, attempting to do a favor for a young couple, looks up his comrade Bakhtiyarov, who is relaxing at the Woodland Fairy restaurant. There, events turn nightmarish, as Denisov envisions his friend Makov frozen to death on a mountaintop, while Bakhtiyarov teases and taunts Denisov, who slips into a state resembling the kind of rational illogic that one experiences in dreams. When he wakes up, he finds that everyone has gone. He calls Lora, who thinks that he has gone out of his mind when he tells her that he was locked in a fairy tale. She herself is in the middle of her own nightmare; having taken Papa to a healer in the country, she left him there, and he ran off in his sleep. The story ends in a poetic passage in which Denisov imagines the old man running through the night, through the forest, up and down hills, in the moonlight, smiling, fast asleep.

"MOST BELOVED"

One of the longer works in Tolstaya's second collection, "Samaia liubimaia" ("Most Beloved"), is set, like many of her stories, in Leningrad and at the dacha. It is a vivid, poignant account of the narrator's recollections of Zhenechka, the woman who has worked for the family as nurse and governess for as long as the children can remember. She has always been there.

The narrator recalls especially the first summer morning at the dacha, when Zhenechka would walk through the house, distribute presents, clear the desk, and get organized for the daily lessons, much resented by the children. Zhenechka is implacable, having taught their mother, and before that, having been their grandmother's childhood friend. Zhenechka wears a hearing aid on her chest that chirrs like a nightingale. Walking with a limp, she wears an orthopedic shoe. She never takes off her amber necklace, because she believes that some sort of healthful electricity emanates from it. She is strict, loving, devoted. Once, Zhenechka gives one of the girls a box, on the cover of which she has written, "Don't wish to be the prettiest; wish to be the most beloved."

The motif of gift giving is present throughout the story. Tolstaya uses this theme as a very effective way of characterizing Zhenechka. As the children grow up, she continues to bring presents when she comes to visit the family, which is all that she has left in the world. Aging, Zhenechka has become tiresome and boring, endlessly retelling her stories of bygone days. Interspersed with incidents from Zhenechka's last years are brief recollections of the first child she ever took care of, a little deaf boy, and of the only love in her life—"short, stunted, meager."

The story closes with a brief description of the deserted dacha, slowly deteriorating as the grasses take over the path, the mold blooms on the porch, and a spider spins the keyhole shut. The children have all grown up; Zhenechka has died. Although the narrator speaks of the old nurse's wish to be the most beloved as being naïve, the implication is clear that she really was just that. The greatest gift was herself, in her unthinking, simple, and total love.

"THE MOON CAME OUT"

"The Moon Came Out" is another story about an elderly figure, this time one named Natasha, born fifty years earlier. The story begins with childhood memories of a dacha near Leningrad, of games played to incantations such as "The moon came out behind the cloud." The parents, breaking all the rules, died, but Grandmother hung on to life. Natasha's adolescence is described in Tolstayan fashion, with nightmarish images of filth and horror. There is a brief interlude when Konovalov is attracted to Natasha, but she feels unworthy and retreats into a world of dreams, which the author describes with images of flowers, wind, sleepy forests, bears, and friendly old women—images straight out of the Russian fairy tales on which Tolstaya draws so frequently and effectively.

Natasha becomes a teacher of geography and never mentions the world in her mind, Queen Maud Land. Natasha lives in a communal flat, crowded, dismal, full of daily humiliations. She goes to Moscow once and falls in love with bearded, joyful Pyotr Petrovich, who has come into the city to shop for his family. As he leaves on the train, quite unaware of Natasha's short-lived devotion, she feels old age gripping her firmly by the shoulder.

"LIMPOPO"

Stories in which cruelty and death are themes include "Sarafim," about a misanthrope who kicks a small dog to death, and "Heavenly Flame," about a pointless practical joke played on a man awaiting death in a sanatorium. These themes are also fully expressed in "Limpopo," again a combination of burlesque and fantasy, reality and ridicule, revolving around the narrator's friends, Judy, from Africa, and Lyonechka, a poet who fights for truth. The dismal lives of Soviet citizens under the rule of the Communist Party are described with all the bite and snap of satire, with macabre humor and bitter irony. The political undertones are clearly present but under the guise of weird and grotesque incidents, such as an inexplicable massacre of innocent people by soldiers of "their own side." This story is Tolstaya's richest in terms of wild fancy, a large group of precisely and concisely delineated characters, a plot of complex and enigmatic events, and numerous and widely ranging literary allusions (to Dante, the Old Testament, Russian fairy tales, Don Juan, Alexander Pushkin, Dr. Doolittle, Søren Kierkegaard, and Homer, to mention only a few).

OTHER MAJOR WORKS

NONFICTION: "In a Land of Conquered Men," 1989; "Intelligentsia and Intellectuals," 1989; "Apples as Citrus Fruit," 1990; "President Potemkin," 1991.

BIBLIOGRAPHY

Gifford, Henry. "The Real Thing." *The New York Review of Books* 36 (June 1, 1989): 3-5. This article contains a review of *On the Golden Porch* and of three books on contemporary Soviet fiction, including *Balancing Acts* by Helena Goscilo, cited below.

Goscilo, Helena, ed. *Balancing Acts: Contemporary Stories by Russian Women*. Bloomington: Indiana University Press, 1989. This 337-page anthology includes one story by Tolstaya, "Peters," and the short-story collection *On the Golden Porch*. Goscilo provides commentary.

_____. *The Explosive World of Tatyana N. Tolstaya's Fiction*. Armonk, N.Y.: M. E. Sharpe, 1996. This is a critical review of Tolstaya's œuvre, covering her whole career to the date of publication.

_____. *Heritage and Heresy: Recent Fiction by Russian Women*. Bloomington: Indiana University Press, 1988. This volume includes three stories by Tolstaya, all published in *On the Golden Porch*, with commentary by Goscilo.

_____. "Monsters Monomaniacal, Marital, and Medical: Tat'iana Tolstaya's Regenerative Use of Gender Stereotypes." In *Sexuality and the Body in Russian Culture*, edited by Jane Costlow, et al. Stanford, Calif.: Stanford University Press, 1993. This chapter discusses Tolstaya's symbolism and sound sources in her prose.

_____. "Tatyana Tolstaia's 'Dome of Many-Colored Glass': The World Refracted Through Multiple Perspectives." *Slavic Review* 47 (Summer, 1988): 280-290. A detailed scholarly analysis of Tolstaya's stories. Includes explanatory and reference footnotes, several of them in Russian and untranslated.

Hamilton, Denise. "A Literary Heiress." *The Los Angeles Times*, May 12, 1992, p. E1. An interview story that provides a brief biographical sketch of Tolstaya's life. Tolstaya contends that she often distorts reality so that it comes back stronger than before and closer to the truth; discusses her collection *Sleepwalker in a Fog*.

See, Carolyn. "In the Russian Tradition." *The Los Angeles Times Book Review*, January 19, 1992, p. 3. A review of *Sleepwalker in a Fog*; suggests that the point in the stories is their timelessness; calls them elegant, overwritten mystical tales that are everything that communism was not.

Trosky, Susan M., ed. *Contemporary Authors* 130. Detroit: Gale Research, 1990. Includes a brief personal history of Tolstaya, a concise summary of her career, and a short general description of her characters.

Wisniewska, Sophia T. "Tat'iana Tolstaia." In *Russian Women Writers*, edited by Christine D. Tomei. New York: Garland. This is a critical biography of Tolstaya and her contribution to Russian literature.

Zalygin, Sergei, comp. *The New Soviet Fiction: Sixteen Short Stories*. New York: Abbeville Press, 1989. This 318-page anthology contains one story by Tolstaya, one of only three women represented. A critical introduction by the compiler analyzes the state of fiction in the Soviet Union during *perestroika* and *glasnost*.

Natalie Harper, updated by
Christine D. Tomei

LEO TOLSTOY

Born: Yasnaya Polyana, Russia; September 9, 1828
Died: Astapovo, Russia; November 20, 1910

PRINCIPAL SHORT FICTION

Sevastopolskiye rasskazy, 1855-1856 (*Sebastopol*, 1887)
Semeynoye schast'ye, 1859 (novella; *Family Happiness*, 1888)
Smert' Ivana Il'icha, 1886 (novella; *The Death of Ivan Ilyich*, 1887)
Kreytserova sonata, 1889 (novella; *The Kreutzer Sonata*, 1890)
The Kreutzer Sonata, The Devil, and Other Tales, 1940
Notes of a Madman and Other Stories, 1943
Tolstoy Tales, 1947

OTHER LITERARY FORMS

Leo Tolstoy is most famous as the author of two superb novels, *Voyna i mir* (1865-1869; *War and Peace*, 1886) and *Anna Karenina* (1875-1878; English translation, 1886). He wrote one other full-length novel, *Voskreseniye* (1899; *Resurrection*, 1899), and a number of novellas, such as *Destvo* (1852; *Childhood*, 1862), *Otrochestvo* (1854; *Boyhood*, 1886), *Yunost'* (1857; *Youth*, 1886), *Kazaki* (1863; *The Cossacks*, 1872), and *Khadzi-Murat* (1911; *Hadji Murad*, 1911). His fiction tends to overshadow his achievement as a dramatist; his plays include *Vlast tmy* (1887; *The Power of Darkness*, 1888) and *Plody prosveshcheniya* (1889; *The Fruits of Enlightenment*, 1891).

ACHIEVEMENTS

Leo Tolstoy is one of the undisputed titans of fiction, recognized by friend and foe alike as a great artist and man. He is Homeric in the epic sweep of *War and Peace* and *Anna Karenina*; in his stress on the primacy of human beings' senses and physical acts; in the clarity, freshness, and gusto with which he presents his world; in his celebration of nature's processes, from brute matter to the stars; in his union of an omniscient perspective with a detached vision.

Unlike Homer, however, he often shows war as wanton carnage resulting from the vainglory and stupidity of a nation's leaders.

While most critical evaluations of Tolstoy's writings are highly laudatory, he has been reproached by some interpreters for his disparagement of science, technology, and formal education, his hostility to aesthetics and the life of the mind, and most of all for his insistence, in his later works, on dictating programs of moral and religious belief to his readers. As a writer, his greatest achievement is to convey an insight into the living moment that renders with unequaled verisimilitude the course of human passions and the pattern of ordinary actions, enabling him to present a comprehensive, coherent, and usually convincing sense of life. His influence, while not as pervasive as that of his rival Fyodor Dostoevski, is evident in the works of Maxim Gorky, D. H. Lawrence, Ernest Hemingway, Giuseppe Tomasi di Lampedusa, Ignazio Silone, Isaac Babel, Mikhail Sholokhov, Aleksandr Solzhenitsyn, and Boris Pasternak when he composed his novel, *Doktor Zhivago* (1957; *Doctor Zhivago*, 1958).

BIOGRAPHY

Leo Nikolayevich Tolstoy was born on September 9, 1828, to a retired army officer, Count Nikolay Ilyich Tolstoy, and a wealthy princess, Maria Nikolaevna Bolkonskaya, who was descended from Russia's first ruling dynasty. His birthplace was a magnificent estate 130 miles south of Moscow, Yasnaya Polyana (serene meadow). Throughout his life, particularly from the late 1850's, when he settled there, this beautiful manorial land, featuring an avenue of lime trees and several lakes, was a romance he kept reinventing, lodged at the center of his self. He disliked urban civilization and industrialization, instead preferring with increasing fidelity the rural simplicities and patriarchal order that had governed the lives of his ancestors and that gave him commanding knowledge of the ways of the landowners and peasants who dominate his writings.

Leo Tolstoy (Library of Congress)

Tolstoy's mother died when he was two, his father when he was nine. He was lovingly brought up by an aunt, Tatyana, who became the model for Sonya in *War and Peace*, just as his parents sat for the portraits of Nicholas Rostov and Princess Maria in that novel. Aunt Tatyana both built the boy's confidence and indulged all his wishes, inclining him to extremes beginning in childhood. He largely wasted several years at the University of Kazan in drinking, gambling, and wenching, then joined an artillery unit in the Caucasus in 1851. That same year, he began working on his first, short novel, *Childhood*, to be followed by *Boyhood* and *Youth*. These works are thinly disguised autobiographical novellas, which unfold a highly complicated moral consciousness.

As a writer, Tolstoy is an inspired solipsist, identifying all other humans in examining his flesh and spirit. His art is essentially confessional, representing the strenuous attempt of a complex and exacting man to reconcile himself with himself. His diary, which he began in 1845, reveals what was to be an inveterate thirst for rational and moral justification of his life. It includes a list of puritanical Rules of Life, which he would update during the tormented periods of guilt that followed his lapses. The biographer Henri Troyat called him "a billy-goat pining for purity." The demands of his senses, mind, and spirit were to contest one another in his character as long as he lived.

Tolstoy served bravely in the Crimean War until 1856, also writing his *Sebastopol* stories as well as a number of other military tales. When he returned to European Russia, he found himself lionized as his country's most promising young author. He passed the years 1856-1861 shuttling between St. Petersburg, Moscow, Yasnaya Polyana, and foreign countries. His two trips abroad disgusted him with what he considered the selfishness and materialism of European bourgeois civilization. In 1859, he founded a school for peasant children at Yasnaya Polyana; in 1862, he launched a pedagogical periodical there; both followed a Rousseauistic model that glorified children's instincts, ignored their discipline, and insisted that intellectuals should learn from the common people, instead of vice versa.

In 1862, the thirty-four-year-old Tolstoy married the eighteen-year-old Sophia Andreyevna Behrs. Family life became his religion, and the union was happy for its first fifteen years, producing thirteen children. He dramatized the stability of marriage and family life in *War and Peace* (written 1863-1869), which his wife was to copy out seven times. Sophia efficiently managed Yasnaya Polyana, often served as Tolstoy's secretary, and nursed him through illnesses. She never recovered from the shock she received, however, a week before their wedding, when he insisted she read every entry of his diary, which recorded not only his moral struggles but also seventeen years of libidinous conduct.

Unhappy times followed the composition of *War and Peace*: the deaths of Aunt Tatyana, a favorite son, and several other relatives; quarrels with Sophia; illness; and depression. *Anna Karenina* (written 1873-1877) is a more somber and moralizing book, with the certainty of death hovering over it, and with sexual passion both given its due and dramatized as destructive to happiness. The male protagonist Levin's search for faith is a pale outline of Tolstoy's own spiritual journey, which next led him to write, between 1879 and 1882, an account of his emotional and ethical pilgrimage entitled *Ispoved* (1884; *A Confession*, 1885).

Shortly after finishing *Anna Karenina*, Tolstoy suffered a shattering midlife crisis that brought him close to suicide. Even though he had much to value— good health, a loving wife, family, fame, wealth, genius—life nevertheless seemed to him a cruel lie, purposeless, fraudulent, empty. For answers, he turned to philosophers, to educated people, and finally to the uneducated but religious peasants whose faith made their lives possible, and he decided to become a religious believer, although rejecting most ecclesiastical dogma.

A Confession is the best introduction to the spiritual struggle that Tolstoy was to wage for his remaining thirty years, which he spent in a glaringly public retirement. Trying to live up to his principles of purity and simplicity, he stripped his personal demands to the barest necessities, dressed and often worked as a peasant, published doctrines of moral improvement in both tracts and tales, signed over to his wife the right to manage his copyrights as well as his property, and renounced (not always successfully) almost all institutions, his title, concert- and theater-going, meat, alcohol, tobacco, hunting, and even sex. He became the high priest of a cult of Christian anarchy, professing the moral teachings of the Gospel and Sermon on the Mount while rejecting the divinity of Christ and the authority of the Church, which excommunicated him for blasphemy in 1901.

Some typical titles of Tolstoy's didactic last years are *V chom moya vera* (1884; *What I Believe*, 1885), "Gde lyubov', tam i Bog" ("Where Love Is, God Is") and "Mnogo li cheloveku zemli nuzhno?" ("How Much Land Does a Man Need?"). His best-known narrative was the tendentious three-part novel *Resurrection*, which is as long as, but far inferior to, *Anna Karenina*. Its protagonist, Nekhlyudov, experiences remorse after having seduced a peasant woman and expiates his transgression by adopting a moral life. Of greatest interest to literary critics is the book-length essay, *Chto takoye iskusstvo?* (1898; *What Is Art?*, 1898), in which Tolstoy rejects all art based on

other than gospel ethics and concludes that only the Old Testament's story of Joseph and primitive popular art will satisfy his standards.

Even in his doctrinaire phase, however, Tolstoy managed to produce great stories and novellas, particularly *The Death of Ivan Ilyich*, "Khozyain i rabotnik" ("Master and Man"), *The Kreutzer Sonata*, and *Hadji Murad*. He also wrote a powerful naturalistic tragedy, *The Power of Darkness*, which featured adultery and infanticide in a somber peasant setting. By contrast, *The Fruits of Enlightenment* is a satiric, farcical comedy revolving around the foibles of the gentry and the land hunger of the peasantry.

Tolstoy's last years were often mired in squabbles with his wife and some of his children, intrigues concerning his legacy, and bitter enmity between Sophia Tolstoy and his chief disciple, Vladimir Chertkov, who became Tolstoy's close confidant. By 1909, the marriage had become extremely stressful, with Countess Tolstoy repeatedly threatening suicide. On November 9, 1910, Leo Tolstoy, driven to distraction, fled his wife and family; on November 13, he was taken ill with what became pneumonia, at the rail junction of nearby Astapovo, and died in the station master's bed there on November 20. His death was mourned as a loss in every Russian family.

ANALYSIS

Leo Tolstoy's ego embraces the world, so that he is always at the center of his fictive creation, filling his books with his struggles, personae, problems, questions, and quests for answers, and above all with his notion of life as an ethical search as strenuous as the pursuit of the Holy Grail. He does not try to puzzle or dazzle; his work is not a clever riddle to be solved or a game to be played but a rich realm to be explored. He disdains the kind of exterior purism practiced by Gustave Flaubert and Henry James among others, which concentrates on the inner lives of individuals—although he is superbly skilled at psychological perception. His aim, rather, is to discover, as far as he can, the essential truth of life's meaning, the revelation to be gained at the core of the vast mesh of human relations. What energizes his work is his conviction that this truth is good, and that, once discovered, it will resolve the discords and conflicts that plague humanity.

In Tolstoy's art, the natural, simple, and true is always pitted against the artificial, elaborate, and false, the particular against the general, knowledge gained from observation against assertions of borrowed faiths. His is the gift of direct vision, of fundamental questions and of magical simplicity—perhaps too simple, as a distinguished historian of ideas has indicated. Isaiah Berlin, in a famous essay titled "The Hedgehog and the Fox," sees Tolstoy as torn between his pluralism (the fox, perceiving reality as varied, complex, and multiple) and monism (the hedgehog, reducing life's fullness to one single truth, the infinity of sensory data to the finite limits of a single mind). Tolstoy, Berlin concludes, was a pluralist in his practice but a monist in his theory, who found himself unable to reconcile the foxiness of his multifarious awareness with his hedgehoglike need to discover one all-embracing answer to its myriad problems.

"THE RAID"

Tolstoy's first stories are set in the Caucasus, where he spent the years 1851 to 1854, with many of the officers and soldiers whom he met serving as thinly disguised models. In "Nabeg: Razskaz volontera" ("The Raid: A Volunteer's Story"), he poses several problems: What is the nature of courage? By what tests does one determine bravery or cowardice? What feelings cause a man to kill his fellow? The first-person narrator discusses these questions with a Captain Khlopov (derived from a Captain Khilkovsky in Tolstoy's diary) and illustrates different types of courage among the military characters. Tolstoy deflates warfare, emphasizing ordinary details and casual, matter-of-fact fortitude rather than dashingly proud heroism. His descriptions of nature are simple, concrete, and expert. The story's most powerful scene has a dying young ensign pass from carefree bravado to dignified resignation as he encounters his end.

SEBASTOPOL SKETCHES

The element of eyewitness reportage is carried over from the Caucasian tales to the three *Sebastopol* sketches, which are fiction passing as war dispatches. Tolstoy took part in the Crimean War (1854-1856) as a sublieutenant, with Russia fighting a complex series of actions against a multiple enemy composed of not only Turkish but also some British, French, and Sardinian troops. While aggressively patriotic, he was appalled by the disorganization of his country's military forces, with the average Russian peasant soldier poorly armed, trained, and led, while many company commanders nearly starved their men by pocketing much of the money allocated for their food.

"Sevastopol v dekabre" ("Sebastopol in December") has no characters and no particular topography. The first-person narrator constructs a guidebook homily out of lived experience, familiarly addressing readers, inviting them to listen to his frontline experiences as he wanders from Sebastopol's bay and dockside to a military hospital filled with shrieking, often multilated soldiers. Says the speaker,

> . . . you will see war not as a beautiful, orderly, and gleaming formation, with music and beaten drums, streaming banners and generals on prancing horses, but war in its authentic expression—as blood, suffering and death.

Tolstoy concludes this sketch with a stirring salute to the epic heroism of Sebastopol's residents and Russian defenders. Yet a somber awareness of death's imminence, as the surgeon's sharp knife slices into his patients' flesh, pervades the sketch.

In "Sevastopol v mae" ("Sebastopol in May"), Tolstoy sharply denounces the vainglory of militarism, stressing the futility of the fighting and the madness of celebrating war as a glorious adventure. The passage describing the death by shellfire of an officer is a superb tour de force, with the author using interior monologue to have the lieutenant crowd his many hopes, fears, memories, and fantasies into a few seconds. The speaker comes to consider war as senseless, horrifying, but also—given human nature—inevitable. He concludes that the only hero he can find is the truth. This is perhaps the finest of Tolstoy's military tales, anticipating the battle and death scenes of *War and Peace*.

In the third narrative, "Sebastopol in August," Tolstoy uses well-developed characters to unify an episodic plot. He focuses on two brothers whose personalities contrast but who are both killed in action. He also strikes a note of shame and anger at Russia's abandonment of the city and the consequent waste of many thousands of lives. He celebrates, however, the quiet heroism of countless common soldiers who risked and often met death with calm nobility.

"TWO HUSSARS"

Before Tolstoy began *War and Peace* in 1863, he wrote a number of long stories or novellas, which he called *povesti*, defined as "A literary narrative of lesser size than a novel." Their compass is usually too small to accommodate the didacticism that his longer works absorb painlessly. One successful story that avoids moralizing is "Dva gusara" ("Two Hussars"). Its first half is devoted to the officer-father, the second to his son. Twenty years apart, they enact the same sequence of card playing, drinking, and philandering, in the same small town, meeting the same people. Their characters, however, differ drastically. The father is gallant, generous, honorable, charming. The son is mean, cold, calculating, cowardly. The father's temperament is natural and open. The son's is contrived and devious, corrupted by decadent society. As always with Tolstoy, he gives his allegiance to the authentic and intuitive, while sardonically scorning the artificial and scheming.

FAMILY HAPPINESS

In *Family Happiness*, Tolstoy treats a problem to which he was to return throughout his career: the place of women, both at home and in society. He had courted a much younger and very pretty girl, Valerya Arseneva, but had become irritated by her fondness for high society and had broken off the relationship. He transforms the experience into a narrative by the young woman, Masha, in the fashion of Charlotte Brontë's novel *Jane Eyre* (1847), which he had read and admired. Now married and a mother, Masha recalls, in the story's first half, her courtship by a man who knew her dead father, considered himself her guardian as she grew up, and was thirty-five to her seventeen when they married. Tolstoy magnificently captures the rapturous chemistry of first love as the girl awakens to womanhood. By the story's second half, however, he undermines her dreams of romantic happiness as she becomes addicted to the whirl of urban high society, driving her husband into rural re-

treat and seclusion. Toward the end, at home in the country after disillusionments in the city, she and he agree to a different sort of marriage than they envisioned at its start, basing it not on passion but on companionship and parenthood. Tolstoy has here sounded some of his most pervasive notes: Sophistication is evil, simplicity is good; the city is decadent, the country is healthy; and romance is dangerous, often a "charming nonsense," while marriage, though a necessary institution, should never be sentimentalized.

"STRIDER"

The story now called "Kholstomer" ("Strider") was originally translated into English as "Kholstomer: The Story of a Horse," because Tolstoy modeled his equine, first-person narrator on a horse by that name celebrated for his enormous stride and speed. The author humanizes his outcast animal, which is consistently stigmatized as a piebald and a gelding, in a keenly compassionate manner, with Strider's sorrowful life made a parable of protest against unjust punishment of those who are somehow different. "He was old, they were young. He was lean, they were sleek; he was miserable, they were gay; and so he was quite alien to them, an outsider, an utterly different creature whom it was impossible for them to pity." Strider's victimization by greedy, selfish owners enables Tolstoy to lash the evils of private property, using an equine perspective to expose its immorality.

The second phase of Tolstoy's production of short fiction follows his two great novels and the tremendous spiritual crisis chronicled in *A Confession*. It was an extremely profound change for an author. The sublime artist comes to repudiate almost all art; the nobleman now lives like a peasant; the wealthy, titled country gentleman seeks to abandon his property, preaching humility and asceticism; the marvelous novelist and story writer prefers the roles of educational reformer, religious leader, social sage, cultural prophet. Yet Tolstoy's artistic instincts refuse to atrophy, and he manages to create different yet also masterful works, less happy and conventional, uncompromising, sometimes perverse, always powerful, preoccupied with purity, corruption, sin, sex, and death. His late stories express his Rousseauistic hostility to such institutions as the state, which forces citizens to pay taxes and serve in the military; the church, which coerces its communicants by fear and superstition; private property, whereby one person owns another; and modern art, which is elitist. The creative gold nevertheless continues to flow from Tolstoy's pen, despite his moralistic resistance to aesthetics, in such novellas as *The Death of Ivan Ilyich*, *The Kreutzer Sonata*, and the story "Master and Man."

THE DEATH OF IVAN ILYICH

The Death of Ivan Ilyich, perhaps his finest story, was Tolstoy's first published work after his conversion. It is more schematic and deliberate than the earlier tales, more selective and condensed in the choice of descriptive and analytic detail. It is a parable of a life badly lived, with Tolstoy here allying his highest art with an exigent passion for establishing the most profound and encompassing truths.

Ivan Ilyich is a cautious, correct, typical representative of his social class. He has achieved success in his profession of judge, in love, in marriage, in his family, and in his friendships, or so appearances indicate. Yet when he reviews his past, confronted with the inescapability of a cancer-ridden death, he slowly arrives at the realization that he has led a life of selfishness, shallowness, smugness, and hypocrisy. Significantly, his surname, Golovin, is derived from the Russian word for "head." He has excluded any deep feelings, as he has lived according to principles of pleasantness and propriety, conforming to the values of his upper-middle-class social sphere in his striving for status, materialism, bureaucratic impersonality and power, decorous appearance, and pleasure.

In part 1, which begins with the announcement of Ivan Ilyich's death, Tolstoy's tone is caustically satiric. Ivan's wife/widow, Praskovya Fedorovna, defines the nature of his loveless home life, grieving formally for her loss and accepting colleagues' condolences while really concerned with the cost of the grave site and the possibility of increasing her widow's pension. Ivan Ilyich, however, deserves no better. He is shown as a prisoner of his cherished possessions who wanted Praskovya primarily for her property, secondarily for her correct social position

and good looks. The density of things dominates Ivan Ilyich's feelings and conduct, pain and pleasure, happiness and misery. His highest moment comes with the furnishing of a new house; and his fall comes from reaching to hang a drape when he is on a ladder. Symbolically, his fall is one from pride and vanity.

The physicians enter to examine Ivan Ilyich's bruised side. They pursue their profession much as he does, from behind well-mannered, ritualistic masks. Ivan Ilyich soon discovers that not only his doctors but also his wife, daughter, colleagues, and friends all refuse him the empathy and compassion that he increasingly needs; they act on the same principle of self-interested pleasure that he has followed. As his physical suffering grows, he experiences the emotional stages that modern psychology accepts as characteristic of responses to lingering terminal illness: denial, loneliness, anger, despondency, and, finally, acceptance. He begins to drop his protective disguises and to realize that his existence has consisted of evasions of self-knowledge, of love, of awareness of the deepest needs of others. His fall into the abyss of death thus brings him to spiritual birth.

At the nadir of Ivan Ilyich's suffering, partial grace comes to him through the care of his servant, Gerasim. He is, like Platon Karataev in *War and Peace*, one of those simple, spontaneous, kindly souls whom Tolstoy venerates. In contrast to the sterile pretensions of Ivan Ilyich's social circle, Gerasim, modest and strong, personifies the Tolstoyan principle of living for others. He is in every sense a "breath of fresh air," showing his master unstinting compassion as he exemplifies the health of youth and naturally loving behavior.

Inspired by Gerasim's devotion, Ivan Ilyich becomes capable of extending compassion to his wife and son. When his condition takes a final, fatal turn, as he feels himself slowly sucked into the bottom of death's sack, he comes to the realization that his life has been trivial, empty, worthless. Two hours before his death, he stops trying to justify it and instead takes pity on his wife, son, and himself. He dies loving rather than hating, forgiving rather than whining, at last surrendering his egoism. Both the story and Ivan Ilyich's life thus end on a note of serenity and joyous illumination. Tolstoy shows that profound consciousness of death can bring one to the communion of true brotherhood. Through his relentless pain, Ivan Ilyich discovers the truth about himself, akin to Prince Andrey in *War and Peace*.

THE KREUTZER SONATA

The Kreutzer Sonata, like *The Death of Ivan Ilyich*, is a condensed masterpiece of harrowing intensity, a poem of the poignant pains of the flesh. Tolstoy presents the nature of marriage more directly and comprehensively than any other writer. In *Family Happiness*, he tries to define its benefits and banes; in *War and Peace*, he celebrates it; in *Anna Karenina*, he upholds yet also questions it; in *The Kreutzer Sonata*, he denounces it vehemently. Though he previously advocated marriage as the morally and socially legitimate release for sexual needs, by the late 1880's, his new views on morality, as well as his own increasingly burdensome marriage, caused him to equate sexuality with hostility and sinfulness and to regard sexual passion as degrading, undermining human beings' spiritual self.

The novella's protagonist, Pozdnyshev, confesses on a train journey that he murdered his wife on suspicion—groundless, as circumstances indicate—of her adultery with an amateur violinist with whom she, a pianist, enjoyed playing duets—such as Ludwig van Beethoven's "Kreutzer Sonata." In the spring of 1888, a performance of this work did take place in Tolstoy's Moscow residence. He proposed to the great realistic painter also present, Ilya Repin, that the artist should paint a canvas, while he would write a story, on the theme of marital jealousy. While Tolstoy fulfilled the bargain, Repin did not. The tale was submitted to the state censor in 1888; Czar Alexander III, who read a copy, issued an imperial banning order. Sophia Tolstoya thereupon removed some of the story's sexual explicitness, and the czar permitted its publication, in bowdlerized form, in 1891. Not until the 1933 Jubilee Edition of Tolstoy's works was the text issued in its original form. Yet even in its toned-down version, it aroused a storm of controversy among readers.

Pozdnyshev relates his conduct to a lightly sketched narrator. His dramatic monologue is powerful and polemical, although his arguments are often exaggerated and inconsistent. The point of his narrative is that sex is sinful, that those who submit to its drives often become vicious and, in Pozdnyshev's case, murderous. Even in marriage, the protagonist insists, sex is ugly, repulsive, and destructive. Despite the deranged character of Pozdnyshev and the manifest injustice of many of his views, the story is disturbing, forceful, and gripping, as he shows how his sexual lust degraded his character and ruined his marriage. Some critics have interpreted the structure of the tale as equivalent to the sonata form, falling into three movements with a slow introduction and the final chapter as a coda. Tolstoy was himself an accomplished pianist.

In a long, uncompromising afterword to the story, Tolstoy addresses the controversy it caused and clearly links Pozdnyshev's views—but not his pathological personality—to his. He argues that carnal love lowers human beings to animalistic conduct, advocates chastity within as well as outside marriage, denounces society for featuring erotic allure, and dismisses marriage itself as a trap for humanity's finest energies. Men and women should replace conjugal relations "with the pure relations that exist between a brother and a sister." Only thus would they behave as true Christians. Tolstoy thus dismisses sex as relevant—let alone fundamental—to human behavior. Rather, he regards it as a diabolic temptation sent to divert human beings' purpose from seeking the kingdom of God on earth.

"MASTER AND MAN"

In his moralistic monograph, *What Is Art?*, Tolstoy asks for writing that is easily understandable, whose subject matter is religious, situations universal, style simple, and technique accessible. None of his successful works embodies these criteria more faithfully than "Master and Man," which is essentially a morality play based on the New Testament. The master is Vasíli Andréevich Brekhunov: selfish, overbearing, coarse, rich, rapacious, the biblical gatherer of wealth who neglects his soul. The servant is Nikíta, a reformed drunkard, who is humane, sensitive, skilled in his work, strong, meek, kindly, rich in spirit though poor in pocket. The contrast between them is stark, with Tolstoy stressing the unambiguous and heavily symbolic nature of the novella: two opposed sorts of men, two opposed sets of moral values, and the conversion of the master to the ethics of his man. The man of flesh and the man of spirit join in the journey of life and the confrontation with death.

Brekhunov, a merchant proud of his ability to drive a hard bargain, sets off with Nikíta on a business trip to make a down payment on a grove. He can consider nothing but his possessions and how to increase them; his relationships to others are governed by materialistic calculations. On their trip, the pair find themselves immersed in a raging snowstorm, which obliterates all landmarks and turns the landscape into a perilous Wood of Error, a moral Wasteland, through which they must make life's passage. Tolstoy masterfully uses the storm for its emblematic qualities. It "buries" the travelers in snowdrifts, is cold like death, turns the substantial into the spectral and vice versa. They lose their way as Brekhunov insists on movements to the left, since men find their reward only on the right hand of God. As Brekhunov urges his horse away from the sled, after having (temporarily) deserted Nikíta, he can only come around in a circle to the same spot, marked by wormwood stalks—wormwood being identified with sin and punishment in Revelation. He is ritualistically confronted with himself in the person of a horsethief, for Brekhunov has been cheating Nikíta of his wages and has stolen a large sum of money from his church to buy the grove.

Nikíta accepts his master's wrong turns without anger or reproof, resigns himself to the snowstorm, and patiently prepares to wait it out when they are forced to settle down for the night in their sled. Around midnight, ill-clad and half-frozen, meekly awaiting likely death before morning, Nikíta asks his master to give the wages owed him to his family and to "Forgive me for Christ's sake!" Finally, moved to pity by Nikíta's words, Brekhunov opens his heavy fur coat and lies down on top of his servant, covering Nikíta with both his coat and body as he sobs.

Just before dawn Brekhunov has a visionary dream, in which "it seemed to him that he was Nikíta and Nikíta was he, and that his life was not in himself but in Nikíta." He wonders why he used to trouble himself so greatly to accumulate money and possessions. At noon the next day, peasants drag both men out of the snow. Brekhunov is frozen to death; Nikíta, though chilled, is alive.

Some critics have faulted the story's ending because Tolstoy has inadequately prepared the reader for Brekhunov's sudden adoption of Christian humility, brotherhood, and self-sacrifice, since he has previously shown not the slightest inclination toward moral regeneration. Be that as it may, most of the tale is enormously impressive in the power of its sensuous description as the snowstorm isolates the couple from ordinary existence, strips them of external comforts, exposes them to the presence of death, forces them to encounter their inmost selves.

Tolstoy's celebration of Brekhunov's redemption through fellowship is his answer to a universe that he has feared all of his life as he confronts the horror of nonexistence conveyed by death. Master and man—or man and man, or man and woman—should cling to each other, love each other, forgive each other. Will such conduct vault their souls into immortality? Tolstoy desperately hopes so.

OTHER MAJOR WORKS

LONG FICTION: *Detstvo*, 1852 (novella; *Childhood*, 1862); *Otrochestvo*, 1854 (novella; *Boyhood*, 1886); *Yunost'*, 1857 (novella; *Youth*, 1886); *Kazaki*, 1863 (*The Cossacks*, 1872); *Voyna i mir*, 1865-1869 (*War and Peace*, 1886); *Anna Karenina*, 1875-1877 (English translation, 1886); *Voskreseniye*, 1899 (*Resurrection*, 1899); *Khadzi-Murat*, 1911 (wr. 1904; *Hadji Murad*, 1911).

PLAYS: *Vlast tmy*, pb. 1887 (*The Power of Darkness*, 1888); *Plody prosveshcheniya*, pr. 1889 (*The Fruits of Englightenment*, 1891); *Zhivoy trup*, pr., pb. 1911 (*The Live Corpse*, 1919); *I svet vo tme svetit*, pb. 1911 (*The Light Shines in Darkness*, 1923); *The Dramatic Works*, pb. 1923.

NONFICTION: *Ispoved'*, 1884 (*A Confession*, 1885); *V chom moya vera*, 1884 (*What I Believe*, 1885); *O zhizni*, 1888 (*Life*, 1888); *Kritika dogmaticheskogo bogosloviya*, 1891 (*A Critique of Dogmatic Theology*, 1904); *Soedinenie i perevod chetyrekh evangeliy*, 1892-1894 (*The Four Gospels Harmonized and Translated*, 1895-1896); *Tsarstvo Bozhie vnutri vas*, 1893 (*The Kingdom of God Is Within You*, 1894); *Chto takoye iskusstvo?*, 1898 (*What Is Art?*, 1898); *Tak chto zhe nam delat?*, 1902 (*What to Do?*, 1887); *O Shekspire i o drame*, 1906 (*Shakespeare and the Drama*, 1906); *The Diaries of Leo Tolstoy, 1847-1852*, 1917; *The Journal of Leo Tolstoy, 1895-1899*, 1917; *Tolstoi's Love Letters*, 1923; *The Private Diary of Leo Tolstoy, 1853-1857*, 1927; *"What Is Art?" and Essays on Art*, 1929; *L. N. Tolstoy o literature: Stati, pisma, dnevniki*, 1955; *Lev Tolstoy ob iskusstve i literature*, 1958; *Leo Tolstoy: Last Diaries*, 1960.

CHILDREN'S LITERATURE: *Azbuka*, 1872; *Novaya azbuka*, 1875; *Russkie knigi dlya chteniya*, 1875.

MISCELLANEOUS: *The Complete Works of Count Tolstoy*, 1904-1905 (24 volumes); *Tolstoy Centenary Edition*, 1928-1937 (21 volumes); *Polnoye sobraniye sochinenii*, 1928-1958 (90 volumes).

BIBLIOGRAPHY

Bayley, John, ed. Introduction to *The Portable Tolstoy*. New York: Viking, 1978. Bayley has written a discerning introduction as well as compiled a comprehensive chronology and select bibliography. This anthology omits the long novels but does excerpt *Childhood, Boyhood*, and *Youth*. The fiction choices are fine. Also included are *A Confession and The Power of Darkness*.

_____. *Tolstoy and the Novel*. London: Chatto & Windus, 1966. Influenced by Henry James's organic conception of the novel, Bayley concentrates on trenchant analyses of *War and Peace* and *Anna Karenina*. He also perceptively examines *Family Happiness, The Kreutzer Sonata*, and *The Devil*.

Berlin, Isaiah. "The Hedgehog and the Fox" and "Tolstoy and Enlightenment." In *Russian Thinkers*. New York: Viking, 1978. The first essay is a famous analysis of Tolstoy's philosophy of history; the second focuses on his indebtedness to Jean-Jacques Rousseau. Both are eloquently written by a distinguished historian and philosopher.

Christian, R. F. *Tolstoy: A Critical Introduction.* Cambridge, England: Cambridge University Press, 1969. Christian is a leading Tolstoyan who is knowledgeable about his subject's sources and influences, writes clearly, and provides particularly helpful interpretations of *Family Happiness* and *The Kreutzer Sonata*.

Jahn, Gary R. *The Death of Ivan Ilich: An Interpretation*. New York: Twayne, 1993. After providing a summary and critique of previous criticism on Tolstoy's most famous story, Jahn examines the context of the story within other works by Tolstoy to argue that the story is an affirmation of life rather than a document of despair.

Orwin, Donna Tussig. *Tolstoy's Art and Thought, 1847-1880*. Princeton, N.J.: Princeton University Press, 1993. Divided into three parts, which coincide with the first three decades of Tolstoy's literary career, Orwin's study attempts to trace the origins and growth of the Russian master's ideas. After focusing on Tolstoy's initial creative vision, Orwin goes on to analyze, in depth, his principal works.

Seifrid, Thomas. "Gazing on Life's Page: Perspectival Vision in Tolstoy." *PMLA* 113 (May, 1998): 436-448. Suggests that the typical visual situation in Tolstoy's fiction is perspectival; argues that Tolstoy's impulse can be linked with the material nature of books and that this linkage has implications for Russian culture as well as for the relation between the verbal and the visual in general.

Simmons, Ernest T. *Introduction to Tolstoy's Writings*. Chicago: University of Chicago Press, 1968. Simmons is the dean of Russian literature studies in the United States and has also written a two-volume biography of Tolstoy. This book is compact, well organized, comprehensive, and reliable. Its style, unfortunately, is pedestrian.

Steiner, George. *Tolstoy or Dostoevsky: An Essay in the Old Criticism*. 2d ed. New Haven, Conn.: Yale University Press, 1996. This welcome reappearance of a classic study of the epic versus the dramatic, first published in 1959, carries only a new preface. In it, however, Steiner makes a compelling case for the reprinting, in the age of deconstructionism, of this wide-ranging study not just

of individual texts, but of contrasting worldviews.
Wasiolek, Edward. *Tolstoy's Major Fiction*. Chicago: University of Chicago Press, 1978. Having written a superb study of Fyodor Dostoevski's fiction, Wasiolek has composed an equally first-rate critique of Tolstoy's. He concentrates on thorough analyses of ten Tolstoyan works, including *Family*

Happiness, The Death of Ivan Ilyich, and "Master and Man." His is a close and acute reading, influenced by Russian Formalists and by Roland Barthes. A twenty-page chronicle of Tolstoy's life and work is illuminating.

Gerhard Brand

JEAN TOOMER

Born: Washington, D.C.; December 26, 1894
Died: Doylestown, Pennsylvania; March 30, 1967

PRINCIPAL SHORT FICTION

Cane, 1923 (prose and poetry)
"Mr. Costyve Duditch, 1928
"York Beach," 1929
The Wayward and the Seeking, 1980 (Darwin T. Turner, editor; prose and poetry)

OTHER LITERARY FORMS

All Jean Toomer's best fiction appears in *Cane*, which also includes fifteen poems. Toomer later wrote fragments of an autobiography and several essays, the most important of which are found in *Essentials: Definitions and Aphorisms* (1931).

ACHIEVEMENTS

Jean Toomer's *Cane*, published in 1923, is considered to be one of the masterpieces of experimental fiction and one of the most important and relevant evocations of African American life in the twentieth century. Toomer's book was rediscovered in the late 1960's after it was reprinted in 1967. *Cane* is represented in most anthologies of American literature, guaranteeing the author a distinguished place in American literary history.

BIOGRAPHY

Born Nathan Eugene Toomer in Washington, D.C., on December 26, 1894, Jean Toomer stayed in

the North for his education, attending the University of Wisconsin and the City College of New York. He began writing and was published in the little magazines of his time before moving South to become a schoolteacher in rural Georgia, an experience which he uses in "Kabnis," the final part of *Cane*. Married twice to whites, Toomer was often equivocal about his blackness, partially because of his involvement in Unitism, the philosophy of George Ivanovitch Gurdjieff. Toomer's later essays and stories expound his version of the philosophy and are often weakened by an excess of mystery and a deficiency of manners. In later life, he lived among the Quakers in Pennsylvania. Toomer died in 1967.

ANALYSIS

Divided into three parts, Jean Toomer's *Cane* consists of short stories, sketches, poems, and a novella. The first section focuses on women; the second on relationships between men and women; and the third on one man. Although capable of being read discretely, these works achieve their full power when read together, coalescing to create a novel, unified by theme and symbol.

CANE

Like all Toomer's work, *Cane* describes characters who have within a buried life, a dream that seeks expression and fulfillment; *Cane* is a record of the destruction of those dreams. Sometimes the dreams explode, the fire within manifesting itself violently; more often, however, the world implodes within the

Jean Toomer (Beineke Rare Book and Manuscript Library, Yale University)

dreamer's mind. These failures have external causes—the inadequacy or refusal of the society to allow expression, the restrictions by what Toomer calls the herd—and internal ones—the fears and divisions within the dreamer himself, as he struggles unsuccessfully to unite will and mind, passion and intellect, what Toomer in the later story, "York Beach," calls the wish for brilliant experience and the wish for difficult experience.

The one limitation on the otherwise thoroughgoing romanticism of this vision is Toomer's rigorous separation of humankind into those who dream, who are worth bothering about, and those who do not. While the struggle of Toomer's characters is for unity, it is to unify themselves or to find union with one other dreamer, never to merge with man in general. Like Kabnis, many find their true identity in recognizing their differences, uniqueness, and superiority. At the end of "York Beach," the protagonist tells his listeners that the best government would be an empire ruled by one who recognized his own greatness.

Toomer's dreamers find themselves in the first and third sections of *Cane* in a southern society which, although poor in compassion and understanding, is rich in supportive imagery. In the second part, set in the North, that imagery is also absent, so the return of the protagonist to the South in part 3 is logical, since the North has not provided a nurturing setting. Although the return may be a plunge back into hell, it is also a journey to an underground where Kabnis attains the vision that sets him free.

The imagery is unified by a common theme: ascent. Kabnis says, "But its the soul of me that needs the risin," and all the imagery portrays the buried life smoldering within, fighting upward, seeking release. The dominant image of the book, the one that supplies the title, is the rising sap of the sugarcane. Cane whispers enigmatic messages to the characters, and it is to cane fields that people seeking escape and release flee. Sap rises, too, in pines, which also whisper and sing; and at the mill of part 1, wood burns, its smoke rising. The moon in "Blood-Burning Moon" is said to "sink upward," an oxymoronic yoking that implies the difficulty of the risin in this book.

A second pattern of imagery is that of flowing blood or water, although generally in the pessimistic *Cane*, water is not abundant. In "November Cotton Flower," dead birds are found in the wells, and when water is present, the characters, threatened by the life it represents, often fear it. Rhobert, in a sketch of that name, wears a diver's helmet to protect him from water, life which is being drawn off. Dreams denied, blood flows more freely than water.

"ESTHER"

"Esther," the most successful story in *Cane*, comes early and embodies many of the book's major themes. It opens with a series of four sentences describing Esther as a girl of nine. In each, the first clause compliments her beauty, the second takes the praise away; the first clauses of each are progressively less strong. Esther represents the destruction of potential by a combination of inner and outer forces. On the outside there is her father, "the richest colored man in town," who reduces Esther to a drab and obsequious life behind a counter in his dry goods store. "Her hair thins. It looks like the dull silk on puny corn ears." Then there is King Barlo, a black giant, who has a vision in the corner of town known as the Spittoon. There, while townspeople gather to watch (and black and white preachers find momentary unity in working out ways to rid themselves of one who threatens their power), Barlo sees a strong black man arise. While the man's head is in the clouds, however, "little white-ant biddies come and tie his feet to chains." The herd in Barlo's vision, as in Toomer's, may destroy the dreamer.

Many, however, are affected by what Barlo has seen, none more so than Esther, who decides that she loves him. The fire begins to burn within. As she stands dreaming in her store, the sun on the windows across the street reflect her inner fire, and, wanting to make it real, Esther calls the fire department. For the next eighteen years, Esther, the saddest of all Toomer's women, lives only on dreams, inventing a baby, conceived, she thinks, immaculately. Sometimes, like many of his characters, sensing that life may be too much for her, knowing that "emptiness is a thing that grows by being moved," she tries not to dream, sets her mind against dreaming, but the dreams continue.

At the end of the story, Esther, then twenty-seven, decides to visit Barlo, who has returned to town. She finds the object of her dream in a room full of prostitutes; what rises is only the fumes of liquor. "Conception with a drunken man must be a mighty sin," she thinks, and, when she attempts to return to reality, she, like many Toomer characters, finds that the world has overwhelmed her. Crushed from without, she has neither life nor dreams. "There is no air, no street, and the town has completely disappeared."

"Blood-Burning Moon"

So, too, in "Blood-Burning Moon," Toomer's most widely anthologized short story and also from the woman-centered first section, is the main character destroyed emotionally. Here, however, the destructive force is primarily internal. Among the most conventional of Toomer's stories, "Blood-Burning Moon" has both a carefully delineated plot and a familiar one at that: a love triangle. What is inventional is the way Toomer manages the reader's feelings about the woman whom two men love. Both men are

stereotypes. Bob Stone is white and repulsively so. Himself divided and content to be, he makes his mind consciously white and approaches Louisa "as a master should." The black, Tom Burwell, is a stereotype too: Having dreams, he expresses his love sincerely, but inarticulately; denied or threatened, he expresses himself violently.

The first two sections open with rhythmic sentences beginning with the word "up"; Louisa sings songs against the omen the rising moon portends, seeking charms and spells, but refusing the simple act of choosing between the two men. Because Louisa does not choose, the story comes to its inevitable violent climax and the death of both men. There is more, however: When Louisa is last seen she too has been destroyed, mentally, if not physically. She sings again to the full moon as an omen, hoping that people will join her, hoping that Tom Burwell will come; but her choice is too late. Burwell is dead, and the lateness of her decision marks the end of her dreams. Like Esther, she is separated from even appropriate mental contact with the world that is.

Cane, Section 2

Barlo's vision (in "Esther"), then, is accurate but incomplete as a description of what happens to Toomer's protagonists. While it is true that the herd will often destroy the dreamer, it is just as likely that the dreamer, from inaction, fear, and division, will destroy himself. The four stories of section 2 all focus on pairs of dreamers who can isolate themselves from the rest of society but who cannot get their dreams to merge. In "Avey" it is the man who, focused on his own dreams, refuses to listen to and accept the value of Avey's. In "Bona and Paul," Paul, a black, takes Bona away from the dance, not, as everyone assumes, to make love to her, but to know her; but knowing a human is denied him because Bona assumes she already knows him, "a priori," as he has said. Knowing he is black, she "knows" that he will be passionate. When he is interested in knowledge before passion, she discovers that to know *a priori* is not to know at all and flees him, denying his dream of knowing her.

In "Theater" the divided main character, sitting half in light, half in shadow, watches another dreamer, the dancer on stage, Dorris. She is dreaming of him, but, although "mind pulls him upward into dream," suspicion is stronger than desire, and by the end of the story John has moved wholly into shadow. When Dorris looks at him, "She finds it a dead thing in the shadow which is his dream." Likewise, in "Box Seat" Muriel is torn between the dreamer Dan, who stands with one hand lying on the wall, feeling from below the house the deep underground rumbling of the subway, literal buried life, and Mrs. Pribby, the landlady, rattling her newspaper, its thin noise contrasting with the powerful below-ground sound. Muriel chooses respectability. At the theater, to which Dan has followed her, she is repelled by a dwarf who offers her a rose; Dan rises to his feet to proclaim that Jesus was once a leper. This last, insistent image, suggesting the maimed sources of beauty that Muriel is too timid to accept, also indicates the overexplicit inflation of claims that damages some of Toomer's fiction. Although in *Cane* most of the stories are under control, some seem rather too sketchy; "Box Seat," however, foreshadows the fault that mars all of Toomer's later fiction: the sacrifice of dramatic ideas in favor of, often pallid, philosophical ones.

"KABNIS"

The last and longest story in *Cane* integrates the themes, making explicit the nature of the destructive forces. The story is "Kabnis," a novella, and the force is sin, a word contained backward in Kabnis's name. It is the story of a black man out of place in the rural South, threatened not so much by whites as by his own people, by his environment, and by his sense of himself.

As the story opens, Kabnis is trying to sleep, but he is not allowed this source of dream; instead, chickens and rats, nature itself, keep him awake. He wants to curse it, wants it to be consistent in its ugliness, but he senses too the beauty of nature, and, because that prevents him from hating it entirely, he feels that even beauty is a curse. Intimidated by nature, Kabnis is also attacked by society, by the local black church, of which the shouting acclamations of faith torture Kabnis, and by the black school superintendent who fires him for drinking. As in "Box Seat," the protagonist is thus caught between expressions of life, which

are yet too strong for him, and its repression, which traps him. So positioned, Kabnis, like Rhobert, is a man drowning, trying vainly to avoid the source of life. From this low point, for the only time in the book, Toomer describes the way up, and Kabnis gains enough strength to throw off his oppression.

He has three friends: Halsey, an educated black who has been playing Uncle Tom; Layman, a preacher, whose low voice suggests a canebrake; and Lewis, a *Doppelgänger* who suggests a version of what a stronger Kabnis might have become and who drops out of the story when Kabnis does indeed become stronger. Once fired, Kabnis takes up residence with Halsey, a Vulcan-like blacksmith who gives him work repairing implements, work for which Kabnis is ill-suited. In his basement, however, Halsey has his own buried life, an old man, Father John, and in the climactic scene, the three men descend into the underground for a dark night of the soul, for the *Walpurgisnacht* on which Kabnis confronts his own demons. Prefiguring the descents in such black fiction as Richard Wright's "Man Who Lived Underground" and Ralph Ellison's *Invisible Man* (1952), this is likewise a descent during which the values of the world above, met on unfamiliar terrain, are rethought. It is a night of debauchery, but also the night when the destructive illusions and fears of the men are exposed.

Father John represents those fears; when he speaks, his message is sin; but Kabnis knows, and for the first time can say, that because of sin the old man has never seen the beauty of the world. Kabnis has, and as he says, "No eyes that have seen beauty ever lose their sight." Kabnis then proclaims a new role for himself: If he is not a blacksmith, he may be, having known beauty, a wordsmith. "I've been shapin words after a design that branded here. Know whats here? M soul." If sin is what is done against the soul and if the soul of Kabnis is what needs the rising, then, as Kabnis says, the world has conspired against him. Now, however, Kabnis acknowledges and confronts that conspiracy, no longer fearing it or Father John. Exhausted by his effort, Kabnis sinks back, but Halsey's sister, Carrie K, does indeed carry K. She lifts him up, and together they ascend the stairs into the daylight, as the risen sun sings a "birth-song" down the streets of the town.

The end is not unequivocally optimistic: It is too small and too tentative a note in this large catalog of the defeated and destroyed. *Cane* does, however, suggest finally that as destructive as dreams may be, once one has seen beauty, if he can free himself from repression, from sin, he may re-create himself. "Kabnis is me," wrote Toomer to Waldo Frank, and he had more in mind than just his use of his experiences. For what Toomer has done in *Cane* is to chart the varieties of sin that society has done to people and, more important, since individuals are always more interesting than society to Toomer, that people have done to themselves. Wholeness is the aim, a wholeness that breaks down barriers between mind and will, man and woman, object and subject, and that allows the potential of dreams to be fulfilled. That the wholeness is so difficult to achieve is the substance of Toomer's short fiction; that Toomer achieves it, both for a character in "Kabnis" and more permanently in his only successful work, a book uniting fiction and poetry, songs and narration, images of fire and water, of descent and ascent, is his testimony that wholeness can be achieved by those who dream of it.

OTHER MAJOR WORKS

PLAY: "Balo," in Alain Locke's *Plays of Negro Life*, pb. 1927.

POETRY: "Banking Coal," in *Crisis*, 1922; *Cane*, 1923 (prose and poetry); "Blue Meridian," in *New American Caravan*, 1936; *The Wayward and the Seeking*, 1980 (Darwin T. Turner, editor; prose and poetry); *The Collected Poems of Jean Toomer*, 1988.

NONFICTION: "Winter on Earth," in *The Second American Caravan*, 1929; "Race Problems and Modern Society," 1929; *Essentials: Definitions and Aphorisms*, 1931; "The Flavor of Man," 1949.

BIBLIOGRAPHY

Bone, Robert. *Down Home: A History of Afro-American Short Fiction from Its Beginnings to the End of the Harlem Renaissance*. New York: Capricorn Books, 1975. Argues that the theater in Toomer's story "The Theater" is an emblem of the two-way, reciprocal relationship of life and art, for there is an osmotic relationship between the life outside and the show inside. "Art-as-transfiguration" is Toomer's theme here; he is concerned with the death of experience and its rebirth as art.

Byrd, Rudolph. *Jean Toomer's Years with Gurdijieff: Portrait of an Artist, 1923-1936*. Athens: University of Georgia Press, 1990. A good introduction to Toomer's years of studying orientalism and the mystical philosophy of George Ivanovitch Gurdjieff. It indicates that, although Toomer was an African American writer, his concerns were primarily spiritual and philosophical rather than social and ethnic. It is a fascinating account of one part of Jean Toomer's life.

_____. "Was He There With Them?" In *The Harlem Renaissance: Reevaluations*. New York: Garland, 1989. This article examines Toomer's tenuous relationship with the writers of the Harlem Renaissance. It asserts that, although Toomer identified with many of the issues and social concerns being addressed by African American writers, his style, techniques, and philosophy made him something of an outsider and gave him a unique position among the major African American writers of the 1920's.

Hajek, Friederike. "The Change of Literary Authority in the Harlem Renaissance: Jean Toomer's *Cane*." In *The Black Columbiad: Defining Moments in African American Literature and Culture*, edited by Werner Sollos and Maria Diedrich. Cambridge, Mass.: Harvard University Press, 1994. Argues that one of the main unifying elements in *Cane* is the concept of changing authority, which occurs in three phrases corresponding to the three sections of the text. Asserts that the work is a swan song for a dying folk culture and a birth chant for a new black aesthetic.

Jones, Robert B. Introduction to *The Collected Poems of Jean Toomer*. Edited by Robert B. Jones and Margery Toomer Latimer. Chapel Hill: University of North Carolina Press, 1988. Although this book is not about Toomer's fiction, the introduction gives an excellent account of Toomer's life and work within the context of the various phases of his writing and philosophical studies. In addition, it discusses the authors and poets who influenced Toomer's life and writings.

Kerman, Cynthia. *The Lives of Jean Toomer: A Hunger for Wholeness*. Baton Rouge: Louisiana State University Press, 1988. This book gives an account of the various stages of Jean Toomer's life and his attempts to find spiritual guidance and revelation throughout his lifetime. An interesting account of a fascinating life.

Moore, Lewis D. "Kabnis and the Reality of Hope: Jean Toomer's *Cane.*" *North Dakota Quarterly* 54 (Spring, 1986): 30-39. Moore's article discusses the elements of "hope" within the context of the characters in *Cane*. In particular, he indicates that despite the repressive aspects of the society in which they live, Toomer's characters are redeemed and indeed triumph over that society by virtue of the positive aspects of their humanity.

Scruggs, Charles, and Lee VanDemarr. *Jean Toomer and the Terrors of American History*. Philadelphia: University of Pennsylvania Press, 1998. Provides critical evaluation of *Cane* and other Toomer works. Includes bibliographical references and an index.

Taylor, Paul Beekman. *Shadows of Heaven*. York Beach, Me.: S. Weiser, 1998. Examines the lives and works of Toomer, George Ivanovitch Gurdjieff, and A. R. Orage.

Wagner-Martin, Linda. "Toomer's *Cane* as Narrative Sequence." In *Modern American Short Story Sequences*, edited by J. Gerald Kennedy. Cambridge, England: Cambridge University Press, 1995. Discusses *Cane* as a modernist tour de force of mixed genre. Examines "Blood-Burning Moon" as Toomer's ideal fiction construct that provides insight into the structural and thematic radicalism of the collection.

Howard Faulkner, updated by
Earl Paulus Murphy

WILLIAM TREVOR
William Trevor Cox

Born: Mitchelstown, County Cork, Ireland; May 24, 1928

PRINCIPAL SHORT FICTION

The Day We Got Drunk on Cake and Other Stories, 1967

The Ballroom of Romance and Other Stories, 1972

The Last Lunch of the Season, 1973

Angels at the Ritz and Other Stories, 1975

Lovers of Their Time and Other Stories, 1978

Beyond the Pale and Other Stories, 1981

The Stories of William Trevor, 1983

The News from Ireland and Other Stories, 1986

Family Sins and Other Stories, 1990

Collected Stories, 1992

Ireland: Selected Stories, 1995

Outside Ireland: Selected Stories, 1995

Marrying Damian, 1995

After Rain, 1996

The Hill Bachelors, 2000

OTHER LITERARY FORMS

Though probably best known as a writer of short stories, William Trevor has also written television and radio scripts, plays, and numerous novels. Among Trevor's novels, *The Old Boys, Miss Gomez and the Brethren, Elizabeth Alone* (1973), *The Children of Dynmouth* (1976), *Fools of Fortune* (1983), *Felicia's Journey* (1994), and *Death in Summer* (1998) have been particularly praised. He has also written two nonfiction works, *A Writer's Ireland: Landscape in Literature* (1984) and *Excursions in the Real World* (1993).

ACHIEVEMENTS

William Trevor is widely regarded as one of the finest storytellers and craftsmen writing in English. In Great Britain, his work has long been widely and favorably reviewed and has frequently been adapted for radio and television broadcast by the British Broadcasting Corporation. In 1964, Trevor's second novel, *The Old Boys*, was awarded the Hawthornden Prize; his fourth collection, *Angels at the Ritz and Other Stories*, was hailed by writer Graham Greene as "one of the finest collections, if not the best, since Joyce's *Dubliners*." In addition, Trevor has won the Royal Society of Literature Award, the Allied Irish Banks' Prize for Literature, and the Whitbread Literary Award; he is also a member of the Irish Academy of Letters. In 1979, "in recognition for his valuable services to literature," Trevor was named an honorary Commander, Order of the British Empire and in the same year received the Irish Community Prize. In 1980 and 1982, he received the Giles Cooper Award for radio plays; in 1983, he received a Jacob Award for a teleplay. He received D.Litt. degrees from the University of Exeter, Trinity College in Dublin, the University of Belfast, and the National University of Ireland in Cork. Trevor received the Sunday Express Book of the Year Award in 1994 for *Felicia's Journey*. In the United States, knowledge of Trevor's work increased markedly when *The Stories of William Trevor*, an omnibus collection, was published in 1983 and received wide and highly enthusiastic reviews.

BIOGRAPHY

Born William Trevor Cox in Ireland's County Cork, William Trevor, the son of a bank manager, spent much of his childhood living in small Irish towns and attending a series of boarding and day schools that included St. Columba's in Dublin. After earning a B.A. in history from Dublin's Trinity College, Trevor, a Protestant, began work as a sculptor and schoolmaster, taking his first job as an instructor of history in Armagh, Northern Ireland. In 1952,

Trevor married Jane Ryan and moved to England, where he spent the next eight years teaching art at two prestigious public schools—first at Rugby and then at Taunton. Between 1960 and 1965, Trevor worked as a copywriter at an advertising agency in London; he simultaneously began devoting an increasing portion of his free time to the writing of fiction. By the early 1970's, following the appearance of several novels and a steady stream of stories in such publications as *Encounter, The New Yorker*, and *London Magazine*, Trevor's reputation was secure. The father of two sons, Trevor settled in Devon and continued to write full time.

ANALYSIS

Like his novels, William Trevor's short stories generally take place in either England or the Republic of Ireland. For the most part, Trevor focuses on middle-class or lower-middle-class figures whose lives have been characterized by loneliness, disappointment, and pain. His stories feature tight organization and lean but detailed prose. Their very "average" characters are made interesting by Trevor's careful attention to the traits and quirks that make them individuals, to the memories and regrets they have of the past. Trevor, often wry and always detached, refuses to sentimentalize any of them; he does not, however, subject them to ridicule. Their struggles reveal the author's deep curiosity about the manifold means by which people foil themselves or, more rarely, manage not to do so. Many of Trevor's characters are trapped in jobs or familial circumstances that are dull or oppressive or both; many retreat frequently to fond memories or romantic fantasies. Trevor rarely mocks the men and women who inhabit his fiction, nor does he treat them as mere ciphers or automatons. In fact, like James Joyce, to whom he is often compared, Trevor assumes a detached authorial stance, but occasionally and subtly he makes it clear that he is highly sympathetic to the plight of underdogs, self-deluders, and the victims of abuse and deceit. Invariably, his principal characters are carefully and completely drawn—and so are the worlds they inhabit. Few contemporary writers of short fiction can render atmosphere and the subtleties of personality as precisely and as tellingly as William Trevor. Few can capture so accurately and wittily the rhythms and nuances of everyday speech. Though its themes can be somber and settings quite bleak, Trevor's brilliantly paced and carefully sculpted fiction consistently moves, amuses, and invigorates.

"THE GENERAL'S DAY"

One of Trevor's earliest stories, "The General's Day," illustrates with particular clarity the darkest side of his artistic vision. Contained in *The Day We Got Drunk on Cake and Other Stories*, "The General's Day" centers on a decorated and now-retired military man who, at seventy-eight, has never quite come to grips with his retirement and so spends his days wandering around the local village looking for something to do. On the day of the story, a sunny Saturday in June, General Suffolk greets the day with energy and resolution but ends by simply killing time in the local tea shop, where he musters what is left of his once-celebrated charm and manages to convince a woman—"a thin, middle-aged person with a face like a faded photograph"—to join him for drinks at the local hotel. There, fueled by gin, General Suffolk flirts so blatantly and clumsily with the woman that she flees, "her face like a beetroot." Fueled by more gin, the lonely man becomes increasingly obnoxious. After suffering a few more rejections and humiliations, he finally stumbles back home, where he is mocked further by his "unreliable servant," Mrs. Hinch, a crude woman who habitually cuts corners and treats herself to secretive swigs of the general's expensive South African sherry. In the story's final scene, General Suffolk, "the hero of Roeux and Monchy-le-Preux," is shown leaning and weeping on his cleaning woman's fat arm as she laughingly helps him back to his cottage. "My God Almighty," General Suffolk, deflated, mutters, "I could live for twenty years."

"AN EVENING WITH JOHN JOE DEMPSEY"

Trevor often portrays older men and women who make stoic adjustments to the present while living principally in the past. He also sometimes focuses on children and adolescents who use vividly constructed daydreams as a means of escaping dreary surroundings or obtuse parents who are themselves sunk in the deadness of their cramped and predictable lives. In "An Evening with John Joe Dempsey," from *The Ballroom of Romance and Other Stories*, Trevor's central figure is a boy of fifteen who lives in a small house in a small Irish town where, daily, he sits in a dull classroom in preparation for a dead-end job at the nearby sawmills. John Joe lives with his widowed mother, a wiry, chronically worried woman, whose principal interest in life is to hover protectively about her only son. John Joe escapes his mother's smothering solicitations by wandering about the town with Quigley, a rather elderly dwarf reputed to be, as one local puts it, "away in the head." Quigley likes to fire John Joe's already active imagination by regaling the boy with detailed descriptions of the sexual vignettes he claims to have witnessed while peeping through area windows. In his own daydreams, John Joe dallies with many of the same sizable matrons whom Quigley likes to portray in compromising positions. One of them, Mrs. Taggart, "the wife of a postman," is a tall, "well-built" woman who in John Joe's fantasies requires repeated rescuing from a locked bathroom in which she stands unblushingly nude. Like many of Trevor's characters, John Joe is thus a convincing mix of the comic and the pathetic. If his incongruous sexual fantasies are humorous, the rest of his life looks decidedly grim. In the story's particularly effective closing scene, Trevor portrays John Joe in his bed, in the dark, thinking again of impossible erotic romps with wholly unobtainable women, feeling

> more alive than ever he was at the Christian Brothers' School . . . or his mother's kitchen, more alive than ever he would be at the sawmills. In his bed he entered a paradise: it was grand being alone.

"NICE DAY AT SCHOOL"

In "Nice Day at School," from the same collection, Trevor's principal character is a girl of fourteen, Eleanor, who lives on a housing estate with her cranky, chain-smoking mother and her father, a former professional wrestler who now works as a nightclub bouncer and likes to claim that his work has made him the trusted friend of many celebrities, including Rex Harrison, Mia Farrow, Princess Margaret, and Anthony Armstrong-Jones. Though Eleanor is embarrassed by her father's obviously exaggerated accounts of his encounters with the rich and famous, she is much given to vivid imaginings of her own. Bombarded daily by saccharine pop songs and the more blatantly sexual chatter of her friends, Eleanor thinks obsessively of her ideal lover:

> a man whose fingers were long and thin and gentle, who'd hold her hand in the aeroplane. Air France to Biarritz. And afterwards she'd come back to a flat where the curtains were the colour of lavender, the same as the walls, where gas fires glowed and there were rugs on natural-wood floors, and the telephone was pale blue.

Subtly, however, Trevor indicates that Eleanor is not likely to find a lover so wealthy and suave. Like her friends and most girls of the same social class, this daughter of a bloated bouncer and a bored, gin-sipping housewife will instead settle for someone like Denny Price, the young butcher's apprentice with "blubbery" lips, who once moved his rough hand up and down her body "like an animal, a rat gnawing at her, prodding her and poking."

"OFFICE ROMANCES"

Trevor often focuses on women who find themselves pursued by or entangled with insensitive or calculating males. In "Office Romances," from *Angels at the Ritz and Other Stories*, Trevor's central character is Angela Hosford, a typist who works quite anonymously in a large London office appointed with "steel-framed reproductions" and "ersatz leather" sofas and chairs. At twenty-six, Angela is pleasant but plain and myopic: She wears contact lenses that give her eyes a slightly "bulgy look." Her pursuer, Gordon Spelle, is, at thirty-eight, tall and "sleek," but his left eyelid droops a bit, and the eye it covers is badly glazed. While watching old films on television when she was fourteen, Angela developed a crush on the American actor Don Ameche and had imagined "a life with him in a cliff-top home she'd invented, in California." Now, she finds herself drawn to the deliberately "old fashioned" Spelle and at one point imagines herself "stroking his face and comforting him because of his bad eye." One day, after his flatteries succeed in rendering Angela both "generous and euphoric," Spelle manages to lure her into a dark

and empty office, where—muttering "I love you" repeatedly—he makes love to her, inelegantly, on the floor. Angela finds this experience "not even momentarily pleasurable, not once," but afterward she basks in the memory of Spelle's heated professions of love. Angela eventually takes a job elsewhere, convinced that Spelle's passion for her "put him under a strain, he being married to a wife who was ill." Like many of Trevor's characters, she understandably decides not to look past her comforting delusions; she refuses to accept the well-known fact that Spelle was "notorious" and "chose girls who were unattractive because he believed such girls, deprived of sex for long periods of time, were an easier bet."

"LOVERS OF THEIR TIME"

The vast gulf that often separates romantic fantasy from unsavory fact is similarly revealed in the title story of *Lovers of Their Time and Other Stories*. In this piece, set in the 1960's, Trevor's lovers are Norman Britt, a mild-mannered travel agent with "a David Niven moustache," and a young woman, Marie, who tends the counter at Green's the Chemist's. Norman and Marie meet regularly in one of Trevor's favorite fictional locations—a dark pub filled with a wide array of drinkers, talkers, and dreamers.

"THE DRUMMER BOY"

In that same place, in "The Drummer Boy," the two listen to Beatles songs and talk of running away with each other to some romantic foreign country—an event they realize is not likely to materialize. Marie is single, but Norman is married to the loud and bawdy Hilda, who spends the better part of her life sipping cheap wine and watching police dramas on the television and who has previously hinted that she is quite content in the odd marital arrangement that Norman loathes. Thus, at Norman's instigation, the two lovers begin to rendezvous more intimately at the nearby hotel, the Great Western Royal. More specifically, they begin to sneak into a large, infrequently used bathroom, "done up in marble," on the hotel's second floor. Here, luxuriating in an enormous tub, they talk hopefully of happier days that, unfortunately, never arrive. Hilda dismisses her husband's request for a divorce by telling him, "You've gone barmy, Norman"; Marie, tired of waiting, weds "a man in a brewery." Thus, as the years pass, Norman is left with a nostalgic longing not only for Marie but also for that brief period in the 1960's when playful risk-taking was much in the air. Often, while riding "the tube" to work, Norman

> would close his eyes and with the greatest pleasure that remained to him he would recall the delicately veined marble and the great brass taps, and the bath that was big enough for two. And now and again he heard what happened to be the sound of distant music, and the voices of the Beatles celebrating a bathroom love, as they had celebrated Eleanor Rigby and other people of that time.

"FLIGHTS OF FANCY"

This allusion to a popular and bittersweet Beatles song is especially appropriate in yet another Trevor story about two thoroughly average and lonely people whose lives have not often been marked by episodes of great passion. In "Flights of Fancy," also from *Lovers of Their Time and Other Stories*, Trevor's principal character, Sarah Machaen, is yet another Rigby-like character destined, one assumes, to spend the rest of her life uneasily alone. Sarah, a clergyman's daughter, is an executive secretary in a large London firm that manufactures lamps; she visits museums, sings in a Bach choir, and is "a popular choice as a godmother." Well into middle age, Sarah is quite content with the externals of her life and gradually has become "reconciled to the fact that her plainness wasn't going to go away." Sometimes, however, she gets lonely enough to daydream of marriage—perhaps to an elderly widower or a blind man. Ironically, the one person who does express a romantic interest in Sarah is another woman, a young and pretty but unschooled factory worker called Sandra Pond. Sarah is shocked at the very idea of lesbianism, yet she cannot stop her mind from "throwing up flights of fancy" in which she pictures herself sharing her flat with Sandra and introducing her to London's many cultural delights. Though her shyness and acute sense of propriety prompt her to reject Sandra's clumsy but clearly genuine professions of love, Sarah is haunted by the sense that she has perhaps passed up her last chance for passion and romance.

"BROKEN HOMES"

"Broken Homes," also from *Lovers of Their Time and Other Stories*, is one of Trevor's most powerful stories. Its principal character, Mrs. Malby, lives with her two budgerigars in a little flat that is scrupulously neat and prettily painted. Mrs. Malby, a widow, lost both of her sons thirty years earlier during World War II; now, at eighty-seven, she has come to terms with her own impending death and wants nothing more than to spend her remaining days in familiar surroundings, her faculties intact. Unfortunately, Mrs. Malby's flat is destroyed and her serenity threatened by a squad of loud and insensitive teenagers from a nearby comprehensive school—"an ugly sprawl of glass and concrete buildings," Mrs. Malby recalls, full of "children swinging along the pavements, shouting obscenities." As part of a community relations scheme, the teenagers have been equipped with mops and sponges and brushes and sent out into the neighborhood in search of good deeds to perform. Mrs. Malby politely asks these obnoxious adolescents to do nothing more than wash her walls, but they treat her with condescension and contempt, and while she is out, they proceed to make a complete mess of her apartment, splattering its walls and floors with bright yellow paint. The students' "teacher," an obtuse and "untidily dressed" bureaucrat, patronizingly assures Mrs. Malby that the damage is slight. He reminds her that, in any event, one must make allowances for the children of "broken homes."

Perhaps more than any of his other stories, "Broken Homes" reveals Trevor's sympathy for the plight of the elderly and his acute awareness of the infirmities and insecurities that accompany old age. The story certainly reveals a strong suspicion that, by the mid-1970's, the British welfare state had become both inefficient and rudely intrusive. Indeed, "Broken Homes" is informed by the subtly expressed sense—not uncommon in Trevor's later fiction—that contemporary Great Britain and Ireland have grown increasingly crass and tacky and that the old social fabric is rapidly and perhaps deleteriously unraveling.

"THE PARADISE LOUNGE"

Arguably, "The Paradise Lounge," from *Beyond the Pale and Other Stories*, is Trevor's most representative story. Set principally in the small bar of Keegan's Railway hotel, in "a hilly provincial town" in the Republic of Ireland, "The Paradise Lounge" shifts its focus between two recognizably Trevoresque figures. One of them, Beatrice, is thirty-two; the other, Miss Doheny, is in her eighties. Beatrice—who wanted to be an actress once—drives often to Keegan's and its adjoining Paradise Lounge to rendezvous with her lover, a middle-aged businessman already married. Miss Doheny, one of the locals, goes regularly to the lounge for a bit of company and several good, stiff drinks. The two have never formally met. Yet Beatrice—observing Miss Doheny from across the room—is convinced that the old woman is an intriguing figure with a fascinating and no doubt satisfyingly romantic past; she does not realize that Miss Doheny is not only lonely but also full of anger and regret. Miss Doheny, in turn, envies Beatrice's freedom—her ability, in a more liberated and enlightened age, to enter into a friendly sexual affair without running the risk of paralyzing guilt and ostracism. She does not realize that the younger woman's affair has grown stale and mechanical and that by her own estimation Beatrice is about to engage in nothing more than a "mess of deception and lies."

AFTER RAIN

The twelve stories of *After Rain* concern how marriage and family ties constrain, bewilder, confound, or, occasionally, help their characters. For instance, a woman's attempt to invigorate the life of her best friend by encouraging an affair ends the friendship; a young man refuses to visit his parents for his birthday because he is jealous of their deep love for each other; a pregnant young woman is forced to marry a man she hardly knows to save the family reputation; a barren wife spends her days drinking herself insensate while fantasizing about her husband's mistress; a Protestant family shrinks in shame when one son claims that a dead Catholic saint has visited him; a retired couple is helpless and dismayed when an old friend, a hopeless reprobate, courts their daughter. As in Trevor's earlier volumes, the central characters, however muddled in their behavior, usually learn some truth about themselves or recognize a fundamental change in their lives. The tone is taut but not

judgmental; the reader is invited to share their emotions rather than laugh at or deplore their plight. The imagery of home, religion, and occupation frequently invests commonplace dramas with broad moral power.

In "The Piano Tuner's Wife," the opening story, a blind piano tuner remarries after his first wife dies. Violet, the second wife, was rejected decades earlier when the piano tuner married her rival, Belle. Now Violet at last succeeds but finds that Belle's memory and style of managing the husband's affairs haunts the marriage at every turn. Violet sets out to efface Belle by contradicting many of the things the first wife told their husband about the countryside and people around them. The piano tuner recognizes her conduct for what it is, self-assertion, and accepts it calmly. In his marriages, as in his work, he seeks harmony. In the title story, "After Rain," Harriet has fled to an Italian resort because of a failed love affair, the same resort that her parents took her to as a child. In the sweltering heat, she feels oppressed by her life. The reader learns of her astonished shock, still disturbing her more than a decade later, at her parents' divorce; she has had previous promising love affairs that all fizzled inexplicably; she cannot be other than distant to her fellow vacationers. To relieve her tedium, she visits a nearby church. There a painting of the Annunciation, vividly colored and showing a rain-swept landscape in the background, lifts her out of her self-absorption. Meanwhile, a hard rain has broken the afternoon heat. Returning to the resort in the refreshing coolness, she suddenly sees her life in a new light, as if she has had an annunciation of her own. She realizes that she has frightened away her lovers by needing too much from love, a reaction to her parents' failed marriage. The annunciation is of her own solitude.

OTHER MAJOR WORKS

LONG FICTION: *A Standard of Behaviour*, 1958; *The Old Boys*, 1964; *The Boarding-House*, 1965; *The Love Department*, 1966; *Mrs. Eckdorf in O'Neil's Hotel*, 1969; *Miss Gomez and the Brethren*, 1971; *Elizabeth Alone*, 1973; *The Children of Dynmouth*, 1976; *Other People's Worlds*, 1980; *Fools of Fortune*,

1983; *Nights at the Alexandra*, 1987; *The Silence in the Garden*, 1988; *Two Lives*, 1991; *Juliet's Story*, 1991; *Felicia's Journey*, 1994*; Death in Summer*, 1998.

PLAYS: *The Elephant's Foot*, pr. 1965; *The Girl*, pr., pb. 1968; *A Night Mrs. da Tanka*, pr., pb. 1972; *Going Home*, pr., pb. 1972; *The Old Boys*, pr., pb. 1971; *A Perfect Relationship*, pr. 1973; *The Fifty-seventh Saturday*, pr. 1973; *Marriages*, pr. 1973; *Scenes from an Album*, pr., pb. 1981; *Beyond the Pale*, 1980.

TELEPLAYS: *The Girl*, pr. 1967; *A Night Mrs. da Tanka*, pr. 1968.

RADIO PLAYS: *Going Home*, pr. 1970; *Scenes from an Album*, pr. 1975.

NONFICTION: *A Writer's Ireland: Landscape in Literature*, 1984; *Excursions in the Real World*, 1993.

EDITED TEXT: *The Oxford Book of Irish Short Stories*, 1989.

BIBLIOGRAPHY

Bonaccorso, Richard. "William Trevor's Martyrs for Truth." *Studies in Short Fiction* 34 (Winter, 1997): 113-118. Discusses two types of Trevor characters: those who try to evade the truth and those who gravitate, often in spite of themselves, toward it; argues that the best indicators of the consistency of Trevor's moral vision may be his significant minority, those characters who find themselves pursuing rather than fleeing truth.

Firchow, Peter, ed. *The Writer's Place*. Minneapolis: University of Minnesota Press, 1974. In this volume, the editor has interviewed a number of contemporary authors from the British Isles, including Trevor, Kingsley Amis, Roald Dahl, Margaret Drabble, John Wain, and Angus Wilson. Trevor discusses such things as writing for radio, his interest in Ireland after living in England, and the then-current British literary scene.

Gitzen, Julian. "The Truth-Tellers of William Trevor." *Critique: Studies in Modern Fiction* 21, no. 1 (1979): 59-72. Gitzen claims that most critics of Trevor's work have found it in the comedic tradition, sometimes dark and at other times more compassionate in its humor, but he argues that, if it is comic, it is also melancholic in its journey from "psychological truth" to "metaphysical mystery."

Haughey, Jim. "Joyce and Trevor's Dubliners: The Legacy of Colonialism." *Studies in Short Fiction* 32 (Summer, 1995): 355-365. Compares how James Joyce's "Two Gallants" and Trevor's "Two More Gallants" explore the complexities of Irish identity; argues that Trevor's story provides an updated commentary on the legacy of Ireland's colonial experience. Both stories reveal how Irish men, conditioned by colonization, are partly responsible for their sense of cultural alienation and inferiority.

MacKenna, Dolores. *William Trevor: The Writer and His Work*. Dublin: New Island, 1999. Offers some interesting biographical details; includes a bibliography and an index.

Morrison, Kristin. *William Trevor*. New York: Twayne, 1993. A general introduction to Trevor's fiction, focusing on a conceptual "system of correspondences" often manifested in Trevor's work by a rhetorical strategy of "significant simultaneity" and a central metaphor of the Edenic garden. Through close readings of Trevor's major works, including such short stories as "Beyond the Pale" and "The News from Ireland," Morrison examines the overall unity of his fiction.

Paulson, Suzanne Morrow. *William Trevor: A Study of the Short Fiction*. New York: Twayne, 1993. This introduction to Trevor's stories examines four common themes from Freudianism to feminism: psychological shock, failed child/parent relationships, patriarchal repressiveness, and materialism in the modern world. Also contains an interview with Trevor and a number of short reviews of his stories.

Rhodes, Robert E. "William Trevor's Stories of the Troubles." In *Contemporary Irish Writing*, edited by James D. Brophy and Raymond D. Porter. Boston: Twayne, 1983. Rhodes claims that, although most of Trevor's fiction had until the 1980's revolved around English characters, his Anglo-Irish stories and protagonists, because of their environment and historical experience, are of greater significance in exploring the complexities of the human condition.

Schirmer, Gregory A. *William Trevor: A Study in His Fiction*. London: Routledge, 1990. One of the first full-length studies of Trevor's fictional writings. Schirmer notes the tension in Trevor's works between morality and the elements in contemporary society that make morality almost an impossibility, with lonely alienation the result. He also discusses Trevor as an outsider, both in Ireland and in England. An excellent study. Includes bibliographical references.

Trevor, William. "A Clearer Vision of Ireland." *The Guardian*, April 23, 1992, p. 25. A personal account of what it means to be an Irish writer. Trevor talks about when he first began consciously to feel Irish and when he first realized what Ireland was really like. Talks about his childhood and youth and his decision to become a writer.

_____, ed. *The Oxford Book of Irish Short Stories*. Oxford: Oxford University Press, 1989. In this collection of Irish short stories from the earliest times through the second half of the twentieth century, Trevor in his introduction makes insightful comments about the significance and context of that literary form to Irish letters and, by implication, discusses his own work.

Brian Murray, updated by
Eugene S. Larson and Roger Smith

FRANK TUOHY

Born: Uckfield, Sussex, England; May 2, 1925
Died: Shepton Mallet, Somerset, England; April 11, 1999

PRINCIPAL SHORT FICTION

The Admiral and the Nuns, with Other Stories, 1962
Fingers in the Door and Other Stories, 1970
Live Bait and Other Stories, 1978
The Collected Stories, 1984

OTHER LITERARY FORMS

In addition to his novels, Frank Tuohy wrote a biography of William Butler Yeats, a travel book on Portugal, numerous articles for British newspapers, and teleplays for British public television.

ACHIEVEMENTS

Frank Tuohy never had a wide general audience, nor did he find favor with academic critics. Still, his writing received high praise from reviewers and from prominent fiction writers. C. P. Snow, Muriel Spark, and Graham Greene all praised Tuohy's fiction.

The high praise from reviewers and fellow writers is reflected in the honors that were bestowed on Tuohy. His first short-story collection, *The Admiral and the Nuns, with Other Stories*, received the Katherine Mansfield-Menton Prize (1960), and *Live Bait and Other Stories* won the William Heinemann Memorial Award (1979).

Tuohy's third novel, *The Ice Saints* (1964), received both the James Tait Black Memorial Prize and the Geoffrey Faber Memorial Prize. In England, Tuohy was elected a Fellow of the Royal Society of Literature in 1965. Two major awards demonstrate the high standing his fiction holds among the literati in the United States. In 1972, the American Institute of Arts and Letters bestowed on him the E. M. Forster Award. In 1995, Tuohy came to New York City to receive the 1994 Bennett Award of twenty thousand dollars from the *Hudson Review*. Eight years earlier, in 1987, he was awarded an honorary doctorate from Purdue University.

BIOGRAPHY

John Francis Tuohy's father was Irish, his mother

Scottish. Tuohy was educated at Stowe School, King's College, Cambridge. He traveled widely and lived for extended periods in Finland, Brazil, Poland, Japan, Portugal, and the United States. The contrast and conflict of manners and cultures became the chief subject of his fiction.

Tuohy was ineligible for military service during World War II because of a defective heart valve, a condition later corrected by surgery. After the war, he spent six years in Brazil as a professor of English language and literature at the University of São Paulo and two years as a visiting professor in Poland at the Jagiellonian University. In the United States he was a visiting writer at various universities, including Purdue University and Texas A&M University. He also lectured at two Japanese universities, from 1983 to 1989, at Rikkyo University, then in the 1990's at Waseda University, both in Tokyo.

Analysis

An initial impression of Frank Tuohy's short stories is likely to be that they are the observations of a sharp-eyed and widely traveled reporter who is filling in the reader on life in such diverse places as Japan, Poland, South America, London, rural England, New England, and New York. Tuohy does have a remarkable talent for direct observation, for bringing before the eyes of his reader the look and feel, the sound, and even the smell of actual places. The gestures of his characters, their speech, and their actions all ring true. Tuohy's accuracy of observation and precision of language, although doubtless a reflection of his own interest in being literally truthful to the physical realities of the places about which he writes, are all part of his strategy for supporting and making real his underlying view of life.

Despite the variety of locales, of character types, and even of subjects, Tuohy's short-story collections are bound together by an overriding vision of the world as a place of moral confusion. Here and there one finds in unlikely places remnants of an older, more civilized way of life, but generally one finds, also in unsuspected places, moral baseness of the sort that would have made a decent man of former times put his hand firmly on his sword. At their most poi-

gnant, Tuohy's stories expose the raw nerves of conflicting cultures, the below-the-surface gnawing of social lesions bloodied by sudden rupture, the confinements within the self caused by differences of custom, of language, of status, of religion.

"The Admiral and the Nuns"

The best people in Tuohy's stories are usually women. In the title story of his first collection, *The Admiral and the Nuns, with Other Stories*, an English woman, the daughter of an English admiral, is living in the interior of a South American country with her Polish husband. The place is a company town; the husband is employed as an engineer at a nearby factory; the neighbors, who are nationals of the country, have developed a deep dislike for the English woman and her husband and have, in effect, instituted a community-wide boycott. The grounds of dislike are these: The English woman is a dreadful housekeeper and cannot discipline her children; her husband drinks too much and pursues women. Tuohy's point is made clear by his narrator, also English, who sees that the woman is charming and valiant, having been formed by her father (the admiral) and trained by the nuns in her convent school. She remains loyal to her husband and, throughout her ordeal (which concludes with their deciding to return to Poland), keeps her chin firmly up.

There is a dreariness, however, in this kind of life and more dreariness ahead, and the narrator's admiration is tempered by what he regards as the woman's limitations: "She was one of those people whom experience leaves untouched. But she was durable. After all, she was an Admiral's daughter." As for the nuns, the narrator "cannot decide whether they had given her the worst, or the best education in the world."

"A Survivor in Salvador"

A more clearly admirable character is the young mulatto woman in "A Survivor in Salvador," the last story in the first collection. The protagonist of this story is an exiled Polish prince who has arrived in San Salvador without money but with a packet of cocaine, which he is attempting to sell. Without friends, liable to deportation if caught with the drug, without food or shelter, he is befriended by a girl who herself has been a victim of various kinds of exploitation, including sexual abuse by the chief of police. The girl, Antonieta, befriends the prince, becomes his mistress, keeps him from starving, and when he is seriously ill from exposure, nurses him back to health. Christophe, the prince, in return, does what he can to show his love for Antonieta.

At thirty-two pages, "Survivor" is easily the longest story in Tuohy's first collection and perhaps his most virtuoso performance in the genre. Always in his three novels and frequently in his stories, he adopts the narrative viewpoints of perceptive European outsiders who are trapped between the shallowness of what they have abandoned and the poverty (in all senses) of what exile has wrought. In "Survivor," Tuohy takes on as naturally as if he were born to it the central intelligence of a down-but-not-quite-out, dispossessed Pole, Prince Krzysztof Wahorski, who has fled Poland after "promises, his title, his bridge game" have all failed. He sees the heroine as his passport back to the noblesse oblige his title, if not his circumstances, ought to bestow. In Tuohy's handling, Antonieta is neither brutalized nor romanticized as she throws the prince a lifeline. This story crosses Joseph Conrad with Guy de Maupassant but ends as pure Frank Tuohy.

"FINGERS IN THE DOOR"

It frequently happens in Tuohy's stories that the main character or characters are exiled Europeans living in a simpler or more integrated culture, in which even the poor are bound together by some mutually shared consciousness. The prince in San Salvador perceives that even the most despised are not as alone as he is. The prince is unusual in Tuohy's fiction, however, for most of Tuohy's exiles are unaware of their loneliness and alienation and are likely to regard those from simpler, more integrated cultures as inferiors to be exploited.

Exploitation of the weak or innocent and the snobbery that appears to be one of its causes are treated in the title story of his second volume of short stories, *Fingers in the Door and Other Stories*. The story takes place on a train traveling to London; the occupants of a first-class carriage are Andrew Ringsett, a successful real estate agent who has moved up in the world, his overdressed wife, their spoiled, teenage daughter, Caroline, and for a time, an elderly woman in an ancient fur, whom the agent's wife Merle recognizes as someone from a higher social class who (she believes) will always snub her (although, as Tuohy remarks, the snobbery is all in Merle's head). The train stops at a station, the husband alights for a few moments, and when he reenters the carriage through an outside door the train lurches suddenly, and the steel door slams shut on his fingers. The husband is in terrific pain, but his wife, embarrassed before someone whom she regards as her social better, apologizes for him to the old woman. The daughter merely stares out the window, outraged that her trip to London has been ruined by her father's accident. The old woman rises from her place in the carriage and addresses the wife, telling her to look after her husband; to the man, she offers her sympathy and the advice to seek immediate medical assistance. It is the husband, however, who exhibits the most admirable behavior. He sees immediately that his wife is embarrassed and humiliated and puts his arm around her and tries to make light of his injury. He has something in common with other Tuohy characters who have not lost the power to feel affection.

LIVE BAIT AND OTHER STORIES

In Tuohy's third collection, *Live Bait and Other Stories*, the theme of exploitation becomes predominant, and as his camera eye moves closer to home, to New England and New York and then to England itself, the sense of moral confusion becomes more acute, the remoteness from human feeling even more profound. In "Summer Pilgrim," a young Japanese teacher visits an elderly English pastoral poet who has been her ideal. At dinner, while his wife is in the kitchen, the venerable poet runs his hand up her leg. The girl, who has been reared to behave dutifully, is too timid and self-effacing either to protest or move away. At a loss what to do, she simply sits there, feeling "rather deaf: . . . like a change in the atmospheric pressure, high up a mountain."

In "Evening in Connecticut" an English visitor is attending a dinner party in the home of a very rich old man, an important benefactor of Barford College, and finds himself in a world which seems detached from reality, a kind of battered Eden in which things are plentiful but life abstract. What the visitor discovers, at last, under the banter and expensive food and drink, is the kind of exploitation Tuohy has found in other times and places but not in so odious a form: The elderly white-haired host informs his English guest that he regularly makes trips to England, where an English doctor, who shares his tastes, has found him a suitable girl of the lower classes, whose parents do not object. The English visitor is outraged but paralyzed by the social conventions and his own timidity. Later he believes that he was on the point of rising to his feet and attacking, but that "surely, was self-delusion." In this kind of society, the sexual exploitation of children appears to be indistinguishable from any other kind of gratification.

The assault on innocence is also the subject of the title story of *Live Bait and Other Stories*. Here, a twelve-year-old boy, a scholarship pupil at a school attended mainly by the rich, accompanies a school acquaintance on a fishing expedition to a lake on the property of an elderly rich aunt and her eccentric son, Major Peverill. The boy is asked about his father's profession and is treated insultingly by both the old woman and her son, who advises the boy, Andrew, to be grateful for being invited into the society of his betters and then, when the boy admits that he is a scholarship student, laughs in his face. Andrew's interest, however, is in the fishing; what in particular excites him is the gardener's account of a twenty-pound pike that inhabits the lake. He contrives to haul off his father's fishing gear and a boat that is usually kept locked away at the lake. His upper-class friend quarrels with him and makes insulting remarks about Andrew's mother; Andrew then fishes for the pike by himself. He hooks the big fish but it breaks his line, and while he is rolling around on the ground in anger, he is watched by Major Peverill, who then attempts to molest him. Andrew escapes but is drawn back to the lake by the hope of catching the pike; this time he is visited by Major Peverill's granddaughter, a strange girl who tries to be friendly until she discovers that Andrew is using a live frog for bait; she then runs off to denounce him to her family. Andrew lands the pike but is

chased by Major Peverill and his laborers, and, from the other side of the lake, by his mother. Andrew is obliged to surrender.

What Tuohy does is to catch, without sentimentalizing, the way a twelve-year-old boy at this particular time and place is himself "live bait" to those about him, who use him to get some strange pleasure, social superiority, adventure, or sensual indulgence. One is made to feel, rather than merely to understand, the meaning of what has happened.

It is impossible to summarize the kind of pleasure afforded by Tuohy's fiction. Each of his stories is like a miniature novel of manners, in which persons of different classes, nationalities, races, religions, political persuasions, and ages are brought into a conflict that reveals an underlying moral conflict as well. There is nothing depressingly cynical or fashionably despairing about Tuohy's stories. Life should be better than this—that is the assumption behind his fiction—and Tuohy is simply an observer-commentator, a truth-teller whose scalpel-like cutting away of pretense reveals the rottenness underneath. His stories are neither about innocents at home nor about innocents abroad, and although they are often about the kind of social incarceration our natures impose on human relationships in alien country, one need not go abroad to find oneself imprisoned. His stories say, in effect, that this is the way life is: awful, incredible, confusing, painful, but, at the same time, fascinating when seen for what it is. The act of experiencing the "bite down on the rotten tooth of fact," is what gives Tuohy's stories their characteristic pleasure. That is the kind of pleasure the best fiction has always given.

Asked by novelist Anthony Burgess which contemporary writers he liked, Graham Greene answered, "I used to read Frank Tuohy" (*Newsweek*, February 4, 1985). Greene's implicit regret that Tuohy had stopped writing novels twenty years earlier with *The Ice Saints* (1964) must bow to praise—again implied—from the master of intrigue—political and religious—in foreign outposts. Did Greene hail his younger contemporary for declining to exploit his experiences in widely differing cultures for exotic effect but rather to illustrate the humiliations that blur human communication on any level and in any milieu? Tuohy's last published story, "A Rainy Season" appearing in *London Magazine* one year before he suffered a fatal coronary attack in the spring of 1999, conveys the unwitting betrayal by local customs in an unnamed country (surely Brazil) of a Miss Bond, an American, a sincere do-gooder on a U.S. State Department mission. The viewpoint character is Marsden, a bystander distinguished in Britain but reduced by the provincialism he finds abroad. The only evolving character is a Canadian, who becomes, via Marsden's account of Miss Bond's disaster, someone who might be saved from his predecessor's folly.

In presenting Tuohy the 1994 Bennett Award in New York, critic Dean Flower observed that "it has become politic . . . these days to speak warmly of Diversity and Multi-Cultural enrichment. Let Frank Tuohy's stories expose the sentimentality and hypocrisy of all that."

OTHER MAJOR WORKS

LONG FICTION: *The Animal Game*, 1957; *The Warm Nights of January*, 1960; *The Ice Saints*, 1964.

NONFICTION: *Portugal*, 1970; *Yeats*, 1976.

BIBLIOGRAPHY

Flower, Dean. "Frank Tuohy and the Poetics of Depression." *The Hudson Review* 49 (Spring, 1996): 87-96. Suggests that such collections of Tuohy's short stories as *Fingers in the Door and Other Stories* and *The Admiral and the Nuns, with Other Stories* may be out of print because most readers probably found them too depressing; concludes that what makes all of Tuohy's works worth reading is their anguished and inconsolable tone.

Hazzard, Shirley. Review of *Fingers in the Door and Other Stories*, by Frank Tuohy. *The New York Times Book Review*, September, 1970, 5. Hazzard asserts that Tuohy writes with Chekhovian simplicity about "the violence we do to others and ourselves" and discusses several of the stories in light of this assertion.

King, Francis. "Obituary: Frank Tuohy." *The Independent*, April 15, 1999, p. 6. A biographical sketch of Tuohy's life and literary career, commenting on his early fiction, his resemblance to W. Somerset Maugham in his attitude toward sex, and his receiving the Katherine Mansfield-Menton Prize for his first volume of short stories.

Prescott, Peter S. "The Whiplash Effect." Review of *The Collected Stories*, by Frank Tuohy. *Newsweek*, February 4, 1985, p. 78. Prescott argues that Tuohy's stories are "extremely pessimistic" but powerful in their portrayal of human pain. Particularly effective, he says, is the "whiplash effect," by means of which Tuohy, having caused the reader to sympathize with a character, suddenly reverses direction and shows the character in an unfavorable light.

Snow, C. P. "Snapshot Album." Review of *Fingers in the Door and Other Stories*, by Frank Tuohy. *Financial Times*, London, May 14, 1970. Snow remarks that Tuohy's "great gifts" are concentration, "intensive exactness," and a language that is "as firm and limpid as English can be." He discusses the "sociology" of Tuohy's stories and demonstrates how in three of these Tuohy's characteristic theme of pain and loneliness is effectively presented.

Wilson, Jason. "Foreigners Abroad: Frank Tuohy's Three Novels." *London Magazine*, July, 1992. Jason Wilson, although writing mostly about Tuohy's long fiction, which he praises as still perceptive about "Britons abroad" even though thirty years out of print, finds his novels "episodic, linked short stories." He says, "The stories cover the same area of exploration [but, because compressed] . . . offer a greater sense of the mystery of people, for there is less need for a plot."

W. J. Stuckey, updated by
Richard Hauer Costa

IVAN TURGENEV

Born: Orel, Russia; November 9, 1818
Died: Bougival, France; September 3, 1883

PRINCIPAL SHORT FICTION

Zapiski okhotnika, 1852 (*Russian Life in the Interior*, 1855; better known as *A Sportsman's Sketches*, 1932)
Povesti i rasskazy, 1856

OTHER LITERARY FORMS

In addition to *A Sportsman's Sketches*, Ivan Turgenev published several other short stories and novellas individually. His main contribution, however, was six novels, some of which are among the best written in Russian, especially *Ottsy i deti* (1862; *Fathers and Sons*, 1867). He also wrote poems, poems in prose, and plays, one of which, *Mesyats v derevne* (1855; *A Month in the Country*, 1924), is still staged regularly in Russian theaters.

ACHIEVEMENTS

Ivan Turgenev's opus is not particularly large, yet with about four dozen stories and novellas and his brief novels, he became one of the best writers not only in Russian but also in world literature. Turgenev was a leading force in the Russian realistic movement of the second half of the nineteenth century. Together with Nikolai Gogol, Fyodor Dostoevski, Leo Tolstoy, and Anton Chekhov, he built the reputation that Russian literature enjoys in the world. Perhaps more than other writers, he was responsible for acquainting foreign readers with Russian literature, and because he spent most of his adult life abroad, he was an esteemed figure in the international literary life.

Turgenev was also instrumental in arousing the sensitivity and consciousness of his compatriots, because he dealt with such burning social issues as the plight of Russian peasantry, in *A Sportsman's Sketches*; the "superfluous man" in Russian society, in "The Diary of a Superfluous Man"; the fixation of Russians with revolution, in *Rudin* (1856; English translation, 1947); the decaying nobility in *Dvoryan-*

skoye gnezdo (1859; *Liza*, 1869; better known as *A House of Gentlefolk*, 1894); and the age-old conflict between generations, in *Fathers and Sons*.

Turgenev also excelled in his style, especially in the use of the language. Albert Jay Nock called him "incomparably the greatest of artists in fiction," and Virginia Woolf termed his works as being "curiously of our own time, undecayed and complete in themselves." His reputation, despite some fluctuations, endures.

BIOGRAPHY

Ivan Sergeyevich Turgenev was born on November 9, 1818, in the central Russian town of Orel, into a small gentry family. His father was a loving, easygoing country squire, while his mother was an overbearing woman of whom Turgenev had many unpleasant memories. He spent his childhood at the family estate, Spasskoe, which he visited every summer even after the family moved to Moscow. He received tutoring at home and later was graduated from the University of St. Petersburg in 1837. He continued his studies in Berlin, acquiring a master's degree in philosophy. His stay in Berlin marks the beginning of a lifelong shuffle between his homeland and the European countries, especially France, Germany, England, and Italy. On one visit to France, he met a French woman, Pauline Viardot, with whom he had a close relationship the rest of his life despite her being married. After serving briefly in the Ministry of Interior, he lived the remainder of his life off his estate income following his parents' death.

Turgenev started to write early, and in 1843, at the age of twenty-five, he published a long narrative poem, *Parasha*, written in imitation of Alexander Pushkin. He soon abandoned poetry for prose, although his reverence for Pushkin and the poetic slant remained constant in his writings. His stories about the dismal life of Russian peasants were much more successful, attracting the attention of readers and critics alike. When the collection of those stories, *A Sportsman's Sketches*, was published in 1852, his reputation as a promising young writer was firmly established. A successful play, *A Month in the Country*, added to his reputation. As his reputation grew, he became friends with many leading writers and critics—Vissarion Belinsky, Nikolai Nekrasov, Tolstoy, Aleksandr Herzen, Dostoevski, and others—but these friendships were often interspersed with heated arguments and enmity. Because of his connections in Europe and a pronounced liberal outlook, he was summoned on several occasions before the investigation committees back in Russia. He was always exonerated, however, and he continued to travel between Russia and Europe.

Turgenev never married, but he had several affairs, while Viardot remained the love of his life, and he was thought to have been the father of a son born to her. The steady stream of successful novels and stories enhanced the esteem in which he was held both at home and abroad. At the same time, he carried on a spirited debate with Russian intellectuals, advocating liberal reforms in Russian society, especially those concerning the plight of peasants, many of whom were still kept as serfs. When they were liberated in 1861, it was believed that not a small merit belonged to Turgenev and his efforts toward their emancipation.

Toward the end of his life, Turgenev kept writing and publishing, though at a slower pace. He also worked on the preparation of his collected works and continued to live in a *ménage á trois* with Viardot and her husband. During his last visit to Russia in the summer of 1881, he visited Tolstoy at Yasnaya Polyana. His health began to deteriorate in 1882, and, after several months of a serious illness, he died at the Viardots' estate in Bougival, near Paris, on September 3, 1883. As his friend Henry James wrote, "his end was not serene and propitious, but dark and almost violent." Turgenev's body was taken to Russia, where he was buried with great honors in St. Petersburg.

ANALYSIS

The reputation of Ivan Turgenev as a short-story writer is based in equal measure on his stories about Russian peasant life and on stories about other seg-

Ivan Turgenev (Library of Congress)

ments of society. Although differing greatly in subject matter and emphasis, they nevertheless share the same mastery of storytelling and style and language. Turgenev wrote stories about the peasants early in his career, revealing his familiarity with life in the countryside and his preoccupation with liberal causes. As he grew older and traveled to Europe, his horizons expanded, and he became more interested in topics transcending his provincial outlook. His acquired cosmopolitanism was also reflected in his turning toward personal concerns of love, alienation, and psychological illumination of his characters. The last story that he wrote, "Klara Milich" ("Clara Milich"), takes him to the realm of the fantastic and supernatural, to life after death, and even to the bizarre twists of the human mind.

A SPORTSMAN'S SKETCHES

Turgenev's stories about Russian peasants are contained primarily in his collection *A Sportsman's Sketches*. As the title implies (the accurate translation is "notes of a hunter"), the twenty-five tales are more like notes and sketches than full-blown stories with plot and characterization. It is one of the few examples in world literature where the entire collection of separate and independent stories has a thematic unity; another example of this unity is Isaac Babel's *Konormiia* (1926; *Red Cavalry*, 1929). The unifying theme is the hard life of Russian peasants—many generations of whom had lived as serfs for centuries—and the neglect of their well-being on the part of their owners. Despite its innocuous title, chosen to mislead the censors, the collection provoked admiration as well as heated debates. It is credited with speeding up the process of the serfs' emancipation.

The stories are set in the countryside around Turgenev's family estate at the middle of the nineteenth century. They are told by the same narrator, a landowner, in fact the thinly disguised author himself. During his tireless hunting trips, Turgenev met various characters, mostly peasants, many of whom told stories worth listening to. The authentic human quality of the settings and marvelous characterization, rather than the social message, make the stories enduring literature.

The author approaches his characters with an open mind. He observes their demeanor "with curiosity and sympathy" and listens to their concerns and complaints without much comment, with a few questions for his own clarification. He refrains from passing judgment and avoids social criticism or satire. Through such unobtrusiveness, he gains the characters' confidence and allows them to talk freely, making the stories more believable. More important, he does not idealize the peasants; instead, he attempts to penetrate the crust of everyday appearances.

The woman in the story "Ermolai i mel'nichikha" ("Yermolai and the Miller's Wife"), whose freedom had been bought by her husband, talks nonchalantly about her hard lot and the lack of love in her life. Yet beneath her story, the reader senses deep melancholy and hopelessness, reinforced by the author's remark to his hunting companion, "It seems she is ailing," and by the companion's retort, "What else should she be?" The burly, taciturn forest warden in the story "Biriuk" ("The Wolf"), who lives alone, excels in protecting the forest from the poachers, and is feared and hated by the peasants, who are not above stealing wood from the landowner. He cannot be bribed and plays no favorites, finding the only pleasure in doing his job. Yet when he catches a poor peasant trying to fell a tree, he lets him go because it is hunger that drove him to thievery. In one of Turgenev's best stories, "Zhivye Moshchi" ("A Living Relic"), a young woman, dying of a fatal illness, gives the impression of total helplessness, yet she is nourished until her untimely death by her naïve religion and love of life. In all these stories, appearances are deceiving and the observer-narrator is able to get to the core of his characters.

Not all characters have an adversarial relationship with their fate. The two friends in "Khor'i Kalynich" ("Khor and Kalynich") epitomize the two halves of a Russian character. Khor is a practical, down-to-earth man who has found success in life. Kalynich is a sensitive soul living in unison with nature, a dreamer who revels in simple pleasures, without worrying about more complex aspects of life. The doctor in "Uezdnyi lekar" ("The Country Doctor"), called to the sickbed of a young girl, falls in love with her, and his love is returned, but he realizes that he cannot save the young girl. He finds solace in the discovery that the girl has satisfied her own craving for love in the last moments of her life. Thus, the results are not as important as the efforts to avoid or alleviate the blows, no matter how unsuccessful the efforts may be.

Peasants are not the only characters drawing the author's attention. The landowners, who wield the power of life and death over their serfs, also appear in several stories. For the most part, they are depicted with much less sympathy and understanding, despite the author's own social origin. In "Dva pomeshchika" ("Two Landowners"), both characters show negative traits: One, a major-general, is a social clown; the other is an insensitive brute, who thinks that a peasant will always be a peasant and who uses a homespun "philosophy" that "if the father's a thief, the son's thief too . . . it's blood that counts." The author seems to be saying that, with such a negative attitude, no improvement of the peasants' lot is possible. "Gamlet

Shchigrovskogo uezda" ("Prince Hamlet of Shchigrovo") offers an even stronger castigation of the serf-owning class. Here, an intelligent and sensitive landowner fails to find understanding among his peers for his attempts to improve the lot of everybody. In a Dostoevskian fashion, he is forced to act like a buffoon in hopes of gaining attention that way. Turgenev's position here sounds very much like a sharp satire against the existing state of affairs, but, as mentioned, he abstains from open and direct criticism, thus making his points even more effective.

Not all of the stories in *A Sportsman's Sketches* are bleak or hopeless. The two best stories of the collection are also the most positive. In "Bezhin lug" ("Bezhin Meadow"), Turgenev relates his evening encounter with five young boys taking care of the horses in the countryside. Sitting by the fire in the evening, they tell one another fantastic stories, to amuse and even frighten one another. The narrator is impressed by the boys' natural demeanor, straightforwardness, bravery, and, above all, rich imagination of which folktales are spun. The author seems to imply that the future of the country is secure if judged by the young who are to inherit it.

The second story, "Pevtsy" ("The Singers"), is even more uplifting. In another chance encounter, the narrator stumbles across an inn in the barely accessible backwoods. He is treated with a singing competition among the inn patrons unlike any other he had experienced. Turgenev uses the diamond-in-the-rough theme to show where the real talent can be found. As the narrator leaves the inn, he hears the people's voices calling each other from one hill to another—a possible explanation of where the marvelous singers learn how to sing. These stories, along with a few others, strike a balance between the negative and the positive aspects of the life depicted in the book.

Surrounded and suffused by nature, Turgenev reacts to it by stating his position concerning human beings in nature. He expresses his admiration for nature by using strikingly detailed descriptions, emphasizing colors, sounds, and scents. His subtlety of observation is complemented by genuine lyricism and careful use of a melodic, rhythmical language. Despite these ornamental features, however, the reader is tempted to view the author's notion of nature as being rather unfeeling and indifferent toward humankind, in the best tradition of Georg Brandes' theory of *la grande indifférante*. A closer look, however, reveals that nature in Turgenev's works shows the difference in degree, not in kind, and that for him, humankind is a part of nature, not outside it. Only in unison with nature can human beings fulfill their potential, in which case nature is not indifferent but, on the contrary, very helpful, as seen in the example of the singers in the aforementioned story.

Other artistic merits of these stories (which Turgenev was able to maintain throughout his writing career) can be found in his careful and delicate choice of suggestive and descriptive words; in the sketchy but pithy psychological portraiture; in the uncomplicated plot structure, consisting usually of an anecdote or episode; in the natural, calm, matter-of-fact narration; and in the effective imagery that is not strained or artificial. Superior craftsmanship goes hand in hand with the "social message" here, preventing the stories from being dated or used for inartistic purposes.

"THE DIARY OF A SUPERFLUOUS MAN"

The second group of Turgenev's tales strikes an altogether different path, although a kinship with his earlier stories can be easily detected. Among many stories outside the cycle of *A Sportsman's Sketches*, eight deserve to be singled out, either for the significance of their contents or for their artistic merit, or both. An early story, "Dnevnik lishnega cheloveka" ("The Diary of a Superfluous Man"), despite its relative immaturity, has a significance that surpasses its artistic quality. It is here that Turgenev coined the phrase "a superfluous man," which would reverberate throughout Russian literature of the nineteenth and twentieth centuries. Even though the superfluous man theme had been used before Turgenev by Pushkin's Eugene Onegin in the novel in verse by the same name and by Mikhail Lermontov's Pechorin in *Geroy nashego vremeni* (1840; *A Hero of Our Times*, 1854), it was Turgenev who made the phrase a literary byword. The story presages Dostoevski's *Zapiski iz podpolya* (1864; *Letters from the Underworld*, 1913;

better known as *Notes from the Underground*, 1918).

Turgenev's "superfluous man" is a young scion of erstwhile wealthy landowners, who writes a diary knowing that he will soon die of a disease. To compound his misery, he is rejected in his love for a beautiful neighbor. The excessive introspection of the "hero" and his inability to cope with reality make this story primarily a psychological character study and not a social statement, as some of Turgenev's works of the same kind would become later.

"MUMU"

Perhaps the best known of Turgenev's stories, "Mumu" comes the closest in spirit to the collection *A Sportsman's Sketches*. A deaf-mute servant loses the girl he loves when he is forced into marrying another woman. Later, he is ordered to kill his beloved dog because its barking is disturbing his mistress's sleep. Drawing the character of the insensitive mistress after his mother, Turgenev castigates the insensitivity of the entire serf-owning class. The story does not sink into sentimental bathos primarily because of the remarkable characterization of the servant as an ultimate sufferer, underscoring the proverbial capacity for suffering of an entire nation. Moreover, by arousing overwhelming pity for the deaf-mute, Turgenev clearly places the blame for this human and social injustice at the door of the unfeeling gentry.

"KING LEAR OF THE STEPPES"

"Stepnoi Korol' Lir" ("King Lear of the Steppes") is another story that in its countryside setting shows kinship with *A Sportsman's Sketches*. Yet it is entirely different in the subject matter, spirit, and atmosphere. In a takeoff on William Shakespeare's tragedy, the story shows children behaving toward their father in a similar manner. The atmosphere here, however, is typically Russian. Harlov, a descendant of a Russianized Swedish family, suffers the same indignity and ingratitude at the hands of his daughters, and he takes similar revenge upon them, but the tragedy is not relieved or ennobled. Turgenev shows a fine sense for plot, and the dialogues—more excessive than usual for him—are in line with the dramatic nature of its model. Artistically, this story is almost a masterpiece, keeping the reader in suspense until the end.

"ASYA"

Love is an overriding theme in Turgenev's later stories. "Asya" ("Asya") and "Pervaya lyubov" ("First Love") are the best representatives of Turgenev's love stories. Both are told in the first person, tempting one to attribute to them autobiographical character, which may not be totally unjustified "Asya" is set in a German town where the narrator (perhaps Turgenev) comes across two compatriots, a brother and a sister.

As the story unfolds, the narrator is increasingly attracted to the woman and develops genuine love feelings, yet he is unable to declare his love openly, vacillating constantly until every chance for consummation is lost. Turgenev was known to have been indecisive in his love affairs, as illustrated by his strange attachment to the Viardot couple. Seen from that angle, the autobiographical element becomes very plausible, but there is more to the story than simply Turgenev's indecisiveness. At this stage of his development, Turgenev had published only one book of short stories and one novel, and he was beset by doubts and indecision, not only in his love relationships but also in his literary aspirations, all too similar to those of the narrator in "Asya." As he himself said,

> There are turning points in life, points when the past dies and something new is born; woe to the man who doesn't know how to sense these turning points and either holds on stubbornly to a dead past or seeks prematurely to summon to life what has not yet fully ripened.

The story reflects the wrenching doubts and soul searching of the protagonist, which did not enable him to take a resolute stance toward the young woman, who herself was searching for a more assuring love. Thus, the love between Asya and the narrator was doomed to failure almost before it began. The two part, and the only thing left is a bittersweet memory of what might have been.

Perhaps Turgenev was not yet ready to give the story the adequate treatment that it deserves. This is evidenced in the fact that Asya, wistful and charming though she may be, is not developed fully as a character. Turgenev will return soon to a similar theme and develop it to the fullest in his novel *A House of Gentlefolk*. It is also worth mentioning that "Asya" is another example of the theme of the superfluous man, which started with "The Diary of a Superfluous Man."

"FIRST LOVE"

"First Love" is a better love story because both the plot and the characters are more fully developed. It involves a rivalry between a young man and his father, vying for the affection of the same woman, Zinaida. In Turgenev's own admission, the story is autobiographical; as he wrote about it in a letter, "It is the only thing that still gives me pleasure, because it is life itself, it was not made up. . . . 'First Love' is part of my experience." Aside from this candid admission, the story has a wide appeal to all, both young and old; to the young because the first love is always cherished the most (the only true love, according to Turgenev), and to the old because it offers a vicarious pleasure of a last triumph.

It invariably evokes a bittersweet nostalgia in everyone. It also presents a plausible, even if not too common, situation. Turgenev controls with a sure hand the delicate relationships between the three partners in this emotional drama fraught with the awakening of manhood in an adolescent, with the amorous playfulness of a young woman who is both a temptress and a victim, and with the satisfaction of a conquest by a man entering the autumn of his life. Similarly, the author handles tactfully a potentially explosive situation between the loving father and adoring son, producing no rancor in aftermath. The story is a throwback to Romanticism, which had already passed in Russian literature and elsewhere at the time of the story's publication. The story ends in a Turgenevian fashion—unhappily for everyone concerned. All these attributes make "First Love" one of the best love stories in world literature.

"THE SONG OF TRIUMPHANT LOVE"

Twenty years later, Turgenev would write another love story, "Pesn' torzhestvuiushchei liubvi" ("The Song of Triumphant Love"), which differs from "First Love" in many respects. It again deals with a love relationship in a *ménage à trois* (it seems that Turgenev was constantly reliving his own predica-

ment with the Viardot couple), but the similarities stop there. The setting is in sixteenth century Ferrara, and the male players—members of ancient patrician families—are on equal footing, even if one is a husband and the other a suitor. The ending is much more than unhappy: It is downright tragic. What makes this story decisively different from other love stories by Turgenev is the introduction of a supernatural element manifesting itself in the woman's conceiving, not by intercourse, but by the platonic desire and the singing of a song by the unsuccessful suitor.

"The Song of Triumphant Love" marks the transition to a more esoteric subject matter in Turgenev's writing. He had written fantastic stories before ("Prizraki," or "Phantoms"), but in the last decade of his life, he employed the supernatural with increasing frequency. In "Stuk . . . stuk . . . stuk . . ." ("Knock . . . Knock . . . Knock . . ."), he deals with a suicidal urge that borders on the supernatural. In his last story, "Clara Milich," he tells of a man who has fallen in love with a woman after her death. Turgenev believed that there is a thin line dividing the real and the fantastic and that the fantastic stories people tell have happened in real life. As he said, "Wherever you look, there is the drama in life, and there are still writers who complain that all subjects have been exhausted." Had he lived longer, most likely he would have tried to reconcile real life with so-called fantasy and the supernatural.

OTHER MAJOR WORKS

LONG FICTION: *Rudin*, 1856 (*Dimitri Roudine*, 1873; better known as *Rudin*, 1947); *Asya*, 1858 (English translation, 1877); *Dvoryanskoye gnezdo*, 1859 (*Liza*, 1869; also as *A Nobleman's Nest*, 1903; better known as *A House of Gentlefolk*, 1894); *Nakanune*, 1860 (*On the Eve*, 1871); *Pervaya lyubov*, 1860 (*First Love*, 1884); *Ottsy i deti*, 1862 (*Fathers and Sons*, 1867); *Dym*, 1867 (*Smoke*, 1868); *Veshniye vody*, 1872 (*Spring Floods*, 1874; better known as *The Torrents of Spring*, 1897); *Nov*, 1877 (*Virgin Soil*, 1877); *The Novels of Ivan Turgenev*, 1894-1899 (15 volumes).

PLAYS: *Neostorozhnost*, pb. 1843 (*Carelessness*, 1924); *Bezdenezhe*, pb. 1846 (*A Poor Gentleman*,

1924); *Kholostyak*, pr. 1849 (*The Bachelor*, 1924); *Zavtrak u predvoditelya*, pr. 1849; *Nakhlebnik*, wr. 1849, pb. 1857; *Razgovor na bolshoy doroge*, pr. 1850 (*A Conversation on the Highway*, 1924); *Mesyats v derevne*, wr. 1850, pb. 1855 (*A Month in the Country*, 1924); *Provintsialka*, pr. 1851 (*A Provincial Lady*, 1934); *Gde tonko, tam i rvyotsya*, wr. 1851, pr. 1912 (*Where It Is Thin, There It Breaks*, 1924); *Vecher v* Sorrente, wr. 1852, pr. 1884 (*An Evening in Sorrento*, 1924); *The Plays of Ivan Turgenev*, pb. 1924; *Three Plays*, pb. 1934.

POETRY: *Parasha*, 1843; *Senilia*, 1882, 1930 (better known as *Stikhotvoreniya v proze; Poems in Prose*, 1883, 1945).

NONFICTION: "Gamlet i Don Kikhot," 1860 ("Hamlet and Don Quixote," 1930); *Literaturnya i zhiteyskiya vospominaniya*, 1880 (*Literary Reminiscences and Autobiographical Fragments*, 1958); *Letters*, 1983 (David Lowe, editor); *Turgenev's Letters*, 1983 (A. V. Knowles, editor).

MISCELLANEOUS: *The Works of Iván Turgenieff*, 1903-1904 (6 volumes).

Bibliography

Allen, Elizabeth Cheresh. *Beyond Realism: Turgenev's Poetics of Secular Salvation*. Stanford, Calif.: Stanford University Press, 1992. Argues that readers should not turn to Turgenev merely for transparent narratives of nineteenth century Russian life; attempts to expose the unique imaginative vision and literary patterns in Turgenev's work. Discusses Turgenev's development of narrative techniques in *A Sportsman's Sketches*, analyzing several of the major stories, such as "Bezhin Meadow" and "The Singers."

Brodianski, Nina. "Turgenev's Short Stories: A Reevaluation." *Slavonic and East European Review* 32, no. 78 (1953): 70-91. In this brief but thorough and stimulating study, Brodianski examines Turgenev's short stories in general, their themes, structure, and psychological illumination of characters, as well as his philosophy (as much as there is of it) and his literary theories about the short story. Inasmuch as it re-evaluates some long-standing opinions about Turgenev, it serves a good purpose.

Brouwer, Sander. *Character in the Short Prose of Ivan Sergeevic Turgenev*. Atlanta: Rodopi, 1996. An excellent look at Turgenev's characters in the short fiction.

Gregg, Richard. "Turgenev and Hawthorne: The Life-Giving Satyr and the Fallen Faun." *Slavic and East European Journal* 41 (Summer, 1997): 258-270. Discusses Hawthorne's influence on Turgenev; comments on the common motif that their "mysterious" stories shared (the uncanny spell, curse, or blight); claims that Turgenev's explicit admiration for those works of Hawthorne in which that motif is to be found attests to a bond of sympathy between the two writers.

Kagan-Kans, Eva. "Fate and Fantasy: A Study of Turgenev's Fantastic Stories." *Slavic Review* 18 (1969): 543-560. Kagan-Kans traces Turgenev's treatment of fantasy and supernatural elements in his stories, as well as the role of fate and dreams. She also examines Turgenev's relationship with other writers, especially the Romanticists, and their influence on him as evidenced in individual stories, especially those dealing with fantasy and the supernatural.

Knowles, A. V. *Ivan Turgenev*. Boston: Twayne, 1988. An excellent introductory study, with a biographical sketch, chapters on the start of Turgenev's literary career, the establishment of his reputation and his first three novels. Subsequent chapters on his later novels, letters, final years, and his place in literature. Includes chronology, notes, and an annotated bibliography.

Lloyd, John Arthur Thomas. *Ivan Turgenev*. 1942. Reprint. Port Washington, N.Y.: Kennikat Press, 1973. A practical, compact biography, tastefully illustrated, treating systematically Turgenev's life and works in a lively, succinct manner. It tends to cling to traditional views about Turgenev, which is useful for comparative purposes.

Magarshack, David. *Turgenev: A Life*. London: Faber & Faber, 1954. An illustrated biography by Turgenev's translator, describing extensively his life. Concentrates on the events that shaped the author's life, his relationships with Russian and foreign writers, and the factual circumstances surrounding his works. A useful introduction to Turgenev and his opus.

Seeley, Frank Friedeberg. *Turgenev: A Reading of His Fiction*. New York: Cambridge University Press, 1991. Seeley prefaces his thorough study of Turgenev's fiction with an outline of Turgenev's life and a survey of his poetry and plays. This volume incorporates later findings and challenges some established views, especially the traditional notion of the "simplicity" of Turgenev's works. Seeley stresses the psychological treatment that Turgenev allotted to his characters.

Sheidley, William E. "'Born in Imitation of Someone Else': Reading Turgenev's 'Hamlet of the Shchigrovsky District' as a Version of Hamlet." *Studies in Short Fiction* 27 (Summer, 1990): 391-398. Discusses the character Vasily Vasilyevych as the most emphatic and the most pathetic of the Hamlet types in *A Sportsman's Sketches*. Contends that in a striking flash of metafictional irony, Vasily recognizes himself as the walking embodiment of the Hamlet stereotype. Sheidley points out the different implications of the Hamlet character in

Elizabethan tragedy and nineteenth century character sketch.

Waddington, Patrick, ed. *Ivan Turgenev and Britain*. Providence, R.I.: Berg, 1995. Essays on Turgenev's reputation in England and in America, including reviews by distinguished critics such as Frank Harris, Virginia Woolf, and Edmund Gosse. Waddington provides a comprehensive introduction, explaining the historical context in which these reviews appeared. With extensive notes and bibliography.

Yarmolinsky, Avrahm. *Turgenev: The Man, His Art, and His Age*. New York: Orion Press, 1959. Reprint. New York: Collier, 1962. Another reliable shorter biography, useful as an introduction to Turgenev. As the title implies, it touches on all important stages in his life and discusses his works as to their geneses, their salient features, and their overall significance for Turgenev and for Russian and world literature. Concludes with a useful chronology and a good bibliography.

Vasa D. Mihailovich

MARK TWAIN
Samuel Langhorne Clemens

Born: Florida, Missouri; November 30, 1835
Died: Redding, Connecticut; April 21, 1910

PRINCIPAL SHORT FICTION

The Celebrated Jumping Frog of Calaveras County, and Other Sketches, 1867
Mark Twain's Sketches: New and Old, 1875
The Stolen White Elephant and Other Stories, 1882
The £1,000,000 Bank-Note and Other New Stories, 1893
The Man That Corrupted Hadleyburg and Other Stories and Essays, 1900

A Double Barrelled Detective Story, 1902
King Leopold's Soliloquy: A Defense of His Congo Rule, 1905
The $30,000 Bequest and Other Stories, 1906
A Horse's Tale, 1907
The Mysterious Stranger and Other Stories, 1916
The Curious Republic of Gondour and Other Whimsical Sketches, 1919
The Adventures of Thomas Jefferson Snodgrass, 1926
The Complete Short Stories of Mark Twain, 1957 (Charles Neider, editor)

Mark Twain (Library of Congress)

Selected Shorter Writings of Mark Twain, 1962
Mark Twain's Fables of Man, 1972 (John S.
   Tuckey, editor)
Life as I Find It, 1977 (Charles Neider, editor)

OTHER LITERARY FORMS

As a professional writer who felt the need for a large income, Mark Twain published more than thirty books and left many uncollected pieces and manuscripts. He tried every genre, including drama, and even wrote some poetry that is seldom read. His royalties came mostly from books sold door to door, especially five travel volumes. For more than forty years, he occasionally sold material, usually humorous sketches, to magazines and newspapers. He also composed philosophical dialogues, moral fables, and maxims, as well as essays on a range of subjects which were weighted more toward the social and cultural than the belletristic but which were nevertheless often controversial. Posterity prefers his two famous

novels about boyhood along the banks of the Mississippi, *The Adventures of Tom Sawyer* (1876) and *Adventures of Huckleberry Finn* (1884), although Twain also tried historical fiction, the detective story, and quasi-scientific fantasy.

ACHIEVEMENTS

Certainly one of the United States' most beloved and most frequently quoted writers, Mark Twain earned that honor by creating an original and nearly inimitable style that is thoroughly American. Although Twain tried nearly every genre from historical fiction to poetry to quasi-scientific fantasy, his novels about boyhood on the Mississippi, *The Adventures of Tom Sawyer* and *Adventures of Huckleberry Finn*, are the works that permanently wove Twain's celebrity status into the fabric of American culture. During his own lifetime, Twain received numerous honors including an M.A., soon followed by an LL.D., from Yale University. The University of Missouri granted him another doctorate in 1902. His proudest moment, however, was in 1907, when the University of Oxford awarded him an honorary LL.D. He was so proud of his scarlet doctor's gown that he wore it to his daughter's wedding.

BIOGRAPHY

After his education was cut short by the death of a stern father who had more ambition than success, at the age of eleven Mark Twain was apprenticed to a newspaper office, which, except for the money earned from four years of piloting on the Mississippi, supplied most of his income until 1868. Then, he quickly won eminence as a lecturer and author before his marriage to wealthy Olivia Langdon in 1870 led to a memorably comfortable and active family life which included three daughters. Although always looking to his writing for income, he increasingly devoted energy to business affairs and investments until his publishing house declared bankruptcy in 1894. After his world lecture tour of 1895-1896, he became one of the most admired figures of his time and continued to earn honors until his death in 1910.

ANALYSIS

Many readers find Mark Twain most successful in briefer works, including his narratives, because they were not padded to fit some extraneous standard of length. His best stories are narrated by first-person speakers who are seemingly artless, often so convincingly that critics cannot agree concerning the extent to which their ingenuousness is the result of Twain's self-conscious craft. While deeply divided himself, Twain seldom created introspectively complex characters or narrators who are unreliable in the Conradian manner. Rather, just as Twain alternated between polarities of attitude, his characters tend to embody some extreme, unitary state either of villainy or (especially with young women) of unshakable virtue. Therefore, they too seldom interact effectively. Except when adapting a plot taken from oral tradition, Twain does better with patently artificial situations, which his genius for suggesting authentic speech make plausible enough. In spite of their faults, Twain's stories captivate the reader with their irresistible humor, their unique style, and their spirited characters who transfigure the humdrum with striking perceptions.

"THE CELEBRATED JUMPING FROG OF CALAVERAS COUNTY"

"The Celebrated Jumping Frog of Calaveras County" is generally regarded as Twain's most distinctive story, although some readers may prefer Jim Baker's bluejay yarn, which turns subtly on the psyche of its narrator, or Jim Blaine's digressions from his grandfather's old ram, which reach a more physical comedy while evolving into an absurdly tall tale. In "The Celebrated Jumping Frog of Calaveras County," Jim Smiley's eagerness to bet on anything in the mining camp may strain belief, but it is relatively plausible that another gambler could weigh down Smiley's frog, Daniel Webster, with quailshot and thus win forty dollars with an untrained frog. Most attempts to find profundity in this folk anecdote involve the few enveloping sentences attributed to an outsider, who may represent the literate Easterner being gulled by Simon Wheeler's seeming inability to stick to his point. The skill of the story can be more conclusively identified, from the deft humanizing of

animals to the rising power and aptness of the imagery. Especially adroit is the deadpan manner of Wheeler, who never betrays whether he himself appreciates the humor and the symmetry of his meanderings. Twain's use of the oral style is nowhere better represented than in "The Celebrated Jumping Frog of Calaveras County," which exemplifies the principles of the author's essay "How to Tell a Story."

"A TRUE STORY"

In 1874, Twain assured the sober *Atlantic Monthly* that his short story "A True Story" was not humorous, although in fact it has his characteristic sparkle and hearty tone. Having been encouraged by the contemporary appeal for local color, Twain quickly developed a narrator with a heavy dialect and a favorite folk-saying that allows a now-grown son to recognize his mother after a separation of thirteen years. While she, in turn, finds scars confirming their relationship on his wrist and head, this conventional plot gains resonance from Rachel's report of how her husband and seven children had once been separated at a slave auction in Richmond. Contemporaries praised "A True Story" for its naturalness, testimony that Twain was creating more lifelike blacks than any other author by allowing them greater dignity, and Rachel is quick to insist that slave families cared for one another just as deeply as any white families. Her stirringly recounted memories challenged the legend of the Old South even before that legend reached its widest vogue, and her spirit matched her "mighty" body so graphically that "A True Story" must get credit for much more craftsmanship than is admitted by its subtitle, "Repeated Word for Word as I Heard It."

"THE FACTS CONCERNING THE RECENT CARNIVAL OF CRIME IN CONNECTICUT"

In "The Facts Concerning the Recent Carnival of Crime in Connecticut," in which Twain again uses first-person narration with a flawless touch for emphasizing the right word or syllable, the main character closely resembles the author in age, experience, habits, and tastes. Of more significance is the fact that the story projects Twain's lifelong struggles with, and even against, his conscience. Here the conscience admits to being the "most pitiless enemy" of its host, whom it is supposed to "improve" but only tyrannizes with gusto while refusing to praise the host for anything. It makes the blunder, however, of materializing as a two-foot dwarf covered with "fuzzy greenish mold" who torments the narrator with intimate knowledge of and contemptuous judgments on his behavior. When beloved Aunty Mary arrives to scold him once more for his addiction to tobacco, his conscience grows so torpid that he can gleefully seize and destroy it beyond any chance of rebirth. Through vivid yet realistic detail, "The Facts Concerning the Recent Carnival of Crime in Connecticut" dramatizes common musings about shame and guilt along with the yearnings some persons feel for release from them. If it maintains too comic a tone to preach nihilism or amorality, it leaves readers inclined to view conscience less as a divine agent than as part of psychic dynamics.

"THE £1,000,000 BANK-NOTE"

The shopworn texture of "The £1,000,000 Bank-Note" reveals Twain's genius for using the vernacular at a low ebb. Narrated by the protagonist, this improbable tale is set in motion by two brothers who disagree over what would happen if some penniless individual were loaned a five-million-dollar bill for thirty days. To solve their argument, they engage in an experiment with a Yankee, Henry Adams, a stockbroker's clerk stranded in London. Coincidence thickens when, having managed by the tenth day of the experiment to get invited to dinner by an American minister, Adams unknowingly meets the stepdaughter of one of the brothers and woos and wins her that very night. Having just as nimbly gained a celebrity that makes every merchant eager to extend unlimited credit, he endorses a sale of Nevada stocks that enables him to show his future father-in-law that he has banked a million dollars of his own. The overall effect is cheerfully melodramatic and appeals to fantasies about windfalls of money; the reader can share Adams's pleasure in the surprise and awe he arouses by pulling his banknote out of a tattered pocket. It can be argued that the story indicts a society in which the mere show of wealth can so quickly raise one's standing, but Twain probably meant Adams to deserve respect for his enterprise and shrewdness when his chance came.

"THE MAN THAT CORRUPTED HADLEYBURG"

"The Man That Corrupted Hadleyburg" is one of the most penetrating of Twain's stories. It achieves unusual depth of character and, perhaps by giving up the first-person narrator, a firm objectivity that lets theme develop through dialogue and incident. It proceeds with such flair that only a third or fourth reading uncovers thin links in a supposedly inescapable chain of events planned for revenge by an outsider who had been insulted in Hadleyburg, a town smugly proud of its reputation for honesty.

Stealthily he leaves a sack of counterfeit gold coins which are to be handed over to the fictitious resident who once gave a needy stranger twenty dollars and can prove it by recalling his words at the time. Next, the avenger sends nineteen leading citizens a letter which tells each of them how to claim the gold, supposedly amounting to forty thousand dollars. During an uproarious town meeting studded with vignettes of local characters, both starchy and plebeian, eighteen identical claims are read aloud; the nineteenth, however, from elderly Edward Richards, is suppressed by the chairman, who overestimates how Richards once saved him from the community's unjust anger. Rewarded by the stranger and made a hero, Richards is actually tormented to death, both by pangs of conscience and by fear of exposure. Hadleyburg, however, has learned a lesson in humility and moral realism and shortens its motto from the Lord's Prayer to run: "Lead Us into Temptation."

"The Man That Corrupted Hadleyburg" exhibits Twain's narrative and stylistic strengths and also dramatizes several of his persistent themes, such as skepticism about orthodox religion, ambivalence toward the conscience but contempt for rationalizing away deserved guilt, and attraction to mechanistic ideas. The story raises profound questions which can never be settled. The most useful criticism asks whether the story's determinism is kept consistent and uppermost—or, more specifically, whether the reform of Hadleyburg can follow within the patterns already laid out. The ethical values behind the story's action and ironical tone imply that people can in fact choose to behave more admirably.

In printing the story, *Harper's Monthly* may well

have seen a Christian meliorism, a lesson against self-righteous piety that abandons true charity. The revised motto may warn that the young, instead of being sheltered, should be educated to cope with fallible human nature. More broadly, the story seems to show that the conscience can be trained into a constructive force by honestly confronting the drives for pleasure and self-approval that sway everyone.

Many of these same themes reappear in quasi-supernatural sketches such as "Extract from Captain Stormfield's Visit to Heaven." Twain never tired of toying with biblical characters, particularly Adam and Eve, or with parodies of Sunday-school lessons. He likewise parodied most other genres, even those which he himself used seriously. In his most serious moods he preached openly against cruelty to animals in "A Dog's Tale" and "A Horse's Tale," supported social or political causes, and always came back to moral choices, as in "Was It Heaven or Hell?" or "The $30,000 Bequest." Notably weak in self-criticism, he had a tireless imagination capable of daringly unusual perspectives, a supreme gift of humor darkened by brooding over the enigmas of life, and an ethical habit of thought that expressed itself most tellingly through character and narrative.

OTHER MAJOR WORKS

LONG FICTION: *The Gilded Age*, 1873 (with Charles Dudley Warner); *The Adventures of Tom Sawyer*, 1876; *The Prince and the Pauper*, 1881; *Adventures of Huckleberry Finn*, 1884; *A Connecticut Yankee in King Arthur's Court*, 1889; *The American Claimant*, 1892; *Tom Sawyer Abroad*, 1894; *The Tragedy of Pudd'nhead Wilson*, 1894; *Personal Recollections of Joan of Arc*, 1896; *Tom Sawyer, Detective*, 1896; *The Mysterious Stranger*, 1916 (revised as *The Chronicle of Young Satan*, 1969, by Albert Bigelow Paine and Frederick A. Duneka); *Mark Twain's Mysterious Stranger Manuscripts*, 1969 (William M. Gibson, editor); *Simon Wheeler, Detective*, 1963.

PLAYS: *Colonel Sellers*, pr. 1874; *Ah Sin*, pr. 1877 (with Bret Harte).

NONFICTION: *The Innocents Abroad*, 1869; *Roughing It*, 1872; *A Tramp Abroad*, 1880; *Life on the Mississippi*, 1883; *Following the Equator*, 1897 (also known as *More Tramp Abroad*); *How to Tell a Story and Other Essays*, 1897; *My Debut as a Literary Person*, 1903; *Extracts from Adam's Diary*, 1904; *Eve's Diary, Translated from the Original Ms*, 1906; *What Is Man?*, 1906; *Christian Science*, 1907; *Extract from Captain Stormfield's Visit to Heaven*, 1909; *Is Shakespeare Dead?*, 1909; *Mark Twain's Speeches*, 1910; *Mark Twain's Letters*, 1917 (2 volumes); *Europe and Elsewhere*, 1923 (Albert Bigelow Paine, editor); *Mark Twain's Autobiography*, 1924 (2 volumes); *Sketches of the Sixties*, 1926 (with Bret Harte); *Mark Twain's Notebook*, 1935 (Albert Bigelow Paine, editor); *Letters from the Sandwich Islands, Written for the Sacramento Union*, 1937; *Letters from Honolulu, Written for the Sacramento Union*, 1939; *Mark Twain in Eruption*, 1940; *Mark Twain's Travels with Mr. Brown*, 1940; *Washington in 1868*, 1943; *The Love Letters of Mark Twain*, 1949; *Mark Twain to Mrs. Fairbanks*, 1949; *Mark Twain of the Enterprise, 1862-1864*, 1957; *Mark Twain-Howells Letters*, 1960; *Mark Twain's Letters to Mary*, 1961; *Letters from the Earth*, 1962; *The Complete Essays of Mark Twain*, 1963; *The Forgotten Writings of Mark Twain*, 1963; *Mark Twain's Letters from Hawaii*, 1966; *Mark Twain's Letters to His Publishers, 1867-1894*, 1967; *Clemens of the Call: Mark Twain in San Francisco*, 1969; *Mark Twain's Correspondence with Henry Huttleston Rogers, 1893-1909*, 1969; *A Pen Warmed-Up in Hell: Mark Twain in Protest*, 1972; *Mark Twain's Notebooks and Journals*, 1975-1979; *Mark Twain Speaking*, 1976 (Paul Fatout, editor).

MISCELLANEOUS: *The Writings of Mark Twain*, 1968 (25 volumes).

BIBLIOGRAPHY

Baender, Paul. "The 'Jumping Frog' as a Comedian's First Virtue." *Modern Philology* 60 (1963): 192-200. Argues that the story does not have the regional emphasis of the typical southwestern frame-story. Retains its interest because of its deadpan delivery rather than its theme of East/West antagonism.

Briden, Earl F. "Twainian Pedagogy and the No-

Account Lessons of 'Hadleyburg.'" *Studies in Short Fiction* 28 (Spring, 1991): 125-234. Argues that within the context of Twain's skepticism about man's capacity for moral education "The Man That Corrupted Hadleyburg" is not a story about a town's redemptive lessons of sin but rather an exposé about humanity's inability to learn morality from either theory or practice, abstract principle or moral pedagogy.

Fishkin, Shelley Fisher. *Lighting Out for the Territory: Reflections on Mark Twain and American Culture*. New York: Oxford University Press, 1996. A broad survey of Mark Twain's influence on modern culture, including the many writers who have acknowledged their indebtedness to him; discusses Twain's use of Hannibal, Missouri, in his writings; charts his transformation from a southern racist to a committed antiracist.

Krause, Sydney J. "The Art and Satire of Twain's 'Jumping Frog Story.'" *American Quarterly* 41 (1964): 562-576. Asserts the story has at least eight levels of story interest, with each having multiple sides. The story is a moral satire on the simplicity of Jim Smiley; but Simon Wheeler, a foil for Smiley, represents the revenge of the West for the trick of the Easterner. The satire is made more complicated by Wheeler's joke on Twain. Thus, Twain has the same relationship to Wheeler that Smiley has to the stranger.

Lauber, John. *The Inventions of Mark Twain*. New York: Hill & Wang, 1990. Very well-written and often humorous, this biography reveals Twain as an extremely complex, self-contradictory individual. Includes an annotated bibliography.

Messent, Peter B. *Mark Twain*. New York: St. Martin's Press, 1997. A standard introduction to Twain's life and works. Provides bibliographical references and an index.

Rasmussen, R. Kent. *Mark Twain A-Z*. New York: Facts on File, 1995. The most impressive reference tool available. Virtually every character, theme, place, and biographical fact can be researched in this compendious volume. Contains the most complete chronology ever compiled.

Sanborn, Margaret. *Mark Twain: The Bachelor Years*. New York: Doubleday, 1990. This biography covers the adventure-filled years from the author's boyhood to marriage in 1870 at age thirty-four. Based on extensive research into letters written to Twain's mother, sister, brothers, and close friends. Includes many letters not referenced by Twain's official biographer, Albert Bigelow Paine. Also includes valuable insights gained from 184 letters written between 1868 and 1870, while courting Olivia Langdon, whom Twain eventually married.

Smith, Henry Nash. *Mark Twain: A Collection of Critical Essays*. Englewood Cliffs, N.J.: Prentice-Hall, 1963. A collection of essays with an introduction by Smith. Among the contributors is W. H. Auden. A chronology of important dates in the author's life is also included.

Wagenknecht, Edward. *Mark Twain: The Man and His Work*. 3d ed. Norman: University of Oklahoma Press, 1967. A thorough revision of the 1935 work in which Wagenknecht considers the vast historical and critical study conducted between 1935 and 1960. He has modified many of his original ideas, most notably, that Mark Twain was "The Divine Amateur." The original chapter with that title has been rewritten and renamed "The Man of Letters."

Wonham, Henry B. *Mark Twain and the Art of the Tall Tale*. New York: Oxford University Press, 1993. Discusses how Twain used the tall-tale conventions of interpretive play, dramatic encounters, and the folk community. Focuses on the relationship between storyteller and audience in Twain's fiction.

Louis J. Budd, updated by Leslie A. Pearl

ANNE TYLER

Born: Minneapolis, Minnesota; October 25, 1941

PRINCIPAL SHORT FICTION

"The Common Courtesies," 1968
"Who Would Want a Little Boy?" 1968
"With All Flags Flying," 1971
"The Bride in the Boatyard," 1972
"The Base-Metal Egg," 1973
"Spending," 1973
"Half-Truths and Semi-Miracles," 1974
"The Geologist's Maid," 1975
"A Knack for Languages," 1975
"Some Sign That I Ever Made You Happy," 1975
"Your Place Is Empty," 1976
"Average Waves in Unprotected Waters," 1977
"Foot-Footing On," 1977
"Holding Things Together," 1977
"Uncle Ahmad," 1977
"Under the Bosom Tree," 1977
"Linguistics," 1978
"Laps," 1981
"The Country Cook," 1982
"Teenage Wasteland," 1983
"Rerun," 1988
"A Woman Like a Fieldstone House," 1989
"People Who Don't Know the Answers," 1991

OTHER LITERARY FORMS

Anne Tyler has published more than a dozen novels, including *Searching for Caleb* (1976), *Earthly Possessions* (1977), *Morgan's Passing* (1980), *Dinner at the Homesick Restaurant* (1982), *The Accidental Tourist* (1985), *Breathing Lessons* (1988), *Saint Maybe* (1991), *Ladder of Years* (1995), and *A Patchwork Planet* (1998). *The Accidental Tourist* was adapted for the screen in 1988, and *Breathing Lessons* was adapted for television's *Hallmark Hall of Fame* in 1994. Tyler has published many nonfiction articles and essays about writing and writers. Her more than 260 book reviews have appeared in national periodicals. She has also written a children's

book, *Tumble Tower* (1993), illustrated by her daughter Mitra Modarressi.

ACHIEVEMENTS

At Duke University, Anne Tyler won the Anne Flexner Award for creative writing. In 1966, she won the *Mademoiselle* magazine award for showing promise as a writer. In 1969 and 1972, she won O. Henry Awards for the short stories "Common Courtesies" and "With All Flags Flying." In 1977, she received a citation from the American Academy of Arts and Letters for her novel *Earthly Possessions*. In 1980, *Morgan's Passing* won her the Janet Heidinger Kafka Prize. In 1982, Tyler was nominated for the Pulitzer Prize for her novel *Dinner at the Homesick Restaurant*, which won a PEN/Faulkner Award for fiction. In 1985, she won the National Book Critics Circle Award for *The Accidental Tourist*, and in 1988, the film version won four Academy Award nominations. That same year Tyler was a National Book Award finalist for *Breathing Lessons*, the novel for which she won the Pulitzer Prize for Literature in 1989. *Breathing Lessons*, *Saint Maybe*, and *Ladder of Years* were Book-of-the-Month Club selections.

BIOGRAPHY

When Anne Tyler was seven, her parents moved to Celo, a Quaker commune in North Carolina, to raise their family in a quiet, isolated environment. Anne and her two brothers were schooled at home. Tyler became an avid reader, and her favorite book was *The Little House* (1942) by Virginia Lee Burton. Unable to support the family adequately at Celo, Tyler's parents moved to Raleigh in 1952, where her father worked as a research chemist, and her mother became a social worker. The Tylers were activists in the Civil Rights movement, opposed the death penalty, and, as Quaker pacifists, opposed U.S. involvement in war. With this background, it is surprising that Tyler's writing reveals no political or social ideology, other than her portrayal of the family as a basic unit in society.

Tyler attended high school in Raleigh, where Mrs. Peacock, her English teacher, taught literature with a dramatic flair and inspired Anne's desire to become a writer. At sixteen, she entered Duke University on scholarship, majoring in Russian studies and literature, and graduated Phi Beta Kappa in 1961. At Duke, Professors Reynolds Price and William Blackburn recognized her talent. Eudora Welty's conversational dialogue, southern settings, and gentle satire also influenced Tyler.

Tyler attended Columbia University but did not finish her master's degree. While working in the library at Duke University, she met Taghi Modarressi, an Iranian medical student, and married him in 1963. He completed his residency in child psychiatry at McGill University in Canada. Then the Modarressis moved to Baltimore, Maryland, where they established a permanent home and produced two daughters, Tezh and Mitra.

As a full-time wife and mother, Tyler wrote and

Anne Tyler (Diana Walker)

published many short stories and book reviews. Always time-oriented and well organized, she wrote when the children were napping or at school. Tyler says her early novels are flawed because normal family distractions interfered with her concentration while she was writing them. In 1970, her novels began to attract readers and critics, and by 1980, her reputation as a mature writer was secure.

Tyler maintains disciplined work methods. She begins writing after breakfast and continues for seven hours daily until late afternoon. She keeps a file of ideas, interesting people, and newspaper articles. Then she plans a story, using charts, pictures, and doodles. She imagines life inside her characters' skins, until they come alive for her. Tyler writes early drafts in longhand because the flow of her pen stimulates creativity; then she writes final drafts on a word processor. When she finishes a project, she rests and enjoys gardening and her family. Her two greatest fears are blindness and arthritis, diseases affecting the senses of sight and touch. As Tyler's skill and success as a novelist has grown, her prolific production of short stories and articles has declined. Tyler, now a widow, settled in Baltimore.

ANALYSIS

Classified by critics as a southern writer, Anne Tyler focuses on modern families and their unique relationships. Her underlying theme is that time inexorably changes the direction of people's lives. The past determines the present and the present determines the future. Her stories show that life moves in generational cycles and that conflicts inevitably arise as time passes and settings change. Within families, the perspective of love evolves, children grow up and leave home, and death and grief sever connections. When a character's freedom is restricted by too many demands on energy or resources, the individual must make choices, adapt to changing circumstances, and endure insecurity and hardship before reaching a temporary equilibrium. Tyler says that life is a "web, crisscrossed by strings of love and need and worry." Her humanistic worldview focuses on individuals, isolated and unable to communicate complex emotions such as love, grief, despair, or guilt. Missed connections, language, social class, age, religious beliefs, ethnicity, and other barriers prevent communication.

Tyler is always aware of the writer/reader connection. What draws a reader are "concrete details, carefully layered to create complexity and depth, like real life." Characters must be individuals with unique qualities, and their dialogue must flow like conversation. Tyler often uses multiple points of view as a third-person observer. She says she is able to assume a convincing masculine persona in her narrative because most human experience has no particular gender. She makes effective use of flashbacks, in which a character's memory travels to the past and links it to the present and future.

"YOUR PLACE IS EMPTY"

The idea for this story occurred when Tyler accompanied her husband, Taghi Modarressi, to Iran to meet her large family. Before the journey, Tyler, like the character Elizabeth, taught herself Persian and spoke it well enough to communicate on a surface level, but she soon discovered that mere words could not express complex emotions or overcome her feelings of being an outsider in a foreign culture.

The situation is reversed in "Your Place Is Empty." Mrs. Ardavi arrives in the United States for a six-month visit with her son Hassan, his American wife Elizabeth, and their small daughter. Hassan has lived in the United States for twelve years and is a successful doctor. Upon arrival at the airport, his mother does not recognize him. She reminds him that his place at home is still empty and urges him to return to Iran. Hassan has not forgotten his heritage, but he has changed, an underlying theme of the story.

Another theme shows how conflicts arise when people from different cultures cannot adapt. At first Elizabeth tries to make Mrs. Ardavi welcome, but soon language and culture become barriers to communication. As Mrs. Ardavi attempts to express her personality and infuse her son's home with Iranian customs, Elizabeth feels resentful and isolated, as if her freedom within her own home is restricted. Food preparation symbolizes their conflict. Elizabeth serves bacon, a taboo food for Mrs. Ardavi, who clutters Elizabeth's kitchen with spices and herbs, pots and pans, as she prepares Hassan's favorite lamb stew. She thinks that Elizabeth's meals are inadequate and that she is a negligent mother. Like an unsuccessful arbiter, Hassan stands between his mother and Elizabeth.

Tyler uses a narrative point of view that shifts between Mrs. Ardavi and Elizabeth. Insight into both women's personalities evokes reader sympathy, especially for Mrs. Ardavi. In flashbacks, she recalls her traditional Muslim girlhood; an arranged marriage to a man she never loved; his prolonged illness and death; grief over her oldest son's unhappy marriage and his untimely death; problems with the spoiled and pregnant wife of her youngest son; and the small comfort of "knowing her place" within the family circle of thirteen sisters who gossip and drink tea each afternoon. Elizabeth expresses resentment at her mother-in-law's interference with icy silence, zealous housecleaning, and private complaints to Hassan. Realizing that the situation has reached an impasse, Hassan suggests that for the duration of her visit, Mrs. Ardavi move to a nearby apartment, away from the intimacy of his family. Unable to find "her place" in her son's American home, Mrs. Ardavi returns to Iran.

"AVERAGE WAVES IN UNPROTECTED WATERS"

This story shows how the passage of time causes physical and emotional changes for Bet, a single mother, and Arnold, her mentally disabled son. Avery Blevins, Bet's "grim and cranky" husband, deserts her after a doctor diagnoses their baby as mentally retarded, the result of a fateful genetic error. Without family (her parents are dead), Bet supports herself and her child at a low-paying job. Arnold's increasingly wild tantrums force her to place him in a state hospital. Bet's landlady and longtime baby-sitter is a kindly woman, who has grown too old to control Arnold's aggressive behavior. His lack of response to her tears and special gift of cookies when he leaves indicates his infantile emotional level. On the train he enjoys watching the conductor scold a black woman for trying to ride without a ticket and cheers loudly as if they are actors in a television comedy. Arnold ignores the hospital setting and the nurse until his mother leaves. Then, like a small child, he screams loudly enough for Bet to hear him in the driveway as she climbs into a taxi. The train is late; so Bet dries her tears and watches strangers draping bunting on a speaker's stand in preparation for a ceremony dedicating the antiquated depot's restoration. She observes their actions while she waits for the train to take her life in a new direction.

Tyler describes how the passage of time erodes concrete objects and compares it to changing human relationships. The shabby boardinghouse has peeling layers of wallpaper, symbolic of passing time and the people who once lived there. Bet is worn down physically and emotionally by Arnold's hyperactive behavior, his short attention span, and his loud, incoherent speech. Marble steps at the mental hospital are worn down by the feet of care-givers and patients who have climbed them. The hospital dormitory is stripped of color and warmth. Only a small, crooked clown picture indicates that children might live there. The nurse disengages emotionally when Bet tries to tell her about Arnold's unique qualities. The train conductor, taxi driver, and station attendant are coldly impersonal, showing lack of empathy for Bet and Arnold. In the past, they have witnessed many arrivals and departures like Bet's and no longer respond to them.

The title "Average Waves in Unprotected Waters" indicates how main characters, Bet and Arnold, adapt to "waves" in their lives. Bet faces disappointments and griefs, just as she once allowed "ordinary" breakers in the ocean to slam against her body, "as if staunchness were a virtue." The waves are not life-threatening; they are unhappy experiences to which she and Arnold must adapt in environments of "unprotected waters." Bet must endure life without family, goals, or resources, and Arnold must endure life in an impersonal mental hospital without his mother's love and protection.

"TEENAGE WASTELAND"

Originally published in *Seventeen* magazine, this story shows how lack of communication between a troubled adolescent and his parents results in tragedy. Tyler's title, "Teenage Wasteland," comes from a popular song by the musical group the Who. Contributing factors to fifteen-year-old Donnie's "wasted"

life include Daisy and Matt's inept parenting skills, a tutor's destructive influence, and Donnie's changing needs as an adolescent. Poor grades, petty thefts, smoking and drinking, and truancy are symptoms of Donnie's low self-esteem.

Tyler tells the story from a third-person point of view, limited to Daisy, a mother who agonizes over her guilt and inadequacies as a parent. Significantly, Matt, the father, does not get directly involved in guiding or disciplining his son. Neither parent is able to talk to Donnie about his personal problems. They focus on academic performance. At first, the parents make strict rules, and Daisy helps Donnie complete his assignments. However, her best efforts result in minimal improvement and cause major emotional storms.

Humiliated and unable to cope, Daisy takes Donnie to see Cal, a young counselor and tutor whose office is in his house, where other students lounge around, playing basketball and listening to rock music by the Who. Cal "marches to a different drummer" and encourages Donnie and other adolescents under his tutelage to rebel from "controlling" adults, like parents and school authorities. Accepting responsibility for one's actions, setting goals, and studying are not part of Cal's agenda. Donnie gradually withdraws from his family in favor of "hanging out" at Cal's with teenagers like himself.

Donnie is expelled from the private school he attends after authorities find beer and cigarettes in his locker, and his academic performance drops even lower. Instead of going home, he runs to Cal's. Donnie claims it was a "frame up," and Cal excuses the boy by saying that the school violated his civil rights. Angry and frustrated, Daisy takes Donnie home and enrolls him in public school, where he finishes the semester. Miserable and friendless, Donnie runs away, his youth wasted, and Daisy wonders what went wrong.

"PEOPLE WHO DON'T KNOW THE ANSWERS"

This story, published in *The New Yorker*, is a revised chapter from Tyler's novel *Saint Maybe*. Doug Bedloe, a recently retired schoolteacher, realizes that nobody has the final answers to life's mysteries. The passage of time changes everything. To fill the void in his life, he tries several boring and unproductive hobbies. Then he becomes interested in some foreign students who live across the street. Like actors in a comedy, they enjoy a casual lifestyle and are fascinated by American gadgets, music, language, and clothing, far different from the "real" life and family responsibilities they have known in distant lands.

Doug compares their experimental lifestyle to his own static existence. Seen through the foreigners' window screen, his house reminds him of a framed needlepoint picture, something "cozy, old-fashioned, stitched in place forever." Yet Doug's family has changed. His wife Bee has become crippled with arthritis. Death has taken their oldest son Danny, whose children now live with them. Beastie, Doug's old dog and companion, is buried under the azalea. Adult siblings, Ian and Claudia, have gradually assumed family authority. Doug feels physically fit, but his life has no anchor. His past is gone, and he must somehow endure the present.

Ian invites his family to a picnic sponsored by the Church of the Second Chance, viewed by some as a cult, or "alternative religion." Brother Emmett and church members have helped Ian endure his overwhelming sense of guilt over Danny's accidental death and support his role as surrogate father to Danny's children. Doug acknowledges that sharing one's joys and sorrows would benefit him, but Bee remains cynical. Doug's past and the present reality make him feel split, like the foreigners' old car, parked half inside their garage with the faulty automatic door bisecting it.

OTHER MAJOR WORKS

LONG FICTION: *If Morning Ever Comes*, 1964; *The Tin Can Tree*, 1964; *A Slipping-Down Life*, 1970; *The Clock Winder*, 1972; *Celestial Navigation*, 1974; *Searching for Caleb*, 1976; *Earthly Possessions*, 1977; *Morgan's Passing*, 1980; *Dinner at the Homesick Restaurant*, 1982; *The Accidental Tourist*, 1985; *Breathing Lessons*, 1988; *Saint Maybe*, 1991; *Ladder of Years*, 1995; *A Patchwork Planet*, 1998.

CHILDREN'S LITERATURE: *Tumble Tower*, 1993 (illustrations by Mitra Modarressi).

BIBLIOGRAPHY

Bail, Paul. *Anne Tyler: A Critical Companion*. Westport, Conn.: Greenwood Press, 1998. Part of a series of reference books about popular contemporary writers, this book contains a biography, literary influences on Anne Tyler, and individual chapters that discuss twelve of Tyler's novels. General analysis includes how her novels fit into southern regional literature, women's literature, and popular culture, as well as critiques from feminist and multicultural points of view. Bail also discusses plot, characters, themes, literary devices, historical settings, and narrative points of view as they apply to individual novels. The book concludes with an extensive bibliography.

Cahill, Susan, ed. *New Women and New Fiction: Short Stories Since the Sixties*. New York: New American Library, 1986. According to Cahill's introduction, the anthology contains twenty-one stories written by unrecognized women geniuses who have created works of art. Their style is minimalist, their humor subtle, and their characters and settings transcend time. Cahill includes a brief biographical sketch of each author preceding her short story. The anthology includes Anne Tyler's "Teenage Wasteland."

Croft, Robert W. *Anne Tyler: A Bio-Bibliography*. Westport, Conn.: Greenwood Press, 1995. Part of a series focusing on American authors, this book is divided into two parts: a biography which includes four chapters, each followed by endnotes. It concludes with an extensive bibliography, divided into primary and secondary sources, with a list of Anne Tyler's papers at Duke University. "A Setting Apart," concerns her childhood in a commune, teen years in Raleigh, college at Duke, and early writing. "The Only Way Out," refers to her feelings of isolation during her early marriage and motherhood and how writing her first novels and short stories kept her in touch with the real world. "Rich with Possibilities" refers to her life in Baltimore, the setting of most of her stories, her book reviews, and discussion of her middle-period novels. "A Border Crossing" deals with Tyler's fame and recurring themes in her novels.

_____. *An Anne Tyler Companion*. Westport, Conn.: Greenwood Press, 1998. A critical study of Tyler's fiction. Includes a bibliography and an index.

Foley, Martha, ed. *The Best American Short Stories 1977*. Boston: Houghton Mifflin, 1977. This volume contains twenty short stories, selected by Martha Foley, founder of *Story* publications. It includes Anne Tyler's "Your Place Is Empty" and stories by other authors that appeared in popular magazines such as the *New Yorker* and *Atlantic Monthly*. Foley's foreword credits mystery writer Rex Stout for leading the 1977 fight for copyright reform that now protects authors from being victimized by publishers.

Kissel, Susan S. *Moving On: The Heroines of Shirley Ann Grau, Anne Tyler, and Gail Godwin*. Bowling Green, Ohio: Bowling Green State University Popular Press, 1996. Topics include Tyler's heroines and her identity as a southern writer. Includes a bibliography and an index.

Murphy, George E., Jr. *The Editor's Choice: New American Series*. Vol. 1. New York: Bantam/Wampeter Press Book, 1985. The introduction contains Murphy's criteria for selection of eighteen popular short stories published in national magazines and nominated to the anthology by fiction editors. Murphy touts the short story as a typically American genre. Selection includes Tyler's "Teenage Wasteland."

Ravenel, Shannon, ed. *The Best American Short Stories 1983*. Boston: Houghton Mifflin, 1983. The introduction, by Anne Tyler, discusses qualities of memorable short stories. She says that they are a unique form, not shortened novels. They must include precise descriptive details, unforgettable characters, and a "moment of stillness . . . the frame through which the reader views all that happens." Plot action is the result of characters' personalities.

_____. *Best of the South*. Chapel Hill, N.C.: Algonquin Books, 1996. The introduction, by Anne Tyler, discusses the importance of settings and how they change over time. To illustrate, she describes the southern town, where she spent her teens: its tree-lined square, statue of a Confederate soldier, the movie theater, dime store with a snack bar, and the department store where Miss Mildred clerked. She compares it to today's scene in Raleigh, North Carolina, with its malls lined with salad bars, maxi-movie theaters, music video stores, fast-food restaurants, and the Gap. She discusses the "yeasty prose" of southern writing with its musical quality and conversational tone, characters who are just as important as what happens, and the narrative point of view and dialogue with which southerners identify.

Quiello, Rose. *Breakdowns and Breakthoughts: The Figure of the Hysteric in Contemporary Novels by Women*. New York: P. Lang, 1996. Discusses the work of Margaret Drabble, Kate O'Brien, and Anne Tyler. Includes a bibliography and an index.

Tyler, Anne. "Still Just Writing." In *The Writer on Her Work: Contemporary Women Writers Reflect on Their Art and Situation*. Edited by Janet Sternberg. New York: Norton, 1980. Tyler's personal essay explains how she keeps her life balanced. Writing fiction draws her into an imaginary world, but being a wife and mother keeps her anchored to the *real* world of home and family. Writing novels takes much time and concentration, so she has gradually given up writing short stories. Revised chapters from some of her novels appear in periodicals as short stories. She has reduced the number of book reviews she writes because she fears her lack of enthusiasm will not give books and authors a fair analysis.

Martha E. Rhynes

U

MIGUEL DE UNAMUNO Y JUGO

Born: Bilbao, Spain; September 29, 1864
Died: Salamanca, Spain; December 31, 1936

PRINCIPAL SHORT FICTION

El espejo de la muerte, 1913
Tres novelas ejemplares y un prólogo, 1920 (*Three Exemplary Novels and a Prologue*, 1930)
San Manuel Bueno, mártir, 1931 (*Saint Manuel Bueno, Martyr*, 1956)
Soledad y otros cuentos, 1937
Abel Sánchez and Other Stories, 1956

OTHER LITERARY FORMS

Miguel de Unamuno y Jugo's works fill sixteen volumes and include plays, several novels, collections of poetry, and hundreds of articles of varying length. His most notable works include the philosophical manifesto *Del sentimiento trágico de la vida en los hombres y en los pueblos* (1913; *The Tragic Sense of Life in Men and Peoples*, 1921), and the literary treatise *Cómo se hace una novela* (1927, *How to Make a Novel*, 1976).

ACHIEVEMENTS

During his lifetime, Miguel de Unamuno y Jugo emerged as a representative voice of the Spanish people, and his heterodox views led to his exile from 1924 to 1930. A professor of Greek, Unamuno was named lifetime rector of University of Salamanca upon his retirement in 1934 and was awarded an honorary doctorate from Oxford University in 1936.

BIOGRAPHY

Miguel de Unamuno y Jugo was born on September 29, 1864, the third of six children. He attended a private school where he was educated in the strict Catholic traditions of the day. As an adolescent,

Unamuno experienced a spiritual crisis that led him into readings of such Catholic philosophers as Jaime Balmes and Juan Donoso. In 1880, he entered the University of Madrid, where he studied under progressive dons and read philosophers like Immanuel Kant, René Descartes, and Georg Wilhelm Friedrich Hegel. He took a licentiate degree in 1883 and a doctorate in 1884 with a thesis on the origins of the Basque people.

Unamuno assumed the chair of Greek language at the University of Salamanca in 1891. That same year, he married his childhood sweetheart, Concepción Lizárraga, with whom he would father nine children. From the mid-1880's onward, Unamuno published articles for local newspapers. His first novel, *Paz en la guerra* (*Peace in War*, 1983), appeared in 1897, and in 1900, he was named rector of the university. Unamuno's literary output grew as the decades passed, as did his reputation as a heretical thinker.

In early 1924, Unamuno left Spain for exile in the Canary Islands, moving on to Paris later that year. He remained in France for six years, awaiting the establishment of the Spanish Republic. He returned to Spain in 1930 and was reappointed to his post in Salamanca the following year. Unamuno died on December 31, 1936, months after the breakout of the Spanish Civil War.

ANALYSIS

Miguel de Unamuno y Jugo is a writer who clearly uses literature as a vehicle for philosophy. His short fiction, though exhibiting some diversity, tends to emphasize broad ideas and characters that verge on caricature or archetype; the plots are simple, and the language is rarely ornate or highly developed. Among the views conveyed in Unamuno's short fiction are his belief in personal responsibility, his cyni-

Miguel de Unamuno y Jugo (Library of Congress)

cism toward the Catholic Church, his basic distrust of doctrine, and his tragic view of life as an experience full of challenges, isolation, and uncertainty. Some of his stories are decidedly romantic and sentimental, such as "El espejo de la muerte" and "El padrino Antonio," with their focus on the infirm, the unhappy, and the elderly. Others are Kafkaesque parables of morality, futuristic visions, and satires on the relationship between the sexes. "Hijos espirituales" is a macabre examination of a marriage in which ambition and infertility lead to madness and tragedy.

For Unamuno, characters determine their own destiny. The concept of self-creation is implicit, and Unamuno offers many characters who have gone abroad to create themselves anew, and others who connive to achieve their shortsighted or selfish goals. The author speculates as well on the powers of human passion and offers individuals who are driven by obsessions or mysteries beyond their control. The psychology of power plays a central role in many stories; Unamuno often poses strong, willful protagonists against weaker, more fearful, or intellectually inferior people around them. Implicit is a sense of the

relativity of morality; Unamuno seems to condemn the weakness and triviality of traditional moralists in favor of the quixotic madness of rebellious and even satanic individualists.

"THE MADNESS OF DOCTOR MONTARCO"

The 1904 short story "La locura del doctor Montarco" ("The Madness of Doctor Montarco") is a simple tale of the downfall of a doctor who publishes bizarre stories, as recounted by a sympathetic onlooker. Dr. Montarco is well regarded as a physician, but his patients begin to distrust him because of his outlandish and amoral tales. He refuses to cease or even explain his writing, though he knows his practice will dwindle and he will be ostracized as a madman. Indeed, he ends up in an asylum where he passes his time dwelling on a passage of Miguel de Cervantes's *Don Quixote de la Mancha* and ranting about goodness and folly. In the end, he dies, melancholy and mute, leaving behind a bulky manuscript and an enigmatic note asking that it be burnt unread. In Dr. Montarco, Unamuno offers an uncompromising, if unlikely, hero, an emblem of individualism and a brand of genius rife with contradiction.

ABEL SÁNCHEZ

Abel Sánchez is an expanded parable of personal obsession. It is the intimate story of the lifelong friendship of Joaquín Monegro and Abel Sánchez. Joaquín becomes a noted doctor and Abel a respected painter; each marries and fathers a child; and their children marry each other and present them with grandchildren in common.

What drives the novella is Joaquín's unflagging jealousy of and obsession with Abel. Here Unamuno draws directly on the Old Testament story of Cain and Abel, and the characters themselves are aware of the parallel. Like his biblical counterpart, Joaquín feels threatened and diminished by his brotherly friend, and feels that he cannot be held responsible for Abel's welfare or ultimate defeat. Through the device of a "confession" that Joaquín creates for his daughter, Unamuno presents the doctor's internal anguish, the deep insecurity beneath a surface of friendship and trust. Joaquín must prove himself better than Abel, yet each time he comes close to doing so, his fears deepen. Abel, in contrast, seems impervious to any sense of rivalry or even comparison. Abel obtains the love of Helena, to whom Joaquín is devoted. Abel basks in the glow of Joaquín's professional tribute, in a speech his friend delivers to undermine him. Joaquín becomes mentor to Abel's son, but he never finds the psychic peace he so deeply desires.

In such a parable, plot is subordinated to the study of character, envy, and obsession. Unamuno, however, is careful not to judge. While Joaquín is portrayed as a lost and pathetic man, the authorial voice presents his feelings and motivations without prejudice. Likewise, Unamuno resists the temptation to portray Abel as a saint; rather, he is a man of flesh and faults, and ultimately he is left outside the inner world of Joaquín's, and the novella's, paranoia.

"TWO MOTHERS"

"Dos madres" ("Two Mothers") is a shrewd and unrelenting portrait of a barren woman determined to have a child whom she can call her own. In his unapologetic fashion, Unamuno presents Raquel, a widow conducting an illicit love affair with a young man named Don Juan. For his part, he would happily and devotedly marry her and adopt a child together. Such might be an attractive option to another widow, but Raquel is more practical. She sees no purpose in such a marriage and convinces him instead to court and win another woman, beget a child and then let her, Raquel, raise it. Raquel is totally straightforward in her plan: She clearly presents it to Don Juan, then chooses the innocent young Berta as his bride and ultimately manipulates them both to obtain their child, her goddaughter Quelina.

Unamuno portrays the psychological anguish of Don Juan and the uncertainty of Berta in contrast to Raquel's cool calculation. The protagonist's name suggests the biblical Rachel, and the story's plot hearkens back to the famous story of King Solomon and the warring mothers. Throughout "Two Mothers," the themes of love, possession, and will are intertwined, and Unamuno places the heartless reality of human striving against the backdrop of legal and religious convention.

"SAINT MANUEL BUENO, MARTYR"

"San Manuel Bueno, mártir" ("Saint Manuel Bueno, Martyr") is one of Unamuno's most hopeful

and humanistic works. It is a portrait, written in the voice of a woman named Angela Carballino, of the inner spiritual life of a revered parish priest named Don Manuel. Throughout the story, Angela relates the magical sway that Manuel seems to have over his parishioners: his wisdom, his humility, the simple power of his voice to inspire and cure. Behind this saintly façade is another reality. Angela gradually comes to see that Manuel's faith is shallow, and his religiosity a mere posture he adopts to satisfy his followers and thereby bind the community together. Angela's brother Lázaro, an unbeliever newly returned from America, learns of Don Manuel's deceit and in turn becomes the priest's devoted acolyte. In the end, both men die, leaving their secret with Angela. The story is also infused with a poetic power: The nearby mountain and the lake become resonating symbols of Manuel's earthbound spirituality, and the town fool Blasillo makes constant appearances as a foil to the priest's anguish and martyrdom. Unamuno appends an epilogue wherein he intimates the authenticity of Angela's account and meditates wryly on the nature of faith.

OTHER MAJOR WORKS

LONG FICTION: *Paz en la guerra*, 1897 (*Peace in War*, 1983); *Amor y pedagogía*, 1902; *Niebla*, 1914 (*Mist: A Tragicomic Novel*); *Abel Sánchez: Una historia de pasión*, 1917 (*Abel Sánchez*, 1947); *La tía Tula*, 1921 (*Tía Tula*, 1976); *Dos novelas cortas*, 1961 (James Russell Stamm and Herbert Eugene Isar, editors).

PLAYS: *La esfinge*, wr. 1898, pr. 1909; *La venda*, wr. 1899, pb. 1913; *La difunta*, pr. 1910; *El pasado que vuelve*, wr. 1910, pr. 1923; *Fedra*, wr. 1910, pr. 1918 (*Phaedra*, 1959); *La princesa doña Lambra*, pb. 1913; *Soledad*, wr. 1921, pr. 1953; *Raquel encadenada*, wr. 1921, pr. 1926; *El otro*, wr. 1926, pr., pb. 1932 (*The Other*, 1947); *Sombras de sueño*, pb. 1930; *El hermano Juan: O, El mundo es teatro*, wr. 1927, pb. 1934; *Teatro completo*, pb. 1959, 1973.

POETRY: *Poesías*, 1907; *Rosario de sonetos líricos*, 1911; *El Cristo de Velázquez*, 1920 (*The Christ of Velázquez*, 1951); *Rimas de dentro*, 1923; *Teresa*, 1924; *Romancero del destierro*, 1928; *Poems*,

1952; *Cancionero*, 1953; *The Last Poems of Miguel de Unamuno*, 1974.

NONFICTION: *De la enseñanza superior en España*, 1899; *Nicodemo el fariseo*, 1899; *Tres ensayos*, 1900; *En torno al casticismo*, 1902; *De mi país*, 1903; *Vida de Don Quijote y Sancho, según Miguel de Cervantes Saavedra, explicada y comentada por Miguel de Unamuno*, 1905 (*The Life of Don Quixote and Sancho According to Miguel de Cervantes Saavedra Expounded with Comment by Miguel de Unamuno*, 1927); *Recuerdos de niñes y de mocedad*, 1908; *Mi religión y otros ensayos breves*, 1910; *Soliloquios y conversaciones*, 1911 (*Essays and Soliloquies*, 1925); *Contra esto y aquello*, 1912; *Del sentimiento trágico de la vida en los hombres y en los pueblos*, 1913 (*The Tragic Sense of Life in Men and Peoples*, 1921); *Cómo se hace una novela*, 1927 (*How to Make a Novel*, 1976); *La agonía del Cristianismo*, 1931 (*The Agony of Christianity*, 1928, 1960); *La ciudad de Henoc*, 1941; *Cuenca ibérica*, 1943; *Paisajes del alma*, 1944; *La enormidad de España*, 1945; *Visiones y commentarios*, 1949.

MISCELLANEOUS: *De Fuerteventura a París*, 1925; *Obras completas*, 1959-1964.

BIBLIOGRAPHY

Barcia, José Rubia, and M. A. Zeitlin, eds. *Unamuno: Creator and Creation*. Berkeley: University of California Press, 1967. An instructive anthology of essays on all aspects of Unamuno's work. Essays examine the author's existentialism, politics, psychology, literary aesthetic, dramatic artistry, and comparisons with Clarín and Cervantes.

Basdekis, Demetrios. *Unamuno and Spanish Literature*. Berkeley: University of California Press, 1967. A somewhat scholarly survey of Unamuno's influence from and place within the Spanish canon. Includes extensive discussion of Cervantes and Quixote; as well as Unamuno's connections with such writers as Clarín, Rodríguez Guillermo Galdós, Antonio Machado, and others.

Earle, Peter G. *Unamuno and English Literature*. New York: Hispanic Institute, 1960. An competent examination of how Unamuno's thinking and writing derives from such writers as Ralph Waldo Emerson; Thomas Carlyle; George Gordon, Lord Byron; Alfred, Lord Tennyson; and William James. Focus is on the development of the individualist and existentialist strains in Unamuno's thought.

Ferrater Mora, José. *Unamuno, a Philosophy of Tragedy*. Translated by Philip Silver. Berkeley: University of California Press, 1962. A updated edition of *Unamuno: Bosquejo de una filosofía* (1944). An excellent investigation into the basics of Unamuno's tragic worldview, emphasizing the nonfiction but including some of the novellas and stories.

Ilie, Paul. *Unamuno: An Existential View of Self and Society*. Madison: University of Wisconsin Press, 1967. An exploration of Unamuno within the existentialist tradition. Offers an insightful examination of Unamuno's debt and response to Friedrich Nietszche, as well as discussion of his interpretation of the Old Testament narrative.

Nozick, Martin. *Miguel de Unamuno: The Agony of Belief*. Princeton, N.J.: Princeton University Press, 1971. From a leading Unamuno scholar, an extremely lucid discussion of Unamuno's oeuvre and philosophy, examining a wide variety of his writings and placing him well within the context of nineteenth and twentieth century world literature.

Rudd, Margaret T. *The Lone Heretic: A Biography of Miguel de Unamuno y Jugo*. Austin: University of Texas Press, 1963. A straightforward and detailed biography that traces the development of Unamuno's thought and artistry in tandem with the events of his life. Full of references to and passages from his writings.

Barry Stewart Mann

JOHN UPDIKE

Born: Shillington, Pennsylvania; March 18, 1932

PRINCIPAL SHORT FICTION

The Same Door, 1959
Pigeon Feathers and Other Stories, 1962
Olinger Stories: A Selection, 1964
The Music School, 1966
Bech: A Book, 1970
Museums and Women and Other Stories, 1972
Too Far to Go: The Maples Stories, 1979
Problems and Other Stories, 1979
Bech Is Back, 1982
Trust Me, 1987
Brother Grasshopper, 1990 (limited edition)
The Afterlife and Other Stories, 1994
Licks of Love: Short Stories and a Sequel, "Rabbit Remembered," 2000

OTHER LITERARY FORMS

A prolific and versatile writer, John Updike is an accomplished novelist, perhaps best known for his "Rabbit" tetralogy, but he is also the author of *The Centaur* (1963), which fuses myth and realism in middle-class America; *Couples* (1968), which examines the social and sexual mores of a modern American town; *The Coup* (1978), in which the narrator is writing, in memoirs, the history of an imaginary African nation; and *Roger's Version* (1986) and *S* (1988), which are creative reworkings of the situation of Nathaniel Hawthorne's *The Scarlet Letter* (1850). His later novels include *Brazil* (1994), *Toward the End of Time* (1997), and *Bech at Bay: A Quasi-Novel* (1998). Updike also published many books of verse and a play (*Buchanan Dying*, 1974), and he has written reviews and critical essays on literature, music, and painting for a few decades. His nonfiction works include *Golf Dreams: Writings on Golf* (1996) and *More Matter: Essays and Criticism* (1999).

ACHIEVEMENTS

The Centaur won for John Updike the National Book Award in 1964. He was elected to the National Institute of Arts and Letters, the youngest man to receive the honor at that time. "The Bulgarian Poetess" won an O. Henry Award in 1966.

Rabbit Is Rich (1981) won an American Book Award and a Pulitzer Prize, while *Hugging the Shore: Essays and Criticism* (1983), a nine-hundred-page volume, won the National Book Critics Circle Award. In 1991, *Rabbit at Rest* won a Pulitzer Prize, and in 1995, it received the Howells Medal. In 1996, Updike's *In the Beauty of the Lilies* (1996) won the Ambassador Book Award, and the next year Updike received the Campion Award. In 1998, he earned the Harvard Arts First Medal and the National Book Medal for Distinguished Contribution to American Letters.

BIOGRAPHY

John Updike was born in 1932, the only child of Wesley Updike, a cable splicer who lost his job in the Depression and had to support his family on a meager teacher's salary ($1,740 per year), and Linda Grace Updike, an aspiring writer. The family moved to Plowville from Shillington, Pennsylvania, in 1945 to live on the farm of Updike's maternal grandparents. Updike recalls that a gift subscription at that time to *The New Yorker*, a Christmas present from an aunt, was a significant factor in his decision to become an artist. In high school, he drew for the school paper, wrote articles and poems, and demonstrated sufficient academic gifts to be awarded a full scholarship to Harvard University, which he entered in 1950.

At college, Updike majored in English, became editor of the prestigious Harvard *Lampoon*, and graduated with honors in 1954. That year, *The New Yorker* accepted a poem and a story, an event that Updike remembered as "the ecstatic breakthrough of my literary life." After graduation, Updike and his wife of one year, Mary Pennington, a fine arts major from Radcliffe, spent 1955 in Oxford, where Updike held a Knox Fellowship. When E. B. White offered him a job as a staff writer with *The New Yorker*, Updike accepted and spent the next two years contributing

John Updike (Davis Freeman)

brief, witty pieces to the "Talk of the Town" section at the front of the magazine. During this time, he worked on the manuscript of a six-hundred-page book, which he decided not to publish because it had "too many of the traits of a first novel." When his second child was born, he believed that he needed a different setting in which to live and work (the literary world in New York seemed "unnutritious and interfering") and moved to Ipswich, Massachusetts, where he found "the space" to write "the Pennsylvania thing," which became the novel *The Poorhouse Fair* (1959), and his first collection of short stories, *The Same Door.*

Choosing to work in a rented office in downtown Ipswich, Updike began an extremely active literary career that would continue for several decades. The first book in the Rabbit series, *Rabbit, Run*, was published in 1960, the same year in which the last of Updike's four children was born. *Rabbit, Run* caught the attention of the reading public with its combina-

tion of sexual candor and social insight, but *The Centaur* was Updike's first real success with serious critics, winning the National Book Award in 1964. That same year, Updike was elected a member of the National Institute of Arts and Letters. During 1964 and 1965, Updike traveled in Eastern Europe, the source for his first story about Henry Bech ("The Bulgarian Poetess"), who became a kind of slightly displaced version of himself in the guise of a Jewish writer from New York. Further travels to Africa led to other Bech stories as well as *The Coup*, but Updike generally remained in Ipswich, involved in local affairs, writing constantly, and using the beach to find the sun, which was the only cure at that time for a serious case of psoriasis. The second Rabbit book, *Rabbit Redux*, was published in 1971, and short-story collections appeared regularly. In the late 1960's, Updike sold the screen rights to his novel *Couples* for a half-million dollars (the film was not produced).

After fifteen years, Updike and his wife ended their marriage, and in 1974 he moved to Boston, returning to the North Shore area in 1976, the year before he married Martha Bernhard. In 1977, Updike published his fifth volume of verse, *Tossing and Turning*, from a major press, and in 1979, two collections of short stories that he had written during the emotional turmoil of the last years of his marriage and its conclusion were issued as *Problems and Other Stories* and *Too Far to Go*. The latter volume included all the stories about a couple named Maples whose lives were a literary transmutation of aspects of Updike's first marriage. Updike continued his energetic and inventive career through the 1980's, writing two novels imaginatively derived from Hawthorne's *The Scarlet Letter*, possibly completing the Rabbit series with *Rabbit at Rest* (1990) and collecting another nine hundred pages of essays in *Odd Jobs* (1991). In 1991, *Rabbit at Rest* won a Pulitzer Prize, and he continued to garner awards throughout the 1990's. He is known as one of the United States' leading writers.

ANALYSIS

From the beginning of his career as a writer, John Updike demonstrated his strengths as a brilliant stylist and a master of mood and tone whose linguistic facility has sometimes overshadowed the dimensions of his vision of existence in the twentieth century. His treatment of some of the central themes of modern times—sexual and social politics, the nature of intimate relationships, the collapse of traditional values, the uncertainty of the human condition as the twentieth century draws to a close—is as revealing and compelling as that of any of his contemporaries. Although he is regarded mainly as a novelist, the short story may well be his true métier, and his ability to use its compressed structure to generate intensity and to offer succinct insight has made his work a measure of success for writers of short fiction, an evolving example of the possibilities of innovation and invention in a traditional narrative form.

THE SAME DOOR *and* PIGEON FEATHERS AND OTHER STORIES

Always eloquent about his aspirations and intentions—as he is about almost everything he observes—John Updike remarked to Charles Thomas Samuels in an interview in 1968 that some of the themes of his work are "domestic fierceness within the middle class, sex and death as riddles for the thinking animal, social existence as sacrifice, unexpected pleasures and rewards, corruption as a kind of evolution," and that his work is "meditation, not pontification." In his short fiction, his meditations have followed an arc of human development from the exuberance of youth to the unsettling revelations of maturity and on toward the uncertainties of old age, a "curve of sad time" (as he ruefully described the years from 1971 to 1978 when his first marriage failed), which contains the range of experience of an extremely incisive, very well-educated, and stylistically brilliant man who has been able to reach beyond the limits of his own interesting life to capture the ethos of an era.

Updike's artistic inclinations were nurtured by his sensitive, supportive parents, who recognized his gifts and his needs, while the struggles of his neighbors in rural Pennsylvania during the Depression left him with a strong sense of the value of community and the basis for communal cohesion in a reliable, loving family. At Harvard, his intellectual capabilities

were celebrated and encouraged, and in his first job with *The New Yorker*, his ability to earn a living through his writing endowed his entire existence with an exhilaration that demanded expression in a kind of linguistic rapture. The 1950's marked the steepest incline in time's curve, and his first two collections, *The Same Door* and *Pigeon Feathers and Other Stories*, while primarily covering his youth and adolescence in the town of Shillington (which he calls Olinger), are written from the perspective of the young man who overcame the limitations of an economically strained and culturally depleted milieu to marry happily, begin a family, and capitalize on his talents in the profession that he adored. There is no false sentimentality about Olinger or the narrowness of some its citizens. Updike always saw right through the fakery of the chamber of commerce manipulators who disguised their bigotry and anti-intellectualism with pitches to patriotism, but the young men in these stories often seem destined to overcome whatever obstacles they face to move toward the promise of some artistic or social reward.

In "Flight," a high school senior is forced to relinquish his interest in a classmate because of his mother's pressures and his social status, but the loss is balanced by his initial venture into individual freedom. "The Alligators" depicts a moment of embarrassed misperception, but in the context of the other stories, it is only a temporary setback, an example of awkwardness that might, upon reflection, contribute to the cultivation of a subtler sensibility. "The Happiest I've Been" epitomizes the author's attitude at a pivotal point in his life, poised between the familiar if mundane streets of his childhood and the infinite expanse of a world beyond, enjoying the lingering nostalgia he feels for home ground, which he can carry in memory as he moves on to a wider sphere of experience. These themes are rendered with a particular power in the often-anthologized "A & P" and in "Wife-Wooing," both from *Pigeon Feathers and Other Stories*.

"A & P"

As in many of his most effective stories, in "A & P" Updike found a voice of singular appropriateness for his narrative consciousness—a boy of nineteen from a working-class background who is working as a checkout clerk at the local A & P grocery store. The store stands for the assembly-line numbness that is a part of the lockstep life that seems to be the likely destiny of all the young men in the town, and it serves as a means of supply for a nearby resort area. When three young women pass the boy's register, he is enchanted by "the queen," a girl who appears "more than pretty," and when she is ordered to dress properly by the store manager on her next visit ("Girls, this isn't the beach"), Sammy feels compelled to deliver a declaration of passionate defense of their innocence. Frustrated by the incipient stodginess and puritanical repression of the entire town and moved by his heart-driven need to make some kind of chivalrous gesture, he finds that his only recourse is to mumble "I quit" as the girls leave the store.

Lengel, the aptly named manager-curmudgeon, speaking for unreasoning minor authority, uses several power trips to maintain his petty tyranny, but Sammy refuses to back down, even when Lengel presents the ultimate guilt ploy, "You don't want to do this to your Mom and Dad." This is an appeal to conformist quiescence, and Sammy, like most of Updike's protagonists, is susceptible to the possibility of hurting or disgracing his family in a small, gossip-ridden community. When Lengel warns him, "You'll feel this for the rest of your life," Sammy recognizes the validity of his threat but realizes that, if he backs down now, he will always back down in similar situations. Frightened and uncertain, he finds the resolve to maintain his integrity by carrying through his gesture of defiance. He knows that he will have to accept the consequences of his actions, but this is the true source of his real strength. Acknowledging that now "he felt how hard the world was going to be to me hereafter," his acceptance of the struggle is at the root of his ability to face challenges in the future. As if to ratify his decision, Lengel is described in the last paragraph reduced to Sammy's slot, "checking the sheep through," his visage "dark gray and his back stiff." If the reward for selling out is a life like Lengel's, then even an act that no one but its agent appreciates (the girls never notice their champion) is better than the defeat of submerging the self in the despair of denial.

"WIFE-WOOING"

"Wife-Wooing" is the real reward for acting according to principle. If the A & P is the symbol of enclosure and the girl a figure for the wonder of the cosmos beyond, then marriage to a woman who incarnates the spirit of wonder contains the possibilities for paradise. The mood of ecstasy is established immediately by the narrator's declaration of devotion, "OH MY LOVE. Yes. Here we sit, on warm broad floor-boards, before a fire. . . ." He is a man whose marriage, in its initial stages, is informed by what seems like an exponential progression of promise. Thus, although he has "won" his mate, he is impelled to continue to woo her as a testament to his continuing condition of bliss, of his exultation in the sensuality of the body's familiar but still mysterious terrain—its "absolute geography." The evocative description of the couple together—framed in images of light and warmth—is sufficient to convey the delight they share, but what makes the story noteworthy is Updike's employment and investigation of the erotics of language as a register of feeling. The mood of arousal becomes a kind of celebration of the words that describe it, so that it is the "irrefutably magical life language leads with itself" that becomes the substance of erotic interest.

Updike, typically, recalls James Joyce, using Blazes Boylan's word "smackwarm" from "the legendary, imperfectly explored grottoes of *Ulysses*" to let loose a chain of linguistic associations beginning with a consideration of the root etymology of "woman"—the "wide w, the receptive o. Womb." Located in a characteristically masculine perspective (inevitable considering Updike's background and the historical context), the narrator envisions himself as a warrior/hunter in prehistoric times, and in a brilliantly imaginative, affectionate parody of Anglo-Saxon alliterative verse, Updike continues to express the husband's exultation through the kind of linguistic overdrive that makes his mastery of styles the focus of admiration (and envy) of many of his peers. Beneath the wordplay and the almost self-congratulatory cleverness, however, there is still another level of intent. Once the element of erotic power in language itself has been introduced, Updike is free to employ that language in an investigation of sensuality that strains at the bounds of what was acceptable in 1960. His purpose is to examine a marriage at the potentially dangerous seven-year point, to recall the sexual history of the couple, and to show how the lessons of mutual experience have enabled them to deepen their erotic understanding as the marriage progressed. Continuing to use language to chart the erogenous regions of the mind and body, Updike arranges a series of puns ("Oh cunning trick") so that the dual fascination of love—for wife, words—is expressed in intertwined images of passion. The story concludes with the husband leaving for work in the cold stone of a city of "heartless things," then returning to the eternal mystery of woman/wooing, where, as Robert Creeley's poem "The Wife" expresses it, he knows "two women/ and the one/ is tangible substance,/ flesh and bone," while "the other in my mind/ occurs."

THE HENRY BECH STORIES

Updike's energetic involvement with the dimensions of life—the domestic and the artistic—crested on a curve of satisfaction for him as the 1950's drew to a close. The chaotic explosion of countercultural diversity that took place in the 1960's fractured the comforting coordinates of a world with which Updike had grown very familiar, and he began to find himself in an adversary position both toward the confines of bourgeois social values and toward the sprawling uncertainty of a country in entropic transition. As a means of confronting this situation at a remove that would permit some aesthetic distance from his displeasure, Updike created Henry Bech, an urban, blocked Jewish writer seemingly the polar opposite of the now urbane Updike but actually only a slight transmutation of his own sensibility. Bech is much more successful in managing the perils of the age than Harry Angstrom, who represents Updike's peevish squareness in *Rabbit Redux*, and the "interview" "Bech Meets Me" (November, 1971) is a jovial display of Updike's witty assessment of his problems and goals.

The individual Bech stories, beginning with "The Bulgarian Poetess" (from *The Music School*), which covers Updike's experiences on a trip to Eastern Eu-

rope sponsored by the State Department, generally work as separate entities, but they are linked sufficiently that there is a clear progression in *Bech: A Book*, while *Bech Is Back* is closer to a novel than a collection of short fiction and *Bech at Bay* is classified as long fiction. Through the personae of Henry Bech and Rabbit Angstrom, among others, Updike maintained a distinct distance from the political and incipient personal turmoil that he was experiencing.

THE MUSIC SCHOOL

In *The Music School*, the stories include fond recollections of a positive, recent past, as in "The Christian Roommates" (which "preserved" aspects of his Harvard experience), or tentative excursions into the malaise of the times, as in the fascinating dissection of psychoanalytic methods offered by "My Lover Has Dirty Fingernails" and in the unusual venture into the possibilities of renewal in a natural setting of "The Hermit." In this story, the prickly, idiosyncratic spirit of the New England individualist and environmentalist Henry David Thoreau is expressed as an urge to escape from the social realities of *success*—an essentially forlorn quest for a larger sense of life than "they" will permit and an attempt to explore the possibility of a mystical essence beyond the attainment of intellectual power.

MUSEUMS AND WOMEN AND OTHER STORIES

While Updike spoke admiringly of the "splendid leafiness" of Pennsylvania and could evoke the mood of Scotland's highland moors (as in "Macbech") with typical facility, his central subject has always been the nature of relationships. In *Museums and Women and Other Stories*, he returned to the consequences of marked changes in the social climate and his personal life that could not be avoided by fictional explorations of subsidiary concerns. The story "When Everyone Was Pregnant" is a paean to an old order passing into history, a celebration of years of relative pleasure and satisfaction that he calls "the Fifties" but which actually encompass the first half of the century. "*My* Fifties," he labels them, positioning himself at the center of a benign cosmos, where tests were passed ("Entered them poor and left them comfortable. Entered them chaste and left them a father") and life was relatively uncomplicated. The paragraphs of the story are like a shorthand list of bounty ("Jobs, houses, spouses of our own"), and the entire era is cast in an aura of innocence, a prelude to a sudden shock of consciousness that utterly changed everything. The factors that caused the shift are never identified, leaving the narrator bewildered ("Now: our babies drive cars, push pot, shave, menstruate, riot for peace, eat macrobiotic"), but the alteration in perception is palpable and its ramifications ("Sarah looks away" after fifteen shared years) unavoidable.

The last section of *Museums and Women and Other Stories* contains five stories under the subhead "The Maples." Updike eventually published seventeen stories about Richard and Joan Maple, a family with four children that might be said to approximate Updike's first marriage, in *Too Far to Go*, and the narrative thread that becomes apparent in the full collection is the transition from optimism and contentment to uncertainty and fracture. A story that registers the process of psychological displacement particularly well is the last one in *Museums and Women and Other Stories*, "Sublimating," in which the Maples have decided to give up sex, which they have mistakenly identified as the "only sore point" in their marriage. Since nearly all that Updike has written on the subject indicates that sex is at the heart of everything that matters in a relationship, the decision—as Updike assumed would be obvious to everyone but the parties involved—was a false solution that could only aggravate the problem. What becomes apparent as the story progresses is that everything in the relationship has become a pretext for disguising true feeling, but the desperation of the participants makes their methods of camouflage sympathetic and understandable.

Unable to accept that change in both parties has permanently altered their position, Richard and Joan repeat strategies that have previously revitalized their marriage, but nothing can be successful, since the actors no longer fit their roles. The procedures of the past cannot be recapitulated, and their efforts produce a series of empty rituals that leave the Maples exhausted and angry. Using external remedies for internal maladies (the purchase of an old farmhouse, impulsive acquisition of trivia), bantering about each

other's lovers to reignite passion, turning their children into would-be allies, exchanging barbed, bitchy, and self-regarding comments, the Maples are more baffled than destructive, but both of them are aware that they will eventually have to confront the fact that they have no solution. Sublimation is ultimately suppression of truth, and Richard Maple's description of the people in a pornographic film house on Forty-second Street in Manhattan as perpetual spectators, who watch unseeing while meaningless acts of obscenity occur in the distance, stands as an emblem of stasis and nullity, a corollary to the paralysis that engulfs the couple. Joan Maple's final comment on their current state, a pathetic observation about the "cleansing" aspects of their nonsensual behavior, brings the story to a conclusion that is warped with tension, a situation that Richard Maple's comment, "we may be on to something," does nothing to relieve.

PROBLEMS AND OTHER STORIES

Updike's next collection, *Problems and Other Stories*, contains a prefatory note that begins, "Seven years since my last short story collection? There must have been problems." The central problem has been the end of Updike's first marriage and the removal of the core of certainty that the domestic structure of his family provided. The unraveling of the threads that were woven through a lifetime of intelligent analysis and instinctual response called everything into question and opened a void that had been lurking near the surface of Updike's work. Updike was far too perceptive ever to assume that a stable family was possible for everyone or that it would provide answers for everything. From the start of the Rabbit tetralogy, the strains inherent in an ongoing marital arrangement were examined closely, but the dissolution of his own primary household drew several specific responses that expanded the range and depth of his short fiction. First, the sad facts of the separation and divorce were handled in the last Maple stories.

"Separating" recounts the parents' attempts to explain the situation to their children. It is written in bursts of lacerating dialogue, a conversation wrought in pain and doubt that concludes with a child posing the tormenting, unanswerable query "*Why?*" to Richard Maple. "Here Come the Maples" presents the ceremony of the divorce as a reverse marriage, complete with programmed statements forcing the couple to agree by saying "I do." The jaunty tone of the proceedings does not totally mask the looming cloud of uncertainty that covers the future. Then, the artist turned toward his work for sustenance. In "From the Journal of a Leper," Updike projects his psychic condition into the life of a potter who is afflicted with a serious skin disease akin to his own. The fear of leprosy stands for all of his doubts before an unknown universe no longer relatively benign; his work provides some compensation but is intricately connected to his psychological stability; a woman with whom he is developing a relationship improves and complicates the situation. The story is open-ended, but in a forecast of the direction Updike has begun to chart for his protagonists, the artist recognizes the necessity of standing alone, dependent ultimately on his own strength. The final words may be more of a self-directed exhortation than a summary of actuality, but they represent a discernible goal: "I am free, as other men. I am whole."

"TRANSACTION"

The difficulties of freedom and the elusiveness of wholeness are explored in "Transaction," one of Updike's most powerful stories. In *The Paris Review* interview with Charles Thomas Samuels, Updike said:

> About sex in general, by all means let's have it in fiction, as detailed as needs be, but real, real in its social and psychological connections. Let's take coitus out of the closet and off the altar and put it on the continuum of human behavior.

The transaction of the title involves a man in his middle years, married but alone in a city labeled "N—," in December at a conference, who somewhat impulsively picks up a prostitute and takes her to his hotel room. What exactly he is seeking is not entirely clear, because the cold, mechanical city and the "raffish army of females" occupying the streets are as much threat as promise and his temporary liberty to act as he chooses is undercut by his feelings of isolation and loneliness. Regarding his actions as a version of an exploratory adventure in which he is curi-

ous about how he will react and tempted not only by lust but also by the desire to test his virility and validity in establishing a human connection with the girl, he is moving into unknown country, where his usual persuasive strategies have no relevance. The "odorless metal" of the room mocks his efforts to re-create the warmth of a home in an anonymous city, and the false bravado of other men around him reminds him of the insecurity that lies beneath the bluster. Even what he calls the "paid moral agent" of his imagination—that is, his mostly vestigial conscience—is summoned briefly only as a source of comforting certainty in the uncharted, shifting landscape he has entered.

His initial investment in the room and in purchasing some aspect of the girl's time does not permit him to exercise any influence on their transaction, a reminder that his generally successful life (marriage, money, status) counts for less than he had thought. The language of commerce that he has mastered does not contain a vocabulary for expressing his current feelings. Ruled by old habits, the preliminary stages of the transaction are a capsule courtship, but he finds that his solicitations are subject to scorn or rebuke. The girl wavers in his imagination between alluring innocence and forbidding authority, an amalgam of a dream lover who accepts him and an indifferent critic who reinforces the mechanical motif by calling his genitals "them" and prepares for their assignation "with the deliberateness of an insult or the routine of marriage." Although Updike uses his extensive abilities of description to render the physical attributes of the girl in vivid detail, she does not seem sexually attractive—an implicit comment on the failure of erotic potential when it is restricted to the external surface, as well as a subtle dig at the magazine *Oui* (a *Playboy* clone), where the story originally appeared. Without the spontaneity of mutual discovery, the transaction becomes clinical and antierotic, an unnatural or perverse use of human capability.

The man is aware of the inadequacy of his supplications. He has been using the strategies of commerce—a mix of supposedly ingratiating self-pity and cold calculation—and when these fail he tries false compliance, then bogus amiability. In desperation, because of a severe reduction in sexual potence, he begins to "make love" to her, and in a shift in tone that Updike handles with characteristic smoothness, the writing becomes lyrical as the man becomes fully involved, and the woman finally responds freely and openly. Old habits intrude, however, and the man's heightened virility causes a reversion to his familiar self. He stops producing pleasure and seeks it again as his due. His excitement has been transformed from authentic passion to calculation, the transaction back on its original terms. Both parties to the agreement have reached a level of satisfaction (he is a successful sexual athlete, and she has met the terms of the contract), and, when she offers to alter the original bargain in a mixture of self-interest and genuine generosity, he is unable to make a further break away from a lifetime of monetary measure. He contents himself with small gestures of quasi gallantry that carry things back toward the original situation of customer and salesperson. Thus, the true cost of real freedom is gradually becoming apparent. He feels an urge to go beyond the transactional to the honestly emotional, but he is hindered by fear, and his instincts are frozen. The residue of the encounter is a dreadful shrinking of his sense of the universe. "She had made sex finite," he thinks, but in actuality, it is only his cramped view of his own possibilities that he sees.

"Trust Me"

"Transaction" marks the beginning of a phase of maturity in Updike's work in which recollection of an earlier time of certitude, confidence, and optimism is still possible, but in which a search for new modes of meaning is gradually taking precedence. "Deaths of Distant Friends," from *Trust Me*, which appeared in an anthology of *Best American Short Stories*, is a finely wrought philosophical meditation—exactly the sort of story cautious anthologists often include, a minor-key minirequiem for a grand past with only a twist of rue at the conclusion to relieve the sentimental mood. "The Egg Race," from *Problems and Other Stories*, is somewhat more severe in its recollection of the past. Here, the origins of the problems of the present are traced with some tolerance of human need back to the narrator's father. The title story, "Trust Me," is closer to the mood of middle-life angst that

informs many of the stories. Again, the narrator reconsiders the past in an effort to determine the cause of the emptiness of the present, but in his attempts to explain the failure of faith in his life, he reveals (to himself) that his parents did not trust each other, that his first wife did not trust the modern world, that his child did not trust him, that with his girlfriend he does not trust himself, and that with a psychotropic agent, he does not (or cannot) trust his senses so he ultimately cannot trust his perceptions. Logically, then, he cannot know, with surety, anything at all. His predicament is a part of a larger vision of loss that directs many stories in the volume, as Updike's characters attempt to cope with a deterioration of faith that revives some of the earlier questions of a religious nature that formed an important dimension of Updike's writing in books such as *The Poorhouse Fair* or *A Month of Sundays* (1975). The situation has changed somewhat, though, since the more traditional religious foundations that Updike seemed to trust earlier have become less specifically viable, even if the theological questions they posed still are important. The newfound or sensed freedom that is glimpsed carries a terrifying burden of singularity.

"Slippage"

"Slippage" conveys this feeling through its metaphors of structural fragility. A "not quite slight earthquake" awakens a man who is "nauseated without knowing why." His wife, a much younger woman, is hidden under the covers, "like something dead on the road," an image of nullity. Blessed or cursed with a memory that "extended so much further back in time than hers," he feels she is preparing them prematurely for senility. At sixty, he sees his life as a series of not-quite-achieved plateaus. His work as a scholar was adequate but not all that it might have been, and his "late-capitalist liberal humanism" now seems passé. Even his delight in the sensual has been shaken, "though only thrice wed." Updike depicts him in his confusion as "a flake of consciousness lost within time's black shale" and extends the metaphor of infirmity to a loose molar and a feeling that his children are "a tiny, hard, slightly shrivelled core of disappointment." In the story's denouement, the man meets a woman at a party; she excites him, but it turns out that she is "quite mad," an ultimate betrayal of his instincts. At the close, he lies in bed again, anticipating another earth tremor and feeling its unsettling touch in his imagination.

"THE CITY"

The aura of discouragement that "Slippage" projects is balanced by another of Updike's most forceful stories, "The City" (also from *Trust Me*). Recalling both "Transaction" with its portrayal of a business traveler alone in an urban wasteland and several later stories in which illness or disease disarms a man, "The City" places Carson—a "victim of middle-aged restlessness—the children grown, the long descent begun"—in a hospital, where he must face a battery of tests to determine the cause of a vague stomach pain. Confronted by doctors, nurses, orderlies, other patients, and fellow sufferers, none of whom he knows, Carson is alone and helpless in an alien environment. The hospital works as a fitting figure for the absurdity and complexity of the postmodern world. The health professionals seem like another species, and Carson's physical pain is a symbol of his spiritual discomfort as he proceeds with the useless repetition of his life's requirements. From the nadir of a debilitating operation, Carson begins to overcome the indignity and unreality of his plight. He becomes fascinated with people who are unknown to him, like a beautiful black nurse whose unfathomable beauty expands the boundaries of his realm. He calls upon his lifelong training as a stoic WASP and determines not to make a fuss about his difficulties. He finds his "curiosity about the city revived" and develops a camaraderie with other patients, a community of the wounded. His removal from the flow of business life—he is a computer parts salesman fluent in techno-babble—helps him regain an ironic perspective that enables him to regard his estranged daughter's ignorance of his crisis as "considerate and loving" because it contributes to the "essential solitude" he now enjoys. In a poetic excursion into Carson's mind, Updike illustrates the tremendous satisfaction available to a person with an artistic imagination capable of finding meaning in any pattern of life's variety. Carson makes the necessary leap of faith required to "take again into himself the miracle of the world"

and seizes his destiny from a mechanized, indifferent cosmos. In a reversal of the curve of decline that was the trajectory of Updike's thought from the problems of the early 1970's through the 1980's, Carson is depicted at the end of "The City" as a version of existential man who can, even amid doubt and uncertainty, find a way to be "free" and "whole"—at least as much as the postmodern world permits.

THE AFTERLIFE AND OTHER STORIES

The central character in many of the stories collected in *The Afterlife and Other Stories* has a superficial autobiographical relationship to Updike, including having moved from the city to the country as a child and having desired to return to the city. In the award-winning "A Sandstone Farmhouse," Joey Robinson visits his mother's farmhouse and watches her die as the farmhouse deteriorates. After she dies, he discovers that the farmhouse was his true home: "He had always wanted to be where the action was, and what action there was, it turned out, had been back there." "The Other Side of the Street" involves a protagonist, Rentschler, returning to his childhood home and seeing it from a house across the street, where he goes to have some papers notarized. He discovers that one of his childhood friends still lives next door to the notary's house. As he leaves, he sees what used to be his house "lit up as if to welcome a visitor, a visitor, it seemed clear to him, long expected and much beloved." He thus experiences a kind of homecoming. The final story in the collection, "Grandparenting," is another tale in the Maple saga. Divorced and married to others, both Richard and Joan (now Vanderhaven) Maple are present when their daughter Judith has her first baby. In spite of the divorce, the Maples still continue as a family.

Central to *The Afterlife and Other Stories* is the family as seen from the perspective of an aging male. Story after story deals with people aging and dying. One, "The Man Who Became a Soprano," treats a group who get together to play recorders. As members of the group begin to form liaisons that end in divorce, and some move away, the group itself agrees to play a concert for an elderly audience at the Congregational church. The concert is a success, but it signals the end of the recorder group.

"The Afterlife," the first story in the collection, focuses on Carter Billings. His and his wife Joan's best friends, the Egglestons, move to England. During the first night of a visit there, Carter awakens and, wandering through the hall, tumbles down the stairs. "Then something—some*one*, he felt—hit him a solid blow in the exact center of his chest," and he finds himself standing on a landing on the stairway. The next morning he decides that he actually bumped into the knob of a newel post. Nonetheless, after the experience his life seems charged with new feeling. It is as though he has had some kind of taste of the afterlife so that he is now "beyond" all earthly matters.

OTHER MAJOR WORKS

LONG FICTION: *The Poorhouse Fair*, 1959; *Rabbit, Run*, 1960; *The Centaur*, 1963; *Of the Farm*, 1965; *Couples*, 1968; *Rabbit Redux*, 1971; *A Month of Sundays*, 1975; *Marry Me: A Romance*, 1976; *The Coup*, 1978; *Rabbit Is Rich*, 1981; *The Witches of Eastwick*, 1984; *Roger's Version*, 1986; *S*, 1988; *Rabbit at Rest*, 1990; *Memories of the Ford Administration*, 1992; *Brazil*, 1994; *In the Beauty of the Lilies*, 1996; *Toward the End of Time*, 1997; *Bech at Bay: A Quasi-Novel*, 1998; *Gertrude and Claudius*, 2000.

PLAYS: *Three Texts from Early Ipswich: A Pageant*, pb. 1968; *Buchanan Dying*, pb. 1974.

POETRY: *The Carpentered Hen, and Other Tame Creatures*, 1958; *Telephone Poles and Other Poems*, 1963; *Verse*, 1965; *Midpoint and Other Poems*, 1969; *Tossing and Turning*, 1977; *Facing Nature*, 1985; *Mites and Other Poems in Miniature*, 1990; *A Helpful Alphabet of Friendly Objects*, 1995.

NONFICTION: *Assorted Prose*, 1965; *Picked-Up Pieces*, 1975; *Hugging the Shore: Essays and Criticism*, 1983; *Self-Consciousness*, 1989; *Just Looking: Essays on Art*, 1989; *Odd Jobs: Essays and Criticism*, 1991; *Golf Dreams: Writings on Golf*, 1996; *More Matter: Essays and Criticism*, 1999.

BIBLIOGRAPHY

Detweiler, Robert. *John Updike*. Boston: Twayne, 1984. Within the confines of the Twayne series format, Detweiler supplies sound, thorough analysis of all Updike's work through the mid-1980's and provides a brief biography and a useful, annotated bibliography.

Donahue, Peter. "Pouring Drinks and Getting Drunk: The Social and Personal Implications of Drinking in John Updike's 'Too Far to Go.'" *Studies in Short Fiction* 33 (Summer, 1996): 361-367. Argues that drinking in the stories moves from a conventional social pastime to an extension of the couple's private discord, significantly changing how they view and interact with each other; their drinking habits expose the degree to which alcohol use is connected to the specific gender roles and family dynamics of the middle-class suburban world the Maples occupy.

Greiner, Donald J. *The Other John Updike: Poems, Short Stories, Prose, Play*. Athens: Ohio University Press, 1981. While devoting a considerable amount of space to other critics, Greiner, who has written three books about Updike, here traces Updike's artistic development in his writing that both parallels and extends the themes of the novels.

Hunt, George W. *John Updike and the Three Secret Things: Sex, Religion, and Art*. Grand Rapids, Mich.: Wm. B. Eerdmans, 1980. An accurate and perceptive (if a bit scholarly in style) examination of the evolution of Updike's thematic focus. Hunt combines psychoanalytical (Jungian), New Critical, and theological approaches in his thesis that Updike's primary concern changed in emphasis during his career.

Luscher, Robert M. *John Updike: A Study of the Short Fiction*. New York: Twayne, 1993. An introduction to Updike's short fiction, dealing with his lyrical technique, his experimentation with narrative structure, his use of the short-story cycle convention, and the relationship between his short fiction and his novels. Includes Updike's comments on his short fiction and previously published critical essays representing a variety of critical approaches.

Macnaughton, William R., ed. *Critical Essays on John Updike*. Boston: G. K. Hall, 1982. A comprehensive, eclectic collection, including essays by writers such as Alfred Kazin, Anthony Burgess, and Joyce Carol Oates, who provide reviews, and various Updike experts who have written original essays. Contains a survey of bibliographies and an assessment of criticism and scholarship.

Newman, Judie. *John Updike*. New York: St. Martin's Press, 1988. A part of the Modern Novelists series, Newman covers the long fiction with facility and insight and offers a solid foundation for understanding Updike's primary concerns throughout his writing. Contains a good, comprehensive introduction and a judicious bibliography.

Pinsker, Sanford. "The Art of Fiction: A Conversation with John Updike." *The Sewanee Review* 104 (Summer, 1996): 423-433. Updike discusses the visual artists who have inspired him, how his academic experiences helped to shape his writing, and how he regards criticism of his work.

Schiff, James A. *John Updike Revisited*. New York: Twayne, 1998. A general introduction surveying all of Updike's work but focusing on his fiction in the late 1990's. The chapter on the short story is relatively brief, with short analyses of such stories as "A & P" and "Separating."

Tallent, Elizabeth. *Married Men and Magic Tricks: John Updike's Erotic Heroes*. Berkeley, Calif.: Creative Arts, 1982. Offers, in Judie Newman's words, "a ground-breaking exploration of the erotic dimensions of selected works." A long-needed analysis that includes a feminist perspective missing from much previous Updike criticism.

Leon Lewis, updated by
Richard Tuerk

V

LUISA VALENZUELA

Born: Buenos Aires, Argentina; November 26, 1938

OTHER LITERARY FORMS

In addition to her novellas, which have been included in collections of her short stories, Luisa Valenzuela is the author of several novels: *Como en la guerra* (1977; *He Who Searches*, 1979), *Cola de lagartija* (1983; *The Lizard's Tail*, 1983), and *Novela Negra con argentinos* (1990; *Black Novel with Argentines*, 1992). She is also the author of the novel *Realidad nacional desde la cama*, 1990.

ACHIEVEMENTS

Luisa Valenzuela won a Fulbright Fellowship in 1969 to attend the University of Iowa Writers' Workshop. She won the Instituto Nacional de Cinematografía Award in 1973 for her first novel *Hay que sonreír* (1966; *Clara*, 1976).

BIOGRAPHY

Born in Buenos Aires in 1938 to a physician father and a prominent writer mother, Luisa Valenzuela grew up in Belgrano, where she had an English tutor and later attended Belgrano Girls School and then an English high school. She received her B.A. degree from the University of Buenos Aires and then wrote for a prominent Argentine magazine. She also worked with Jorge Luis Borges at the National Library of Argentina.

In 1958, Valenzuela went to Paris to become a correspondent for the Argentine newspaper *El Mundo*. While in France she became involved with the structuralist literary theory group known as *Tel Quel*, returning to Buenos Aires with her husband and her daughter in 1961. After her divorce, she attended the University of Iowa Writers' Workshop on a Fulbright grant in 1969. In 1975, she returned to Buenos Aires and joined the staff of the journal *Crisis*. She has conducted writing workshops and taught Latin American literature at universities in the United States.

ANALYSIS

Luisa Valenzuela has become the darling of feminist critics, making a place for herself as a female writer who has exposed and challenged the Hispanic sexist world, which has historically discriminated against women; typically she relates domestic sexual domination and abuse alongside political repression and torture. The fact that Valenzuela was highly influenced by the psychoanalyst Jacques Lacan during her period of schooling in France has also provided critics with a ready-made set of critical terms with which to approach her fiction.

In many ways Valenzuela's work is a conventional extension of the Magical Realism that characterized writers of the so-called Latin American boom, such as Jorge Luis Borges, Julio Cortázar, and Gabriel García Márquez. Making using of folklore from South America, as well as modern anthropology and psychoanalysis, Valenzuela creates hallucinatory worlds of sadistic men and repressed and autistic

Luisa Valenzuela (©Miriam Berkley)

women. However, Valenzuela is more a stylist than a political philosopher, focusing on how the story is told rather than what it says. It is in "the articulation between the narrated anecdote and the style of narration" that the secret of the text resides, says Valenzuela.

"I'M YOUR HORSE IN THE NIGHT"

"De noche soy tu caballo" ("I'm Your Horse in the Night") opens mysteriously with the young female protagonist being awakened by her doorbell, concerned it might be some threatening "them." However, it is an equally mysterious and unidentified "him" that she meets "face to face, at last." He embraces her and pulls out "potential clues" that elude her, such as a bottle of liquor and a record. The song they listen to is "I'm Your Horse in the Night," which she translates slowly to bind him into a spell, telling him he is the horse of the spirit who is riding her. He tells her, however, that she is always getting carried away with esoteric meanings, that she is his horse as a sexual creature only.

The phone wakes her up and a voice says that the man, Beto, has been found dead in the river, his body decomposed after six days in the water. When the police arrive, she says they will not find anything, for her only real possession was a dream and "they can't deprive me of my dreams just like that." The police want to know where the mysterious man is, but she will say only that he abandoned her. Insisting that, even if they torture her she will not tell them her dreams, she says, "The man simply vanished. I only run into him in my dreams, and they're bad dreams that often become nightmares."

The story is about the interrelationship between dream and reality in which the sexual encounter is oneiric while its aftermath is frightening real. "I'm Your Horse in the Night" sets up several typical Valenzuela dichotomies. Even as the horse is the nightmare horse of myth, it is a cultural sign of female submission. While the sexual union is romantic/erotic, it is also a primal animal encounter. Basically, this is a story about the objectification of woman's desire for transcendence above the ordinary world of "mere facts."

"UP AMONG THE EAGLES"

"Donde viven las águilas" ("Up Among the Eagles") is one of Valenzuela's most straightforward philosophical fantasies, presenting her treatment of the split between the sacred and the profane in a relatively uncluttered way. The basic situation of the story is that of a young woman who has gone into the country, "up among the eagles," where the people speak a strange language whose meaning they themselves have forgotten. They speak her language only when dealing with trivial matters of everyday reality; otherwise, their world focuses on the sacred, for which they use a language of silence.

The people have no concept of time as a linear progression, living instead in the realm of mythic time of eternal recurrence. The woman secretly takes Polaroid photos of herself, a sequence that reflects her existence in the realm of linear time. She fears that if the people find the photos they will either abominate her for being susceptible to age or adore her as if she were like a statue, forever captive and contained.

The story ends with her taking the last photo on her roll of film, hoping to recover her being. However, the picture "gradually reveals the blurred image of a stone wall." She climbs a mountain to reach the city of the dead where she will put the successive faces of her photos on the mummies there so she will be free to go down, taking with her her last photo, in which she is herself and she is stone. The basic dichotomy is between mutable flesh and the transcendence of ultimate desire.

"OTHER WEAPONS"

Called by feminist critics a landmark in Latin American feminine literature for its critique of Western patriarchal practices, "Cambio de armas" ("Other Weapons") is a depiction of woman as wife-whore-slave in the extreme, for the female in the story is reduced to total passivity by torture at the hands of her male master. In an almost autistic state of isolation, her consciousness effaced, the woman feels completely isolated in time and space, cut off from the past, with no hope for a future.

The story falls within a tradition of sadistic Blue-beard stories, stories in which a powerful male figure uses the woman as a sex object, keeps her shut off from the world and imprisoned within herself. The story is told in a fragmentary fashion, in third person but from the woman's perspective, as she haltingly tries to "find herself out." Complete with whips and voyeuristic peep holes where the man's colleagues can watch the man sexually dominate the woman, "Other Weapons" is a paradigm of the sadistic male who uses the phallus as a weapon to subdue the woman.

The final revelation of the story comes when he tells her that she was a revolutionary who had been ordered to kill him but was caught just when she was aiming at him. He says everything he did was to save her, for he forced her to love him, to depend on him like a newborn baby. "I've got my weapons, too," he repeats over and over. However, when he starts to leave, she remembers what the gun is for, lifts it and aims. Called by feminist critics a horrible symbolic embodiment of the "happy" housewife, the woman in the story reflects the common Valenzuela theme of equating marriage law with political imprisonment.

"SYMMETRIES"

Valenzuela has said that "Simetrías" ("Symmetries"), the title story of her 1993 collection, is like a symmetrical counterpart to the earlier story "Other Weapons." Both stories reflect Valenzuela's insistence that political aggression mirrors sexual aggression. The story is told as a series of monologues which alternate back and forth between the torturer and the tortured. The other significant symmetry in the story, however, takes place in time, alternating between a story that takes place in 1947, which involves a woman becoming obsessively fascinated with an orangutan in a zoo, and one in 1977, which recounts the parallel obsession that a man has with his tortured female victim.

In the first story, the woman's husband, a colonel in the army, becomes so jealously infuriated because of her infatuation with the animal that he kills it. In the second story, the colonel is sent away on a mission by his superiors so that the woman with whom he has become so involved can be destroyed. At the end of "Symmetries," the two stories and the two time periods become one; the bullet that kills the orangutan and the one that kills the torturer's beloved victim seems to be the same. When the woman returns to the zoo and the man returns to the prison and they find the objects of their obsessive desires dead, "they both find a thread of terror creeping up their spine and they find a hatred that will grow with the days."

OTHER MAJOR WORKS

LONG FICTION: *Hay que sonreír*, 1966 (*Clara*, 1976); *El gato eficaz*, 1972; *Como en la guerra*, 1977 (*He Who Searches*, 1979); *Cola de lagartija*, 1983 (*The Lizard's Tail*, 1983); *Novela Negra con argentinos*, 1990 (*Black Novel with Argentines*, 1992); *Realidad nacional desde la cama*, 1990 (*Bedside Manners*, 1995).

BIBLIOGRAPHY

Bach, Caleb. "Metaphors and Magic Unmask the Soul." *Americas* 47 (January/February, 1995): 22-28. Notes that Valenzuela is distressed by the cultural banality common the world over. Says that her prose involves the reader by posing questions rather than suggesting simplistic solutions; claims her books are not for the lazy reader.

Logan, Joy. "Southern Discomfort in Argentina: Postmodernism, Feminism, and Luisa Valenzuela's *Simetrías*." *Latin American Literary Review* 24 (July-December, 1996): 5-17. Argues that in the fairy-tale section of *Symmetries*, Valenzuela's critique of Western patriarchal practices is most clear. Claims that the collection is a textual performance of the interplay between postmodernism and feminism.

Magnarelli, Sharon. "Simetrías: 'Mirror, Mirror, on the Wall. . . .'" *World Literature Today* 69 (Autumn, 1995): 717-726. Argues that the collection *Symmetries* is organized around motifs of language and power. Analyzes "Tango," "Transfigurations," and the title story "Symmetries" in terms of the motif of parallel situations and responses.

Marting, Diane. "Female Sexuality in Selected Short Stories by Luisa Valenzuela: Toward an Ontology of Her Work." *Review of Contemporary Fiction* 6 (Fall, 1986): 48-54. Discusses how three stories from *Strange Things Happen Here* treat female sexuality in terms of figurative and mimetic modes of narration.

_____. "Gender and Metaphoricity in Luisa Valenzuela's 'I'm Your Horse in the Night.'" *World Literature Today* 69 (Fall, 1995): 702-708. A survey and critique of previous interpretations of the story, accompanied by a close reading in which Marting argues that the story criticizes the man for his retrograde treatment of the woman who loves him.

Morello-Frosch, Maria. "'Other Weapons': When Metaphors Become Real." *Review of Contemporary Fiction* 6 (Fall, 1986): 82-87. Discusses the story "Other Weapons" as one in which the protagonist creates her own vision of the world in opposition to the political establishment. Says the story presents sexual and political repression in terms of communication with one's past.

Rubio, Patricia. "Fragmentation in Luisa Valenzuela's Narrative." *Salmagundi*, nos. 82/83 (Spring/Summer, 1989): 287-296. Argues that the objective of Valenzuela's writing is not the mimetic representation of reality, but the creation of a fictive world that witnesses its own mutation. Discusses Valenzuela's use of the fragment and the various acts of fragmentation in her fiction.

Valenzuela, Luisa. Interview by Marie-Lise Gazarian Gautier. In *Interviews with Latin American Writers*. Elmwood Park, Ill.: Dalkey Archive Press, 1989. In this composite interview, Valenzuela discusses rebellion and freedom in her work, the effect of censorship, writers who have influenced her, the relationship between fantasy and reality in her fiction, and her interest in magic. Valenzuela says she prefers the short story over the novel.

Charles E. May

GUY VANDERHAEGHE

Born: Esterhazy, Saskatchewan, Canada; April 5, 1951

PRINCIPAL SHORT FICTION

Man Descending, 1982
The Trouble with Heroes, and Other Stories, 1983
Things as They Are?, 1992

OTHER LITERARY FORMS

Guy Vanderhaeghe's first novel, *My Present Age* (1984), was a finalist for the Booker McConnell Prize and has been translated into several languages. *Homesick* (1989) won the City of Toronto Book Award. Despite these honors, Vanderhaeghe's short stories were generally more critically esteemed than his novels. This changed when, in 1996, Vanderhaeghe's novel *The Englishman's Boy*, set in Saskatchewan in the 1870's and Hollywood in the 1920's, won the coveted Governor-General's Award for Fiction. In the late 1990's, international publishers became more interested in Canadian novels, especially in the wake of the success of the film version of Michael Ondaatje's novel *The English Patient* (1992). It was hoped that *The Englishman's Boy*, with its similar title, would become both a popular and critical success. This did not happen, though the novel sold moderately well. The short-story form, more immune to marketing, may still be the leading forum for Vanderhaeghe's distinct and incisive talent. Vanderhaeghe has also written two plays, *I Had a Job I Liked Once* (1992) and *Dancock's Dance* (1996).

ACHIEVEMENTS

Man Descending, Guy Vanderhaeghe's first collection of short stories, won the Geoffrey Faber Memorial Prize in 1982. His longer fiction also won the Governor-General's Award and the City of Toronto Book Award, as well as being nominated for the Booker McConnell Prize. He has been awarded an honorary Litt. D. by the University of Saskatchewan.

BIOGRAPHY

Guy Vanderhaeghe was born in Esterhazy, Saskatchewan, about 150 kilometers from the city of Regina. He received his B.A. (1971) and M.A. (1975), both in history, from the University of Saskatchewan; he also received a B.Ed. from the University of Regina in 1978. He worked in various academic jobs as well as doing occasional writing, editing, and archival work until the publication of his first story collection, *Man Descending*. During the mid-1980's, he was a writer-in-residence at the Saskatchewan Public Library. Despite holding a part-time teaching job in the national capital of Ottawa, Vanderhaeghe for the most part continued to reside, teach, and write in his native Saskatchewan.

ANALYSIS

Guy Vanderhaeghe is a Canadian prairie writer, the prairie provinces being those of Alberta, Saskatchewan, and Manitoba. Prairie writing tends to be largely realistic, though not without symbolic and experimental overtones. Vanderhaeghe's social realism is given heft by both a sense of place and a sense of style. He is particularly known for his portrayal of male characters living in contemporary times.

Vanderhaeghe's stories have some similarities to those of American writers a decade or so senior to him, such as Richard Ford and Raymond Carver. Like Ford and Carver, Vanderhaeghe often focuses on alienated male protagonists who are bewildered by the contemporary universe in which the time-honored rules of masculinity seem no longer operative. He differs from them, though, in that his perspective is more comic, less gritty than theirs. Vanderhaeghe's stories are more philosophical than the norm, even if the philosophy is more practical than theoretical. For instance, in the story "Sam, Soren, and Ed," Vanderhaeghe uses the thought of the Danish philosopher Søren Kierkegaard to illuminate issues in his protagonist's development, though this reference is in the spirit of fun as much as erudition. Also, Vanderhaeghe does not affect the artlessness possessed at times by American writers; his stories are finely crafted, and, despite their often contemporary Canadian setting, are in the twentieth century tradition of the short story as art form. Vanderhaeghe's gently humorous tone and his agility at making wry comments and observing odd details assist him in putting his own stamp upon the form.

MAN DESCENDING

Man Descending concerns a married couple, Ed and Victoria. Ed is monopolizing the bathroom, smoking and drinking, and generally trying to maintain traditional male modes of excess. Victoria is distressed by this and is generally upset about the state of her marriage, especially because Ed is unemployed. Ed feels his wife's love for him has been diminished by what should be the external factor of his present joblessness, and he strongly suspects she is having an affair with Howard, a pompous professional man.

Using the example of a child prodigy, whose life ended at four and a half basically because he had no more worlds to conquer, Ed hypothesizes that everyone's life follows the same curve, after a certain point descending from its peak. Ed feels that, though only thirty, he is losing out to less manly, more negotiable men, such as Howard. Ed is not a blue-collar worker; indeed, he is intellectual enough to use words like "innuendo" and to work in an adult-education program, but he is skeptical of the bureaucratic jargon bandied about in his workplace, and this seems to represent a general dissent from the overly formalized living conditions of postmodern humanity.

Ed and Victoria go to a party, where Ed sees that Victoria and Howard are obviously flirtatious. He gets involved in a physical fight with Howard, in which Howard bests him. Howard is about to beat Ed to a pulp when Victoria suddenly intervenes on Ed's behalf. Moved by Victoria's gesture, Ed pledges to reform himself, to get a job, and to treat his wife better. Victoria, though, seems skeptical of these promises, and, it is implied, the reader should be as well.

Vanderhaeghe skillfully balances the reader's sympathies between husband and wife. Ed is shown to be self-pitying; he acts as if Howard, though 'superior' to him in being employed, is less of a 'man's man' than is Ed himself, but the fact that Howard wins the fight demonstrates that this is not so. Victoria at first seems to be callously not sticking by her husband, but her intervention in Ed's favor makes her more sympathetic. The overall impression is that the problems in this marriage have grown too large for these two flawed people to solve.

It is interesting that, even though Vanderhaeghe is often seen not only as a male writer but also as one who is sympathetic with the plight of contemporary men, he nonetheless shows neither Ed nor Howard in a positive light. Indeed, Vanderhaeghe comes across as much as a "male feminist" as a defender of archaic gender roles, although the concrete predicaments of his characters make either generalization seem fatuous.

"THE WATCHER"

"The Watcher" begins with a classic short-story premise: the young child as observer, onlooker, both failing to understand the adults around him and providing a perspective on them. Charlie is a sickly boy in the late 1950's, who often is bedridden from bronchitis, enabling him to hear a lot of gossip about his family's friends and neighbors. Charlie moves in with his grandmother, who is the only rock of stability in an otherwise dysfunctional family; Grandma Bradley is a strong, self-reliant woman. A new element is introduced by the arrival of Charlie's aunt, Evelyn, and her lover, an eccentric, disreputable intellectual named Robert Thompson. Aunt Evelyn is a cocktail waitress, who is always criticized by the overbearing Grandma Bradley. She finds self-definition in her relationship with Thompson, a graduate student from British Columbia, who admires the American Beat writers, even though Thompson beats her and exploits her sexually. Charlie, too, has a weird fascination with the raffish Thompson, who provides a model of virility lacking in his immediate family. Charlie even gratuitously strangles his grandmother's chicken in emulation of Thompson's sadistic control of Aunt Evelyn, underscoring how Thompson's masculine self-expression is characterized by violence and abuse. Grandma Bradley tries everything to keep the sponging Thompson from becoming a permanent resident of her home. After a particularly obtrusive display of lovemaking on the couple's part, Grandma decides that Thompson must go. She hires two local thugs from the auto body shop to beat up Thompson; at first, he is supposed to come to them, but when Thompson does not fall to the ruse, the attackers come to the Bradley house and assault him. Later on, Thompson is taken into custody by the police, who tell him to leave town, both because Grandma Bradley is a local and because Thompson has, after all, beaten his girlfriend. Evelyn does not come with him, not because she does not want to but because she sees that the forces of authority are on her mother's side.

More interesting to the reader is the evolving stance of Charlie. Asked by the police if he witnessed the assault, Charlie lies and says he did not because he is still too young to be deprived of his grandmother's protection. As a child, Charlie is in the category of vulnerable women like Evelyn, whose life choices are controlled by others. If maturing as a man entails becoming like Thompson, however, the transition from watching to acting, which Charlie will make as an adult male, will not necessarily be benign.

"THE EXPATRIATES' PARTY"

"The Expatriates' Party" starts with a fifty-seven-year-old Canadian man visiting his adult son in London in 1977. Joe has not seen his son Mark in two years. Upon meeting him at the airport, he is disconcerted not only by his son's changed demeanor but also by the way England itself does not conform to his stereotype of it, acquired in his years of teaching English poetry to generations of Canadian schoolchildren. (Vanderhaeghe here is commenting upon Canada's residual colonial posture toward Britain.) Joe's wife, Marie, has just died, and, traumatized by his recent loss, Joe punches one of his students, a boy named Wesjik, representative of the slack youth whom he cannot reach and who do not appreciate the sacrifices made by his generation. Joe is forced to resign from the school for this incident but is not prosecuted. After talking about current politics with his son and his London friends, most of whom are Canadian expatriates, Joe remembers his wife's final decaying years, and what he sees as his own pointless,

unrewarding career as a schoolteacher. Though Mark and his friends are expatriates in a literal sense, perhaps, Joe thinks, he is one as well, having never found a true "home" in his life even though he has lived all the time in one place. The last words of the story are Joe's as he muses, "Je me souviens." This phrase means "I remember" in French, but in a Canadian context it is the national motto of the province of Québec. Joe's personal memories cannot be separated from the condition of his country. Other allusions, to the monarchy and to the ethnic diversity of contemporary Britain and Canada contribute to Vanderhaeghe's interweaving of past and present, universal feeling and Canadian content.

OTHER MAJOR WORKS

LONG FICTION: *My Present Age*, 1984; *Homesick*, 1989; *The Englishman's Boy*, 1996.

PLAYS: *I Had a Job I Liked Once*, 1992; *Dancock's Dance*, 1996.

BIBLIOGRAPHY

Gray, Alasdair. "Varieties of Contempt." In *The New York Times Book Review* (October 13, 1985): 28. Vanderhaeghe was fortunate to have his first public exposure to American readers mediated through this distinguished Scottish novelist, who praises his Canadian counterpart for the "variety of voices" and "special sort of rage and hatred" evoked by his characters.

Hillis, Doris. "An Interview with Guy Vanderhaeghe." *Wascana Review* 19, no. 1 (1984): 11-28. This interview of Vanderhaeghe by a respected local critic is largely taken up with discussion of the stories in *Man Descending*.

Keahey, Deborah. *Making It Home: Place in Canadian Prairie Literature*. Winnipeg: University of Manitoba Press, 1998. This critical comment on Vanderhaeghe is divided into specialized articles in academic journals and brief mentions in overall surveys on Canadian literature. This is a good example of the latter category, importantly situating Vanderhaeghe in his regional milieu and considering later as well as earlier work.

Prober, Kenneth G. *Writing Saskatchewan: Twenty*

Critical Essays. Regina: University of Regina, 1989. Includes several comments on Vanderhaeghe's early stories.

Van Herk, Aritha. Review of *Man Descending*, by Guy Vanderhaeghe. *Western American Literature*

18, no. 3 (November, 1983). This early review by a major contemporary of Vanderhaeghe is a valuable consideration of his themes and techniques.

Nicholas Birns

GIOVANNI VERGA

Born: Catania, Sicily; September 2, 1840
Died: Catania, Sicily; January 27, 1922

PRINCIPAL SHORT FICTION

Primavera ed altri racconti, 1876

Vita dei campi, 1880 (*Under the Shadow of Etna*, 1896)

Novelle rusticane, 1883 (*Little Novels of Sicily*, 1925)

Per le vie, 1883

Vagabondaggio, 1887

I ricordi del capitano D'Arce, 1891

Don Candeloro e Cia., 1894

Del tuo al mio, 1905 (adaptation of his play)

Cavalleria Rusticana and Other Stories, 1926

The She-Wolf and Other Stories, 1958

OTHER LITERARY FORMS

The published works of Giovanni Verga are of only two kinds, fiction and drama. Since he considered his primary vocation to be that of novelist, all his earliest publications are novels. His first play, written when he was twenty-nine, was never produced and remained unpublished until after his death. Eventually he wrote seven plays, all of them derived from his own works of fiction. He first turned to short fiction with a relatively lengthy story called *Nedda*. It was long enough, at any rate, to be accorded separate publication in a tiny volume in 1874 but was clearly not of standard novel length. This publication is generally regarded as the start of his interest in the short story as a literary form.

Two years later he published his first collection of short stories, and that volume also included the previously published *Nedda*. Thereafter, he practiced this new literary form assiduously enough to make his short stories as important a part of his total achievement as were his novels. Verga is a rarity among writers of fiction in that he published no poetry—not even in his youth—and no literary criticism or travel books. Aside from his novels, short stories, and plays, only selections from his personal letters have ever appeared in print.

ACHIEVEMENTS

As a socially conscious writer, Giovanni Verga is considered the most determined spokesman of the conditions in which the poor of his native Sicily lived. A master writer of novels and short stories and the leader of an innovative realistic and naturalistic literary current known as *Verismo*, Verga in his works explored the struggle of humankind to survive in adverse circumstances. He emphasized the importance of family, work, and basic moral and religious values, and he focused on the fundamental role these values play in overcoming difficult times. To enrich his highly humanitarian themes, Verga developed an intense dramatic expression characterized by detailed descriptive features and original linguistic solutions. Along with being widely recognized as one of the best Italian writers, Verga was bestowed with several official honors by the Italian government, while his works continue to endure lasting success as modern classics.

Giovanni Verga (Library of Congress)

BIOGRAPHY

The city of Catania, where Giovanni Verga spent the first twenty-five years of his life, was a cultural center for Sicily and even possessed a university; but it was geographically so remote from the mainstream of Italy's cultural life and so small a place, that its atmosphere was nevertheless provincial and in some ways even primitive. Verga's family were well-to-do landowners in a society that was agricultural at its base and still feudal in its organization. Verga was fortunate in his schooling to have come under the influence of a teacher who was a writer and who also encouraged his literary bent; at the age of seventeen, Verga completed his first novel. Although he embarked on the study of law a year later, he quickly found he had no taste for the subject and dropped out of the university to pursue a literary career. He tried founding a journal and published a novel at his own expense, but Catania proved an impossible base from which to launch a literary career. In 1865, he went to Florence, where he became part of a circle of young writers, and a few years later he moved to Milan, which was even more active as a center of the arts.

During the 1870's, Verga was living in Milan, publishing novels and short stories, winning a small reputation, and seeking a new literary voice for himself which would express his ideal of what fiction should be. Because of illness in his family, he made frequent trips back to Catania during that period. From these factors emerged the Verga who would be recognized as one of Europe's master storytellers. The decision to write about his native Sicily, and the development of a new, disciplined style, produced in quick succession the short-story collection *Under the Shadow of Etna* in 1880 and the novel *I Malavoglia* (1881; *The House by the Medlar Tree*, partial translation, 1890, 1953; complete translation, 1964). Both volumes won quick recognition as masterpieces and inaugurated the most productive decade of Verga's career, when he was at the height of his powers and acknowledged as the leader of the new literary aesthetic called *Verismo*, an Italian version of the realism and naturalism which dominated the writing of fiction everywhere in Europe during the second half of the nineteenth century.

Verga's success in the 1880's failed to make him happy. His basic view of life was pessimistic, he was always something of a loner, and while he pursued many love affairs, he always avoided marriage. He grew restless and discontent with life in a great literary center, found himself spending more and more time in his native region, and by 1894 had resettled permanently in Catania. His literary output slowed to a trickle thereafter, and he lived out his years in quiet isolation. His eightieth birthday was officially celebrated in 1920, and honors were bestowed upon him by the Italian government, but he disdained to participate in any of the public ceremonies. He died two years later of a cerebral hemorrhage.

ANALYSIS

Giovanni Verga's first experiments with the short-story form in the 1870's were quite conventional in theme and offered no originality of form or technique. At best, critics have discerned in this work the struggles of a writer in a period of crisis seeking a new basis for his art. The publication of the group of stories about Sicily, under the title *Under the Shadow of Etna*, demonstrated that he had found that new basis. For these stories he developed a new literary language and a new style: Description and rhetoric were reduced to the barest minimum possible, and characters and action were portrayed in terse, nervous prose which was more impressionistic notation than precise narrative, and which often reproduced, as direct or indirect discourse, the speech patterns of the characters themselves.

"RUSTIC CHIVALRY"

The most renowned of these stories, "Cavalleria rusticana" ("Rustic Chivalry"), exemplifies this new style fully. The opening paragraph informs the reader that the story's hero, Turiddu Macca, having completed his military service, is trying unsuccessfully to attract the attention of his former beloved, Lola, by peacocklike antics in the public square. When he learns that she has betrothed herself to another during his absence, Turiddu swears that he will destroy his rival, and Verga makes this known to the reader by switching in mid-sentence to implied indirect discourse, in which Turiddu's own characteristic language, including curses, is abruptly intruded into a normal third-person narrative sentence: "When Turiddu first got to hear of it, oh, the devil! he raved and swore!—he'd rip his guts out for him, he'd rip 'em out for him, that Licodia fellow!" (Although D. H. Lawrence's translation is less than accurate, it nevertheless conveys the effect of the mixed narrative mode well enough.) A few paragraphs later Verga reports a direct conversation between Turiddu and Lola, and their words include local proverbial expressions, coarse language, and rough, ungrammatical constructions—all designed to communicate impressionistically but with great economy of means the nature of the characters and of their world.

Brevity and suggestion are the keynotes of Verga's prose style. Much is left unsaid, and transitions are abrupt, unelaborated, and unexplained. Thus, after the early conversation between Turiddu and Lola, Verga quickly states that Lola married the man from Licodia, and Turiddu swore he would get even "right under her eyes, the dirty bitch" (in Giovanni Cec-

chetti's much more accurate translation). Without the least probing of psychological motives, Verga then recounts Turiddu's cruel courtship of a girl named Santa, who lives across the street from Lola's house, to arouse Lola's jealousy and the abrupt success of the maneuver when Lola invites Turiddu to become her lover. Swiftly and relentlessly, the action moves to its inevitable climax; there is always a minimum of explanation or analysis from the narrator and as much as possible through the vehicle of direct or reported speech by the four principal characters. The jilted Santa tells Lola's husband, Alfio, that he has been cuckolded by Turiddu. In accordance with the crude customs of local "chivalry," Alfio challenges Turiddu to a "duel" to the death, with clasp knives. The violent fight is rapidly and vividly recounted in half a page, much of it dialogue, at the end of which Alfio is seriously wounded, and Turiddu is dead, having lost the fight when Alfio suddenly threw dirt in his face, blinding him. The ironic intention in the title of the story becomes especially clear in this last circumstance: In a primitive Sicilian village, the savage, violent, animalistic resolution of an "affair of honor" provides a mocking parody of the aristocratic traditions of chivalry. The Sicilian behavior is not admirable, but it is instinctive and entirely natural, compared to the ritualistic and artificial modes of chivalry.

"THE SHE-WOLF"

Verga's grasp of the essentially instinctive nature of Sicilian peasant behavior is even more starkly presented in "La Lupa" ("The She-Wolf"). The title figure in this narrative is a middle-aged peasant woman of imperious sexuality who makes a sexual slave of her own son-in-law, as though she has cast a spell over him that he is incapable of resisting, in spite of his revulsion and hatred of her. The role of primitive superstition in the relationship is emphasized by Verga's incantatory repetition of the proverbial phrase, *fra vespero e nona* ("between the hours of nones and vespers"), that time of the most intense heat in the late afternoon, when all work stops, and when Pina, the she-wolf, would come to the threshing-floor to make love with her son-in-law. The story concludes with the unforgettable vision of the son-in-law, desperate to be rid of her torment, advancing on his mother-in-law with an axe, while she unflinchingly strides toward her death, holding a bouquet of red poppies, and devouring him with her black eyes. Both are the victims of uncontrollable instinct, beyond the reach of reason, and in the story's final moment, both acquire a kind of grim, tragic heroism.

Under the Shadow of Etna

Superstition and the dark force of instinct dominate most of the stories in *Under the Shadow of Etna*. In "L'amante di Gramigna" ("Gramigna's Mistress"), for example, the story concerns a girl of good family who suddenly abandons her respectable life to follow the notorious bandit, Gramigna, because he seems to her to embody her ideal of manhood. In "Rosso Malpelo" (the title is the nickname of the hero and means "the redheaded evil-haired one"), a young boy's character and fate are inevitably shaped by the local superstition that people born with red hair are evil and must be ostracized. Perhaps the greatest accomplishment of Verga's new style of writing in *Under the Shadow of Etna* was the immediacy with which he was able to plunge his readers into the violent emotional atmosphere of the Sicilian social system. By Verga's technique, the reader experiences this unfamiliar but fascinating world as directly as possible and with almost unnoticed mediation from the narrator.

"Property"

Similar themes and similar techniques marked the new collection of short stories which Verga published three years after *Under the Shadow of Etna* under the title *Little Novels of Sicily*. Again he dealt with the raw passions of the Sicilian peasants, although now with a diminished sense of their heroism and with a heightened sense of the bitterness of their lives. The best-known story in this collection, "La roba" ("Property"), analyzes an instance of obsessive behavior in a man who has, in an exaggerated form, the traditional and instinctive peasant attachment to the land. Mazzarò has devoted all of his energy and all of his means to the acquisition of land, denying himself any pleasure or indulgence in this single-minded pursuit which has dominated his whole life. The impressive opening paragraph outlines the astonishing expanse of property which had come under Mazzarò's ownership by his middle years, and the story goes no to explore, from within, the compulsions and obsessive drives which overwhelm Mazzarò's reason and his humanity, turning him into nothing more than an acquisitive machine. The story concludes, as it must, with the vision of desperation in Mazzarò when he finally realizes that his death is close and that he will have to give up his property which has been so painfully accumulated. He reels crazily about his own courtyard, killing his ducks and turkeys, and screaming: "Roba mia, vientene con me!" ("My property, come with me!").

"The Last Day"

Verga applied the same techniques to urban themes in a collection of stories about Milan, entitled *Per le vie*. Critics generally have considered these stories somewhat less intense and therefore less effective than the Sicilian stories, but such a tale as "L'Ultima giornata" ("The Last Day") is surely in no way artistically inferior to "Rustic Chivalry" or to "The She-Wolf." It tells the story of the last hours of a vagabond who, in desperation, ends his hopeless life by throwing himself under the wheels of a train. The technical brilliance of the story lies in its indirection: It begins with an account of some well-to-do train passengers whose enjoyment is disturbed by a bump just as the train is passing through the outskirts of Milan; the next day, the newspapers report that a dead body has been found on the tracks, and soon the police investigate, following the few clues and tracking down witnesses so that a proper report can be filed on whether or not a murder for money had been involved since the victim's pockets have been found empty. The gradual unfolding of the victim's desperate plight is accomplished by the perfunctory efforts of the police, ironically operating on the wrong assumption, and in this way the final day of the suicide's life is reconstructed, clue by pathetic clue, for the reader. The story concludes with glimpses of the way various people react to "the day's suicide," demonstrating how little their lives are really touched by the event and emphasizing the melancholy truth that life goes grimly and obliviously on.

In the decade after 1883, Verga wrote more short stories; although some of them are fine, most of them mark a decline in his creative powers. By 1894, when he returned to live in isolation in Catania, his work as a short-story writer was virtually complete. In about fifteen years of peak productivity, however, Verga had truly created the art of the modern short story in Italy and had left as his legacy nearly two dozen stories of the highest excellence, as well as another two dozen or more stories of lesser quality, as models for his successors. In doing so, Verga renewed and brought up to the artistic standards of modernity a literary tradition that had been dormant in Italy since its distinguished beginnings with Giovanni Boccaccio in the fourteenth century.

OTHER MAJOR WORKS

LONG FICTION: *I carbonari della montagna*, 1861-1862 (also as *I carbonari della montagna: Sulle lagune*, 1975; includes *Sulle lagune*); *Sulle lagune*, 1863 (serial), 1975 (book); *Una peccatrice*, 1866; *Storia di una capinera*, 1871; *Eva*, 1873; *Eros*, 1874; *Tigre reale*, 1875; *I Malavoglia*, 1881 (*The House by the Medlar Tree*, partial translation 1890, 1953, complete translation 1964); *Il marito di Elena*, 1882; *Mastro-don Gesualdo*, 1889 (English translation, 1893, 1923); *Dal tuo al mio*, 1906.

PLAYS: *Cavalleria rusticana*, pr., pb. 1884 (based on his short story; *Cavalleria Rusticana: Nine Scenes from the Life of the People*, 1893); *In portineria*, pb. 1884 (based on his short story "Il canario del N. 15"); *La Lupa*, pr., pb. 1896 (based on his short story); *La caccia al lupo*, pr. 1901 (based on his short story; *The Wolf Hunt*, 1921); *La caccia alla volpe*, pr. 1901; *Dal tuo al mio*, pr. 1903; *Teatro*, pb. 1912; *Rose caduche*, pb. 1928 (wr. 1873-1875).

NONFICTION: *Lettere al suo traduttore*, 1954; *Lettere a Dina*, 1962, 1971; *Lettere a Luigi Capuana*, 1975.

BIBLIOGRAPHY

Adams, Robert Martin. "The Godfather's Grandfather." *The New York Review of Books* 31 (December 20, 1984): 46-49. A discussion of Verga's works, including *The She-Wolf and Other Stories*; notes that his reputation stems from the sparse, realistic stories of Sicilian peasants that he wrote in the 1880's; claims that Verga's haunting studies of the destructive power of sex and money retain much of their impact.

Alexander, Foscarina. *The Aspiration Toward a Lost Natural Harmony in the Work of Three Italian Writers: Leopardi, Verga, and Moravia*. Lewiston: The Edwin Mellen Press, 1990. Provides biographical notes and bibliography.

Bergin, Thomas Goddard. *Giovanni Verga*. New Haven, Conn.: Yale University Press, 1931. A well-organized study that traces a definite line of development from Verga's first published work to his last. Includes a useful bibliography and an informative commentary on Verga's style.

Cecchetti, Giovanni. *Giovanni Verga*. Boston: Twayne, 1978. An extensive study on Giovanni Verga and his work. Provides an overview of the most complex characteristics of the author.

_____. Introduction to *The She-Wolf and Other Stories*, by Giovanni Verga. Berkeley: University of California Press, 1958. This volume contains the best of Verga's short fiction available in translation. The book is divided in two parts, with selections of stories from Verga's early and late period. Cechetti emphasizes that this translation was made "as literal as possible" in order to "render the spirit as well as the letter of the original." The translator has made every effort to "convey Verga's style and the rhythm of his sentences."

Kalasky, Drew, ed. *Short Story Criticism: Excerpts from Criticism of the Works of Short Fiction Writers*. Vol. 21. Detroit, Mich.: Gale Research, 1996. A thoughtful collection of criticism of works by Verga, Jean Rhys, William Sansom, William Saroyan, and others.

Lane, Eric. Introduction to *Short Sicilian Novels*, by Giovanni Verga, translated by D. H. Lawrence. London: Daedalus Books, 1984. Lane's introduction provides the reader with an accurate historical overview and with perspicacious critical observations. The three-page chronology proves to be useful and informative and one of the best ever compiled on Verga. Lawrence's translation is by far the bestknown and can be considered a commendable attempt to render Verga into English.

Lucente, Gregory. "The Ideology of Form in Verga's 'La Lupa': Realism, Myth, and the Passion of Control." *Modern Language Notes* 95 (1980): 105-138. Lucente argues that the interaction of realistic and mythic structures in "She Wolf" determines its logic; contends that within the social world of the story, the basic opposition of passion and control (irrational/rational, nature/culture, libido/superego) is pushed to a transcendent realm in terms of pure expression and absolute repression.

Patruno, Nicholas. *Language in Giovanni Verga's Early Novels*. Chapel Hill: University of North Carolina Press, 1977. An excellent study that examines, analyzes, and determines the linguistic norm of the early works of Giovanni Verga, namely *Una peccatrice, Eva, Tigre reale*, and *Eros*. Particular attention is given to Verga's Florentine period, between 1866 and 1875. This work comprises a historical introduction and an explanation of phonology and lexicon used by Verga in his early novels.

*Murray Sachs, updated by
Rosaria Pipia*

VERGIL
Publius Vergilius Maro

Born: Andes, near Mantua, Italy; October 15, 70 B.C.E.

Died: Brundisium (now Brindisi), Italy; September 21, 19 B.C.E.

PRINCIPAL SHORT FICTION

Eclogues, 43-37 B.C.E. (also known as *Bucolics*; English translation, 1575)

Georgics, c. 37-29 B.C.E. (English translation, 1589)

Aeneid, c. 29-19 B.C.E. (English translation, 1553)

OTHER LITERARY FORMS

There are several minor poems attributed with varying degrees of cogency to Vergil. Among these are the *Culex* (c. 50 B.C.E.; *The Gnat*, 1916), *Ciris* (c. 50 B.C.E.; the seabird), and *Aetna* (c. 50 B.C.E.).

ACHIEVEMENTS

More than any other poet of his age, Vergil adopted traditional Greek forms of poetry and adapted them to the Roman spirit. His *Eclogues* were inspired by the *Idylls* of Theocritus (third century B.C.E.), although they included allusions to real persons and events that would have been familiar to Vergil's audience. The *Georgics* transformed the style of didactic poetry seen in the works of Hesiod and Aratus into an idealization of the Italian landscape and rustic way of life; unlike earlier didactic poetry, the *Georgics* provides less practical instruction and more celebration of agriculture and the Roman farmer. The *Aeneid* contains many scenes and images inspired by the *Iliad* and the *Odyssey* but focuses upon a hero who embodies the ideals of Augustan Rome.

In addition, Vergil's poetry imbued traditional literary forms with the author's own devotion to the Roman virtues of *humanitas* (compassion for humanity) and *pietas* (sense of duty). Because of the influence of Vergil's works, especially the *Aeneid*, upon later periods, these virtues have become part of the entire Western literary tradition.

Vergil also interpreted, in a fictional and symbolic form, the most important moment in the history of ancient Rome: the transformation, under Augustus, of the Republic into the Empire. Vergil's Aeneas is, in many ways, an idealized image of the emperor Augustus himself. The view that later ages would have of Rome's first emperor was thus largely determined by Vergil's depiction of Rome's founder. Moreover, the *Aeneid* is also a profoundly patriotic poem, illus-

Vergil (Library of Congress)

trating the belief of Vergil and Augustus that the founding of Rome fulfilled the will of the gods.

BIOGRAPHY

Vergil (Publius Vergilius Maro) was born near Mantua in Northern Italy in what was then Cis-alpine Gaul on October 15, 70 B.C.E. His father's name is of Etruscan origin, a fact of some modest significance, perhaps, in one's understanding of the Italian wars depicted in the *Aeneid*. His boyhood was spent in relatively simple surroundings, but when he reached fifteen (putting on the toga virilis on the day that his greatest Latin predecessor, Lucretius, is said to have died), he went to Milan and then Rome to study rhetoric (a journey passed in reverse direction by St. Augustine four centuries later). His public career was limited and unsuccessful, however, for philosophy and science were his true interests. He joined the cultural circle of the Epicurean philosopher, Siro, near Naples (it is important to note that the *Aeneid* in large measure supports the Stoic, not the Epicurean, view

of life). The influence of other prominent Romans not only made amends for the confiscation of his family's land following the Battle of Philippi (43 B.C.E.) but also introduced the poet, already in the midst of the composition of the *Eclogues*, to Octavian, the heir of Caesar, eventually to be called Caesar Augustus. Following the advice of Maecenas, the eponymous archetype of enlightened patronage, Vergil began the *Georgics*, a work which took seven years to complete, chiefly because of the care with which he composed, producing some lines in the morning and reducing them to a small number of perfected verses by the end of the day. Having celebrated first pastoral and then agricultural life, Vergil turned with the active encouragement of Octavian to the active life of the hero. The *Aeneid* slowly developed (with books 2, 4, and 6 the first to be completed) but it was never finished as Vergil hoped; he died with the request that the partly imperfect epic should be burned, but his executors and Augustus himself overrode his last wish and a central text of the Western imagination was thus preserved.

ANALYSIS

Vergil's works can be considered in the light of two relationships: his literary connection with the Greek poetry on which his works are modeled, and his personal and ideological connection with the builders of the Roman Empire. Vergil, like most Roman artists, worked within genres invented by the Greeks, but he also left on his works a uniquely Roman imprint. It was his great genius that he was able to combine both Greek and Roman elements so effectively.

AENEID

The *Aeneid* of Vergil is an epic poem combining historical and mythical elements in twelve books celebrating the origin and destiny of the Roman people. It owes much to Homer, something to Apollonius Rhodius, and even something to the first Latin epic writer, Ennius. At the heart of the poem is a success story made poignant by the careful delineation of the great price of that success. Indeed, it is precisely this sense of loss which hovers over the successful plot line which makes the *Aeneid* a more richly ambiguous poem than its predecessors and all of its successors save *Paradise Lost* (1667).

In outline, the *Aeneid* tells the story of a Trojan prince Aeneas, the son of the goddess Venus and the mortal Anchises, from the time he leaves the burning city of Troy to his conquest on the site of the new Troy in Italy. In between he has many adventures, endures several temptations, displays little variety in personality, but emerges with a character experienced in Stoic fashion and representative or emblematic of the ideal Roman leader—in fact, not unlike Augustus, putatively descended from Trojan ancestors, as he seemed to some. The poem therefore displays both the unity of long fiction and the generic traits of early short fiction—for many of the individual episodes can stand alone but together tell the larger story.

Book 1 begins as epic poems should, *in medias res*, with the storm-tossed Trojans and their captain Aeneas driven onto the coast of North Africa not far from Carthage. The storm was prompted by Juno, ever hostile to the Trojans from the time Paris, the Trojan prince, had made his famous judgment in favor of Venus, not Juno or Minerva (to continue the Latin names); but Venus in disguise provides her son with helpful background information. He enters Carthage and sees in the newly constructed temple painted with scenes of the now-famous struggles of Achilles, Priam, Hector, and even himself. He meets the Carthaginian Queen Dido, who is hospitable to the wandering Trojans, chiefly because she has known what it is to suffer as a refugee. Indeed, her statement which has moved countless readers, moved especially another sufferer and student of suffering, Sigmund Freud, who kept her lines on his desk ("My own acquaintance with misfortune has been teaching me to help others who are in distress"). Dido orders a celebratory banquet and, already smitten with love for Aeneas, asks him to tell the entire story of the fall of Troy.

Book 2 is Aeneas's narrative of the destruction of Troy in which ruin he lost his wife, Creusa, and with difficulty persuaded his father, Anchises, to flee along with Aeneas and his son, Ascanius (also called Iulus). This book has firmly imprinted itself in the Western imagination. Among the most vivid episodes

are Sinon's treachery; the death of Laocoon and his sons; the murder of Priam by Pyrrhus (see William Shakespeare's *Hamlet*, 1600-1601); the appeal of Creusa and the flaming sign about the head of little Ascanius; and most especially, Aeneas carrying his aged father, a necessary link with the Trojan past, and holding in his right hand little Ascanius, the necessary link with the future, struggling to keep up with his short steps to the strides of his heroic father. Meanwhile the wife, Creusa, significantly follows behind this trio of males and finally is lost in the flames of Troy. It is Creusa whose death frees Aeneas to meet the temptation of Dido and the opportunity of Lavinia, and whose ghost assures Aeneas that all is for the best as the gods have ordered it and that happiness and a kingdom await him in the West.

Book 3 continues Aeneas's tale of his wanderings, and along with book 10 shows most the signs that Vergil would have revised or polished it if he had lived. Among the adventures are the meeting with Andromache, the widow of Hector, another of the grieving women in this masculine world; the advice of the seer Helenus to look for the huge white sow with its thirty young as a sign guaranteeing the proper place for the founding of the new Troy; the counsel to avoid Scylla and Charybdis; the description and appearance of Polyphenus; and finally, the death of Anchises in Sicily, the last landfall before the arrival in Carthage.

Book 4, the most humanly moving, the most romantic, the saddest, and the most Vergilian segment of the poem, involves the love and death of Dido. Vergil's presentation with sympathetic understanding of the defeated moved Augustine to tears, reduced Aeneas in the eyes of readers immemorial to a mere instrument of the gods rather than a feeling human being, and tempted Milton to repeat the story in the form of Adam and Eve with an antithetical resolution. Like John Milton after him, Vergil had some difficulty in succeeding with the tactic of criticizing by authorial statement the all-too-moving conduct he depicts. The image of Rumor is especially memorable, but even it pales in comparison to the final lamentation and suicide of Dido, betrayed by Aeneas and destiny.

Book 5 is a relaxation between the two most powerful books, 4 and 6; its funeral games are a more morally sophisticated version of the games in book 23 of the *Iliad* (c. 800 B.C.E.). Although there is a relaxation in narrative tension, symbolic significance remains high, for the book is framed by two deaths. It opens with Aeneas, as his fleet heads for Sicily, looking backward at the walls of Troy which reflect the flames from Dido's funeral pyre, and it ends with the sacrificial death by drowning of the Trojan helmsman Palinurus. Both Dido and to a lesser degree Palinurus represent the cost in human terms of political obligation. Of the several events in the funeral games themselves, the most memorable is the boxing match between the huge braggart Dares and the old champion Entellus, whose initial humiliation and ultimate regeneration reveal in small the fortunes of the Trojans in large. The psychological understanding and symbolic patterning show Vergil at his best. This book and this episode are important influences upon the imagery, structure, and theme of Milton's drama, *Samson Agonistes* (1671).

Book 6, with Aeneas's descent into the underworld guided by the Sibyl, is the greatest of the books of the poem in terms of vision and poignancy. The obstacles and dangers which Aeneas avoids in the underworld are another version of the hurdles he has had to clear throughout his career presented in the first five books. Among the memorable scenes are Palinurus with his appeal for a proper burial, and Dido, marble cold in her scorn of Aeneas's exculpatory explanation, an episode described by T. S. Eliot as the most "civilized" in Western literature. Aeneas finally reaches that part of the underworld called the Land of Joy, where his father Anchises provides a vision of the destiny of his descendants, that is, a vision of the Roman future, a future already history to Vergil's contemporary audience. Of all the Roman heroes, the young Marcellus, son to Octavia and nephew to Augustus, is the last, and his tragic, early death foretold in the poem and experienced only recently by his readers led to his mother's swooning when Vergil read aloud the passage to her.

The sixth book brings an end to the "Odyssean" part of the *Aeneid*; Aeneas's wanderings are at an end. The last six books constitute the "Iliadic" *Aeneid*, concerned primarily with battles and the preparation for battle. As Vergil's nature was not very martial, his success in the last part of the work seems less memorable, although his profound insight into human character and into the inescapably tragic, nature of existence has allowed him to create two unforgettable characters only less memorable than Dido herself. These are Turnus, the young king of the Rutulians who plays the role of the vanquished Hector to that of the avenging Achilles of Aeneas, and Mezentius, the savage tyrant, grieving at the loss of his son, indomitable in defeat. That Vergil's three most memorable characters should all suffer loss and defeat is not without significance in any analysis of the poet's sensibility and humanity.

Book 7 tells of Aeneas's landing in Latium, of his dealings with King Latinus, who obeys an oracle and offers Aeneas the hand of his daughter Lavinia. By the intervention of the ever hostile Juno, however, war is created between the Trojans and the Latins. Latinus does not oppose Aeneas but Turnus does, claiming Lavinia for himself.

Book 8 has Aeneas acquire allies in the form of Evander and his son Pallas, their troops, and the Etruscan troops and their leader Tarchon. Most celebrated is the description of the shield which Vulcan forges for Aeneas. On it are depicted scenes from a Roman history, the very beginning of which Aeneas is fighting to create. At the center of the shield is depicted the Battle of Actium and the consequent triumph of Augustus.

Book 9 presents the siege of the Trojan camp nearly successful in the absence of Aeneas and costing the lives of the two young men Nisus and Euryalus, who perish through the rashness of Euryalus and the profound loyalty of Nisus. Vergil stops his narrative at their deaths to expostulate on their happy fate of dying together and to argue for their immortality through his poetry. The intensity of this celebration of male bonding should not obscure the artistry with which Vergil has prepared this episode, for during the funeral games of book 5, Nisus, who is an apparent winner in the footrace, unexpectedly slips and in that slip saves victory for Euryalus by interfering with his rival Salius. His apparent triumph in book 9 should be compared with his sacrificial return to help his less able friend.

In book 10 the Trojan siege is relived, and in a great battle Pallas is killed, as are Lausus and Mezentius, son and father. The death of Mezentius is described in a particularly powerful manner, and the despoiling of Pallas by Turnus proves, like that of the Rutulians by Euryalus, to be the cause of the death of the conqueror.

Book 11 provides a temporary truce and the suggestion of single combat between Aeneas and Turnus. Turnus wishes to continue the war, but in the fight loses his most valuable ally Camilla, a warrior-maiden slain by a javelin while watching another whose resplendent armor she fancies. Like Euryalus before her and Turnus after her, she dies partly through her desire for spoil.

Book 12 brings Turnus and Aeneas into single combat for the hand of Lavinia and the possession of the city of Latium. Aeneas defeats Turnus, who asks for mercy. Aeneas begins to grant Turnus his request but sees the spoils of Pallas worn by Turnus and in a fit of rage kills the Rutulian king. On this note the epic ends and in its oddly un-Vergilian close provides further argument that the poet had left his work in need of some revision or addition.

The traditional Homeric devices of epic construction appear throughout the poem: the invocation to the muse, the beginning of the poem *in medias res*, the use of flashbacks, repetition by epithets and formulas, the catalogues, and the epic similes. All these devices contribute to a written work which, while lacking the power of its Homeric, oral predecessors, surpasses them in its psychological insights and structural subtleties. Modern readers perhaps no longer share Vergil's conception of the Roman imperium, of the moral supremacy of Stoicism, or even of the nature of the hero, but the broad drama of personal desire and political obligation, of the tension between the individual and the state, remains current. Even if it were the case that apolitical readers should come to the poem, they would find there the essential sadness of things expressed in language as close to perfect as language can be.

BIBLIOGRAPHY

Anderson, William S. *The Art of the "Aeneid."* Englewood Cliffs, N.J.: Prentice-Hall, 1969. An excellent, though very brief, general introduction to the *Aeneid*, including information on the author's life and historical background. Also contains a short commentary on the *Aeneid* itself. A good place for the general reader to begin.

Benestad, J. Brian. "Paterno on Vergil: Educating for Service." *America* 170 (April 2, 1994): 15-17. In this speech, Benestad comments on Penn State's head football coach, Joe Paterno, and his autobiographical comments on the enormous impression made on him as a student by studying Vergil's *Aeneid*. For Paterno, a central message of the epic is that a man's first commitment is not to himself but to others, for Aeneas was the ultimate team player.

Bernard, John D., ed. *Vergil at 2000: Commemorative Essays on the Poet and His Influence.* New York: AMS Press, 1986. Fifteen essays by noted scholars, concerning most aspects of Vergilian scholarship, including the author's life and style and his historical background and influence.

Hardie, Philip R. *Virgil.* Oxford, England: Oxford University Press, 1998. Offers interpretation and criticism of the *Aeneid* and the *Georgics*.

Levi, Peter. *Virgil: His Life and Times.* New York: St. Martin's Press, 1999. A thorough introduction to Vergil. For the beginning student.

Martindale, Charles, ed. *The Cambridge Companion to Virgil.* Cambridge, England: Cambridge University Press, 1997. An excellent reference tool for students of Vergil.

Otis, Brooks. *Vergil: A Study in Civilized Poetry.* Oxford, England: Clarendon Press, 1963. One of the best, and most influential, general studies of Vergil's poetry. Contains a discussion of the author's background and style, as well as a brief analysis of all of his works. Traces the influences of Hesiod, Aratus, and Theocritus as well as Homer upon Vergil and presents Aeneas as the ideal of the Augustan individual.

Pöschl, Viktor. *The Art of Vergil*, translated by Gerda Seligson. Ann Arbor: University of Michigan

Press, 1962. A detailed study of metaphor and symbolism in the poetry of Vergil, with special attention paid to the influence of Homer on the *Aeneid*.

Verbart, Andre. "Milton on Vergil: Dido and Aeneas in *Paradise Lost*." *English Studies* 78 (March, 1997): 111-126. Discusses the relationship between Vergil and Milton's Adam and Eve; notes that in Milton's epic Adam's first words to Eve echo Aeneas's last words to Dido; notes four other parallels that have never been noted and com-

ments on how Vergil's work has affected the structure of Milton's epic.

Wiltshire, Susan Ford. *Public and Private in Vergil's "Aeneid."* Amherst: University of Massachusetts Press, 1989. An influential study of the theme of duty and public destiny, as well as a consideration of the cost of duty upon the individual in the *Aeneid*. Examines the ways in which the lessons of the *Aeneid* are relevant to the modern world.

Rosemary Barton Tobin, updated by
Jeffrey L. Buller

HELENA MARÍA VIRAMONTES

Born: East Los Angeles, California; February 26, 1954

PRINCIPAL SHORT FICTION
The Moths and Other Stories, 1985

OTHER LITERARY FORMS

Helena María Viramontes is the author of *Under the Feet of Jesus*, a novel that she dedicated to the memory of civil rights activist César Chávez. She coedited with María Herrera-Sobek two anthologies, *Chicana Creativity and Criticism: Creative Frontiers in American Literature* and *Chicana (W)rites: On Word and Film* (1995).

ACHIEVEMENTS

Helena María Viramontes won a National Endowment for the Arts grant in 1989 and received the John Dos Passos Prize for Literature for 1995.

BIOGRAPHY

Helena María Viramontes was born on February 26, 1954, in East Los Angeles, California, a city that has served as the setting for most of her short fiction. One of nine children in the family, she learned the value of work from an early age. Her father was a construction worker, her mother a homemaker. The Viramontes household was often filled with friends

and relatives who had crossed the Mexican border looking for work. In her fiction Viramontes draws on the memories of the stories she heard from these immigrants. As a student at Immaculate Heart College, where she was one of only five Chicanas in her class, Viramontes worked twenty hours a week while carrying a full load of classes. She received a B.A. in 1975 with a major in English literature. In 1977 her short story "Requiem for the Poor" won first prize for fiction in a contest sponsored by *Statement Magazine* of California State University, Los Angeles. In 1978 "The Broken Web" was the first-place winner, and in 1979 "Birthday" won first prize in the Chicano Literary Contest at the University of California at Irvine. "The Broken Web" and "Birthday" appear in her collection of short stories *The Moths and Other Stories*. She received an M.F.A. in the creative writing program of the University of California at Irvine. She became an assistant professor of English at Cornell University in Ithaca, New York. She has served as editor of the cultural magazine *Chismearte* and coordinator of the Los Angeles Latino Writers Association.

ANALYSIS

In her short stories Helena María Viramontes provides a vision of Hispanic women in American society, presenting female characters whose lives are limited by the patriarchy of Hispanic society and the imposition of religious values. She provides a humanistic and caring approach to the poor and downtrodden women who inhabit the working-class world of her fiction. She deals with the issues of abortion, aging, death, immigration, divorce, and separation. The stories in *The Moths and Other Stories* are arranged in the order of the stages in a woman's life, beginning with the story of a young girl in "The Moths" moving on to stories of women in the later stage of life. Near the end of the collection, "Snapshots" is the story of a divorced woman who feels that she has wasted her life in the mundane and demanding trivia of housework. "Neighbors" depicts an elderly woman, isolated and living in fear of the young men in the neighborhood.

"THE MOTHS"

"The Moths" is the story of a young Chicana girl who finds a safe refuge in caring for her aging grandmother, her Abuelita. Constantly in trouble at home, fighting with her sisters, and receiving whippings, the rebellious fourteen-year-old girl finds a purpose for her life as she works with her grandmother to plant flowers and grow them in coffee cans. Viramontes describes in detail how the two women nurture the plants as they form a world of their own, away from the dominating force of the girl's father.

The story contains elements of the Magical Realism that characterizes much contemporary Third World American literature. When her more feminine sisters call her "Bull Hands" because her hands are too large and clumsy for the fine work of embroidery or crocheting, the girl feels her hands begin to grow. As her grandmother soothes the hands in a balm of dried moth wings and Vicks, the girl feels her hands shrink back to normal size. Another example of Magical Realism occurs at the end of the story, when the image of the moths is realized as they fly out of the dead grandmother's mouth.

The women exist in a world of wild lilies, jasmine, heliotrope, and cilantro, working with mayonnaise jars and coffee cans. The vines of chayotes wind around the pillars of the grandmother's house, climbing to the roof and creating the illusion that the house is "cradled" in vines, safe and protected. In her own home the girl's Apá, her father, forces her to go to church by banging on the table, threatening to beat her, and lashing out at her mother, her Amá. In one brief scene Viramontes is able to portray the brutal hold the father has on the family. In contrast to this household, the grandmother's house, devoid of a masculine presence, is a place of peace and growth. When the grandmother dies, the girl finds her, and she bathes her grandmother's body in a ceremony. As she performs this ritual, the girl sees the old scars on the woman's back, evidence that she, too, had suffered beatings.

"SNAPSHOTS"

As the story opens, Olga Ruiz, a woman whose husband has left her, reflects on her life and admits that it was the "small things in life" that made her happy: "ironing straight arrow creases" on her husband's work shirts and cashing in coupons. Now that she has reached middle age, she realizes that she has wasted her life in the pursuit of housework with nothing to show for all her efforts. Now that she is alone, a hopeless lethargy has set in, and she seems unable to cope with her new circumstances. Marge, her daughter, tries to get her involved with projects, pleading "Please. Mother. Knit. Do something."

As she pores over the snapshots in family albums, Olga sees that she has been "longing for a past that never actually existed." The title of the story refers to more than the actual snapshots. Olga sees snapshots as ghosts and feels "haunted by the frozen moments." She remembers her grandmother's fear that snapshots would steal a person's soul, and she recounts how her grandfather tried to take a family picture with his new camera; not knowing how to operate it, he took the film out and expected it to develop in the sunlight. As the story ends, Olga, fearing that her grandmother was right, decides that if she finds a picture of her grandmother, she will destroy it.

Viramontes paints a portrait of a woman who has devoted her life to being a good wife and mother, cooking, cleaning, taking care of others, and then in her middle years has been abandoned. Her husband has remarried, and her son-in-law is tired of her calls to her daughter, Marge. At one point he takes the phone away from Marge and says, "Mrs. Ruiz, why don't you leave us alone." A few minutes later, Dave, her former husband calls and asks her to "leave the kids alone." After a lifetime of hard work, Olga has been left alone, feeling that her life was worthless.

"NEIGHBORS"

"Neighbors," the last story in the collection, tells the story of Aura Rodriguez, an isolated seventy-three-year-old woman who lives in fear of the young men in her neighborhood, who have vowed to get even with her for calling the police on them. Realizing that she must take care of herself, she gets a gun and sits in a chair facing the door, ready to protect herself. This story opens with a description of a neighborhood that has "slowly metamorphosed into a graveyard." Aura believes in living within her own space and expects her neighbors to do the same.

In the words of Fierro, Aura's old neighbor, Viramontes repeats the metaphor of the graveyard that she used at the beginning of the story. Fierro remembers the quiet hills and old homes that existed before the government destroyed the houses and covered the land with "endless freeway" that "paved over his sacred ruins, his secrets, his graves . . . his memories." The story is filled with realistic details such as the description of Aura's "Ben Gay scented house slipper."

"THE CARIBOO CAFÉ"

Conflict in Central America is the focus of "The Cariboo Café," in which a woman from El Salvador has suffered the loss of her child at the hands of government officials. Interwoven with the story of her grief is the story of the cook, who suffers from loneliness after losing his wife and son, and the terrified illegal immigrants who fear capture by the police. The woman from El Salvador, who has been mourning the loss of her small son for several years, mistakenly believes that one of the immigrants in the café is her son.

In the first segment of this three-part story, Sonya and her brother Macky, children of illegal immigrants, are frightened when they see a police officer seizing a man on the street. Trained to fear the police, the children run to the café for protection. In the second part, the narrator is the cook, who has shown immigration agents where the immigrants are hiding even though they have been regular customers. The narrator of the third part is the Salvadoran woman

whose young son was taken by army officials. After numerous attempts to find her son, the woman moved across the Mexican border to the United States. In the final, violent confrontation when the police enter the café, the woman fights them, identifying them with the army officials who took her son. Viramontes tells this complex story through shifting points of view to reveal different perspectives as she shows the power of oppressive governments.

OTHER MAJOR WORKS

LONG FICTION: *Under the Feet of Jesus*, 1995; *Their Dogs Came with Them*, 2000.

NONFICTION: "Nopalitos: The Making of Fiction," 1989; "Why I Write," 1995.

EDITED TEXTS: *Chicana Creativity and Criticism: Charting New Frontiers in American Literature*, 1987, rev. 1996 (with María Herrera-Sobek); *Chicana (W)rites: On Word and Film*, 1995 (with Herrera-Sobek).

BIBLIOGRAPHY

Green, Carol Hurd, and Mary Grimley Mason. *American Women Writers*. New York: Continuum, 1994, 463-465. The editors provide a brief biographical sketch as well as an analysis of the short stories in *Moths*. They emphasize the portrayal of Chicana women with their strengths and weaknesses as they struggle with the restrictions placed on them because they are women. They note that many of the characters pay a price for rebelling against traditional values.

Richards, Judith. "Chicano Creativity and Criticism: New Frontiers in American Literature." *College Literature* 25 (Spring, 1998): 182. In this review of the anthology edited by Viramontes and María Herrera-Sobek, Richards argues that the book provides a good starting place for those who want to evaluate the Chicana literary movement. Points to the emergence of urban working-class women as protagonists, the frequent use of child and adolescent narrators, and autobiographical formats that focus on unresolved issues as characteristics of Chicana literature.

Saldivar-Hull, Sonia. "Helena María Viramontes."

Dictionary of Literary Biography. Chicano Writers series. Detroit: Gale Research, 1992. Summarizes and analyzes several stories from *Moths*, stressing the cultural and religious traditions that restrict women's lives. Discusses the patriarchal privileges that the father assumes in the story when he shouts at his daughter "'Tu eres mujer'" (you are a woman) in order to control her. Calls "Snapshots" a "scathing critique of the politics of housework" and refers to the divorced Olga as "an alienated laborer whose value has decreased."

Yarbo-Bejarano, Yvonne. *Introduction to "The Moths and Other Stories."* Houston, Tex.: Arte Público Press, 1995. Discusses Viramontes's portrayal of women characters who struggle against the restrictions placed on them by the Chicano culture, the church, and the men in these women's lives. Provides a brief analysis of each story in the collection, showing that the stories deal with problems Chicana women face at various stages of their lives. Notes that, although Viramontes addresses the problems of racial prejudice and economic struggles, the emphasis is on the cultural and social values that shape these women and suggests that most of stories involve the conflict between the female character and the man who represents an oppressive authority figure.

Judith Barton Williamson

GERALD VIZENOR

Born: Minneapolis, Minnesota; October 22, 1934

PRINCIPAL SHORT FICTION

Anishinabe Adisokan: Stories of the Ojibwa, 1974
Wordarrows: Indians and Whites in the New Fur Trade, 1978
Earthdivers: Tribal Narratives on Mixed Descent, 1981
Landfill Meditation: Crossblood Stories, 1991

OTHER LITERARY FORMS

Best known for his novels, especially *Griever: An American Monkey King in China* (1987), Gerald Vizenor has also published several volumes of poetry, many of them devoted to haiku. He also wrote the screenplay *Harold of Orange* (1983) and a number of nonfiction volumes, including *Manifest Manners: Postindian Warriors of Survivance* (1994) and *Postindian Conversations* (1999), which champion the Native American cause.

ACHIEVEMENTS

Winner of the Fiction Collective Award (1987), the American Book Award (1988), California Arts Council Literature Award (1989), and the PEN/Oakland Book Award (1990), Gerald Vizenor has become a prominent voice in Native American Literature despite the difficulty of his works. His academic recognition has included the J. Hill Professorship at the University of Minnesota and the David Burr Chair at the University of Oklahoma.

BIOGRAPHY

On October 22, 1934, Gerald Robert Vizenor was born to La Verne Peterson Vizenor and Clement Vizenor, who was murdered twenty months later. Thereafter, Gerald was reared partly by his father's Anishinaabe relatives. At age fifteen, he joined the National Guard and at eighteen the U.S. Army—an experience he found intellectually stimulating, particularly during his station in Japan. In 1955, at the end of his enlistment, he entered New York University, then transferred in 1956 to the University of Minnesota. He married Judith Horns in 1959 and graduated the year his son Robert was born in 1960. He began graduate work until his writings as social worker and activist won him a position as a reporter for the *Minneapolis Tribune* (1968–1969). From 1970 to 1971, he taught at Lake Forest College in Illinois; from 1971 to 1972, he directed the Indian Studies Program at Bemidji State University, Minnesota; in 1973, he attended Harvard University; and in 1974, he joined the *Tribune*'s editorial staff. His career continued in a similarly nomadic fashion. Particularly notable was his time spent teaching at Tianjin University in China, which inspired the writing of *Griever*. He was divorced in 1969 and remained single until his marriage to Laura Hall in 1981.

ANALYSIS

Like much postcolonial literature, Gerald Vizenor's short fiction refuses to accept the science–based worldview of the Occident, instead employing a Magical Realism that fuses Native American religious beliefs with modern images. This was already the case in his early, relatively more conventional short narratives (including *Wordarrows*) and has subsequently led to even freer fantasy. He is also postcolonial in that his engagé position inclines him toward satire, playful diatribes, and seemingly pedantic documentation that interweave the conventions of factual and fictional literature, so as to comment on actual events but without letting their seriousness constrain his sense of humor.

He undermines the distinction between fact and fiction because it is based on the dichotomy of objective and subjective, which colonialism used to subordinate the supposedly superstitious emotionalism of "primitive" people to its own "objectivity." Similarly, colonialism (in the guise of the Bureau of Indian Affairs, for example) long tried to replace oral traditions with bureaucratic literacy, taught by a school system that forbade the use of Native American languages. Despite a decreasing market for short fiction (except in poorly paid academic journals), Vizenor produced many brief works, a practice congruent with the oral

tradition he seeks to preserve; his craftsmanship cannot be separated from his politics.

"THE PSYCHOTAXIDERMIST"

This story is a self–reflexive account of a generation. Its narrator, Colonel Clement Beaulieu, is a persona of Vizenor, who combined the first name of his father with the last of his grandmother. Beaulieu recalls an anecdote about Newcrows, a shaman whose imagination could bring dead animals to life. In a satire of white society, the shaman is arrested for performing this miracle on a golf course. Then, he infests the prosecutor and judge with magical ticks, thereby ending the trial. In an epilogue, Beaulieu begins telling the story to a group of nuns, with its protagonist changed to Sister Isolde. The point is that oral narratives are altered for each audience. Only through such imaginative adaptation can the tales themselves become psychotaxidermists, not merely preserving past forms but reanimating them.

WORDARROWS

The preface to this work compares the ancient use of arrows to the modern employment of words in the defense of the tribe. Most of the stories are vignettes from the time when Vizenor was executive director of the American Indian Employment and Guidance Center in Minneapolis. As he has acknowledged, some of these vignettes might seem racist except for Vizenor's being a Native American. For instance, "Roman Downwind" portrays a teenager who barely passes his driving test on the third try, celebrates until he had exhausted his cash and family, then talks an agency into giving him enough money so that he can meet a white woman and be comfortable for one more day. In "Marleen American Horse," such self–defeating behavior is diagnosed as the result of Native Americans' accepting colonial stereotypes, which produces guilt that leads to substance abuse and more guilt in a vicious circle.

"LANDFILL MEDITATION"

First published in a slightly different version in 1979, this story provides a title for *Landfill Meditation*. The tale's importance derives from its primary image: society's treating Native Americans as garbage. A trickster able to profit from this racism, Nose Charmer becomes rich by dumping toxic waste on wetlands he is trying to claim as sacred grounds. His story is being told "backward" by Clement Beaulieu—a pun on the stereotype of "backward" Native Americans. Another of Beaulieu's anecdotes concerns "Belladonna Winter Catcher." Her fatal flaw is a predilection for "terminal creeds," a phrase that Vizenor uses repeatedly to signify any humorless conception of life. The other Native Americans murder her, as they have poisoned many of those guilty of the same fault. After telling these loosely related parables, Beaulieu floats out the window, buoyed by his laughter.

EARTHDIVERS

This collection takes its name from the widely distributed myth that dry land was created by divers who brought it from the bottom of the sea. To Vizenor, the situation of having to create the ground of one's existence particularly suits "mixedbloods," who are between cultures. In the preface, where he discusses this myth, Vizenor derides cultural critic Alan Dundes's Freudian interpretation, which Vizenor considers the quintessence of humorless, colonial reduction of Native American creativity to filth. Vizenor's stories celebrate trickster figures who manage, for a while at least, to find a place for themselves in the wasteland of urban civilization. In "The Chair of Tears," for instance, academia is arrayed against the Native American Studies Department, whose chair must have publications and other credentials to please the establishment but quite the opposite to satisfy the radical students. Knowing that he has no safe ground on which to proceed, the seventh appointee makes a series of startling innovations, such as establishing a Department of Undecided Studies, likely, given student procrastination, to become the largest and potentially most powerful unit on campus. The volume concludes, however, not with the success of such mediating tricksters but with a group of stories about a collapse in racial relations because of unsuccessful attempts to halt the execution of a Native American.

"LUMINOUS THIGHS: MYTHIC TROPISMS"

This story's protagonist, Griever de Hocus, also is the center of Vizenor's novels *Griever*, a surrealistic fictionalization of Vizenor's teaching at Tianjin University, and *The Trickster of Liberty: Tribal Heirs to a*

Wild Baronage (1988), largely about Griever's family. Although Vizenor's persona in his earlier books, Clement Beaulieu, had appeared in episodes of a Magical Realist bent, he was a more transparent and believable version of Vizenor than Griever, who seeks to turn himself into myth as a defense against the urbanized world. This self-transformation involves "tropisms," a word previously used by Nathalie Sarraute, who defined them as the psychological patterns with which people jockey for control over one another. To her, these behaviors are futile but to Vizenor, they are "mythic," bestowing a sense of connection to primordial meaning. "Luminous Thighs: *Mythic Tropisms*" opens with one of these mythic tropisms. To annoy the man next to him on a train, Griever tells a preposterous story about driving a novelist's car into a river so that the novelist, after being rumored to be dead, could have the pleasure of publicly declaring himself to be alive. This metaphor of rebirth through water, present in Griever's other discourses, is meant to unsettle anyone near him (since stereotypes left unsettled are likely to turn against him in a white society). The luminous thighs themselves are sexually unsettling because they are of an androgynous statue. They give a title not only to the story but also to a screenplay Griever hopes to make with actor Robert Redford (Vizenor worked at Redford's Sundance Institute). The story's digressive conclusion is a denunciation of the novel *Hanta Yo* (1979), a book that pandered to the public's desire for myths and imposed humorless stereotypes on Native Americans. For Vizenor's tale to wander into a review of it is perhaps more unsettling than any of his previous expansions of the short-story genre.

OTHER MAJOR WORKS

LONG FICTION: *Darkness in Saint Louis Bearheart*, 1978 (rev. as *Bearheart: The Heirship Chronicles*, 1990); *Griever: An American Monkey King in China*, 1987; *The Trickster of Liberty: Tribal Heirs to a Wild Baronage*, 1988; *The Heirs of Columbus*, 1992; *Dead Voices: Natural Agonies in the New World*, 1992; *Chancers*, 2000.

SCREENPLAY: *Harold of Orange*, 1983 (film released in 1984).

POETRY: *Matsushima: Pine Islands*, 1984 (originally pub. as four separate volumes of haiku during the 1960's).

NONFICTION: *Thomas James White Hawk*, 1968; *The Everlasting Sky: New Voices from the People Named the Chippewa*, 1972; *Tribal Scenes and Ceremonies*, 1976; *Crossbloods: Bone Courts, Bingo, and Other Reports*, 1990; *Interior Landscapes: Autobiographical Myths and Metaphors*, 1990; *Manifest Manners: Postindian Warriors of Survivance*, 1994; *Postindian Conversations*, 1999.

MISCELLANEOUS: *Summer in the Spring: Ojibwe Lyric Poems and Tribal Stories*, 1981 (rev. as *Summer in the Spring: Anishinaabe Lyric Poems and Stories*, 1993); *The People Named the Chippewa: Narrative Histories*, 1984; *Shadow Distance: A Gerald Vizenor Reader*, 1994.

BIBLIOGRAPHY

Blaeser, Kimberly. *Gerald Vizenor: Writing in the Oral Tradition*. Norman: University of Oklahoma Press, 1996. Blaeser emphasizes Vizenor's own awareness of ironic contrasts between his eclecticism and his sense of continuity with the tribal past.

Haseltine, Patricia. "The Voices of Gerald Vizenor: Survival Through Transformation." *American Indian Quarterly* 9, no. 1 (Winter, 1985): 31. In discussing Vizenor's multiplicity, Haseltine suggests that one strata of it arises from dream vision experience.

Isernhagen, Hartwig. *Momaday, Vizenor, Armstrong: Conversations on American Indian Writing*. American Indian Literature and Critical Studies series 32. Norman: University of Oklahoma Press, 1999. Although Vizenor has given many interviews, this work brings him into the context of N. Scott Momaday's works, which have been a major influence on Vizenor's.

Monsma, Bradley John. "'Active Readers . . . Obverse Tricksters': Trickster-Texts and Cross-Cultural Reading." *Modern Language Studies* 26 (Fall, 1996): 83-98. Monsma investigates to what extent Vizenor's use of the trickster theme expects both the readers and the author to be tricksters.

Owens, Louis, ed. *Studies in American Indian Literatures: The Journal of the Association for the Study of American Indian Literatures* 9 (Spring, 1997). This special issue devoted to Vizenor contains articles on his contrasts between tribal and legal identity, the way Samuel Beckett, John Bunyan, and he use the past in comparable ways, his employment of Buddhist and wasteland imagery, as well as his changing poetic vision.

Vizenor, Gerald. "An Interview with Gerald Vizenor." Interview by Neal Bowers and Charles L. P. Silet. *Melus* 8, no. 1 (1981): 41-49. Vizenor relates the multiplicity, constant change, deliberate provocation, even contradiction in his own works to the traditional function of oral tales as a vivid dialogue between performer and audience, an activity he calls "word cinema."

_____. "Mythic Rage and Laughter: An Interview with Gerald Vizenor." Interview by Dallas Miller. *Studies in American Indian Literatures: The Journal of the Association for the Study of American Indian Literatures* 7 (Spring, 1995): 77-96. This interview explores the twin poles of anger and laughter in Vizenor's writing.

_____. "On Thin Ice, You Might as Well Dance: An Interview with Gerald Vizenor." Interview by Larry McCaffery and Tom Marshall. *Some Other Fluency: Interviews with Innovative American Authors*. Philadelphia: University of Pennsylvania Press, 1996. Vizenor considers that the precariousness of his situation has spurred his artistry.

_____. "'I Defy Analysis': A Conversation with Gerald Vizenor." Interview by Rodney Simard, Lavonne Mason, and Ju Abner. *Studies in American Indian Literatures: The Journal of the Association for the Study of American Indian Literatures* 5 (Fall, 1993): 42–51. Vizenor protests against critics' attempts to classify him.

James Whitlark

VOLTAIRE

François-Marie Arouet

Born: Paris, France; November 21, 1694
Died: Paris, France; May 30, 1778

PRINCIPAL SHORT FICTION

Le Monde comme il va, 1748 (revised as *Babouc: Ou, Le Monde comme il va*, 1749; *Babouc: Or, The World as It Goes*, 1754, also as *The World as It Is: Or, Babouc's Vision*, 1929)

Memnon: Ou, La Sagesse humaine, 1749 (*Memnon: Or, Human Wisdom*, 1961)

La Lettre d'un Turc, 1750

Le Blanc et le noir, 1764 (*The Two Genies*, 1895)

Jeannot et Colin, 1764 (*Jeannot and Colin*, 1929)

L'Histoire de Jenni, 1775

Les Oreilles du Comte de Chesterfield, 1775 (*The Ears of Lord Chesterfield and Parson Goodman*, 1826)

OTHER LITERARY FORMS

Voltaire's writings are vast, spanning more than one hundred volumes of letters, literature, and scholarship. He wrote in both French and English, publishing his works in several countries, depending on the prevailing political climate.

Voltaire has been remembered most for his incisive short stories, which convey complex philosophical ideas. During his own age, however, he was noted as a political satirist, playwright, and poet. He was a master of the epic poem, and his *La Henriade* (1728; a revision of *La Ligue*; *Henriade*, 1732) revived the popularity of this genre. His plays were renowned throughout France, and *Œdipe* (1718; *Oedipus*, 1761), produced when Voltaire was only twenty-four, received critical acclaim. His major philosophical work, *Dictionnaire philosophique portatif* (1764; *A Philosophical Dictionary for the Pocket*, 1765; also as *Philosophical Dictionary*, 1945), was an ambitious compendium of philosophical ideas and terms. In addition, his historical writings, such as *Le Siècle de Louis XIV* (1751; *The Age of Louis XIV*, 1752), have earned for him a reputation as one of the first modern historians.

ACHIEVEMENTS

During his lifetime, Voltaire was both revered and rejected. He was alternately honored by kings for his brilliance and exiled or imprisoned for his radical political views. He was welcomed into the courts of George I and Princess Caroline of England, Frederick II of Prussia, and Louis XV of France. Louis XV appointed him as Royal Historiographer and as Ordinary Gentleman of the King's Bedchamber in the 1740's. In 1746, Voltaire realized one of his greatest ambitions when he was elected to the prestigious Académie Française. In the 1750's, Frederick II gave him a medal of merit, made him a chamberlain, and considered Voltaire to be his personal tutor and court philosopher until a bitter disagreement caused Voltaire to leave Prussia.

Voltaire's scathing attacks on intolerance, injustice, and superstition scandalized many of the powerful in the government and the French Roman Catholic Church, but his humor, imagination, and daring in expressing his opinions won for him numerous followers as well. When he was living in Switzerland in his later years, people made pilgrimages to his home and stood outside it hoping to catch a glimpse of him. At the end of his life, Voltaire returned to Paris to the acclaim of crowds of admirers. Yet, even in death, he stirred controversy: His body had to be smuggled out of Paris to allow him the decent burial in consecrated ground that the French Catholic hierarchy denied him.

Voltaire was one of the foremost philosophes of the French Enlightenment, and his influence went far beyond his long and successful lifetime. His ideas on the freedom and dignity of the individual are credited with having had a strong influence on the French Revolution of 1789. His satirical and irreverent wit gradually eroded some of the religious and political intolerance of eighteenth century France. Many who have fought for toleration, justice, and equality have looked back to the spirit of Voltaire's writings. He summarized his own sense of satisfaction about the successes of his and other philosophes' writings in a letter to Jean Le Rond D'Alembert dated July 18, 1766, in which he rejoiced that

> the Church of Wisdom is beginning to develop in our neighborhood where, twelve years ago the most somber fanaticism ruled. The provinces are becoming enlightened, the young magistrates are thinking boldly. . . . One is astonished by the progress that human reason has made in so few years.

BIOGRAPHY

Voltaire was born François-Marie Arouet on November 21, 1694, the son of a *grand bourgeois* lawyer. From 1704 to 1711, he attended a Jesuit boarding school, after which he pursued the study of law until his political writings earned for him his first exile from Paris in 1716 and his first imprisonment in the Bastille in 1717. From that time on, he devoted himself to his writing, beginning with plays and poetry and expanding to literature, philosophy, and history. He was socially and intellectually precocious, associating with many aristocratic and libertine men in the Société du Temple (Society of the Temple) by the time he was twelve. Voltaire was brilliant, witty, a talented writer, and in later years, a social activist. Yet he could also be impulsive and hotheaded, which resulted in his arrest on several further occasions. Voltaire lived in various parts of France, England, Holland, Prussia, and Switzerland, moving in and out of these countries as his political sentiments and personal temperament made it unwise or impossible for him to stay where he was. He spent the last years of his life near the Swiss border, between his French homeland and the freer intellectual environment of Geneva, allowing himself an escape route to either country.

Voltaire was as untraditional in his personal life as in his political and philosophical ideas. His freedom from the norms of society, however, seemed to sustain his creative energies. In 1734, Voltaire met Madame Émilie du Châtelet, who would be his mistress and intellectual partner for the next fifteen years. He moved in with her and her husband at their estate at Cirey, where he wrote and studied with the "divine Émilie." Even after Voltaire's widowed niece, Ma-

Voltaire (Library of Congress)

dame Denis, had become his new mistress, he maintained an intellectual relationship with Madame du Châtelet which would inspire him until her death in 1749. Her death saddened and depressed Voltaire for many years, contributing to the growing skepticism about the goodness of the world that is evident in his later fictional works, such as *Candide: Ou, L'Optimisme* (1759; *Candide: Or, All for the Best*, 1759). Throughout his life, Voltaire had suffered from bouts with ill health and severe hypochondria. He lived to be eighty-three, however, and was one of the most energetic and prolific authors in history.

ANALYSIS

Voltaire's wit and insight into the human condition found a memorable forum in his short stories. These stories were not merely entertaining fantasies but were works of philosophical and social reflection as well. By allowing his readers to see the world through his characters' eyes, Voltaire taught new ways of thinking about the attitudes and situation of humanity.

Voltaire's fiction ranges from extremely short pieces to the longer works *Zadig: Ou, La Destinée, Histoire orientale* (1748; originally as *Memnon: Histoire orientale*, 1747; *Zadig: Or, The Book of Fate*, 1749), *Le Micromégas* (1752; *Micromegas*, 1753), *Candide*, and *L'Ingénu* (1767; *The Pupil of Nature*, 1771; also as *Ingenuous*, 1961). While those longer works are the primary stories for which he is remembered, his shorter tales contain many of the same themes in a tightly crafted and inventive form.

Voltaire was fascinated throughout his life with the issues of good and evil, freedom and determinism, and the nature of Providence. A Deist to the end of his life, convinced that God had created the world and left it to run according to an original plan, Voltaire yet struggled with the concepts of fate and Providence from the human perspective. The view of Gottfried Wilhelm Leibniz and others that this is the best of all possible worlds fit with Voltaire's Deism but not with his experience of the world. Voltaire's stories show a continually deepening sense of the evil and folly in life, in which it is difficult to find the good. His protagonists often undertake long and bizarre journeys, on which they learn tolerance from the experience of the universality of human suffering. Human goodness does not seem to be rewarded in the long run, and no obviously overarching plan shows itself to his heroes. It appears that existence is a pointless interplay of events in which evil people seem to be quite happy and successful, and the good often suffer miserably. Yet Voltaire always allows for the possibility that some good may be present in the worst of situations, even if that good is well hidden.

ZADIG

Within Voltaire's longer stories, this theme is quite obvious. In *Zadig*, the protagonist encounters a continually changing cycle of fortunes and misfortunes until he finally decides in despair that goodness will never be rewarded. An angel in disguise teaches him that the ways of Providence are inscrutable and all that happens in life creates the best possible world as a whole. Once Zadig realizes that the evil in the world is part of the divine plan, and that the world would be imperfect without it, he is freed from his ig-norance and becomes the happy man that he had always believed he would be. He ends up a king, ruling more justly and compassionately because of the wisdom gained from his misfortunes.

CANDIDE

In the later work, *Candide*, Voltaire's growing pessimism is evident. Candide is an innocent and optimistic young man who undergoes an incredible series of cruel and painful disasters. Considering the enormity of the ills which meet him from all sides—he is exiled, drafted, beaten, robbed, and continually loses the woman he loves—he is amazingly slow to question his optimistic view of the world. By the end of his life, however, Candide settles down on a small farm with the woman he sought all his life (now grown quite ugly and disagreeable), and he brushes aside his original belief that things are all ordered for the best. He recognizes that the attempt to try to ignore the inevitability of suffering and evil in life leads to a tragic failure: the failure to try to improve the world in whatever ways are possible. He is now more content with the attitude that "we must cultivate our garden," thus abandoning the question of the good of the whole universe for the task of alleviating the misery of existence in his small corner of the world.

BABOUC

In Voltaire's shorter tales *Babouc* and *Memnon*, the issue of the apparent dominance of evil over good receives an answer similar to that given by *Zadig* in 1747. As in the novel *Zadig*, the protagonists learn that this world is imperfect but that it plays its appointed role in a universe that is ordered by Providence.

In *Babouc*, the jinni Ithuriel descends to earth to send Babouc on a fact-finding journey to Persia. Babouc is to travel throughout Persepolis to see if the Persians are worthy of punishment or destruction because of their evil actions. Babouc sets off and soon finds himself in the midst of a war between Persia and India. This war, begun over a petty dispute, has been ravaging the country for twenty years. Babouc witnesses bloody battles, treachery, and cruelty on both sides. He also witnesses many amazing acts of kindness and humanity. His journey continues in this vein. For every set of abuses in religion, politics, sexual conduct, and education, he finds also some good and noble elements. His cry of surprise echoes throughout the piece: "Unintelligible mortals! . . . How is it that you can combine so much meanness with so much greatness, such virtues with such crimes?"

By the end, he agrees with a wise man whom he meets that evil is prevalent and good people are rare, yet the best is hidden from a visitor and needs to be sought more diligently. As he examines the society, he finds that those who have obtained positions of power through corrupt means are capable of devotion to their work and often pursue their careers with devotion and justice. He gains compassion for the people and their leaders and devises a way in which to communicate what he has learned to the jinni. He has a metalsmith fashion a statue out of every kind of stone, earth, and metal and takes this figure back to Ithuriel, asking, "Will you break this pretty little image, because it is not all gold and diamonds?" Ithuriel immediately comprehends and pardons the Persians, deciding not to interfere with "the way the world goes." Even though the world is not fully good, it contains enough good to merit its continued existence.

MEMNON: OR, HUMAN WISDOM

In *Memnon: Or, Human Wisdom* (not to be confused with *Memnon: Histoire orientale*, the original title of *Zadig*), Voltaire takes a different path to a similar moral. In this humorous tale, a young man named Memnon plans to become perfectly wise by ridding himself of all of his passions. He decides to renounce love, drinking, wasting money, and arguing. He is assured that this will lead him to financial and emotional security, remove all hindrances to the exercise of his reason, and thus make him happy. After he forms this plan, he looks out his window and sees a young woman in tears. He rushes to counsel her, sheerly out of compassion, and ends in her embrace. Her uncle enters, and only a large sum of money convinces him not to kill Memnon. Memnon then has dinner with his friends and consoles himself by getting drunk and gambling, which leads to an argument in which he loses an eye. "The wise Memnon is carried back home drunk, with no money, and minus an

eye." He recovers a bit, only to find that his investors have bankrupted him.

He ends up sleeping on a pile of straw outside of his house and dreams that a six-winged heavenly creature, his good jinni, comes to him. Memnon wonders where his good jinni was the night before and is told that he was with Memnon's brother, who was blinded and imprisoned. Memnon comments that it is worthwhile "to have a good genie in a family, so that one of two brothers may be one-eyed, the other blind, one lying on straw, the other in prison." The jinni helpfully points out that the situation will get better if Memnon abandons his ridiculous attempt to be perfectly wise. This world is only one of many others, all of which are ordered by degrees of perfection, and the earth is far down near the craziest end of the scale. All is well, the jinni assures him, when one considers the arrangement of the universe as a whole. Memnon says that he will believe that all is well when he can see that it is with both eyes.

JEANNOT AND COLIN

Although Voltaire's fiction depicts a crazy world where fortunes are uncertain, evils abound, and goodness does not ensure happiness, there are two things which are valued in most of his stories—the search for knowledge and the companionship of trusted friends. In *Jeannot and Colin*, Voltaire examines the worth of friendship and learning over the illusory happiness to be gained from wealth and power.

Jeannot and Colin are friends and roommates at school until Jeannot's father sends for him to come home and enjoy the new family wealth. Jeannot does so, scoring his old friend and turning with relish to his new life of leisure. His mother and father discuss his future with a tutor, but each area of study, whether philosophy, mathematics, or history, is judged of no use to a young man of society who now has servants to do as he wishes. They decide to teach him to dance and be attractive, so that he can shine in social graces. He becomes a vaudeville singer and charms all the ladies of breeding. This, however, does not last: His father is bankrupted, his mother forced to become a servant, and Jeannot himself is homeless. In a state of distress, he runs into his old friend, Colin, whom he had snubbed. Colin is overjoyed to see him and offers to take Jeannot into his home and his business and to help Jeannot's mother and father out of their difficulties. Colin's kindness and forgiveness change Jeannot's heart and allow Jeannot's natural goodness to grow, free from the ravages of society. Jeannot lives happily, assisting his parents and marrying Colin's equally sweet-tempered sister.

Philosophical reflections and social satire weigh down the plots of some later stories, such as *The Ears of Lord Chesterfield and Parson Goodman*, making them tedious. These stories show the drier side of Voltaire's satire. At his best, however, Voltaire offered his readers richly woven tales which critiqued society, satirized pretensions, expressed new philosophical ideas, and simply entertained. The stories include much humor and piercing insight into the common follies of humanity. These philosophical tales succeeded, as no straightforward philosophy could, in offering many people new perspectives on reason, experience, and humanity.

OTHER MAJOR WORKS

LONG FICTION: *Zadig: Ou, La Destinée, Histoire orientale*, 1748 (originally as *Memnon: Histoire orientale*, 1747; *Zadig: Or, The Book of Fate*, 1749); *Le Micromégas*, 1752 (*Micromegas*, 1753); *Histoire des voyages de Scarmentado*, 1756 (*The History of the Voyages of Scarmentado*, 1757; also as *History of Scarmentado's Travels*, 1961); *Candide: Ou, L'Optimisme*, 1759 (*Candide: Or, All for the Best*, 1759; also as *Candide: Or, The Optimist*, 1762; also as *Candide: Or, Optimism*, 1947); *L'Ingénu*, 1767 (*The Pupil of Nature*, 1771; also as *Ingenuous*, 1961); *L'Homme aux quarante écus*, 1768 (*The Man of Forty Crowns*, 1768); *La Princesse de Babylone*, 1768 (*The Princess of Babylon*, 1769).

PLAYS: *Œdipe*, pr. 1718 (*Oedipus*, 1761); *Artémire*, pr. 1720; *Mariamne*, pr. 1724 (English translation, 1761); *L'Indiscret*, pr., pb. 1725 (verse); *Brutus*, pr. 1730 (English translation, 1761); *Ériphyle*, pr. 1732; *Zaïre*, pr. 1732 (English translation, 1736); *La Mort de César*, pr. 1733; *Adélaïade du Guesclin*, pr. 1734; *L'Échange*, pr. 1734; *Alzire*, pr., pb. 1736 (English translation, 1763); *L'Enfant prodigue*, pr. 1736 (verse; prose translation *The Prodigal*, 1750?); *La Prude: Ou, La Grandeuse de Cassette*, wr. 1740, pr., pb. 1747 (verse; based on William Wycherley's play *The Plain Dealer*); *Zulime*, pr. 1740; *Mahomet*, pr., pb. 1742 (*Mahomet the Prophet*, 1744); *Mérope*, pr. 1743 (English translation, 1744, 1749); *La Princesse de Navarre*, pr., pb. 1745 (verse; music by Jean-Philippe Rameau); *Sémiramis*, pr. 1748 (*Semiramis*, 1760); *Nanine*, pr., pb. 1749 (English translation, 1927); *Oreste*, pr., pb. 1750; *Rome sauvée*, pr., pb. 1752; *L'Orphelin de la Chine*, pr., pb. 1755 (*The Orphan of China*, 1756); *Socrate*, pb. 1759 (*Socrates*, 1760); *L'Écossaise*, pr., pb. 1760 (*The Highland Girl*, 1760); *Tancrède*, pr. 1760; *Don Pèdre*, wr. 1761, pb. 1775; *Olympie*, pb. 1763; *Le Triumvirat*, pr. 1764; *Les Scythes*, pr., pb. 1767; *Les Guèbres: Ou, La Tolérance*, pb. 1769; *Sophonisbe*, pb. 1770 (revision of Jean Mairet's play); *Les Pélopides: Ou, Atrée et Thyeste*, pb. 1772; *Les Lois de Minos*, pb. 1773; *Irène*, pr. 1778; *Agathocle*, pr. 1779.

POETRY: *Poème sur la religion naturelle*, 1722; *La Ligue*, 1723; *La Henriade*, 1728 (a revision of *La Ligue*; *Henriade*, 1732); *Le Mondain*, 1736 (*The Man of the World*, 1764); *Discours en vers sur l'homme*, 1738 (*Discourses in Verse on Man*, 1764); *Poème de Fontenoy*, 1745; *Poème sur les événements de l'année 1744*, 1745; *Poème sur la loi naturelle*, 1752 (*On Natural Law*, 1764); *La Pucelle d'Orléans*, 1755, 1762 (*The Maid of Orleans*, 1758; also as *La Pucelle: Or, The Maid of Orleans*, 1785-1786); *Poème sur le désastre de Lisbonne*, 1756 (*Poem on the Lisbon Earthquake*, 1764); *Le Pauvre Diable*, 1758; *Épître à Horace*, 1772.

NONFICTION: *An Essay upon the Civil Wars of France . . . and Also upon the Epick Poetry of the European Nations from Homer Down to Milton*, 1727; *Histoire de Charles XII*, 1731 (*The History of Charles XII*, 1732); *Le Temple du goût*, 1733 (*The Temple of Taste*, 1734); *Letters Concerning the English Nation*, 1733; *Lettres philosophiques*, 1734 (originally published in English as *Letters Concerning the English Nation*, 1733; also as *Philosophical Letters*, 1961); *Discours de métaphysique*, 1736; *Éléments de la philosophie de Newton*, 1738 (*The Elements of Sir Isaac Newton's Philosophy*, 1738); *Vie de Molière*, 1739; *Le Siècle de Louis XIV*, 1751 (*The Age of Louis XIV*, 1752); *Essai sur les mœurs*, 1756, 1763 (*The General History and State of Europe*, 1754, 1759); *Traité sur la tolérance*, 1763 (*A Treatise on Religious Toleration*, 1764); *Dictionnaire philosophique portatif*, 1764, 1769 (enlarged as *La Raison par alphabet*, also known as *Dictionnaire philosophique*; *A Philosophical Dictionary for the Pocket*, 1765; also as *Philosophical Dictionary*, 1945); *Commentaires sur le théâtre de Pierre Corneille*, 1764; *Avis au public sur les parracides imputés aux calas et aux Sirven*, 1775; *Correspondence*, 1953-1965 (102 volumes).

MISCELLANEOUS: *The Works of M. de Voltaire*, 1761-1765 (35 volumes), 1761-1781 (38 volumes); *Candide and Other Writings*, 1945; *The Portable Voltaire*, 1949; *Candide, Zadig, and Selected Stories*, 1961; *The Complete Works of Voltaire*, 1968-1977 (135 volumes; in French).

BIBLIOGRAPHY

Aldridge, A. Owen. *Voltaire and the Century of Light*. Princeton, N.J.: Princeton University Press, 1975. A teacher and student of comparative literature, Aldridge reexamines the life and career of Voltaire within the context of European intellectual and political history, providing many useful insights in a pleasant style equally suited to the specialist as to the general reader. Also offered are stimulating readings of *Candide* and other selected works, together with a valuable bibliography.

Havens, George R. *The Age of Ideas*. New York: Henry Holt, 1955. Often reprinted and providing a model and inspiration for many writers, Havens's witty, informed overview of the Enlightenment and its precursors remains authoritative as a guide to trends and thinkers of the period. Contains groups of chapters devoted to Charles de Montesquieu, Voltaire, Denis Diderot, and Jean-Jacques Rousseau. The four chapters devoted to Voltaire provide an excellent introduction to the man and his work, with brief but perceptive readings of such texts as *Zadig* and *Candide*.

Hearsey, John E. N. *Voltaire*. New York: Barnes & Noble Books, 1976. Rich in anecdote and incident, Hearsey's biography sets out to bring Voltaire, his friends, and his enemies back to life for the benefit of the contemporary reader. On balance, Hearsey succeeds in his task, but the result often more closely resembles a novel than a serious study. The select bibliography is quite brief, of use only to the most general of readers.

Howells, Robin. *Disabled Powers: A Reading of Voltaire's Contes*. Amsterdam: Éditions Rodopi, 1993. A good examination of the works. Includes a bibliography.

_____. "Pleasure Principles: Tales, Infantile Naming, and Voltaire." *The Modern Language Review* 92 (April, 1997): 295-307. Suggests that one of the characteristics of the eighteenth century French prose tale is repetition, which includes "infantile naming"—repetitious or "nonsensical" phonetic practices typical of young children. Argues that naming in these tales by Voltaire and others offers various types of regressive satisfaction.

Mason, Haydn Trevor. *Candide: Optimism Demolished*. New York: Twayne, 1992. Divided into two parts: the literary and historical context (including critical reception); and a reading (the book's view of history, philosophy, personality, structure, and form). With notes and an annotated bibliography.

_____. *Voltaire*. New York: St. Martin's Press, 1975. Not to be confused with the biography published six years later and cited below, Mason's comprehensive monograph, intended for the interested undergraduate or general reader, steers clear of the traditional chronological approach in order to present Voltaire's work by genre, treating first his drama and dramatic criticism, proceeding thereafter to deal with historiography, short fiction, poetry, and polemics. Mason's approach, however unorthodox, proves quite effective, especially when dealing with the short fiction. Supplemented by a useful if brief bibliography.

_____. *Voltaire: A Biography*. Baltimore: The Johns Hopkins University Press, 1981. Building on the strengths implicit in his earlier, genre-oriented study of Voltaire's works, Mason here presents a concise but lively survey of his subject's life, clearly relating the major works to their context, including inspiration and/or (as is especially pertinent in the case of Voltaire) provocation. Closely documented, useful both as biography and as criticism, this volume is recommended to the student and to the general reader alike; those in search of a bibliography are, however, advised to consult Manson's earlier study cited above.

Vartanian, Aram. "*Zadig:* Theme and Counter-theme."

In *Dilemmas du roman*, edited by Catherine Lafarge. Saratoga, Calif.: Anima Libri, 1990. Argues that the philosophic theme of impersonal fate is counterpoised against a background theme which creates a contrapuntal movement of the narrative structure. Asserts the story is told in such a way that its overall meaning emerges from a network of tensions felt among its various elements.

Mary J. Sturm, updated by
David B. Parsell

KURT VONNEGUT

Born: Indianapolis, Indiana; November 11, 1922

PRINCIPAL SHORT FICTION

Canary in a Cat House, 1961
Welcome to the Monkey House, 1968
Bagombo Snuff Box: Uncollected Short Fiction, 1999
God Bless You, Dr. Kevorkian, 1999

OTHER LITERARY FORMS

Kurt Vonnegut has published numerous volumes, including essays, short stories, the plays *Happy Birthday, Wanda June* and *Between Time and Timbuktu: Or, Prometheus-5, a Space Fantasy* (1972), and the novels on which his reputation is principally based. His best-known novels include *The Sirens of Titan* (1959), *Cat's Cradle* (1963), *Slaughterhouse-Five: Or, The Children's Crusade, a Duty-Dance with Death* (1969), and *Breakfast of Champions* (1973), and he published *Timequake* in 1997.

ACHIEVEMENTS

For many years, the popular success of the writing of Kurt Vonnegut exceeded critical recognition of his work. With his earlier work labeled as science fiction and published in paperback editions and popular magazines such as *Ladies' Home Journal* and *The*

Saturday Evening Post, critical attention was delayed. In 1986, Vonnegut received the Bronze Medallion from Guild Hall.

BIOGRAPHY

Although not specifically an autobiographical writer, Kurt Vonnegut has frequently drawn on facts and incidents from his own life in his writing. The youngest in a family of three children, Kurt Vonnegut, Jr., was born and reared in Indianapolis, Indiana. While serving in the army as an infantry scout during World War II, he was taken prisoner by the Germans and interned at Dresden, Germany, at the time of the 1945 Allied firebombing of the city that cost 135,000 lives. He survived only through the ironic circumstance of being quartered in an underground meat locker. This episode contributed much toward his authorial distance: After returning to that meat locker forty-three years later in 1998, Vonnegut commented that he is one of the few who could recall the destruction of an Atlantis.

Although the destruction of Dresden became a recurring motif in Vonnegut's work, not until twenty-three years later could he bring himself to write the novel of his war experiences, *Slaughterhouse-Five*. After the war, Vonnegut worked in public relations for General Electric in Schenectady, New York

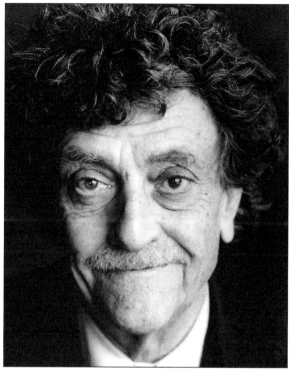

Kurt Vonnegut, Jr. (Jill Krementz)

(called "Ilium" in his fiction), before leaving in 1950 to devote himself full-time to his writing. In 1945, he married Jane Marie Cox, settling in Cape Cod, where they reared their own three children and the three children of Vonnegut's deceased sister, Alice. In 1972, he moved to New York City and was divorced from Cox early in 1974. He was married to the photographer Jill Krementz in November, 1979, and they adopted a daughter, Lily. They were divorced in 1991.

ANALYSIS

After the publication of his masterpiece, *Slaughterhouse-Five*, however, the work of Kurt Vonnegut received increasingly serious critical commentary. He has emerged as a consistent commentator on American culture through the second half of the twentieth century. His short stories range from satiric visions of grotesque future societies, which are extensions of modern societies, and portrayals of ordinary people, which reassert the stability of middle-class values. In his novels, the social satire predominates, and Vonnegut blends whimsical humor and something approaching despair as he exposes the foibles of American culture and a world verging on destruction through human thoughtlessness. As in the short stories, however, attention to an unheroic protagonist doing his or her best and to the value of "common human decency" persists.

Best known for his novels, Vonnegut has acknowledged the ancillary interest of short stories for him. In the preface to his collection of short stories *Welcome to the Monkey House*, he describes the stories as "work I sold in order to finance the writing of the novels. Here one finds the fruits of Free Enterprise." Vonnegut's blunt comment, however, does not imply that the stories can be dismissed out of hand. The themes of the stories are the themes and concerns of all his work. Again, in the preface to *Welcome to the Monkey House*, Vonnegut describes those concerns in a characteristically tough style. He recalls a letter his brother sent him shortly after bringing his firstborn home from the hospital: "Here I am," that letter began, "cleaning the shit off of practically everything." Of his sister, Vonnegut tells us that she died of cancer: "her dying words were 'No pain.' Those are good dying words. . . . I realize now that the two main themes of my novels were stated by my siblings: 'Here I am cleaning the shit off of practically everything' and 'No pain.'" These terms apply equally well to the themes of Vonnegut's short stories. His muckraking is frequently social satire; his concern is with the alleviation of human suffering.

Vonnegut's short stories generally fall into two broad categories: those that are science fiction, and those that are not. The science fiction characteristically pictures a future society controlled by government and technology, whose norms have made human life grotesque. The protagonist is often an outlaw who has found such norms or conventions intolerable.

In contrast, Vonnegut's stories that are not science fiction regularly affirm social norms. Ordinary life in these stories is simply not threatened by large-scale social evil. Some of these stories indeed depict the victims of society—refugees, displaced persons, juvenile delinquents—but primarily they show such people's efforts to recover or establish conventional lives. It is within the context of conventional life that Vonnegut's protagonists can achieve those qualities which in his view give a person stability and a sense of worth. These are the qualities of modesty, considerateness (which he often calls common human decency), humor, order, and pride in one's work. They are values interfered with, in the science-fiction stories, by governmental and technological controls.

Vonnegut has resented any dismissal of his work merely because it is science fiction, a kind of writing he describes as incorporating "technology in the human equation." In the novel, *God Bless You, Mr. Rosewater* (1965), Eliot Rosewater speaks for Vonnegut when he delivers an impassioned, drunken, and impromptu defense of the genre before a convention of science-fiction writers:

> I love you sons of bitches. . . . You're all I read any more. . . . You're the only ones with guts enough to *really* care about the future, who *really* notice what machines do to us, what wars do to us, what cities do to us, what big, simple ideas do to us, what tremendous misunderstandings, mistakes, accidents and catastrophes do to us.

In Eliot Rosewater's opinion, society's "greatest prophet" is an obscure writer of science fiction named Kilgore Trout, a recurring character in Vonnegut's fiction. His masterpiece, the work for which he will be revered in the far future, is a book entitled *2BR02B*, a rephrasing of Hamlet's famous question.

"WELCOME TO THE MONKEY HOUSE"

The story of *2BR02B*, in Vonnegut's précis, corresponds closely to his own short story, "Welcome to the Monkey House." Vonnegut writes of his fictional character, "Trout's favorite formula was to describe a perfectly hideous society, not unlike his own, and then, toward the end, to suggest ways in which it could be improved." The approach describes Vonnegut's writing as well. *2BR02B* predicates an America crippled by automation and overpopulation. Machines have taken over most jobs, leaving people idle and feeling "silly and pointless." The government's solution has been to encourage patriotic suicide. Ethical Suicide Parlors have been widely estab-

lished, each identifiable by its purple roof and each located next to a Howard Johnson's restaurant (with its orange roof), where the prospective client is entitled to a free last meal.

This is also the world of "Welcome to the Monkey House." The story takes place in Cape Cod in an unspecified future time. Fourteen Kennedys, by now, have served as presidents of the United States or of the world. There is a world government; in fact, in this world, Vonnegut writes, "practically everything was the Government." Most people look twenty-two years old, thanks to the development of antiaging shots. The population of the world numbers seventeen billion people. For Vonnegut, the world's dilemma is the result of advanced technology combined with backward human attitudes. Suicide is voluntary, but everyone, under law, must use "ethical" birth control pills that, in fact, control not birth but sexuality. Their effect is to make people numb below the waist, depriving them not of the ability to reproduce, "which would have been unnatural and immoral," but rather of all pleasure in sex. "Thus did science and morals go hand in hand," Vonnegut ironically concludes.

The kind of morality that could produce these pills is exemplified in J. Edgar Nation, their inventor. Walking through the Grand Rapids Zoo with his eleven children one Easter, he had been so offended by the behavior of the animals that he promptly developed a pill "that would make monkeys in the springtime fit things for a Christian family to see." In the opinion of Billy the Poet, a renegade in this society, throughout history those people most eager "to tell everybody exactly how God Almighty wants things here on Earth" have been unaccountably terrified of human sexuality.

Billy the Poet's special campaign is to deflower hostesses in Ethical Suicide Parlors, who are all, as part of their qualifications for the job, "plump and rosy" virgins at least six feet tall. Their uniform is a purple body stocking "with nothing underneath" and black leather boots. In this world, only death is permitted to be seductive. Billy's modus operandi is to single out a hostess and send her some bawdy doggerel, calculated to offend (and to excite) narrow sensibilities. Nancy McLuhan, his present target, is more intrigued than she will admit to herself. Billy kidnaps her and takes her to his current hideout, the old Kennedy compound at Hyannis Port, now "a museum of how life had been lived in more expansive times. The museum was closed." The original lawn is now green cement; the harbor is blue cement. The whole of the compound is covered by an enormous plastic geodesic dome through which light can filter. The only "light" in which an earlier graciousness can now be seen is colored by the world's pervasive vulgarity. The current world president, named "Ma" Kennedy but not the "real thing," keeps a sign reading "Thimk!" on the wall of her office in the Taj Mahal.

Nancy's encounter with Billy is not the licentious orgy she expects but an approximation of an old-fashioned wedding night. Billy explains to her that most people only gradually develop a full appreciation of their sexuality. Embarrassed and confused, she tries conscientiously to resist her comprehension of his motives. As he leaves, Billy offers Nancy another poem, this time the famous sonnet by Elizabeth Barrett Browning that begins "How do I love thee? Let me count the ways." The implication is that sexuality is one dimension of human love sorely lacking in their world. Far from being obscene, that love pursues a larger "ideal Grace," in the words of the poem, wholly unavailable either to the vulgarity of "Ma" Kennedy or to the narrow-minded purity of J. Edgar Nation. Billy also leaves with Nancy a bottle of birth-control pills that will not hamper sexual enjoyment. On the label are printed the words "WELCOME TO THE MONKEY HOUSE." If Browning's poem risks sentimentality, the story ends in a comic readjustment of the reader's sense of proportion. Sex need not be humorless; the reader need not view himself and the human condition with the chilling seriousness and inflated self-importance of J. Edgar Nation. The reader is left with the impression that Nancy McLuhan has begun her conversion. There is a measure of hope in this world where, as Billy assures her, the "movement is growing by leaps and bounds."

"HARRISON BERGERON"

Governmental domination of private life is nearly total, however, in the world of "Harrison Bergeron,"

whose inhabitants are tortured and shackled as a matter of course, all in the name of equality. In the United States of 2081, equality of all persons has been mandated by the 211th, 212th, and 213th Amendments to the Constitution. People are not merely equal under the law, but "equal every which way." Those people of "abnormal" capacities must wear equalizing handicaps at all times. Hazel Bergeron is a person of average intelligence, which means that "she couldn't think about anything except in short bursts." Her husband, George, however, as a man of superior intelligence, has to wear a "mental handicap radio" in his ear which broadcasts at twenty-second intervals strident noises designed to break his concentration: burglar alarms, sirens, an automobile collision, or a twenty-gun salute. A strong man as well, George wears "forty-seven pounds of bird shot in a canvas bag" padlocked around his neck.

Neither George nor his wife is able to recall that their fourteen-year-old son, Harrison, has just been arrested. They are watching on television a performance by ballerinas also weighted down with bird shot and masked to disguise their beauty. As a law-abiding couple, George and Hazel have only fleeting suspicions that the system is a bad one. If not for such handicaps, George says, "pretty soon we'd be right back to the dark ages again, with everybody competing against everybody else." When the television announcer cannot deliver a news bulletin because he—"like all announcers"—has a serious speech impediment, Hazel's response is a well-meaning platitude, "he tried. That's the big thing." A ballerina, disguising her "unfair" voice, reads the announcement for him: Harrison Bergeron, "a genius and an athlete," has escaped from jail.

Suddenly Harrison bursts into the television studio. A "walking junkyard," he wears tremendous earphones, thick glasses, three hundred pounds of scrap metal, a rubber ball on his nose, and black caps on his teeth. In this reductio ad absurdum of the ideal of equality, the technology is pointedly silly. "I am the Emperor!" Harrison cries, and tears off his handicaps, revealing a man who "would have awed Thor, the god of thunder." Harrison is rival to the gods. A ballerina joins him as his empress. Freed of her restraits, she is "blindingly beautiful." Whatever the reader may perceive as ultimate human beauty, Harrison and the ballerina are that. Together the two of them dance in "an explosion of joy and grace" equally as fantastic as the shackles they have thrown off. They leap thirty feet to kiss the ceiling and hover midair to embrace each other, "neutralizing gravity with love and pure will." They have defied the laws of the land, the law of gravity, the laws of motion. They dance out the soaring aspiration of the human spirit, for a moment made triumphantly manifest.

The United States Handicapper General, ironically named Diana Moon Glampers, then breaks into the television studio and shoots them both. Her ruthless efficiency is in marked contrast to the bumbling capabilities of everyone else. The reader is suddenly aware that the idea of equality has been made an instrument of social control. Clearly some are allowed to be more equal than others. In their home, Harrison's parents are incapable of either grief or joy. They resume their passive, acquiescent lives, having forgotten the entire scene almost as soon as they witnessed it.

If the conventional life depicted in Vonnegut's work other than his science fiction has not been made this grotesque by technology and government, it is, nevertheless, also humdrum and uninspiring. These limitations, however, are more than compensated for by the fact that ordinary people feel useful, not superfluous, and they are capable of sustaining love. This dynamic is especially true of "Poor Little Rich Town," first published in *Collier's* and reprinted in *Bagombo Snuff Box*. In this story an entire village rejects the wisdom of an efficiency expert, Newell Cady. The bonds of community love win over logic, because the townspeople do not want the postmistress to lose her job.

"Go Back to Your Precious Wife and Son"

In "Go Back to Your Precious Wife and Son" the narrator's occupation is selling and installing "aluminum combination storm windows and screens" and occasionally a bathtub enclosure. He marks as "the zenith of [his] career" an order for a glass door for a film star's bathtub specially fixed with a life-sized picture of the film star's face on it. He is comically intent on installing the enclosure and on doing the job

well, even as the star's household disintegrates around him. Yet if it is funny, the narrator's pride in his mundane work is also the basis of stability in his life, a stability visibly lacking in the apparently glamorous life of Gloria Hilton, the film star. Also installing two windows for her, he says about them,

> The Fleetwood Trip-L-Trak is our first-line window, so there isn't anything quick or dirty about the way we put them up. . . . You can actually fill up a room equipped with Fleetwoods with water, fill it clear up to the ceiling, and it won't leak—not through the windows, anyway.

While the narrator is at work in the bathroom, Gloria Hilton is engaged in dismissing her fifth husband. She speaks to him, as she always speaks, in a series of fatuous clichés. She tells him, "You don't know the meaning of love," after earlier seducing him away from his family with the words, "Dare to be happy, my poor darling! Oh, darling, we were *made* for each other!" She had then promptly announced to the press that the two of them were moving to New Hampshire "to find ourselves." In the narrator's (and the reader's) only glimpse of Gloria Hilton, she is without makeup ("she hadn't even bothered to draw on eyebrows") and dressed in a bathrobe. He decides, "that woman wasn't any prettier than a used studio couch." Her actual commonplaceness and utter self-absorption are patent.

Her hapless fifth husband is a writer, George Murra, of whom she had expected no less than "the most beautiful scenario anybody in the history of literature has ever written for me." In the constant publicity and tempestuousness of their lives together, however, he has been unable to work at all. He had been lured by a hollow glamour, she by the possibility of greater self-glorification. The superficiality of their marriage is revealed in his references to her as "Miss Hilton," and her contemptuous parting words: "Go on back to your precious wife and your precious son."

In a long drinking session together after Gloria leaves, Murra explains to the narrator his earlier dreams of breaking free from the petty marital squabbles, the financial worries, the drab responsibility and sameness of conventional life. The narrator momentarily and drunkenly succumbs to the appeal of the glamorous life; when he staggers home he immediately offends his wife. Murra is now repentant and nearly desperate for the forgiveness of his son, living at a nearby preparatory school. When the boy arrives to visit his father, it is apparent that the hurt and bitterness of his father's desertion have made him rigid with intolerant rectitude. The situation looks hopeless until the narrator (back to finish his job) suggests to Murra that he topple the boy from his pedestal with a kick in the pants. The gambit works, the family is reconciled, and the narrator returns home, having agreed to exchange bathtub doors with Murra. He finds his own wife gone and his own son stuffily self-righteous; but his wife returns, her equanimity restored. The new bathtub enclosure with Gloria's face on it amuses his wife. She is exactly Gloria's height; when she showers, the film star's face on the door forms a "mask" for her. Gloria's glamour is all mask and pose; but his wife's good humor is genuine. The ordinary lives of the narrator and his wife have provided them with exactly what Gloria lacks and what Murra and his son need to recover: the saving grace of humor, tolerance, and a sense of proportion.

BAGOMBO SNUFF BOX

The 1999 publication of *Bagombo Snuff Box* presented again several of the previous stories, plus others that achieved magazine exposure in the 1950's and 1960's but had since been forgotten. In the introduction to this volume, Vonnegut explains that his stories are "a bunch of Buddhist catnaps" designed to slow the pulse and breathing and allow one's troubles to fade away. He also provides his eight rules for writing stories in this introduction. Only three of the twenty-three stories here could be construed as futuristic. The title story focuses on a braggart who attempts to win favor with a former wife by false exaggeration of the exotic snuffbox, which her son quickly identifies as a common item. As in his previous work, the high and mighty are deflated and the average person is ennobled. George M. Helmholtz, a band director, is the qualified hero of three of these stories. An authorial "coda" at the end of the volume argues for the importance of the "Middle West" of Ohio and Indiana.

Despite the fact that most of Vonnegut's short stories are not science fiction and similarly applaud conventional life, the happy triumph of kindness and work seems contrary to the thrust of his novels. What he values remains the same, but the prospect of realizing those values becomes more desperate as the vision of normalcy recedes. The crises of the planet are too extreme and the capabilities of technology too great for Vonnegut to imagine a benign society in the future which could foster those values.

Vonnegut's novels are often described as "black humor," wholly unlike the generous good humor of "Go Back to Your Precious Wife and Son." This is another label that annoys the author ("just a convenient tag for reviewers"), but his description of black humor recalls his own lonely rebels whose cause is seriously overmatched by the monolithic enemy: "Black humorists' holy wanderers find nothing but junk and lies and idiocy wherever they go." Vonnegut has said that the writer functions like the canaries coal miners took with them into the mines "to detect gas before men got sick." He must serve society as an early-warning system so that one can work to improve the human condition while one still may.

OTHER MAJOR WORKS

LONG FICTION: *Player Piano*, 1952; *The Sirens of Titan*, 1959; *Mother Night*, 1961; *Cat's Cradle*, 1963; *God Bless You, Mr. Rosewater: Or, Pearls Before Swine*, 1965; *Slaughterhouse-Five: Or, The Children's Crusade, a Duty-Dance with Death*, 1969; *Breakfast of Champions: Or, Goodbye Blue Monday*, 1973; *Slapstick: Or, Lonesome No More!*, 1976; *Jailbird*, 1979; *Deadeye Dick*, 1982; *Galápagos*, 1985; *Bluebeard*, 1987; *Hocus Pocus*, 1990; *Timequake*, 1997.

PLAY: *Happy Birthday, Wanda June*, pb. 1970.

TELEPLAYS: *Between Time and Timbuktu: Or, Prometheus-5, a Space Fantasy*, 1972.

NONFICTION: *Wampeters, Foma, and Granfalloons (Opinions)*, 1974; *Palm Sunday: An Autobiographical Collage*, 1981; *Conversations with Kurt Vonnegut*, 1988; *Fates Worse than Death: An Autobiographical Collage of the 1980's*, 1991.

CHILDREN'S LITERATURE: *Sun Moon Star*, 1980 (with Ivan Chermayeff).

BIBLIOGRAPHY

Broer, Lawrence R. *Sanity Plea: Schizophrenia in the Novels of Kurt Vonnegut*. Ann Arbor, Mich.: UMI Research Press, 1988. This volume focuses on the theme of social neurosis, with emphasis on schizophrenic behavior in the main characters of the novels through *Bluebeard*. The thesis has relevance to a number of the short stories and gives insight into the evolution of Vonnegut's fiction.

Giannone, Richard. *Vonnegut: A Preface to His Novels*. Port Washington, N.Y.: Kennikat, 1977. Treats the novels up to *Slapstick* and the play *Happy Birthday, Wanda June*, in the context of Vonnegut's life and times. Emphasizes developing themes and techniques connecting the novels, with chapters devoted to individual novels.

Klinkowitz, Jerome, Julie Huffman-Klinkowitz, and Asa B. Pieratt, Jr. *Kurt Vonnegut, Jr.: A Comprehensive Bibliography*. Hamden, Conn.: Archon Books, 1987. An authoritative bibliography of works by and about Vonnegut. Lists Vonnegut's works in all their editions, including the short stories in their original places of publication, dramatic and cinematic adaptations, interviews, reviews, secondary sources, and dissertations.

_____. *"Slaughterhouse-Five": Reforming the Novel and the World*. Boston: Twayne, 1990. This book contains the most thorough and most modern treatment available of *Slaughterhouse-Five*. With care and insight, Klinkowitz debunks earlier, fatalistic interpretations of the novel. Features a comprehensive chronology, a thorough bibliography, and an index.

_____. *Vonnegut in Fact: The Public Spokesmanship of Personal Fiction*. Columbia: University of South Carolina Press, 1998. Klinkowitz makes a case for Vonnegut as a sort of redeemer of the novelistic form, after writers such as Philip Roth declared it dead. He traces Vonnegut's successful integration of autobiography and fiction in his body of work. Provides an extensive bibliography and an index.

_____, and David L. Lawler, eds. *Vonnegut in America: An Introduction to the Life and Work of Kurt Vonnegut*. New York: Delacorte Press, 1977. A collection of essays ranging from biography and an "album" of family photographs to Vonnegut as satirist, science-fiction writer, and short-story writer. Discusses his reputation in the Soviet Union and Europe. Contains an authoritative bibliography.

_____, and John Somer, eds. *The Vonnegut Statement*. New York: Delacorte Press, 1973. A collection of essays by various authors, which establishes the nature and sources of Vonnegut's reputation at this important juncture. Analyzes his career from his college writing to the short fiction, and through the novels to *Slaughterhouse-Five*. Includes an interview and a bibliography. The most important accounting of his career through its first two decades.

Merrill, Robert, ed. *Critical Essays on Kurt Vonnegut*. Boston: G. K. Hall, 1990. A comprehensive collection of essays on Vonnegut's works and career, which includes reviews, previously published essays, and articles commissioned for this work. The extensive introduction traces in detail Vonnegut's career and critical reception from the beginnings to 1990.

Nuwer, Hank. "Kurt Vonnegut Close Up." *The Saturday Evening Post* 258 (May/June, 1986): 38-39. A biographical sketch which discusses Vonnegut's writing career, noting that his work often deals with the subject of man's inability to cope with technology.

Reed, Peter J. *The Short Fiction of Kurt Vonnegut*. Westport, Conn.: Greenwood Press, 1997. A critical study of the author's short fiction. Includes a bibliography and an index.

_____, and Marc Leeds, eds. *The Vonnegut Chronicles: Interviews and Essays*. Westport, Conn.: Greenwood Press, 1996. Vonnegut discusses, among other topics, postmodernism and experimental fiction. Includes a bibliography and an index.

Schatt, Stanley. *Kurt Vonnegut, Jr.* Boston: Twayne, 1976. Discusses the first eight novels, with separate chapters on the short stories and on the plays. Includes a chronology, a biography, and a bibliography up to 1975.

Stone, Brad. "Vonnegut's Last Stand." *Newsweek* 130 (September 29, 1997): 78. A biographical sketch that focuses on *Timequake*, which Vonnegut has called his last book.

Vonnegut, Kurt, Jr. Interview by Wendy Smith. *Publishers Weekly* 228 (October 25, 1985): 68-69. Vonnegut discusses his writing career, censorship, and his work; notes that Vonnegut is an ardent foe of book censorship and has strong words for those who seek to limit the free speech of others.

Martha Meek, updated by Peter J. Reed
and Scott D. Vander Ploeg

W

JOHN WAIN

Born: Stoke-on-Trent, Staffordshire, England; March 14, 1925
Died: Oxford, England; May 24, 1994

OTHER LITERARY FORMS

John Wain built his reputation as a novelist in the 1950's, his first novel being *Hurry on Down* (1953), which was published in the United States as *Born in Captivity* in 1954 and which was followed in subsequent decades by *Where the Rivers Meet* (1988), *Comedies* (1990), and *Hungry Generations* (1994). His further efforts include several volumes of poetry, criticism, and literary biography. Among his plays is *Johnson Is Leaving: A Monodrama* (pb. 1994). He also wrote *Sprightly Running: Part of an Autobiography* (1962) in which he declared, "I would be a short-story writer [over being a novelist] if it weren't so impossible to make a living at it."

An influential essayist, editor, critic, and literary biographer, Wain believes his poetry to be his most important literary contribution.

ACHIEVEMENTS

John Wain won the Somerset Maugham Award in 1958 for *Preliminary Essays* (1957), the James Tait Black Memorial Prize and Heinemann Bequest Award in 1975 for *Samuel Johnson* (1974) and the Whitbread Literary Award in 1985 for *Young Shoulders* (1982; pb. in U.S. as *The Free Zone Starts Here*, 1982). In 1973, he was elected the twenty-seventh professor of poetry at the University of Oxford. He holds honorary degrees from the University of Keele and the University of Loughborough and became an honorary fellow of St. John's College, Oxford University, in 1985.

BIOGRAPHY

John Barrington Wain was born in Staffordshire, England, in 1925, the son of a dentist. After he was found unfit to join the armed forces because of poor eyesight, he went in 1943 to St. John's College, Oxford, being graduated in 1946 and staying on for three years as a Fereday Fellow. At Oxford he began to publish his first verse and met Kingsley Amis and Philip Larkin, both of whom spoke both respectfully and venomously of him in conversation and memoir. He left teaching and became a full-time writer in 1955. In 1953, he served as host of the British Broadcasting Corporation's "First Reading" program, which became a springboard for the British movement poets. Although he objected to being classified as one of the "Angry Young Men," the label stuck. Because Wain, Amis, and John Osborne, all near thirty years old, were writing social protest and caustic humor, they were inevitably—if artificially—grouped by critics. Despite their individual differences, they did have the collective effect of sharpening England's social sensibility and invigorating its literature. Wain and his second wife Eirian James had three sons; she died in 1988. He married Patricia Dunn the next year. In 1994, Wain died of a stroke.

ANALYSIS

Though frequently categorized as one of the "Angry Young Men" of the 1950's, John Wain claims that his work is not decidedly bitter. Still, his reputation as a debunker of rigid English society and an apologist for the alienated young man has persisted. While

Wain's short stories are disciplined and energetic, he is at times an acerbic social critic and frequently writes with a strong moral cast. Typically, Wain's stories concern the internal conflict of a first-person narrator. The narrator usually is not very perceptive, whether for lack of intelligence or maturity. A frequent effect of Wain's stories is that a conflict is well developed, human narrowness is scourged with satire, and a thematic irony is made unmistakably clear. His early stories reflected his "angry" mood of the 1950's but also show concern for a wide range of topics.

"MASTER RICHARD" AND "A MESSAGE FROM THE PIG-MAN"

Two stories from Wain's first collection *Nuncle and Other Stories* provide insight into his early short fiction. Both "Master Richard" and "A Message from the Pig-Man" are dominated by the perceptions of their child-protagonists. Richard, a five-year-old prodigy, is the narrator of his story. It develops by means of the diary convention, with Richard recording his observations secretly in a notebook. The boy gauges his maturity of mind at roughly thirty-five because the conversation of adults is easily comprehensible. Such a voice puts considerable strain on the narrative credibility of the story.

Richard reads, writes, and types with the facility of an adult. Wain makes a few concessions to the age of his narrator: He faces pain and cries like any other child and throws china cups to get attention. At the other extreme, the boy has a sense of perspective that belies that of the most precocious child. He carries out a long conditioning process to prepare his parents gradually for the realization that he has learned to read on his own. The very notion of patience over a long period of time is alien to the mind of even a very bright child. Further, Richard makes jokes and uses a vocabulary of slang that cannot be accounted for, since these abilities come almost entirely from experience. The greatest breach of credibility occurs when Richard speaks of the absurd and of insanity, constructs that only time and experience—not precocity—can bring to the consciousness. The problem is that no clear frame of reference is established for the reader. The narrator's situation, environment, and

John Wain (AP/Wide World Photos)

comments are based on the presumption of conventional reality as the norm of the story; Richard's unique perception, however, forces the reader to view the story as somewhat surrealistic. The narrative exhibits both realism and surrealism but is committed consistently to neither, and the ambivalence is disconcerting.

Richard's crisis comes with the birth of a younger brother, whom he hates jealously. As a result of his contempt for his own cruelty to his brother and for his parents, who cannot understand him, he coolly decides to commit suicide. This conclusion, which has not been prepared for in the development of the story, is more convenient than satisfying.

Unlike "Master Richard," "A Message from the Pig-Man" is thoroughly believable. Eric, the viewpoint character, is also five years old, but the narrative is third-person, giving Wain more room to maneuver in disclosing the story. The thematic function of the boy's sensibility in the story is to comment on the need to confront fear. Eric finally faces the Pig-man, whom he assumes to be a grotesque creature rather than an old man simply collecting scraps for his pigs. He goes out with some scraps at his mother's insistence and tells himself, "It was the same as getting into icy cold water. If it was the end, if the Pig-man seized him by the hand and dragged him off to his hut, well, so much the worse."

Although his fear has a comic effect, it teaches the central lesson of the story. Once he has faced the Pig-man and found him harmless, he returns home to be put off when he asks his mother and his new stepfather why his father cannot live with them. Lacking Eric's courage to face up to problems, they hedge instead of answering. The viewpoint of the child generates humor and provides insight into the deeper weaknesses of adults; still the concluding irony is too heavy.

"KING CALIBAN"

This powerful story may well be Wain's most widely read on both sides of the Atlantic. Originally published in *The Saturday Evening Post*, it leads off *Death of the Hind Legs and Other Stories*, his second collection, just as it does his fourth, *King Caliban and Other Stories*. Despite a predictable outcome, the story is effective because of the flashback narration of the cocky, street-smart Bert, who takes on caretaker duties for Fred, his older brother ("as strong as three men and as honest as daylight"). "Short of grey matter," Fred works as a handyman in the same office managed by his wife Dorene. To make more money, brother and wife inveigle the gentle Fred into professional wrestling as King Caliban ("some kind of monster on a desert island"). Neither can understand Fred's simple moral outrage at the gratuitous violence and bloodthirsty taunting. First, the anguished Fred injures an opponent and later nearly kills a heckler. Bert walks away from the situation unscathed and uncomprehending, leaving his bewildered brother to face the consequences. The strength of "King Caliban" is its deft interlocking of two major themes, -corruption-of-innocence and innocence-of-corruption, within the narrative without commentary.

DEATH OF HIND LEGS AND OTHER STORIES

Death of Hind Legs and Other Stories also contains two stories of adultery—"Come in Captain Grindle" and "Further Education"—in which Wain captures the casual, amoral sordidness of contemporary mores. The issue is not simply sexual. At their core—in "King Caliban" too—is the willingness to manipulate people for personal ends. In "Giles and Penelope," a young woman comes to realize that her lover uses her as a pawn. In the end she demands to be treated as what she in fact is—a kept woman. At first appalled, Giles finally accepts, excited by the prospect of using, then discarding, Penelope, when it suits him.

The stories in *The Life Guard*, Wain's last important collection (his third) are more sophisticated than the earlier ones. In the title story there is overdone irony in the death of Hopper, who actually drowns when he is supposed to be acting out the part to make Jimmy look necessary as lifeguard. Despite the unrestrained turn of plot, the story achieves substance and interest as the narrative lets the reader see Jimmy's desperation. As a dull boy, he is in his element when he gets the job of lifeguard at the beach. He fears the future and lacks ambition, but he has skill and confidence in the water. Eager to prove that he is useful on the calm shore, Jimmy decides to win attention by appearing to save Hopper's life. When he sees that Hopper really is in trouble, he is faced with exactly the kind of test he had been waiting for all summer, only he fails, and Hopper dies. In Jimmy's moral and physical agony as he brings Hopper to land, there is considerable dramatic energy—almost enough to make the reader overlook the predictable conclusion.

"WHILE THE SUN SHINES"

Another story from the collection, "While the Sun Shines," shows considerable control and is one of Wain's best stories by far. The conflict here between the tractor driver, the unnamed first-person narrator, and Robert, the son of the absent farm owner, is well drawn. First-person narration is particularly appropriate because the external conflict of the story is secondary to what goes on in the narrator's mind. Another man was seriously injured when the tractor overturned as he tried to mow a dangerously steep hill. When Robert orders the narrator to try the same task, he refuses more out of spite than fear. Later, however, he takes on the challenge, not for Robert's sake, but for his own, and possibly to impress Robert's roving wife Yvonne. The appeal she holds for the narrator adds a subtle dimension to the story. Although he knows she is a woman who uses men, she appeals to him more than he will admit. Thus in retrospect there is a question as to whether the narrator mastered the hill entirely for himself, as he thinks, or for Yvonne as well. Because he professes contempt for her throughout the story, his yielding to her at the end is a surprise, but a very effective one. The man who tells the story is ironically unaware of his own motives. He concludes, "What could I do? Another time, I'd have gone straight back to Mary and the kids. But today I was the king, I'd won and it was a case of winner take all." He goes from the tractor to her bed, and there is some question as to who has really won the day. The strength of the piece lies in what Wain does not say outright.

There is no doubt that Wain's concern as a writer is well placed; the problems he chooses to present are significant. The weakness in his short stories is a lack of restraint. When he makes the necessary effort to say less explicitly and more implicitly, his stories gain the light touch and resonance that mark good writing.

OTHER MAJOR WORKS

LONG FICTION: *Hurry on Down*, 1953 (pb. in U.S. as *Born in Captivity*, 1954); *Living in the Present*, 1955; *The Contenders*, 1958; *A Travelling Woman*, 1959; *Strike the Father Dead*, 1962; *The Young Visitors*, 1965; *The Smaller Sky*, 1967; *A Winter in the Hills*, 1970; *The Pardoner's Tale*, 1978; *Young Shoulders*, 1982 (pb. in U.S. as *The Free Zone Starts Here*, 1982); *Where the Rivers Meet*, 1988; *Comedies*, 1990; *Hungry Generations*, 1994.

PLAYS: *Harry in the Night: An Optimistic Comedy*, pr. 1975; *Johnson Is Leaving: A Monodrama*, pb. 1994.

TELEPLAY: *Young Shoulders*, 1984 (with Robert Smith).

RADIO PLAYS: *You Wouldn't Remember*, 1978; *A Winter in the Hills*, 1981; *Frank*, 1982.

POETRY: *Mixed Feelings*, 1951; *A Word Carved on a Sill*, 1956; *A Song About Major Eatherly*, 1961; *Weep Before God: Poems*, 1961; *Wildtrack: A Poem*, 1965; *Letters to Five Artists*, 1969; *The Shape of Feng*, 1972; *Feng: A Poem*, 1975; *Poems for the Zo-*

diac, 1980; *Thinking About Mr. Person*, 1980; *Poems, 1949-1979*, 1981; *The Twofold*, 1981; *Open Country*, 1987.

NONFICTION: *Preliminary Essays*, 1957; *Gerard Manley Hopkins: An Idiom of Desperation*, 1959; *Sprightly Running: Part of an Autobiography*, 1962; *Essays on Literature and Ideas*, 1963; *The Living World of Shakespeare: A Playgoer's Guide*, 1964; *Arnold Bennett*, 1967; *A House for the Truth: Critical Essays*, 1972; *Samuel Johnson*, 1974; *Professing Poetry*, 1977; *Samuel Johnson 1709-1784*, 1984 (with Kai Kin Yung); *Dear Shadows: Portraits from Memory*, 1986.

CHILDREN'S LITERATURE: *Lizzie's Floating Shop*, 1981.

EDITED TEXTS: *Contemporary Reviews of Romantic Poetry*, 1953; *Interpretations: Essays on Twelve English Poems*, 1955; *International Literary Annual*, 1959, 1960; *Fanny Burney's Diary*, 1960; *Anthology of Modern Poetry*, 1963; *Selected Shorter Poems of Thomas Hardy*, 1966; *Selected Shorter Stories of Thomas Hardy*, 1966; *Thomas Hardy's "The Dynasts,"* 1966; *Shakespeare: Macbeth, a Casebook*, 1968; *Shakespeare: Othello, a Casebook*, 1971; *Johnson as Critic*, 1973; *The New Wessex Selection of Thomas Hardy's Poetry*, 1978 (with Eirian James).

BIBLIOGRAPHY

Amis, Kingsley, *Kingsley Amis: Memoirs*. New York: Summit Books, 1991. Gives a vivid glimpse of infighting among aspiring writers. Amis hints wryly that Wain envied the bestsellerdom of *Lucky Jim* that placed his own first novel, *Hurry on Down*, into the shade.

Bayley, John. "Obituary: John Wain." *The Independent*, May 25, 1994, p. 14. In this biographical sketch of Wain's life and literary career, Bayley compares him with Kingsley Amis and praises his biography of Samuel Johnson.

Burgess, Anthony. *The Novel Now: A Guide to Contemporary Fiction*. New York: W. W. Norton, 1967. Expanded from an earlier study, Burgess's work groups Wain with other class-conscious British fiction writers.

Gerard, David E. *John Wain*. Westport, Conn.: Meckler, 1987. Contains a comprehensive annotated bibliography of Wain's work. Lists materials of critical and biographical interest, including radio, television, and sound recordings.

Gindin, James J. *Postwar British Fiction: New Accents and Attitudes*. Berkeley: University of California Press, 1962. Gindin's chapter "The Moral Center of John Wain's Fiction" discusses Wain's use of morality as a thematic and structural device and claims that each novel contains a central statement of the moral worth of the individual.

Heptonstall, Geoffrey. "Remembering John Wain." *Contemporary Review* 266 (March, 1995): 144-146. A brief discussion of Wain's central themes of faithlessness and the assumption that there are no assumptions; discusses Wain's rejection of realism and his intention to speak imaginatively.

Pickering, Jean. "The English Short Story in the Sixties." In *The English Short Story, 1945-1960*, edited by Dennis Vannatta. Boston: Twayne, 1985. The most comprehensive study of Wain as a writer of short fiction.

Salwak, Dale. *John Wain*. Boston: Twayne, 1981. Part of Twayne's English Authors series, this work is the first book-length study of Wain and is a useful introduction to Wain's career.

Walzer, Michael. "John Wain: The Hero in Limbo." *Perspective* 10 (Summer/Autumn, 1958): 137-145. In his consideration of Wain's first three novels, Walzer maintains that Wain develops a new kind of picaresque hero.

James Curry Robison, updated by Jerry Bradley and Richard Hauer Costa

---

ALICE WALKER

Born: Eatonton, Georgia; February 9, 1944

PRINCIPAL SHORT FICTION

In Love and Trouble: Stories of Black Women, 1973
You Can't Keep a Good Woman Down, 1981
The Complete Stories, 1994

OTHER LITERARY FORMS

Alice Walker is known for her achievements in both prose and poetry; in addition to her short-story collections, she has published several novels, volumes of poetry, collections of essays, and children's books. Her novels *The Third Life of Grange Copeland* (1970), *Meridian* (1976), *The Color Purple* (1982), *The Temple of My Familiar* (1989), *Possessing the Secret of Joy* (1992), and *By the Light of My Father's Smile* (1998) examine the struggles of African Americans, especially African American women, against destruction by a racist society. Her poetry is collected in *Once: Poems* (1968), *Five Poems* (1972), *Revolutionary Petunias and Other Poems* (1973), *Goodnight, Willie Lee, I'll See You in the Morning: Poems* (1979), *Horses Make a Landscape Look More Beautiful* (1984), and *Her Blue Body Everything We Know: Earthling Poems, 1965-1990* (1991). *In Search of Our Mothers' Gardens: Womanist Prose* (1983) is a collection of essays important to an understanding of Walker's purposes and methods as well as the writers influential on her fiction. A later collection of nonfiction prose is *Living by the Word: Selected Writings, 1973-1987* (1988). Walker also wrote *Langston Hughes: American Poet* (1974), *To Hell with Dying* (1988), and *Finding the Green Stone* (1991) for children. The anthology she edited entitled *I Love Myself When I Am Laughing . . . and Then Again When I Am Looking Mean and Impressive: A Zora Neale Hurston Reader* (1979) did much to revive interest in the fiction of Zora Neale Hurston, the writer she considers one of the major influences on her fiction.

ACHIEVEMENTS

From the beginning of her career, Alice Walker has been an award-winning writer. Her first published essay, "The Civil Rights Movement: What Good Was It?" won first prize in *The American Scholar*'s annual essay contest in 1967. That same year she won a Merrill writing fellowship. Her first novel was written on a fellowship at the MacDowell Colony in New Hampshire. In 1972, she received a Ph.D. from Russell Sage College. *Revolutionary Petunias and Other Poems* was nominated for a National Book Award and won the Lillian Smith Award of the Southern Regional Council in 1973. *In Love and Trouble* won the Richard and Hinda Rosenthal Award from the American Institute of Arts and Letters in 1974. *The Color Purple*, which remained on *The New York Times* list of best-sellers for more than twenty-five weeks, was nominated for the National Book Critics Circle Award and won both an American Book Award and the Pulitzer Prize for Fiction. Walker's many honors include a National Endowment for the Arts grant in 1969 and 1977, a Radcliffe Institute Fellowship in 1971-1973, and a John Simon Guggenheim Memorial Foundation Fellowship in 1977-1978. In 1984, she received a Best Books for Young Adults citation from the American Library Association for *In Search of Our Mothers' Gardens*. She has also won the O. Henry Award (1986), the Langston Hughes Award (1989), the Nora Astorga Leadership Award (1989), the Fred Cody Award for lifetime achievement (1990), the Freedom to Write Award (1990), the California Governor's Arts Award (1994), and the Literary Ambassador Award (1998).

BIOGRAPHY

Alice Malsenior Walker was born in Eatonton, Georgia, to sharecropper parents on February 9, 1944. She attended Spelman College in Atlanta on scholarship, transferring to Sarah Lawrence College in New York, from which she was graduated in 1965. While working in the Civil Rights movement in Mississippi in the summer of 1966, she met Melvyn Rosenman Levanthal, an attorney, whom she married in 1967. After residing for seven years in Jackson, Mississippi, the couple returned to the East in 1974,

Alice Walker (Jeff Reinking/Picture Group)

where Walker served as a contributing editor to *Ms.* magazine. The two were divorced in 1976, sharing joint custody of a daughter, Rebecca. Walker cofounded a publishing house in Navarro, California, Wild Trees Press. She has been a writer-in-residence and a teacher of black studies at Jackson State College (1968-1969), a lecturer in literature at Wellesley College and the University of Massachusetts at Boston (1972-1973), a distinguished writer in the African American studies department at the University of California at Berkeley (1982), and a Fannie Hurst Professor of Literature at Brandeis University (1982). She coproduced a 1992 film documentary, *Warrior Marks*, directed by Pratibha Parmar, a film she narrated and for which she wrote the script. Walker settled in Mendocino, California, where she continued to write and remained politically active.

ANALYSIS

The heroism of black women in the face of turmoil of all kinds rings from both volumes of Alice

Walker's short stories like the refrain of a protest song. *In Love and Trouble* reveals the extremes of cruelty and violence to which poor black women are often subjected in their personal relationships, while the struggles in *You Can't Keep a Good Woman Down* reflect the social upheavals of the 1970's.

IN LOVE AND TROUBLE

Such subjects and themes lend themselves to a kind of narrative that is filled with tension. The words "love" and "trouble," for example, in the title of the first collection, identify a connection that is both un-expected and inevitable. Each of the thirteen stories in this collection is a vivid confirmation that every kind of love known to woman brings its own kind of suffering. Walker is adept at pairing such elements so as to create pronounced and revealing contrasts or in-tense conflicts. One such pair that appears in many of these short stories is a stylistic one and easy to see: the poetry and prose that alternate on the page. An-other unusual combination at work throughout the short fiction may be called the lyrical and the socio-logical. Like the protest song, Walker's stories make a plea for justice made more memorable by its poetic form. She breathes rhythmic, eloquent language into the most brutish and banal abuses.

These two elements—similarity of subject matter and the balance of highly charged contraries—pro-duce a certain unity within each volume. Yet beyond this common ground, the stories have been arranged so as to convey a progression of interconnected pieces whose circumstances and themes repeat, alter-nate, and overlap rather like a musical composition. The first three stories of *In Love and Trouble*, for ex-ample, are all about married love; the next two are about love between parent and child; then come three stories in which black-white conflict is central; the fourth group concerns religious expression; and the last three stories focus on initiation. Other themes emerge and run through this five-set sequence, link-ing individual motifs and strengthening the whole. Jealousy is one of those motifs, as is the drive for self-respect, black folkways, and flowers, in particu-lar the rose and the black-eyed Susan.

Four stories suggest the breadth of Walker's imag-ination and narrative skills. "Roselily" strikes an an-ticipatory note of foreboding. "The Child Who Fa-vored Daughter" is an equally representative selection, this time of the horrific destruction of the black woman. "The Revenge of Hannah Kemhuff" is as cool and clear as "The Child Who Favored Daugh-ter" is dark and fevered. The narrator recounts a tale of Voodoo justice, specifically crediting Zora Neale Hurston, author of *Mules and Men* (1935). The final story in this collection, "To Hell with Dying," is an affirmative treatment of many themes Walker has de-veloped elsewhere more darkly.

"ROSELILY"

"Roselily" takes place on a front porch sur-rounded by a crowd of black folk, in sight of High-way 61 in Mississippi during the time it takes to perform a wedding ceremony. As the preacher in-tones the formal words, the bride's mind wanders among the people closest to her there—the bride-groom, the preacher, her parents, sisters, and chil-dren. The groom's religion is note the same as hers, and she knows that he disapproves of this gathering. She speculates uneasily about their future life to-gether in Chicago, where she will wear a veil, sit on the women's side of his church, and have more ba-bies. She is the mother of four children already but has never been married. He is giving her security, but he intends, she realizes, to remake her into the image he wants. Even the love he gives her causes her great sadness, as it makes her aware of how unloved she was before. At last, the ceremony over, they stand in the yard, greeting well-wishers, he completely alien, she overcome with anxiety. She squeezes his hand for reassurance but receives no answering signal from him.

Poetic and fairy tale elements intensify the ambiv-alence felt by the bride in this magnetic mood piece. First, there are the ceremonial resonances of the words between the paragraphs of narrative, stately and solemn like a slow drumbeat. As these phrases alternate with Roselily's thoughts, a tension devel-ops. At the words *"Dearly Beloved,"* a daydream of images begins to flow, herself a small girl in her mother's fancy dress, struggling through "a bowl of quicksand soup"; the words *"we are gathered here"* suggest to her the image of cotton, waiting to be weighed, a Mississippi ruralness she knows the bride-groom finds repugnant; *"in the sight of God"* creates in her mind the image of God as a little black boy tugging at the preacher's coattail. Gradually, a sense of foreboding builds. At the words *"to join this man and this woman"* she imagines "ropes, chains, hand-cuffs, his religion." The bridegroom is her rescuer, like Prince Charming, and is ready to become her Pygmalion. Like Sleeping Beauty, Roselily is only dimly aware of exchanging one form of confinement, of enchantment, for another. At the end of the cere-mony, she awakes to his passionate kiss and a terrible sense of being wrong.

"THE CHILD WHO FAVORED DAUGHTER"

While "Roselily" is a subtle story of a quiet inner life, "The Child Who Favored Daughter" records the circumstances of a shocking assault. It begins, also, on a front porch. A father waits with a shotgun on a hot afternoon for his daughter to walk from the school bus through the front yard. He is holding in his hand a letter she had written to her white lover. Real-izing what her father knows, the girl comes slowly down the dusty lane, pausing to study the black-eyed Susans. As his daughter approaches, the father is re-minded of his sister, "Daughter," who also had a white lover. His intense love for his sister had turned to bitterness when she gave herself to a man by whom he felt enslaved; his bitterness poisoned all of his re-lationships with women thereafter. He confronts the girl on the porch with the words "White man's slut!" then beats her with a stable harness and leaves her in the shed behind the house. The next morning, failing to make her deny the letter and struggling to suppress his "unnameable desire," he slashes off her breasts. As the story ends, he sits in a stupor on the front porch.

This story of perverted parental love and warring passions explores the destructive power of jealousy and denial. Its evil spell emanates from the father's unrepented and unacknowledged desire to possess his sister. He is haunted by her when he looks at his own daughter. Once again, a strongly lyrical style height-ens the dominant tone, in this case, horror. Short lines of verse, like snatches of song interspersed with the narrative, contrast sharply in their suggestion of pure feeling with the tightly restrained prose. The daugh-ter's motif associates her with the attraction of natural beauty: *"Fire of earth/ Lure of flower smells/ The sun."* The father's theme sounds his particular resig-nation and doom: *"Memories of years/ Unknowable women—/ sisters/ spouses/ illusions of soul."* The re-sulting trancelike confrontation seems inevitable, the two moving through a pattern they do not control, do not understand.

"THE REVENGE OF HANNAH KEMHUFF"

In "The Revenge of Hannah Kemhuff," a woman who has lost husband, children, and self-respect, all because a charity worker denied her food stamps, comes to the seer Tante Rosie for peace of mind. Tante Rosie assures the troubled woman that the combined powers of the Man-God and the Great Mother of Us All will destroy her enemy. Tante Rosie's apprentice, who narrates the story, teaches Mrs. Kemhuff the curse-prayer printed in Zora Neale Hurston's *Mules and Men*. Then she sets about to col-lect the necessary ingredients for the conjure: Sarah Sadler Holley's feces, water, nail parings. Her task seems to become almost impossible when her mentor tells her that these items must be gained directly from the victim herself. Nevertheless, with a plan in mind, the young woman approaches Mrs. Holley, tells her that she is learning the profession from Tante Rosie, and then asks her to prove that she, as she claims, does not believe in "rootworking." It is only a short while until Mrs. Kemhuff dies, followed a few months later by Mrs. Holley, who had, after the visit of the apprentice, taken to her bedroom, eating her nails, saving her fallen hair, and collecting her excre-ment in plastic bags and barrels.

This is the first story in the collection in which the black community comes into conflict with the white. It is a conflict of religious traditions and a strong statement in recognition of something profound in African folkways. Mrs. Holley failed Mrs. Kemhuff years before in the greatest of Christian virtues, that of charity. Mrs. Kemhuff, though now reconciled to her church, cannot find peace and seeks the even greater power of ancient conjure to restore her pride. Like other African American writers who have han-dled this subject, Walker first acknowledges that Voodoo is widely discounted as sheer superstition, but then her story argues away all rational objections. Mrs. Holley does not die as the result of hocus-pocus but because of her own radical belief, a belief in spite of herself. There is something else about this story that is different from those at the beginning of the collection. Instead of a dreamy or hypnotic action, alert characters speak and think purposefully, clearly, one strand of many evolving patterns that emerge as the stories are read in sequence.

"To Hell with Dying"

"To Hell with Dying" is the last story in the collection and a strong one. A more mellow love-and-trouble story than most preceding it, it features a male character who is not the villain of the piece. Mr. Sweet Little is a melancholy man whom the narrator has loved from childhood, when her father would bring the children to Mr. Sweet's bedside to rouse him from his depression with a shout: "To hell with dying! These children want Mr. Sweet!" Because the children were so successful in "revivaling" Mr. Sweet with their kisses and tickling and cajoling ways, they were not to learn for some time what death really meant. Years pass. Summoned from her doctoral studies in Massachusetts, the twenty-four-year-old narrator rushes to Mr. Sweet's bedside, where she cannot quite believe that she will not succeed. She does induce him to open his eyes, smile, and trace her hairline with his finger as he once did. Still, however, he dies. His legacy to her is the steel guitar on which he played away his blues all those years, that and her realization that he was her first love.

It is useful to recognize this story as an initiation story, like the two that precede it, "The Flowers" and "We Drink the Wine in France." Initiation stories usually involve, among other things, an unpleasant brush with reality, a new reality. A child, adolescent, or young adult faces an unfamiliar challenge and, if successful, emerges at a new level of maturity or increased status. Always, however, something is lost, something must be given up. As a very small girl, the narrator remembers, she did not understand quite what was going on during their visits to the neighbor's shack. When she was somewhat older, she felt the weight of responsibility for the dying man's sur-

vival. At last, after she has lost her old friend, she is happy, realizing how important they were to each other. She has successfully negotiated her initiation into the mysteries of love and death, as, in truth, she had already done to the best of her ability at those earlier stages. This often-reprinted story is a culmination of the struggle between Death and Love for the lives of the girls and women, really for all the blacks of *In Love and Trouble*, one which well represents Walker's talent and demonstrates her vision of blacks supporting and affirming one another in community.

You Can't Keep a Good Woman Down

You Can't Keep a Good Woman Down is her salute to black women who are pushing ahead, those who have crossed some barriers and are in some sense champions. There are black women who are songwriters, artists, writers, students in exclusive Eastern schools; they are having abortions, teaching their men the meaning of pornography, coming to terms with the death of a father, on one hand, or with the meaning of black men raping white women, on the other. Always, they are caught up short by the notions of whites. In other words, all the political, sexual, racial, countercultural issues of the 1970's are in these stories, developed from what Walker calls the "womanist" point of view.

This set of stories, then, is somewhat more explicitly sociological than the first and somewhat less lyrical, and it is also more apparently autobiographical, but in a special sense. Walker herself is a champion, so her life is a natural, even an inescapable, source of material. Walker-the-artist plays with Walker-the-college-student and Walker-the-idealistic-teacher, as well as with some of the other roles she sees herself as having occupied during that decade of social upheaval. Once a writer's experience has become transformed within a fictive world, it becomes next to impossible to think of the story's events as either simply autobiography or simply invention. The distinction has been deliberately blurred. It is because Walker wants to unite her public and private worlds, her politics and her art, life as lived and life as imagined, that, instead of poetry, these stories are interspersed with autobiographical parallels, journal entries, letters, and other expressions of her personality. There are three stories that deserve special attention, "Nineteen Fifty-Five," "Fame," and "Source." To begin with, they serve as checkpoints for the collection's development, from the essentially simple and familiar to the increasingly complex and strange, from 1955 to 1980. Furthermore, these stories are independently memorable.

"NINETEEN FIFTY-FIVE"

The opening story, "Nineteen Fifty-Five," is presented from the perspective of a middle-aged blues singer, Gracie Mae Still, whose signature song, recorded by a young white man named Traynor, brings him fame and fortune. Gracie Mae records her impressions of Traynor in a journal, beginning with their first meeting in 1955 and continuing until his death in 1977. Over the years, the rock-and-roll star (obviously meant to suggest Elvis Presley) stays in touch with the matronly musician, buying her lavish gifts—a white Cadillac, a mink coat, a house—and quizzing her on the real meaning of her song. From the army, he writes to tell her that her song is very much in demand, and that everyone asks him what he thinks it means, really. As time goes by and his life disappoints him, he turns to the song, as if it were a touchstone that could give his life meaning. He even arranges an appearance for himself and Gracie Mae on the variety show hosted by Johnny Carson, with some half-developed notion of showing his fans what the real thing is and how he aspires to it. If he is searching for a shared experience of something true and moving with his audience, however, he is to be disappointed again. His fans applaud only briefly, out of politeness, for the originator of the song, the one who really gives it life, then squeal wildly for his imitation, without any recognition of what he wanted them to understand. That is the last time the two musicians see each other.

In part, this story is about the contribution that black music made to the spirit of the times and how strangely whites transformed it. The white rock-and-roll singer, who seems as much in a daze as some of the women of *In Love and Trouble*, senses something superior in the original blues version, but he misplaces its value, looking for some meaning to life that can be rolled up in the nutshell of a lyric. In contrast

to the bemused Traynor, Gracie Mae is a down-to-earth champion, and her dialect looks forward to Walker's masterful handling of dialect in *The Color Purple*. She repeatedly gives Traynor simple and sensible advice when he turns to her for help, and she has her own answer to the mystery of his emptiness: "Really, I think, some peoples advance *so* slowly."

"FAME"

The champion of "Fame" is Andrea Clement White, and the events take place on one day, when she is being honored, when she is being confronted by her own fame. She is speaking to a television interviewer as the story begins. The old woman tells the young interviewer that in order to look at the world freshly and creatively, an artist simply cannot be famous. When reminded by the young woman that she herself is famous, Andrea Clement White is somewhat at a loss. As the interview continues its predictable way, the novelist explaining once again that she writes about people, not their color, she uneasily asks herself why she does not "*feel* famous," why she feels as though she has not accomplished what she set out to do.

The highlight of the day is to be a luncheon in her honor, at which her former colleagues, the president, and specially invited dignitaries, as well as the generally detested former dean, will all applaud her life accomplishments (while raising money). All the while, the lady of the hour keeps a bitingly humorous commentary running in her mind. Her former students in attendance are "numbskulls," the professors, "mediocre." Out loud, she comments that the president is a bore. No matter how outrageous her behavior, she is forgiven because of her stature; when she eats her Rock Cornish hen with her hands, the entire assembly of five hundred follows suit. At last, however, the spleen and anxious bravado give way to something out of reach of the taint of fame: a child singing an anonymous slave song. Recalled to her dignity, the honored guest is able to face her moment in the limelight stoically.

In this comic story of the aggravations and annoyances that beset the publicly recognized artist, Walker imagines herself as an aging novelist who does not suffer fools gladly. She puts the artist's inner world on paper so that something of her gift for storytelling and her habits of mind become visible. The stress of the occasion and being brought into forced contact with her former president and dean trigger her aggressive imagination, and her innate narrative gift takes over. She visualizes using her heavy award as a weapon against the repulsive, kissing dean, hearing him squeal, and briefly feels gleeful. The story, however, is something more than simply a comic portrait of the artist's foibles. When Andrea Clement White questions herself about her own sense of fame, admits her own doubts, she is searching for something certain, as Traynor is searching in "Nineteen Fifty-five," though not so blindly. Like him, she is called out of the mundane by a meaningful song.

"SOURCE"

The last story of *You Can't Keep a Good Woman Down* is "Source," which connects the social conscience of an antipoverty worker in Mississippi with the expanding consciousness of the alternative lifestyle as practiced on the West Coast. Two friends, Irene and Anastasia had attended college together in New York. When funding for Irene's adult-education project was cut, she traveled to San Francisco for a change of scene, to be met by Anastasia, living on welfare with some friends named Calm, Peace, and their baby, Bliss, all under the guidance of a swami named Source. The two young women had been unable to find any common ground, Irene believing in collective action and Anastasia believing that people choose to suffer and that nothing can be changed. After walking out on a meeting with Source, Irene was asked to leave. Years later, the two meet again in Alaska, where Irene is lecturing to educators. Anastasia is now living with an Indian and passing for white. This time, the two women talk more directly, of color, of Anastasia's panic when she is alone, of her never being accepted as a black because of her pale skin. Irene is brought to face her own part in this intolerance and to confess that her reliance on government funding was every bit as insecure as had been Anastasia's reliance on Source. Their friendship restored and deepened, the two women embrace.

The title of this story suggests a theme that runs throughout the entire collection, the search for a center, a source of strength, meaning, or truth. This source is very important to the pioneer, but it can be a false lure. When Irene recognizes that she and Anastasia were both reaching out for something on which to depend, she states what might be taken as the guiding principle for the champion: "*any* direction that is away from ourselves is the wrong direction." This final portrait of a good woman who cannot be kept down is a distinctively personal one. Women who are not distracted by external influences and who are true to themselves and able to open themselves to one another will triumph.

Walker's short fiction adds a new image to the pantheon of American folk heroes: the twentieth century black woman, in whatever walk of life, however crushed or blocked, still persevering. Even those who seem the most unaware, the most poorly equipped for the struggle, are persevering, because, in their integrity, they cannot do otherwise. The better equipped know themselves to be advocates. They shoulder their dedication seriously and cheerfully. They are the fortunate ones; they understand that what they do has meaning.

"EVERYDAY USE"

One of the more widely anthologized of Walker's stories, "Everyday Use" addresses the issues of identity and true cultural awareness and attacks the "hyper-Africanism" much in vogue during the 1960's and 1970's as false and shallow. The occasion of the story is Dee's brief trip back to her home, ostensibly to visit with her mother and her sister, Maggie, who was left seriously scarred in the fire of suspicious origin that destroyed their home years earlier. Dee's real purpose, however, is to acquire some homemade quilts and other artifacts of her culture so that she can display them in her home as tokens of her "authenticity," her roots in the soil of rural Georgia. She wears a spectacular dashiki and wishes to be called by an "African" name; she is accompanied by a man who likewise affects "African" dress, hairstyle, naming tradition, and handshaking routines. Walker's tongue is firmly in her cheek as she portrays these two characters in vivid contrast with Mama and Maggie, whose lives are simple, close to the earth, and genuine. Despite (or perhaps because of) Mama's sacrifices and hard work to send Dee off to acquire an education in the outside world, Dee reveals a fundamental selfishness and lack of understanding of her culture and family and, her purposes thwarted, leaves without the quilts in a cloud of dust and disdain. Mama and Maggie sit in their neat yard, its dirt surface carefully raked, enjoying the shade and their snuff together "until it was time to go in the house and go to bed."

Walker's control of style and tone is nowhere more certain than in this powerful and economical story. Here she shows that family, tradition, and strength are to be found in the items of everyday use that have survived the fires of prejudice, from whatever source, and illuminate the true meaning of family and love and forgiveness. Despite the truth of Dee's parting statement that "it really is a new day for us," Walker leaves no doubt that the promise of that new day will be dimmed if traditions are exploited rather than understood and cherished. Maggie, after all, learned how to quilt from her grandmother and her great aunt and thus has a much surer sense of her own identity than her sister.

OTHER MAJOR WORKS

LONG FICTION: *The Third Life of Grange Copeland*, 1970; *Meridian*, 1976; *The Color Purple*, 1982; *The Temple of My Familiar*, 1989; *Possessing the Secret of Joy*, 1992; *By the Light of My Father's Smile*, 1998.

POETRY: *Once: Poems*, 1968; *Five Poems*, 1972; *Revolutionary Petunias and Other Poems*, 1973; *Goodnight, Willie Lee, I'll See You in the Morning: Poems*, 1979; *Horses Make a Landscape Look More Beautiful*, 1984; *Her Blue Body Everything We Know: Earthling Poems, 1965-1990*, 1991.

NONFICTION: *In Search of Our Mothers' Gardens: Womanist Prose*, 1983; *Living by the Word: Selected Writings, 1973-1987*, 1988; *Warrior Marks: Female Genital Mutilation and the Sexual Blinding of Women*, 1993; *The Same River Twice: Honoring the Difficult*, 1996; *Anything We Love Can Be Saved: A Writer's Activism*, 1997; *The Way Forward Is with a Broken Heart*, 2000.

CHILDREN'S BOOKS: *Langston Hughes: American*

Poet, 1974; *To Hell with Dying*, 1988; *Finding the Green Stone*, 1991.

EDITED TEXT: *I Love Myself When I Am Laughing . . . and Then Again When I Am Looking Mean and Impressive: A Zora Neale Hurston Reader*, 1979.

BIBLIOGRAPHY

Awkward, Michael. *Inspiriting Influences: Tradition, Revision, and Afro-American Women's Novels*. New York: Columbia University Press, 1989. Though dense, Awkward's book may be useful in placing Walker within the context of her African American literary heritage and in providing some possibilities for interpreting *The Color Purple* and for understanding the connections among Zora Neale Hurston, Jean Toomer, and Walker. The book is laden with critical jargon but is nevertheless important in placing Walker in context historically, thematically, and politically. Awkward emphasizes the creative spirit of African American females and their search for self in a non-patriarchal community as themes of Walker's fiction. Endnotes may lead researchers to other useful materials on Walker's fiction as well as on works by and on other African American women.

Bauer, Margaret D. "Alice Walker: Another Southern Writer Criticizing Codes Not Put to 'Everyday Use.'" *Studies in Short Fiction* 29 (Spring, 1992): 143-151. Discusses parallels between Walker's *In Love and Trouble* and stories by William Faulkner, Katherine Anne Porter, Eudora Welty, and Flannery O'Connor. Argues that Walker, like these other southern writers, examines the tendency to support social and religious codes at the expense of individual fulfillment.

Bloom, Harold, ed. *Alice Walker*. New York: Chelsea House, 1989. An important collection of critical essays examining the fiction, poetry, and essays of Walker from a variety of perspectives. The fourteen essays, including Bloom's brief introduction, are arranged chronologically. Contains useful discussions of the first three novels, brief analyses of individual short stories, poems, and essays, and assessments of Walker's social and political views in connection with her works and other African

American female authors. A chronology of Walker's life and a bibliography may be of assistance to the beginner.

Bloxham, Laura J. "Alice [Malsenior] Walker." In *Contemporary Fiction Writers of the South*, edited by Joseph M. Flora and Robert Bain. Westport, Conn.: Greenwood Press, 1993. A general introduction to Walker's "womanist" themes of oppression of black women and change through affirmation of self. Provides a brief summary and critique of previous criticism of Walker's work.

Borgmeier, Raimund. "Alice Walker: 'Everyday Use.'" In *The African-American Short Story: 1970 to 1990*, edited by Wolfgang Karrer and Barbara Puschmann-Nalenz. Trier, Germany: Wissenschaftlicher Verlag Trier, 1993. A detailed discussion of the generic characteristics of one of Walker's best-known stories. Analyzes the tension between the typical unheard-of occurrence and everyday reality as well as the story's use of a central structural symbol.

Butler-Evans, Elliott. *Race, Gender, and Desire: Narrative Strategies in the Fiction of Toni Cade Bambara, Toni Morrison, and Alice Walker*. Philadelphia: Temple University Press, 1989. Focusing on the connections between gender, race, and desire, and their relationship to the narrative strategies in the fiction of these three contemporary writers, Butler-Evans argues that Walker's works are "structured by a complex ideological position" oscillating between "her identity as 'Black feminist' or 'woman-of-color' and a generalized feminist position in which race is subordinated." Useful discussions of Walker's first three novels are included. Although no attention is given to short fiction, the student may receive assistance with understanding Walker's "womanist" position in all her works. Includes somewhat lengthy endnotes and a bibliography.

Davis, Thadious M. "Alice Walker's Celebration of Self in Southern Generations." *Southern Quarterly* 21 (1983): 39-53. Reprinted in *Women Writers of the Contemporary South*, edited by Peggy Whitman Prenshaw. Jackson: University Press of Mississippi, 1984. An early but still-useful general introduction to the works and themes of Walker, emphasizing particularly her concern for a sense of identity/self and her folk heritage. Davis discusses most significant works briefly, points out the sense of outrage at injustice in Walker's fiction, including several short stories, and also makes frequent references to her essays.

Gates, Henry Louis, Jr., and K. A. Appiah. *Alice Walker: Critical Perspectives Past and Present*. New York: Amistad, 1993. An examination of African American women in Walker's work. Includes a bibliography and an index.

Gentry, Tony. *Alice Walker*. New York: Chelsea, 1993. Examines the life and work of Walker. Includes bibliographical references and index.

McKay, Nellie. "Alice Walker's 'Advancing Luna—and Ida B. Wells': A Struggle Toward Sisterhood." In *Rape and Representation*, edited by Lynn A. Higgins and Brenda R. Silver. New York: Columbia University Press, 1991. Shows how the story allows readers to see how women's cross-racial relationships are controlled by systems of white male power. The story helps its audience understand why black women fail to provide group support for feminists of the antirape movement in spite of their own historical oppression by rape.

Mills, Sara, Lynne Pearce, Sue Spaull, and Elaine Millard. *Feminist Readings, Feminists Reading*. Charlottesville: University Press of Virginia, 1989. Analyzes Walker as a feminist writer from a feminist perspective. The book devotes the discussion of Walker mostly to *The Color Purple*, which is interpreted as an example of "authentic realism" designed for a female audience and as part of a female tradition beginning in the nineteenth century. More important, Walker is a part of the "self-conscious women's" revisionist tradition that has been evident since the early 1980's. Contains endnotes and a bibliography, as well as a glossary of terms related to feminist literary criticism and to literary theory in general.

Petry, Alice Hall. "Walker: The Achievement of the Short Fiction." In *Alice Walker: Critical Perspectives Past and Present*, edited by Henry Louis Gates, Jr., and K. A. Appiah. New York: Amistad,

1993. A skeptical analysis of Walker's short fiction that contrasts the successful and focused achievement of *In Love and Trouble* (1973) with the less satisfying *You Can't Keep a Good Woman Down* (1981). Petry argues that the latter collection suffers in many places from unfortunate unintentional humor, trite and clichéd writing, and reductionism, and a confusion of genres that perhaps owe much to her being a "cross-generic writer."

Pryse, Marjorie, and Hortense J. Spillers, eds. *Conjuring: Black Women, Fiction, and Literary Tradition*. Bloomington: Indiana University Press, 1985. This useful book contains brief analyses of several Walker short stories as well as her first three novels; most of the discussion of Walker is, however, devoted to *The Color Purple*. Tracing the roots of Walker's works to folk tradition, this study, a collection of essays on various African American female authors, emphasizes the influence of Zora Neale Hurston as well. Although no

essay is devoted entirely to Walker, the book would be of some help in understanding Walker's literary tradition and heritage.

Wade-Gayles, Gloria. "Black, Southern, Womanist: The Genius of Alice Walker." In *Southern Women Writers: The New Generation*, edited by Tonette Bond Inge. Tuscaloosa: University of Alabama Press, 1990. An excellent, thorough introduction to the life and literary career of Walker. Placing emphasis on Walker's voice as a black, southern woman throughout her works and arguing that Walker's commitment is to the spiritual wholeness of her people, Wade-Gayles examines several essays that are important to an understanding of her fiction and beliefs, her first three novels, both collections of short stories, and her collections of poetry. Supplemented by a bibliography of Walker's works, endnotes, and a useful secondary bibliography.

Rebecca R. Butler, updated by D. Dean Shackelford
and Theodore C. Humphrey

ROBERT WALSER

Born: Biel, Switzerland; April 15, 1878
Died: Herisau, Switzerland; December 25, 1956

PRINCIPAL SHORT FICTION

Fritz Kochers Aufsätze, 1904
Aufsätze, 1913
Geschichten, 1914
Kleine Dichtungen, 1914
Der Spaziergang, 1917 (*The Walk and Other Stories*, 1957)
Kleine Prosa, 1917
Prosastücke, 1917
Poetenleben, 1918
Seeland, 1919
Die Rose, 1925

Eine Ohrfeige und Sonstiges, 1925 (*A Slap in the Face Et Cetera*, 1985)
Selected Stories, 1982 (foreword by Susan Sontag)
Aus dem Bleistiftgebiet: Mikrogramme aus den Jahren 1924-1925, 1985
Masquerade and Other Stories, 1990

OTHER LITERARY FORMS

Robert Walser's reputation as a prose miniaturist long obscured his achievement as a novelist. He published three novels, *Geschwister Tanner* (1907; the Tanner siblings), *Der Gehülfe* (1908; the assistant), and *Jakob von Gunten* (1909; English translation, 1969). The latter is generally acknowledged to be the most impressive work. *Der "Räuber"-Roman* (1972;

the "bandit" novel), a boldly personal, experimental work, was published posthumously. His most important dramatic works were published in the volume *Komödie: Theatralisches* (1919; comedy: theatrical writings). He also wrote poetry, the merit of which has been the subject of some controversy.

ACHIEVEMENTS

In the early decades of the twentieth century, critics praised the psychological complexity and stylistic finesse of Robert Walser's stories and essays. The novelist Robert Musil even asserted that Franz Kafka's first book, *Betrachtung* (1913; *Meditation*, 1940) was a "special case of the Walser type." Walser's fiction appeared both in avant-garde reviews and in newspaper *feuilletons*. By the 1920's, however, his increasingly experimental prose had begun to alienate the editors and newspapers on whom he depended for a living. After he ceased writing in 1933, his work fell into oblivion.

Critics in Germany and Switzerland rediscovered Walser in the 1960's. The edition of collected works by Jochen Greven, which began appearing in 1966, gathered together for the first time all the short fiction that had appeared in scattered newspapers and reviews. Readers could at last appreciate the range and versatility of his prose. Walser is now widely regarded as one of the most significant writers in twentieth century German literature. Although English translations by Christopher Middleton appeared as early as 1957, what brought Walser's work to the attention of English-speaking readers was the publication in 1982 of the *Selected Stories*, with a foreword by Susan Sontag.

One of Walser's greatest gifts as a writer was his ability, as Christian Morgenstern put it, to "see the world as a continuous wonder." He made no attempt to separate perceptions that are "significant" from those that are "trivial." While some readers find this rejection of conventional discriminations frustrating, others find its heterodoxy refreshing. In a brief but now classic essay of 1929, Walter Benjamin evoked the enigma of Walser's seemingly artless art: "While we are used to seeing the mysteries of style emerge out of more or less fully developed and purposeful

works of art, here we are faced with language running wild in a manner that is totally unintentional, or at least seems so, and yet that we find attractive and compelling. A letting go, moreover, that ranges through all forms from the graceful to the bitter."

BIOGRAPHY

Robert Otto Walser was born in Biel, Switzerland, on April 15, 1878. His father, Adolf Walser, a bookbinder by trade, was, by all accounts, a convivial individual, if a rather lackluster businessman. His mother, whose maiden name was Elisa Marti, was socially ambitious but psychically labile. She died in 1894, when Robert was sixteen.

Walser spent his active years as a writer in four cities: Zurich (1896-1905), Berlin (1905-1913), then his native Biel (1913-1921), and, finally, Bern (1921-1929). His work falls into four phases, which coincide with the periods he spent in those cities. Frequently switching both jobs and addresses, he lived on what he himself described as "the periphery of bourgeois existences." He sold much of his short fiction to newspapers and reviews, some of which he later published in book form. He supplemented this meager income mostly through menial clerical jobs. While in Berlin, he attended a school for servants. For a brief period he was employed as a butler at Dambrau Castle in Upper Silesia.

The years in Berlin were crucial for his artistic development. Through his brother Karl, a painter and illustrator, he came into contact with leading intellectual figures. Yet, although cosmopolitan Berlin left its mark on his increasingly sophisticated prose, he never lost the outsider's contempt for the established order. His relations with the writers Hugo von Hofmannsthal and Frank Wedekind and the industrialist and politician Walter Rathenau were stormy.

Walser's three Berlin novels attracted some favorable critical attention but relatively few readers. He could not interest publishers in further novels, and some manuscripts were lost. After his return to Biel in 1913, he turned his back on the novel and continued writing *feuilleton* essays and short stories. During his lifetime he wrote more than thirteen hundred individual pieces of short prose. In 1921 he moved to

Bern, claiming that he wished to make his prose more cosmopolitan in outlook. His style became increasingly experimental, and editors began to reject his submissions. In the mid-1920's his anxiety about writing literally paralyzed his hand, leading him to invent what he called his "pencil method" of composition. In a tiny script, he wrote texts now known as microgrammes. A selection of hitherto unpublished microgrammes, which had been deciphered painstakingly by scholars in Zurich, was published in 1985 under the title *Aus dem Bleistiftgebiet* (from the pencil territory).

By the late 1920's, Walser was leading the life of a recluse and hearing persecuting voices from which he could find no escape. On January 25, 1929, he was admitted to the Waldau asylum near Bern. At first, he appears to have reached almost thankfully for the new role of inmate, which he was to play diligently, mending sacks and refusing special concessions, for the remaining twenty-seven years of his life. Yet, at times, he longed to be set free. In 1933, in apparent protest against his transfer from Waldau to the asylum at Herisau, in the canton of Appenzell-Ausserrhoden, he gave up writing altogether. He died at the age of seventy-eight on Christmas Day, 1956.

ANALYSIS

Robert Walser's early reputation as a miniaturist was misleading. His essays and stories actually form the nucleus of a larger work, which he once described as a "sliced-up or torn-apart novel of myself." The main protagonist in this autobiographical "novel" is not so much Walser as his poetic self. This self adopts a wide variety of roles, such as that of the servant, the artist, and the child. Yet Walser never identifies for long with these fictional alter egos. His stance toward them is ironic, haughty, or nonchalant. Having adopted them with the flick of a pen, he can discard them just as swiftly. More crucial than their individual identities is their unmistakable voice, which remained remarkably constant throughout his career. By turns effusive and reticent, self-effacing and self-inflating, long-winded and laconic, solitary and convivial, this voice determines the cadences of his prose.

Throughout his career, Walser struggled to reconcile his modernist practice with his conservative ideals. His literary values were firmly rooted in Swiss literary tradition. Among Walser's idols was the civic-minded nineteenth century novelist Gottfried Keller, who is renowned for his lyrical realism. Walser's own prose, however, is closer to the self-conscious experimentation of modernists such as Virginia Woolf.

FRITZ KOCHERS AUFSÄTZE

While not a major achievement, his first book, *Fritz Kochers Aufsätze* (Fritz Kocher's essays), is a characteristic product of the Zurich phase. Walser adopted the persona of a schoolboy writing compositions on hackneyed themes such as friendship and nature. These neo-Romantic effusions are tongue-in-cheek, but tiresome nevertheless. Walser's stylistic dexterity only becomes apparent when he lets the schoolboy mask slip. Alternating with the purple prose of Fritz Kocher are stretches of sophisticated and self-conscious writing, which poke fun not only at the convention of schoolboy essays but also at language itself.

The tone becomes more urgent in the final piece in the collection "Der Wald" (the forest). Kocher intimates that he is driven into the forest by unspecified woes, but this oblique confession ends abruptly. Kocher claims that he must be careful not to divulge too much about himself. Here he is clearly speaking on behalf of Walser himself, the Walser who does not want readers to recognize the self lurking behind his numerous personas. This attitude is stated unequivocally in "Das Kind" ("The Child"): "Nobody has the right to treat me as if he knew me."

It has been said of Kafka's stories that they are alienated fairy tales. This is true also of Walser's. His two Zurich fairy tales in free verse are indispensable for an understanding of his short prose. In *Aschenbrödel* (1901; *Cinderella*, 1985) and *Schneewittchen* (1901; *Snowwhite*, 1985), which Benjamin called "one of the most profound compositions in recent literature," Walser's heroines rebel against the script of the Grimm Brothers by refusing to allow themselves to be rescued. They owe their creativity to the sisters and stepmother who torment them. Without that hostility, they would be lost. Happiness and reciprocated love would destroy what they most prize in themselves. Thus, they chase away the Prince Charmings.

"A STRANGE CITY"

There are examples in the short prose both of this bleak vision and of a radiant counterpoint. In "Seltsame stadt" ("A Strange City"), for example, Walser conjures up a utopian society. The inhabitants of this singular city are dolls, relatives, perhaps, of the graceful puppets that Heinrich von Kleist describes in his essay "Über das Marionettentheater" ("The Marionette Theater"). They revere life and treasure the senses and can thus dispense with preachers and artists. Surfacing here is the conviction that in a truly civilized society the professional artist would be superfluous. The narrator dwells in a rather fetishistic manner on the shoes and trousers of the women. These obsessions recur in the short prose, most flagrantly, perhaps, in "Hose" ("Trousers"), which is less about women's emancipation than about Walser's trousers fetish.

"OSKAR"

The story "Oskar" is uncharacteristically forthright. Written in Biel but reflecting on the Zurich years, it describes the origins of Walser's stylization of himself as a self-denying hermit. Oskar discovers within himself a need for solitude. He is not content to satisfy this need, and he feels compelled to make life harsher by denying himself such creature comforts as a warm room in winter. His shaping of this idiosyncratic persona is partly involuntary, partly willed. The rationale for his seemingly masochistic behavior is aesthetic. He expects the solitude to sharpen his appetite for life. As Oskar's isolation intensifies, however, the narrator intimates the human cost of his wayward odyssey.

In Berlin, Walser retained the pose of the naïve provincial, but his prose became increasingly sophisticated. The theater stimulated his imagination, and he wrote frequently for the influential review *Die Schaubühne*. Although he was ostensibly commenting on the plays of Wedekind, Gerhart Hauptmann, and others, his real subject was the self-impersonation that he himself practiced in the medium of prose. Ideally, he wanted his fiction to enact an ap-

pealing version not only of himself but also of life itself. He was, however, fully aware that this quest for life in art raises tortuous epistemological questions. Even as early as 1902, in the dramatic sketch *Die Knaben* (1902; the boys), an actor is chided for confusing life with appearances and "the body with its reflexes."

"RESPONSE TO A REQUEST"

In "Beantwortung einer anfrage" ("Response to a Request"), Walser illustrates graphically the exploitation of the self on which his art is based. The narrator offers advice to an actor who has asked him for a sketch that he can perform. Instead of giving the actor a script, the narrator advises him to use his body as his material. Carefully choreographed gestures will enable him to manipulate the audience's response. If physical pain is to horrify the spectator, then it must be elegantly enacted. The uncharacteristically violent self-immolation at the end of the story anticipates the lurid effects of the later expressionists. More important, however, the execution of this sketch mirrors the workings of Walser's prose. It, too, manipulates images of the self, relying for its effects on emotional dissonance and stylistic incongruity.

In Biel, Walser regressed stylistically. He did not always distance himself successfully from the neo-Romantic clichés that once again invaded his prose. In "Die einfahrt" (the entrance), for example, the description of his return to the fatherland aboard a train full of noble workers is downright mawkish. Nature affords him a screen onto which he can all too easily project the fulfillment of secret desires. In "Der wald" (the wood), the forest becomes the setting for an illusionary erotic encounter. This sketch could be contrasted with the less self-indulgent treatment of the same motif in *Fritz Kochers Aufsätze*.

"THE WALK"

The Walk and Other Stories is an exceptional chronicle of the Biel years. Walser is more candid than elsewhere about the darker emotions underlying his surface exuberance. The title "The Walk" evokes both a physical activity and a philosophy of life, as "the Way" evokes Christianity and Taoism. The narrator, a writer, begins his walk in a romantically adventurous mood, wishing to escape gloomy brooding over a blank sheet of paper in his study, for, as he says, writers who truly understand their profession like to lay their pens aside from time to time: "Uninterrupted writing fatigues, like digging," he says. Repeatedly, the narrator rhapsodizes over what he sees on his walk—a dog, children, a shop—loving all that he sees with a "fiery love," telling himself that he will write down a sort of fantasy about his stroll, which he will entitle "The Walk."

When challenged by the inspector of taxes that he is always seen out for a walk, the narrator says he could not write another word or produce the smallest poem without walking, for he would be dead and his profession destroyed. Insisting that a walk advances him professionally and also provides him with amusement and joy, he says a walk always is filled with significant phenomena. The man who walks, says the narrator, must be able to bow down and look at the smallest everyday thing: "Mysterious and secretly there prowl at the walker's heels all kinds of beautiful subtle walker's thoughts."

William H. Gass has suggested that Walser's is the perfect "stroller's psychology," for to him all that he sees is equal; everything is fresh and astonishing and a pleasant puzzle. Gass says Walser loved his long peaceful walks in the woods about which he creates a picture postcard world. However, if the postcard shows a pretty inn on the edge of a village in the Alps, one senses that behind the window is a weeping woman. Gass argues that Walser's prose "strolls," for it follows the contours of its subject. There is no narrative here, for the narrator simply stops at various points, thinks about what he sees, and then moves on.

Although "The Walk" seems a discursive ramble of a romantic and nondiscriminating observer/narrator, it is undercut by parody and play in which Walser uses a number of different prose styles, making it difficult for the reader to know which descriptions and ruminations are serious and which are parodies. As Susan Sontag says about "The Walk," the soliloquies that make up the work are both gleeful and rueful. Walser's art, she says, assumes terror and depression, in order to accept it, "ironize over it, lighten it."

Walser is no ordinary voyeur, says William H. Gass, for he follows each thought and feeling with both a fond and a skeptical regard. Because he is an author he not only focuses on the process of seeing but also must attend to the writing of the page, transforming characters he encounters into words that reflect on themselves. In this way, Gass says, Walser was a postmodernist before the fashion, a fiction writer very much aware of how fictions create their authors as well as their ostensible subjects.

A SLAP IN THE FACE ET CETERA

Eine Ohrfeige und Sonstiges (1925; *A Slap in the Face Et Cetera*, 1985) is one of the most provocative texts of the Bern years. It is hard to assign it to any one genre. Walser showers the reader with an assortment of diary-like entries, anecdotes, aphorisms, fragmentary stories and miniature fairy tales. The opening paragraph forces the reader to plunge immediately into a narrative that juxtaposes events as if they were elements in a collage. Elsewhere in his final collection, *Die Rose* (the rose), Walser suggests that this freewheeling method of composition allows him to play on "the instrument of his fancies."

The opening lines of *A Slap in the Face Et Cetera* represent clipped renderings of actual impressions prompted by a brief visit to Biel. Instead of developing the initial allusions to a schoolteacher and a sergeant, however, the narrator flits into the tiny auditorium of a theater, which immediately suggests its opposite, a giant railway station he has recently observed. He teases the reader by withholding key information, such as the name of the playwright, who turns out to be Oscar Wilde. Walser perceives an affinity between his fate and that of the Irishman. Later, in the middle of a meditation on the vagaries of the literary marketplace, he invokes the eighteenth century poet Friedrich Hölderlin, who suffered a mental breakdown and spent the last thirty-six years of his life in seclusion.

Walser strews fragmentary fictions amid diary-like entries of this kind. One of these miniature stories is a grotesque fairy tale about a mother, Lady Hypocrite, and her son, "little trouserlegs." Walser is playing here on the register of unacknowledged childhood traumas. Lurking beneath such fairy-tale figures as the passionately wicked mother is an autobiographical substratum that he banishes from the surface of his prose. Instead, he finds refuge in his own playfulness, indulging in whimsical allusions to high culture and reveling in his own power to mold the fairy tale any way he chooses. He clings to this high-wire exuberance, which cannot, however, entirely distract the attention of the reader from the abyss below.

These fragmentary fictions often reveal as much as they conceal. In a final fiction, introduced by a banner headline, Walser develops the motif of the romantic triangle toward an ingenious anticlimax. His heroes often have a weakness for Platonic relationships in which they can indulge their fantasies without fear of losing them to a paltry reality. In this fragment, the narrator's totally imaginary infatuation with a married woman, whom he has never met, suggests the fragility of the threads linking an isolated dreamer—the narrator and behind him, Walser himself—to the world of others.

Skepticism about the epistemological status of fiction had been a feature of Walser's prose ever since the Zurich years, but the debate within him about his poetic principles intensified in the mid-1920's. The incomprehension that greeted the verbal playfulness of the Bern prose affected him deeply. He edged slowly toward silence. In *A Slap in the Face Et Cetera*, he could still transmute his skepticism about fiction into verbal high jinks, but by the late 1920's his tone had changed. In "Brief an einen besteller von novellen" ("Letter to a Commissioner of Novellas"), he explains somewhat defensively why he cannot deliver works that conform to the traditional genre. In mock-bureaucratic language, he argues that traditional novellas can no longer do justice to contemporary life, which has turned into "something tentative, cautiously groping." In "Für die Katz" ("For Zilch") he wryly conceded the pointlessness of his literary productivity. In 1933, he renounced literature for good.

OTHER MAJOR WORKS

LONG FICTION: *Geschwister Tanner*, 1907; *Der Gehülfe*, 1908; *Jakob von Gunten*, 1909 (English translation, 1969); *Der "Räuber"-Roman*, 1972.

PLAYS: *Aschenbrödel*, pr. 1901 (fairy-tale play;

Cinderella, 1985); *Schneewittchen*, pr. 1901 (fairy-tale play; *Snowwhite*, 1985); *Die Knaben*, pr. 1902 (sketch); *Komödie: Theatralisches*, pb. 1919.

POETRY: *Gedichte*, 1909; *Unbekannte Gedichte*, 1958.

MISCELLANEOUS: *Das Gesamtwerk*, 1966-1975 (13 volumes); *Robert Walser Rediscovered: Stories, Fairy-Tale Plays, and Critical Responses*, 1985.

BIBLIOGRAPHY

Avery, George. *Inquiry and Testament: A Study of the Novels and Short Prose of Robert Walser*. Philadelphia: University of Pennsylvania Press, 1968. This introduction to Walser is aimed at both the general reader and the student of German literature. Deals with the themes, the style, and the structure of the Swiss writer's fiction in the context of European literary developments of the early twentieth century.

Cardinal, Agnes. *The Figure of Paradox in the Work of Robert Walser*. Stuttgart: H.-D. Heinz, 1982. Cardinal's astute examination of Walser's technique is informative and interesting. Includes a bibliography.

Gass, William H. "Robert Walser." In *Finding a Form*. New York: Alfred A. Knopf, 1996. Gass argues that Walser's narrators frequently split their point of view between surface reality and a picture-postcard world; the result, Gass contends, is a complex prose style that reveals Walser to be a postmodernist long before the fashion.

Hamburger, Michael. "Explorers: Musil, Robert Walser, Kafka." In *A Proliferation of Prophets: Essays on German Writers from Nietzsche to Brecht*. Manchester, England: Carcanet Press, 1983. Views "freedom and ambivalence" as hallmarks of Walser's art, claiming that he combines the freedom of the essay and the poem with the art of prose fiction.

Harman, Mark, ed. *Robert Walser Rediscovered: Stories, Fairy-Tale Plays, and Critical Responses*. Hanover, N.H.: University Press of New England, 1985. Along with translations, some previously published, are commentaries by major critics, contemporary and modern. Followed by a chronology, notes, a select bibliography, and an index of Walser's works. Essential reading.

_____. "Stream of Consciousness and the Boundaries of Self-Conscious Fiction: The Works of Robert Walser." *Comparative Criticism* 6 (1984): 119-134. Views the fairy tales, short prose, and novels of Walser as parts of an "autobiographical construct." In spite of their confessional aspects, Walser's works are products of craftsmanship and reflection.

Hinson, Hal. "Brothers of Invention." *The Washington Post*, April 18, 1996, p. G1. In this review/interview, Stephen and Timothy Quay discuss their film adaptation of Walser's novella "Jakob von Gunten"; they talk about what drew them to Walser's work and how they tried to adapt Walser's theme and style to film.

Sontag, Susan. Foreword to *Selected Stories*, by Robert Walser. Translated by Christopher Middleton, et al. Manchester, England: Carcanet New Press, 1982. Views Walser as a "miniaturist" in short prose and comments on the "refusal of power" and compassionate despair of his work. See also Christopher Middleton's "Postscript," pp. 191-194.

Mark Harman, updated by Anna M. Wittman and Charles E. May

WANG ANYI

Born: Shanghai, China; 1954

PRINCIPAL SHORT FICTION

Leng tu, 1982 (novella)

Liu shi, 1982 (novella; *Lapse of Time*, 1988)

Xiao bao zhuang, 1985 (novella; *Baotown*, 1989)

Huang shan zhi lian, 1986 (novella; *Love on a Barren Mountain*, 1991)

Xiao cheng zhi lian, 1986 (novella; *Love in a Small Town*, 1988)

Jin xiu gu zhi lian, 1987 (novella; *Brocade Valley*, 1992)

Lapse of Time, 1988

Hai shang fan hua meng, 1996

Xianggang de qing yu ai, 1996

OTHER LITERARY FORMS

Wang Anyi published a travelogue entitled *Mu nü tong you mei li jian* (mother and daughter traveling together in America) in 1986. Addressed to a Chinese audience, this book is essentially derived from notes and observations written during the author's tour of the United States. Her first novel, *Chang hen ge*, was published in 1996.

ACHIEVEMENTS

Wang Anyi first started publishing her work in November, 1976; in less than a decade, she had already been recognized as a prolific writer of substantial achievement. Her short story "Ben ci lie che zhong dian zhan" ("Destination") was chosen for the Chinese National Award for Short Stories in 1982, and her novellas *Lapse of Time* and *Baotown* won the National Award for Short Novels in 1983 and 1986 respectively. *Baotown* was the topic of a seminar hosted by the Writers' Association of Shanghai shortly after its publication in 1985. The Three Loves Trilogy, written in 1986, has attracted attention as a controversial work because of its depiction of illicit or extramarital love affairs—a sensitive issue that, in China, is considered to be a "forbidden territory."

BIOGRAPHY

Wang Anyi was born in Shanghai in 1954. Her mother, Ru Zhijuan, is an accomplished writer whose career began in 1947. Thanks to her cultured family background, Wang was exposed to music, art, and literature as a child. She finished her junior high school education in 1969, the third year of the Cultural Revolution, a period during which a cataclysmal chaos extended all over China as civil and human rights were severely restricted by the Communist regime.

In 1970, like many other teenagers across the Chinese nation, Wang was sent to a rural area in the province of Anhui to join a production brigade as a "young intellectual" (high school graduate) to be "re-educated by the poor and lower-middle peasants." In 1972, however, she managed to find a position in the orchestral troupe of the Xuzhou City Commission for Literature and Arts in the province of Jiangsu; it was during this period that she started writing. In 1978, as the political climate began to change for the better, Wang was transferred back to Shanghai, where she started working in the editorial department of *Childhood* magazine. In 1980, she enrolled in the Fifth Annual Writers' Workshop hosted by the Writers' Association of China. Upon graduation at the end of the year, Wang returned to her editorial work and emerged rapidly as an important writer.

ANALYSIS

Wang Anyi's career coincides with an important historical juncture in contemporary Chinese literature. Prior to the death of Mao Zedong and the fall of the Gang of Four in 1976, Chinese writers were required to play a subservient role and serve the immediate interests of the government. After the introduction of the economic reform in 1978, however, a relatively ameliorated environment allowed writers to pursue authentic and diversified means of expression with a certain amount of liberty. Wang is one of the young writers who seized such an opportunity. Although she once regarded herself as independent of literary movements, she admits that she has benefitted from trends such as the Literature of Wound, the Literature of Transvaluation, the Literature in Search of Roots, and the Quest for Urban Awareness. These tendencies are evident in her works, but her style is peculiarly her own, and in the end, they also culminate in a uniquely lyrical form of humanistic expression.

"AND THE RAIN PATTERS ON"

Representative of Wang's short stories is "And the Rain Patters On," which is reminiscent of the Litera-

ture of Wound, a groundbreaking literary trend that has as its theme the injuries, injustices, sufferings, and aftermaths of the Cultural Revolution. In this story, meticulously crafted from lyrical flashbacks, symbols, and motifs, Wenwen, a woman sent to the countryside as an "educated youth," returns to Shanghai and finds herself to be a spinster and out of place in a world being transformed by modernity. Unable to catch up with the latest fashions, she finds romance to be elusive. While her family has been trying to arrange for her to meet and date a marriageable man (Xiao Yan), she dreamily yearns for a relationship that would somehow be different. One rainy night, after missing the last bus home, she is given a ride on a bike by a man about whom she feels ambivalent. The man is simply an ordinary good Samaritan who happened to pass by, but Wenwen is touched by his casual remark about the beauty of street lamps in the rain and by his account about his having been saved by another good Samaritan. She begins to hope and even trust that she will run into this stranger again. Claiming that she has found a boyfriend, Wenwen rejects Xiao Yan, though to the chagrin of her family it is clear that she is simply daydreaming. Toward the end of the story, the narrator asserts that there are many pleasures in life, and dreaming is one of them; one has to insist on believing that dreams will come true, or else life would be unbearable. Encouraging and disturbing at the same time, this message exemplifies the tensions between the ideal and the real, and the conflicts between the inner life and the outer world. "And the Rain Patters On" also typifies Wang's persistent efforts in juxtaposing idealistic yearnings and realistic pressures, combining these opposites into a new humanism through lyrical expression and psychological representation.

"DESTINATION"

Such efforts can be found in most of the short stories in *Lapse of Time*—for example, in "Destination." In this award-winning piece, because of the mundane pressures of life in Shanghai, Chen Xin is confronted with his family's suggestion that he arrange to marry any woman who has a room to offer as dowry. Realizing, however, that "ahead of him there would be another ten, twenty, and thirty years" and that "he must give his future some serious thought," Chen Xin refuses to compromise and is embroiled in a familial conflict, which is left unresolved at the end of the story. In spite of this conflict, however, the story contains an important touch of humanism as the family, fearing that he may commit suicide, comes searching for him after he has disappeared into the streets for the entire night after a quarrel. Finally, Chen Xin is described as being reconciled to the thought that he will be in search of his true destination—a paradox typical of Wang Anyi's fiction in that her protagonists are deprived materialistically and yet remain spiritually unvanquished.

"THE BASE OF THE WALL"

Whether consciously or otherwise, in many of her stories Wang's new humanism focuses on the pervasive phenomenon of alienation under the socialist regime, though in an existential manner she decides that her protagonists are capable of rising or staying above the mire. For example, in one of her most triumphant stories, "The Base of the Wall," A'nian (son of a working-class family)—chooses to befriend and assist Duxing (daughter of a supposedly antireactionary family from the other side of the broken wall) after he has had a glimpse, through a diary that he has stolen, into the inner life of the sensitive, intelligent, and ostracized "class enemy" whom he and the other kids used to abuse. By eliminating the bigotry from the children of his own neighborhood and by bringing children from both sides of the wall closer to one another, A'nian has dismantled the barrier arbitrarily set up to pit one part of humanity against another.

LAPSE OF TIME

All the above themes—tensions between the ideal and the real, conflicts between the inner life and the outer world, the paradox between spirituality and materiality, the triumph of humanism over alienation under socialism—are explored to a fuller extent in *Lapse of Time*. The novella is a series of sketches chronicling the awakening, growth, and transformation of a housewife during the Cultural Revolution. Duanli, a college graduate, is married to Wenyao, the son of a Shanghai businessman. At the beginning of the Cultural Revolution, the properties of the family are seized by the Red Guards. Wenyao is a superflu-

ous man incapable of meeting the new challenges of life; his brother, Wenguang, for fear of being implicated, distances himself from his father. The responsibility of caring for the family of nine falls on the shoulders of Duanli, who finds it difficult to cope with poverty. No longer a "bourgeois lady of the house," she learns the meaning of life anew, starting from the basics of survival. Gradually, Duanli has in effect become the "guardian" of the household. Upon restitution and the return of the family properties after the Cultural Revolution, fortune again seems to smile on the family, and everyone feels complacent and justified in demanding a better life to make up for the losses of the fateful decade. Duanli, who has become a practical person, feels the same and quits working, but after two years of tiresome and unauthentic social life, she is troubled by the loss of her sense of vitality previously gained from the fateful decade. In the end, she decides to resume her job at the factory, not only to fight boredom but also to continue with her search for the meaning of life and to prevent life from lapsing into oblivion. Full of details about quotidian struggles and the sordid nature of life in contemporary China, the novella most likely will pluck at the heartstrings of millions of readers who, having emerged from a decade of hardships, find themselves entrenched in a whole series of struggles not only to achieve a better economic life but also to establish a significance for themselves.

BAOTOWN

Whereas *Lapse of Time* enlarges on urban consciousness as a condition for the definition of humanity in an alienated society, *Baotown* is an attempt to explore the historical, cultural, and symbolic dimensions of humanity in a rustic and remote corner of rural China. The legend of King Yu of Xia (c. 21-16 B.C.E.), the tamer of the great flood and the founder of the first dynasty in Chinese history, is invoked, somewhat ironically, in the preface, in order to situate Baotown in a mythical and historical context. A folk ballad on numbers, which contains quasi-nonsensical cliché references to random events in Chinese history, recurs throughout the story as a leitmotif. The nonlinear plot is constructed intricately around an odd assortment of two dozen characters, four of whom are responsible for the major event in the history of Baotown. The first of these is Picked-Up. Having been reared by his "aunt," an unmarried woman who claims that she picked him up as a baby from the street, he runs away and settles in Baotown to cohabit with, and slave for, a widow, but he is despised by the community. The second is Bao Fifth Grandfather, an old man who has become an "end-of-the-liner" upon the death of his grandson and only descendant. He is befriended by Dregs, the third character and the youngest son of Bao Yanshan. This little boy, in the end, loses his life for the sake of Bao Fifth Grandfather during a flood, but his body is salvaged by Picked-Up. The fourth character is Bao Renwen, a young man whose aspiration to be a writer is fulfilled when he provides a written account about the accident for broadcast on radio. Unknowingly, he not only immortalizes Dregs but also helps to create a sense of importance for Bao Yanshan and to dignify Picked-Up. Written with a mixed sense of humor, irony, satire, sympathy, and lament, *Baotown* is a dazzling work thanks to its technical experimentation and its penetration into the human psyche as it is shaped by the historical and cultural conditions of China. The mythmaking process occurring in both the preface and the conclusion of the novella is especially thought-provoking.

THREE LOVES TRILOGY

Just as *Baotown* was still arousing much enthusiasm among its readers, Wang moved on to transcend herself even further, in 1986, by turning out the controversial Three Loves trilogy. The three novellas share the common theme of unorthodox love, but each work has its unique focus. In *Love on a Barren Mountain*, which deals with extramarital love and sex, Wang focuses on the intensity of an obsessive relationship between a talented but superfluous man and a seductive woman of questionable reputation. They can each be described as married to the right person of their choice, until their fatal encounter tells each of them that the other could have been a better match. It is a poignant tragedy of desire which ends in the lovers' suicide, though death itself does not seem to constitute a real resolution. The omniscient narrator is careful not to take a judgmental stand, as if to suggest that love of such intensity is beyond any ordinary sense of right and wrong or good and evil.

The second piece in the trilogy, *Love in a Small Town*, deals with the strange relationship between two dancers of a sleazy troupe. Both performers have been deformed as a result of improper training, the woman being larger and the man smaller in size than normal. Their relationship is full of sadomasochistic contradictions: They both hate and crave each other so intensely that if they are not trying to beat each other's brains out, they are burning with desire for each other. They are condemned to a relationship that amounts to mutual punishment and destruction through either sexual contact or physical combat. Such a consuming affair drags both parties deeper and deeper into a quagmire. Eventually, actually contemplating suicide, the woman, who has been evading the man for a long period, decides to satiate her desire for the last time as if she were going to die in a battle. Miraculously, this last union makes the woman pregnant and gives her the courage to live for herself and her twins as an unmarried mother and an outcast, whereas the man sinks so low that he becomes a good-for-nothing gambler and alcoholic. The solution to the contradictions in the story is therefore polarized between the rise above and the fall below the line that sets humanity apart from bestiality. In this stunning story, which reads like a parable if not a pathological case study, it seems that the author is raising the question of what to do with the inherent deformity or deficiency of human nature itself.

The third piece of the trilogy, *Brocade Valley*, differs sharply from the first and the second in that here the focus is on an extramarital relationship that is the result of phantasmagoria. In the story, an editor takes part in a conference held in the Lushan Mountains, a scenic tourist resort. With household chores behind her, she is distanced from her contempt-breeding husband, who has become all too familiar. Surrounded by men of talent, she feels that she has fallen in love with a writer who she thinks is also in love with her. Although the romantic scenery intimates that the romance is real, nothing has actually transpired. Returning to live her life of daily routines, for a while she hopes that the "romance" will materialize even if it entails a terrible scandal, but finally she is reconciled to the thought that it would suffice only to have a wonderful impression of the valley. This dreamy story is a subtle exploration of the distinctive nature of feminine desire and sexual difference in the context of married life in contemporary China. At issue is not whether the woman and her husband love each other, but rather how love itself can stay uncontaminated by the practical concerns of everyday life and survive the wear and tear of familiarity.

The three stories of the trilogy are independent of one another but also interrelated. They constitute a progression toward the resolution of the question of love, sex, and marriage on psychological rather than moral grounds. In these stories, every single character has gone on trial; although in the end no one really triumphs, readers begin to sense that the author's examination of the characters' innermost thoughts, feelings, desires, and secrets, however perverse, has sharpened and deepened their understanding of humanity itself. As none of the characters is given a name, the trilogy seems to be inviting readers to witness the introspections of the characters themselves and, in the process, start an introspection of the anonymous man and woman within the reader's own psyche.

XIANGGANG DE QING YU AI

The development of Wang's short stories can be divided into three periods. The writings of the first two periods are represented respectively in *Lapse of Time* and the Three Loves trilogy. In 1996, Wang edited ten of her stories written in the 1990's into a collection entitled *Xianggang de qing yu ai* (love and sentiment in Hong Kong). The collection signifies the climax of Wang's short-fiction writing. The collection contains the love stories "Miaomiao," "'Wenge' yishi" (anecdotes of the 'Cultural Revolution'), and *Xianggang de qing yu ai*, as well as the critically acclaimed novellas *Beitong zhidi* (a land of tragedy), *Shushu de gushi* (our uncle's story), and *Shangxin Taipingyang* (sadness for the Pacific).

In this collection, Wang continues her quest for the meaning of love. In "Miaomiao," a cleaning maid in a small-town hotel has the daring spirit to adopt the dress style of the big city and explore the meaning of sex and love; ironically, her fashionable dress is seen as "backwardness" in the town and she is repeatedly used and abandoned by men as an object of sex. It does not matter what sexuality means: beauty or adultery. Miaomiao is left with unspeakable loneliness. In "'Wenge' yishi" it is not sexual desire or love but a shared sense of loneliness that binds a couple together. *Xianggang de qing yu ai*, a story of an old rich Hong Kong businessman and his young mistress from Mainland China, examines the idea that the balance in a relationship between a man and a woman depends on equal exchange. Spiritual needs can be exchanged for financial independence. The relationship between the businessman and young woman is sincere but businesslike.

In China, Wang is also known as a regional writer. The majority of her stories are set in Shanghai. In her earlier writings, Shanghai was largely portrayed as a land of exquisite culture and taste, new trends, and passionate love. However, in *Beitong zhidi*, Shanghai becomes a nightmarish labyrinth of alienation and persecution for outsiders. Liu Desheng, a peasant from Shangdong, misread the market and attempted to sell bags of ginger in Shanghai. Apart from his business failure, he completely lost his bearing in Shanghai. Groping his way in the maze of residential lanes, he was seen as an alien and chased as a "criminal." He was eventually cornered by a mob and the police at the top of a building from which he accidentally fell to his death. Such a sense of alienation worms its way into the story *Shushu de gushi* as the corroding power of melancholy. The uncle, who had become alienated from his wife and his environment, became a source of alienation with the rise of his fame and power. His son was so estranged from him that he attempted to kill him. In *Shangxin Taipingyang*, individual melancholy gains historical and global significance. Melancholy becomes a distinctive mode of narration. It adds sobriety and multilayers of depth to an otherwise simple story.

Having grown up privileged and yet given opportunities to experience and sympathize with the conditions of the deprived in both urban and rural China during a tumultuous age, Wang is a dynamic and conscientious writer equipped with a wide variety of technical resources, including lyricism, cinematic flashes, and psychological realism. Assessing her own career, she has stated that the overall theme that she has been attempting to formulate, after much rational deliberation, is that humankind's greatest enemy is itself. According to this proposition, Wang believes that a human being has to struggle against not only the world outside but also, more important, the self within. Furthermore, she observes that such a struggle is by definition a solitary and lifelong campaign, but in the sense that it is experienced by all human beings on different battlefronts, it is also a collective endeavor that can be shared. The short stories and novellas analyzed above certainly bear out her characterization of the human struggle. Her preoccupation with such a struggle offers a unique humanistic vision perfectly adapted to the social, political, historical, and cultural conditions of contemporary Chinese literature.

OTHER MAJOR WORKS

LONG FICTION: *Chang hen ge*, 1996.

NONFICTION: *Mu nü tong you mei li jian*, 1986; *Piaobo de yuyan*, 1996.

BIBLIOGRAPHY

Hung, Eva. Introduction to *Love in a Small Town*. Hong Kong: Chinese University of Hong Kong, 1988. Contains an overview of Wang's life and career up to 1987, focusing on Wang's views on women and the authorities' condemnation of the sexuality in the Three Loves trilogy.

_____. Introduction to *Love on a Barren Mountain*. Hong Kong: Chinese University of Hong Kong, 1991. An informed discussion and analysis of the backgrounds, issues, themes, and techniques of the three novellas in the Three Loves trilogy both individually and as a progression. Argues that Wang Anyi has adopted a woman-centered attitude in her treatment of relationships between men and women.

Kinkley, Jeffrey. Preface to *Lapse of Time*. San Francisco: China Books and Periodicals, 1988. An introductory overview of Wang Anyi's short fiction translated for collection in *Lapse of Time*. Focusing on the humanism by which Wang's works are informed, Kinkley provides brief but useful analyses of their historical background and social contexts, as well as the author's motivations, preoccupations, themes, techniques, and style.

Leung, Laifong. "Wang Anyi: Restless Explorer." *Morning Sun Interviews with Chinese Writers of the Lost Generation*. New York: Sharpe, 1994. An insightful interview revealing how Wang searches for new subjects and different styles in fictional representation.

Li Ziyun. Preface to *Best Chinese Stories, 1949-1989*. Beijing: Chinese Literature Press, 1989. An extremely useful analysis of the development of short fiction as an engaging art form in the postliberation era. Major trends, along with representative authors and works, are identified and discussed in the context of the political movements in contemporary China.

See, Carolyn. "Cultural Evolution." Review of *Baotown*, by Wang Anyi. *Los Angeles Times*, January 14, 1990, p. 1. Discusses *Baotown*, Wang's fictional account of her exile to a small village during the Chinese Cultural Revolution of the 1970's; discusses the quality of stubbornness and curiosity that underlies the survival of the workers and peasants there.

Tang Xiaobing. "Melancholy Against the Grain: Approaching Postmodernity in Wang Anyi's Tales of Sorrow." *Boundary* 24 (Fall, 1997): 177-199. Examines the origin and content of Wang's tales of sorrow, most notably her critically acclaimed novella *Shangxin Taipingyang*, an imaginative rewriting of an earlier, simpler short story; argues that this rewriting is motivated by an unresolvable sadness, a global desolation that lies at the heart of Wang's melancholy imagination.

Wang Anyi. "Biographical Note—My Wall." In *Lapse of Time*. San Francisco: China Books and Periodicals, 1988. The author identifies the wall separating the neighborhood of the deprived from the neighborhood of the privileged (she grew up in the latter) as the spiritual source of her art. Wang explains how, because of the symbolic impact of the wall, she can be likened to an acrobat walking a tightrope both in her life and in her fiction.

Zhong, Xueping. "Sisterhood? Representations of Women's Relationships in Two Contemporary Chinese Texts." In *Gender and Sexuality: Twentieth-Century Chinese Literature and Society*. Edited by

Tonglin Lu. Albany: State University of New York Press, 1993. A detailed comparison of Wang Anyi's "Brothers" with Jiang Zidan's "Waiting for the Twilight."

Balance Chow, updated by
Qingyun Wu

SYLVIA TOWNSEND WARNER

Born: Harrow, England; December 6, 1893
Died: Maiden Newton, England; May 1, 1978

PRINCIPAL SHORT FICTION

Some World Far from Ours, and Stay Corydon, Thou Swain, 1929
Elinor Barley, 1930
Moral Ending and Other Stories, 1931
The Salutation, 1932
More Joy in Heaven, and Other Stories, 1935
The Cat's Cradle Book, 1940
A Garland of Straw and Other Stories, 1943
The Museum of Cheats, 1947
Winter in the Air, and Other Stories, 1955
A Spirit Rises, 1962
A Stranger with a Bag, and Other Stories, 1966 (U.S. edition, *Swans on an Autumn River: Stories*, 1966)
The Innocent and the Guilty: Stories, 1971
Kingdoms of Elfin, 1977
Scenes of Childhood, 1981
One Thing Leading to Another: And Other Stories, 1984
Selected Stories of Sylvia Townsend Warner, 1988

OTHER LITERARY FORMS

In addition to the short stories for which Sylvia Townsend Warner is best known, she wrote seven novels: *Lolly Willowes: Or, The Loving Huntsman* (1926), *Mr. Fortune's Maggot* (1927), *The True Heart* (1929), *Summer Will Show* (1936), *After the Death of*

Don Juan (1938), *The Corner That Held Them* (1948), and *The Flint Anchor* (1954). She also wrote several collections of poetry, which were published as *Collected Poems* (1982), a biography, a travel guidebook, and a volume of literary criticism, and she translated two books from French into English.

ACHIEVEMENTS

In 1926, Sylvia Townsend Warner's first novel, *Lolly Willowes*, was the first Book-of-the-Month Club selection; her second novel, *Mr. Fortune's Maggot*, was a selection of the newly formed Literary Guild. Her later novels did not attain the same popularity, but her short stories, 144 of which were published in *The New Yorker* over a period of four decades, gained for her a wide readership.

In 1967, she became a Fellow of the Royal Society of Literature (she wryly commented that it was the first public acknowledgment she had received since she was expelled from kindergarten) and in 1972, an honorary member of the American Academy of Arts and Letters. Her short story "The Love Match" was awarded the Prix Menton for 1968.

No full-length critical assessment of Warner's achievement as novelist, short-story writer, and poet has been produced. John Updike noted in a favorable review that her "half century of brilliantly varied and superbly self-possessed literary production never won for her the flaming place in the heavens of reputation that she deserved." As far as her achievement in the short story is concerned, however, she certainly ranks alongside H. E. Bates and V. S. Pritchett, her two British contemporaries, whose work most resembles her own.

BIOGRAPHY

Sylvia Townsend Warner was born in Harrow, Middlesex, on December 6, 1893. She was educated mostly at home (her father was a schoolmaster), having been considered a disruptive influence in kindergarten. Her early talent was for music, and in 1914 she was set to travel to Vienna to study under Arnold Schönberg, but the outbreak of World War I prevented it. In 1916, after the death of her father, she moved to London and was a member of the editorial committee which compiled the ten-volume *Tudor Church Music* (1922-1929). Her first publication was a collection of poetry, *The Espalier*, in 1925, a time when she thought of herself primarily as a poet. In the 1920's, she met the novelist T. F. Powys, who proved to be influential on her early poetry and fiction. In 1930, Warner moved to the country and lived with her friend Valentine Ackland in a Dorset village. During the 1930's, she and Ackland became involved in left-wing politics, joining the Communist Party and serving with the Red Cross in Barcelona during the Spanish Civil War. In subsequent years, Warner lived the quiet life of an English gentlewoman in rural Dorset, managing to sustain her literary output up to her final years. She died in 1978.

ANALYSIS

One of the notable features of Sylvia Townsend Warner's short stories is her elegant, precise, epigrammatic, and witty prose. These qualities are particularly noticeable when she focuses on what she knows best: the niceties of English middle- and upper-class life as they reveal themselves in day-to-day domestic and social routines, and the sudden disruption of those routines. As in the novels of her British contemporary, Barbara Pym, her detached and humorous observance of the oddities of humanity is one of the chief pleasures to be gained from her stories. She has a sharp but sympathetic eye for eccentricity of all kinds, and her stories cover a wide range of situations and points of view.

Perhaps because of the variety of her fiction, it would be misleading to pinpoint specific themes or leading ideas. Warner's stories do not reveal a consistent or dominant mood or atmosphere. She does not espouse a philosophy or champion a cause. Her subject matter is the infinite variety of human nature: its follies, regrets, hopes, deceits, compromises, its small defeats and victories, the tidy chaos of the average human life. The stories frequently develop out of an apparently insignificant event or chance encounter or an incident or memory from the protagonist's past, which resurfaces to affect the present. A sudden rift is produced in the otherwise smooth fabric of daily life, and often an ironic twist at the end will reveal a new dimension to a relationship or to the inner life of the protagonist.

Warner is a traditionalist. She does not experiment with modern techniques (her chief technical device is the flashback); her stories succeed through strong characterization and plotting. There is an old-fashioned quality about her and her fictional world. Almost all of her stories are set in England, with a carefully evoked spirit of place (perhaps this accounts in part for her success in *The New Yorker*, since she usually portrays a timeless, civilized England that popular American culture has tended to idealize).

"HEE-HAW!"

Warner has a Thomas Hardy-like awareness of the ironies of fate (Hardy was a major influence on her early poetry) and of the tricks that time plays. Many of her stories (for example, "The Sea Is Always the Same," "Johnnie Brewer," and "A Second Visit") center on the protagonist's return, after a gap of many years, to a former home or place of memories. In "*Hee-Haw!*" from *Winter in the Air, and Other Stories*, Mrs. Vincent returns to the village in Cornwall, where for three years, thirty years previously, she had lived turbulently with her first husband, Ludovick, a young artist who was later to gain eminence. The first sound she hears on her return is the unchanging, regular sound of the foghorn from the lightship (*Hee Haw! Hee Haw!*), which seems to span the thirty years of her absence, giving a sense of permanence and familiarity to the external environment. What of her internal environment? She is introduced to an old man in the hotel bar, who needs little prompting to recall the famous artist. His recollections, however, shock her. He tells her that Ludovick and his wife (or girlfriend, he did not know which) were the happiest couple he had ever seen, and he relates several incidents in which they were playing and laughing together. Mrs. Vincent, however, knowing how stormy her relationship with Ludovick was, assumes without question that the old man must be referring to another woman. In a wave of jealousy, she realizes that she has discovered, thirty years after the event, her husband's infidelity. She is left to her anger and her melancholy; an old wound has been reopened in a way that she would not have imagined possible.

The strength of "*Hee-Haw!*" is in the contrast between the ease with which the reader guesses the truth (although the truth is never overtly established) and the inability of Mrs. Vincent to recognize that her relationship with Ludovick might have looked quite different from the outside. It is at once a poignant tale of reminiscence and a reminder of the subjectivity of the experience of life. Appearances are not what they seem, and memory is only shifting sand.

"WINTER IN THE AIR"

"Winter in the Air" also focuses on a return. A middle-aged woman, Barbara, returns to live in London after a twelve-year absence, following the breakup of her marriage. The story consists of a series of flashbacks to the final stages of her marriage two months previously, interspersed with Barbara's thoughts as she arranges the furniture in her new apartment. The reader is given a minimum of clues regarding the reasons for the divorce, and the chief interest of this otherwise slight, although typical story, lies in the fact that nine-tenths of its emotional force lies below the surface. Deep emotions surface only momentarily.

What Barbara really feels, though, is contained in the half-remembered snatches of a quotation from William Shakespeare's *The Winter's Tale* (1623) which flash into her mind: the dignified, despairing speech of Hermione, the wronged wife, whose chief comfort in life, the favor of her husband, has gone, though she does not know how or why it went. As Barbara sits down to write to Willie, she knows that

in real life one does not say such things, and all she is prepared to commit to paper is a platitude about her new charwoman; this, however, is as unsatisfactory to her as confessing her true feelings and she tears up the letter and throws it away. Neither truth nor platitude can be uttered, and the deeper emotional terrain of her life must remain as silent as the silence which she notices enveloping her new apartment. Silence will hide secrets and heal pain, and life will go on. The story finishes with Barbara projecting herself into the mundane thoughts of the charwoman about the weather: Winter is in the air. This final thought has a slightly ominous connotation; whether it hints at Barbara's future loneliness, old age, or simply the demise of emotional honesty and communication, Warner rightly leaves it to the reader to decide.

"A LOVE MATCH"

Swans on an Autumn River contains what is often regarded as Warner's finest story, "A Love Match." It centers on a quiet conservative couple, Justin Tizard and his elder sister Celia. Justin returns on leave after the Battle of the Somme in 1916, in which Celia's fiancé has been killed. He stays at her apartment in London, but during his sleep he relives the terrible scenes of battle, raving incoherently. Celia, sleepless, listens in horror in the adjoining room. The following day, as they stroll casually around London, an old woman mistakes them for man and wife. The incident is one of several foreshadowings of what is to come. Two nights later, Celia is again awakened by Justin's ravings. She goes to his side to comfort him, and the combination of her compassion and his distress drives them into the physical expression of love.

Afterward, they feel no regret, and as the years go by they find happiness together. They possess an intuitive insight into each other's feelings, feel no need to impress each other, and are not particularly concerned with each other's likes and dislikes. Their common childhood memories act as a bond between them. They also become practiced at shielding their true relationship from their neighbors in Hallowby, the English village to which they move in 1923, and soon become one of the most respectable of couples.

Their lives are upset in the 1930's when Celia, who has become bored with local society and has developed a reputation for supporting unusual causes, receives a series of anonymous letters which claim that her secret is common knowledge in the village. The letters turn out to be only idle gossip from one of Justin's disappointed female admirers, and he soon puts a stop to them. Nothing has changed, and the secret remains intact.

The final outcome is carefully developed to produce the maximum effect. During World War II, Hallowby is bombed. Rescue workers entering a bombed house find a bedroom floor deep in rubble. Slates from the roof have fallen on the bed, crushing the two bodies that lay there. One of the villagers at the scene offers the opinion that Justin went into Celia's bedroom to comfort her. Others agree, and the coroner accepts this hypothesis as truth.

Warner's comment that the story's success was a victory for "incest and sanity" was only partly tongue in cheek. Rarely has incest been so sympathetically portrayed. Warner places subtle emphasis on the ease with which the lovers communicate and the depth of their love. The very criminality of their liaison adds to its preciousness for them. The ambiguity of the conclusion is also important. It is not made explicit whether the villagers genuinely believe their own explanation, whether they simply cannot comprehend the implications of what they see, or whether they guess the truth but, out of common human decency, desire to shield the lovers from shame. The openendedness of this conclusion reflects the necessary mixture of emotions which the story has raised and left unresolved. The image of the two lovers in death, locked together in the tenderness of their illegal union and surrounded by the debris of their ruined house, remains vividly in the reader's mind.

"SWANS ON AN AUTUMN RIVER"

"Swans on an Autumn River" also culminates in a strong visual image, which juxtaposes opposites to suggest the unattainable nature of an ideal. Norman Repton, an engineer in his late sixties, visits Ireland for the first time on a business trip. It is a country for which he has always felt a romantic longing, fueled by the poetry of William Butler Yeats. The country does not meet his expectations, however, and he soon discovers that he is an alien in an unfamiliar land.

Repton is attracted to the river, which is one of two central symbols in the story. It is as if the river has power to compensate him for his old age, his weak physical condition, and the dissatisfaction with life that he feels. At night, he leaves the curtain of his room undrawn, so he can see the river, which also casts its lightly dancing reflection on the ceiling. In spite of this, he is aware of neither, being alternately sunk heavily in sleep or at the mercy of his bladder and digestion. His low vitality is a strong contrast to everything that the flowing river and its reflection suggests. In its ease, serenity, and sparkling movement, it represents another realm of being, but it is a realm which is forever closed to him, however much he longs for it.

This theme is restated and developed by another powerful symbol in the climax of the story. When he wakes in the morning, he sees a gathering of swans on the river. He looks at them enraptured, as if they were his own treasure. He grabs some bread and rushes out of the hotel, by which time eighteen swans have collected. The swans come flocking toward him as he excitedly tosses them the bread. He notes how skillfully they swim "without check or collision" (unlike his own troubled and unsatisfactory life). When the feeding is interrupted by a swarm of gulls competing for the bread, Repton strikes at one of them and becomes so angry that he loses all thought of where he is. He only succeeds in making a fool of himself, falling down and hitting his head on the pavement. To two passersby, he is nothing more than a corpulent old Englishman behaving eccentrically, and the story ends with a policeman arranging for an ambulance to take him away.

The poetry of Yeats may well have been in Warner's mind when she wrote this story. The swans resemble those in "The Wild Swans at Coole" which "drift on the still water,/ Mysterious, beautiful." In their effortlessness, they seem to belong to a realm of eternity, and they are contrasted in the story with the frequent emphasis on the limitations and restrictions of ordinary bodily life. Repton himself calls to mind the lines from Yeats's "Sailing to Byzantium": "An aged man is but a paltry thing,/ A tattered coat upon a stick, unless/ Soul clap its hands and sing! . . ." Repton cannot clap his hands and sing, however, and he cannot be gathered into the "artifice of eternity" which the swans on the river symbolize. "Swans on an Autumn River" thus becomes a tragic story of the disparity between the infinity of human desire and the finite realities within which it must operate.

THE INNOCENT AND THE GUILTY

The Innocent and the Guilty is the only one of Warner's collections to be organized under a specific theme. She had confessed to an "obsessive" concern with this theme, but the title is wholly ironic ("Perhaps one day, I shall . . . write a story where the innocent are charming and the guilty nauseating"). The ironic purpose is clear from "Truth in the Cup," in which a group of self-righteous villagers, celebrating in the local hotel on a stormy night, lament the moral decay of the young. Like sinful man in Genesis, however, they become victims of a catastrophic flood. It is also clear in "The Quality of Mercy," in which a drunken young woman and the local toughs who help her home are more virtuous than the "respectable" sister who greets them with abuse and recrimination.

"BUT AT THE STROKE OF MIDNIGHT"

The distinctions between innocence and guilt become blurred in "But at the Stroke of Midnight," one of Warner's most ambitious stories. It is a mysterious tale, with a hint of the supernatural, and it centers on the motif of rebirth. The protagonist is Lucy Ridpath, an undistinguished middle-aged woman who escapes from her dull marriage to seek a new life. Adopting the name Aurelia, she goes through a number of adventures in London and becomes like "a nova—a new appearance in the firmament, the explosion of an aging star." She has a powerful effect on everyone she meets. A clergyman sees her as a tranquil, spiritual woman; others find themselves curiously attracted to her and do her unexpected favors.

Leaving London to stay at a guesthouse, she adopts a stray cat and calls it Lucy. (Cats appear with somewhat alarming frequency in Warner's fiction.) She moves to a country cottage and successfully tries her hand at being a landscape artist. It seems that her rebirth is accomplished. The title, however, with its Cinderella connotations, suggests that it will not last. So it turns out. One cold wet night, Lucy returns late,

mortally injured, and the moment the cat dies, Aurelia realizes that she is no longer Aurelia but Lucy Ridpath once more. When morning breaks, she goes outside to bury the cat, but she finds herself immersed in floodwater. Walking toward the road, she has a half-conscious desire to drown, and as she wades deeper in the water, she falls and is swept away by the current.

This curious but stimulating story, a mixture of realism and fantasy, is one of Warner's very few attempts to deal with an archetypal theme. It does not entirely succeed. The ending is abrupt and the reason for Lucy's death is unexplained. The cat, it seems, mysteriously embodies her former self, to which she must return when the cat dies. It is quite possible that Warner intended such a supernatural implication. In one of her early stories, "Early One Morning," from the collection *The Salutation*, an old woman dies and her soul immediately passes into one of the local greyhounds. Perhaps the tragedy of "But at the Stroke of Midnight" is that having once known rebirth, Lucy cannot lapse back into a former state. Caught between two selves, the old and the new, she can be neither.

"OXENHOPE"

In "Oxenhope," Warner returns to a favorite theme, the effects of the passing of time, as experienced by a protagonist who returns to former haunts. As the story develops, it becomes a subtle meditation on the presence of mortality and the longing for immortality.

William, a man in his sixties, returns to the village where he had stayed for a month when he was seventeen. As he drives through, he recognizes everything in the landscape. He thinks about the old shepherd he had known, with his prodigious memory that seemingly would never die, and he wants to know all the changes that the unchanging valley has seen. As he reminisces, the narrative passes freely between present event and past remembrance; past and present seem to merge. He finds the gravestone of the woman who had befriended him and cleans it so that the name stands out, just as he had done with the other family gravestones so many years previously. He notices, however, that the most recent name is the least visible, as if the woman had not expected to be remembered.

Fully aware of the imprint of mortality, he decides that the past is irrecoverable and that there is no purpose in staying. Then comes the ironic twist in the tale, so characteristic of Warner. He meets a local boy, who talks to him about local legends. One story is of a man who "set fire" to the loch and sent flames leaping up around his boat. William immediately realizes that the man was him—out in a rowing boat he had taken a match to bubbles of marsh gas as they rose to the surface of the water, and the fire had been the result. He leaves the village satisfied, with no need even of a backward glance, realizing that he is lodged in the collective memory of the locality, which lends him a kind of immortality. The subtlety of the observed paradox and its implications reveal Warner's fiction at its best. Human life remains embedded in the past even when the past has seemed to vanish or to be vanishing, and yet the knowledge of this fact paradoxically frees the present from the past's stifling grip.

KINGDOMS OF ELFIN

Two more collections are worthy of comment. *Kingdoms of Elfin* is a collection of fantasies about fairy kingdoms. The product of Warner's final creative years, these stories display considerable ingenuity (and Warner clearly relishes the telling of them), but few rank with her best work. The fantasy setting does not supply the moral bearings necessary in order to feel and respond fully to the odd adventures of the fairy protagonists. Warner invents her own fairy lore with considerable aplomb, but the kingdoms she describes are not mythical or otherworldly. On the contrary, they tend to parallel human institutions, particularly the hierarchical structure of medieval or Renaissance society. In consequence, much of the pleasure to be gained from them is in the occasional acid comment about the superstitions of religion, or in the gentle mocking of the social pretenses and snobbery and the political plotting and maneuvering that bedevil both human and fairy worlds.

SCENES OF CHILDHOOD

Scenes of Childhood is a posthumous collection of Warner's reminiscences about her upbringing in Edwardian England, a time "when there was a Tzar in Russia, and scarcely an automobile or a divorced person in Mayfair." Impressionistic sketches rather than fully developed stories, they display her epigrammatic style to best advantage. Extracting much harmless fun from the eccentricities of upper-middle-class English life, she parades an assortment of odd characters ranging from her parents to great aunts, nannies, retired majors, French teachers, and a butler whose smile was so ghastly that he had to be got rid of (he revenged himself by joining the fire brigade and ruining the Warner's kitchen while putting out a minor fire).

At their best, Sylvia Townsend Warner's short stories constitute a quiet exploration of the oddities and ironies of the human condition, as it unfolds itself in time, fate, and circumstances. She is an acute observer, but she is careful not to judge. Her humor, always tart, is never malicious. She is a realist, and few of her stories end in unqualified optimism. She is aware of the pain of loss and the mockery that time makes of human ideals. She notes the human capacity for self-deceit but also the ability to make peace with limitations. Rarely faltering in the smoothness of her controlled, elegant, economical prose, she is a craftswoman whose finely wrought stories entertain and delight.

OTHER MAJOR WORKS

LONG FICTION: *Lolly Willowes: Or, The Loving Huntsman*, 1926; *Mr. Fortune's Maggot*, 1927; *The True Heart*, 1929; *Summer Will Show*, 1936; *After the Death of Don Juan*, 1938; *The Corner That Held Them*, 1948; *The Flint Anchor*, 1954.

POETRY: *The Espalier*, 1925; *Time Importuned*, 1928; *Opus 7*, 1931; *Whether a Dove or a Seagull: Poems*, 1933; *Boxwood*, 1957; *Twelve Poems*, 1980; *Collected Poems*, 1982.

NONFICTION: *Jane Austen*, 1951; *T. H. White: A Biography*, 1967; *Letters*, 1982.

BIBLIOGRAPHY

Ackland, Valentine. *For Sylvia: An Honest Account.* New York: W. W. Norton, 1985. A brief but poignant autobiography by Warner's lover, detailing the years with Warner and the painful separation caused by Ackland's struggle with alcoholism. Bea Howe's lengthy foreword discusses her first-hand understanding of the influence of Ackland on Warner's personal and professional life.

Brothers, Barbara. "Through the 'Pantry Window': Sylvia Townsend Warner and the Spanish Civil War." In *Rewriting the Good Fight: Critical Essays on the Literature of the Spanish Civil War*, edited by Frieda S. Brown et al. East Lansing: Michigan State University Press, 1989. Places Warner in the context of her contemporaries regarding the period of the Spanish Civil War. Bibliography.

Dinnage, Rosemary. "An Affair to Remember." *The New York Times*, March 7, 1999. A review of *Selected Letters of Sylvia Townsend Warner and Valentine Ackland*; comments on Warner's offbeat short stories from *The New Yorker*, claiming the short story was well suited to her whimsy; discusses her lesbian relationship with Valentine Ackland.

Harmon, Claire. *Sylvia Townsend Warner: A Biography*. London: Chatto & Windus, 1989. An even and thorough biography with illustrations, a bibliography, and an index. Deals openly and prominently with the relationship between Valentine Ackland and Warner. Gives a biographical and historical context of Warner's work but with little critical detail.

Loeb, Marion C. "British to the Core." *St. Petersburg Times*, August 6, 1989, p. 7D. A review of *The Selected Stories of Sylvia Townsend Warner*; notes that her stories deal with the world of civil servants, vicars' wives, and pensioners; comments on her graceful, lyrical style.

Maxwell, William, ed. Introduction to *Letters: Sylvia Townsend Warner*. New York: Viking, 1982. The novelist and editor for *The New Yorker* and Warner's longtime personal friend shows great admiration for Warner's work. Maxwell notes her historical astuteness, her "ironic detachment," and her graceful formalism of language. Maxwell also considers the letters in the light of their being a writer's "left-over energy" and written without the inhibition of editorial or critical judgment. Includes a brief biographical sketch.

Perenyi, Eleanor. "The Good Witch of the West." *The New York Review of Books* 32 (July 18, 1985): 27-30. Argues that Warner's writing reputation has suffered from the inability of critics to categorize her writings, which include dozens of short stories and seven novels; notes that the publication of her letters has sparked new interest and that their talk of dreams and visitations suggests that Warner harbored "more than a touch of the witch."

Strachan, W. J. "Sylvia Townsend Warner: A Memoir." *London Magazine* 19, no. 8 (November, 1979): 41-50. An overview of Warner's fiction, with a close look at the elements of fantasy and realism. *Kingdoms of Elfin* and *Lolly Willowes*, for example, seem incongruent given Warner's activity during World War I, but such realistic works as *The Flint Anchor* demonstrate her earthy, pragmatic quality. Even her most fantastic works reveal reason "firmly in control."

Tomalin, Claire. "Burning Happiness." *The New York Times*, February 18, 1996. A review of *The Diaries of Sylvia Townsend Warner*; discusses the nature of her feminism and her communism; notes the passion of her grief for Valentine Ackland after Ackland's death.

Updike, John. "Jake and Olly Opt Out." *The New Yorker* 55 (August 20, 1979): 97-102. In this comparative review of Kingsley Amis's *Jake's Thing* (1978) and Warner's *Lolly Willowes*, Updike looks at the role of nature in Warner's work and discerns a subtle strain of feminism. He argues that, unlike Amis and other former poets-turned-novelists, Warner's poetic style retains elements of "magic and music" and that her talent merits a much greater recognition than she has received.

Bryan Aubrey, updated by
Lou Thompson

ROBERT PENN WARREN

Born: Guthrie, Kentucky; April 24, 1905
Died: West Wardsboro, near Stratton, Vermont; September 15, 1989

PRINCIPAL SHORT FICTION
  Blackberry Winter, 1946
  The Circus in the Attic and Other Stories, 1947

OTHER LITERARY FORMS

In addition to his short fiction, Robert Penn Warren published ten novels, several volumes of poetry, a play, a biography, two collections of critical essays, three historical essays, three influential textbooks, several children's books, two studies of race relations in America, one memoir, and several book-length treatises on literature. He won a host of distinguished awards, including three Pulitzer Prizes, two for poetry and one for fiction. Three of his novels have been filmed, and one of them, *All the King's Men* (1946), has been presented in operatic form.

ACHIEVEMENTS

Honored as a major American poet and novelist, Robert Penn Warren displayed uncommon versatility in significant contributions to almost every literary genre. His work has been translated worldwide, and his short stories are widely anthologized. While he is best known for his novel *All the King's Men*, which won the Pulitzer Prize, he was most prolific as a poet whose awards included two Pulitzer Prizes and an appointment as America's first poet laureate.

The subject of Warren's fiction, and much of his poetry, is southern rural life in the late nineteenth and early twentieth centuries. He reveals a rootedness in his subject and its values, a concern for moral issues, and a gift for dialogue and environmental detail that lends distinctiveness to his work. His short stories, for example, are set down in rich, vigorous style, and they delineate the flow of time, the influence of past on present, and the painful necessity of self-knowledge.

BIOGRAPHY

Robert Penn Warren was educated at Guthrie High School and was graduated from Vanderbilt University in Nashville, Tennessee (B.A., 1925), where he was associated with the Fugitive Group of poets; he did graduate work at the University of California (M.A., 1927), Yale University, and Oxford, and as a Rhodes scholar (D.Litt., 1930). In 1930, he contributed an essay, *I'll Take My Stand*, to the Agrarian symposium. Between 1935 and 1942, he was an editor of the *Southern Review* and was influential in the articulation and practice of the New Criticism. After an active career as a professor of English at a number of American colleges and universities, he retired from Yale in 1973. His first marriage to Emma Brescia in 1930 ended in divorce in 1950. He and his second wife, the writer Eleanor Clark, herself a National Book Award winner, had one son and one daughter.

Warren won the Pulitzer Prize for Fiction in 1947, the Pulitzer Prize for Poetry in 1958 and 1979, and the National Book Award in 1958. From 1944 to 1945, he was the second occupant of the Chair of Poetry at the Library of Congress. In 1952 he was elected to the American Philosophical Society; in 1959 to the American Academy of Arts and Letters; and in 1972 to the American Academy of Arts and Sciences. In 1967, he received the Bollingen Prize in Poetry, and in 1970 the National Medal for Literature and the Van Wyck Brooks Award. In 1974, he was chosen to deliver the third Annual Jefferson Lecture in the Humanities. In 1975 he received the Emerson-Thoreau Award of the American Academy of Arts and Sciences; the next year the Copernicus Award from the Academy of American Poets; and in 1977 the Harriet Monroe Prize for Poetry. Other awards included the Shelley Memorial Prize and the Presidential Medal of Freedom. In 1986, Warren achieved the unique distinction of becoming the first poet laureate (by act of Congress) of the United States. Warren's life spanned almost the whole twentieth century. After producing a rich final harvest of work from the mid-1970's to the mid-1980's, he died in 1989 at age

Robert Penn Warren (©Washington Post; reproduced by permission of the D. C. Public Library)

eighty-four at his summer residence in Vermont. He left to posterity a canon of outstanding creative effort.

ANALYSIS

Many of Robert Penn Warren's stories feature an adult protagonist's introspective, guilty recollections of imperishable childhood events, of things done or left undone or simply witnessed with childish innocence.

"BLACKBERRY WINTER"

"Blackberry Winter" (the literal reference is to an unseasonable, late spring cold snap) opens with a nine-year-old boy's unbroken, secure world, a small community permeated with the presence and warmth of protective loved ones. A vaguely sinister city-clothed stranger happens by and is given a job burying drowned chicks and poults by the boy's mother. Later the boy watches with his father and neighboring farmers as a dead cow, the yoke still around her neck, bobs down a flooding creek past fields of ruined to-bacco plants. Then the boy finds a somehow shocking heap of litter washed out from under the house of his father's black help. Dellie, who lives there, is sick in bed with "woman-mizry," and after calling him to her side, gives her son little Jebb a sudden, "awful" slap. Big Jebb predicts that the cold snap will go on and that everything and everyone will die, because the Lord is tired of sinful people.

Later on, when the boy's father explains that he cannot afford to hire any help now but offers the stranger fifty cents for a half day's work, the stranger curses the farm and leaves, followed by the curious boy, whom he also curses. "You don't stop following me and I cut yore throat, you little son-of-a-bitch." "But I did follow him," the narrator tells us, "all the years." At the end of the story all the sureties of the boy's world have been threatened, and in the epilogue we learn that the farm was soon lost, his parents died, and little Jebb has gone to prison. The narrator has learned that the essence of time is the passing away of things and people; he has been exposed to natural and moral evil.

"WHEN THE LIGHT GETS GREEN"

"When the Light Gets Green" (the reference is to a peculiar, ominous shade of greenish light just before a storm) recalls "Blackberry Winter" in its setting, characterization, and theme, as well as in its retrospective point of view. The story's first two sentences display the technique: "My grandfather had a long white beard and sat under the cedar tree. The beard, as a matter of fact, was not very long and not very white, only gray, but when I was a child. . . ." Grandfather Barden had served as a Confederate cavalry captain in the Civil War; he had been a hero, but now he is old and thin and his blue jeans hang off his shrunken hips and backside. During a bad hailstorm in the summer of 1914 which threatens his son-in-law's tobacco crop, the old man has a stroke and collapses, and later upstairs in his room waits to die— unloved, as he believes. His is the necessarily uncomprehending and hopeless fight that love and pride put up against time and change. His grandson, who visits him but cannot speak, suffers the guilt of having tried and failed both to feel and to communicate the impossible love the old man needed.

Mr. Barden, as we learn in the epilogue, lived until 1918, by which time other catastrophes had intervened—the farm sold, his son-in-law fighting in France, where he would soon be killed, his daughter working in a store. "I got the letter about my grandfather, who died of the flu," the story concludes, "but I thought about four years back, and it didn't matter much." The now adult narrator is puzzled and shamed by his failure and betrayal of his grandfather. In the dual perspective of the story Warren infuses a self-condemnatory ambivalence toward the old man which gives to the narrative the quality of expiation.

"Prime Leaf"

"Prime Leaf," Warren's first published story, derives from the Kentucky tobacco wars of the first decade of the twentieth century, in which tobacco farmers organized in an attempt to secure higher prices from the tobacco buyers. The focus of the story is upon contention within the Hardin family, most directly between Old Man Hardin and Big Thomas, his son, but also involving Thomas's wife and young son. Old Man Hardin leaves the farmers' association rather than support the use of force against those members who object to the association's price fixing. Big Thomas, whom he had originally convinced to join the association, refuses to resign immediately. Their reconciliation occurs only after Big Thomas wounds one of a party of barn-burning night riders raiding the Hardins' property. Big Thomas decides that he will wait at home for the sheriff, but his father urges him to ride into town to justice, and on the way Big Thomas is ambushed and killed. The opposition of father and son is a contest between idea and fact, between idealism and pragmatism. Old Man Hardin is a kind and morally upright man but is also notably detached, remote, and unyielding. To his idealism is opposed his son's stubborn practicality, born of hard experience.

In delineating the conflict of the two men, with its tragic and ironic outcome, Warren did not espouse the beliefs of either, but focused on the incompleteness of each. Old Man Hardin, embodying the rock-like integrity of the gentleman-farmer tradition, places an unwise reliance on what he still—despite much evidence to the contrary—takes to be the due processes of law. He cannot save his son and is in a way responsible for his death. Big Thomas, firing at the night riders until his rifle jams, before yielding to his father, does not resolve in acceptable fashion the problem of ends and means.

"The Circus in the Attic"

"The Circus in the Attic" is a long and crowded tale about the meaning—or apparent meaninglessness—of history. It features, appropriately enough, a would-be local historian, Bolton Lovehart, a frail, frustrated man of aristocratic antecedents, whose deepest desire is simply to be free and himself. The only child of a weak father and an almost cannibalistically possessive mother, Bolton as a boy makes several doomed gestures of resistance. To his mother's subsequent horror, he participates in a riverbank baptismal ceremony; later he runs off with a carnival but is immediately retrieved. During his first year at college his now widowed mother has a heart attack; such at least is her story, although she will not allow a specialist to examine her and treats her son's suggestion as treason. In any event, Bolton does not return to college and life closes in on him. He begins to see a young woman, but, realizing that Bolton's mother has the stronger hold, she deliberately seduces and then abandons him.

Establishing the context of local history back to the first white settlers, Warren provided a series of vivid and ironic vignettes, one of which distinguishes between the official, heroic, United Daughters of the Confederacy version of the Civil War battle of Bardsville and the half-comic, half-sordid truth of the unremarkable little affair. One of the heroes, Cash Perkins, full of liquor, climbed on the wrong horse, a particularly mean one, and was carried, helpless and roaring, directly into Yankee rifle range. The truth of the other memorialized hero, Seth Sykes, was somewhat more involved. He cared nothing for Secession, said so publicly, and lost a stomp-and-gouge fight over it. Then he said he hoped the Yankees would come, which they soon did, to take his corn, for which they offered him a note. He would have none of it; he had offered them meat but not his corn. He resisted and was killed. Of the official, patriotic versions of these two deaths, Warren wrote, ". . . people always believe what truth they have to believe to go on being the way they are."

Bolton Lovehart's major resource and consolation is the painstaking creation of a tiny circus—complete with animals and clowns and trapeze artists and a lion tamer—which he carves in the attic office where he is supposedly composing his study of local history. Upon his mother's death (finally, she does have a heart attack), it appears that he may at last enter into a life of his own. Shortly before World War II, Bolton marries, finds a hero in his braggart stepson, a posthumous Medal of Honor winner, and becomes for a time in his reflected energy and glory a current affairs expert and historian of sorts. His wife, however, who has been unfaithful to him, is killed in an automobile crash, his stepson is taken from him, and at last he returns to the creation of those small, inanimate, innocent, wooden objects whose world alone he cherishes, controls, and understands. Bolton Lovehart's is less a fully human life than a kind of pathetic facsimile. His study of Bardsville's past—and by extension, humans' study of history—seems to assert that historical causation and "truth" are unknowable, that all humans are equally unimportant, and that all people are trapped in their own dark compulsions.

Warren is commonly identified as a southern writer and associated with such other premier representatives of that area as William Faulkner and Eudora Welty. So long as "southern" is not equated with "regionalist" in the limiting sense of that term, the description is accurate if not very illuminating. In another sense, however, as is apparent in his short fiction, Warren was a provincial, at least insofar as he retained an attachment to and an awareness of generally humanistic values—moral, social, and theological—often regarded as a vital part of the region's heritage. Thus the frequently noticeable tension between stylistic understatement (apparent in passages quoted earlier) and thematic intensity characteristic of the stories seems a reflection of a pull between the old humanistic conception of human wholeness and a naturalistic belief in the fragmented and unintegrated nature of human experience.

Warren published his last short story, "The Circus in the Attic," in 1947; thereafter he published as stories fourteen prepublication excerpts from his novels. Although in his nearly twenty years as a short-story writer Warren produced some fine work, both the author and a good many of his readers have found his achievement in short fiction less satisfying than that in other genres, notably poetry and the novel.

Explanations for his limited success in and satisfaction with short fiction might start with the fact that when he wrote many of the stories collected in *The Circus in the Attic and Other Stories*, he was a beginner, at least in fiction. It is also the case, as Warren conceded, that he wrote for the quick buck, which did not come. Most of the stories did not represent major efforts; as Arthur Miller has said of his own short stories, they were what came easier. Finally, and most importantly, the form itself seems to have inhibited Warren's natural talents and inclinations.

In writing stories in the 1930's and 1940's, Warren appears to have backed into what was for him an unhappy compromise; stories were neither long enough nor short enough, offered neither the satisfying extensive scope of the novel nor the demanding intensive concision of the poem. Short stories might occasionally serve as sketches for novels ("Prime Leaf," discussed earlier, is the prototype of Warren's first published novel, *Night Rider*, 1939), but Warren found that the overlap between the short story and the poem was bad for him, that stories consumed material that would otherwise have become poems. Thus he said, "Short stories are out for me."

Despite such demurs, however, Warren's achievement in the short story is that of a major talent. Warren's ear never failed him; the voices from the past and of the present always ring true. No one writing in his day had a better ear—one could almost say recollection, if one did not know Warren's age—for the voices of late nineteenth and early twentieth century America. His eyes were open to both the panorama and to the smallest evocative detail: from the trapper looking across the mountains to the West to the cracked and broken shoe of a tramp. He was intensely alive to the natural world. This is not to say simply that the natural backgrounds of the stories are vividly realized and accurately observed, although Warren was here the equal of Ernest Hemingway or Faulkner, but that such observation and realization provide the bases for those effects characteristic of his stories, for the evocation of atmosphere, for tonal modulation, and for symbolic representation.

OTHER MAJOR WORKS

LONG FICTION: *Night Rider*, 1939; *At Heaven's Gate*, 1943; *All the King's Men*, 1946; *World Enough and Time: A Romantic Novel*, 1950; *Band of Angels*, 1955; *The Cave*, 1959; *Wilderness: A Tale of the Civil War*, 1961; *Flood: A Romance of Our Time*, 1964; *Meet Me in the Green Glen*, 1971; *A Place to Come To*, 1977.

PLAYS: *Proud Flesh*, pr. 1947; *All the King's Men*, pr. 1958.

POETRY: *Thirty-six Poems*, 1935; *Eleven Poems on the Same Theme*, 1942; *Selected Poems 1923-1943*, 1944; *Brother to Dragons: A Tale in Verse and Voices*, 1953; *Promises: Poems 1954-1956*, 1957; *You, Emperors, and Others: Poems 1957-1960*, 1960; *Selected Poems: New and Old, 1923-1966*, 1966; *Incarnations: Poems 1966-1968*, 1968; *Audubon: A Vision*, 1969; *Or Else—Poem/Poems 1968-1974*, 1974; *Selected Poems, 1923-1975*, 1976; *Now and Then: Poems 1976-1978*, 1978; *Brother to Dragons: A New Version*, 1979; *Being Here: Poetry 1977-1980*, 1980; *Ballad of a Sweet Dream of Peace*, 1980 (with Bill Komodore); *Rumor Verified: Poems 1979-1980*, 1981; *Chief Joseph of the Nez Percé*, 1983; *New and Selected Poems, 1923-1985*, 1985.

NONFICTION: *John Brown: The Making of a Martyr*, 1929; *Modern Rhetoric*, 1949 (with Cleanth Brooks; better known as *Fundamentals of Good Writing: A Handbook of Modern Rhetoric*); *Segregation: The Inner Conflict of the South*, 1956; *Selected Essays*, 1958; *The Legacy of the Civil War: Meditations on the Centennial*, 1961; *Who Speaks for the Negro?*, 1965; *Democracy and Poetry*, 1975; *Portrait of a Father*, 1988; *New and Selected Essays*, 1989.

EDITED TEXT: *An Approach to Literature: A Collection of Prose and Verse with Analysis and Discussions*, 1936 (with Cleanth Brooks and John Thibaut Purser); *Understanding Poetry: An Anthology for College Students*, 1938, (with Brooks); *Understanding Fiction*, 1943, (with Brooks); *Faulkner: A Collection of Critical Essays*, 1966; *Randall Jarrell, 1914-1965*, 1967 (with Robert Lowell and Peter Taylor); *American Literature: The Makers and the Making*, 1973 (with R. W. B. Lewis).

BIBLIOGRAPHY

Blotner, Joseph. *Robert Penn Warren: A Biography.* New York: Random House, 1997. Blotner's is the first of what will almost certainly be many biographies following Warren's death in 1989. Blotner began his work while Warren was still alive and had the good fortune to have the cooperation not only of his subject but also of the larger Warren family. Blotner's book is straightforward and chronological; it makes a good beginning.

Bohner, Charles. *Robert Penn Warren.* 1962. Rev. ed. Boston: Twayne, 1981. This lucid survey encompasses details of Warren's literary career and an analysis of his major themes. Also provides a study of the development of his art as evidenced in his novels and short fiction, his poetry (through *Being Here: Poetry 1977-1980*), and his major essays. The survey also includes a detailed chronology and a valuable select bibliography.

Clark, William Bedford, ed. *Critical Essays on Robert Penn Warren.* Boston: G. K. Hall, 1981. A comprehensive collection of criticism by leading literary scholars of Warren's major work as novelist, poet, biographer, and essayist. Among the contributors are Harold Bloom, Malcolm Cowley, Carlos Baker, John Crowe Ransom, and Randall Jarrell. The collection includes a valuable 1969 interview with Warren by Richard Sale.

Dietrich, Bryan. "Christ or Antichrist: Understanding Eight Words in 'Blackberry Winter.'" *Studies in Short Fiction* 29 (Spring, 1992): 215-220. Discusses the final line of the story, "But I did follow him, all the years," by analyzing and critiquing previous critical interpretations of the line and by providing a religious reading of the tramp as Antichrist; suggests that the young protagonist of the story follows in the footsteps of disillusionment.

Ferriss, Lucy. "Sleeping with the Boss: Female Subjectivity in Robert Penn Warren's Fiction." *The*

Mississippi Quarterly 48 (Winter, 1994/1995): 147-167. Part of a special issue on Warren; suggests a feminist reading of Warren's fiction, discussing significant women characters who have sexual liaisons with men of power and wealth; argues that Warren's ability to risk the profound disruption of masculine authority either by admitting female "selves" or by exposing the self-other dialectic as unreliable demonstrates his faith in the continuing resilience of interpretation.

Guttenberg, Barnett. *Web of Being: The Novels of Robert Penn Warren*. Nashville: Vanderbilt University Press, 1975. Guttenberg examines nine novels of Warren from *Night Rider* through *Meet Me in the Green Glen* with emphasis on the existential element. He advances the premise that through all the novels the individual struggles to attain the true being of selfhood through self-awareness.

Justus, James H. *The Achievement of Robert Penn Warren*. Baton Rouge: Louisiana State University Press, 1981. A cogent study of Warren's work from the premise that the latter largely derives from the cultural circumstances of time and place in his career. The book is divided into four sections dealing, respectively, with Warren's themes, poetry, nonfiction prose, and novels.

Millichap, Joseph R. "Robert Penn Warren and Regionalism." *The Mississippi Quarterly* 48 (Winter, 1994/1995): 29-38. Discusses Warren's insistence that regional writing should aim at meanings that transcend mere parochialism; notes Warren's constant effort to reshape his relationship to his regional roots.

Nakadate, Neil. *Robert Penn Warren: A Reference Guide*. Boston: G. K. Hall, 1977. This helpfully annotated reference guide to significant scholarship on Warren and his work encompasses writings by Warren from 1929 to 1977, and about him from 1925 to 1975. A checklist of doctoral dissertations and master's theses on Warren is also included.

Ruppersburg, Hugh. *Robert Penn Warren and the American Imagination*. Athens: University of Georgia Press, 1990. Ruppersburg considers the Warren opus an attempt to define a national identity. Subscribing to Warren's notion that he was not a historical writer, Ruppersburg attempts to place Warren in a contemporary context, emphasizing such modern American concerns as civil rights and nuclear warfare.

Strandberg, Victor. *The Poetic Vision of Robert Penn Warren*. Lexington: University Press of Kentucky, 1977. A thorough and lively discussion of Warren's poetry offering elucidation of major poems and an examination of the development of the poet's three major themes: "Poems of passage, the undiscovered self, and mysticism." The study supersedes Strandberg's *A Colder Fire* (1965).

Watkins, Floyd C., John T. Hiers, and Mary Louise Weaks, eds. *Talking with Robert Penn Warren*. Athens: University of Georgia Press, 1990. A collection of twenty-four interviews, extending from 1953 to 1985, in which Warren talks about his work with characteristic honesty, openness, folksiness, and wit from the joint perspective of writer, interpreter, and critic. The group of interviewers includes Ralph Ellison, Marshall Walker, Bill Moyers, Edwin Harold Newman, Floyd C. Watkins, and Eleanor Clark.

Allen Shepherd, updated by
Christian H. Moe

JEROME WEIDMAN

Born: New York, New York; April 4, 1913
Died: New York, New York; October 6, 1998

PRINCIPAL SHORT FICTION

The Horse That Could Whistle "Dixie," 1939
The Captain's Tiger, 1947
My Father Sits in the Dark, 1961
Nine Stories, 1963
The Death of Dickie Draper, and Nine Other
    Stories, 1965

OTHER LITERARY FORMS

Jerome Weidman's published works include plays, essays, travelogues, more than twenty novels, autobiographical sketches, one autobiographical volume, and numerous short-story collections and uncollected short stories. He is probably best known for his dramatic scripts, including the musicals *Fiorello!* (produced in 1959, published in 1960) and *Tenderloin* (produced in 1960, published in 1961), done in collaboration with George Abbott, and a musical version of his first novel, *I Can Get It for You Wholesale* (1937), produced and published in 1962.

ACHIEVEMENTS

As a fiction writer, Jerome Weidman is known best for his unpleasant, sometimes brutal, portrayal of Jewish characters in novels such as *I Can Get It for You Wholesale* and *What's in It for Me?* (1938), and in short stories such as "The Kinnehórrah," "Chutzbah," and "The Horse That Could Whistle 'Dixie.'" He portrays characters more sensitively in his novels *Fourth Street East: A Novel of the Way It Was* (1971) and *The Enemy Camp* (1958) and in his stories "My Father Sits in the Dark" and "Movable Feast." Many of the settings in his novels and short stories are drawn from the areas in which he grew up—New York's Lower East Side and the Bronx, and many of the activities his characters pursue are drawn from his own experiences as a child growing up in the slums and from his experiences as an office boy, an accountant, a law student, and a writer. Weidman

won a Pulitzer Prize in 1960 for his collaboration on *Fiorello!*

BIOGRAPHY

Educated in stints at City College, New York, 1931-1933; Washington Square College, 1933-1934; and New York University Law School, 1934-1937, Jerome Weidman married Elizabeth Ann Payne and has three children. He was cowinner of the Pulitzer Prize in drama and winner of the New York Drama Critics Circle Award and the Antionette Perry ("Tony") Award, all for *Fiorello!* in 1960. He is a member of the Authors Guild and Dramatists Guild of Authors League of America of which he served as president from 1969 to 1974, and the Writers Guild of America West. Settling in the San Francisco area in the early 1990's, Weidman's work on a second autobiographical volume and short stories and sketches are also drawn from his Lower East Side childhood and his young adulthood living in the Bronx.

ANALYSIS

While Jerome Weidman's novels, *I Can Get It for You Wholesale* and *What's in It for Me?*, are often neglected because of his brutally realistic treatment of unsavory Jewish characters, his short stories are frequently humorous, good-natured jabs at not only the Jewish community but also the world as a whole. His early stories, particularly those in *The Horse That Could Whistle "Dixie,"* are remarkably well constructed and display the work of a writer who has a clear conception of what he portrays. His later work, often marred by hasty writing and commercialism, retains the same sense of humor, but often lapses into the maudlin and into fits of bathos. Such flaws should be no surprise in the stories of a man who freely admits that his primary aim in writing is to make money.

Weidman draws extensively on his life as a child and young man trying to survive in the slums of New York, first on Fourth Street East and later in the Bronx. In fact, he claims that all of his short stories, even those with female protagonists, are more or less autobiographical. The people of Weidman's stories are almost universally playing the game of life, and Weidman's stories reflect the gamesmanship of their situations. The puzzles to be pieced together and the games to be played by Weidman's characters are the puzzles and games that all people have played at one time or another and, as such, Weidman's stories become something of a mirror of life. The mirror is faceted and reflects many pieces of a whole, however, and it is making those pieces reflect a steady image that is the challenge for the reader and for the characters alike.

"MY FATHER SITS IN THE DARK"

It is the task, set for himself, of the youngster in "My Father Sits in the Dark" to "figure out" why his father, night after night, sits quietly alone in his darkened house. None of the pieces the young man sorts out seems to fit. The family is poor, but his father would not worry about money. He would not worry about the family's health, either. None of the conventional answers fits. It is not until the young man confronts his father in the dark kitchen of the house that the pieces seem to fit. His father is an immigrant. His home in Austria did not have electricity, which made him familiar with the dark, so dark now provides for him a comfortable, nostalgic feeling. When the son asks the father why he sits in the dark, his father replies that it helps him think. When asked what he thinks about, he replies, "Nothing." The implication is that the old man does not have to have a more rational reason to sit in the dark and that the son, with his rationalized, fabricated understanding of the situation, has come to an incomplete understanding, but an understanding nevertheless. The fact that Weidman is playing the conflicts of modern society against the idyllic Old World is evident, but he does not belabor the point; he only reveals the exultant son going back to bed after he finally accepts his father's explanation for sitting in the dark. The outcome makes both happy, but there is no real resolution for the reader.

"THREE-TWO PITCH"

The same sort of puzzle appears in "Three-Two Pitch." Harry Powell is a bright young graduate on a

Jerome Weidman (Library of Congress)

three-month internship with the office of the best public relations specialist in New York. Powell, from Cleveland, is considered a "hick," but he takes his father's advice to ingratiate himself with the secretary of the office in order to succeed. His success is such that he is prepared to marry the secretary before the action begins. D. J., Powell's employer, has a yearly commitment to have lunch with his Cleveland high school teacher, Doc Hapfel, but this year, after making the arrangements, he gets "tied up" and tells Harry to meet Hapfel and begin without him. In the course of the lunch, during which Doc becomes drunker and drunker, a series of calls from D. J.'s office (from the secretary Powell is thinking of marrying) relate that D. J. will be later and later, and after every call, Doc seems to know, intuitively, what has been said—as if he were going through a familiar ritual. When Doc finally collapses and Powell is forced to cope with the situation, he begins to put the pieces together. The lunch happens every year; D. J. always sends his intern to lunch with Doc; D. J. is always tied up; he will always come later. Doc finally admits he has not seen D. J. for years, and when Powell discovers, fortuitously, that D. J. has not been in town all day, but is in Detroit, he realizes that he has been duped and used to pacify the expectations of an old man.

Weidman stresses the conflict between "hick" Cleveland and sophisticated New York, but the principal theme is the puzzle which Powell must put together. The pieces are the secretary, D. J., Doc Hapfel, and Harry Powell himself. Before Harry can solve the puzzle, he must assimilate all of the pieces and come to an understanding of the situation and of himself. When he does solve the puzzle, the solution is devastating. He understands he has no place in New York, that he has been used, and that his self-esteem has blinded him to all of these realities. Only by returning to Cleveland and entering law school, as his father counseled him to do at the start of the story, can Powell provide a definitive, if somewhat unsatisfactory, solution to the whole puzzle.

"I KNEW WHAT I WAS DOING"

"I Knew What I Was Doing" presents life as more of a game than a puzzle, but the same unsavory undertone attaches itself to the outcome. Throughout the story, Myra, a fashion model, plays one potential escort against another until she works herself up from a mere stock clerk to a wealthy clothing buyer. By portraying her game of enticement and entrapment, Weidman shows her as a cold, calculating woman who succeeds at the game because she knows the rules so well. The irony of her role is that her chumps, the men in her life, fall so predictably within the rules of the game. One of them, however, nearly upsets the game plan when he falls in love with Myra and proposes marriage almost simultaneously with her conquest of the rich clothing buyer. She retains her composure, however, and tells this, the most ensnared chump, to "paste it [a marriage license] in your hat." Weidman's characters in this story are little more than pawns being played by the queen. Weidman is not particularly interested in character here, but rather in the progress of the match. The story is, perhaps, the epitome of Weidman's depiction of game playing.

"THE HORSE THAT COULD WHISTLE 'DIXIE'"

At the other end of the spectrum is "The Horse That Could Whistle 'Dixie.'" Rather than flat, featureless characters, Weidman gives us a thoroughly reprehensible father playing the age-old game of growing up with his unwilling son. After watching many children ride the ponies at the zoo pony ride and sneering fatuously at those who only ride in the horse cart and not astride the beasts, the father drags the son to the ponies and forces him to ride. Despite the child's tearful entreaties and the sensible suggestions of the attendant, who can see that the child is terrified, the father forces the child to ride not once, but four times. At the end, the child is a "whipped, silent mass of tear-stained quivering fright" who has finally satisfied his father's sense of propriety. Here the game has no winner, no ending, and no understanding. The son does not understand the father's motives, the father does not understand the son's reluctance, and the crowd watching the events does not want to understand. This is the most undesirable of Weidman's games, in which a person is forced to play by someone else's rules.

From the gentle "My Father Sits in the Dark," to the savage "The Horse That Could Whistle 'Dixie,'" Weidman portrays, fabricates, and manipulates the games people play and the puzzles that they are. If readers are to understand the games and puzzles, they must abandon credulity and prepare themselves for the inconsistencies that the games-master builds into the game.

OTHER MAJOR WORKS

LONG FICTION: *I Can Get It for You Wholesale*, 1937; *What's in It for Me?*, 1938; *I'll Never Go There Anymore*, 1941; *The Lights Around the Shore*, 1943; *Too Early to Tell*, 1946; *The Price Is Right*, 1949; *The Hand of the Hunter*, 1951; *Give Me Your Love*, 1952; *The Third Angel*, 1953; *Your Daughter Iris*, 1955; *The Enemy Camp*, 1958; *Before You Go*, 1960; *The Sound of Bow Bells*, 1962; *Word of Mouth*, 1964; *Other People's Money*, 1967; *The Center of the Action*, 1969; *Fourth Street East: A Novel of the Way It Was*, 1971; *Last Respects*, 1972; *Tiffany Street*, 1974; *The Temple*, 1975.

PLAYS: *Fiorello!*, pr. 1959 (with George Abbott); *Tenderloin*, pr. 1960 (with Abbott); *I Can Get It for You Wholesale*, pr. 1962; *Cool Off!*, pr. 1964; *Pousse-Café*, pr. 1966; *Ivory Tower*, pr. 1968 (with James Yaffe); *The Mother Lover*, pr. 1969; *Asterisk! A Comedy of Terrors*, pr., pb. 1969.

NONFICTION: *Letter of Credit*, 1940; *Traveler's Cheque*, 1954; *Back Talk*, 1963; *Praying for Rain*, 1986.

BIBLIOGRAPHY

Bannon, Barbara A. "Authors and Editors." *Publishers Weekly* 196 (July 28, 1969): 13-15. Uses the publication of Weidman's *The Center of the Action* as a starting point for a treatment of his literary career. The article discusses aspects of the relationship between Weidman's fiction and his life. Accompanied by a photograph of Weidman.

Barkham, John. "The Author." *Saturday Review* 45 (July 28, 1962): 38-39. This interview, concerning Weidman's fiction and theater work, accompanies a review of Weidman's novel *The Sound of Bow Bells*. Barkham's essay examines some of Weidman's ideas about the way stories should be written and treats Weidman's daily schedule as a writer. A photograph of Weidman accompanies the review.

Hawtree, Christopher. "Chronicles of the Lower East Side." *The Guardian*, October 20, 1998, p. 22. A brief sketch of Weidman's life and literary career; concludes with a comment on his story "Monsoon," which he compares to a story by Eudora Welty in its treatment of racism.

Liptzin, Sol. *The Jew in American Literature*. New York: Bloch, 1966. This volume discusses Weidman in the context of American literature. Liptzin briefly compares Weidman to Budd Schulberg in connection with their treatment of "the Jewish go-getter" and of "unpleasant Jewish money-grubbers."

Sherman, Bernard. *The Invention of the Jew: Jewish-American Education Novels, 1916-1964*. New York: Yoseloff, 1969. Treats Weidman's *I Can Get It for You Wholesale* as a rogue-hero novel. Sherman places the work in a tradition beginning with *The Rise of David Levinsky* by Abraham Cahan and running through *Haunch, Paunch, and Jowl* by Samuel Ornitz and *What Makes Sammy Run* (1941) by Budd Schulberg.

Weidman, Jerome. Interview by Lisa See. *Publishers Weekly* 230 (September 12, 1986): 72-73. Uses the publication of Weidman's autobiographical volume, *Praying for Rain*, as a point of departure for surveying his literary career. Also treats some of Weidman's ideas about composition. Includes a photograph of Weidman.

Clarence O. Johnson, updated by
Richard Tuerk

DENTON WELCH

Born: Shanghai, China; March 29, 1915
Died: Crouch, Kent, England; December 30, 1948

PRINCIPAL SHORT FICTION

Brave and Cruel, 1948
A Last Sheaf, 1951
The Stories of Denton Welch, 1985

OTHER LITERARY FORMS

Besides his short-story collections, Denton Welch published several novels, an unfinished novel, journals, and uncollected poems. Both the unfinished novel and the short-story collections were published after his death.

ACHIEVEMENTS

Denton Welch's fiction has been favorably compared to that of Jean Cocteau, Marcel Proust, André Gide, Christopher Isherwood, and Truman Capote. Few writers began their career with the kind of precocious brilliance and searing honesty that characterized the early works of Welch. Dead at age thirty-three after thirteen years of debilitating pain resulting from a bicycle accident in 1935, Welch had been known primarily as a painter until he began writing only six years before his death. His first work garnered high critical praise from a number of respected and established British literary figures, such as Edith Sitwell, Sir Herbert Read, and Cyril Connolly, to name but a few. His direct narrative manner, sexual openness, and dazzling prose style contrasted greatly with the highly realistic war fiction that was being produced throughout the 1940's. Much of his short fiction documents the fall from innocence to experience that oversensitive young boys undergo when they lose a parent or a friend through death or misunderstanding. A number of his later stories are also superb portraits of the initial stirrings of artistic impulse and demonstrate how creative adolescents learn to trust their imaginations and begin to become artists. An authentically original voice, Welch writes in a style that appears completely nonderivative.

Few writers have dramatized so precisely the agony of adolescence, a phase he labeled as "sordid and fearful."

BIOGRAPHY

Denton Welch was born in Shanghai, China, into a family of wealth and privilege. His father was a prosperous rubber merchant, and his American-born mother a devoted Christian Scientist. He spent much of his youth traveling back and forth between Asia and Europe in the company of his mother, to whom he was inordinately devoted because of his father's absence. To his great disappointment, he was enrolled in one of England's finest boarding schools, Repton, which his two older brothers attended. The typical lifestyle of an English boys' school brought traumatic change in the young boy's life, especially in the wake of the casual days spent with his mother traveling throughout the world. He so detested Repton that he ran away, preferring to visit well-known cathedrals at Salisbury and Exeter. He finally found satisfaction at the Goldsmith School of Art in London, where he was able to develop his considerable talent as a painter and where he enjoyed the relaxed and open atmosphere of an art school.

Two experiences profoundly altered Welch's relatively secure and happy life: The first was the death of his beloved mother when he was eleven years old, and the second, at age twenty, was a catastrophic bicycle accident that left him a permanent invalid and contributed to his early death at the age of thirty-three. The last thirteen years of his life were spent in great pain and discomfort but were, ironically, his most artistically productive years.

From his early published writings, Welch found great and encouraging praise from Edith Sitwell, who called him "a born writer." Renowned literary editors such as Cyril Connolly and Sir Herbert Read found his work fresh and completely original. In an age that rarely allowed mention of sexual matters, Welch's candor about his homosexuality disturbed a number of England's conservative literary intelligentsia. More disturbing to them, however, was the originality of his writing style and its apparent artlessness and absence of any discernible literary influences.

ANALYSIS

Denton Welch's early stories deal with the recurrent theme of the loss of an innocent vision of the world. There is usually a fall of some kind in which an innocent young boy learns some devastating information that alters, or will soon alter, the way he feels about his life thereafter.

"THE COFFIN ON THE HILL"

One of Welch's finest stories, "The Coffin on the Hill," documents an eight-year-old boy's first serious confrontation with mortality. The story concerns an Easter voyage of a family on a boat up a river in China. The story is told through the eyes of the eight-year-old as he experiences the mysteries of the Orient. The ship is, obviously, a symbol of an ark floating on the river of life, and life on the ship is Edenic. Welch is an unashamedly symbolic writer.

The cooks on the ship playfully tease the young boy with stories about drowned people in the river who, if he fell into the water, would pull him down to the bottom. His response is to return to his cabin, assume the fetal position, and hug his strange doll, which he has named "Lymph Est." The family then visits an ancient Chinese graveyard, where the boy sees, while off on his own, an open grave with a rotting corpse in it. He is so stunned by the sight that he returns to his family but is unable to separate the lesson of death from the fear and the sure knowledge that even his dear mother will someday become mere dust and ashes. Though he is only eight, his sensitive nature already has begun to torment him: "For I knew that she would come to it at last; and that knowledge was unbearable." His last act is to throw his favorite doll into the river as a sign of his growing maturity but also as a kind of propitiatory sacrifice that might somehow appease the gods of necessity and fate.

"AT SEA"

"At Sea" can be viewed as a further development of the same themes found in "The Coffin on the Hill." Again, there is a sea journey of a young boy, Robert, with his mother, but in this story the boy is pathologi-

cally attached to her to such an extent that their relationship becomes the major focus of the story. There is no father in the story at all. There is, however, a male character named Mr. Barron, who expresses some interest in Robert's mother and asks her to dance at a party. Robert's Oedipal jealousy so enrages him that he wets himself and publicly humiliates himself and his embarrassed mother. The reader discovers that his mother is showing signs of some eventual illness that seems fatal and, as in "The Coffin on the Hill," the youthful protagonist is forced to face the inevitable death of his mother.

Welch introduces a princess and her little dog, who tries repeatedly to break his leash and gain freedom, characters presenting fairly obvious mirror images of Robert chained to his mother's love. Some critics see Mr. Barron's name as a pun on Charon, the mythical guide and personification of death, who is leading Robert's beloved mother in a dance of death. The title of the story also foreshadows the plight of the boy after his mother's death, when he will surely be "at sea" or alone and lost. One of the strange rituals that the boy practices is writing elaborate letters in spite of the fact that he can neither read nor write, so that the reader sees him as someone who also cannot "read" or interpret the signs or portents of the catastrophe of his mother's impending death.

The narrative ends with a highly emotional loss of innocence as the boy realizes that his mother is ill. As he views her in a semiconscious state, he says: "He wanted to sing something so consummate and wonderful that his mother would turn over and smile and be happy forever; but he knew that she was dying and that she could not save herself." It is fairly clear that both of these extremely well-crafted stories are, if not blatantly autobiographical, at least fictive expressions of the deep and abiding loss that Welch experienced during his mother's lingering illness and eventual death when he was eleven years old.

His mother was a strict Christian Scientist and refused medication throughout her fatal illness, a fact that embittered Denton Welch against the beliefs and practices of that religion. Indeed, he quotes hymns and some of Mary Baker Eddy's writings at the conclusion of "At Sea." Not only does this story and several of his novels record young children's loss of innocence, but also it particularly records the disappearance of the core of his emotional being, the love of his mother.

"WHEN I WAS THIRTEEN"

"When I Was Thirteen" is, unquestionably, one of his most accomplished stories; it certainly is his most famous and most frequently anthologized one. The reader sees only the beginning of a fall from innocence to knowledge. The major character experiences a violent beating from his brother after spending a day and night with an older lad named Archer. He has absolutely no understanding of the names his brother is calling him: "Bastard, Devil, Harlot, Sod!"—except "Devil."

The story details a holiday trip that the unnamed narrator and his older brother, William, a student at Oxford, spend in Switzerland. William prefers the company of his fellow Oxford students and virtually abandons his young brother, who rather enjoys his solitude. Shortly after his brother leaves for an extended ski trip, the thirteen-year-old meets the handsome, charming, and friendly Archer, who is the same age as William. The younger boy is flattered by the attention of the attractive Archer, and they spend time together eating, skiing, and drinking. The younger boy is exhilarated by the contact and states quite honestly: "I had never enjoyed myself quite so much before. I thought him the most wonderful companion, not a bit intimidating, in spite of being rather a hero . . . and thought that, apart from my mother, who was dead, I had never liked anyone so much as I liked Archer." They get somewhat drunk together, bathe in the same water, and give each other body rubs. Nothing overtly sexual takes place, and though the language describing their contact is highly sensual, even sexual, innocence prevails. Indeed, the evening ends with Archer singing "Silent Night" in German and: "I began to cry in the moonlight with Archer singing my favorite song; and my brother far away up in the mountain."

Though the boy sleeps at Archer's that night, he awakens with a hangover the next morning and goes back to his hotel just as his brother, William, returns from his ski trip. Once William hears about the boy's

escapades, he assumes that Archer has sexually seduced his brother and proceeds to beat his innocent brother, plunging his head in a basin of ice water and plunging his fingers down his brother's throat forcing him to vomit. Welch has so brilliantly constructed the story that the reader, not the boy, experiences the fall from innocence to knowledge, anticipating the boy's fall when he discovers what those words mean in the future. What the thirteen-year-old will find out is that what he experienced as genuine love, affection, and care from Archer is labeled, by the world, as sodomy and prostitution. Welch also cleverly uses the name "Archer" as a possible mythic echo of Cupid whose arrows cause people to fall in love.

Welch has further indicted types such as William and his friends who hate and fear Archer but do not know why. Robert Phillips, the most reliable critic on Welch, theorizes that William may be projecting his own fear of his homosexual feelings toward Archer. This fear, in turn, causes him to read homosexual undertones in perfectly innocent relationships. Archer is probably homosexual, but he is also rich, independent, and comfortable in his sexuality. It could also simply be that William's violent response to his brother's friendship is jealousy. The story is so rich in its construction that Welch enables the reader to interpret it in many equally valid ways. This story is one of his first to document various steps in a young boy's rite of passage from childhood to the more manly ceremonies of smoking and drinking with an older male whom he admires and wants to imitate.

"THE JUDAS TREE"

"The Judas Tree" is another story that is thematically related to "The Coffin on the Hill" and "At Sea" insofar as all three show how young people perceive the pain and loneliness of old age and begin to feel within themselves foreshadowings of their own dwindling powers. Specifically, this story concerns a young art student who is pursued by Mr. Clinton, a retired schoolmaster. They meet on the street of an English town as the older man offers to let the younger man sniff the bouquet of hyacinths, narcissus, and daffodils that he is carrying. The figure of Mr. Clinton carries echoes of Oscar Wilde, who frequently carried flowers, and the ominous pervert from James Joyce's "An Encounter," who persisted in trying to engage a boy in sexual conversation. There is also a suggestion of the strangers that the closeted Aschenbach from Thomas Mann's "Death in Venice" kept encountering on his trip south.

The obviously lonely retired schoolmaster begs the art student to paint for him a picture of Judas actually hanging on the tree where he committed suicide, since of all the pictures that he has collected of Judas, none portrays him actually in the throes of death. He also proposes that he give the young man voice lessons as payment for the picture. The young man promises to paint the picture but then decides that there is something deeply disturbing in their relationship and tells the man that he has no time. The desperate older man immediately rejects the art student's friendship, treating him as one who has "betrayed" his promise, a Judas figure, and the story concludes on a despairing note as the art student declares: "How old and mad and undesirable he must be feeling!" The reader is left with the distinct impression that he is also describing himself in his inevitable later years.

Welch's next story, "The Trout Stream," could certainly be considered a novella, since it is divided into three major sections and runs to about twenty-six pages. In this well-constructed piece, a young boy sets out on another voyage of discovery with his sensitive and beautiful mother. This time it is a land voyage to an Edenic setting of an English manor presided over by Mr. Mellon. It is also a story of the fall of a great house, a genre that was particularly popular in British and American fiction throughout the nineteenth century.

The central character, Mr. Mellon, is the lord of his manor but is also paralyzed from the waist down and must be confined to a wheelchair. The large house is strangely sterile and lifeless, and the young narrator keeps finding artifacts such as a beautifully carved ivory piece of a beggar covered with rats, an object that symbolizes the servant class that surrounds Mr. Mellon and attends to his needs. The name Mellon is also used to suggest the American family of the same name known for their fabulous wealth. The young boy becomes friendly with the housekeeper, Mrs. Slade, and her daughter, Phyllis. An unattractive, blunt girl, Phyllis takes the young boy on a tour of the grounds to show him the artificial trout stream that Mellon has built. The trout, like the characters in the story, are controlled and trapped by Mellon's pervasive power and wealth. The story concludes with Mellon building a more impressive estate, which is even more sterile than the first. Part 3 shows the narrator, now a young man, returning to the ruins of the estate after Mrs. Slade has drowned herself in the trout stream because Mellon rejected her, and after Phyllis has run away with the handsome chauffeur, Bob. All Mellon's effort to create his own little human "trout stream" or regenerated Eden has failed, and he is left lonely and helpless at the story's conclusion. Welch's novella has become another parable of the ravages of time even on the rich and powerful.

"BRAVE AND CRUEL"

"Brave and Cruel," the title story of Welch's first short-story collection, is one of his most compelling creations. The major characters are both artists of a sort. David, the narrator, is a painter, but Micki Beaumont is a con artist par excellence. Micki Beaumont claims to be a returning hero after World War II and entertains the local crowd with fascinating tales of his bravery as a fighter pilot. Everyone believes him because of his charm and good looks. He asks the quiet Katherine Warde to marry him, and she accepts. The major theme of the story is appearance versus reality, or how normal people see what they want to see even though the artist, David, suspects Micki's stories from the beginning. As the story unfolds, the community discovers that Micki's real name is Potts, not Beaumont—that is, a little pot rather than a "beautiful mountain" (the literal translation of the French *beau mont*). Though everyone knows that Micki is a charming con artist, the Warde family, strangely enough, stays in contact with him throughout his embarrassing arrest and disgrace. The snobbish David sees him years later on a bus, dressed in expensive clothes and seemingly prosperous. "Brave and Cruel" is certainly one of Welch's best constructed stories and also discusses on a very sophisticated level how people need their fictions, even though they know them to be fictions, to vivify their banal lives. The necessity of art and illusion becomes, in this story, one of Welch's most serious themes.

"THE FIRE IN THE WOOD"

Many critics consider the short story "The Fire in the Wood" to be his finest work. Again, the main character, Mary, a virgin, is an artist who cannot seem to find a subject that engenders enthusiasm or "fire" in her imagination. Her name obviously evokes the Blessed Virgin but also suggests "sea," or the primordial repository of archetypes that artists use for inspiration. The plot also shows strong affinities with a number of D. H. Lawrence's tales in which dried-up artist types meet sexually charged primitive innocents whose naturalness and physical energy revitalize their artistic powers. *Lady Chatterley's Lover* (1928) is the prototype of such stories. Mary, the artist, meets Jim, the woodsman or Adam figure, in an artificial woods that a wealthy man had designed to surround his proposed mansion but died before it could be completed. Like the trout stream in the story of the same name, the "wood" becomes a human-made, regenerated Eden in which Mary tempts the innocent Jim into an adulterous affair. Jim, however, has saved Mary not only by becoming her lover but also, more important, by becoming a model for her reawakened artistic energies. At the story's conclusion, reality intrudes as Mary discovers that what appeared to be innocent and noble is merely another sordid tale of madness, greed, and retribution. The important "fall" in the tale is Mary's coming into reality and leaving her adolescent dreamworld. The fall then is a *felix culpa*, or "happy fall," because Mary may now be able to ground her imagination in reality rather than fantasy.

"THE HATEFUL WORD" AND "THE DIAMOND BADGE"

Two stories in Denton Welch's second collection stand out as exceptionally well wrought: "The Hateful Word" and "The Diamond Badge." "The Hateful Word" bears a strong resemblance to "The Fire in the Wood": Both stories use a female narrator, or what several critics call an Albertine voice—that is, the female voice through which Proust speaks in much of his fiction even though the speaker in the actual story

is a male. Both Proust and Welch used this device as a method of covering their homosexuality. In "The Hateful Word," an aging woman offers a gardening job to a young German prisoner named Harry Diedz. Her name, Flora Pinkston, symbolizes her passionate (pink) nature and her desire that Harry "till" her garden. Her first name means "flower." The obvious Freudian overtones are difficult to overlook. The plot is also very Laurentian insofar as it describes a frustrated but passionate woman married to a dull lawyer who has not been able to satisfy her sexual needs. The young, handsome German gardener is paid to come each day and revive her neglected garden. Flora momentarily loses control of herself and passionately kisses the sensuous but polite young man. Though embarrassed by her pass, he tries, nevertheless, to explain that he feels toward her the way he feels toward his mother. He states: "You are like mother to me— my English mother." The word "mother"—the hateful word—devastates Flora and simultaneously awakens her to the harsh reality of her middle years, ushering away any residual illusions of appealing to young males.

The final story in *A Last Sheaf*, "The Diamond Badge," is one of Welch's most sophisticated psychological tales, involving issues of control and manipulation. Susan Innes writes to the author of a book that she has just finished reading and succeeds in getting an invitation to visit him. She does not know that the author, Andrew Clifton, is terribly deformed and is taken care of by a young, handsome man named Tom Parkinson. Obviously, Clifton loves Parkinson very deeply. Susan is shocked by Clifton's deformity, a fact that changes her whole attitude toward him. She stays the night but experiences a nightmare during which Tom Parkinson comes into her room to comfort her. She is very attracted to Tom and decides to "accidentally" leave a beautiful diamond pin or badge behind to ensure further contact and, perhaps, another invitation. Finally, after months of silent waiting, she reads a new story by Andrew Clifton called "The Diamond Badge" and realizes that the story is really about her attempt to manipulate both Andrew and Tom. Shortly after reading the story, she receives her diamond badge back without a comment. Andrew had not even sent it registered mail. Susan's attempt to control the lives of these two men merely exposed her selfish and mean-spirited attitude toward both of them.

The majority of the stories in Welch's collection *Brave and Cruel* deal with the crises of childhood and adolescence and particularly with falls from a childish innocence into the painful knowledge of emerging adulthood. The second collection, *A Last Sheaf*, concerns the specific difficulties that young artists experience when they first attempt to practice their creative talents. In both collections, the protagonists are overly sensitive, introspective, and isolated. They feel profoundly separated from the normal world and suffer terribly from that alienation. As time passes, they experience increased desperation and take dangerous and, sometimes, self-destructive steps to alleviate their emptiness.

OTHER MAJOR WORKS

LONG FICTION: *Maiden Voyage*, 1943; *In Youth Is Pleasure*, 1944; *A Voice Through a Cloud*, 1950 (unfinished novel).

POETRY: *Dumb Instrument: Poems and Fragments*, 1976.

NONFICTION: *I Left My Grandfather's House*, 1958; *The Journals of Denton Welch*, 1984.

BIBLIOGRAPHY

Crain, Caleb. "It's Pretty, but Is It Broken?" *The New York Times*, June 20, 1999. Discusses Welch as the "champion of preciousness," fascinated with picnics and antiques. Comments on the relationship of Welch's homosexuality and physical disability to his writing.

De-la-Noy, Michael. *Denton Welch: The Making of a Writer.* New York: Viking, 1984. This standard biography uses much material never before published. The biographer uses many of Welch's letters, letters to Welch from his friends, and materials from personal recollections of those who knew him.

Gooch, Brad. "Gossip, Lies, and Wishes." *The Nation* 240 (June 8, 1985): 711-713. Gooch praises Welch for his ability to make even the smallest objects into mementos by the precision of his writing. Though Welch seems haunted by death and time, he is never morbid and can, at times, be flippant about tombs and graveyards.

Hollinghurst, Alan. "Diminished Pictures." *The Times Literary Supplement*, no. 4264 (December 21, 1984): 1479-1480. Hollinghurst finds Welch's aestheticism anything but precious. It helped him focus his attention on art objects during times of great physical and mental pain. He wrote to save himself and to enrich his life.

Phillips, Robert. *Denton Welch.* New York: Twayne, 1974. The only book-length critical treatment of all Welch's work. Phillips's interpretations are thorough, though he tends to find Freudian and Jungian patterns most helpful. He also intelligently points out some of the affinities that Welch shared with D. H. Lawrence and James Joyce.

Skenazy, Paul. "The Sense and Sensuality of Denton Welch." *The Washington Post Book World*, April 6, 1986, p. 1. A review of *The Stories of Denton Welch* that comments on Welch's focus on the texture of social rituals rather than narrative structure and plot tension; asserts one reads Welch not for character revelation but to experience his sensibility; notes that nearly all the stories concern a confused outsider seeking security and love.

Updike, John. "A Short Life." In *Picked-Up Pieces.* New York: Alfred A. Knopf, 1975. Updike calls Welch an authentic existential writer insofar as his agony enabled him to create a world particle by particle. He sees Welch's autobiographical account of his terrible accident as "a proclamation of our terrible fragility."

Patrick Meanor

FAY WELDON

Born: Alvechurch, Worcestershire, England; September 22, 1931

PRINCIPAL SHORT FICTION

Watching Me, Watching You, 1981
Polaris and Other Stories, 1985
Moon Over Minneapolis: Or, Why She Couldn't Stay, 1991
Angel, All Innocence, and Other Stories, 1995
Wicked Women: A Collection of Short Stories, 1997
A Hard Time to Be a Father, 1998

OTHER LITERARY FORMS

Fay Weldon is a prolific author of novels and teleplays. Her best-known novel, *The Life and Loves of a She Devil* (1983), was made into a British Broadcasting Corporation (BBC) drama and a Hollywood film. Her numerous plays for television, primarily the BBC, include a 1971 award-winning episode of *Upstairs, Downstairs* and a 1980 dramatization of Jane Austen's novel *Pride and Prejudice* (1813). Weldon has also written plays for radio and the theater, plus nonfiction and the children's books *Wolf the Mechanical Dog* (1988), *Party Puddle* (1989), and *Nobody Likes Me* (1997).

ACHIEVEMENTS

Fay Weldon's novel *The Heart of the Country* (1987) won the 1989 *Los Angeles Times* book prize. Two other novels, *Praxis* (1978) and *Worst Fears* (1996), were finalists for the Booker McConnell Prize and the Whitbread Literary Award, respectively.

BIOGRAPHY

No doubt Fay Weldon's life has influenced her work, which often contains autobiographical elements. Her characteristic subjects—the lives of contemporary women and relations between women and men—reflect the extremes of her early life, spent almost exclusively among females, and her adult life, spent mostly in the company of males.

Born Fay Birkinshaw, Weldon grew up in Britain and New Zealand, where her parents emigrated when she was an infant and then divorced when she was six. When Weldon was fourteen, her mother took her and her sister back to London, where they lived in an all-female household with her grandmother. There, Weldon attended Hampstead High, a girls' school. In 1949 Weldon received a scholarship to attend Scotland's coeducational St. Andrews University, from which she received an M.A. in economics and psychology in 1952. By 1955 she had had a child (Nicholas) and was struggling to earn a living. Her assortment of jobs included writing propaganda for the British Foreign Office and later writing copy for advertising firms, a career in which she gradually moved up and prospered. She also visited a psychoanalyst, which suggested the scene for a number of her stories.

In 1960 she married Ronald Weldon, an antiques dealer, and became a suburban wife and mother in Primrose Hill, outside London. The Weldons had three sons, Daniel (1963), Thomas (1970), and Samuel (1977). The last pregnancy, when Weldon was forty-six, was difficult, and she thought she might die. The Weldons had moved to beautiful but distant Somerset in 1976, to an old country house where Weldon felt isolated—another familiar scene in some of her stories. Eventually the marriage broke up, and Weldon returned to London to preside as the literary lioness she had become.

ANALYSIS

Fay Weldon could be called the contemporary Jane Austen, an entertaining, satiric chronicler of today's rude manners centered around sex and self. As befits an admirer of Jane Austen, Weldon focuses on the matings of women and men, almost always from the women's point of view. In keeping with the contemporary world, the matings are often shallow, insecure, and unhappy. Awful events occur in Weldon's short fiction: seductive women break up marriages, pregnant women are abandoned, babies are abused, and ghosts rattle through old houses. Yet, for the most part, Weldon maintains a comic tone, though again her black comedy is consistent with the times.

Weldon is able to deal with awful events and still maintain a comic tone through manipulation of narrative technique and voice. She experiments with discontinuous and fragmented narration, making sudden leaps in her characters' lives. To attain this out-of-breath pace, she sometimes sacrifices depth of characterization, especially of the male characters. What else is an author to do in an age of shallow people? The shallowness of her characters may be seen as another symptom of the times. Her narrative techniques also reflect her background in writing advertising copy—the transfer of sound bite technology to short fiction. Her stories would probably not be convincing enough to entertain if they were not also narrated in highly believable human voices, the colloquial, confused voices of single mothers, suburban housewives, daughters, and feminists.

Fay Weldon (AP/Wide World Photos)

Since the voices in Weldon's writing are almost always female, she has sometimes been claimed as a feminist writer. Her writing does not, however, express a consistent feminist ideology or agenda. There is no shortage of oppressive men in Weldon's writing, but neither is there a shortage of wicked women. In fact, some of the targets of Weldon's satire are misguided women who have constructed their identity around feminist ideology and who behave accordingly. Weldon's work does not so much express an ideology as, in the classic mode, hold a mirror up to nature.

"WATCHING ME, WATCHING YOU"

"Watching Me, Watching You," which gives its title to Weldon's first collection of short fiction, is ostensibly a ghost story, the first of several stories set in old houses where strange noises and happenings occur. The ghost here is rather lethargic, mostly reacting to stranger happenings among the house's living inhabitants. Echoing stories by Nathaniel Hawthorne and Edgar Allan Poe, curtains rustle, wine glasses tip, walls sweat and cry, and mirrors crash to the floor only to comment on human behavior. The real story is of how Vanessa steals Anne's husband Maurice and marries him, only to have Audrey steal Maurice from her in the end, as if some crude sense of cosmic justice operates in the old house cursed by human failings. Meanwhile, two children are born to suffer, and Maurice does not make a good impression himself. The gothic conventions are used to justify the narration, which covers fifteen years, since presumably the ghost can see the past, present, and future all at once. The story's comic tone is rather tentative, except in the characterization of the ghost and in a little satire at the end, in which Anne and Vanessa are communing with each other amid posters "calling on women to live, to be free, to protest, to re-claim the right, demand wages for housework, to do anything in the world but love."

MOON OVER MINNEAPOLIS

Perhaps Weldon's most popular collection of short fiction, *Moon Over Minneapolis* represents the variety of her work. As in some of her other collections, the variety is indicated by groupings of stories under subheadings: "Stories of Working Life," "Four Tales from Abroad," "Tales of the New Age," "Stories for Christmas," "Three Tales of Country Life" (showing the Somerset influence), and "As Told to Miss Jacobs" (stories narrated to a silent psychoanalyst).

One of the tales from abroad is a favorite of literary anthologists, "Ind Aff or Out of Love in Sarajevo." The puzzling abbreviation in the title is one John Wesley, founder of Methodism, used for "inordinate affection," a sin "which bears the spirit away from God towards the flesh." In the story a twenty-five-year-old Cambridge graduate student feels "inordinate affection" for her professor and thesis director, even to the extent of sharing a vacation with him in Sarajevo and paying for her share. The aptly named Professor Peter Piper, a forty-six-year-old married man and father of three, is a male chauvinist pig of the old school. While the peerless Peter imposes his opinions on his young charge, from tastes in food to theories of history, he does not pay any attention when she speaks. The setting finally brings her to her senses when they reflect on the local hero Gavrilo Princip, the young assassin credited with starting World War I by shooting the Archduke Francis Ferdinand, and when a handsome young waiter smiles at her:

> I smiled back, and instead of the pain in the heart I'd become accustomed to as an erotic sensation, now felt, quite violently, an associated yet different pang which got my lower stomach. The true, the real pain of Ind Aff!

"Ind Aff" can be interpreted as a prototypical feminist story, but other stories in *Moon Over Minneapolis* poke fun at extreme feminist attitudes. In "Subject to Diary" a middle-aged career woman, who is close only to her diary, cancels her third abortion at the last minute on a sudden motherly impulse. In "I Do What I Can and I Am What I Am" a daughter disappoints her feminist mother by being sweet, by getting an A in her housecraft course and F's in chemistry and physics, by dressing in frilly women's clothes instead of pants, and by becoming an airline stewardess and winning the Miss Skyways Competition. Finally, in "Au Pair" a "big-busted, bovine" Danish girl gets a position with the Beaver family in England, cleans up

the messy house, starts cooking good meals, takes care of the children, starts sleeping with the husband, and eventually replaces the neurotic Mrs. Beaver.

The title story, "Moon Over Minneapolis," is disappointing, which is probably what one should expect from a title that contrasts with the romantic song title "Moon Over Miami." In the story, romance fails when an English woman calls off her wedding to a Minneapolis man in order to return home and take care of her dependent extended family. This story, like others in the collection, makes use of some interesting techniques, such as symbolic uses of settings, plays on names, and experiments with narration. "Moon Over Minneapolis," for example, is narrated by the English woman to her psychoanalyst, Miss Jacobs, and "Au Pair" is narrated secondhand by the girl's mother back in Copenhagen (assisted by letters and phone calls) while the mother entertains sailors from around the world in bed.

"PAINS"

"Pains," subtitled "A Story of Most Contemporary Women, 1972," appears in the collection *Wicked Women*. Like some other stories in the collection, it uses engaging women's voices and narrative techniques, but the fireworks are perhaps most brilliant here. The story features not just one woman's voice but a whole cacophony, as the local Women's Liberation Group meets downstairs while upstairs, in ironic juxtaposition, Paula undergoes labor and eventually delivers a son. At the very moment she gives birth, her husband is downstairs trying to kiss a neighbor woman. These ironic situations are only the framework for the dazzling display of voices ranging from radical-sounding feminists who quote Vladimir Ilich Lenin to Audrey, the neighbor woman, who opines,

> I *like* being a woman . . . I mean, what's wrong with it? I mean, it's all a bit ridiculous, isn't it, all this bra-burning and why do they make themselves so *plain*. Present company excepted, of course.

A HARD TIME TO BE A FATHER

A Hard Time to Be a Father, a collection of nineteen stories, continues with some of Weldon's familiar subjects and techniques. Even some of the titles are reminiscent of earlier stories, but the stories here are just as entertaining as earlier ones. Jealousy and revenge are still a part of "Once in Love in Oslo," in which a former wife seeks retribution against a present one, and in "Come on Everyone," in which the protagonist returns years later to savage her popular college roommate. The media's feeding frenzies are satirized in "What the Papers Say" and prenatal testing in "A Libation of Blood." Other stories, however, have less of a satirical edge, as if Weldon is willing to concede the possibility of happy turns of fate, if only by luck or chance. Such stories include "Spirits Fly South," "Noisy into the Night," the title story, and "GUP—Or Falling in Love in Helsinki," in which a young woman meets her long-lost father, and GUP means "Great Universal Paradox."

OTHER MAJOR WORKS

LONG FICTION: *The Fat Woman's Joke*, 1967 (pb. in U.S. as *. . . And the Wife Ran Away*, 1968); *Down Among the Women*, 1971; *Female Friends*, 1974; *Remember Me*, 1976; *Words of Advice*, 1977 (pb. in England *Little Sisters*, 1978); *Praxis*, 1978; *Puffball*, 1980; *The President's Child*, 1982; *The Life and Loves of a She-Devil*, 1983; *The Shrapnel Academy*, 1986; *The Rules of Life*, 1987; *The Hearts and Lives of Men*, 1987; *The Heart of the Country*, 1987; *Leader of the Band*, 1988; *The Cloning of Joanna May*, 1989; *Darcy's Utopia*, 1990; *Growing Rich*, 1992; *Life Force*, 1992; *Affliction*, 1993 (pb. in U.S. as *Trouble*, 1993); *Splitting*, 1995; *Worst Fears*, 1996; *Big Girls Don't Cry*, 1997 (pb. in England as *Big Women*, 1997); *Rhode Island Blues*, 2000.

PLAYS: *Permanence*, pr. 1969; *Time Hurries On*, pb. 1972; *Words of Advice*, pr., pb. 1974; *Friends*, pr. 1975; *Moving House*, pr. 1976; *Mr. Director*, pr. 1978; *Action Replay*, pr. 1979 (also known as *Love Among the Women*); *After the Prize*, pr. 1981; *I Love My Love*, pr. 1981 (also known as *Wordworm*); *The Four Alice Bakers*, pr. 1999.

TELEPLAYS: *Wife in a Blonde Wig*, 1966; *The Fat Woman's Tale*, 1966; *What About Me*, 1967; *Dr. De Waldon's Therapy*, 1967; *Goodnight Mrs. Dill*, 1967; *The Forty-fifth Unmarried Mother*, 1967; *Fall of the Goat*, 1967; *Ruined Houses*, 1968; *Venus Rising*, 1968; *The Three Wives of Felix Hull*, 1968; *Hippy Who Cares*, 1968; *£13083*, 1968; *The Loophole*, 1969; *Smokescreen*, 1969; *Poor Mother*, 1970; *Office Party*, 1970; *On Trial*, 1971 (in *Upstairs, Downstairs* series); *Old Man's Hat*, 1972; *A Splinter of Ice*, 1972; *Hands*, 1972; *The Lament of an Unmarried Father*, 1972; *A Nice Rest*, 1972; *Comfortable Words*, 1973; *Desirous of Change*, 1973; *In Memoriam*, 1974; *Poor Baby*, 1975; *The Terrible Tale of Timothy Bagshott*, 1975; *Aunt Tatty*, 1975 (adaptation of Elizabeth Bowen's story); *Act of Rape*, 1977; *Married Love*, 1977 (in *Six Women* series); *Pride and Prejudice*, 1980 (adaptation of Jane Austen's novel); *Honey Ann*, 1980; *Watching Me, Watching You*, 1980 (in *Leap in the Dark* series); *Life for Christine*, 1980; *Little Miss Perkins*, 1982; *Loving Women*, 1983; *Redundant! Or, the Wife's Revenge*, 1983.

RADIO PLAYS: *Spider*, 1972; *Housebreaker*, 1973; *Mr. Fox and Mr. First*, 1974; *The Doctor's Wife*, 1975; *Polaris*, 1978; *Weekend*, 1979 (in *Just Before Midnight* series); *All the Bells of Paradise*, 1979; *I Love My Love*, 1981.

NONFICTION: *Letters to Alice on First Reading Jane Austen*, 1984; *Rebecca West*, 1985; *Sacred Cows: A Portrait of Britain, Post-Rushdie, Pre-Utopia*, 1989.

CHILDREN'S LITERATURE: *Wolf the Mechanical Dog*, 1988; *Party Puddle*, 1989; *Nobody Likes Me*, 1997.

EDITED TEXTS: *New Stories Four: An Arts Council Anthology*, 1979 (with Elaine Feinstein).

BIBLIOGRAPHY

Barreca, Regina, ed. *Fay Weldon's Wicked Fictions.* Hanover, N.H.: University Press of New England, 1994. A collection of eighteen critical essays, five by Weldon herself, dealing with leading themes and techniques in her fiction and various issues raised by it, such as her relation to feminism and her politics and moral stance. A few essays focus on specific novels, but others are relevant to both her short and long fiction. Includes "The Monologic Narrator in Fay Weldon's Short Fiction," by Lee A. Jacobus. Essays by Weldon include "The Changing Face of Fiction" and "On the Reading of Frivolous Fiction."

Dowling, Finuala. *Fay Weldon's Fiction*. Rutherford, N.J.: Fairleigh Dickinson University Press, 1998. An examination of the themes and techniques in Weldon's fiction, with emphasis on the novels but relevance to the short fiction as well.

Faulks, Lana. *Fay Weldon*. Twayne's English Authors series 551. Boston: Twayne, 1998. An introduction to Weldon's life and work. Focusing on the novels, Faulks sees Weldon's work as "feminist comedy" contrasting with feminist writing that depicts women as oppressed. Also examines Weldon's experiments with narrative techniques.

Salzmann-Brunner, Brigitte. *Amanuenses to the Present: Protagonists in the Fiction of Penelope Mortimer, Margaret Drabble, and Fay Weldon*. New York: Peter Lang, 1988. Examines the women in these authors' works, with opportunities for some comparisons and contrasts.

Harold Branam

H. G. WELLS

Born: Bromley, Kent, England; September 21, 1866
Died: London, England; August 13, 1946

PRINCIPAL SHORT FICTION

The Stolen Bacillus and Other Incidents, 1895
The Plattner Story and Others, 1897
Thirty Strange Stories, 1897
Tales of Space and Time, 1899
The Vacant Country, 1899
Twelve Stories and a Dream, 1903
The Country of the Blind and Other Stories, 1911
A Door in the Wall and Other Stories, 1911
The Short Stories of H. G. Wells, 1927 (also pb. as *The Complete Stories of H. G. Wells*, 1966)
The Favorite Short Stories of H. G. Wells, 1937 (also pb. as *The Famous Short Stories of H. G. Wells*, 1938)

OTHER LITERARY FORMS

Beginning with *The Time Machine: An Invention* (1895) and ending with *The War in the Air, and Particularly How Mr. Bert Smallways Fared While It Lasted* (1908), H. G. Wells wrote nine fantastic, often futuristic novels, which he called scientific romances. Works like *The Invisible Man: A Grotesque Romance* (1897), *The War of the Worlds* (1898), and *The First Men in the Moon* (1901), which now fall under the rubric of science fiction, earned Wells the informal place that he shares with Jules Verne as a cofounder of that genre. Wells also wrote more than thirty realistic novels, of which the three most famous are *Kipps: The Story of a Simple Soul* (1905), *Tono-Bungay* (1908), and *The History of Mr. Polly* (1910). His fiction became increasingly speculative and utopian (or dystopian) after 1920. Wells, assisted by specialists, wrote three encyclopedic works devoted to the history of the universe, to biology, and to economics. The first, *The Outline of History: Being a Plain History of Life and Mankind* (1920), became a staple of home libraries throughout the world.

ACHIEVEMENTS

George Orwell declared that the twenty-five years between *The Time Machine* and *The Outline of History* should bear Wells's name. In fact, the reputation of H. G. Wells gave rise to a term, "Wellsian," whose mention conveys "the shape of things to come." Perhaps critic Walter Allen summed up best Wells's virtues and their defects:

I still think [Wells] had the largest natural talent of any English writer of the century. He did not always use it well, but he was a positive cornucopia of ideas. . . . Almost certainly he will look much greater in the future than he does now.

Wells anticipated the League of Nations with his World State and forecast the atom bomb thirty years before Hiroshima.

BIOGRAPHY

One of the most amply self-documented lives in the annals of English literature began on September 21, 1866, when to Sarah Neal Wells, a lady's maid, and to Joseph Wells, an unsuccessful tradesman though accomplished cricketer, was born the last of three sons, Herbert George (Bertie) Wells. The infant first "squinted and bubbled at the universe" in a shabby bedroom over a china shop in Bromley, in a residence called Atlas House. Bertie Wells's escape from the drab life of his two siblings was astonishing though brief. Her older sons safely apprenticed, Sarah Wells took thirteen-year-old Bertie with her to an estate called Uppark, where she hired on as a housekeeper in 1880. The change in outlook from shopkeeper's window to below stairs in a manor house was lifesaving. It lasted a year, during which the boy encountered great books for the first time—the satires of Voltaire, the saga of Gulliver, the liberating air of Plato's *Politeia* (388-368 B.C.E.; *Republic*, 1701).

The young Wells's education was fragmentary, alternating with dismal apprenticeships one after another. He escaped anonymity through an unlikely door. He began to pass examinations and to show unusual ability in science. At eighteen he won a scholarship to the Normal School of Science, London, to train to be a teacher. His zoology professor was Thomas H. Huxley, brilliant essayist, evolutionist, and public spokesperson for Charles Darwin and the theory of evolution. It was Huxley's example and lectures that provided Wells with vital links between the traditional religious beliefs in which he had been brought up and the scientific ideas he absorbed as a student. Huxley's fears about the pitfalls of natural selection if left unchecked by ethical and social progress took form in his student's imagination in such cosmic phenomena as colliding comets, invading

H. G. Wells (Library of Congress)

Martians, and monstrous creatures seen by his time traveler.

The year 1895 was crucial on domestic and literary fronts. He divorced his first wife, a cousin; happily married a teacher, Amy Catherine Robbins; and published *The Time Machine*, which brought him a fervent readership and contracts from England's leading editors for stories only he could write. He published upward of sixty tales in magazines and in five collections, most of them written before he was thirty-five, and *The Complete Stories of H. G. Wells* has remained steadily in print. They were products of the astonishing outburst of creative energy that turned Wells from an obscure science tutor into one of the most admired and discussed writers of his time, "the most influential writer in the English-speaking world," according to Anatole France.

The great crisis in Wells's life as a writer and a man came in his early forties when, with thirty volumes published and status as a public figure well in hand, he chose to become a force recognizable only in his own time. Wells began to write utopian blueprints disguised as novels, long tracts calling for elitist utopias, encyclopedias of knowledge which were really propaganda. He continued to publish essays, even novels, almost into his final—his eightieth—year. He died one year after the dropping of the atomic bomb, an event he had predicted thirty years earlier.

ANALYSIS

By the 1890's, the golden age of the English short story had begun. Edgar Allan Poe and his theory that every story should strive for a single effect had become a pattern for imitation. Rudyard Kipling's stories of Indian life were opening a new and exotic dimension to readers worldwide. A flourishing discipleship of Guy de Maupassant, later to be led by W. Somerset Maugham, had come into existence on the English side of the channel. Wells's range is narrower than Kipling's, only rarely does Wells achieve macabre effects anywhere near Poe's, and he is incapable of the irony underlying the deceptively anecdotal stories of the French master Maupassant. However, from these three H. G. Wells learned the technique of the short story. "I was doing my best to write as the others wrote," Wells acknowledged, "and it was long before I realized that my exceptional origins and training gave me an almost unavoidable freshness of approach."

Often a story "starts as a joke," Wells observed in retrospect. "There is a shock of laughter in nearly every discovery." H. E. Bates, himself a master of short fiction, was one of the first to see the twinkle in the storyteller's eye. He praises Wells as

> a great Kidder, a man who succeeded in telling more tall stories than any writer of his generation yet, by a genius for binding the commonplace to some astounding exploration of fancy, succeeded in getting them believed.

A close friend, the novelist and memoirist Frank Swinnerton, believes that of Wells's rich variety of writings "the short stories may well be the most characteristic."

The spellbinding tale-teller felt right at home in an end-of-century cultural anxiety—a late-Victorian sense of crisis which seemed to inhibit the large statement. The major self-contained fictions of the 1890's were mood-inducing novellas such as Oscar Wilde's *The Picture of Dorian Gray* (1891), Henry James's *The Turn of the Screw* (1898), and *The Time Machine*. "Anything is possible" became the rule.

"THE MAN WHO COULD WORK MIRACLES"

A famous story, "The Man Who Could Work Miracles," is not only Wells at his playful best but also a paradigm for a vast literature about humble souls unexpectedly endowed with the power to upset their worlds. The clerk Fotheringay's supreme windfall lies in being able to conjure up miracles. Like so many who lack the proper combination of dash and restraint for the proper use of divine powers, Fotheringay lets his reach exceed his grasp. Requesting that the earth stop rotating, he precipitates a scene of comic confusion as every object about him falls off into space.

"THE LORD OF THE DYNAMOS"

From the first paragraph of this story, the reader is *shown*, never *told*, Wells's hatred of Empire. The reader is introduced to Holroyd, the uncivilized-civilized white man, the characteristically wooden product of technological society, and to Azuma-zi, the "burden" who will rise against oppression and destroy. Holroyd, the chief attendant of the dynamos that keep an electric railway going, and his helper, who has come from the "mysterious East," are opposed at all points. Holroyd delivers a theological lecture on his big machine soon after Azuma-zi's arrival. "Where's your 'eathen idol to match 'im?" he shouts. Azuma-zi hears only a few words above the din: "Kill a hundred man. . . . That's something like a Gord!" Azuma-zi learns to worship the dynamo. Under Holroyd's sneering tutorship, the native obeys only too well. By tribal custom, he must ritualize the dynamo. One night Azuma-zi grasps the lever and sends the armature in reverse. There is a struggle; Holroyd is electrocuted. His death is taken to have been accidental, and a substitute arrives. For Azuma-zi, the newcomer is to be a second sacrifice. This time the Asian is foiled; to avoid capture, he kills himself by grabbing the naked terminals. The conclusion is phrased in mythic terms: "So ended prematurely the worship of the Dynamo Deity, perhaps the most short-lived of all religions. Yet withal it could at least boast a Martyrdom and a Human Sacrifice." The story echoes Joseph Conrad and Kipling, but it can be read simply as a good story or for wider implications beneath the parable.

"THE COUNTRY OF THE BLIND"

More effectively than anywhere except in certain of the scientific romances and in the last pages of *Tono-Bungay*, Wells's finest novel, "The Country of the Blind" blends the riches of the storyteller and the mystic. To the mythmaker at the heart of Wells, no imagery proved so obsessive. From his student days under Huxley down to his deathbed conviction that humankind had played itself out, Wells viewed humankind darkly: as struggling in an evolutionary whirl to fulfill its promise, but always forced back into some sealed-off country of the blind.

Essentially, the story is a pessimistic restatement of Plato's Allegory of the Cave. The mountaineer Nunez comes unawares on a fastness deep in the Andes, where for centuries the inhabitants have been sightless and where the idea of seeing has disappeared. At first, Nunez brazenly assumes the truth of the proverb "In the country of the blind, the one-eyed man is king," and he confidently expects to become master. However, he finds that the blind inhabitants have developed other faculties; that in a land where no one sees, the sighted are actually the disabled. Eventually Nunez is forced to submit, and his submission includes giving up his eyes, regarded by the blind as grievous and useless appendages. As Nunez rebels and endeavors to escape over the mountains, he is obliged to leave behind the woman, Medina, he has come to love.

Like the prisoners of Plato's cave, the blind have made the remote valley a symbol of self-imposed limits. They can no more conceive of a world outside their valley than the chained cave dwellers can imagine anything beyond the flickering shadows on the wall. The blind world, like the world Wells sought to reform, goes on, self-satisfied.

"THE DOOR IN THE WALL"

By the time Wells stopped writing stories, he had tired of any notion of "art for art's sake." A harassed Wells insisted to his onetime American admirer, Henry James, that he would rather be called a jour-

nalist than an artist. James broke with Wells, seeking to protect his precious territory, the novel, from the brash invasion of his younger and better-selling peer. The latter's expressed determination "to have all of life" embraced by fiction ran up against James's charges that writers like Wells "saturated" fiction.

One of Wells's least characteristic stories touches on a theme that James worked into several stories and his own favorite of his novels, *The Ambassadors* (1903), namely, the unlived life. In "The Door in the Wall," Lionel Wallace, a wealthy and famous cabinet minister, finds himself haunted by a childhood memory of a door that leads into a garden containing all the things that success has denied him—peace, delight, beauty. Three times Wallace rejects the door before yielding to its promise and stepping fatally into an excavation pit. Much of the story is told between quotation marks, but the unidentified narrator maintains a tone which suggests he has been mesmerized by Wallace's conviction into a reluctant acceptance:

> And it was at school that I heard first of the 'Door in the Wall'—and that I was to hear of a second time only a month before his death. To him at least [it] was a real door, leading through a real wall to immortal realities . . .

Bernard Bergonzi, whose *The Early H. G. Wells* (1961) is still unsurpassed in its linking of Wells's stories and scientific romances to the search for new enchantments at the turn of the century, presents a convincing case for the beautiful garden behind the closed door as a symbol of the imagination, and Wallace as a projection of Wells's split persona.

"THE BEAUTIFUL SUIT"

Three years after "The Door in the Wall," in 1909, Wells published in *Collier's* another story in the same spirit. A boy is presented by his mother with a shining suit but is constrained from wearing it, except on special occasions, by the poor woman's innate caution—a reference perhaps to Wells's own mother and to her sense of Victorian propriety. The boy dreams of the fuller life he believes wearing the suit will bring him. One moonlit night he unwraps the precious gift, dons it, and in an ecstasy of fulfillment, plunges into what was by day a duck pond but which to his night sense "was a great bowl of silver moonshine . . . amidst which the stars were netted in tangled reflections of the brooding trees upon the bank." To the boy's starry eyes, his suit equips him for his journey, but next morning his body is found in the bottom of a stone pit,

with his beautiful clothes a little bloody, and foul and stained with the duckweed from the pond [but] his face . . . of such happiness . . . that you would have understood indeed . . . he had died happy.

OTHER MAJOR WORKS

LONG FICTION: *The Time Machine: An Invention*, 1895; *The Wonderful Visit*, 1895; *The Island of Dr. Moreau*, 1896; *The Wheels of Chance: A Holiday Adventure*, 1896; *The Invisible Man: A Grotesque Romance*, 1897; *The War of the Worlds*, 1898; *When the Sleeper Wakes: A Story of the Years to Come*, 1899; *Love and Mr. Lewisham*, 1900; *The First Men in the Moon*, 1901; *The Sea Lady*, 1902; *The Food of the Gods, and How It Came to Earth*, 1904; *Kipps: The Story of a Simple Soul*, 1905; *In the Days of the Comet*, 1906; *Tono-Bungay*, 1908; *The War in the Air, and Particularly How Mr. Bert Smallways Fared While It Lasted*, 1908; *Ann Veronica: A Modern Love Story*, 1909; *The History of Mr. Polly*, 1910; *The New Machiavelli*, 1910; *Marriage*, 1912; *The Passionate Friends*, 1913; *The Wife of Sir Isaac Harman*, 1914; *The World Set Free: A Story of Mankind*, 1914; *Bealby: A Holiday*, 1915; *The Research Magnificent*, 1915; *Mr. Britling Sees It Through*, 1916; *The Soul of a Bishop—A Novel—with Just a Little Love in It—About Conscience and Religion and the Real Troubles of Life*, 1917; *Joan and Peter: The Story of an Education*, 1918; *The Undying Fire: A Contemporary Novel*, 1919; *The Secret Places of the Heart*, 1922; *Men like Gods*, 1923; *The Dream*, 1924; *Christina Alberta's Father*, 1925; *The World of William Clissold: A Novel at a New Age*, 1926 (3 volumes); *Meanwhile: The Picture of a Lady*, 1927; *Mr. Blettsworthy on Rampole Island*, 1928; *The King Who Was a King: The Book of a Film*, 1929; *The Autocracy of Mr. Parham: His Remarkable Adventure in*

This Changing World, 1930; *The Buplington of Blup*, 1933; *The Shape of Things to Come: The Ultimate Resolution*, 1933; *The Croquet Player*, 1936; *Byrnhild*, 1937; *The Camford Visitation*, 1937; *Star Begotten: A Biological Fantasia*, 1937; *Apropos of Dolores*, 1938; *The Brothers*, 1938; *The Holy Terror*, 1939; *Babes in the Darkling Wood*, 1940; *All Aboard for Ararat*, 1940; *You Can't Be Too Careful: A Sample of Life, 1901-1951*, 1941.

NONFICTION: *Text-Book of Biology*, 1893 (2 volumes); *Honours Physiography*, 1893 (with Sir Richard A. Gregory); *Certain Personal Matters*, 1897; *A Text-Book of Zoology*, 1898 (with A. M. Davis); *Anticipations of the Reaction of Mechanical and Scientific Progress upon Human Life and Thought*, 1902 (also known as *Anticipations*); *The Discovery of the Future*, 1902; *Mankind in the Making*, 1903; *A Modern Utopia*, 1905; *Socialism and the Family*, 1906; *The Future in America: A Search After Realities*, 1906; *This Misery of Boots*, 1907; *New Worlds for Old*, 1908; *First and Last Things: A Confession of Faith and Rule of Life*, 1908; *The Great State: Essays in Construction*, 1912 (also known as *Socialism and the Great State*); *The War That Will End War*, 1914; *An Englishman Looks at the World: Being a Series of Unrestrained Remarks upon Contemporary Matters*, 1914 (also known as *Social Forces in England and America*); *God, the Invisible King*, 1917; *The Outline of History: Being a Plain History of Life and Mankind*, 1920; *Russia in the Shadows*, 1920; *The Salvaging of Civilization*, 1921; *A Short History of the World*, 1922; *Socialism and the Scientific Motive*, 1923; *The Open Conspiracy: Blue Prints for a World Revolution*, 1928; *Imperialism and the Open Conspiracy*, 1929; *The Science of Life: A Summary of Contemporary Knowledge About Life and Its Possibilities*, 1929-1930 (with Julian S. Huxley and G. P. Wells); *The Way to World Peace*, 1930; *What Are We to Do with Our Lives?*, 1931 (revised edition of *The Open Conspiracy*); *The Work, Wealth, and Happiness of Mankind*, 1931 (2 volumes); *After Democracy: Addresses and Papers on the Present World Situation*, 1932; *Evolution, Fact and Theory*, 1932 (with Huxley and G. P. Wells); *Experiment in Autobiography: Discoveries and Conclusions of a Very Ordinary*

Brain Since 1866, 1934 (2 volumes); *The New America: The New World*, 1935; *The Anatomy of Frustration: A Modern Synthesis*, 1936; *World Brain*, 1938; *The Fate of Homo Sapiens: An Unemotional Statement of the Things That Are Happening to Him Now and of the Immediate Possibilities Confronting Him*, 1939; *The New World Order: Whether It Is Obtainable, How It Can Be Attained, and What Sort of World a World at Peace Will Have to Be*, 1940; *The Common Sense of War and Peace: World Revolution or War Unending?*, 1940; *The Conquest of Time*, 1942; *Phoenix: A Summary of the Inescapable Conditions of World Reorganization*, 1942; *Science and the World Mind*, 1942; *Crux Ansata: An Indictment of the Roman Catholic Church*, 1943; *'42 to '44: A Contemporary Memoir upon Human Behaviour During the Crisis of the World Revolution*, 1944; *Mind at the End of Its Tether*, 1945.

CHILDREN'S LITERATURE: *The Adventures of Tommy*, 1929.

BIBLIOGRAPHY

Batchelor, John. *H. G. Wells*. Cambridge, England: Cambridge University Press, 1985. An important examination of Wells's work. Includes an index and a bibliography.

Bates, H. E. *The Modern Short Story*. Boston: The Writer, Inc., 1941. Himself one of England's finest short-story writers, Bates accords high rank to Wells in the genre and rebuts charges that Wells's style lacks beauty. Calls Wells a "literary [Thomas] Edison."

Bergonzi, Bernard. *The Early H. G. Wells: A Study of the Scientific Romances*. Toronto: University of Toronto Press, 1961. Still the most knowledgeable account of the remarkable affinity of Wells's early fantasies, including his short stories, with the search for new worlds and behavior that characterized the turn of the century. Bergonzi, in a long third chapter, "The Short Stories," links "The Country of the Blind" and "The Door in the Wall" to Freudian-Jungian tendencies in Wells.

Costa, Richard Hauer. *H. G. Wells*. Boston: Twayne Publishers, 1985. A thorough study of Wells's work. Includes notes, references, and a bibliography.

_____. "Wells and the Cosmic Despair." *The Nation* (September, 12, 1966): First essay on "The Country of the Blind" to compare the original version (1904), written in his thirties, with a revision done in his seventies. Wells changes the ending to permit the hero Nunez and his blind lover Medina to escape together to the sighted—the civilized—world, only to find that the woman, her life saved by Nunez's vision, prefers the simplicity of the valley of the blind to the fearfully complicated Nunez world "that may be beautiful but terrible to *see*." Wells's cosmic pessimism may thus be symbolized.

Rainwater, Catherine. "Encounters with the 'White Sphinx': Poe's Influence on Some Early Works of H. G. Wells." *English Literature in Transition* 26, no. 1 (1983). Wells follows Edgar Allan Poe in blurring the distinction between his characters and their imaginings. Rainwater demonstrates Wells's debt with "The Red Room," a Wellsian ghost story which, like Poe's stories, depends upon a narrator's altered state of consciousness for its effects.

Richard Hauer Costa

EUDORA WELTY

Born: Jackson, Mississippi; April 13, 1909

PRINCIPAL SHORT FICTION

A Curtain of Green and Other Stories, 1941
The Wide Net and Other Stories, 1943
The Golden Apples, 1949
Short Stories, 1950
Selected Stories of Eudora Welty, 1954
The Bride of the Innisfallen and Other Stories,
    1955
The Collected Stories of Eudora Welty, 1980
Moon Lake and Other Stories, 1980
Retreat, 1981

OTHER LITERARY FORMS

In addition to her many short stories, Eudora Welty has published novels, essays, reviews, an autobiography, a fantasy story for children, and a volume of photographs of Mississippi during the Depression, *One Time, One Place: Mississippi in the Depression, A Snapshot Album* (1971), taken during her stint as photographer and writer for the Works Progress Administration.

ACHIEVEMENTS

Eudora Welty possesses a distinctive voice in southern, and indeed in American, fiction. Her vibrant, compelling evocation of the Mississippi landscape, which is her most common setting, has led to comparisons between her work and that of other eminent southern writers such as William Faulkner, Carson McCullers, and Flannery O'Connor. Welty's graceful, lyrical fiction, however, lacks the pessimism that characterizes much of established southern writing, and though her settings are distinctly southern, her themes are universal and do not focus on uniquely southern issues.

The honors and awards that Welty has amassed throughout her long career are so many as to defy complete listing in a short space. Among her major achievements are four O. Henry Awards for her short stories (first prizes in 1942, 1943, and 1968, and a second prize in 1941), two Guggenheim Fellowships (1942, 1949), honorary lectureships at Smith College (1952) and the University of Cambridge (1955), election to the National Institute of Arts and Letters (1952) and to the American Academy of Arts and Letters (1971), honorary LL.D. degrees from the University of Wisconsin (1954) and Smith College (1956), a term as Honorary Consultant to the Library of Congress (1958-1961), the William Dean Howells Medal of the American Academy of Arts and Letters for *The Ponder Heart* (1954), the Gold Medal for Fiction of the National Institute of Arts and Letters (1972), the Pulitzer Prize in fiction (awarded in 1973 for her 1972 novel *The Optimist's Daughter*), the National Medal of Literature and Medal of Freedom (1981), the National Medal of Arts (1986), the naming of the Jackson Public Library in her honor (1986), and a Rea Award (1992).

BIOGRAPHY

Eudora Welty was born on April 13, 1909, in Jackson, Mississippi. In the Welty household, reading was a favorite pastime, and Welty recalls in her autobiography, *One Writer's Beginnings* (1984), both being read to often as a young child and becoming a voracious reader herself. Her recollections of her early life are of a loving and protective family and of a close, gossip-prone community in which she developed her lifelong habit of watching, listening to, and observing closely everything around her. Her progressive and understanding parents encouraged her in her education, and in 1925, she enrolled at the Mississippi State College for Women. After two years there, she transferred to the University of Wisconsin and was graduated with a B.A. in English in 1929.

Welty subsequently studied advertising at the Columbia University Business School; her father had recommended to her that if she planned to be a writer, she would be well advised to have another skill to which she could turn in case of need. During the Depression, however, she had little success finding employment in the field of advertising. She returned to

Eudora Welty (Richard O. Moore)

Mississippi and spent the next several years working variously as a writer for radio and as a society editor. In 1933, she began working for the Works Progress Administration, traveling throughout Mississippi, taking photographs, interviewing people, and writing newspaper articles. She later credited this experience with providing her with much material for her short stories as well as sharpening her habit of observation. During these working years, she wrote short stories and occasionally traveled to New York in an effort to interest publishers in her work, with little success. Her first short story, "Death of a Traveling Salesman," was published in 1936 by a "little" magazine called *Manuscript*. Her ability as a writer soon attracted the attention of Robert Penn Warren and Cleanth Brooks, editors of *The Southern Review*, and over the next years her writing appeared in that magazine as well as in *The New Yorker*, *The Atlantic Monthly*, and *The Sewanee Review*.

Her first collection of short stories, *A Curtain of Green and Other Stories*, appeared in 1941, with a preface by Katherine Anne Porter. Welty's reputation as an important southern writer was established with this first volume, and, at the urging of her editor and

friend John Woodburn, who encouraged her to write a longer work of fiction, she followed it with her fabular novel *The Robber Bridegroom* in 1942. Thenceforth, she continued with a fairly steady output of fiction, and with each successive publication, her stature as a major American writer grew. Although fiction is her primary field, she has written many essays and critical reviews and has dabbled in the theater. In addition to stage adaptations of *The Robber Bridegroom* and *The Ponder Heart*, she has collaborated on a musical (never produced) entitled *What Year Is This?* and has written several short theatrical sketches. In 1984, her autobiography, *One Writer's Beginnings*, appeared and quickly became a best-seller.

Welty has spent most of her life living in, observing, and writing about Jackson and the Mississippi Delta country. Her frequent visits to New York, and her travels in France, Italy, Ireland, and England (where she participated in a conference on American studies at the University of Cambridge in 1955) have provided her with material for those few stories that are set outside her native Mississippi. From time to time, she has lectured or taught but in general has preferred the quiet and privacy of her lifelong home of Jackson.

ANALYSIS

Although some dominant themes and characteristics appear regularly in Eudora Welty's fiction, her work resists categorization. The majority of her stories are set in her beloved Mississippi Delta country, of which she paints a vivid and detailed picture, but she is equally comfortable evoking such diverse scenes as a Northern city or a transatlantic ocean liner. Thematically, she concerns herself both with the importance of family and community relations and, paradoxically, with the strange solitariness of human experience. Elements of myth and symbol often appear in her work, but she uses them in shadowy, inexplicit ways. Perhaps the only constant in Welty's fiction is her unerring keenness of observation, both of physical landscape and in characterization, and her ability to create convincing psychological portraits of an immensely varied cast of characters.

"DEATH OF A TRAVELING SALESMAN"

One of her earliest stories, "Death of a Traveling Salesman," tells of a commercial traveler who loses his way in the hill country of Mississippi and accidentally drives his car into a ravine. At the nearest farm dwelling, the salesman finds a simple, taciturn couple who assist him with his car and give him a meal and a place to stay for the night. The unspoken warmth in the relationship of the couple is contrasted with the salesman's loneliness, and he repeatedly worries that they can hear the loud pounding of his heart, physically weakened from a recent illness and metaphorically empty of love. When he leaves their house in the morning, his heart pounds loudest of all as he carries his bags to his car; frantically he tries to stifle the sound and dies, his heart unheard by anyone but himself.

"A WORN PATH"

Another relatively early story, "A Worn Path," recounts an ancient black woman's long and perilous journey on foot from her remote rural home to the nearest town. The frail old woman, called Phoenix, travels slowly and painfully through a sometimes hostile landscape, described in rich and abundant detail. She overcomes numerous obstacles with determination and good humor. Into the vivid, realistic description of the landscape and journey, Welty interweaves characteristically lyrical passages describing Phoenix's fatigue-induced hallucinations and confused imaginings. When Phoenix reaches the town, she goes to the doctor's office, and it is revealed that the purpose of her journey is to obtain medicine for her chronically ill grandson. A poignant scene at the story's close confirms the reader's suspicion of Phoenix's extreme poverty and suggests the likelihood that her beloved grandson will not live long; old Phoenix's dignity and courage in the face of such hardship, however, raise the story from pathos to a tribute to her resilience and strength of will. Like her mythical namesake, Phoenix triumphs over the forces that seek to destroy her.

"WHY I LIVE AT THE P.O."

"Why I Live at the P.O." is a richly comic tale of family discord and personal alienation, told in the first person in idiomatic, naturalistic language that captures the sounds and patterns of a distinctive southern speech. It is one of the earliest examples of Welty's often-used narrative technique, what she calls the "monologue that takes possession of the speaker." The story recounts how Sister, the intelligent and ironic narrator, comes to fall out with her family over incidents arising from her younger sister Stella-Rondo's sudden reappearance in their small southern town, minus her husband and with a two-year-old "adopted" child in tow.

Welty's flair for comedy of situation is revealed as a series of bizarrely farcical episodes unfolds. Through the irritable Stella-Rondo's manipulative misrepresentations of fact and Sister's own indifference to causing offense, Sister earns the ire of her opinionated and influential grandfather Papa-Daddy, her gullible, partisan mother, and her short-tempered Uncle Rondo. Sister responds by removing all of her possessions from communal use in the home and taking up residence in the local post office, where she is postmistress. Inability to communicate is a recurrent theme in Welty's short fiction; in this case, it is treated with a controlled hilarity that is chiefly comic but that nevertheless reveals the pain of a family's disunity. This story is one of the best examples of Welty's gift for comic characterization, her gentle mockery of human foibles, and her ear for southern idiom and expression.

"KEELA, THE OUTCAST INDIAN MAIDEN"

Although Welty disliked having the term "gothic" applied to her fiction, "Keela, the Outcast Indian Maiden" has a grotesque quality that characterizes much of southern gothic writing. Steve, a former circus sideshow barker, has enlisted the help of Max in finding a small, clubfooted black man who used to be exhibited in the sideshow as "Keela, the Outcast Indian Maiden." As a sideshow freak, he was forced to behave savagely and eat live chickens. Max has brought Steve to the home of Little Lee Roy, who is indeed the man Steve seeks.

As Little Lee Roy looks on, Steve tells Max the disgusting details of the sideshow act and explains how Little Lee Roy was ill-treated by the circus until a kind spectator rescued the victim from his degrading existence. Although he persistently refers to Little Lee Roy as "it" and, unlike Max, refuses to address Little Lee Roy directly, Steve expresses guilt and regret over his role in Little Lee Roy's exploitation. There are subtle resonances of the South's troubled legacy in the way the obviously culpable Steve tries to diminish his role in this ugly episode of oppression by pleading ignorance. He claims that he never knew that the sideshow freak was a normal man and not the savage beast that he was displayed as being in the circus.

The simpleminded Little Lee Roy, however, reacts to these reminders of his bizarre past with uncomprehending glee; he seems to have forgotten the pain and unpleasantness of his life with the circus and remembers it only as a colorful adventure. Steve cannot expiate his guilt; he has nothing to offer Little Lee Roy to compensate him for his brutal treatment. He says awkwardly to Max, "Well, I was goin' to give him some money or somethin', I guess, if I ever found him, only now I ain't got any." After the white men's departure, Little Lee Roy's children return, but they hush him when he tries to tell them about the visitors who came to talk to him about "de old times when I use to be wid de circus." The ugly incidents have left no scar on their simple victim; rather, it is the victimizer who suffers an inescapable burden of guilt and shame.

"The Wide Net"

"The Wide Net" is a fabular tale of the mysteries of human relationships and the potency of the natural world. Young William Wallace returns home from a night on the town to find a note from his pregnant wife saying that she has gone to drown herself in the river. William Wallace assembles a motley collection of men and boys to help him drag the river. The river's power as a symbol is apparent in the meaning that it holds for the many characters: To youngsters Grady and Brucie it is the grave of their drowned father; to the rough, carefree Malones, it is a fertile source of life, teeming with catfish to eat, eels to "rassle," and alligators to hunt; to the philosophical and somewhat bombastic Doc, it signifies that "the outside world is full of endurance." It is also, the river-draggers discover, the home of the primeval "king of the snakes."

Throughout the story, Welty deliberately obscures the nature of William Wallace's relationship with his wife, the history behind her threat, and even whether William Wallace truly believes his wife has jumped in the river. Characteristically, Welty relies on subtle hints and expert manipulation of tone rather than on open exposition to suggest to her readers the underpinnings of the events that she describes. This deliberate vagueness surrounding the facts of the young couple's quarrel lends the story the quality of a fable or folktale. The young lover must undergo the test of dragging the great river, confronting the king of snakes, and experiencing a kind of baptism, both in the river and in the cleansing thunderstorm that drenches the searchers, before he is worthy of regaining his wife's love.

Like a fable, the story has an almost impossibly simple and happy ending. William Wallace returns from the river to find his welcoming wife waiting calmly at home. They have a brief, affectionate mock quarrel that does not specifically address the incident at all, and they retire hand in hand, leaving the reader to ponder the mystery of their bond.

"Livvie"

"Livvie" has a lyrical, fabular quality similar to that of "The Wide Net." Livvie is a young black woman who lives with her elderly husband, Solomon, on a remote farm far up the old Natchez Trace. The strict old husband is fiercely protective of his young bride and does not allow her to venture from the yard or to talk with—or even see—other people. The inexperienced Livvie, however, is content in Solomon's comfortable house, and she takes loving care of him when his great age finally renders him bedridden. One day, a white woman comes to her door, selling cosmetics. Livvie is enchanted with the colors and scents of the cosmetics but is firm in her insistence that she has no money to buy them. When the saleswoman leaves, Livvie goes into the bedroom to gaze on her ancient, sleeping husband. Desire for wider experience and a more fulfilling life has been awakened in her, and as her husband sleeps, she disobeys his strictest command and wanders off down the Natchez Trace.

There, she comes upon a handsome, opulently

dressed young man named Cash, whom she leads back to Solomon's house. When Solomon awakes and sees them, he is reproachful but resigned to her need for a younger man, asking God to forgive him for taking such a young girl away from other young people. Cash steals from the room, and as Livvie gazes on the frail, wasted body of Solomon, he dies. In a trancelike shock, Livvie drops Solomon's sterile, ticking watch; after momentary hesitation, she goes outside to join Cash in the bright light of springtime.

"Livvie" is almost like a fairy tale in its use of simple, universal devices. The beautiful young bride, the miserly old man who imprisons her, the strange caller who brings temptation, and the handsome youth who rescues the heroine are all familiar, timeless characters. Welty broadens the references of her story to include elements of myth and religion. Young Cash, emerging from the deep forest dressed in a bright green coat and green-plumed hat, could be the Green Man of folklore, a symbol of springtime regeneration and fertility. In contrasting youth with age and old with new, Welty subtly employs biblical references. Old Solomon thinks rather than feels but falls short of his Old Testament namesake in wisdom. Youthful Cash, redolent of spring, tells Livvie that he is "ready for Easter," the reference ostensibly being to his new finery but suggesting new life rising to vanquish death. The vague, dreamy impressionism of "Livvie," which relies on image and action rather than dialogue to tell the story (except in the scenes featuring the saleswoman), adds to this folktalelike quality.

"A Still Moment"

In "A Still Moment," Welty uses historical characters to tell a mystically imaginative tale. Lorenzo Dow, the New England preacher, James Murrell, the outlaw, and John James Audubon, the naturalist and painter, were real people whom Welty places in a fictional situation. Dow rides with an inspired determination to his evening's destination, a camp meeting where he looks forward to a wholesale saving of souls. With single-minded passion, he visualizes souls and demons crowding before him in the dusky landscape. Dow's spiritual intensity is both compared and contrasted to the outlook of the outlaw Murrell,

who shadows Dow along the Natchez Trace. Murrell considers his outlawry in a profoundly philosophical light, seeing each murder as a kind of ceremonial drawing out and solving of the unique "mystery" of each victim's being. Audubon, like Dow and Murrell, has a strange and driving intensity that sets him apart from other men. His passion is the natural world; by meticulously observing and recording it, he believes that he can move from his knowledge to an understanding of all things, including his own being.

The three men are brought together by chance in a clearing, each unaware of the others' identities. As they pause, a solitary white heron alights near them in the marsh. As the three men stare in wonder at the snowy creature, Welty identifies for the reader the strange similarity of these outwardly diverse men: "What each of them had wanted was simply *all*. To save all souls, to destroy all men, to see and record all life that filled this world." The simple and beautiful sight of the heron, however, causes these desires to ebb in each of them; they are transfixed and cleansed of desire. Welty uses the heron as a symbol of the purity and beauty of the natural world, which acts as a catalyst for her characters' self-discovery. Oddly, it is Audubon, the lover of nature, who breaks the spell. He reaches for his gun and shoots the bird, to add to his scientific collection. The magic of the moment is gone, and the lifeless body of the bird becomes a mere sum of its parts, a dull, insensate mass of feathers and flesh.

Audubon, his prize collected, continues on his way, and the horrified Dow hurries away toward his camp meeting, comforted by the vivid memory of the bird's strange beauty. The dangerous Murrell experiences an epiphanic moment of self-realization; the incident has reminded him poignantly of all men's separateness and innocence, a thought that reconfirms in him his desire to waylay and destroy. It is only through a brief but intense moment of shared feeling and experience that the men can recognize their essential loneliness. As in "The Wide Net" and "Livvie," the most important communication must be done without words.

"Moon Lake"

"Moon Lake" is from the collection *The Golden*

Apples, the stories of which are nearly all set in or around the mythical community of Morgana, Mississippi, and feature a single, though extensive, cast of characters. Thematically, it shares with "A Still Moment" the sense of the paradoxical oneness and interconnectedness of the human condition. The story describes a sequence of events at a camp for girls at the lake of the story's title. The characteristically lushly detailed landscape is both beautiful and dangerous, a place where poisonous snakes may lurk in the blackberry brambles and where the lake is a site for adventure but also a brown-watered, bug-infested morass with thick mud and cypress roots that grasp at one's feet.

The story highlights the simultaneous attraction and repulsion of human connection. Antipathies abound among the group assembled at the lake: The lake's Boy Scout lifeguard, Loch, feels contempt for the crowd of young girls; the Morgana girls look down on the orphan girls as ragged thieves; rivalry and distrust crops up among individual girls. The sensitive Nina yearns for connection and freedom from connection at the same time; she envies the lonely independence of the orphans and wishes to be able to change from one persona to another at will, but at the same time she is drawn to Easter, the "leader" of the orphans, for her very qualities of separateness and disdain for friendship.

Nina and her friend Jinny Love follow Easter to a remote part of the lake in an unsuccessful attempt to cultivate her friendship, and when they return to where the others are swimming, Easter falls from the diving platform and nearly drowns. The near-drowning becomes a physical acting out of the story's theme, the fascinating and inescapable but frightening necessity of human connection. Without another's help, Easter would have died alone under the murky water, but Loch's lengthy efforts to resuscitate the apparently lifeless form of Easter disgust the other girls. The quasi-sexual rhythm of the resuscitation is made even more disturbing to the girls by its violence: Loch pummels Easter with his fists, and blood streams from her mud-smeared mouth as he flails away astride her. The distressing physical contact contrasts with the lack of any emotional connection during this scene. One orphan, a companion of Easter, speculates that if Easter dies she gets her winter coat, and gradually the other girls grow bored of the spectacle and resent the interruption of their afternoon swim. Jinny Love's mother, appearing unexpectedly at the camp, is more concerned with the lewdness that she imputes to Loch's rhythmic motions than with Easter's condition and she barks at him, "Loch Morrison, get off that table and shame on you." Nina is the most keenly aware of the symbolic significance of the incident and of the peril of connection; she reflects that "Easter had come among them and had held herself untouchable and intact. For one little touch could smirch her, make her fall so far, so deep."

"THE WHOLE WORLD KNOWS"

Another story from *The Golden Apples* is "The Whole World Knows," which features the adult Jinny Love Stark, whom readers have met as a child in "Moon Lake," and Ran McLain, who appears briefly in "Moon Lake" and other stories in this collection. The story addresses the inescapable net of personal and community relations and the potentially stifling and limiting nature of small-town life. Welty uses a monologue form similar to the one in "Why I Live at the P.O.," but in this story, told by Ran, the tone is lamenting and confessional rather than comically outraged.

Ran and Jinny are married but have separated, ostensibly over Jinny's infidelity. They both remain in the claustrophobically small town of Morgana, living in the same street and meeting occasionally in the town's bank, where Ran works alongside Jinny's lover, Woody Spights. On the surface, the story centers on Ran's developing relationship with a Maideen Sumrall, a foolish, chattering young country girl with whom he has taken up as a way of revenging himself on his wayward wife. The true focus, however, is on the causes of the deterioration of Ran's marriage to the lively, enthusiastic Jinny, revealed obliquely through other events in the story. The reasons for Jinny's initial infidelity are only hinted at; her irrepressibly joyous and wondering outlook is contrasted with Ran's heavy and brooding nature, indicating a fundamental incompatibility. Ran's careless and selfish use of Maideen, to whom he is attracted because she seems a young and "uncontaminated" version of Jinny, suggests a dark side to his nature that may be at the root of their estrangement. There is a vague suggestion, never clearly stated, that Ran may have been unfaithful to Jinny first. The merry, carefree Jinny baffles and infuriates Ran, and he fantasizes about violently murdering both Jinny and her lover, Woody. His true victim, however, is Maideen, the vulnerable opposite of the unflappable, independent Jinny. After Ran roughly consummates his shabby affair with the semi-willing Maideen, he wakes to find her sobbing like a child beside him. Readers learn in another story that Maideen eventually commits suicide. The story ends inconclusively, with neither Ran nor Jinny able or even entirely willing to escape from their shared past, the constricted community of Morgana being their all-knowing "whole world" of the story's title. As in "Moon Lake," true connection is a paradox, at once impossible, inescapable, desirable, and destructive.

"WHERE IS THE VOICE COMING FROM?"

"Where Is the Voice Coming From?" was originally published in *The New Yorker*, and it remained uncollected until the appearance of the complete *The Collected Stories of Eudora Welty* in 1980. In it, Welty uses a fictional voice to express her views on the civil rights struggle in the South. The story, written in 1863 in response to the murder of Medgar Evers in Welty's hometown of Jackson, is told as a monologue by a southern white man whose ignorance and hate for African Americans is depicted as chillingly mundane. He tells how, enraged by black activism in the South, he determines to shoot a local civil rights leader. He drives to the man's home late on an unbearably hot summer night, waits calmly in hiding until the man appears, and then shoots him in cold blood. The callous self-righteousness of the killer and his unreasoning hate are frighteningly depicted when he mocks the body of his victim, saying "Roland? There was only one way left for me to be ahead of you and stay ahead of you, by Dad, and I just taken it. . . . We ain't never now, never going to be equals and you know why? One of us is dead. What about that, Roland?" His justification for the murder is simple: "I done what I done for my own

pure-D satisfaction." His only regret is that he cannot claim the credit for the killing.

Welty scatters subtle symbols throughout the story. The extremely hot weather, which torments the killer, reflects the social climate as the civil rights conflict reaches a kind of boiling point. To the killer, the street feels as hot under his feet as the barrel of his gun. Light and dark contrast in more than just the black and white skins of the characters: The stealthy killer arrives in a darkness that will cloak his crime and he finds light shining forth from the home of his prey, whose mission is to enlighten. When the killer shoots his victim, he sees that "something darker than him, like the wings of a bird, spread on his back and pulled him down."

Unlike most of Welty's fiction, "Where Is the Voice Coming From?" clearly espouses a particular viewpoint, and the reader is left with no doubt about the writer's intention in telling the story. The story, however, embodies the qualities that typify Welty's fiction: the focus on the interconnections of human society; the full, sharp characterization achieved in a minimum of space; the detailed description of the physical landscape that powerfully evokes a sense of place; the ear for speech and idiom; and the subtle, floating symbolism that insinuates rather than announces its meaning.

OTHER MAJOR WORKS

LONG FICTION: *The Robber Bridegroom*, 1942; *Delta Wedding*, 1946; *The Ponder Heart*, 1954; *Losing Battles*, 1970; *The Optimist's Daughter*, 1972.

NONFICTION: *Music from Spain*, 1948; *The Reading and Writing of Short Stories*, 1949; *Place in Fiction*, 1957; *Three Papers on Fiction*, 1962; *One Time, One Place: Mississippi in the Depression, A Snapshot Album*, 1971; *A Pageant of Birds*, 1974; *The Eye of the Story: Selected Essays and Reviews*, 1978; *Ida M'Toy*, 1979; *Miracles of Perception: The Art of Willa Cather*, 1980 (with Alfred Knopf and Yehudi Menuhin); *One Writer's Beginnings*, 1984; *Eudora Welty: Photographs*, 1989; *A Writer's Eye: Collected Book Reviews*, 1994 (Pearl Amelia McHaney, editor) *Country Churchyards*, 2000.

CHILDREN'S LITERATURE: *The Shoe Bird*, 1964.

BIBLIOGRAPHY

Evans, Elizabeth. *Eudora Welty.* New York: Frederick Ungar, 1981. This accessible survey discusses both Welty's fiction and her essays and reviews. The brief literary biography of Welty in the opening chapter is useful and offers interesting information on Welty's relationship with her publishers and editors in the early part of her long literary career.

Georgia Review 53 (Spring, 1999). A special issue on Welty celebrating her ninetieth birthday, with articles by a number of writers, including Doris Betts, as well as a number of critics and admirers of Welty.

Kaplansky, Leslie A. "Cinematic Rhythms in the Short Fiction of Eudora Welty." *Studies in Short Fiction* 33 (Fall, 1996): 579-589. Discusses the influence of film technique on Welty's short fiction; argues that in taking advantage of cinematic rhythm in her stories, Welty developed her mastery of technique and style.

Mississippi Quarterly 50 (Fall, 1997). A special issue on Welty, with essays comparing Welty to William Faulkner, Edgar Allan Poe, and Nathaniel Hawthorne, and discussions of the women in Welty's stories, her political thought, her treatment of race and history.

Mortimer, Gail L. *Daughter of the Swan: Love and Knowledge in Eudora Welty's Fiction.* Athens: University of Georgia Press, 1994. Concentrates primarily on the short stories.

Prenshaw, Peggy Whitman, ed. *Conversations with Eudora Welty.* Jackson: University Press of Mississippi, 1984. A collection of interviews with Welty spanning the years 1942-1982. Welty talks frankly and revealingly with interviewers such as William F. Buckley, Jr., and Alice Walker about her fiction and her life, addressing such topics as her methods of writing, her southern background, her love of reading, and her admiration for the works of writers such as William Faulkner, Elizabeth Bowen, and Katherine Anne Porter.

Vande Kieft, Ruth M. *Eudora Welty.* 1962. Rev. ed. Boston: Twayne, 1987. This comprehensive examination of Welty's fiction offers detailed explications of many of Welty's works as well as chapters on particular aspects of her writing, such as elements of comedy and Welty's deliberate desire to "mystify" her readers.

Waldron, Ann. *Eudora Welty: A Writer's Life.* New York: Doubleday, 1998. The first full-length biography of Welty, but one that was done without her authorization or permission; provides a great deal of detail about Welty's life and literary career but derives commentary about Welty's work from reviews and other previous criticism.

Westling, Louise. *Sacred Groves and Ravaged Gardens: The Fiction of Eudora Welty, Carson McCullers, and Flannery O'Connor.* Athens: University of Georgia Press, 1985. Westling examines Welty's fiction, along with the work of other eminent female southern writers, as part of a tradition of southern women's writing. Westling brings a feminist perspective to bear on such aspects of southern women's writing as myth, sexuality, and the symbolic power of place. Welty's fiction is analyzed as a feminine celebration of a matriarchal society in which women can find freedom and fulfillment outside the social strictures of traditional southern life.

Weston, Ruth D. *Gothic Traditions and Narrative Techniques in the Fiction of Eudora Welty.* Baton Rouge: Louisiana State University Press, 1994. Discusses Welty's use of the gothic tradition in her fiction; provides original readings of a number of Welty's short stories.

Catherine Swanson

GLENWAY WESCOTT

Born: Kewaskum, Wisconsin; April 11, 1901
Died: Rosemont, New Jersey; February 22, 1987

PRINCIPAL SHORT FICTION

. . . Like a Lover, 1926
Good-bye, Wisconsin, 1928
The Babe's Bed, 1930
Twelve Fables of Aesop, 1954

OTHER LITERARY FORMS

Glenway Wescott honed his writing skills early in his career by writing poetry: *The Bitterns* (1920) and *Natives of Rock* (1925). He went on to write three novels, *The Apple of the Eye* (1924), *The Grandmothers* (1927), and *Apartment in Athens* (1945), and two volumes of essays, *Fear and Trembling* (1932) and *Images of Truth* (1962). Additional works include a hagiography entitled *A Calendar of Saints for Unbelievers* (1932) and a nonfiction volume, *The Best of All Possible Worlds: Journals, Letters, and Remembrances, 1914-1937* (1975).

ACHIEVEMENTS

Of all the expatriated Americans who were living in Europe during the 1920's, Glenway Wescott is most notable for the pursuit of his theme. Regardless of whether Wescott was writing about his native Wisconsin or Europe, he always returned to his theme of returning home. In a sense, Wescott's single novella, three novels, and numerous short stories can be viewed as a journey in search of the source of the creative self.

Because Wescott stopped writing fiction at the age of forty-four, some critics have classified him as a writer who had the qualities needed for great achievement but who failed to live up to the promise of his early works. Although Wescott's body of work is relatively small, his technical achievements were significant. Not only was he a master of the carefully turned aphorism, but also he invented the technique of the participating narrator. Wescott may not be a major American writer, but he still ranks as one of the most distinctive prose stylists in twentieth century American fiction.

BIOGRAPHY

Glenway Wescott's life is made up of two diametrically opposed phases. He was born on a farm in Kewaskum, Wisconsin, on April 11, 1901. Glenway was very close to his mother, who nurtured his interests in music, acting, and literature. He soon, however, proved to be a great disappointment to his father, Bruce Peters Wescott, because he hated the drudgery of farmwork. When Glenway was thirteen, his relationship with his father became openly hostile as the result of a minor incident, and he was shunted from relative to relative. During his last two years at Waukesha High School, Glenway lived with his father's brother, a preacher named William Samuel Wescott. His uncle's vast library opened an entirely new world for the young man, which he continued to explore in the literary society to which he belonged in high school.

By the time Wescott was sixteen, his experiences were no longer like those of other boys who had grown up on Wisconsin farms. After graduating from high school in 1917, Wescott went to Chicago. While he was living with the wealthy mother of his uncle's wife, Wescott attended the University of Chicago. His new experiences, like his previous ones on the farm in Wisconsin, were later to serve as material for his fiction. Wescott had no interest in a literary career when he first entered the university, but his distaste for required courses led him to enroll in several literature courses during his first semester. His enthusiasm for literature soon led to his involvement in the university's newly formed Poetry Club. Through the imagistic poetry that he wrote as a college student, Wescott learned how to solidify an intense moment and to etch it into the consciousness with sharp imagery.

In 1918, Wescott went to New Mexico to recover from a failed homosexual relationship that had driven him to attempt suicide. Between 1918 and 1920, he began writing poetry based on his New Mexico experiences and published it in a volume entitled *The Bitterns*. Harriet Monroe was so impressed with Wescott's work that she hired him to work for *Poetry* in 1921. It was also in 1921 that Wescott published his first short story, "Bad Han," which launched his career as a prose writer. Wescott's developing style was influenced by writers whom he met while working for the magazine, including Edwin Arlington Robinson.

It was during the summer of 1921 that Wescott traveled to Europe with his friend Monroe Wheeler. During the next eleven years, Wescott produced the fiction that established him as a midwestern prodigy. He became financially solvent following the publication in Europe of two novels, *The Apple of the Eye* and *The Grandmothers*, and a collection of short stories, *Good-bye, Wisconsin*. He was less successful with his two departures from fiction, *Fear and Trembling* and *A Calendar of Saints for Unbelievers*, both written in 1932.

Convinced that Europe had become a "rat trap" for him, Wescott returned to the United States in 1933 and settled in New York. While he was growing accustomed to living in the United States again, Wescott produced no fiction at all until 1940. In many ways, World War II shocked him into writing again. *The Pilgrim Hawk: A Love Story*, which continued to be his most popular work, changed the minds of those critics who believed that he had "written himself out." In 1945, he wrote *Apartment in Athens* in an attempt to convince his publisher that he was still a "valuable property."

Despite the success of *Apartment in Athens*, Wescott produced no more works of fiction, even though he did begin several projects. In 1962, a collection of essays entitled *Images of Truth* established him as one of the most influential critics in the United States, because he was writing to the cultivated general reader, not to the most sophisticated and highbrow critics. Wescott's profiles of six writers whom he admired offered a memorable insight into how his own fiction-writer's mind perceived the world. Although this, his final work, did not totally satisfy his faithful coterie of admirers, who had looked forward

Glenway Wescott (Library of Congress)

to the kind of a large complex novel that they believed he had the ability to write, it eloquently confirmed his faith in the literary life. It was a fitting end to the career of this melancholy yet tantalizing literary figure.

ANALYSIS

Glenway Wescott's short fiction employs many of the same themes and techniques that he used in his first two novels. The two major themes continue to be the self and love. A technical innovation that he first used in *The Grandmothers*, the participating narrator, also appears in his short fiction. His use of symbols is also similar to what he had done in his first two novels. The bird remained his favorite symbol and was usually placed at the center of the story. Except for *The Babe's Bed*, the short stories that appear after *Good-bye, Wisconsin* are inferior in quality and demonstrate how Wescott lost his enthusiasm for a literary form once he had mastered it. The next short form with which he experimented, the novella, perfected certain techniques of prose fiction that he used with mixed results in his short stories.

Wescott shaped a number of his early experiences into short stories in which he employed impressionistic techniques instead of the mere transcription of events.

GOOD-BYE, WISCONSIN

To a certain extent, the ten short stories and title essay in *Good-bye, Wisconsin* illustrate reasons why Wescott could not stay in Wisconsin. They cannot, however, be dismissed simply as regional stories in that the universal truths of which they speak could be found anywhere.

Several of the stories that deal, in one way or another, with the search for the self illustrate the ways in which rural Wisconsin impedes that search. "The Sailor" goes beyond being a regional story in the way that it also includes the theme of love. Terrie, who is another of Wescott's expatriates, has joined the navy to escape the depressing surroundings of rural Wisconsin. After spending some time in France, he recounts his adventures there to his brother, Riley. By the time Terrie has finished his narration, he has revealed that he has been severely traumatized by a failed love affair that he had with a French prostitute named Zizi. Riley, however, sees the stories as nothing more than tales of whiskey and women. Sensing Riley's lack of understanding, Terrie is filled with a thirst that cannot be quenched at home. Emotions such as the ones that Terrie encountered in Europe are foreign to Wisconsin.

Wisconsin serves primarily as the setting for a transition from innocence to experience in "In a Thicket." Lilly is a fifteen-year-old girl who lives with her senile grandfather in a house surrounded by a thicket. After hearing about a black convict who escaped the night before from a nearby prison, she stays up all night waiting for him to appear. When she finally sees him at the door, she stands transfixed until he walks away. The three-inch gash that she finds in the screen door the next morning symbolizes the figurative loss of her virginity. The sexual side of her nature has been awakened by the intruder, and she emerges from the thicket of her childhood into the world of the senses.

Like "In a Thicket," "The Whistling Swan" takes place in Wisconsin, but it focuses instead on the theme of love. Like Terrie in "The Sailor," the protagonist of "The Whistling Swan," Hubert Redd, is an expatriate. He is, however, closer to Wescott himself in that he is an artist, a composer, and a sophisticate who is aware of both the advantages and drawbacks of living in Europe and the United States. He returns to his hometown in Wisconsin after his wealthy patrons withdraw their support on the grounds that he is immoral and untalented. The love that he feels for his childhood sweetheart complicates his life because it conflicts with his desire to return to Europe and resume his artistic pursuits. Redd's inner conflict is resolved when he impulsively shoots a swan and simultaneously kills that part of himself that draws him to Paris. The intentional ambiguity of the ending poses the possibility that he is sobbing, not because he has killed the swan, but because he has destroyed the creative impulse that made him unhappy in Wisconsin.

"A Guilty Woman" traces a woman's progression from a type of love that enslaves to the type that liberates. Evelyn Crowe is a forty-five-year-old ex-convict who served six years in prison for murdering her lover, Bill Fisher. Fisher had been initially attracted to her because he relished the challenge of corrupting and abandoning an "old maid." Upon her release from prison, she is taken in by her friend Martha Colvin to live on her farm in Wisconsin. While living there, Evelyn is attracted to Martha's bachelor friend, Dr. John Bolton. She resists the romantic impulse that is building up inside her until she realizes that the passionless life to which she had returned was a form of pride. No longer content to be a self-sufficient spinster, she finally allows herself to fall in love. Wescott finds a kind of courage in Evelyn's flexibility, which he believed was discouraged by small-town America.

The short story that merited the most critical acclaim was "Like a Lover." Like Lilly in "In a Thicket," Alice Murray is an isolated girl who is mesmerized by a man, in this case, an older man named Hurst. Despite her mother's protests, she marries him. The assortment of whips and clubs that her husband keeps in the house, however, terrifies her and drives her back to her mother's house. She remains in isolation for seven years until she learns that Hurst is to marry Mrs. Clayburn, a widow. Even though Mrs. Clayburn believes Alice's words of warning, she admits that she is unable to break the spell that he holds over her. For two months following Mrs. Clayburn's marriage, Alice is tormented by ominous nightmares that foretell the woman's murder. The story concludes with the appearance of Alice's friend, Mary Clifford, riding frantically from the Hurst farm, waving her arms. Shocked by what she knows has happened to the new Mrs. Hurst, Alice faints and falls backward on the porch. Ostensibly, "Like a Lover" exploits the same kind of scandalous material that Wescott used in "A Guilty Woman." The godlike power that the men in both stories have over women, however, illustrates Wescott's belief, discussed in depth two years later in *A Calendar of Saints for Unbelievers*, that the love for God is similar to the love for a man or a woman in that both forms of affection render a person completely helpless.

THE BABE'S BED

The Babe's Bed, which is a thirty-five-page short story published as a book in Paris, is, in a sense, a postscript to the introductory essay in *Good-bye, Wisconsin*. Both were written after Wescott returned to Wisconsin for a short visit and concern an expatriated American who compares the Midwest to Europe. In both works, Wisconsin and the United States in general are found to retard the development of the self.

The story is told from the limited point of view of a nameless bachelor who returns home. As in other stories by Wescott, dramatic tension is created through the narrator's conflicting impulses. The bachelor becomes so lost in fantasies involving his sister's baby that he becomes detached from reality. He begins by imagining that the baby is his and then convinces himself that his married sister is his mother. The climax occurs at the dinner table when the baby screams at being placed in the harness that serves as its bed. The baby's bed, which is the story's central symbol, bears a close resemblance to the mental web that has ensnared the bachelor. Before he attacks everyone at the table, he realizes that he has been living in a fantasy world and directs his anger toward himself before he can do any real harm to his loved ones.

THE PILGRIM HAWK

With the publication of *The Pilgrim Hawk: A Love Story*, Wescott created what many critics have referred to as a genuine short masterpiece. The novella differs from most of Wescott's previous fiction in that it concerns expatriated Americans living in France instead of rural midwestern Americans. The story is retold in 1940 by the protagonist, Alwyn Tower, who interrupts his first-person narrative to comment on such matters as love, marriage, religion, alcoholism, and individual and artistic freedom. The events that he recalls took place during one day in May of 1928 or 1929 in France at the house of Alexandra Henry, a great friend of Tower. The story focuses on the arrival of Madeleine and Larry Cullen, a rich, handsome couple from Ireland who arrive unexpectedly with their chauffeur, Ricketts, and Madeleine Cullen's falcon, Lucy. For the most part, the action of the novella takes the form of a conversation among the four main characters.

As the Cullens chat about money and neighbors, it becomes clear that the hawk symbolizes the Cullens' relationship and the Cullens themselves. Madeleine resembles the feathered predator in the way she uses her charms to capture and hold her prey, Larry, who is too weak to escape the hold that she has on him. Both she and her husband, however, are hawklike in that they are prisoners of their own appetites. Although the hawk is consistent with the bird symbolism in Wescott's other stories and novels, it differs in the way it revolves, taking on different meanings in different situations.

Tower continues to attach symbolic meanings to the hawk until it comes to stand for himself and Alexandra as well. Eventually, he builds a tower of symbolic meanings that blinds him to the "petty" facts that constitute reality. The process continues until Cullen, in a drunken stupor, attempts to kill someone; Madeleine, who reports the event just before she and her husband leave for Paris, never makes it clear whether Larry tried to kill himself or Ricketts in a fit of jealous rage. This violent turn of events shocks Tower back to reality, enabling him to descend from the symbolic tower that he has constructed. He recognizes that the "whisper of the devil" is the fear that he has attached the wrong meanings to things in order to make life more meaningful.

OTHER MAJOR WORKS

LONG FICTION: *The Apple of the Eye*, 1924; *The Grandmothers: A Family Portrait*, 1927; *The Pilgrim Hawk: A Love Story*, 1940; *Apartment in Athens*, 1945.

POETRY: *The Bitterns: A Book of Twelve Poems*, 1920; *Natives of Rock: XX Poems, 1921-1922*, 1925.

NONFICTION: *Elizabeth Madox Roberts: A Personal Note*, 1930; *Fear and Trembling*, 1932; *A Calendar of Saints for Unbelievers*, 1932; *Images of Truth: Remembrances and Criticism*, 1962; *The Best of All Possible Worlds: Journals, Letters, and Remembrances, 1914-1937*, 1975.

EDITED TEXTS: *The Maugham Reader*, 1950; *Short Novels of Colette*, 1951.

BIBLIOGRAPHY

Baker, Jennifer Jordan. "'In a Thicket': Glenway Wescott's Pastoral Vision." *Studies in Short Fiction* 31 (Spring, 1994): 95-187. Explores the paradox of the Midwest as both isolating and repressive as well as simple and idyllic in one of Wescott's best-known stories, "In a Thicket." Shows how Wescott treats this tension with narrative conventions and the narrative perspective of traditional pastoral.

Benfey, Christopher. "Bright Young Things." *The New York Times*, March 21, 1999, sec. 7, p. 9. A review of *When We Were There: The Travel Albums of George Platt Lynes, Monroe Wheeler, and Glenway Wescott*; comments on Wescott's fussy style but claims that his novella *The Pilgrim Hawk* is a brilliant work that can stand comparison with William Faulkner or D. H. Lawrence; asserts the central image of the novella comes from Wescott's relationship with George Platt Lynes.

Calisher, Hortense. "A Heart Laid Bare." *The Washington Post*, January 13, 1991, p. X5. In this review of Wescott's journals, *Continual Lessons*, Calisher provides a brief biographical sketch of Wescott; claims that he was not a true original as a novelist, but rather he was a reporter of a non-

fictive kind; contends the image we have from the journals is a writer not quite in the closet and not quite out of it.

Johnson, Ira. *Glenway Wescott: The Paradox of Voice*. Port Washington, N.Y.: Kennikat Press, 1971. Johnson has written what is by far the most incisive look into Wescott's career. The book explicates and criticizes each of Wescott's works in detail. He also demonstrates how each work reflects Wescott's development as a writer. The book does not, however, provide sufficient insight into Wescott's early life to qualify as a biographical study.

Kahn, Sy Myron. *Glenway Wescott: A Critical and Biographical Study*. Ann Arbor, Mich.: University Microfilms, 1957. Much of the biographical information that is included in Kahn's dissertation cannot be found anywhere else. By showing how Wescott's experiences influenced each of his major works, Kahn has made an indispensable contribution to Wescott scholarship.

Rosco, Jerry. "An American Treasure: Glenway Wescott's *The Pilgrim Hawk*." *The Literary Review* 15 (Winter, 1988): 133-142. Rosco's analysis of Wescott's famous novella is taken from information provided by Wescott himself during his last interview. Wescott's personal reflections regarding how he wrote the story and how he was influenced by W. Sommerset Maugham are particularly revealing.

Rueckert, William H. *Glenway Wescott*. New York: Twayne: 1965. In this work, which is the first book-length appraisal of Wescott, Rueckert attempts to revise Wescott's reputation as a man of letters who produced only one minor masterpiece. Although Rueckert's analysis is perceptive, he does not examine each work in enough depth to support his premise that Wescott is a major artist who deserves more attention.

Wescott, Glenway. *Continual Lessons: The Journals of Glenway Wescott, 1937-1955*. Edited by Robert Phelps and Jerry Rosco. New York: Farrar, and Straus Giroux, 1990. Wescott's diaries provide a glimpse of his life.

Alan Brown

JESSAMYN WEST

Born: North Vernon, Indiana; July 18, 1902
Died: Napa, California; February 23, 1984

PRINCIPAL SHORT FICTION

The Friendly Persuasion, 1945
Cress Delahanty, 1953
Love, Death, and the Ladies' Drill Team, 1955
*Except for Me and Thee: A Companion to the
    Friendly Persuasion*, 1969
Crimson Ramblers of the World, Farewell, 1970
The Story of a Story and Three Stories, 1982
Collected Stories of Jessamyn West, 1986

OTHER LITERARY FORMS

Best known for her first collection of short stories, *The Friendly Persuasion*, Jessamyn West also published eight novels during her long literary career, including *Leafy Rivers* (1967), set on the frontier in nineteenth century Ohio, and *South of the Angels* (1960), set, like many of her short stories, in Southern California. West also published an opera libretto based on the life of John James Audubon, *A Mirror for the Sky* (1948), and a collection of poems, *The Secret Look: Poems* (1974). Among her screenplays was that for the film *Friendly Persuasion* (1956), written in collaboration. Her autobiographical writings include an account of the production of that film, *To See the Dream* (1957); *Hide and Seek: A Continuing Journey* (1973), the story of her early life; *The Woman Said Yes: Encounters with Life and Death—Memoirs* (1976), dealing with her illness with tuberculosis and her sister's sickness and suicide; and *Double Discovery: A Journey* (1980), a travel diary. She edited *The Quaker Reader* in 1962.

ACHIEVEMENTS

Ever since the publication of her first book, Jessamyn West has had a large and loyal following. Critics praise her craftsmanship: her clear prose, her vivid realization of the natural setting, her historical accuracy, her effective creation of characters who are complex human beings beneath their seemingly sim-

ple surface. Her accomplishments have been recognized by the Indiana Authors' Day Award in 1957, the Thormod Monsen Award in 1958, and the Janet Kafka Prize in 1976, as well as by the awarding of honorary doctorates both in her native Midwest and in her longtime home, California. West's works are divided between the midwestern frontier of her family's past and the new frontier of twentieth century Southern California. The fact that her fiction is authentically regional does not limit her appeal, however, for her themes transcend local color, dealing as they do with survival as a moral and loving being in a difficult and dangerous world.

BIOGRAPHY

Jessamyn West was born in North Vernon, Indiana, on July 18, 1902. After moving with her parents to California, she completed her education at Fullerton High School, at Whittier College, where she received a B.A. in English in 1923, and at the University of California, Berkeley. Although she had published short stories based on her family's Quaker past, she did not collect them in a book until 1945, thus publishing her first book at the age of forty-three. Later, she taught at numerous universities and at Breadloaf. Her last book, *The State of Stony Lonesome* (1984), was completed shortly before her death, on February 23, 1984, at her longtime home in Napa, California.

ANALYSIS

Jessamyn West's short stories fall into two categories: those which treat various episodes in the lives of a single family and are gathered in a single volume, and those which more conventionally are quite separate in plot and character, gathered in the customary collections. The books *The Friendly Persuasion*, *Except for Me and Thee: A Companion to the Friendly Persuasion*, and *Cress Delahanty* fall into the first category. Although some critics have called them novels, the sketches of which each volume is composed are obviously separate. The fact that an ac-

Jessamyn West in 1945 (Library of Congress)

knowledgment preceding *The Friendly Persuasion* refers to "stories in this book" which had been published in various magazines makes West's own assumptions clear. In the introduction to *Collected Stories of Jessamyn West*, Julian Muller calls those earlier volumes "novels," while admitting that the chapters could stand alone, and thus he omits those sketches from his collection. A complete analysis of West's short fiction, however, must include the consideration of those works on an individual basis, even though a study of her long fiction might also include them.

The *Collected Stories of Jessamyn West* included all the stories from two previous volumes, *Love, Death, and the Ladies' Drill Team* and *Crimson Ramblers of the World, Farewell*, along with eight additional stories which Jessamyn West wished to have included. According to the editor, those stories which were omitted, West believed, needed revision.

"99.6"

The focus in all West's work is a basic tension in human life. On the one hand, humans yearn to be free of restraints; on the other hand, they desire to love and to please the beloved, thus voluntarily to accept limitations on their individuality. The beloved is not just their human partner: The term also suggests divinity, speaking to the spirit directly, in the Quaker tradition. Although social or religious groups may presume to judge the conduct of West's characters, the final judgment must be their own, guided by their separate and sacred consciences. According to the editor of the *Collected Stories of Jessamyn West*, West's first published story was "99.6." Set in a tuberculosis sanatorium, the story reflects West's own experience. The protagonist, Marianne Kent, desperately watches her temperature, hoping for the change which would signal some improvement in her health. Aware of her own feverish condition, the consumption which is truly consuming her, she wishes that the nurse would help her with an illusion, with the suggestion that perhaps the heat she feels comes from warmer weather outside, not from her own fever. Although the obvious antagonists are Marianne Kent and her disease, at the conclusion of the brief story the protagonist turns to God, pleading with Him for some sign of hope, for some reduction from 99.6. Thus, the real struggle is a spiritual one. Mrs. Kent must accept what divinity permits.

THE FRIENDLY PERSUASION

In *The Friendly Persuasion* stories, set in the nineteenth century among the Indiana Quakers of the Ohio River Valley, conscience is always a consideration. The Irish Quaker Jess Birdwell, a devout man but one who has a mind of his own, is married to Eliza Cope Birdwell, a stricter Quaker—in fact, a Quaker minister, who must consider the community's judgment of her as well as God's. "Music on the Muscatatuck" illustrates the stresses on the relationship between Jess and Eliza, which result from their differences in temperament and convictions. After describing the natural beauty of the Birdwell farm, the comfort and plenty of their pretty home, the goodness of Eliza as a wife, and Jess's own prosperity, West sets the problem: Jess likes music; as a Quaker, he is supposed to have nothing to do with it.

Jess's temptation comes when, like Eve in the Garden, he is separated from his mate. On a business trip to Philadelphia, he meets an organ salesman; already seduced by his own love of music, he stops by the store. The result is inevitable: He orders an organ.

When Jess returns home, he cannot find the words to tell Eliza, who follows the Quaker teachings about music, what he has done. Unfortunately, when the organ arrives, Eliza makes a miscalculation about Jess's male pride: She commands him to choose between the organ and her. Jess moves the organ in the house, and Eliza is left in the snow, pondering her next course of action. Fortunately, Eliza knows the difference between her domain and that of the Lord. She compromises, and the organ goes in the attic. All goes well until a church committee comes to call just when the Birdwell's daughter Mattie has slipped up to the attic to play on the organ. Surely God inspires Jess Birdwell in this crucial situation, for he prays and continues praying until the music stops. The committee concludes that angels have provided the accompaniment; Jess suspects that the Lord, who has kept him praying for so long, has made His statement. Just as Eliza is about to announce her triumph, however, the music once again comes from the attic, and Jess again responds.

The story is typical of West. The human beings involved live close to their natural setting; they are ordinary people, neither rich nor poor. Although they may disagree with one another and although they often have much to learn, they are usually basically good, and at the end of the story, some resolution of their conflict with one another and with their spiritual scruples is suggested. The tone is also typical. Perhaps one reason for West's popularity is that, in an age when many writers do not seem to like their own characters, and for good reason, she is honestly fond of hers. As a result, she laughs at their foibles and follies, their deficiencies in wisdom, and their mistakes in judgment without negating the fact of their basic goodness.

One of the endearing qualities of the Birdwell family is that, despite their strict religious convictions, they accept differences within the family; each member is expected, above all, to follow his or her own conscience. In the Civil War story "The Battle of Finney's Ford," what was supposed to be a fight against Morgan's raiders proves to be no fight at all, because Morgan's raiders change their route. In the meantime, however, the Birdwell boys must decide whether to fight. One of them, Joshua, says that he is willing to kill, if necessary; the other, Labe, will not join the town's defenders. Ironically, at the end of the story, Josh says that the reason he must fight is that he so dislikes fighting, while Labe admits that he must not fight because he truly enjoys fighting. Thus the real "The Battle of Finney's Ford" has been a battle of conscience for the boys and, for the parents, a struggle to let them make their own decisions. The slightness of the external plot, typical of many of West's stories, does not reduce the magnitude of the internal action. For Jess, Eliza, Josh, and Labe, there is a major spiritual battle; as usual, the element of love is present in the resolution of the conflict.

CRESS DELAHANTY

Although *Cress Delahanty* is set in twentieth century California rather than nineteenth century Indiana, and although it lacks the specific Quaker religious background, the importance of the natural setting, the basic goodness of the characters, and the emphasis on spiritual problems are similar to the stories in *The Friendly Persuasion*. For example, "Fifteen: Spring" deals with Cress's selfish encounter with death, just as in the previous volume "The Meeting House" had followed Jess Birdwell through a similar crisis. In "Fifteen: Spring," Cress has developed a schoolgirl crush on a dying man, the father of sons her age. In her egotism, she wishes to be important to him, even to die in his place, if necessary, but after a visit to his home, after realizing that God is in charge, not Cress, she learns that she is not of major importance to her beloved, nor is her love of any help to him. Ironically, the final consolation comes from his wife, who recalls her own lost youth and, from her own tragic situation, finds pity for foolish Cress.

"A TIME OF LEARNING"

Many of West's stories deal with young people who are being initiated into life. In *Love, Death, and the Ladies' Drill Team*, "A Time of Learning" describes the encounter of nineteen-year-old Emmett Maguire, a talented sign- and housepainter, with his first love, Ivy Lish. Emmett loves the seemingly perfect girl with all of his heart. When he paints her picture, it is an act of total commitment. Unfortunately,

Emmett must learn that the beloved is not always worthy of the emotion she inspires. As other men know, Ivy is consistently unfaithful. When Emmett learns that she has given his painting to another lover, his immediate impulse is toward revenge: He will paint her on the barn, as ugly as she has proved herself to be, for all to see. Then comes his spiritual crisis. Somehow, he finds, he cannot paint ugliness, or perhaps he cannot hate. When he paints a larger-than-life picture of her on the barn, he finally forgets about her in the joy of realizing that he is indeed a good painter. Thus, finally, his love of art is more important than her betrayal of him, and his wish to love defeats his temptation to hate.

"Neighbors"

West clearly believes, however, that it is not just the young who must learn about life. One of the optimistic elements in her stories is the suggestion that life is learning itself. Because most of her major characters are willing to expand their consciousnesses, anxious to revise their judgments, they are appealing. Thus, in *Except for Me and Thee: A Companion to the Friendly Persuasion*, the Quaker preacher Eliza Birdwell, a stubborn woman with a strict conscience, must deal with the issue of fugitive slaves. In the long story "Neighbors," Eliza not only must decide whether to obey the law, as her religion dictates, by turning over the fugitive slaves who seek refuge with her or to hide them and defy the law of her country but also must come to terms with Jess's involvement in running slaves to freedom, at the risk of his life and his liberty. The decision is not easy, but in changing her mind about the law and in acquiescing to the demands of Jess's conscience, Eliza herself grows spiritually.

Crimson Ramblers of the World, Farewell

Not all of West's stories have so hopeful a conclusion. In "The Condemned Librarian," from *Crimson Ramblers of the World, Farewell*, an embittered teacher, who believes that she has not been able to realize her dreams, consults a woman doctor who, against all odds, has risen from being a high school librarian to her present profession. Perversely, the teacher refuses to reveal her symptoms to the doctor,

and, despite all of her efforts, the doctor fails to diagnose tuberculosis. As a result, the teacher nearly dies, but to her delight, the doctor must abandon her practice and go back to being a high school librarian. The title "The Condemned Librarian" makes it clear that hatred has, in this situation, had a great triumph, but ironically, the person most trapped is the bitter teacher, who must live with the knowledge that she herself is condemned. Although she feels happy thinking of the doctor's misery, she admits that the old magic is gone from her teaching. Clearly, by her spite she has corroded her own soul.

Other stories of that collection, however, end with understanding and reconciliation. For example, "Live Life Deeply" begins with the disappearance of fourteen-year-old Elspeth Courtney, who has turned up at the maternity ward of the local hospital. Her distraught father, pursuing her, discovers that she had been on Reservoir Hill early that morning, contemplating suicide because, as she confided to the troubled man she met there, a teacher she admired had made fun of her for a composition entitled "Live Life Deeply." The stranger had been worrying about his wife's cesarean section, while Ellie had been worrying about her humiliation. When the baby is born, the stranger's problem is solved. Then, the new father solves Ellie's problem by pointing out that she wants to live life fully and that her pain is as much a part of a full life as the excitement and joy of the birth. Convinced, Ellie begins to plan her next composition, which will deal with her experiences in the maternity ward. Now that she understands that pain and joy are both a part of life and that both are necessary to make life interesting, she can move ahead, accepting even her setbacks.

In all of Jessamyn West's stories, whether the setting is the past or the present, Indiana or California, an individual, young or old, has the opportunity to grow spiritually. If, like the teacher in "The Condemned Librarian," one chooses to hate instead of to love or if one refuses to permit freedom of conscience to others, one's life will be miserable. Many ordinary people, however, live lives as meaningful and as exciting as those of Jess Birdwell, Cress Delahanty, and Elspeth Courtney. In her carefully crafted accounts of everyday life, Jessamyn West has revealed the drama of spiritual conflict in these later centuries as compellingly as did the productions of *Everyman* in medieval times.

OTHER MAJOR WORKS

LONG FICTION: *The Witch Diggers*, 1951; *Little Men*, in *Star Short Novels*, 1954; *South of the Angels*, 1960; *A Matter of Time*, 1966; *Leafy Rivers*, 1967; *The Massacre at Fall Creek*, 1975; *The Life I Really Lived*, 1979; *The State of Stony Lonesome*, 1984.

PLAY: *A Mirror for the Sky*, pb. 1948 (libretto).

SCREENPLAY: *Friendly Persuasion*, 1956.

POETRY: *The Secret Look: Poems*, 1974.

NONFICTION: *To See the Dream*, 1957; *Love Is Not What You Think*, 1959; *Hide and Seek: A Continuing Journey*, 1973 (autobiography); *The Woman Said Yes: Encounters with Life and Death—Memoirs*, 1976; *Double Discovery: A Journey*, 1980.

EDITED TEXT: *The Quaker Reader*, 1962.

BIBLIOGRAPHY

Barron, James. "Jessamyn West, Author of Stories About Quakers in Indiana, Dies." *The New York Times*, February 24, 1984, p. B16. In this obituary of West, Barron briefly traces her personal and literary life and comments on her focus on Quakers.

Betts, Doris. "Skillful Styles from Two Storytellers." *Los Angeles Times*, February 26, 1987. A review of *Collected Stories of Jessamyn West*; comments on her narrators as observers, her characters as eccentrics, and her animals as lovable.

Farmer, Ann Dahlstrom. *Jessamyn West: A Descriptive and Annotated Bibliography*. Lanham, Md.: Scarecrow, 1998. A helpful tool for students of West. Includes an index.

Prescott, P.S. "The Massacre at Fall Creek." *Newsweek*, April 14, 1975, 86. According to Prescott, the ingredients in a "good old-fashioned novel" combine suspense, violence, and villainy with sentiment. *The Massacre at Fall Creek* is a concrete example of this genre. Jessamyn West's expertise, according to Prescott, extends not only to the "good old-fashioned novel" but also to other literary forms as well.

Shivers, Alfred S. *Jessamyn West*. Rev. ed. New York: Twayne, 1992. This biography of Jessamyn West probes the religious influences of her Quaker beliefs on her literary endeavors, thus providing an essential clue to her character and personality. Shivers incorporates his literary criticism of her works.

Welty, Eudora. "A Search: Maddening and Infectious." *The New York Times Book Review*, January 14, 1951, 5. Welty discusses the characterizations and plot of *The Witch Diggers*, which she embeds in the metaphor of a game of charades. She states that both contain elements of the known and the unknown bound into a solvable puzzle so that this game is a clever metaphor for *The Witch Diggers*.

West, Jessamyn. *Double Discovery: A Journey*. New York: Harcourt Brace Jovanovich, 1980. West's own memoir incorporates her youthful letters and journals from her first trip abroad with her later rediscovery of that long-lost youthful self. This autobiography gives readers a glimpse of a woman's description of the development of her adult self.

_____. *The Woman Said Yes: Encounters with Life and Death*. New York: Harcourt Brace Jovanovich, 1980. West's account of her experiences as a survivor of tuberculosis is intermingled with an account of her mother's life. This amalgamation of two lives lets interested readers delve into another facet of West's intellectual and artistic development.

Yalom, Marilyn, and Margo B. Davis, eds. *Women Writers of the West Coast: Speaking of Their Lives and Careers*. Santa Barbara, Calif.: Capra Press, 1983. Jennifer Chapman's chapter discusses the role of religion—in this case, Quakerism—in West's life and work.

Rosemary M. Canfield Reisman, updated by Maxine S. Theodoulou

EDITH WHARTON
Edith Newbold Jones

Born: New York, New York; January 24, 1862
Died: St.-Brice-sous-Forêt, France; August 11, 1937

PRINCIPAL SHORT FICTION

The Greater Inclination, 1899
Crucial Instances, 1901
The Descent of Man, 1904
The Hermit and the Wild Woman, 1908
Tales of Men and Ghosts, 1910
Xingu and Other Stories, 1916
Here and Beyond, 1926
Certain People, 1930
Human Nature, 1933
The World Over, 1936
Ghosts, 1937
The Collected Short Stories of Edith Wharton,
    1968

OTHER LITERARY FORMS

Edith Wharton's prolific career includes the publication of novels, novellas, short stories, poetry, travel books, criticism, works on landscaping and interior decoration, a translation, an autobiography, and wartime pamphlets and journalism. Her novel *The Age of Innocence* (1920) was awarded the Pulitzer Prize in 1921. Several of her works have been adapted for the stage, including *The Age of Innocence* and the novels *Ethan Frome* (1911), *The House of Mirth* (1905), and *The Old Maid* (1924). The dramatization of *The Old Maid* was awarded the Pulitzer Prize for drama in 1935. Films based on Edith Wharton's works include *The House of Mirth, The Glimpses of the Moon* (1922), and *The Old Maid*.

ACHIEVEMENTS

Edith Wharton's talent in affording her reader an elegant, well-constructed glance at upper-class New York and European society won for her high esteem from the earliest years of her career. The novel *The House of Mirth* was her first best-seller and, along with *Ethan Frome* and *The Age of Innocence*, is con-

sidered to be one of her finest works. During World War I, Wharton served the Allied cause in Europe by organizing relief efforts and caring for Belgian orphans, work for which she was inducted into the French Legion of Honor in 1916 and the Order of Leopold (Belgium) in 1919. In the United States, the 1920's would see Wharton's literary career flower. In 1921, she became the first woman to receive the Pulitzer Prize, awarded to her for *The Age of Innocence*; in 1923, she also became the first female recipient of an honorary degree of doctor of letters from Yale University; in 1927, she was nominated for the Nobel Prize in Literature; in 1928, her novel *The Children* was the Book-of-the-Month Club selection for September. By 1930, Wharton was one of the most highly regarded American authors of the time and was elected to the American Academy of Arts and Letters. After Wharton's death in 1937, her fiction was not as widely read by the general public as it was during her lifetime. Feminist literary scholars, however, have reexamined Wharton's works for their unmistakable portrayal of women's lives in the early 1900's.

BIOGRAPHY

Edith Newbold Jones was born into the highest level of society. Like most girls of her generation and social class, she was educated at home. At the age of twenty-three she married a wealthy young man, Edward Wharton; they had no children. Wharton divided her time between writing and her duties as a society hostess. Her husband, emotionally unstable, suffered several nervous breakdowns, and in 1913, they were divorced. Wharton spent a great deal of time in Europe; after 1912 she returned to America only once, to accept the honorary degree of doctor of letters from Yale University in 1923. During World War I, Wharton was very active in war work in France for which she was made a Chevalier of the Legion of Honor in 1916. Realizing that after her death her friends would suppress much of her real personality in their accounts of her life, and wanting the truth to be told, Wharton willed her private papers to Yale University, with instructions that they were not to be published until 1968. These papers revealed a totally unexpected side of Wharton's character: passionate, impulsive, and vulnerable. This new view of the author has had a marked effect on subsequent interpretations of her work.

ANALYSIS

Because many of Edith Wharton's characters and themes resemble those of Henry James, her work has sometimes been regarded as a derivative of his. Each of these authors wrote a number of stories regarding such themes as the fate of the individual who challenges the standards of society, the effect of commercial success on an artist, the impact of European civilization on an American mentality, and the confrontation of a public personality with his own private self. Further, both James and Wharton used ghost stories to present, in allegorical terms, internal experiences which would be difficult to dramatize in a purely realistic way. Wharton knew James and admired him as a friend and as a writer, and some of her early short stories—those in *The Greater Inclination* and *Crucial Instances*, for example—do resemble James's work. As she matured, however, Wharton developed an artistic viewpoint and a style which were distinctly her own. Her approach to the themes which she shared with James was much more direct than his: She took a more sweeping view of the action of a story and omitted the myriad details, qualifications, and explanations which characterize James's work.

It is not surprising that Wharton and James developed a number of parallel interests. Both writers moved in the same rather limited social circle and were exposed to the same values and to the same types of people. Not all their perceptions, however, were identical since Wharton's viewpoint was influenced by the limitations she experienced as a woman. She was therefore especially sensitive to such subtle forms of victimization as the narrowness of a woman's horizons in her society, which not only denied women the opportunity to develop their full potential but also burdened men with disproportionate

Edith Wharton (Library of Congress)

responsibilities. This theme, which underlies some of her best novels–*The House of Mirth* is a good example—also appears in a number of her short stories, such as "The Rembrandt."

"THE REMBRANDT"

The narrator of "The Rembrandt" is a museum curator whose cousin, Eleanor Copt, frequently undertakes acts of charity toward the unfortunate. These acts of charity, however, often take the form of persuading someone else to bear the brunt of the inconvenience and expense. As "The Rembrandt" opens, Eleanor persuades her cousin to accompany her to a rented room occupied by an elderly lady, the once-wealthy Mrs. Fontage. This widowed lady, who has suffered a number of financial misfortunes, has been reduced from living in palatial homes to now living in a dingy room. Even this small room soon will be too expensive for her unless she can sell the one art treasure she still possesses: an unsigned Rembrandt. The supposed Rembrandt, purchased under highly romantic circumstances during the Fontages' honeymoon in Europe, turns out to be valueless. The curator, however, is moved by the dignity and grace with which

Mrs. Fontage faces her situation, and he cannot bring himself to tell her that the painting is worthless. He values it at a thousand dollars, reasoning that he himself cannot be expected to raise that much money. When he realizes that his cousin and Mrs. Fontage expect him to purchase the painting on behalf of the museum, he temporizes.

Meanwhile, Eleanor interests an admirer of hers, Mr. Jefferson Rose, in the painting. Although he cannot really spare the money, Rose decides to buy the painting as an act of charity and as an investment. Even after the curator confesses his lie to Rose, the young man is determined to relieve Mrs. Fontage's misery. The curator, reasoning that it is better to defraud an institution than an individual, purchases the painting for the museum. The only museum official who might question his decision is abroad, and the curator stores the painting in the museum cellar and forgets it. When the official, Crozier, returns, he asks the curator whether he really considers the painting valuable. The curator confesses what he has done and offers to buy the painting from the museum. Crozier then informs the curator that the members of the museum committee have already purchased the painting privately, and beg leave to present it to the curator in recognition of his kindness to Mrs. Fontage.

Despite its flaws in structure and its somewhat romantic view of the business world, "The Rembrandt" shows Wharton's concern with the relationship between helpless individuals and the society which produced them. Her portrait of Mrs. Fontage is especially revealing—she is a woman of dignity and breeding, whose pride and training sustain her in very difficult circumstances. That very breeding, however, cripples Mrs. Fontage because of the narrowness which accompanies it. She is entirely ignorant of the practical side of life, and, in the absence of a husband or some other head of the family, she is seriously handicapped in dealing with business matters. Furthermore, although she is intelligent and in good health, she is absolutely incapable of contributing to her own support. In this very early story, Wharton applauds the gentlemen who live up to the responsibility of caring for such women. Later, Wharton will censure the men and the women whose unthinking conformity to social stereotypes has deprived women like Mrs. Fontage of the ability to care for themselves and has placed a double burden on the men.

"THE EYES"

As Wharton matured, her interest in victimization moved from the external world of society to the internal world of the individual mind. She recognized the fact that adjustment to life sometimes entails a compromise with one's private self which constitutes a betrayal. One of her most striking portrayals of that theme is in "The Eyes." This tale employs the framework of a ghost story to dramatize an internal experience. The story's aging protagonist, Andrew Culwin, has never become part of life, or allowed an involvement with another human being to threaten his absolute egotism. One evening, as his friends amuse themselves by telling tales of psychic events they have witnessed, Culwin offers to tell a story of his own. He explains that as a young man he once flirted with his naïve young cousin Alice, who responded with a seriousness which alarmed him. He immediately announced a trip to Europe; but, moved by the grace with which she accepted her disappointment, Culwin proposed to her and was accepted. He went to bed that evening feeling his self-centered bachelorhood giving way to a sense of righteousness and peace. Culwin awakened in the middle of the night, however, and saw in front of him a hideous pair of eyes. The eyes, which were sunken and old, had pouches of shriveled flesh beneath them and redlined lids above them, and one of the lids drooped more than the other. These eyes remained in the room all night, and in the morning Culwin fled, without explanation, to a friend's house. There he slept undisturbed and made plans to return to Alice a few days later. Thereupon the eyes returned, and Culwin fled to Europe. He realized that he did not really want to marry Alice, and he devoted himself to a self-centered enjoyment of Europe.

After two years, a handsome young man arrived in Rome with a letter of introduction to Culwin from Alice. This young man, Gilbert Noyes, had been sent abroad by his family to test himself as a writer. Culwin knew that Noyes's writing was worthless, but he temporized in order to keep the handsome youth with him. He also pitied Noyes because of the dull clerk's job which waited for him at home. Finally, Culwin told Noyes that his work had merit, intending to support the young man himself if necessary. That night, the eyes reappeared; and Culwin felt, along with his revulsion, a disquieting sense of identity with the eyes, as if he would some day come to understand all about them. After a month, Culwin cruelly dismissed Noyes, who went home to his clerkship; Culwin took to drink and turned up years later in Hong Kong, fat and unshaven. The eyes then disappeared and never returned.

Culwin's listeners perceive what the reader perceives: The eyes that mock Culwin's rare attempts to transform his self-centered existence into a life of involvement with someone else are in fact his own eyes, looking at him from the future and mocking him with what he would become. The eyes also represent Culwin's lesser self, which would in time take over his entire personality. Even in his youth, this lesser self overshadows Culwin's more humane impulses with second thoughts of the effect these impulses are likely to have on his comfort and security. The story ends as Culwin, surprised by his friends' reaction to his story, catches sight of himself in a mirror, and realizes the truth.

"AFTER HOLBEIN"

Wharton's twin themes of social and self-victimization are joined most effectively in a later story which many readers consider her best: "After Holbein." The title refers to a series of woodcuts by Hans Holbein the Younger, entitled "The Dance of Death." They show the figure of death, represented by a skeleton, insinuating himself into the lives of various unsuspecting people. One of these engravings, entitled "Noblewoman," features a richly dressed man and woman following the figure of death.

The story begins with a description of an elderly gentleman, Anson Warley, who has been one of the most popular members of New York society for more than thirty years. In the first three pages of the story, the reader learns that Warley fought, long ago, a battle between his public image and his private self; and the private self lost. Warley gradually stopped staying at home to read or meditate and found less and less

time to talk quietly with intellectual friends or scholars. He became a purely public figure, a frequenter of hot, noisy, crowded rooms. His intellect gave itself entirely to the production of drawing-room witticisms, many of them barbed with sarcasm. On the evening that the story takes place, Warley finds himself reminded of one of these sallies of his. Some years earlier, Warley, who had been dodging the persistent invitations of a pompous and rather boring society hostess, finally told his circle of friends that the next time he received a card saying "Mrs. Jasper requests the pleasure," he would reply, "Mr. Warley declines the boredom." The remark was appreciated at the time by the friends who heard it; but in his old age Warley finds himself hoping that Mrs. Jasper never suffered the pain of hearing about it.

At this point in the story, Wharton shifts the scene to a mansion on Fifth Avenue, where a senile old woman prepares herself for an imaginary dinner party. She wears a grotesque purple wig, and broad-toed orthopedic shoes under an ancient purple gown. She also insists on wearing her diamonds to what she believes will be another triumph of her skill as a hostess. This woman is the same Mrs. Jasper whom Warley has been avoiding for years. She is now in the care of an unsympathetic young nurse and three elderly servants. Periodically, the four employees go through the charade of preparing the house and Mrs. Jasper for the dinner parties which she imagines still take place there.

While Mrs. Jasper is being dressed for her illusory dinner party, Anson Warley is preparing to attend a real one. Despite his valet's protests concerning his health, Warley not only refuses to stay at home but also insists on walking up Fifth Avenue in the freezing winter night. Gradually he becomes confused and forgets his destination. Then he sees before him Mrs. Jasper's mansion, lighted for a dinner party, and in his confusion, he imagines he is to dine there. He arrives just as Mrs. Jasper's footman is reading aloud the list of guests whom Mrs. Jasper thinks she has invited.

When dinner is announced, Warley and Mrs. Jasper walk arm in arm, at a stately processional gait, to the table. The footman has set the table with heavy blue and white servants' dishes, and he has stuffed newspapers instead of orchids into the priceless Rose Dubarry porcelain dishes. He serves a plain meal and inexpensive wine in the empty dining room. Lost in the illusion, however, Warley and Mrs. Jasper imagine that they are consuming a gourmet meal at a luxuriously appointed table in the presence of a crowd of glittering guests. They go through a ritual of gestures and conversation which does indeed resemble the *danse macabre* for which the story is named. Finally, Mrs. Jasper leaves the table exhausted and makes her way upstairs to her uncomprehending and chuckling nurse. Warley, equally exhausted and equally convinced that he has attended a brilliant dinner party, steps out into the night and drops dead.

"After Holbein" is a powerful story primarily because of the contrasts it establishes. In the foreground are the wasted lives of Warley and Mrs. Jasper, each of whom has long given up all hope of originality or self-realization for the sake of being part of a nameless, gilded mass. The unsympathetic nurse, who teases Mrs. Jasper into tears, acts not from cruelty but from her inability to comprehend, in her own hopeful youth, the tragedy of Mrs. Jasper's situation. This nurse is contrasted with Mrs. Jasper's elderly maid, Lavinia, who conceals her own failing health out of loyalty to her mistress, and who is moved to tears by Mrs. Jasper's plight. Even the essential horror of the story is intensified by the contrasting formality and restraint of its language and by the tight structuring which gives the plot the same momentum of inevitability as the movements of a formal dance.

Warley and Mrs. Jasper have been betrayed from within and from without. They have traded their private selves for public masks, and have spent their lives among others who have made the same bargain. Lavinia's recollections suggest to the reader that Mrs. Jasper subordinated her role as mother to her role as hostess; and her children, reared in that same world, have left her to the care of servants. Her friends are dead or bedridden, or they have forgotten her. She exists now, in a sense, as she has always existed: as a grotesque figure in a world of illusion.

Warley, too, has come to think of himself only in terms of his social reputation—he will not accept the reality of his age and infirmity. Thus, as he drags one leg during his icy walk along Fifth Avenue, he pictures a club smoking room in which one of his acquaintances will say, "Warley? Why, I saw him sprinting up Fifth Avenue the other night like a two-year-old; that night it was four or five below." Warley has convinced himself that whatever is said in club smoking rooms by men in good society is real. None of the acquaintances, however, to whom he has given his life is with him when he takes that final step; and it would not have mattered if anyone had been there. Warley is inevitably and irrevocably alone at last.

Wharton's eleven volumes of short stories, spanning thirty-nine years, record her growth in thought and in style. They offer the entertainment of seeing inside an exclusive social circle which was in many respects unique and which no longer exists as Wharton knew it. Some of Wharton's stories are trivial and some are repetitive; but her best stories depict, in the inhabitants of that exclusive social world, experiences and sensations which are universal.

OTHER MAJOR WORKS

LONG FICTION: *The Touchstone*, 1900; *The Valley of Decision*, 1902; *Sanctuary*, 1903; *The House of Mirth*, 1905; *The Fruit of the Tree*, 1907; *Madame de Treymes*, 1907; *Ethan Frome*, 1911; *The Reef*, 1912; *The Custom of the Country*, 1913; *Summer*, 1917; *The Marne*, 1918; *The Age of Innocence*, 1920; *The Glimpses of the Moon*, 1922; *A Son at the Front*, 1923; *Old New York*, 1924 (4 volumes; includes *False Dawn*, *The Old Maid*, *The Spark* and *New Year's Day*); *The Mother's Recompense*, 1925; *Twilight Sleep*, 1927; *The Children*, 1928; *Hudson River Bracketed*, 1929; *The Gods Arrive*, 1932; *The Buccaneers*, 1938.

POETRY: *Verses*, 1878; *Artemis to Actæon*, 1909; *Twelve Poems*, 1926.

NONFICTION: *The Decoration of Houses*, 1897 (with Ogden Codman, Jr.); *Italian Villas and Their Gardens*, 1904; *Italian Backgrounds*, 1905; *A Motor-Flight Through France*, 1908; *Fighting France from Dunkerque to Belfort*, 1915; *French Ways and Their Meaning*, 1919; *In Morocco*, 1920; *The Writing of Fiction*, 1925; *A Backward Glance*, 1934; *The Letters* of *Edith Wharton*, 1988; *The Uncollected Critical Writings*, 1997 (Frederick Wegener, editor).

BIBLIOGRAPHY

Banta, Martha. "The Ghostly Gothic of Wharton's Everyday World." *American Literary Realism: 1870-1910* 27 (Fall, 1994): 1-10. An analysis of Wharton's ghost story "Afterward" and her novella *Ethan Frome* as illustrative of the nineteenth century craving for a circumscribed experience of the bizarre. Claims Wharton's stories illustrate Walter Benjamin's concept of the threshold, for they embody a moment when dream is replaced by history.

Beer, Janet. *Kate Chopin, Edith Wharton, and Charlotte Perkins Gilman: Studies in Short Fiction*. London: Macmillan, 1997. Beer devotes two chapters of Wharton's short fiction, focusing primarily on the novellas in one chapter and the regional stories about New England in the other.

Bell, Millicent, ed. *The Cambridge Companion to Edith Wharton*. Cambridge, England: Cambridge University Press, 1995. Essays on the works, as well as on Wharton's handling of manners and race. Bell gives a critical history of Wharton's fiction in her introduction. Includes a chronology of Wharton's life and publications and a bibliography.

Bendixen, Alfred, and Annette Zilversmit, eds. *Edith Wharton: New Critical Essays*. New York: Garland, 1992. Studies of the works, as well as on Wharton's treatment of female sexuality, modernism, language, and gothic borrowings. There is an introduction and concluding essay on future directions for criticism.

Benstock, Shari. *No Gifts from Chance: A Biography of Edith Wharton*. New York: Charles Scribner's Sons, 1994. Although Benstock applies a feminist perspective to Wharton's life, she does not claim that Wharton was a feminist. Using primary materials not previously available, she provides a detailed account on Wharton's early life. Also discusses her literary relationship with Henry James, whose work she admired.

Fracasso, Evelyn E. *Edith Wharton's Prisoner of Consciousness: A Study of Theme and Technique in the Tales*. Westport, Conn.: Greenwood Press, 1994. Analyzes stories from three periods of Wharton's career. Focuses on her technique in treating the theme of imprisonment. Deals with people trapped by love and marriage, imprisoned by the dictates of society, victimized by the demands of art and morality, and paralyzed by fear of the supernatural.

Lewis, R. W. B. *Edith Wharton: A Biography*. New York: Harper & Row, 1975. The definitive biography on Wharton. Uses the previously inaccessible papers of the Yale Collection to provide a meticulous portrait of the author.

McDowell, Margaret B. *Edith Wharton*. Boston: Twayne, 1975. A perceptive biography and analysis of Wharton's body of writings. Chapter 6 discusses her most important short fiction.

Nevius, Blake. *Edith Wharton: A Study of Her Fiction*. Berkeley: University of California Press, 1961. Examines two recurrent themes in Wharton's fiction: the tension that arises between an individual's public and private selves, and the desire for individual freedom and the need to assume social responsibility.

Olin-Ammentorp, Julie. "'Not Precisely War Stories': Edith Wharton's Short Fiction from the Great War." *Studies in American Fiction* 23 (Autumn, 1995): 153-172. Rather than being stories of action and heroism or tedious hours in the trenches, Wharton's war stories were suggested by her experiences, observations, and reflections on the war and on the home-front culture that it produced.

Young, Judy Hale. "The Repudiation of Sisterhood in Edith Wharton's 'Pomegranate Seed.'" *Studies in Short Fiction* 33 (Winter, 1996): 1-11. Argues that the story is an indictment of the woman writer who perpetuates the state of noncommunication among women; claims the story is Wharton's anti-manifesto of female writing. In it, she presents her notion of just what the woman who writes must not do.

Joan DelFattore, updated by
Mary F. Yudin

E. B. WHITE

Born: Mount Vernon, New York; July 11, 1899
Died: North Brooklin, Maine; October 1, 1985

PRINCIPAL SHORT FICTION

The Second Tree from the Corner, 1954

OTHER LITERARY FORMS

Though best remembered for two children's books, *Charlotte's Web* (1952) and *Stuart Little* (1945), E. B. White was noted during his lifetime for humorous essays and light poetry. His phenomenally successful revision and expansion of William Strunk's textbook *The Elements of Style* (1979) is a publishing legend. In 1981, a miscellany, *Poems and Sketches of E. B. White*, was published.

ACHIEVEMENTS

E. B. White received numerous awards and honorary doctorates. He was awarded the National Institute of Arts and Letters Gold Medal for Essays and Criticism in 1960, the Presidential Medal of Freedom in 1963, the National Institute of Arts and Letters National Medal for Literature in 1971, and a Pulitzer Prize special citation in 1978.

BIOGRAPHY

Elwyn Brooks White was born in Mount Vernon, New York, on July 11, 1899. He graduated from Cornell University, where he had discovered his love for literature and served as editor-in-chief of the *Cornell Daily Sun*. The most important event in his career was being hired by *The New Yorker* in 1926. He was largely responsible for shaping this famous magazine's sophisticated tone with his prose and painstaking editing. At *The New Yorker* he met James Thurber, an important literary influence, and Katharine Sergeant Angell, his wife, collaborator, and inspiration until her death in 1977. Known to millions only as the author of *Stuart Little* and *Charlotte's Web*, White was one of America's finest essayists. Thurber, himself a perfectionist, praised "those silver and crystal sentences which have a ring like the ring of no-

body else's sentences in the world." One of White's often quoted statements is: "The whole duty of a writer is to please and satisfy himself, and the true writer always plays to an audience of one." Fleeing the stress of New York City, this shy, retiring individualist spent much of his later life on a farm in Maine. He died on October 1, 1985.

ANALYSIS

E. B. White's most important literary influence was Henry David Thoreau, author of *Walden: Or, Life in the Woods* (1854), the only book White really cared about owning. The influence of Thoreau's subtle humor and individualistic philosophy can be seen in White's writing, including his short fiction. Like Thoreau, White believed that "the mass of men lead lives of quiet desperation," that most people spend their lives getting ready to live but never actually living. White's short stories usually deal with the quiet desperation of life in the big city, where human beings trapped in an unnatural environment are beset by stress and anxiety, often temporarily alleviated by alcohol, meaningless social activities, and unfulfilling work.

Whereas Thoreau wrote about the joy of living close to nature, White, as a *New Yorker* contributor, had to deal with the reverse side of the picture—the anomie of life in one of America's most crowded, most competitive cities. When he managed to effect a Thoreauvian escape from New York to the peace and quiet of Maine, White lost interest in writing short stories.

White, like Thoreau, never lost his sense of humor even when dealing with depressing subjects. Most characteristic of White's short stories is their strange mixture of humor and emotional distress. In this he resembles his friend and collaborator James Thurber, who defined humor as "emotional chaos remembered in tranquillity." Thurber was a major influence on White, just as White was a major influence on Thurber. White's stories would seem too morbid without their leavening of humor. White and Thurber were

E. B. White in 1945 (AP/Wide World Photos)

both admirers of Henry James, and that older writer's high literary standards and dedication to his craft are obviously reflected in White's short stories.

"THE DOOR"

White's most frequently anthologized story is an interior monologue reminiscent of the stream-of-consciousness technique pioneered by James Joyce. White's harrowing but courageously humorous story concerns a lonely individual having a nervous breakdown. The only other character is an unnamed receptionist who says, "We could take your name and send it to you." Her unnerving—and ungrammatical—statement suggests that the protagonist, having lost his identity, must wait for someone to tell him who he is. He feels disoriented in a city whose friendly landmarks are being replaced by cold, forbidding modern buildings without character. He mentally equates the city with those cages in which psychologists condition laboratory rats to behave according to certain arbitrary rules, then drive them crazy by changing the rules. The protagonist goes on to reflect that he is not the only victim of "progress."

. . . and I am not the only one either, he kept thinking—ask any doctor if I am. The doctors, they know how many there are, they even know where the trouble is only they don't like to tell you about the prefrontal lobe because that means making a hole in your skull and removing the work of centuries.

"The Door" is a very personal story. White tried psychotherapy after a nervous breakdown but was disappointed, as evidenced in another autobiographical story, "The Second Tree from the Corner." "The Door" also shows White's concern about the corruption of the English language through crass commercialism and general vulgarization of culture. He was appalled by the proliferation of ugly, newly coined words which this story mimics with his own coinages such as "flexsan," "duroid," and "thrutex." For White such perversions of language were symptomatic of the destruction of human values by the blind onrush of science and technology driven by avarice and consumerism.

"THE SECOND TREE FROM THE CORNER"

White described this story as "the one where the fellow says goodbye to sanity." Here the nameless protagonist of "The Door" is called Trexler and has gotten past the receptionist into the psychiatrist's inner sanctum. The humor is contained in the contrast between materialistic doctor and idealistic patient. Little is accomplished during five sessions, until the psychiatrist asks, "What do you want?" Trexler puts the doctor on the defensive by asking the same question. The doctor thinks he knows what he wants: ". . . a wing on the small house I own in Westport. I want more money, and more leisure to do the things I want to do." Trexler refrains from asking, "And what are those things you want to do, Doctor?" The overworked psychiatrist has no idea what he really wants—and everyone is in the same boat. This insight ends psychotherapy. Outside, when Trexler notices the remarkable beauty of the second tree from the corner, he experiences an epiphany. Intentionally echoing the conclusion of Henry James's short story "The Beast in the Jungle," White writes:

He felt content to be sick, unembarrassed at being afraid; and in the jungle of his fear he glimpsed (as he had so often glimpsed them before) the flashy tail feathers of the bird courage.

"The Second Tree from the Corner" is a humorous way of dramatizing Thoreau's painful truth that "most men lead lives of quiet desperation." White found contentment by moving from the bedlam of Manhattan to a farm in Maine. There he discovered what he really wanted: peace, quiet, and simplicity, work to occupy his hands, and a rational way of life close to nature.

PREPOSTEROUS PARABLES

White wrote many satirical pieces he called "preposterous parables." "The Hour of Letdown" is a spinoff of countless jokes in which a man brings a talking dog into a saloon. Instead of a dog, the stranger brings a chess-playing machine, which has many human characteristics, including a thirst for rye whiskey. White was foretelling the future. Computers do not yet need alcoholic beverages, but they can now beat world chess champions. Intelligent machines are becoming indispensable to modern society, while displacing millions from jobs and creating new problems as fast as they help solve the old. Electronic engineers are experimenting with improvements to make computers superior to humans in more ways. At the end of the story the stranger leaves in his car with the machine driving. This may have seemed absurd in 1951, but computers now operate automobiles on freeways and perform better in stressful traffic conditions than their owners.

"The Morning of the Day They Did It" is narrated by a space orbiter who survived the nuclear holocaust that destroyed all life on earth. It might be described as a cautionary science-fiction story, warning readers what would happen if science and technology advanced faster than human moral and spiritual development. White advocated a democratic world government to create universal peace and prosperity.

In "Quo Vadimus" (Latin for "Where are we going?"), two strangers stop on a Manhattan sidewalk and begin an impromptu philosophical discussion in the midst of pedestrians rushing in both directions. It turns out that one man was hurrying to deliver a note regarding a petty change in a salesman's instruction book. The other confesses that he was on his way to the office to write an article about complexity, which nobody may have time to read. Both agree they have lost sight of what is essential and are trapped in lives of quiet desperation. The man planning to write the article predicts that modern life can only get more complicated. By implication, the scurrying pedestrians blindly jostling them on the sidewalk are all on equally trivial errands.

White's "Preposterous parables," like most of his stories, have a common theme: Man is becoming dehumanized by his own inventions. Progress is a double-edged sword. Consumerism does not lead to happiness but to anxiety and wage slavery. The problems that troubled White during the relatively simple period when he was writing for *The New Yorker* continue to grow more ominous and perplexing in the new millennium.

OTHER MAJOR WORKS

POETRY: *The Lady Is Cold*, 1929; *The Fox of Peapack and Other Poems*, 1938.

NONFICTION: *Is Sex Necessary? Or, Why We Feel the Way We Do*, 1929 (with James Thurber); *Letters of E. B. White*, 1976; *The Elements of Style*, 1979; *Essays of E. B. White*, 1979.

CHILDREN'S LITERATURE: *Stuart Little*, 1945; *Charlotte's Web*, 1952; *The Trumpet of the Swan*, 1970.

ANTHOLOGY: *A Subtreasury of American Humor*, 1941 (edited with Katherine Sergeant White).

MISCELLANEOUS: *Poems and Sketches of E. B. White*, 1981.

BIBLIOGRAPHY

Angell, Roger. "The Making of E. B. White." *The New York Times Book Review* (August 3, 1997): 27. White's stepson Angell, an editor and writer for *The New Yorker*, describes life on the Maine farm, White's need for independence and privacy, his Thoreauvian love of nature and respect for honest manual labor. In spite of withdrawing from New York City, White kept informed and concerned about world events.

Elledge, Scott. *E. B. White: A Biography*. New York: W. W. Norton, 1984. This first full-length biography describes White's childhood, his years at Cornell, his struggle to find himself as a writer, his friendships with humorist James Thurber and *New Yorker* editor Harold Ross, his half-century marriage to Katharine Angell White and analyzes the relationship between his life and his writings.

Root, Robert L., Jr., ed. *Critical Essays on E. B. White.* C. K. Hall, 1994. Varying perspectives by prominent authors who are easy to read and worth knowing, including Diana Trilling, Joseph Wood Krutch, Irwin Edman, Malcolm Cowley, James Thurber, Clifton Fadiman, and John Updike. Contains discussions of "The Door," "The Second Tree from the Corner," and other stories.

Root, Robert L., Jr. *E. B. White: The Emergence of an Essayist.* Iowa City: University of Iowa Press, 1999. Analyzes the "four fairly pronounced periods" in White's literary career, his painstaking method of writing and revising, and the influence of Henry David Thoreau, Michel Eyquem de Montaigne, and others. Focuses on White's dedication to his craft and developing technique as a prose stylist, with minimal attention to his personal life.

Sampson, Edward C. *E. B. White.* Twayne's United States Authors series. New York: Twayne, 1974. This early study contains a wealth of valuable information in compressed form, including a chronology, a literary biography, an appraisal of White's significance, references, and selected bibliography.

Updike, John. "MAGNUM OPUS: At E. B. White's Centennial, Charlotte Spins On." *The New Yorker* 75 (July 12, 1999): 74-78. Updike, noted for his sensitive short stories, was strongly influenced by White's standards while working under him at *The New Yorker* early in his career. In this tribute, Updike recounts personal memories and analyzes *Charlotte's Web* as White's "disguised autobiography."

Bill Delaney

JOHN EDGAR WIDEMAN

Born: Washington, D.C.; June 14, 1941

PRINCIPAL SHORT FICTION

Damballah, 1981
Fever: Twelve Stories, 1989
All Stories Are True, 1992
The Stories of John Edgar Wideman, 1992

OTHER LITERARY FORMS

John Edgar Wideman's career began officially in 1967 with the appearance of his first novel, *A Glance Away.* Since this first publication, he has repeatedly returned to the novelistic form in works such as *Hurry Home* (1970); *The Lynchers* (1973); *Hiding Place* (1981), intended as the middle volume of the Homewood Trilogy; *Sent for You Yesterday* (1983), the final volume in the trilogy; *Reuben* (1987); *Philadelphia Fire* (1990); *The Cattle Killing* (1996); and *Two Cities* (1998). In addition, Wideman has written works of autobiographical nonfiction, *Brothers and Keepers* (1984), in which he compares his own life to that of his troubled younger brother, serving a lifetime jail sentence, and *Fatheralong: A Meditation on Fathers and Sons, Race, and Society* (1994). Wideman has also written regularly on African American topics for *The New York Times Book Review* and has published scholarly work on African American predecessors such as Charles Waddell Chesnutt and W. E. B. Du Bois.

ACHIEVEMENTS

John Edgar Wideman has distinguished himself both as a strong contemporary voice within the African American literary tradition and as a serious scholar examining the legacy of his predecessors in that tradition. His early fictional technique reflects

John Edgar Wideman (University of Wyoming)

his aesthetic debt to Anglo-American narrative experimentation, ranging from the originators of the English novel in the eighteenth century to the great modernists of the twentieth century; racial concerns, while evident, did not predominate in his first works. With the 1980's, however, Wideman deliberately began exploring African American literary forms in accordance with his growing desire to reengage his own racial identity and reach out more directly to an African American readership. Accordingly, he published the three works that constitute the Homewood Trilogy as trade paperbacks rather than in initial hardcover, so as to increase their accessibility. The trilogy's third volume, *Sent for You Yesterday*, received the PEN/Faulkner Award for Fiction for its innovative fusion of subject matter and novelistic technique. The traumatic experience of a brother's crime and punishment, which was an important source for the 1983 novel, also prompted the nonfictional *Brothers and Keepers*, in which Wideman's quest for forms adequate to the polyphonic character of the African American experience takes on great personal urgency; the autobiography was nominated for the National Book Award. Wideman has also been awarded

the John Dos Passos Award, the Lannan Literary Award, the John D. and Catherine T. MacArthur Foundation ("genius") Award, the Rea Award, and an honorary doctorate from the University of Pennsylvania. He edited *The Best American Short Stories 1996*.

BIOGRAPHY

John Edgar Wideman was the first of five children born to Bette French and Edgar Wideman. His youth was spent in the African American community of Homewood, within the city of Pittsburgh, Pennsylvania, and his fiction draws heavily upon the experiences of his family across a century of Homewood history. As a youth, Wideman demonstrated the same blend of athletic and academic ambition that often distinguishes his fictional characters and dramatizes their divided allegiances. Upon graduation as Peabody High School valedictorian, Wideman received a Benjamin Franklin scholarship to the University of Pennsylvania and subsequently played for its basketball team, hoping someday to be drafted by the National Basketball Association. Selected for the Philadelphia Big Five Basketball Hall of Fame and tapped for Phi Beta Kappa, Wideman also won a Rhodes scholarship; upon completion of his B.A. at the University of Pennsylvania in 1963, he attended Oxford University, where, in 1966, he earned a B.Phil. as a Thouron Fellow. Having been an active writer since his undergraduate years, Wideman secured a Kent Fellowship from the University of Iowa Writers' Workshop in 1966. His first novel, *A Glance Away*, appeared in 1967, winning for him immediate attention as a significant new voice in contemporary American letters.

Alongside his creative endeavors, Wideman steadily pursued an academic career. In 1966, he accepted a teaching position at the University of Pennsylvania, where he later headed the African American studies program from 1971 to 1973 and rose to the rank of professor of English; he was also assistant basketball coach from 1968 to 1972. Academic appointments brought him to Howard University, the University of Wyoming at Laramie, and the University of Massachusetts at Amherst. The National Endowment for the Humanities in 1975 named him a Young Humanist Fellow; in 1976, the U.S. State Department selected him for a lecture tour of Europe and the Near East. That same year, he held a Phi Beta Kappa lectureship. Wideman married Judith Ann Goldman in 1965, and together they had three children: Daniel, Jacob, and Jamila. The family tragedy of his youngest brother, Rob, who was convicted in 1978 of armed robbery and murder, was grimly reiterated in 1988, when Wideman's son Jacob received a life sentence for the 1986 murder in Arizona of a teenage traveling companion.

In speaking about the formative influences upon his writing, Wideman asserts that his creative inclinations underwent a transformation upon his arrival as a new faculty member at the University of Pennsylvania, where students of color assumed him to be as well versed in the African American literary legacy as he was in the Anglo-American tradition. His responsiveness to their concerns prompted him not only to create the university's African American studies program but also to recover the cultural identity that he had self-consciously minimized in pursuit of the dominant culture's standards of academic excellence. His subsequent writing, fiction and nonfiction alike, repeatedly sounds the autobiographical theme of "coming home," and Wideman not only dissects the obstacles that thwart such return but also espouses the belief that art can at least make possible a temporary reconciliation between past and present. By paralleling his own multigenerational family history and the community history of Homewood, Wideman fuses personal and collective memory to create a mythology of the human condition at once particular and universal.

ANALYSIS

John Edgar Wideman's avowed artistic end is the creation of characters whose rich inner lives testify to a "sense of themselves as spiritual beings" that challenges the deterministic simplicities often dominant in literary depictions of the African American sensibility. Like Richard Wright, Ralph Ellison, and James Baldwin before him, Wideman insistently links naturalistic detail to an existential quest for meaning and

integrity that is complicated by the peculiar difficulties of sustaining one's humanity under the degradations of racism. While the material consequences of racist injustice are ever-present in his stories, Wideman makes clear that his most pressing concern is the threat posed to the souls of its victims. In turn, he suggests that the renewal of contemporary African American society, increasingly ravaged by hopelessness and self-destructiveness, lies in a self-conscious recovery of, and healing through, the cultural identity he so rigorously documents in his evocation of Homewood. Thus in Wideman's fiction the struggle of individual souls in an absurd and dehumanizing world does not unfold in a completely existential void; his characters move within a community whose past vitality derived from history, traditions, language, and relationships linking generations back beyond the darkness of slavery. The imaginative architecture that unifies the Homewood Trilogy employs interpenetrating plot lines, family trees, and community legends to make clear that Wideman's real subject is the communal survival once made possible by its citizens' heroic decency against great odds.

DAMBALLAH

Damballah, the collection of twelve short stories that begins the trilogy, announces Wideman's intentions aesthetically as well as thematically. The fugue-like polyphony of voices achieved by bringing together separate narratives drawn from a wide spectrum of Homewood personalities and historical moments captures not only the community's diversity but also the power of oral culture in all of its forms— speech, music, storytelling—to nourish and sustain it in the midst of unrelenting racial hostility. In "The Chinaman," a narrative "I" identified elsewhere as John (and quite evidently an autobiographical presence) explains that the funeral of his maternal grandmother, Freeda, had reconnected him with old family legends that he had years earlier set aside as unworthy of serious literary treatment. Listening months later to his own mother describe Freeda's death and thereby complete a story he had been unable to finish alone, he concludes, "The shape of the story is the shape of my mother's voice." Wideman's narrator repeatedly explains that this text is a collaborative project in which narratives culled from the collective memory of his family are woven together through the mediating agency of his own consciousness to reveal a design that affirms the faith in human possibility now leaching away in the ruins that were once Homewood.

Wideman's preoccupation with the crisis of black men in modern America—a crisis vividly depicted in his own estrangement from his origins and his brother Rob's criminality and imprisonment—explains the placement of his maternal grandfather, John French, at the center of these stories. French's defiant courage, loyalty, quick wit, tough-minded devotion to his family, and acute survival instincts make him a model of masculine virtue for a new generation desperately in need of his example. He stands in seemingly obvious contrast to his equally talented but blighted grandson Tommy Lawson, the narrator's drug-addicted brother, whose crimes destroy his future and who is the counterbalancing focus of the last third of the collection. Yet, French lives on in Tommy's rebellious energy and probing mind, making the youth's current circumstances all the more tragic.

Wideman also records the voices of the strong women who have sustained the community throughout the crises surrounding their men and whose emotional anguish reflects the complex emotional dynamic between black men and women in Wideman's fiction. Freeda Hollinger French, the text's matriarch, proves herself capable of swift, violent intervention to safeguard her child or her husband in "Lizabeth: The Caterpillar Story." Lizabeth French Lawson actually gives birth to the narrator in "Daddy Garbage," within a story line juxtaposed to the grim discovery of another infant's frozen corpse and the moral imperative of the two old men who find it and insist upon a decent burial. As the future is denied to one child and extended to another, one perceives a subtle echo of the divergent paths Lizabeth's own sons will pursue in later years.

Wideman's sensitivity to the orality of African American culture leads him to seek linguistic approximations for the music and talk-story patterns at the heart of African American imaginative expression. His prose resonates with the jazz rhythms of African American vernacular and often quotes directly from the musical yoking of human misery and triumph in what is called the blues. In "The Songs of Reba Love Jackson," a successful Gospel singer admits that her artistry expresses emotional nuances beyond the power of language alone: "Couldn't speak about some things. She could only sing them. Put her stories in the songs she had heard all her life so the songs became her stories." In the closing piece of the volume, "The Beginning of Homewood," the narrator creates a wall of sound from the voices he has unloosed in the preceding stories; writing to his brother Tommy in prison, he acknowledges that his real task as a writer has been to hear and synthesize those women's testimonials to the community's history of defeat and transcendence:

> The chorus wailing and then Reba Love Jackson soloing. I heard May singing and heard Mother Bess telling what she remembers and what she had heard about Sybela Owens. I was thinking the way Aunt May talks. . . . her stories exist because of their parts and each part is a story worth telling . . . the voice seeks to recover everything, that the voice proclaims *nothing is lost*, that the listener is not passive but lives like everything else within the story.

Wideman's most immediate purpose here is to tell the story of the slave woman Sybela Owens who, together with her white master/lover, fled the South, settled on Bruston Hill, the symbolic navel of Homewood, and began the family line that has produced his own family. By embedding Sybela's story of physical and spiritual redemption within a mediation on his brother's grim circumstances, the narrator conveys the continued urgency of such issues for African Americans; he also engages in the metafictional self-reflexiveness that characterizes his generation of American writers as he muses over the act of writing and its problematic relationship to lived events. Wideman has even bigger aims with Sybela, however, for his imaginative energy also transforms her into a mythic female progenitor who becomes a thematic counterpart to the African slave Orion ("Ryan") introduced in the first (and title) story, "Damballah." Like Sybela, Orion resists the degradation of his circumstances, so much so that his unyielding integrity leads to his execution by enraged whites who accuse him of sexual crimes. Before his death, however, he inspires an American-born slave boy with the mysterious power of his native religious beliefs, having taught him to chant to Damballah, the "good serpent of the sky" and a paternal deity whose wisdom and benign oversight make of the cosmos one transcendent family. Despite Wideman's sophisticated postmodernist affinity for refracting illusions of "reality" through multiple conflicting subjectivities, he seeks, finally, an integrative vision in which the mythical and the historical coalesce to offer the hope of spiritual renewal.

FEVER

While *Damballah* draws its cumulative power from its unifying narrative sensibility and its consistent focus upon the citizens past and present of Homewood, *Fever: Twelve Stories* demonstrates a much looser internal logic grounded in thematic rather than storytelling interlacings. Once again, Wideman uses the short story to escape the constraints of novelistic continuity and reconfigure—this time through unrelated voices—motifs that literally assume international proportions. His most striking theme correlates the historical catastrophes of American slavery, the Holocaust, and modern international terrorism, thereby suggesting a common pattern of scapegoating and racist antagonism that transcends the experience of any single group of victims.

"The Statue of Liberty" and "Valaida," for example, both demonstrate how episodes of interracial miscommunication and self-indulgent fantasizing about the imaginary "Other" continually compromise the possibility of real human engagement. Moreover, in the latter story, a Jewish Holocaust survivor relates to his black maid a story of the jazz performer, whose actions in a wartime concentration camp saved his life; her droll response resists the intended empathy he has attempted to build between them: "Always thought it was just you people over there doing those terrible things to each other." In "Hostages," an Israeli expatriate and daughter of Auschwitz survivors reflects on her first marriage to an Israeli Arab and her current marriage to a wealthy businessman who

offers a prime target for Muslim terrorists; finally she sees herself as a hostage to the comfortable but isolated life she leads and meditates on the Talmudic lesson of the Lamed-Vov, or "God's hostages," predestined "sponges drawing mankind's suffering into themselves."

"Fever," the volume's title story—and one of its most accomplished—depicts the 1793 yellow fever epidemic in Philadelphia, a crisis attributed to African slaves brought up north from the Caribbean but in fact resulting from the internally bred corruption of the swamp-ridden city. A metaphor for the pervasive racial contagions of this ironically dubbed "City of Brotherly Love," the fever levels all distinctions of race, gender, and class even as it triggers responses affirming them. The story's protagonist, Richard Allen, is a minister exhausting himself in Christian service to dying whites and blacks alike. Eventually confronted by the angry monologue of an infected Jewish merchant unimpressed by his humanity, he too is told of the Lamed-Vov, the implication being that Allen has been arbitrarily selected "to suffer the reality humankind cannot bear," enduring an unimaginable and unrelieved burden of "earth, grief and misery." A nihilistic voice in the text, Abraham deconstructs Allen's faith and further magnifies the din of conflicting perspectives—past and present, conciliatory and confrontational—that make the story the touchstone of the volume's exploration of compassion as a limited but essential response to incomprehensible suffering, be its origins cosmic or human—or both.

Elsewhere, Wideman contrasts vision versus blindness ("Doc's Story" and "When It's Time to Go") to illustrate very different positionings by African Americans within the racially charged dominant culture through which they try to move. Wideman's attunement to the musical textures of African American culture again asserts itself, as does his interest in the drama of the individual alienated from his root culture by his ambitions. "Surfiction" offers an exercise in postmodern pastiche that is both a self-conscious parody of the imaginative stasis to which contemporary critical and aesthetic practice can lead and a serious study of the ways in which human determination to communicate across the void poignantly subverts even the most sophisticated intellectual distancing devices. Finally, then, the reader of this volume is left musing on the cultural incompatibilities institutionalized by ideologies of difference—racial, gender, ethnic, nationalistic—and the heroic folly of the Richard Allens of the world, who resist them against all odds.

ALL STORIES ARE TRUE

Like Wideman's earlier stories, these stories experiment with an associative narrative technique and are also sometimes based on Wideman's family in Homewood. Whether set in Homewood or elsewhere, however, all of these stories put the individual in the context of larger social conditions in America. The title story, which returns us to Homewood and a visit by a middle-aged man to his mother, soon shifts scenes to the dehumanizing conditions of the modern American prison, where his brother fights endlessly to gain parole. For both his mother and his imprisoned brother, faith—whether Muslim or Christian—becomes a way to endure the harsh realities of their lives. Yet another story of a mother and a wayward son is "Everybody Knew Bubba Riff," a free-form examination of the life and death of an aggressive young man named Bubba, whose indulgent mother and punitive stepfather cannot understand the reasons for his bad outcome. By story's end, the reader sees that the problem may have been less with his parents, however, than with the prevailing American myth of the empowered individual, which led Bubba to see himself as a footloose, free agent with no obligation or connection to his past or its traditions, whose only measure of manhood was in violence. Another story, "Backseat," returns to Homewood and to Wideman's dying grandmother. In reviewing Martha Wideman's life, John Edgar Wideman discovers his grandmother's origins as an illegitimate child of a white man and sees that for her, sexuality was always part of larger issues such as race, marriage, parenthood, male domination, and female subservience. This discovery of his grandmother's complicated sexual life contrasts with Wideman's own memories of shallow adolescent sexual adventures in the backseat of his car. Other aspects of black life are explored in such stories as "Newborn Thrown in Trash and Dies," inspired by an article in *The New York Times*. This story adopts the perspective of an infant who has been thrown by its mother down a trash chute. As the baby hurtles past the floors, the narrative flashes forward to the various indignities and deprivations of contemporary inner city life to which it would have been exposed. Far from urban decay, the issue of racism nevertheless surfaces even in better circumstances. In such stories as "Signs," a young black woman in graduate school, on her way to a successful life, finds menacing notes addressed to her which make her realize that racial prejudice has not been eradicated in her privileged environment. Eventually the reader learns that the young woman has composed these signs of racial antagonism herself, suggesting that memories of racism are so ingrained that the individual may not be able to overcome them.

OTHER MAJOR WORKS

LONG FICTION: *A Glance Away*, 1967; *Hurry Home*, 1970; *The Lynchers*, 1973; *Hiding Place*, 1981; *Sent for You Yesterday*, 1983; *The Homewood Trilogy*, 1985 (includes *Damballah*, *Hiding Place*, and *Sent for You Yesterday*); *Reuben*, 1987; *Philadelphia Fire*, 1990; *The Cattle Killing*, 1996; *Two Cities*, 1998.

NONFICTION: *Brothers and Keepers*, 1984; *Fatheralong: A Meditation on Fathers and Sons, Race, and Society*, 1994.

BIBLIOGRAPHY

Bell, Bernard W. *The Afro-American Novel and Its Tradition*. Amherst: University of Massachusetts Press, 1987. Bell provides a short but incisive overview of Wideman's evolving concerns as an African American as well as a postmodernist innovator. He also notes Wideman's evocative uses of history as an imaginative paradigm and identifies as his major theme "the conflict between [his protagonists'] ascribed and achieved identities as black men."

Bennion, John. "The Shape of Memory in John Edgar Wideman's *Sent for You Yesterday*." *Black American Literature Forum* 20 (1985): 143-150. While the sole analytic emphasis of this essay is the novel that closes the Homewood Trilogy, it nevertheless offers a useful introduction to major themes in Wideman's fiction.

Berben, Jacqueline. "Beyond Discourse: The Unspoken Versus Words in the Fiction of John Edgar Wideman." *Callaloo* 8 (1985): 525-534. Although this essay is primarily a study of the novel *Hiding Place*, the second volume in the Homewood Trilogy, Berben also discusses the mythic character of Homewood as it unfolds in *Damballah*. Berben's argument that Wideman regularly evaluates his characters according to their ability to deal with truth and break free from self-delusion offers useful insight into all Wideman's writing.

Byerman, Keith Eldon. *John Edgar Wideman: A Study of the Short Fiction*. New York: Twayne, 1998. A critical look at Wideman's short fiction, including interview material. Includes a bibliography and an index.

Coleman, James W. *Blackness and Modernism: The Literary Career of John Edgar Wideman*. Jackson: University Press of Mississippi, 1990. Coleman regards the personal pattern of Wideman's alienation from and return to Homewood as reiterated in his aesthetic movement "from an uncritical acceptance of the forms and themes of mainstream modernism . . . to a black voicing of modernism and postmodernism that is consistent with Afro-American perspectives." The book deals with all Wideman's work through 1989, includes a later interview with him, and appends a brief bibliography of critical sources.

Gysin, Fritz. "John Edgar Wideman: 'Fever.'" In *The African-American Short Story: 1970 to 1990*, edited by Wolfgang Karrer and Barbara Puschmann-Nalenz. Trier, Germany: Wissenschaftlicher Verlag, 1993. A detailed discussion of the title story of Wideman's 1989 collection. Provides historical background for the 1793 Philadelphia yellow fever epidemic and the part African American citizens played in fighting the epidemic. Analyzes the collage structure of the story and Wideman's use of formal narrative devices of compression, repetition, and telescoping of experiences.

Mbalia, Doreatha D. *John Edgar Wideman: Reclaiming the African Personality*. Selinsgrove: Susquehanna University Press, 1995. Discusses, among other topics, Wideman's narrative technique. Includes a bibliography and an index.

O'Brien, John, ed. *Interviews with Black Writers*. New York: Liveright, 1973. In this early interview, Wideman sets forth his interest in aesthetic experimentation at the expense of fictional realism, his penchant for fabulation, and the relationship between his racial subjects and his artistic choices in rendering them.

Samuels, Wilfred D. "Going Home: A Conversation with John Edgar Wideman." *Callaloo* 6 (1983): 40-59. Samuels asks Wideman to discuss his movement from a Eurocentric literary aesthetic to one grounded in African American culture, language, and art forms. Central to that shift has been his imaginative "return to Homewood" and his increasing preoccupation with the emotional complexity of growing up black and male in the United States.

TuSmith, Bonnie, ed. *Conversations with John Edgar Wideman*. Jackson: University Press of Mississippi, 1998. Includes nineteen interviews with Wideman, from 1963 to 1997; covers a wide range of topics about the sources of Wideman's fiction, his perspectives on race in America, his philosophic thought, and his writing technique.

Wideman, John Edgar. "John Edgar Wideman." In *Conversations with American Novelists*, edited by Kay Bonetti, Greg Michaelson, Speer Morgan, Jo Sapp, and Sam Stowers. Columbia: University of Missouri Press, 1997. In this interview by Kay Bonetti, Wideman discusses the oral tales told to him by his aunt, which he developed into the stories in the Homewood Trilogy. Talks about the politics of writing in America, the risks writers have to take to write truthfully about themselves and those they love, and his fiction's concern with brotherhood and sisterhood.

Barbara Kitt Seidman, updated by
Margaret Boe Birns

MARIANNE WIGGINS

Born: Lancaster, Pennsylvania; November 8, 1947

PRINCIPAL SHORT FICTION

Herself in Love and Other Stories, 1987
Learning Urdu, 1990
Bet They'll Miss Us When We're Gone, 1991

OTHER LITERARY FORMS

During Marianne Wiggins's career, she has produced several novels: *Babe* (1975), *Went South* (1980), *Separate Checks* (1984), *John Dollar* (1989), *Eveless Eden* (1995), and *Almost Heaven* (1998).

ACHIEVEMENTS

Marianne Wiggins's works have produced considerable critical comment and recognition. In 1989, she received fiction grants from both the National Endowment for the Arts and the Whiting Foundation. Based on her novels and short stories written since 1989, Wiggins is classified as one of the most imaginative and daring writers of fiction.

BIOGRAPHY

Marianne Wiggins was born November 8, 1947, in Lancaster, Pennsylvania, the daughter of John Wiggins (a grocer and a preacher who also tried farming) and Mary Klonis. Probably because she was born in the Amish region of Pennsylvania, Wiggins has always had a fascination with "utopian" communities. She considered her father the classic American "lost father"; an unsuccessful grocer and a farmer who lost his land, he eventually committed suicide. He was a stern and religious man who attended the church founded by his father. Wiggins's mother, rather paradoxically, was an exotic Greek woman whose family had emigrated to Virginia.

For the first years of Wiggins's life, she was reared as a fundamentalist Christian. Then, at age nine, she was baptized into the Greek Orthodox Church but now professes no religion. Often ill as a child—she had hepatitis and later had a kidney removed—Wiggins spent much of her time reading.

She first married at age seventeen, to Brian Porzak, a film distributor, on June 6, 1965, and they had one child, Lara. Wiggins and Porzak were divorced in 1970, after which Wiggins had a brief career as a stockbroker, trying to support her daughter as a single parent.

On January 23, 1988, Wiggins married Salman Rushdie, a well-known author living in England. Their life together was thrown into disarray, however, with the publication of Rushdie's *The Satanic Verses*, in 1988. With the ensuing uproar that this novel produced in the Islamic world and the subsequent death sentence issued by the Ayatollah Ruhollah Khomeini in Iran, Wiggins and Rushdie had to leave their London home and go into hiding, at times separately, and Wiggins had to cancel a tour promoting her novel *John Dollar*. This enforced exile undermined their relationship, and in 1991, Wiggins came out of hiding and acknowledged that the marriage had failed. That same year, her short-fiction collection *Bet They'll Miss Us When We're Gone*, which contains some of her most autobiographical work, was published.

ANALYSIS

Marianne Wiggins's work focuses largely on the decisions that women face—and make—throughout their lives. For example, most of the characters in Wiggins's *Herself in Love and Other Stories* (1987) are women searching for the meaning of life. Through her skill of expression with the magic and mystery of words, Wiggins creates her own distinctive language and uses her originality and diversity to make eccentric characters and implausible plots seem believable. In addition, when writing a collection of stories, she challenges herself to write a better, more in-depth plot for each subsequent story. Her writing is based on the belief that "it's the role of writers to touch the nerve that otherwise, untouched, lulls [people] to complacency." She has stated that she writes about what she fears, a tenet that she believes is the underlying provocation in the role of the writer.

"Kafkas"

Perhaps one of Wiggins's greatest fears is that of going mad. In "Kafkas," the mental condition of a young woman with a doctorate (presumably in philosophy) deteriorates noticeably while searching for a man by the last name of Kafka who will discuss philosophy with her. She goes about her search by calling information in major cities throughout the United States and asking for all the listings of male Kafkas. She then calls each one, looking for her soul mate, explaining that she is searching for a husband who can give her the name Fran Kafka.

When her sister, Dina, discovers (by way of a seven-hundred-dollar telephone bill) what Fran is doing, she confronts Fran. It becomes clear at this point, however, that regardless of whether this project started off as a mere amusement, it has become very serious indeed. When Dina tells Fran that she must leave, Fran replies that she cannot, "They'll kill me, Dina. Can't you hear them? There are Indians out there."

"Green Park"

Similarly, an undercurrent of violence and madness runs through "Green Park," in which a woman takes back her married lover (who had left her for his wife) only to plan a way of avenging her previous hurts. The power of the story lies in the chilling way in which the main character never lets on to her lover the pain and rage that she is feeling.

As her lover carefully shaves her legs, the main character thinks to herself about what it would be like if he cut her. The reader is held in thrall waiting for the slip that will lead to the

> red ribbon, a bright racine vine in the water, a shimmering curtain, her blood, unfurling itself like a shoot, turning the water not crimson or brilliant, but soft pink and pearly and rose.

His comment that he "gardened like hell to forget" her leads to her thought that there is "an instant when she might have said that he's cut her."

"Among the Impressionists"

"Among the Impressionists" also speaks about lost love, although it is love of a much more fleeting, imaginary kind. Lucy is an elderly woman who fanta-

sizes during her daily trip to the National Gallery (the story is set in London) that she meets a different artist (and sometimes more than one) each day. One day, it is Edgar Degas; another, it is Camille Pissarro. To each artist whom she meets, Lucy tells him—or her, for Lucy often meets Mary Cassatt—that she is meeting her lover.

Lucy's rendezvous, however, is nothing more than a pathetic re-creation of a onetime meeting with a young man whom she dismissed rather abruptly, being too shy to converse with him. Her missed chance has left her, fifty years later, worn down by "haunting regrets." As a love story, "Among the Impressionists" is extremely tragic: a life wasted on a memory. Wiggins finishes the story with Lucy's description to Édouard Manet of what she and her lover do each day when they meet:

> We look at each other. We stare and we stare until the edges of the things around us start to grow invisible. . . . Until the world itself begins to grow invisible, until the only thing we see is what exists between two lovers.

With this fantasy, Lucy has been able to insulate herself from the disappointments of her life, unlike the character Fran, in "Kafkas," who is becoming separated from reality in a much more painful way. Fran stares at her sister, although she is "looking less at Dina than at the *distance* that the walls define, the way they seem to form a ring around their voices."

Bet They'll Miss Us When We're Gone

In *Bet They'll Miss Us When We're Gone*, one of Wiggins's greatest fears is of being left alone. This volume of fiction, set mostly in the United States but also in London, Wales, Amsterdam, and Spain, is a collection of thirteen articulate, remarkably realized stories that portray Wiggins's original, challenging, and eloquent style. Wiggins's ability to move through myriad different perspectives, to use a convincing voice through very different characters, and to manipulate language in a surprising, sometimes shocking manner, is portrayed in this volume of short fiction. By trusting the intelligence of the reader, Wiggins enhances the reader's participation as these stories unfold. Some stories use the backdrop of world events, such as the 1991 Gulf War and the 1986 nuclear accident at Chernobyl, while others focus on family sorrows and the struggle to forgive. Despite the fact that the stories were written over an extended period of time, 1979 to 1990, and deal with a wide variety of scenarios, at the end there is a general thematic relationship that ties them all together: the role that memory plays in human life and behavior, sometimes persisting and sometimes failing.

Each story ends with the date and place where it was written, many of them chronicling the travels and travails of Wiggins's life in exile with Rushdie. These stories are very autobiographical, despite Wiggins's assertion in a 1990 interview that she could not write about their life in hiding for personal and safety reasons.

"Croeso i Gymru" begins with a forceful announcement, the first part of which reads, "We were on the lam in Wales." This sentence perhaps most succinctly sums up Wiggins's feelings from this period (though using different words, she has stated similar ideas during interviews). In addition, when her first-person main character says, "I depend on books for meaning. I depend on them for definition," the reader can believe that the key to Wiggins's emotional survival during this time was, in fact, being able to read and to continue writing.

The strain of the time that Wiggins spent in hiding comes through best in "Croeso i Gymru." There was the worry that people would recognize who she is, for she was allowed to go out (although presumably Rushdie was not). She occupied her time learning Welsh, reading the local, very rural newspapers, and walking among the meadows, inhabited only by sheep and British military personnel out playing war games as Harrier jump jets swooped by overhead. Most of all, however, she and her protectors sit and "wait for one aged psychopath to die."

"Balloons'n Tunes" is an intriguing story about the sorrow of an old man, Carl Tanner, and his interaction with his neighbor, Dolores. After the death of his wife, Tanner realizes how much he misses her and continues to carry on conversations with her as though she were still alive. Dolores, a curious, nosy, but concerned neighbor, is worried and upset by Tanner's babblings. The story centers around their mu-

tual search for meaning in life and for understanding of each other.

As with many of Wiggins's other short fictional stories, "Balloons'n Tunes" seems rather adroit and sometimes haunting. The story appears to be a reflection of losses suffered in Wiggins's own life, including her two divorces, and how to cope with those losses. Left alone and confronted by an apparently interfering neighbor, Tanner must fill the void in his life left by the reality of losing his wife. At times, his memory plays tricks on him, as he tries to forget her death by continuing to talk with her as though she were present. He has a difficult time trying to understand and accept her death, and the lonely, temporary nature of mortality stares him in the face, as those around him, particularly Dolores, perturb his life without understanding him. By taking loved ones for granted when alive, then painfully missing them after their deaths, this story can be interpreted as a literal realization of the title of the book.

Probably the most obviously autobiographical of the *Bet They'll Miss Us When We're Gone* stories, "Grocer's Daughter," was written long before the troubles of 1989, in Martha's Vineyard, in May of 1979. Yet, perhaps it was this rough period that caused Wiggins to remember earlier hurts and hardships. The story interweaves a matter-of-fact narrative with lists and describes Wiggins's father, John, a man whom "life defeated." Wiggins describes him as a man who told her "strange, portenting things: if I ate too much bread, I'd get dandruff." She goes on to flesh out his description with the statement, "He read *Reader's Digest*, *Coronet*, and *Pageant* and didn't believe in evolution."

Yet, this piece is not all humorous anecdotes; Wiggins's motive in writing was also to achieve a healing in herself, for she says,

> There were times I didn't like him. He left abruptly. He left me much unfinished business. . . . I'd like to turn to him today and say, "I love you: too late: I'm sorry: you did the best you could: you were my father: I learned from you: you were an honest man."

Wiggins's writing is at its strongest with these heartfelt remembrances and regrets, for it speaks to the universal feelings that many adult children have upon their parents' deaths. The dedication page for *Bet They'll Miss Us When We're Gone* reads only "remembering my father," but it is this motivation that gives the warmth that infuses the best of Wiggins's work.

OTHER MAJOR WORKS

LONG FICTION: *Babe*, 1975; *Went South*, 1980; *Separate Checks*, 1984; *John Dollar*, 1989; *Eveless Eden*, 1995; *Almost Heaven*, 1998.

BIBLIOGRAPHY

Field, Michele. "Marianne Wiggins." *Publishers Weekly* 235 (February 7, 1989): 57-58. Written just prior to the uproar over *The Satanic Verses*, this article supplies many biographical details, many of which help to give a background for interpreting Wiggins's work. The article also provides a synopsis of Wiggins's writing career as well as what has motivated her "explicit and frightening" writing.

Garrett, George. "On the Lam in Wales." *The New York Times*, June 30, 1991. A review of *Bet They'll Miss Us When We're Gone* that discusses Wiggins's focus on the persistence and failure of memory, the magic and mystery of language, and the pathetic limits of thinking.

James, Caryn. "Marianne Wiggins and Life on the Run." *The New York Times*, April 9, 1991, p. C13. This brief article is partly a discussion of *Bet They'll Miss Us When We're Gone* and partly a commentary on the reasons why Wiggins believed that it was necessary, ultimately, to leave Rushdie. It discusses Wiggins's feelings while in hiding and how the experience affected her writing, especially by increasing and intensifying its autobiographical nature.

_____. "Wiggins: Author, Feminist, and Wife of Rushdie." *The New York Times*, April 4, 1990, p. C17. This article gives biographical details and talks about Wiggins's life in London, her marriage to Salman Rushdie, and her writings in *Herself in Love and Other Stories*. Written early in Wiggins's exile, it reveals much of Wiggins's character and personality. Most notable about her frame of mind at that time was her determination to stand by Rushdie and not to be cowed by anyone.

Kakutani, Michiko. "Life on the Lam with Rushdie." *The New York Times*, June 14, 1991, p. C23. A review of *Bet They'll Miss Us When We're Gone* that praises three of the stories—"Angel," "Rex," and "Grocer's Daughter"—and criticizes the rest as being of interest only because of Wiggins's experience as the wife of exiled Salman Rushdie.

Phillips, Andrew. "A Life in Hiding." *Maclean's* 102 (August 21, 1989): 30. This article is most useful for a brief but clear picture of the events that forced Wiggins and Rushdie into hiding. It also discusses, however, the disruption to Wiggins's life and career, notably that as she seemed poised on the brink of success, she was forced to withdraw from the limelight, and it notes the repercussions that this withdrawal had on her career.

Jo-Ellen Lipman Boon, updated by Alvin K. Benson

JOY WILLIAMS

Born: Chelmsford, Massachusetts; February 11, 1944

PRINCIPAL SHORT FICTION

Taking Care: Short Stories, 1982
Escapes: Stories, 1990
"Craving," 1991
"The Route," 1992
"Marabou," 1993
"Honored Guest," 1994

OTHER LITERARY FORMS

Although Joy Williams is known mainly for her short fiction, she is also the author of the novels *State of Grace* (1973), *The Changeling* (1978), *Breaking and Entering* (1988), and *The Quick and the Dead* (2000) and a book of nonfiction *Florida Keys: A History and Guide* (1986). She has also written travel articles for *Esquire* magazine, including "How to Do and Undo Key West" (February, 1996), "Nantucket Now" (September, 1996), "Desert Flower" (January, 1997), "No Place Like Home" (March, 1997).

ACHIEVEMENTS

Joy Williams has established herself as one of the preeminent practitioners of the short-story form in the United States. Along with Raymond Carver, Richard Ford, and a handful of other writers, she has perfected a style and content which accurately render life in late twentieth century America. It is not a pretty picture she paints: In Williams's stories, characters cannot communicate, couples cannot connect, and children are being abandoned or reared by others.

Williams has been the recipient of numerous awards in her career, including a John Simon Guggenheim Memorial Foundation Fellowship in 1974. Her stories regularly appear in the leading U.S. literary journals–*Esquire*, *The New Yorker*, *Grand Street*—and many have been collected in the annual *The Best American Short Stories* or *Prize Stories: The O. Henry Awards* collections and in other prime anthologies of contemporary American fiction.

BIOGRAPHY

Born in 1944, Joy Williams grew up in the small Maine town of Cape Elizabeth, where both her father and her grandfather were Congregational ministers. She holds degrees from Marietta College, in Ohio, and from the University of Iowa. Married to Rust Hills, the writer and fiction editor at *Esquire*, she has one daughter, Caitlin. She has taught in the writing programs at several leading U.S. universities (including the University of California at Irvine and the University of Arizona) and has settled into homes in Arizona and Florida.

ANALYSIS

Joy Williams is a short-story writer with a dark vision encased in a clean prose style. While a few of her stories have an experimental, almost surrealistic form, and often a wry, ironic tone, the bulk fall into what can be called the realist mode, minimalist division: Williams deals with American family life in the last third of the twentieth century, focusing on troubles, handicaps, and incompletions. She interests readers in these subjects without divulging all the information that they might ordinarily want or need about the characters and their situations. What further distinguishes her stories is a prose style that is clean but highly metaphorical, for the images and motifs of the stories often carry the meaning more deeply than the action or exposition.

Hers is not a reassuring portrait of contemporary American life. The families are often dysfunctional, physically as well as psychologically: parents abandon children, by leaving or by dying, and children wander in life without guidance. Alcohol is a cause of the unhappiness as well as its hoped-for cure. In nearly all her stories, love is being sought but is rarely found and nearly as rarely expressed. Characters seem unable to ask the questions that might free them from their unhappiness; the best they can hope for is an escape to some other state, physical or emotional. Disabilities, addictions, dead animals, arguments in restaurants, and car accidents abound in Williams's stories.

Williams's first collection *Taking Care* contains stories published in the 1970's and early 1980's in *The New Yorker*, *Partisan Review*, *The Paris Review*, *Esquire*, *Ms.*, and other leading vehicles of contemporary American fiction. These stories show a firmness and subtlety that have marked Williams's style over her entire career (although there was probably more range here than in her second collection). The themes that would mark that career are clearly established in this first collection. While many of the stories are riveting in their subject matter, they leave readers with a sense of hollowness and futility. There are few resolutions in Williams, even early in her career, but there are the tensions, violence, and disconnections that mark most of her stories.

"TAKING CARE"

In the title story, Jones, a preacher, is "taking care" of two generations: a wife dying of leukemia and a six-month-old baby girl whom his daughter has left him to care for before fleeing to Mexico. Jones baptizes his granddaughter and then brings his wife back from the hospital; in the last line of the story, "Together they enter the shining rooms"—rooms made "shining" by Jones's love and care. This epiphanic ending, however, cannot erase all the abandonment and death. Jones is surely "taking care" of more than his required load in this life, and there is a heaviness, a spiritual sadness, that is expressed appropriately in Williams's flat, terse prose style.

Other stories in *Taking Care* have similar themes and forms. In "Traveling to Pridesup," three sisters in their eighties and nineties, "in a big house in the middle of Florida," find a baby abandoned in a feed bag on their mailbox. In the journey in their old Mercedes to find someone to help, Lavinia gets them lost, drives hundreds of miles in circles, and finally crashes. In a tragicomic mix reminiscent of Flannery O'Connor, the story ends with a painful revelation, "the recognition that her life and her long, angry journey through it, had been wasteful and deceptive and unnecessary."

"Winter Chemistry," features two students who spy on their teacher every night and inadvertently kill him when they are caught. "Shepherd" concerns a young woman who cannot get over the death of her

German shepherd and who will probably lose her boyfriend because of it. ("'We are all asleep and dreaming, you know,'" he tells her in a speech that might apply to characters in other stories in *Taking Care*. "'If we could ever actually comprehend our true position, we would not be able to bear it, we would have to find a way out.'") In "The Farm," alcohol, infidelities, and the accidental killing of a hitchhiker will destroy the central couple. "Breakfast," too, has many of the stock Williams ingredients: parents who abandon their children, a half-blind dog, and characters who are both alcoholic and lacking direction.

Possibly the only difference in *Taking Care* from Williams's later fiction is that there appears to be more humor in these early stories, and more effort by Williams to perfect a wry, ironic style. ("The Yard Boy," for example, is a surreal caricature of a kind of New Age spiritual character.) Yet the other landmarks are there as well: The style is often flat and cryptic, events and incidents seem to have more a symbolic than a representational quality, and people pass by one another without touching or talking. There is little love in these stories (even in those that are supposedly love stories), but often a violence beneath the surface that is constantly threatening to bubble up and destroy the characters or kill their animals (as in "Preparation for a Collie" or "Woods"). People rarely have names; rather, they are "the woman," "her lover," "the child." Williams writes easily about children, but hers are children who are wandering in an adult world without supervision or love (as in "Train" or "The Excursion.") Williams works here in the great American tradition of Sherwood Anderson's *Winesburg, Ohio* (1919), in which characters become what Anderson called "grotesques." Williams writes of grotesques as well, of bizarre characters who are lost or losing or obsessive, and whom nothing, apparently, will save.

ESCAPES

These elements can be found throughout the title story of Williams's second collection, *Escapes*. The narrator, a young girl, describes the time when her alcoholic mother (abandoned by the father) took her to see a magician. The mother, drunk, wanders onto the stage and has to be removed. Layers of escape, both literal and metaphorical, characterize this story: the father's abandonment of his dysfunctional family; the magician's illusions ("Houdini was more than a magician, he was an escape artist"); the mother's addiction to alcohol; and the daughter's dreams of escaping her lot: "I got out of this situation," Lizzie writes in the last line of the story, "but it took me years."

Williams's later short fiction is unique not only for this bleak view of human nature, in which people are shown trapped and searching for some inexpressible transcendence, but also for a prose style that is both less and more than it appears: less because, like other minimalists whom Williams resembles (such as Raymond Carver and Ann Beattie), she draws only the outlines of the action and leaves the characters' backgrounds to the reader's imagination and more because Williams manipulates metaphors and motifs in such a way that they carry a heavy weight of meaning in her stories. In "Escapes," for example, the old magician's illusion of sawing a woman in half becomes the vehicle for the story's theme: The alcoholic mother tells her daughter that she witnessed that trick performed by Houdini when she was a child. She wanted to be that lady, "sawed in half, and then made whole again!" Her subsequent intrusion into the show by walking onstage is her attempt to escape by realizing that dream, "to go and come back," but the dream is impossible to realize and therefore self-destructive. The usher escorts mother and daughter out of the theater, assuring the drunken woman that she can "pull [herself] through." She will not, however, succeed in reconstructing herself and her life, and in the end, the reader suspects, the daughter will escape only by abandoning the mother.

The stories in *Escapes* thus seem to work at cross-purposes: While the prose style is clean and uncluttered, the motifs and metaphors lead readers to meanings beneath the surface, to a depth that is full of horror and despair. In the second story, "Rot" (first reprinted in the O. Henry Prize collection of 1988), these concerns and formal characteristics continue. Dwight persuades his wife, who is twenty-five years younger than he is, to allow him to park the vintage Thunderbird he has just bought in their living room.

The car is full of rot and rust—a symbol, readers may suspect, of the couple's marriage. The reader learns little about these characters, what they do or where they are headed; instead, symbolism replaces information: The rusting car was found in a parking lot with its owner dead inside it; now Dwight sits in the car in the living room and looks dead.

The other stories in *Escapes* take a similar approach: "The Skater," which was chosen to appear in the 1985 collection *Best American Short Stories*, presents a family, parents and a daughter, on a tour of East Coast prep schools. It slowly becomes apparent that the sickness at the heart of this family is the memory of the daughter—like the skater of the title who glides in and out of the story at several points—who died the previous year; the parents simply want Molly to be away from the sadness of their home.

The young woman in "Lulu" puts an old couple to bed after all three have gotten drunk one morning; she then attempts to drive off with their boa constrictor, apparently searching for love (she wonders, "Why has love eluded me"). In "Health," a twelve-year-old girl is undergoing ultraviolet treatments to help her recover from tuberculosis but is surprised by a man who walks in during one of her tanning sessions, as she lies naked on the couch. The grandmother of "The Blue Men" tries, in part through use of alcohol, to assuage her grief over her dead son, who was executed for murdering a police officer. "The Last Generation," the collection's closing story, depicts a father, numbing his pain over his wife's death through drink and work and neglecting his own children.

Williams's bleak vision is mitigated only by the sureness of her prose and the symbolic poetry of her language. "Bromeliads," in which a young mother abandons her new baby to her parents, becomes the central metaphor of the story's meaning. As the young woman explains, bromeliads are "thick glossy plants with extraordinary flowers. . . . They live on nothing. Just the air and the wind"—a perfect description of the mother herself.

In "White," a couple has moved from Florida to Connecticut to escape the memory of their two babies, who have died. They cannot, however, escape their grief, even in alcohol and evasion. At a party they throw for a departing Episcopal priest, the husband describes a letter that the couple has recently received from the woman's father; after the greeting, the letter contains nothing, "just a page, blank as the day is long." The letter becomes a symbol for the missed communication, the things that are not said and that may in fact be inexpressible, abandonment and death among them.

In the end, readers are left with the bleakness of Williams's stories—despite a minimalist style and a use of metaphor that almost negates that vision. Only "Honored Guest" differs in that it implies affirmation of life through a character's likening those alive to honored guests. Nevertheless, Williams remains one of the more highly regarded short-fiction writers in modern-day America, often anthologized and the recipient of numerous awards. Along with Raymond Carver, Ann Beattie, Richard Ford, and a handful of other contemporaries, she continues to produce works that are read by university students and the general public alike, and younger writers emulate her polished style.

OTHER MAJOR WORKS

LONG FICTION: *State of Grace*, 1973; *The Changeling*, 1978; *Breaking and Entering*, 1988; *The Quick and the Dead*, 2000.

NONFICTION: *Florida Keys: A History and Guide*, 1986.

BIBLIOGRAPHY

Cooper, Rand Richards. "The Dark at the End of the Tunnel." *The New York Times*, January 21, 1990. In this detailed review of *Escapes*, Cooper focuses on the quirky, ominous world they create; discusses several stories, arguing that "The Blue Men" and the title story are the strongest.

Fox, Linda A. "Excellent Guide Unlocks the Mysteries of the Keys." *The Toronto Sun*, January 14, 1998, p. 55. A discussion of Williams's travel guide, *The Florida Keys: A History and a Guide*; notes that Williams's book is full of useful information about wildlife, sea life, and local folklore.

Heller, Zoe. "Amazing Moments from the Production Line." *The Independent*, July 21, 1990, p. 28. In this review of *Escapes*, Heller complains that Williams's style has become a mannerism, but singles out "In the Route" as a story that is more interesting than the other formulaic pieces in the collection.

Hills, Rust. Review of *State of Grace*. *Esquire* 80 (July, 1973): 26, 28. Hills recognizes that Williams has a problem with structure but praises her language: ". . . open the novel to virtually any page and you'll instantly see it—a kind of strange phosphorescent style describing disquieting, dark and funny goings-on. Sentences are brilliant, gorgeous, surprising. . . ."

Kirkus Reviews. Review of *Escapes*. 57 (November 15, 1989): 1633. This anonymous reviewer recognizes that "Williams' weird, seemingly anesthetized, protagonists are usually in flight: from inexorable fate, from the oppressive past, from reality itself."

Kornblatt, Joyce. "Madness, Murder, and the Surrender of Hope." Review of *Taking Care*. *The Washington Post Book World*, March 21, 1982, 4. Nothing her similarity to Flannery O'Connor and Joyce Carol Oates, the reviewer here sees the redemptive qualities of Williams's work, for in the "fragile gestures" of these stories, "we glimpse, merely glimpse, an order of being that eschews randomness, that ascribes value, that insists on love in the face of destructiveness."

Malinowski, Sharon. "Joy Williams." In *Contemporary Authors*, edited by Deborah A. Straub. Vol. 22. Detroit: Gale Research, 1988. A good summary of Williams's career, including long passages from reviews of her novels and her short-story collections through 1982. "In Williams's fiction, the ordinary events of daily life are susceptible to bizarre turns of horror and individuals are lost in their private selves, unable to comprehend the forces which shape their lives. Although Williams occasionally alleviates her bleak vision with humor, a sense of hopelessness and despair remains central to her work."

Williams, Joy. "Joy Williams." Interview by Molly McQuade. *Publishers Weekly* 237 (January 26,

1990): 400-401. This brief but wide-ranging interview allows Williams to talk about her career and her sense of her own writing; words, for example, are intended "to affect the reader in unexpected, mysterious, subterranean ways. The literal surface has to be *very* literal—smooth and exact—yet what makes it strange is what's teeming underneath. Stories should be something other than they appear to be. . . . They should make you uncomfortable."

David Peck, updated by
Mary H. Bruce

TENNESSEE WILLIAMS

Born: Columbus, Mississippi; March 26, 1911
Died: New York, New York; February 25, 1983

PRINCIPAL SHORT FICTION
One Arm and Other Stories, 1948
Hard Candy: A Book of Stories, 1954
The Knightly Quest: A Novella and Four Short Stories, 1967
Eight Mortal Ladies Possessed: A Book of Stories, 1974
Collected Stories, 1985

OTHER LITERARY FORMS
In addition to his three dozen collected and uncollected stories, Tennessee Williams wrote two novels, a book of memoirs, a collection of essays, two volumes of poetry, numerous short plays, a screenplay, and more than twenty full-length dramas. Among the most important of his plays are *The Glass Menagerie* (1944), *A Streetcar Named Desire* (1947), *Cat on a Hot Tin Roof* (1955), and *The Night of the Iguana* (1961).

ACHIEVEMENTS
Tennessee Williams's most obvious achievements in literature lie in the field of drama, where he is considered by many to be America's greatest playwright, a standing supported by two Pulitzer Prizes, a Commonwealth Award, a Medal of Freedom (presented by President Jimmy Carter), and an election in 1952 to a lifetime membership in the National Institute of Arts and Letters. Williams himself, however, felt that his short fiction contained some of his best writing. Indeed, besides stories appearing in his own collections, Williams published stories in many of America's most prestigious magazines, including *The New Yorker* and *Esquire*, and many have been selected for various anthologies, including three in Martha Foley's *Best American Short Stories* annual anthologies. Williams's short stories and plays alike dramatize the plight of the "fugitive," the sensitive soul punished by a harsh, uncaring world; in the stories, however, readers find specific and frequent voice given to a theme and subject only hinted at in Williams's drama, at least until his later, less memorable, plays: the plight of the homosexual in a bigoted society.

BIOGRAPHY
Descended on his mother's side from a southern minister and on his father's from Tennessee politicians, Thomas Lanier (Tennessee) Williams moved with his family from Mississippi to St. Louis shortly after World War I. He attended the University of Missouri and Washington University, finally graduating from the University of Iowa. After odd jobs in the warehouse of a shoe factory, ushering at a movie house, and even a stint screenwriting in Hollywood, he turned full-time writer in the early 1940's, encouraged by grants from the Group Theatre and Rockefeller Foundation. Despite purchasing a home in Key West, Florida, in 1950, Williams spent most of the remainder of his life living for short periods in a variety of locales in Europe, the United States, and Mexico.

His two Pulitzer Prizes early in his career, plus four Drama Critics Circle Awards, solidified Williams's reputation as a playwright; the quality of his writing declined, however, after the early 1960's, in great part as a result of drug dependency. He died, alone, in a New York City hotel room in 1983.

ANALYSIS

Although during his lifetime Tennessee Williams was commonly held to be without peer among America's—many would say the world's—playwrights, he began his career writing short fiction, with a story entitled "The Vengeance of Nitocris" in *Weird Tales* in 1928. As late as 1944, when his first theatrical success was in rehearsal, George Jean Nathan reportedly observed that Williams "didn't know how to write drama, that he was really just a short-story writer who didn't understand the theatre." In proportion to the worldwide audience familiar with Williams's dramas, only a handful know more than a story or two, usually from among the ones later transformed into stage plays. Seven of Williams's full-length dramas, in fact, had their genesis in the fiction: *The Glass Menagerie* in "Portrait of a Girl in Glass"; *Summer and Smoke* (1947) in "The Yellow Bird"; *Cat on a Hot Tin Roof* in "Three Players of a Summer Game"; *The Night of the Iguana* and *Kingdom of Earth* (1968) in stories of the same names; *The Milk Train Doesn't Stop Here Anymore* (1963) in "Man Bring This Up Road"; and *Vieux Carré* (1977) in "The Angel in the Alcove" and "Grand."

"THE NIGHT OF THE IGUANA"

The play *The Night of the Iguana* is sufficiently different from its progenitor to indicate how Williams rethought his material in adapting it to another medium. Both works portray a spinsterish artist, Miss Jelkes; but while Hannah in the play has fought for and achieved inner peace, Edith's harsher name in the story belies her edginess, neurosis, and lack of "interior poise." Having channeled her own "morbid energy" into painting, she discerns in the contrasting "splash of scarlet on snow . . . a flag of her own unsettled components" warring within her. When a servant at the Costa Verde hotel tethers an iguana to the veranda, Edith recoils hysterically from such brutal-

Tennessee Williams (Sam Shaw, courtesy of New Directions Publishing Corp.)

ity against "one of God's creatures," taking its suffering as proof of a grotesque "universe . . . designed by the Marquis de Sade."

This picture of cosmic indifference, even malevolence, occurs in a handful of Williams's stories, most notably in "The Malediction," in which the lonely Lucio exists in a meaningless universe verging on the absurd, ruled by a God "Who felt that something was wrong but could not correct it, a man Who sensed the blundering sleep-walk of time and hostilities of chance" and "had been driven to drink." Edith finds God personified in a violent storm "like a giant bird lunging up and down on its terrestrial quarry, a bird with immense white wings and beak of godlike fury."

Her fellow guests at the hotel are two homosexual writers. Squeamish and yet attracted by the forbidden nature of their relationship, Edith insinuates herself into their company only to become the object of a desperate attack on her "demon of virginity" by the older of the two. Although she has earlier hinted that she always answers, with understanding, cries for help from a fellow sufferer, she ferociously fends off his pathetic advances, metaphorically associated with the predatory "bird of blind white fury." Afterward, however, once the younger man has mercifully cut loose the iguana, Edith feels her own "rope of loneliness had also been severed," and—instead of drawing back in "revulsion" from "the spot of dampness" left on her belly by the older writer's semen—exclaims "Ah, life," evidently having reached through this epiphanic moment a new acceptance and integration of her sexuality. Yet, unlike Hannah, whose compassionate response to Shannon in the play is for him a saving grace and who can affirm, along with Williams, that "Nothing human disgusts me unless it's unkind, violent," Edith's inability to answer unselfishly the older man's need—the cardinal sin in Williams—may have permanently maimed him by destroying his self-respect.

Williams does not always capitalize fully on his gift for writing dialogue in his stories. For all its interest in light of the later play, the pace of "The Night of the Iguana" is curiously desultory and enervated, which might not have been true if the story had been written from Edith's point of view. Williams does indeed prove adept at handling first-person narration in several autobiographical tales, whose content seems hardly distinguishable at times from the sections of the *Memoirs* (1975).

"THE RESEMBLANCE BETWEEN A VIOLIN CASE AND A COFFIN"

He can, however, become annoyingly self-conscious when, in authorial intrusions analogous to the nonrepresentational techniques that deliberately destroy the illusion of reality in his dramas, he breaks the narrative line in a dozen or so stories to interject comments about himself as writer manipulating his materials, sometimes apologizing for his awkwardness in handling the short-story form, or for playing too freely with chronology or radically shifting tone. At times these stories provide some notion of Williams's aesthetic theories and practice, as when, in "Three Players of a Summer Game," for example, he discusses the method by which the artist orders experience by a process that distorts and "yet . . . may be

closer than a literal history could be to the hidden truth of it." These "metafictional" asides might indicate his conception of character portrayal. On that point—while without qualms at employing clinical details when necessary—Williams insists, in "Hard Candy," on the need for "indirection" and restraint rather than "a head-on violence that would disgust and destroy" if he is to remain nonjudgmental and respect the "mystery" at the heart of character.

An almost identical comment occurs in "The Resemblance Between a Violin Case and a Coffin," part of a small group of *rites de passage* stories in the Williams canon. The story centers on a love triangle of sorts as the young narrator faces the destruction of the "magical intimacy" with his pianist sister as she enters adolescence—that "dangerous passage" between the "wild country of childhood" and the "uniform world of adults"—and turns her attentions towards a fellow musician, Richard Miles. It is as if she has deserted the narrator and "carried a lamp into another room [he] could not enter." He resents the "radiant" Richard, but also feels a frightening prepubescent physical attraction for the older boy. Like many of Williams's adult neurotics whose libidinous desires rebel against their Puritan repressions, the narrator longs to touch Richard's skin, yet recoils in shame and guilt from the boy's offer of his hand as if it were somehow "impure." Seeing Richard play the violin, however, provides an epiphany as the narrator "learns the will of life to transcend the single body" and perceives the connection between Eros and Thanatos. For the narrator equates the act of playing the phallic violin with "making love," and the violin case to "a little black coffin made for a child or doll." He mourns the loss of youth and innocence and the birth of the knowledge of sin and death.

Tom, the authorial voice in *The Glass Menagerie*, confesses to "a poet's weakness for symbols," and one of Williams's own hallmarks has always been an extensive use of visual stage symbolism—"the natural speech of drama." As he remarks in one of his essays, it can "say a thing more directly and simply and beautifully than it could be said in words"; he employs symbols extensively, however, in only a handful of stories, although he does rely heavily on figurative language. In the earlier stories the imagery is ordinarily controlled and striking, as, for example, in this line (reminiscent of Karl Shapiro's "cancer, simple as a flower, blooms") describing the doctor's tumor from "Three Players of a Summer Game": "An awful flower grew in his brain like a fierce geranium that shattered its pot." In the more recent tales, however, Williams's diction frequently becomes overwrought and demonstrates some lack of control, falling into what he criticizes elsewhere in the same essay as "a parade of images for the sake of images."

If the mood of "The Resemblance Between a Violin Case and a Coffin" is tender and elegiac, the tone of a much later *rite de passage* story, "Completed," is chilling, but no less haunting and memorable. Miss Rosemary McCord, a student at Mary, Help a Christian School, is a withdrawn debutante subjected by her unsympathetic mother to a pathetic and bizarre coming-out dance. The onset of menstruation has been late in coming for Rosemary, and when it finally does arrive, she is pitifully unprepared for it. Ironically, the fullness of physical development in Rosemary coincides with a death wish; her only "purpose in life is to complete it quick." Her one understanding relative, the reclusive Aunt Ella, deliberately retreats from the external world through morphine; the drug brings her comforting apparitions of the Virgin Mary and tears of peace. Rosemary goes to live with her, aware that she has been taken captive and yet willingly submissive, ready to be calmed through drugs and her own reassuring visions of the Virgin. Her life—apparently the latest of several variations on that of Williams's own sister—is over before it began. Perhaps it is, however, only in such a sheltered, illusory life that this fragile, sensitive girl can exist.

"SABBATHA AND SOLITUDE"

The other "passage" that threads through Williams's stories is that from life to death, obsessed as he is with what he terms "a truly awful sense of impermanence," with the debilitating effects of time on both physical beauty and one's creative powers, and the sheer tenacity necessary if one is to endure at least spiritually undefeated. In "Sabbatha and Solitude," the aging poetess (undoubtedly semi-autobiographical) finds that the process of composition is a

trial not unlike the Crucifixion that results only in "a bunch of old repeats," while in the picaresque "Two on a Party," the blond and balding queen and hack screenwriter exist at the mercy of that "worst of all enemies . . . the fork-tailed, cloven-hoofed, pitchfork-bearing devil of Time."

"COMPLETED"

"Completed" is one of Williams's few later stories—"Happy August the Tenth" is another—that can stand alongside some of his earliest as a fully successful work. Just as there was a noticeable diminution in the power of his later dramas compared with the ones from *The Glass Menagerie* through *The Night of the Iguana*, so, too, each successive volume of short fiction was less impressive than its predecessor. As Williams's vision of the universe darkened and became more private, the once elegiac tone acquired a certain stridency and sharp edge; and as Williams developed a tough, self-protective shell of laughter as a defense against his detractors, some of the dark humor—what he once called the "jokes of the condemned"—became directed towards the pathetic grotesques who increasingly peopled his works, whereas once there was only compassion.

"DESIRE AND THE BLACK MASSEUR"

Thus, two of the most representative stories, "One Arm" and "Desire and the Black Masseur," neither of which, significantly, has ever been dramatized, appeared in his first collection. Unquestionably the most macabre of all his tales is "Desire and the Black Masseur," which details the fantastic, almost surreal sadomasochistic relationship between the insecure, sexually repressed Anthony Burns and an unnamed black masseur at a men's bath. Burns, whose name blends that of a Christian saint with the suggestion of consummation by fire—here metaphoric—suffers from an overly acute awareness of his own insignificance, as well as of his separateness and lack of completeness as a human being. Williams views the latter as an inescapable fact of the human condition and proposes three means available to compensate for it: art, violent action, or surrendering oneself to brutal treatment at the hands of others. Burns chooses the third path, submitting himself as if in a dream, finding at the punishing hands of the masseur first pain, then orgasmic pleasure, and ultimately death. Although the masseur thus secures a release from his pent-up hatred of his white oppressors, this tale should not be construed as a social comment reflecting Williams's attitude toward black/white relations, hardly even peripherally a concern in his work, despite his being a southern writer.

Blacks figure importantly in only two other stories. In the ribald "Miss Coynte of Greene," the title character's long-frustrated female eroticism erupts into nymphomania, her pleasure intensified by the dark skin of her sexual partners. In "Mama's Old Stucco House," Williams's gentlest foray into the black/white terrain, the failed artist Jimmy Krenning is cared for physically and emotionally after his own mother's death by the black girl Brinda and her Mama, the latter having always functioned as his surrogate mother.

That "Desire and the Black Masseur" is to be read on levels other than the literal appears clear when Williams places its climax at the end of the Lenten Season. The death and devouring of Burns becomes a ritual of expiation, a kind of black mass and perversion of the sacrifice on Calvary, even accomplished in biblical phraseology. Indeed, counterpointed with it is a church service during which a self-proclaimed Fundamentalist preacher exhorts his congregation to a frenzy of repentance. What Williams has written, then, is not only a psychological study of man's subconscious desires and an allegory of the division between innocence and evil within all men but also a parable exposing how excessive emphasis on guilt and the need for punishment at the hands of a vengeful God have destroyed the essential New Testament message of love and forgiveness. So Burns's strange rite of atonement stands as a forceful indictment of a Puritanism that creates a dark god of hate as a reflection of one's own obsession with evil, which is one of the recurrent emphases in almost all of Williams's important dramas, especially *Suddenly Last Summer* (1958) and *The Night of the Iguana*.

"ONE ARM"

Something of the obverse, the possibility for transcending one's knowledge of evil and isolation, occurs in "One Arm," the quintessential—and perhaps the finest—Williams story, in which can be discerned nearly all the central motifs that adumbrate not only his fiction but also his plays. Oliver Winemiller, a former light heavyweight champion who in an accident two years earlier lost an arm, is one of Williams's "fugitive kind," a lonely misfit, cool, impassive, now tasting, like Brick in *Cat on a Hot Tin Roof*, "the charm of the defeated." Since all he possessed was his "Apollo-like beauty," after his physical mutilation he undergoes a psychological and emotional change; feeling that he has lost "the center of his being," he is filled with self-loathing and disgust. He enters on a series of self-destructive sexual encounters, finally committing a murder for which he is sentenced to die.

While in confinement awaiting execution, he receives letters from all over the country from his male lovers, confessing that he had aroused deep feelings in them, that he had effected a "communion" with them that would have been, if he had only recognized it, a means of "personal integration" and "salvation." If it was not until very late in his dramas that Williams openly treated homosexuality with sympathy, in his stories his unapologetic and compassionate attitude existed from the very first. Oliver's epiphany, that he had been loved, liberates him from his self-imposed insularity; ironically, however, this rebirth makes his approaching death harder to accept. On the eve of his execution, he recognizes that the Lutheran minister who visits him has used religion as an escape from facing his own sexuality, and he desperately hopes that by forcing the minister to come to terms with himself and his "feelings" he can thereby somehow repay his debt to all those who had earlier responded to him with kindness. The minister, however, recognizing a forbidden side of himself and still suffering guilt over his adolescent sexual awakening during a dream of a golden panther, which Oliver reminds him of, refuses to give Oliver a massage and rushes from his cell. Oliver goes to his execution with dignity, gripping the love letters tightly between his things as a protection from aloneness.

The doctors performing the autopsy see in Oliver's body the "nobility" and purity of an "antique sculpture." Yet Williams reminds his readers in the closing line that "death has never been much in the way of completion." Although the work of art is immutable, it is not alive as only the emotionally responsive person can be, for the true artist in Williams is the person who goes out unselfishly to answer the cry for help of others, and the real work of art is the bond of communion that is formed by that response. Thus "One Arm" incorporates virtually all of Williams's major attitudes, including his somewhat sentimental valuation of the lost and lonely; his romantic glorification of physical beauty and worship of sexuality as a means of transcending aloneness; his castigation of Puritan repression and guilt that render one selfish and judgmental; and his Hawthornian abhorrence of the underdeveloped heart that prevents one from breaking out of the shell of the ego to respond with infinite compassion to all God's misbegotten creatures.

Although Williams's stories, with their frequent rhetorical excesses, their sometimes awkward narrative strategies, and their abrupt shifts in tone, technically do not often approach the purity of form of Oliver's statue, they do, nevertheless—as all good fiction must—surprise the reader with their revelations of the human heart and demand that the reader abandon a simplistic perspective and see the varieties of human experience. What in the hands of other writers might seem a too specialized vision, frequently becomes in Williams's work affecting human and humane.

OTHER MAJOR WORKS

LONG FICTION: *The Roman Spring of Mrs. Stone*, 1950; *Moise and the World of Reason*, 1975.

PLAYS: *Battle of Angels*, pr. 1940; *This Property Is Condemned*, pb. 1941 (one act); *The Lady of Larkspur Lotion*, pb. 1942 (one act); *The Glass Menagerie*, pr. 1944; *Twenty-seven Wagons Full of Cotton*, pb. 1945 (one act); *You Touched Me*, pr. 1945 (with Donald Windham); *Summer and Smoke*, pr. 1947; *A Streetcar Named Desire*, pr., pb. 1947; *American Blues*, pb. 1948 (collection); *Five Short Plays*, pb. 1948; *The Long Stay Cut Short: Or, The Unsatisfactory Supper*, pb. 1948 (one act); *I Rise in Flame, Cried the Phoenix*, pb. 1951 (one act); *The Rose Tat-*

too, pr., pb. 1951; *Camino Real*, pr., pb. 1953; *Cat on a Hot Tin Roof*, pr., pb. 1955; *Orpheus Descending*, pr. 1957 (revision of *Battle of Angels*); *Suddenly Last Summer*, pr., pb. 1958; *The Enemy: Time*, pb. 1959; *Sweet Bird of Youth*, pr., pb. 1959 (based on *The Enemy: Time*); *Period of Adjustment*, pr. 1959; *The Night of the Iguana*, pr., pb. 1961; *The Milk Train Doesn't Stop Here Anymore*, pr. 1963 (revised); *The Eccentricities of a Nightingale*, pr., pb. 1964 (revision of *Summer and Smoke*); *Slapstick Tragedy: The Mutilated and The Gnädiges Fräulein*, pr., 1966 (one acts); *The Two-Character Play*, pr. 1967; *The Seven Descents of Myrtle*, pr., pb. 1968 (as *Kingdom of Earth*); *In the Bar of a Tokyo Hotel*, pr. 1969; *Confessional*, pb. 1970; *Dragon Country*, pb. 1970 (collection); *The Theatre of Tennessee Williams*, pb. 1971-1981 (7 volumes); *Out Cry*, pr. 1971 (revision of *The Two-Character Play*); *Small Craft Warnings*, pr., p6 1972 (revision of *Confessional*); *Vieux Carré*, pr. 1977; *A Lovely Sunday for Creve Coeur*, pr. 1979; *Clothes for a Summer Hotel*, pr. 1980; *A House Not Meant to Stand*, pr. 1981.

SCREENPLAYS: *The Glass Menagerie*, 1950 (with Peter Berneis); *A Streetcar Named Desire*, 1951 (with Oscar Saul); *The Rose Tattoo*, 1955 (with Hal Kanter); *Baby Doll*, 1956; *The Fugitive Kind*, 1960 (with Meade Roberts, based on *Orpheus Descending*); *Suddenly Last Summer*, 1960 (with Gore Vidal); *Stopped Rocking and Other Screenplays*, 1984.

POETRY: *In the Winter of Cities*, 1956; *Androgyne, Mon Amour*, 1977.

NONFICTION: *Memoirs*, 1975; *Where I Love: Selected Essays*, 1978.

BIBLIOGRAPHY

Falk, Signi Lenea. *Tennessee Williams*. 2d ed. Boston: Twayne, 1978. Though devoting most of her attention to Williams's plays, Falk addresses many of the short stories. Falk's discussions of "One Arm," "Desire and the Black Masseur," and "Portrait of a Girl in Glass" are especially interesting. Contains a useful, though dated, bibliography.

Leverich, Lyle. *The Unknown Tennessee Williams*. New York: Crown Publishers, 1995. This first volume of a two-volume biography traces Williams's life for the first thirty-three years. Draws on previously unpublished letters, journals, and notebooks. Discusses Williams's focus on how society has a destructive influence on sensitive people and his efforts to change drama into an unrealistic form.

Martin, Robert A., ed. *Critical Essays on Tennessee Williams*. New York: G. K. Hall, 1997. An excellent, accessible collection of criticism of Williams's works.

Roudané, Matthew C., ed. *The Cambridge Companion to Tennessee Williams*. Cambridge, England: Cambridge University Press, 1997. Contains copious amounts of information on Williams and his works.

Spoto, Gary. *The Kindness of Strangers: The Life of Tennessee Williams*. Boston: Little, Brown, 1985. Spoto's study is the closest to a definitive biography of Williams. Provides, however, only passing mention of the short stories. A brief bibliography follows the text.

Tharpe, Jac, ed. *Tennessee Williams: A Tribute*. Jackson: University Press of Mississippi, 1977. A collection of fifty-three essays on various aspects of Williams's art. Many note Williams's short fiction in passing, and four are fully (or in the main) devoted to the short fiction. Contains a bibliography.

Vannatta, Dennis. *Tennessee Williams: A Study of the Short Fiction*. Boston: Twayne, 1988. The only book-length study of Williams's short fiction. Contains a selection of essays concerning Williams's short fiction by various scholars and a selection of Williams's own letters, essays, and reviews.

Woodhouse, Reed. *Unlimited Embrace: A Canon of Gay Fiction, 1945-1995*. Amherst: University of Massachusetts Press, 1998. Includes a chapter on Williams's gay short stories; claims the most astonishing thing about the stories is their lack of special pleading, that while they are not graphic, they are not apologetic for their homosexuality. Provides an extended analysis of the story "Hard Candy."

Thomas P. Adler, updated by Dennis Vannatta

WILLIAM CARLOS WILLIAMS

Born: Rutherford, New Jersey; September 17, 1883
Died: Rutherford, New Jersey; March 4, 1963

PRINCIPAL SHORT FICTION
The Knife of the Times and Other Stories, 1932
Life Along the Passaic River, 1938
Make Light of It: Collected Stories, 1950
The Farmers' Daughters: The Collected Stories of William Carlos Williams, 1961
The Doctor Stories, 1984

OTHER LITERARY FORMS

Best known as a poet, William Carlos Williams nevertheless wrote in a variety of literary forms (some of them defying categorization) including poetry, novels, short stories, prose poetry, essays, autobiography, and plays. *Paterson*, his extended poem published in four separate volumes (1946-1951), with a fifth volume serving as a commentary (1958), is his most famous and enduring work.

ACHIEVEMENTS

William Carlos Williams received numerous awards, including the Dial Award in 1926, the National Book Award in 1950, the Bollingen Award in 1953, and, posthumously, the Pulitzer Prize in poetry in 1963.

BIOGRAPHY

After attending public schools in New Jersey,

spending time in Europe, and then finishing high school in New York, William Carlos Williams enrolled in the University of Pennsylvania's Medical School in 1902. While completing his M.D. there, he met Ezra Pound, Hilda Doolittle, and the painter Charles Demuth. In 1910, he began work as a general practitioner in Rutherford, New Jersey; in addition to this practice, from 1925 on he became a pediatrician at Passaic General Hospital. Williams held these positions until several strokes forced him to retire in 1951. His medical and literary careers always coexisted. In 1909, he had his first volume, *Poems*, privately published. As his reputation grew, he traveled to Europe several times and encountered such writers as James Joyce, Gertrude Stein, and Ford Madox Ford. He married Florence Herman in 1912, and they had two sons. Williams died on March 4, 1963, in his beloved Rutherford.

ANALYSIS

William Carlos Williams was one of the major figures of literary modernism whose peers included Ezra Pound and Wallace Stevens. Highly influenced by the visual arts and the imagist movement, Williams's work was marked by a rejection of metaphysics, characterized by his famous dictum: "No ideas/ But in things." Williams's objective approach to literature is reflected in the coarse realism of his short stories. His prose shares the basic principles of his poetic theory: use of an American idiom, adherence to a locale, communication through specifics, and belief in organic form. The pastiche effects of Williams's poetry and prose had a profound influence on the next generation of American literary modernists, particularly the so-called Objectivist School, which included Louis Zukofsky, George Oppen, Carl Rakosi, and Charles Reznikoff.

M. L. Rosenthal claims that William Carlos Williams's short stories "are often vital evocations of ordinary American reality—its toughness, squalor, pathos, intensities." As such, this short fiction tends to exhibit distinctive characteristics. First, its style is the American idiom, with heavy reliance on dialogue and speech rhythm. Second, Williams inevitably writes of his own locale and stresses the Depression's dramatic effect on ordinary working people. Third, as he shows in his poem "A Sort of a Song," there should be "No ideas/ But in things"; in other words, details should suggest underlying ideas, not vice versa. Fourth, Williams himself is often present, but as a doctor, never as a poet; thus biography and autobiography constitute important plot elements. Last, the author allows plot to develop organically, which affects length (the tales range from one to thirty pages) and structure (the stories may appear diffuse or highly compressed).

Williams published two main short-story anthologies: *The Knife of the Times and Other Stories* and *Life Along the Passaic River*. In 1950, he collected these and other stories into a single volume called *Make Light of It*; then, in 1961, this was superseded by his complete collected stories entitled *The Farmers' Daughters*. Although these stories may indicate progressive technical sophistication or experimentation, they all treat "the plight of the poor" (as Williams says on several occasions) or the physician's frequently ambiguous role of healing the sick within an infected society.

"OLD DOC RIVERS"

On the choice of title for his first short-story anthology, Williams observes "The times—that was the knife that was killing them" (the poor). A typical story is "Old Doc Rivers," which provides a full background on one rural general practitioner. It also contains a strong autobiographical element because the narrator is a younger doctor (apparently Williams). An enormously complex picture emerges of Doc Rivers: efficient, conscientious, humane, yet simultaneously crude, cruel, and addicted to drugs and alcohol. The story builds this portrait by piling up specifics about the physician's personal and professional lives and interweaving case studies among the young doctor-narrator's comments. The narrator is astonished by River's psychological sharpness, intuition for the correct diagnosis, and ability to inspire blind faith in his patients. As with many Williams tales, the reader's moral response is ambiguous, for when sober, Rivers is not a good doctor, yet when drunk or doped, he is at least as good as anyone else. The plot follows a roughly chronological structure which charts Rivers's gradual mental and physical decline. This story's particular strengths are its narrator voice, concrete details, re-creation of dialogue, and exploration of the doctor-patient relationship.

"JEAN BEICKE"

Williams further considers the physician-patient relationship in "Jean Beicke" and "A Face of Stone," representative of his second short-fiction collection. Told by a pediatrician-narrator (but this time an established, not a beginning, doctor), "Jean Beicke" is set in a children's ward during the Depression and recounts the story of a "scrawny, misshapen, worthless piece of humanity." Although Jean is desperately ill, she wins the hearts of the physicians and nurses by her sheer resilience: "As sick as she was," the narrator marvels, "she took her grub right on time every three hours, a big eight ounce bottle of milk and digested it perfectly." Yet little Jean's symptoms puzzle the medics, and despite initial improvement, she finally dies. Up to this point, doctors and readers alike have been ignorant of her previous history, but when her mother and aunt visit the dying infant, it is learned that she is the third child of a woman whose husband deserted her. As her aunt says, "It's better off dead—never was any good anyway." After the autopsy, the doctors discover they have completely misdiagnosed Jean. The storyteller ends the tale like this:

> I called the ear man and he came down at once. A clear miss, he said. I think if we'd gone in there earlier, we'd have saved her.
> For what? said I. Vote the straight Communist ticket. Would it make us any dumber? said the ear man.

Williams thought "Jean Beicke" was "the best short story I ever wrote." One reason is its involved narrator, whose sophisticated social conscience (why cure these Depression babies only to return them to a sick society?) contrasts with the nurses' instinctive (but perhaps naïve) humanitarianism. The story's careful structure takes us from external details—Jean's misshapen body, tiny face, and pale blue eyes—to internal ones—in the postmortem—and so suggests that beneath society's superficial ills lie fundamental, perhaps incurable, troubles. Once again, Williams shows his skill for catching the speech patterns of ordinary Americans, especially in the monologue of Jean's aunt. Finally, the author's main achievement is to individualize yet not sentimentalize Jean and to dramatize her life-and-death struggle so that it matters to him—and to the reader.

"A FACE OF STONE"

In "A Face of Stone," the doctor-narrator becomes the main character. A harried family doctor, he finds himself at the end of a busy morning confronted by a young Jewish couple. The husband, one of "the presuming poor," insists that he examine their baby, while the wife maintains an expressionless, stony face. As the doctor approaches the baby boy, his mother clutches him closer and is extremely reluctant to relinquish him. Frustrated and tired, the doctor is brusque and patronizing. When he eventually looks at the child, he discovers that it is quite healthy. During the winter, the people request a house call, but he refuses to go; then, in the spring, they return and still protest that the child is unwell. Conquering his annoyance at their persistence, the family doctor checks the boy and says that he simply needs to be fed regularly and weaned.

Now the physician expects the consultation to finish, but the young Jew asks him to examine his wife. The doctor is by this time exhausted and furious; however, he starts to check this passive, poverty-stricken, physically unattractive woman. Then, almost accidentally, he discovers she is a Polish Jew who has lost her whole family. Immediately, he forgets her ugliness, grasps her intense anxiety for her baby, and realizes the strong bond between wife and husband: "Suddenly I understood his half shameful love for the woman and at the same time the extent of her reliance on him. I was touched." The woman smiles for the first time when the doctor prescribes painkillers for her varicose veins and she senses that she can trust him.

This story effectively dramatizes the shifting reactions between patients and doctors as they try to establish a viable relationship. Often, a physician may exploit his position of power (as this one does at the beginning) and forget that his clients are human. If he does, he turns into Doc Rivers at his worst. The best relationship occurs when both parties move beyond stereotypes to view each other as individuals. Because the doctor narrates the tale, the reader follows his process of discovery, so when he stops stereotyping the couple, the reader does too. Williams once again successfully uses dialogue to convey character interaction. Also, as in "Jean Beicke," he reveals people through detail (such as the woman's ripped dress, bowlegs, and high-heeled, worn-out shoes).

"THE FARMERS' DAUGHTERS"

Williams composed few notable short stories after *Life Along the Passaic River*, mainly because he diverted his energies into longer projects (novels, plays, and *Paterson*). From the early 1940's to the mid-1950's, however, he worked on a long short story which he eventually called "The Farmers' Daughters" (and whose title he used for his collected short fiction). The title characters are Helen and Margaret, two southern women who have been (and continue to be) betrayed by their men. Their similar background and experience form the basis of an enduring, unshakable friendship that terminates only with Margaret's death. Technically, this is one of Williams's best stories: It unfolds quickly in a "paragraph technique" as the narrator—once more a doctor—re-creates the women's conversations and letters, then links them chronologically with his own comments. The teller refers to himself in the third person, so that most of the time the story progresses through dialogue. This extract, in which Margaret and the doctor chat, illustrates the strength of using direct, idiomatic speech:

What's your favorite flower, Margaret?
Why?
I just want to know.
What's yours?
No. Come on—don't be so quick on the trigger so early in the evening. I think I can guess. Petunias! (emphasizing the second syllable.) God knows I've seen enough of them. No. Red roses. Those are really what I love.

Unlike Williams's previous stories, "The Farmers' Daughters" relies on complex character depiction and development rather than on plot or theme.

Most short-story writers merely write, but Wil-liams left behind theoretical as well as practical evidence of his interest in the genre. *A Beginning on the Short Story (Notes)* (1950) outlines his basic tenets: truthfulness, unsentimentality, and simplicity. "The finest short stories," he states, "are those that raise . . . one particular man or woman, from that Gehenna, the newspapers, where at last all men are equal, to the distinction of being an individual." From the herd of humanity, Williams succeeds in individualizing Doc Rivers, little Jean Beicke, the Jewish couple, Margaret, Helen, and all his various doctor-narrators.

OTHER MAJOR WORKS

LONG FICTION: *The Great American Novel*, 1923; *A Voyage to Pagany*, 1928; *White Mule*, 1937; *In the Money*, 1940; *The Build-Up*, 1952.

PLAYS: *A Dream of Love*, pb. 1948; *Many Loves and Other Plays*, pb. 1961.

POETRY: *Poems*, 1909; *The Tempers*, 1913; *Al Que Quiere!*, 1917; *Kora in Hell: Improvisations*, 1920; *Sour Grapes*, 1921; *Spring and All*, 1923; *Last Nights of Paris*, 1929 (translation with Elena Williams); *Collected Poems, 1921-1931*, 1934; *An Early Martyr and Other Poems*, 1935; *Adam & Eve & the City*, 1936; *The Complete Collected Poems of William Carlos Williams, 1906-1938*, 1938; *The Broken Span*, 1941; *The Wedge*, 1944; *Paterson*, 1946-1958; *The Clouds*, 1948; *Selected Poems*, 1949; *Collected Later Poems*, 1950, 1963; *Collected Earlier Poems*, 1951; *The Desert Music and Other Poems*, 1954; *A Dog and the Fever*, 1954 (translation with Elena Williams); *Journey to Love*, 1955; *Pictures from Brueghel*, 1962; *Selected Poems*, 1985; *The Collected Poems of William Carlos Williams: Volume I, 1909-1939*, 1986; *The Collected Poems of William Carlos Williams: Volume II, 1939-1962*, 1988.

NONFICTION: *In the American Grain*, 1925; *A Novelette and Other Prose*, 1932; *A Beginning on the Short Story (Notes)*, 1950; *The Autobiography of William Carlos Williams*, 1951; *Selected Essays of William Carlos Williams*, 1954; *The Selected Letters of William Carlos Williams*, 1957; *I Wanted to Write a Poem: The Autobiography of the Works of a Poet*, 1958; *The Embodiment of Knowledge*, 1974; *A Recognizable Image*, 1978; *William Carlos Williams,*

John Sanford: A Correspondence, 1984; *William Carlos Williams and James Laughlin: Selected Letters*, 1989.

BIBLIOGRAPHY

Dietrich, R. F. "Connotations of Rape in 'The Use of Force.'" *Studies in Short Fiction* 3 (Summer, 1966): 446-450. Argues that the language of the story suggests a sexual encounter: The wooden spatula is a phallic symbol; the girl's bleeding is a violation; the idea of its being a pleasure to attack her suggests rape. Contends the sexual connotations suggest the savagery of human nature that lies close to the surface.

Gish, Robert. *William Carlos Williams: A Study of the Short Fiction*. Boston: Twayne, 1989. A very fine single-volume study of Williams's substantial contributions to the short story and the essay.

Gregory, Elizabeth. *Quotation and Modern American Poetry: Imaginary Gardens with Real Toads*. Houston, Tex.: Rice University Press, 1996. Studies of Williams, T. S. Eliot, and Marianne Moore. Includes bibliographical references and an index.

Kenner, Hugh. *A Homemade World: The American Modernist Writers*. New York: Alfred A. Knopf, 1975. A useful introduction to Williams and his work. Establishes the author's significance within the milieu of his fellow modernist writers.

Lowney, John. *The American Avant-Garde Tradition: William Carlos Williams, Postmodern Poetry, and the Politics of Cultural Memory*. Lewisburg, Pa.: Bucknell University Press, 1997. A good examination of postmodernism and Williams's poetry and literature.

Murphy, Margueritte S. *A Tradition of Subversion: The Prose Poem in English from Wilde to Ashbery*. Amherst: University of Massachusetts Press, 1992. Devotes a chapter to Williams's improvisations in *Kora in Hell*. Discusses Williams's debt to the French for his prose improvisational genre; discusses the unpredictable nature of the genre and how it works against the reader's expectations.

Paul, Sherman. *The Music of Survival: A Biography of a Poem by William Carlos Williams*. Urbana: University of Illinois Press, 1968. One of the best introductory monographs on Williams's poem "The Desert Music." This volume is useful because it lucidly examines Williams's poetic methods, which were also utilized in his prose.

Sayre, Henry M. *The Visual Text of William Carlos Williams*. Urbana: University of Illinois Press, 1983. Sayre ably demonstrates the influence that modernist painters and photographers had on Williams's poetry and prose, and he examines the visual effects of the graphic presentation of Williams's poetry on the printed page.

Vendler, Helen, ed. *Voices and Visions: The Poet in America*. New York: Random House, 1987. A well-written introduction to the American literary modernists. Includes a substantial chapter on Williams. This book is tied to the Public Broadcasting Service television series of the same name.

Wagner, Linda W. "Williams' 'The Use of Force': An Expansion." *Studies in Short Fiction* 4 (Summer, 1967): 351-353. Disagrees with the rape interpretation of the story, arguing that nothing could be further from the Doctor's intention and that his use of force can be attributed to other reasons.

Whitaker, Thomas R. *William Carlos Williams*. 1964. Rev. ed. Boston: Twayne, 1989. Whitaker's discussion of the short stories in chapter 6 of this general introduction to Williams's life and art focuses primarily on the stories in *The Knife of the Times*; includes a brief discussion of the oral style of the stories and the transformation of their anecdotal core.

*Kathryn Zabelle Derounian, updated by
William E. Grim*

ANGUS WILSON

Born: Bexhill, East Sussex, England; August 11, 1913

Died: Bury St. Edmunds, Suffolk, England; June 1, 1991

PRINCIPAL SHORT FICTION

The Wrong Set and Other Stories, 1949
Such Darling Dodos and Other Stories, 1950
A Bit off the Map and Other Stories, 1957
Death Dance: Twenty-five Stories, 1969

OTHER LITERARY FORMS

Although Angus Wilson enjoyed initial success with the publication of his first two short-story collections, he is better know as a novelist, particularly for *Anglo-Saxon Attitudes* (1956) and *The Old Men at the Zoo* (1961). Wilson is also an important literary critic, having published studies of Émile Zola, Charles Dickens, and Rudyard Kipling. He also wrote a play, a study of the influence of television on the arts, and a book on the relationship between his life and his fiction.

ACHIEVEMENTS

Angus Wilson was a guest lecturer, honorary fellow, and professor at a number of universities in England and America. In 1958, his third novel, *The Middle Age of Mrs. Eliot*, won the James Tait Black Memorial Prize and the French Prize for Best Foreign Novel. He was made a Fellow of the Royal Society of Literature in 1958 and was Chairman of England's National Book League between 1971 and 1974. He was made Companion of the Order of the British Empire in 1968 and Chevalier de l'Ordre des Arts et des Lettres in France in 1972. He was awarded a knighthood in 1980.

BIOGRAPHY

Angus Frank Johnstone Wilson was born on August 11, 1913, in the small resort town of Bexhill near Hastings on England's south coast. Although his father was descended from a wealthy Scottish family,

the Wilsons lead a somewhat threadbare existence after World War I, moving from hotel to hotel. As a result, Wilson attended a number of different schools until he enrolled in a preparatory school run by an older brother. In 1927, he entered Westminster School as a day student, living with his parents in London in a small hotel. With the assistance of a legacy he received after his mother's death, he went to Merton College, Oxford University, in 1932 to study medieval history.

From 1936 through the early 1950's Wilson worked for the British Museum's Department of Printed Books. During World War II, he was assigned to the Foreign Office and came close to suffering a nervous breakdown. After the war, when he returned to the British Museum, he was put in charge of replacing the thousands of books destroyed in the bombings. In the late 1940's, Wilson began publishing short stories in a number of journals before putting them together in two collections published in 1949 and 1950. As a result of his increasing literary recognition, he quit the museum to devote himself to writing in 1955, moving out of London to a cottage in a village in Suffolk. In his last years, he traveled widely and taught at several American universities, particularly in California.

ANALYSIS

Angus Wilson has most often been recognized as a satirist and an author of comedy-of-manners fiction; however, there has been some disagreement among critics as to whether he has the moral stance for satire or whether his work is more lightweight social comedy. Wilson himself said he preferred to think of himself as the author of comedy of manners.

Wilson once said he believed a short story is closer to a play or a poem than to a novel. Indeed, his stories are like one-act drawing-room comedies. Instead of probing complexities of individual psychology or establishing elaborate symbolic structures, Wilson is more interested in setting up dramatic situations in which relatively easy targets are exposed to

Angus Wilson (Camera Press Ltd./Archive Photos)

his witty ridicule. However, even as Wilson deftly reveals the pretensions of his characters—be they upper-class snob, lower-class climber, or middle-class bureaucrat—he does not dehumanize them. Beneath the laughter, there is always a subtle groan of sympathy.

"TOTENTANZ"

"Totentanz," which means "dance of death," focuses on a Scottish couple, Brian Capper, who has been appointed to a chair of art history in London, and his wife, Isobel, who has received a legacy of half a million pounds from an uncle and aunt. In London, she cultivates four people: Professor Cadaver, Lady Maude, Guy Rice, and Tanya Mule. The will by which she has inherited her money includes a clause which insists that two seven-foot marble monuments be set in the room of her house, where she entertains friends. She and her husband devise a scheme by which they will give one party and then get rid of the monuments.

People come to the party dressed in costume: Mrs. Mule as a vampire, Lady Maude as Marie Antoinette, Professor Cadaver as a corpse eater, and Guy Rice as the suicide of the poet Thomas Chatterton. Fulfilling these disguises, Guy kills himself because he is being blackmailed; Lady Maude dies like a queen, decapitated by a young man with an ax; Cadaver breaks his neck in a cemetery when he begins to clear away a freshly dug grave; and Mrs. Mule plays the vampire. The deaths mark the end of Isobel's social aspirations. The story is one of Wilson's most popular combinations of farce, pathos, and the grotesque. As critic Averil Gardner has suggested, it is a black comedy worthy of Evelyn Waugh.

"REALPOLITIK"

Wilson's most frequently anthologized story, "Realpolitik" is a classic example of his social satire. This comic set piece is structured like a one-act play, in which the central character, John Hobday, who has recently been made head of an art gallery, holds forth for an audience of the gallery staff. It becomes immediately apparent that Hobday is a big-mouthed bureaucrat who knows nothing about art but has vulgar and grandiose plans to boost traffic in the modest gallery. The story is primarily made up of Hobson's theatrical posturing and uncouth-salesman approach, as he sets forth plans for the gallery to compete with the cinema, football, and the fireside radio.

Throughout the story, Hobson is mildly interrupted by the staff, who plainly disapprove of his plans, but who obviously have little or no power to stop him. The final straw occurs when Hobson says he is going to bring in students from universities and experts from other museums to work at the gallery, all of which may necessitate some revisions in seniority. When one of the older staff members says that if so they will resign, Hobson, happily anticipating this, shows them out. The story ends with Hobson's secretary chiding him for lying to the staff and warning him that he is getting too fond of bullying. However, when she leaves the room, he thinks that for all her loyalty she knows him too well and that perhaps a graduate-student secretary would be more suitable for him.

"WHAT DO HIPPOS EAT?"

The final story in Wilson's collection *Such Darling Dodos*, "What Do Hippos Eat?" focuses on Maurice Legge, a fifty-five-year-old former officer, who is past his prime and down on his luck, living in a boardinghouse and having an affair with the land-lady, Greta, who is below him in class and twenty years younger; she has joined forces with Legge in the hope that he will teach her some of his upper-class manners. The story centers on a trip to the zoo, which in various ways allows Wilson to expose Legge's pompous posturing and Greta's money-grubbing vulgarity.

Although Greta genuinely likes Legge and he is sentimentally fond of her, their selfish needs get in the way of any real caring; the tension between them is exacerbated by the fact that he has not paid the rent in the past two months. Greta takes great pride in Legge when he shows off by telling small children about his adventures with tigers in India, and he in turn basks in her admiration; however, the mood changes when, at the monkey cage, Legge is upstaged by a young man with more knowledge about the ani-mals than he possesses.

When the resulting argument deteriorates to the issue of the unpaid two-months' rent, Legge loses face even more. The story ends with final humiliation when Legge is embarrassed by a young zookeeper he tries to patronize and when Greta says in front of the young man that she is going to buy Legge a new suit, as if he were an old man in her care. In the final ironic scene, Legge puts his hands on Greta's waist and con-siders pushing her in the hippo pool; however, she thinks it is a gesture of affection and tries to reestab-lish his egoistic superiority by asking in a childlike way, "What *do* hippos eat, darling?"

The story quite deftly sets up a situation to satirize the efforts of the lower class to emulate their betters and rise in social esteem, while the upper class, with-out money to support their snobbishness, are reduced to empty posturing. As a result, the reader is not sure which is the more repellent or pathetic—Legge's boasting swagger or Greta's toadying mendacity. This story is typical of Wilson's satire, for his charac-ters engage the reader's sympathy and judgment at once.

OTHER MAJOR WORKS

LONG FICTION: *Hemlock and After*, 1952; *Anglo-Saxon Attitudes*, 1956; *The Middle Age of Mrs. Eliot*, 1958; *The Old Men at the Zoo*, 1961; *Late Call*, 1964; *No Laughing Matter*, 1967; *As If by Magic*, 1973; *Setting the World on Fire*, 1980.

PLAY: *The Mulberry Bush*, pr., pb. 1956.

NONFICTION: *Émile Zola: An Introductory Study of His Novels*, 1952; *The Wild Garden: Or, Speaking of Writing*, 1963; *The World of Charles Dickens*, 1970; *The Strange Ride of Rudyard Kipling*, 1977.

BIBLIOGRAPHY

Brooke, Allen. "The Mimetic Brilliance of Angus Wilson." *New Criterion* 15 (October, 1996): 28-37. In this biographical essay, Brooke describes Wilson's childhood and youth, his early literary career, his homosexual relationship with Tony Garrett, his disillusionment with communism, and his declining final years.

Drabble, Margaret. *Angus Wilson: A Biography*. New York: St. Martin's Press, 1995. A detailed biogra-phy of Wilson in which his friend Margaret Drab-ble shows the autobiographical sources of much of his fiction in his early years. Drabble describes Wilson's long-term homosexual relationship with Anthony Garrett and analyzes his obsession with the nature of evil in relationship to his mother's Christian faith.

Faulkner, Peter. *Angus Wilson: Mimic and Moralist*. London: Secker and Warburg, 1980. Discusses the satirist's negative judgment on the patterns of life around him in Wilson's early stories. Provides summary analyses of many of the stories in Wil-son's first two collections, focusing on his devel-oping satiric style.

Gardner, Averil. *Angus Wilson*. Boston: Twayne, 1985. In this general introduction to Wilson's life and art, Gardner devotes one chapter to *The Wrong Set* and *Such Darling Dodos*. Argues that the central reality of his stories is the world of people; neither nature nor the divine nor the eter-nal is very important in them. Says that the unity of Wilson's stories lies in their milieu of personal uncertainty, social precariousness, and emotional ambivalence, which allows people to be funny and pathetic at once.

Gransden, K. W. *Angus Wilson*. Essex: Longmans,

Green, 1969. A pamphlet-length introduction to Wilson's work; argues that the success of his early stories depends on their satirical analyses of people's vulnerability, failure, and self-deception. Suggests that many of his stories begin realistically and then are pushed to a farcical climax that involves violence or hysteria.

Halio, Jay L. *Angus Wilson*. London: Oliver and Boyd, 1964. Discusses the character types and situations in *The Wrong Set* and *Such Darling Dodos*, such as the Raffish Old Sport, the Intense Young Woman, and the Widow Who Copes. Argues that Wilson is primarily interested in the success or failure of people to understand who they are and what they are doing; provides a detailed analysis of "Heart of Elm."

_____. *Critical Essays on Angus Wilson*. Boston: G. K. Hall, 1985. A collection of reviews, interviews, and criticism covering Wilson's literary ca-reer. Includes influential reviews by Edmund Wilson, V. S. Pritchett, Kingsley Amis, and Anthony Burgess, as well as important essays by Malcolm Bradbury, A. S. Byatt, and Margaret Drabble. Halio's overview essay is a concise survey of Wilson's work and a critique of the criticism of it.

Vanatta, Dennis, ed. *The English Short Story: 1945-1980*. Boston: Twayne, 1985. In his article on the English short story between 1945 and 1950, John Stinson says that Wilson's characters cannot come to terms with themselves or the reality of their social situation; argues that in miniature portraits, Wilson captures psychological and social nuance through skillful irony. Dean Baldwin, in his essay on the 1950's English short story, says Wilson is often classed with nineteenth century novelists such as Charles Dickens; discusses his themes of social cruelty and his eye for detail.

Charles E. May

LARRY WOIWODE

Born: Carrington, North Dakota; October 30, 1941

PRINCIPAL SHORT FICTION
The Neumiller Stories, 1989
Silent Passengers: Stories, 1993

OTHER LITERARY FORMS

For the most part, Larry Woiwode is a writer of fiction, primarily the novel. His several novels, which have received critical acclaim, are, however, closely related to his short stories in style, setting, and characters. He has also written poetry and the nonfiction works *Acts* (1993), *Aristocrat of the West: The Story of Harold Schafer* (2000), and *What I Think I Did: A Season of Survival in Two Acts* (2000).

ACHIEVEMENTS

In 1970, Larry Woiwode received the William Faulkner Foundation First Novel Award and a notable book award from the American Library Association for *What I'm Going to Do, I Think* (1969). He received a John Simon Guggenheim Memorial Foundation Fellowship (1971-1972), and in 1976 his *Beyond the Bedroom Wall: A Family Album* (1975) was a finalist for both the National Book Award and the National Book Critics Circle Award and won the award in fiction from the Friends of American Writers. North Dakota State University awarded him an honorary doctorate in 1977; in 1977 and 1978, he received Bush Foundation Fellowships. In 1980 Woiwode won an Ernest Hemingway Foundation Award and that same year received an award in fiction from the American Academy of Arts and Letters.

BIOGRAPHY

Larry Alfred Woiwode was born on October 30, 1941, in Carrington, North Dakota, and grew up in nearby Sykestown. His father, Everett Woiwode, taught high school English, and when Woiwode was ten, his father moved the family to Manito, Illinois. In high school, Woiwode wrote poems for a local newspaper, and while attending the University of Illinois at Urbana-Champaign (1959-1964), he continued his writing, was published often, won some writing prizes, and gained an associate degree in rhetoric. After leaving college, he worked briefly in Florida with a theatrical company, before moving to New York, where he began his professional writing career.

According to Woiwode, William Maxwell, an editor for *The New Yorker*, was responsible for shifting his writing from what he calls "postmodernism" to a concern for an authentic voice, one rooted in his past. At Maxwell's urging, he became a freelance writer and published stories and poems in such journals as *The Atlantic Monthly, The New Yorker*, and *Harper's*. Four of those stories formed the nucleus of *What I'm Going to Do, I Think*, his first novel. He spent 1973 and 1974 as writer-in-residence at the University of Wisconsin. *Beyond the Bedroom Wall: A Family Album*, his second novel, features narrative shifts, unconventional, nonliterary material, and many Neumiller characters. It, too, received critical acclaim.

Before he continued the Neumiller saga in *Born Brothers* (1988), he wrote two other books: *Even Tide* (1977), a collection of poems, and *Poppa John* (1981), an atypical Woiwode novel about the plight of an elderly, out-of-work soap opera actor. Both works reflect Woiwode's deepening religious faith. Woiwode, reared as a Roman Catholic, and his wife joined the Orthodox Presbyterian church in 1977, and his writing has continued to focus on religious issues and to employ Christian symbols, allusions, and myths. *Born Brothers*, in fact, is a conscious reworking of the Jacob and Esau story with an overlay of the Cain and Abel tale. After deciding that New York was not the place for family life, Woiwode and his family lived, by his admission, in about ten states before settling on a ranch in North Dakota.

ANALYSIS

Larry Woiwode has used his life and his North Dakota and Illinois childhood to create a series of fictional autobiographical works, rooted in a narrowly

Larry Woiwode (Nancy Crampton)

circumscribed region peopled by a family that spans several generations. Like his southern counterparts William Faulkner and Flannery O'Connor, he is a regionalist whose depiction of his characters' values, religion, and family transcends the immediate and topical because his themes—memory, death, guilt, identity—are universal. Even when his characters leave the Midwest, they take those values with them, and the clash of those values with more urban ones is at the root of some of Woiwode's best fiction. That fiction is expressed in a style that encompasses shifting points of view and the inclusion of materials such as diaries, letters, lists, and prose, creating a sense of a prose photograph, an image caught in time.

THE NEUMILLER STORIES

Woiwode's short fiction has appeared in a number of magazines, most notably *The New Yorker*, where he received the encouragement and guidance of William Maxwell. After the stories' publication, many of them were revised and included in *Beyond the Bedroom Wall: A Family Album*, a long, multigenerational novel that resembles an album, or scrapbook, because it contains lists, diaries, and descriptions of photographs, the last a recurrent motif in his fiction. The sprawling nature of his novel accommodated the altered Neumiller stories, which were reworked again for their appearance in *The Neumiller Stories*.

Although *The Neumiller Stories* is divided into three parts representing three phases of Woiwode's literary career (1964-1967, 1968-1972, and 1982-1989), the collection seems unified in character, setting, and theme, and while the stories do not progress sequentially from the first North Dakota Neumillers to the last, there is novel-like development, with flashbacks, and the last three stories focus on the latest Neumillers. Moreover, the collection begins and ends with a male attempting to deal with the death of Alpha Neumiller, who serves as the center of the collection of stories—the date of her death becomes the point from which the time and setting of each story is measured and located.

"Deathless Lovers," the first story, occurs within a year of Alpha's death and concerns a brief conversation between an unnamed boy, probably Jerome, and his grandmother. Unlike the rest of the stories, it is written in the present tense, a literary device Woiwode used in his early stories but soon abandoned because of its limits. In this six-page story, the present tense is workable and appropriate because it suggests the temporary suspension of time, the sense of the snapshot, the moment not to be forgotten. Even though the boy is with his maternal grandmother, his thoughts are of his mother.

Half the story concerns the turbulent relationship between the grandmother and grandfather, which the boy accurately perceives as love because of the "so, so" she croons to her invalid husband. Her love for the boy is not stated but is reflected in her "so, so" assurance to the boy as she takes him in her arms. The smell of her dress is "a smell he will remember in its layers of detail . . . whenever he loves a woman, fears that he'll lose her, and his love becomes so smothering and possessive that she runs from him." The grandmother is the mother, who in turn becomes all women he loves and fears losing, and that fear is encapsulated in his memory as a moment, a smell that will recur throughout his life.

A nine-year-old serves as the first-person narrator of "Beyond the Bedroom Wall," which concerns his perception of the events surrounding Alpha's death. One of Woiwode's literary strengths is his ability to capture a child's thoughts, apprehensions, and sense of isolation. In this story, Jerome's physical isolation in his windowless bedroom mirrors his isolation from the adult world. The "wall" is both physical and emotional. After dreaming about being unable to follow his mother, Jerome wakes to find a "wall" on the wrong side of his bed: "If there was a wall where I was convinced there was none, I couldn't imagine what waited for me in that emptiness where the wall should be." Jerome senses the "emptiness" is his mother's death, which has yet to happen but which will always stay with him.

In both "The Visitation" and "Pheasants," memory is associated, metaphorically and literally, with a photograph. Through a metaphorical photograph, the visit by Jerome's uncles becomes a "visitation" as Conrad, Elling, and Alpha become spirits: "As if he were viewing a photograph that had been snapped of them at that moment, and began receding into his mind . . . retreating like spirits he had taken by surprise." In "Pheasants," Alpha's memory of "her mother's favorite photograph of her, taken when she was a child of five or six" is juxtaposed with her current situation as hopes are juxtaposed to reality. What might have been, symbolized by the attractive neighbor, differs from what is and makes her "capable of doing serious harm to her sons," the physical manifestations of her constricted situation.

"The Beginning of Grief," which ends the first part of Woiwode's book, also uses optical imagery to describe the diminished world in which Martin, Alpha's husband, lives after her death, "imprisoned within the sphere of his eye." Alpha, "at the periphery of every thought," lives on in the gestures and "averted eyes" of their children, who also attempt, with varying degrees of success, to cope with their mother's death. In this story, Woiwode shifts the focus from Jerome to Charles, the second son, whose bad behavior is caused by Alpha's death. Martin, who seems unaware that he, too, is affected by his wife's death, loses control and kicks Charles, but the two are eventually reconciled—not verbally, for both are incapable of expressing their feelings in words, but physically, through reaching out to each other.

The second five stories, written between 1968 and 1972, are more varied, though family history links them together. "The Suitor" recounts Martin's proposal to Alpha in 1939; "Pneumonia," interesting because of a dramatic shift in point of view, concerns their son Charles's narrow escape from death. While "The Old Halvorson Place" is also about Martin, Alpha, and their family, it incorporates not only the Neumiller saga but also a history of the house, which Alpha realizes is not really theirs. As in "Beyond the Bedroom Wall," the house seems alive, throbbing with memories that impinge on the lives and actions of the children. From the start, the attic is off limits to the children, who nevertheless play there, thereby tampering "with the heart of the house." While the rest of the house "was becoming Alpha's," the "heart" of the house is not hers; when Father James Russell, whose family had also lived at the Halvorson Place, appears to tell her about his family's life there, Alpha is defeated: "now the Russells, as well as the Halvorsons, would always occupy a part of their house."

The past also lives on in "Marie," a story told from the perspective of Martin and Alpha's older daughter, who has unconsciously assumed her dead mother's role. Her borrowed identity is threatened by Laura, a widow Martin will soon marry. As she reviews the family situation at the Christmas holidays, Marie turns to the favorite photograph of her mother and prays, "Oh, Mom, come back, come back." She looks at the family album but finds that the "pattern had been lost." Marie wants to preserve the status quo, to keep things the way they are, and to preserve her identity: "I was just starting to find out where I belong in this family." At the end of the story, Marie has so thoroughly identified with her mother that her father's impending marriage is a rejection of her mother and, more significantly, of her.

"Burial," the last of the second five stories, is both a beginning and an end, for it is a flashback containing information about the first North Dakota Neumiller, Otto, and also an account of how Charles,

Otto's son, not only buries his father but also comes to terms with the past and closes a chapter of his life. Exhausted and suffering from a hangover, Charles returns to North Dakota to bury his father and make arrangements for his aunt Augustina. After he arrives, he must confront not only his father's dead body, which he prepares for burial, but also the legacy that his father left: a community mistakenly convinced that Otto "owes" them money. In his father's house, he meets his father's "presence": "It was the height of his father. The presence turned a new side in Charles's direction." Only by obeying his father's wishes for burial can the Hamlet-like Charles exorcize his father's ghost and be free.

The last three of *The Neumiller Stories*, written between 1982 and 1989, do form the basis for another of the Neumiller novels. All three involve Charles, Martin, Martin's wife Katherine, Alpha's son, and their life in New York City. Like F. Scott Fitzgerald's protagonists, they are Westerners in a corrupt East, where they are "disenfranchised," alienated from others, one another, and themselves. "Firstborn," narrated through Charles's consciousness, depicts him as an egocentric young man who feels trapped into marriage, guilty of the death of his newborn son, and only after the birth of his fourth child "freed into forgiveness" and able to "begin again to see." Charles's forgiveness comes only after his prayer, "Good God, forgive me," and reflects the Christian influence on Woiwode's writing.

"A Brief Fall," which alludes to Katherine's affair, concerns her second pregnancy, but the story is told from her perspective, and the portrait of Charles reveals him as an insecure person using sex to counterbalance his loss of youth. When she meets Robert F. Kennedy, Katherine sees "a picture of the shattering end of his brother, the President, which seemed the end of youth, and of Charles." At the end of the story, however, a waiting Katherine looks in the mirror, another "frame" like the artist's "frame" that incorporates art and perhaps reality, and sees "a new and untraceable geography of weighty beauty."

This upbeat ending is followed by "She," the last of the stories. In it, the first-person narrator is a writer who tells a story within the story itself. Using

Estrelaria, an Indian from Guatemala, he returns again to his mother's death: "These incidents began to interconnect . . . because of my mother." At the end of the story, the narrator reflects on the emotional and geographical identification between land, mother, and (the last words of the book) "my wife." Thus, it is the mother's "legacy" that enables Charles to persevere, that allows him to structure experience, and that provides Woiwode with a center for his multigenerational fictional world.

SILENT PASSENGERS

In *Silent Passengers* Woiwode abandons the Neumillers and focuses on new characters, though they live in familiar Woiwode territory and reenact parent/child relationships and memories. "Confessionals," the only spiritually explicit story, is a first-person account of a person's, probably Woiwode's, conversion from Catholicism to Protestantism; but the narrator uses the Abraham and Isaac story to identify himself as the sacrificial son waiting for the father's redemption. In "Owen's Father," the son's glimpse of his father's fifteen-year-old passport forces him to relive the events surrounding his father's suicide and to move from identifying with his father to discovering his own identity. By comparing the son's insights with the bare-bones newspaper account of the father's death, Woiwode shows the reader how reliving or rethinking the past can free one from that past.

In "Black Winter," a retired and weary professor returns to his family home to manual, rather than intellectual, labor and reexamines his childhood. At the end of the story he is "past the pale of existence," where he discovers, with the aid of a "presence as powerful as his father," that he had "subverted" his childhood by assuming that his father did not care "one whit" what he did. A similar reworking of the past occurs in "Summer Storms," in which the narrator, a writer like Woiwode (in fact, in these stories the traditional distinction between author and narrator seems almost to be obliterated), is reminded of a summer storm that occurred when he was thirteen. Despite a terrible storm, he rides his horse to a birthday party for Siobhan, a flirtatious girl he idolizes. When she discovers that he is the "only damn person

here" because of the storm, Siobhan "dismisses" him. However, he comes to realize that her "dismissal" also acknowledges his tenacity and his ability to survive.

Parents in Woiwode's fiction affect their children, but they also learn from them. In "Blindness," Mel's temporary blindness, a physical infirmity that reminds him of his aging father's limitations, enables him to see a new world, "the world of his daughter," who now leads him. Similarly, Steiner, the protagonist in "Silent Passengers," is redeemed from his guilt by his injured son, who returns to pet the horse who maimed him. The son, who has a way with "pardon," provides his father with a vision, one of those suspended moments in Woiwode's fiction that promises forgiveness for one of Woiwode's fallen characters.

OTHER MAJOR WORKS

LONG FICTION: *What I'm Going to Do, I Think*, 1969; *Beyond the Bedroom Wall: A Family Album*, 1975; *Poppa John*, 1981; *Born Brothers*, 1988; *Indian Affairs*, 1992.

POETRY: *Poetry North: Five North Dakota Poets*, 1970 (with Richard Lyons, Thomas McGrath, John R. Milton, and Antony Oldknow); *Even Tide*, 1977.

NONFICTION: *Acts*, 1993; *Aristocrat of the West: The Story of Harold Schafer*, 2000; *What I Think I Did: A Season of Survival in Two Acts*, 2000.

BIBLIOGRAPHY

Block, Ed, Jr. "An Interview with Larry Woiwode." *Renascence: Essays on Value in Literature* 44 (Fall, 1991): 17-30. Woiwode discusses the writer's task, the importance of his own family to his work, his current writing projects, his personal life, and his opinion of several young writers.

Flower, Dean. Review of *The Neumiller Stories*, by Larry Woiwode. *The Hudson Review* 43 (Summer, 1990): 311. Flower's extensive and perceptive review of Woiwode's stories examines the early stories, their alterations in novel form, and their "ungathering," revising, and "unrevising" in *The Neumiller Stories*. For Flower, the stories form a "superb family chronicle," with the three new stories adding new layers to the Neumiller characters. Of particular interest is Flower's comment on the way Woiwode "expands the frame" at the end of the story and leaves his readers with an image that resembles a snapshot, a moment caught in time.

Moritz, Charles. *Current Biography Yearbook*. New York: H. W. Wilson, 1989. The essay on Woiwode traces his life and literary work and reviews critical responses to his novels. For the most part, the novels are discussed in terms of their autobiographical content, especially of the characters, including those who most resemble Woiwode himself. Although it does not contain much criticism about Woiwode's work, this essay is particularly helpful, since it identifies and evaluates the available secondary sources. Includes a bibliography.

Siconolfi, Michael T. Review of *The Neumiller Stories*, by Larry Woiwode. *America* 163 (December 1, 1990): 434-435. In this lengthy, informative review, Siconolfi discusses the reworkings of stories as they become parts of novels and then resurface as the short stories in this collection. He maintains that while Woiwode's stories can stand on their own, they also are interrelated "like distant branches of a family tree," an apt comparison since the stories are rooted in family. While Sinconolfi mentions several of the stories, he focuses on Woiwode's gift at working the "nurturing, eternal feminine" and on the novelist's acknowledging of his grandmother's influence.

Tallent, Elizabeth. "Before the Bedroom Wall." Review of *The Neumiller Stories*, by Larry Woiwode. *The New York Times Book Review* (December 17, 1989): 17. Tallent points out that ten of the thirteen stories had appeared before, once in journals and once in revised form, in Woiwode's *Beyond the Bedroom Wall: A Family Album*. In their latest form, the stories seem, to Tallent, to lack some of the immediacy and detail they had in the novel. Her review is of special interest because she notes that Alpha Neumiller's death in childbirth is the pivotal event in the collection and that the collection begins and ends with a boy's, then a man's, projection of Alpha's persona onto another female character.

Woiwode, Larry. Interview by Michele Field. *Publishers Weekly* 234 (August 5, 1988): 67-68. Woiwode discusses his life, his career, and the relationship between biographical fact and fiction.

_____. "An Interview with Larry Woiwode." *Christianity and Literature* 29 (Winter, 1979): 11-18. Woiwode discusses the autobiographical nature of his work, the Jacob/Esau biblical framework of *Born Brothers*, the "mechanics of memory," his religious rebirth, the influence of William Maxwell, and his future writing plans. This frank, informative interview contains a considerable amount of biographical information, most of which is applied to Woiwode's writing, and some perceptive comments about the Christian themes of *Born Brothers*.

_____. "The Reforming of a Novelist." Interview by Timothy K. Jones. *Christianity Today* 36 (October 26, 1992): 86-88. In this interview Woiwode discusses his conversion experience, his church service, the role of faith in his writing, and reactions to his books.

Thomas L. Erskine

THOMAS WOLFE

Born: Asheville, North Carolina; October 3, 1900
Died: Baltimore, Maryland; September 15, 1938

PRINCIPAL SHORT FICTION

From Death to Morning, 1935
The Hills Beyond, 1941
The Complete Short Stories of Thomas Wolfe, 1987

OTHER LITERARY FORMS

While some novelists are failed poets, a tradition that began with Cervantes in the early seventeenth century, Thomas Wolfe was a failed playwright. None of his plays was accepted for commercial production. Wolfe is most famous (his fame in the 1930's was international) for his early novels. His first editor unfortunately persuaded him to stay away from the novella or short novel form, and the editor of his posthumous novels essentially pieced them together out of shorter pieces that Wolfe saw as short novels, not as parts of a rambling, protean novel. Hugh Holman's collection of Wolfe's short novels and Richard Kennedy's study of his last editor's stewardship are beginning to establish Wolfe's very real talent for the shorter forms.

The best-known of Wolfe's novels are *Look Homeward, Angel* (1929) and *You Can't Go Home Again* (1940). Wolfe's notebooks are also very informative, not only to scholars but also to young writers interested in the processes through which a writer refines experience (and Wolfe was more able to do this than his first wave of admirers would admit). It is particularly fascinating to see how the "real" incident that inspired one of the scenes in "Death the Proud Brother" became transformed into that scene.

ACHIEVEMENTS

It can be argued that Thomas Wolfe did not write short stories at all and that his "stories" were only fragments torn from the single great body of his life's work. Even Francis E. Skipp, the editor of *The Complete Short Stories of Thomas Wolfe*, acknowledges that Wolfe or his editors cut and shaped these frag-

ments into discrete units to suit monetary or publishing needs as opportunities presented themselves. Since Wolfe seldom if ever seriously applied himself to writing individual stories rather than pieces belonging to the grand epic of his own self-expression, it is unfair to hold him rigorously to the standards of the modern story.

Wolfe's reputation was at one time enormous both at home and abroad. He has often been the writer that young writers read; age and artistic maturity, however, usually dampen that youthful enthusiasm. Although many critics praised his work, a reaction against Wolfe set in even during his lifetime. Among his detractors was Bernard De Voto, who, in a 1936 essay called "Genius Is Not Enough," attacked Wolfe, citing his first two novels as books full of "long, whirling discharges of words, unabsorbed in the novel, unrelated to the proper business of fiction, badly if not altogether unacceptably written. . . ." The controversy continues. Wolfe's real strength, formerly obscured by the hands of his editors, may indeed lie in the novella or short-novel form. Whatever the critical opinion, Wolfe will always have supporters. William Faulkner said, "My admiration for Wolfe is that . . . he was willing to throw away style, coherence, all the rules of preciseness, to try to put all the experience of the human heart on the head of a pin. . . ."

BIOGRAPHY

Thomas Clayton Wolfe was the youngest child of Julia Elizabeth Westall and William Oliver Wolfe, a Pennsylvania mason and stonecutter who went south to find work. One of Wolfe's brothers, Benjamin Harrison Wolfe, died at age eighteen, as does the brother in *Look Homeward, Angel*. Although Wolfe's mother did run a tourist home, The Old Kentucky Home, it is important to remember that his family was very prosperous; one scholar estimates that they were financially in the upper two percent of the town's population. Although this fact does not mean that an affluent adolescent cannot suffer the torments of the damned, it nevertheless somewhat negates the concept of Thomas Wolfe as the poor, suffering, and morbidly sensitive child, which was fashioned by the early members of his literary cult. The Wolfes were German, an unusual ethnic origin in that part of Carolina, where most of the people were Scotch-Irish or English, and they lived in the western, mountain end of North Carolina, which had more in common with East Tennessee, Appalachian Ohio, and mountain Pennsylvania than with eastern North Carolina, the Tidewater of Virginia, or even northern Mississippi (the setting of Faulkner's stories). Both ethnic background and geographic environment are reflected strongly in Wolfe's works.

Wolfe was enrolled at the University of North Carolina at Chapel Hill; at that time it was the university's only campus and was restricted to males during his first two years. He majored in the classics and in English literature, and he began his writing career as a playwright with the Carolina Playmakers. By college age, Wolfe had achieved his full growth (he was six feet, six inches tall and later, as a slightly older man, weighed two hundred and fifty pounds) and in appearance was a man of epic proportions as well as epic ambitions. Wolfe went to Harvard University in 1920 to study under George Pierce Baker at the drama workshop; he left Harvard in 1923, after earning an M.A. in English and writing *Welcome to Our City*, later performed in 1947, and *The Mountains* (1970), about a family feud.

From 1924 to 1930 he led a rather unhappy existence as an English instructor at New York University, a private university on Washington Square. He was not able to find a producer for *Welcome to Our City* or *Mannerhouse* (1948), a play about the Civil War. In 1925, he met Aline Bernstein, and their stormy relationship became the most important one in his short life. Aline Frankau Bernstein was almost twenty years older than Wolfe. When she was still nineteen, she had married a broker, Theodore Bernstein, and became interested in making sets and costumes for her friends in Neighborhood Playhouse when it was founded in 1915, soon becoming the first woman member of United Scenic Artists. As her biographer says, "without intending to, she rather took

Thomas Wolfe (Library of Congress)

the color out of those men at hand." In 1925, she met Wolfe; a relationship developed which Wolfe described as "the met halves of the broken talisman." In 1926, he went to Europe with Aline and began *Look Homeward, Angel*, with some assistance, both literary and financial, from her. In 1928, after another trip abroad with Aline and a breakup with her, he finished *Look Homeward, Angel*, and Scribner's showed interest in the manuscript. The editor who found Wolfe's gigantic manuscript and who greatly helped him during his early career was Maxwell Perkins. With Perkins's constant help, Wolfe published *Look Homeward, Angel*, which sold fifteen thousand copies and earned for Wolfe about six thousand dollars. Although Wolfe, at this point in his career, wanted to publish two shorter novels, one of which had already been partly set in type, Perkins gave Wolfe what modern scholars conclude was "unfortunate" advice and leadership; he advised him to work on yet another big novel. Upon Perkins's advice, he concentrated on *Of Time and the River* (1935); three years after its publication he died of tuberculosis of the brain, a rare condition that had not immediately been diagnosed. Although he had been working in his last years toward shorter and more controlled stories which used different viewpoint techniques, when he died, Edward C. Aswell at Harper's gave the public what they wanted: He created the "old" Wolfe by piecing together two more gigantic novels. There is no doubt that Wolfe needed editing and that he placed himself at the mercy of those who edited his works, and the massive amount of material written prior to his death became the basis from which Aswell would create *The Web and the Rock* (1939) and *You Can't Go Home Again* (1940).

ANALYSIS

Some of Thomas Wolfe's short stories were printed in *The Hills Beyond*, a posthumous volume compiled by Edward C. Aswell after he had published Wolfe's two "novels" of his own creation. The tough-minded old Confederate general of the story "The Dead World Relived" mourns a South ten times as full of frauds after the Civil War as before it; the story is unforgettable and furnishes a much-needed corrective to the myth that southerners in the American literary renaissance of the 1920's and 1930's could hardly wait to start writing about the old Colonels.

"A KINSMAN OF HIS BLOOD"

"A Kinsman of His Blood" is a short, concise, and moving story in its subtly achieved pathos and its nostalgia for what life and history are, rather than for what we might want them to be, and is probably the best story in *The Hills Beyond*. The action takes place entirely in the foreground, and the story is really that of Arthur Pentland, also known from the beginning of the story as Arthur Penn. The viewpoint through which the reader sees Arthur is that of the ubiquitous Eugene Gant; the third character in the story is Eugene's uncle, Bascom Pentland, who appears in *Of Time and the River*. It could be the tale of any three men related to each other; Arthur is the son of Bascom and the only one "who ever visited his father's house; the rest were studiously absent, saw their father only at Christmas or Thanksgiving." Even so, the relation between Bascom and Arthur is "savage and hostile."

Arthur is a huge, obese, dirty, disheveled, grubby, distraught man who has trouble speaking clearly and coherently. The reader is told nothing of the history of his problems, or of Eugene's background, and knows only that the conflict is stark, ugly, and dramatic. Some of Arthur's behavior is clearly sociopathic. His table manners are not only embarrassing but also offensive. On one occasion, he tells an anecdote about a Harvard man who climbed into a cage with a gorilla; although the man knew fourteen languages, the gorilla killed him. Arthur's summation of the incident is as frightening as anything in European fiction which tries to depict the mindless, anarchic malevolence of the crazy or the revolutionary.

Arthur decides that his grammar school teacher really loves him; even though the woman ignores his protestations of love, then tries to silence him with rudeness, he persists. He refuses to believe his mother when she tells him the woman does not really care for him, and he storms out "like a creature whipped with furies." Finally, he goes to California to see the woman. Arthur is a pitiful, subnormal, obviously seriously disturbed creature, but frightening in his obesity, his filth, his animal-like inability to understand human beings. The story ends with Eugene, out walking in the rain through the South Boston slums, spotting Arthur as he shuffles along, a bundle of old newspapers under one arm. Eugene, a nice man, is glad to see him and offers to shake his hand. Arthur denies twice that he is Arthur Pentland, then says he is Arthur Penn and screams out in terror, begging Eugene to leave him alone. There is no sentimentality here; this is tragedy, however small and prosaic.

"NO DOOR"

The only collection of short fiction Wolfe prepared himself and saw through publication was *From Death to Morning*; it contains the stories "No Door" and "Death the Proud Brother."

"No Door" is about a writer and his short acquaintance with "well-kept people who have never been alone in all their life," in this case a man who lives in a penthouse near the East River furnished with several sculptures by Jacob Epstein, rare books and first editions, and a view of Manhattan which displays its "terrific frontal sweep and curtain of starflung towers, now sown with the diamond pollen of a million lights." The writer is told by these people how marvelous it is to live alone with creatures of the slums. Their remarks trigger recollections of the lower depths of stinking, overcrowded, working-class Brooklyn. The writer hangs around, partly amused, partly chagrined, partly in awe of the rich man and his mistress, thinking that *they* may be the ones who will open the door to the life of glamour and ease for which he, as a poor writer, yearns. Even as he hopes, however, he knows it is useless: These creatures are foreign to him. He tells of the agony and senselessness and brutality and sordidness of his existence, and the man and his mistress condescendingly and patronizingly wish his lot were theirs. Finally, at the end of the evening, he returns to Brooklyn and hears two old people discussing the death of a priest, and the story ends on a note of desperation and impotent fury.

The effect of the story depends on the consciousness of the narrator, here appearing in the first person although the reader sees him through the second person, an almost unheard-of viewpoint in English. Wolfe makes his points subtly, the length is a rather modest one for him, his satirical eye is sharp, and the rhetoric meshes with the inner turmoil lying just beneath the surface of conversation. If Wolfe had written more stories like this he might have been one of the giants of the American short story.

"DEATH THE PROUD BROTHER"

"Death the Proud Brother" is a very long, almost unstructured, 22,000-word novella which attempts to present as a unified narrative several unrelated incidents of death and loneliness. Wolfe said of this story, "It represents *important* work to me." The story's thematic unity arises from the narrator's successful unifying of all the incidents within his own consciousness, drawing the world to him, exercising implicit rights of selection, unlike the third-person, omniscient narrators of Wolfe's last novels. This story is a masterpiece in its conjunction of viewpoint and material. Only this viewpoint could master this material, and only disjointed, logically discrete material such as the story presents requires a first-person viewpoint.

There is no plot, but there is some structure. Wolfe describes three violent deaths. The fourth death is that of an old bum on a bench, and it occurs quietly, imperceptibly, anonymously—he is a "cipher." His death, which takes up the bulk of the novella, furnishes Wolfe with a chance to study America. If it is true that everybody talks about America but nobody can find it, then Wolfe came closest in this last movement of the novella, which was his favorite. The story is typically Wolfean in many ways; by the passion and the wise guile of his rhetoric, Wolfe becomes so thoroughly a part of the writing that he, too, becomes a cipher—the transparent narrator. It surely is no accident that the death which moves the narrator so profoundly is the death of an urban Everyman. This is the kind of story, perhaps even the story itself, that caused Faulkner to say that Wolfe had tried to put all of life on the head of a pin.

OTHER MAJOR WORKS

LONG FICTION: *Look Homeward, Angel*, 1929; *Of Time and the River*, 1935; *The Web and the Rock*, 1939; *You Can't Go Home Again*, 1940; *The Short Novels of Thomas Wolfe*, 1961 (C. Hugh Holman, editor).

PLAYS: *The Mountains*, pr. 1921, pb. 1970; *Welcome to Our City*, pr. 1923 (published only in German as *Willkommen in Altamont*, 1962); *Mannerhouse*, pb. 1948.

POETRY: *The Face of a Nation: Poetical Passages from the Writings of Thomas Wolfe*, 1939; *A Stone, a Leaf, a Door: Poems by Thomas Wolfe*, 1945.

NONFICTION: *The Story of a Novel*, 1936; *Thomas Wolfe's Letters to His Mother*, 1943; *The Portable Thomas Wolfe*, 1946; *The Letters of Thomas Wolfe*, 1956; *The Notebooks of Thomas Wolfe*, 1970; *The Thomas Wolfe Reader*, 1982; *The Autobiography of an American Novelist: Thomas Wolfe*, 1983; *Beyond Love and Loyalty: The Letters of Thomas Wolfe and Elizabeth Nowell*, 1983; *My Other Loneliness: Letters of Thomas Wolfe and Aline Bernstein*, 1983.

BIBLIOGRAPHY
Bassett, John Earl. *Thomas Wolfe: An Annotated Critical Bibliography*. Lanham, Md.: Scarecrow

Press, 1996. A helpful tool for the student of Wolfe. Indexed.

Bentz, Joseph. "The Influence of Modernist Structure in the Short Fiction of Thomas Wolfe." *Studies in Short Fiction* 31 (Spring, 1994): 149-162. Argues that while Wolfe's novels owed much to the nineteenth century novel tradition, his short stories were heavily influenced by the modernism of the 1920's and 1930's. Discusses the nonlinear, open-ended nature of such stories as "No Cure for It" and "The Lost Boy."

Bloom, Harold, ed. *Thomas Wolfe.* New York: Chelsea House, 1987. Several essays are devoted to *Look Homeward, Angel,* but Wolfe's other works are covered as well, with an introduction, chronology, and bibliography.

Donald, David Herbert. *Look Homeward: A Life of Thomas Wolfe.* Boston: Little, Brown, 1987. Donald's painstakingly thorough examination of the huge volume of Wolfe's papers, including the published and unpublished manuscripts, and of Wolfe criticism has produced a work that, in its scope, depth, and readability, makes it the essential biography, replacing such earlier works as Elizabeth Nowell's *Thomas Wolfe: A Biography* (1960) and Andrew Turnbull's *Thomas Wolfe* (1968). A distinguished historian, Donald is on less solid ground when he ventures into the more literary concerns of interpretation and criticism. The questions surrounding the roles of Wolfe's editors and the legitimacy of the published texts are explored if not resolved. Contains exhaustive notes but no formal bibliography.

Field, Leslie A., ed. *Thomas Wolfe: Three Decades of Criticism.* New York: New York University Press, 1968. This collection contains landmark essays by many of the most important critics in the field of Wolfe criticism; revealed are the central issues and the range of critical response provoked by Wolfe's work, from its first publication through the mid-1960's.

Idol, John Lane, Jr. *A Thomas Wolfe Companion.* New York: Greenwood Press, 1987. An expression of the resurgence of interest in Wolfe by an unabashed devotee, this handy book is a potpourri of Wolfeana with glossaries of characters and places, genealogical charts of Wolfe's fictional families, a descriptive and "analytic" bibliography of primary works, and an annotated bibliography of secondary materials. Also contains information on the various collections of Wolfe material, The Thomas Wolfe Society, The Thomas Wolfe Review, and even times and prices of tours of the holy sites.

Johnston, Carol Ingalls. *Of Time and the Artist: Thomas Wolfe, His Novels, and the Critics.* Columbia, S.C.: Camden House, 1996. Looks at Wolfe's autobiographical fiction and the critical response to it.

McElderry, Bruce R. *Thomas Wolfe.* New York: Twayne, 1964. An excellent basic introduction to Wolfe's life and work, McElderry's study provides lucid analysis well supported by standard critical opinion, including a chapter on the shorter fiction. Contains a useful chronology and annotated select bibliographies of primary and secondary sources.

Phillipson, John S., ed. *Critical Essays on Thomas Wolfe.* Boston: G. K. Hall, 1985. Contains twenty-three essays, most formerly published, written between 1970 and the early 1980's. Arranged by genre, the book contains seven essays on Wolfe's short fiction.

John Carr, updated by Douglas Rollins

TOBIAS WOLFF

Born: Birmingham, Alabama; June 19, 1945

PRINCIPAL SHORT FICTION

In the Garden of the North American Martyrs,
   1981
Back in the World, 1985
The Stories of Tobias Wolff, 1988
The Night in Question, 1996

OTHER LITERARY FORMS

Besides short stories, Tobias Wolff has published
a novella, *The Barracks Thief* (1984), and a memoir,
This Boy's Life (1989). He also edited short-story anthologies, including *The Best American Short Stories
1994* (1994).

ACHIEVEMENTS

The quality of his work has earned for Wolff much
critical respect and numerous literary prizes. He received a Wallace Stegner Fellowship in 1975-1976 to
study creative writing at Stanford University, and
even before he published his first book, he won creative writing grants from the National Endowment
for the Arts (1978, 1985), a Mary Roberts Rinehart
grant (1979), and an Arizona Council on the Arts and
Humanities fellowship in creative writing (1980). He
has also won several O. Henry Awards (1980, 1981,
and 1985) and a John Simon Guggenheim Memorial
Foundation Fellowship (1982). Wolff's *In the Garden
of the North American Martyrs* received the St. Lawrence Award for Fiction (1982), his *The Barracks
Thief* (1984) took the PEN/Faulkner Award for Fiction (1985), and he won the Rea Award for short stories (1989). His *This Boy's Life: A Memoir* (1989)
won *The Los Angeles Times* book prize for biography
and the Ambassador Book Award of the English-
Speaking Union and was a finalist for the National
Book Critics Circle Award. *In Pharaoh's Army:
Memories of the Lost War* (1994) won *Esquire*-Volvo-
Waterstone's Prize for Nonfiction and was a finalist
for both the National Book Award (1994) and *The
Los Angeles Times* Book Award for biography

(1995). He has also received a Whiting Foundation
Award (1990), a Lila Wallace-*Reader's Digest* Award
(1994), and a Lyndhurst Foundation Award (1994).

BIOGRAPHY

Readers are lucky to have two prime sources dealing with Tobias Jonathan Ansell Wolff's parents and
Wolff's early life: Wolff's own memoir and a recollection of his father entitled *The Duke of Deception:
Memories of My Father* (1979), written by Wolff's
older brother, the novelist Geoffrey Wolff. Together,
these works portray a remarkable family, though
Rosemary Loftus Wolff, Wolff's mother, wryly observed that, if she had known so much was going to
be told, she might have watched herself more closely.

The one who bore watching, however, was
Wolff's inventive father, a genial Gatsby-like figure
who, in pursuit of the good life, forged checks, credentials, and his own identity. He began as Arthur
Samuels Wolff, a Jewish doctor's son and boarding-
school expellee, but later emerged as Arthur
Saunders Wolff, an Episcopalian and Yale University
graduate. A still later reincarnation was as Saunders
Ansell-Wolff III. On the basis of forged credentials,
he became an aeronautical engineer and rose to occupy an executive suite. During his time, however, he
also occupied a number of jail cells. Still, he showed
remarkable creativity in his fabrications, so perhaps it
is not surprising that both his sons became writers of
fiction. Family life with him was something of a
roller coaster, exciting but with many ups and downs.
Eventually, this instability led to the family's breakup
in 1951: Twelve-year-old Geoffrey remained with the
father, while the mother took five-year-old Tobias,
who had been born June 19, 1945, in Birmingham,
Alabama, one of several locations where the family
had chased the American Dream. Henceforth reared
separately, sometimes a country apart, the two boys
were not reunited until Geoffrey's final year at
Princeton University.

Meanwhile, Tobias and his mother lived first in
Florida, then in Utah, and finally in the Pacific North-

west, where his mother remarried. The stays in Utah and the Pacific Northwest are recounted in *This Boy's Life*, which covers Wolff's life from the age of ten until he left for Hill School in Pottstown, Pennsylvania, (where he faked his references to be accepted). He attended Hill School for a time but did not graduate and instead ended up joining the military. From 1964 to 1968, Wolff served in the U.S. Army Special Forces and toured Vietnam as an adviser to a South Vietnamese unit, experiences he recounted in his second volume of memoirs, *In Pharaoh's Army*. After this service, deterred by the antiwar movement in the United States, he traveled to England, where he enrolled at Oxford University. He received a B.A., with first class honors, from Oxford University in 1972.

Returning to the United States, he worked first as a reporter for *The Washington Post*, then at various restaurant jobs in California, and finally entered the Stanford University creative writing program. He received an M.A. from Stanford in 1978. While at Stanford, he met and became friends with other writers, including Raymond Carver, and taught for a period of time. While pursuing his own writing, Wolff has taught creative writing at Goddard College, Arizona State University, and Syracuse University. In 1975, he married Catherine Dolores Spohn, a teacher and social worker; they had two sons, Michael and Patrick.

Analysis

Tobias Wolff is an outstanding contemporary craftsman of the American short story. Working slowly, sometimes taking months and countless drafts, he polishes each story into an entertaining, gemlike work that reads with deceptive ease. He has said, in interviews, that he needs time to get to know his characters but that the finished story no longer holds any surprises for him. For the reader, the result is full of surprises, insights, humor, and other line-by-line rewards, particularly in character portrayal and style. The influences on his work—his friend Raymond Carver and earlier masters such as Guy de Maupassant, Anton Chekhov, Sherwood Anderson, Ernest Hemingway, and Flannery O'Connor—indicate the company Wolff intends to keep.

No overriding theme, message, or agenda seems to unite Wolff's work—only his interest in people, their quirks, their unpredictability, their strivings and failings, and their predicaments as human beings. Despite their dishonesty and drug use, most of his characters fall within the range of a very shaky middle-class respectability or what passes for it in contemporary America. Although most of them do not hope for much, many still have troubles separating their fantasies from reality. Despite their dried-up souls, vague remnants of Judeo-Christian morality still rattle around inside their rib cages, haunting them with the specter of moral choice (Wolff himself is a Catholic). It is perhaps emblematic that a considerable amount of action in his stories occurs inside automobiles hurtling across the landscape (except when they break down or fly off the road).

Wolff himself has called his stories autobiographical (just as his memoirs are somewhat fictionalized), but this seems true only in a broad sense. Wolff goes on to say that many of his characters reflect aspects of himself and that he sometimes makes use of actual events. According to Wolff, "The Liar" mirrors himself as a child: The story is about a boy who reacts to his father's death by becoming a pathological liar. A story that appears to make use of an actual event is "The Missing Person," about a priest who, to impress his drinking buddy, fabricates a story about killing a man with his bare hands. Before he knows it, the buddy has spread the news to the nuns. Wolff related a similar story about himself in an *Esquire* magazine article ("Raymond Carver Had His Cake and Ate It Too," September, 1989), recalling his friend Carver after Carver's death from cancer. In a tale-swapping competition with Carver, known for his bouts with alcohol, Wolff bested his friend by fabricating a story about being addicted to heroin; aghast, Carver repeated the story, and people began regarding Wolff with pity and sorrow.

"Our Story Begins"

A truly autobiographical story titled "Our Story Begins" (a double or triple entendre) probably gives a more typical view of Wolff's sources of inspiration: uncanny powers of observation and a good ear. In this story, Charlie, an aspiring writer, who barely supports himself by working as a busboy in a San Francisco restaurant, is discouraged and about ready to quit. On his way home through one of those notorious San Francisco fogs, however, he stops at a coffeehouse. There he overhears a conversation between a woman, her husband, and another man. The man tells a story about a Filipino taxi driver's fantastic love obsession with a local woman, and the trio are identified as a love triangle themselves. Charlie soaks it all in with his cappuccino, then, newly inspired by these riches, heads home through the fog. Wolff brings these stories to a close with a patented ending: A Chinese woman carrying a live lobster rushes past, and a foghorn in the bay is likewise an omen that "at any moment anything might be revealed."

IN THE GARDEN OF THE NORTH AMERICAN MARTYRS

Wolff's patented ending is an updated open version of O. Henry's surprise ending, which wrapped things up with a plot twist. Wolff's endings are usually accomplished with a modulation of style, a sudden opening out into revelation, humor, irony, symbolism, or lyricism. Such an ending is illustrated by "Next Door," the first story of *In the Garden of the North American Martyrs*. A quiet couple are scandalized by the goings-on next door, where everybody screams and fights and the husband and wife make love standing up against the refrigerator. To drown out these raucous neighbors, the couple turns up their television volume, goes to bed, and watches the film *El Dorado*. Lying next to his wife, the husband becomes sexually aroused, but she is unresponsive. The seemingly uneventful story ends when the husband suddenly imagines how he would rewrite the movie—an ambiguous ending that suggests both his desire for some of the lusty, disorderly life next door (and in the movie) and the quiet, passionless fate that he is probably doomed to endure.

The next story, "Hunters in the Snow," perhaps Wolff's best, is much more eventful and has an unforgettable ending. The story is set in the wintry fields of the Northwest, where three deer hunters, supposedly old buddies, rib and carp and play practical jokes on one another. The ringleader, Kenny, who is driving his old truck, is unmerciful to Frank and especially to

Tub. Tub, however, wreaks a terrible revenge when one of Kenny's practical jokes backfires and, through a misunderstanding, Tub shoots him, inflicting a gruesome gut wound. Frank and Tub throw Kenny into the back of the pickup truck and head off over unfamiliar country roads for the hospital fifty miles away. After a while, Frank and Tub become cold from the snow blowing through a hole in the windshield and stop at a tavern for a beer, where they strike up a sympathetic conversation with each other. Leaving the directions to the hospital on the table, they hit the road again. A little farther on, Frank and Tub have to stop at the next tavern for another beer and, this time, a warm meal. Self-absorbed, they continue their discoveries that they have much in common and become real pals. Meanwhile, Kenny is cooling in the back of the truck, and the story ends when they get under way again:

> As the truck twisted through the gentle hills the star went back and forth between Kenny's boots, staying always in his sight. "I'm going to the hospital," Kenny said. But he was wrong. They had taken a different turn a long way back.

The title story, "In the Garden of the North American Martyrs," shows that academics can be just as cruel as hunters (or, in this case, the Iroquois Indians). The story's protagonist is Mary, a mousy historian who has a terrible teaching job at a college in the rainy Northwest. She is invited by her friend Louise—who is a member of the history faculty of a posh college in upstate New York, Iroquois country—to interview for a job opening there. When Mary arrives on campus, she finds that she has been cruelly exploited: The interview was only a setup to fulfill a college requirement that a woman be interviewed for every job opening. As the story ends, Mary changes the topic of her demonstration lecture and—before horrified faculty and students assembled in the college's modernized version of the long house—delivers a grisly account of how the Iroquois "took scalps and practiced cannibalism and slavery" and "tortured their captives."

Two other memorable stories in Wolff's first collection explore the bittersweet possibilities of relationships that never come to fruition. In "Passenger," the strictly behaved protagonist, Glen, is conned into giving a ride to the aging flower child Bonnie and her dog Sunshine. They become a working unit in the car, like an informal but close-knit family, and the reader sees that they are good for each other but realizes that the relationship probably would not last much longer than the day's journey; the probability is symbolized by a hair-raising incident along the way, when the dog leaps on the driver, Glen, causing the car to go spinning down the wet highway out of control. In "Poaching," a real family gets together again, briefly: A divorced woman visits her former husband and their small son. It is clear that husband and wife should reunite for their own good and the good of the child, but neither will make the first move—even though they sleep together in the same bed. The state of their relationship is symbolized by an old beaver who tries to build his lodge in a pond on the property and is quickly shot.

BACK IN THE WORLD

The stories in *Back in the World*, Wolff's second collection, are not quite as finished as the ones in his first but include several worth noting. The title is a phrase used by American soldiers in Vietnam to refer to home. Ironically, from Wolff's stories it appears that "back in the world" is also a crazy battle zone. Besides "The Missing Person" and "Our Story Begins," other stories that stand out are "Coming Attractions," "Desert Breakdown, 1968," and "The Rich Brother."

"Coming Attractions," the collection's first story, showcases a precocious teenage girl who is every parent's nightmare. She shoplifts and makes random anonymous phone calls late at night: For example, she calls and wakes an unfortunately named Mr. Love, sixty-one years old, and gets him excited about winning a big contest. First, however, he has to answer the question: "Here's the question, Mr. Love. I lie and steal and sleep around. What do you think about that?" Still, she reveals another side of herself at the end, when she dives to the bottom of an ice-cold swimming pool in the middle of the night and fishes out an abandoned bike for her little brother.

The two other stories feature cars. In "Desert Breakdown, 1968," the car of a young family fresh back from Germany—a former American soldier, his pregnant German wife, and their first child—breaks down at an isolated service station in the Mojave desert. The locals do not lift a hand to help, except for a woman who runs the station, and the husband is tempted to abandon his young family there. The story demonstrates that men cannot be depended on, but women are quite capable of taking care of themselves: The German wife beats up one of the local cowboys, and the station operator goes out and shoots rabbits for dinner. In "The Rich Brother," the collection's last story, the lifestyles of two brothers clash. The rich brother drives to a distant religious commune to rescue his young brother, but on the way home, they quarrel, and the rich brother abandons the young one along the roadside. As the story ends, however, the rich brother is having second thoughts, afraid to get home and face the questions of his wife: "Where is he? Where is your brother?"

THE NIGHT IN QUESTION

The fifteen stories in *The Night in Question* again display Wolff's command of dialogue, expressive detail, and meticulous plotting. The plots frequently turn on situational irony, and the endings show the principal characters suffering unexpectedly because of their behavior. That behavior devolves from self-delusion. The disparity between characters' intentions and the consequences of their actions creates conflict that at times skirts the bizarre but is moving and provocative in the end.

The "Other Miller" illustrates Wolff's use of a surprise ending to reveal the source of self-delusion. Miller, a young soldier, is told that his mother has died. He is delighted because he believes that the authorities have mistaken him for another Miller in his battalion. He plays along in order to get emergency leave and amuses himself with the sympathy of other soldiers. He never believes his mother has died because she is young and, more important, he is obsessed with punishing her for remarrying after his father's death. His enlistment, in fact, had been meant to punish her. Not until he opens the door to his home does the truth force its way through his childish spite. The only mistake, all along, has been his; his mother now dead, he has only punished himself with his bitter love.

In some stories the ending is foreshadowed, gradually intensifying for the reader the emotional state of the protagonists. "The Life of the Body" concerns an aging preparatory school English teacher. A romantic, he loves the classics and is liberal in applying their themes to modern social problems. The story opens in a bar. He is drunk, makes a pass at a pretty young veterinarian, and is beaten up by her boyfriend. The next day, heroically bruised, he does not correct the rumors among his students that he has been mugged by a gang. He tells the truth to a friend and admits his foolishness but continues to pursue the veterinarian despite her hostility and dangerous boyfriend. As the story ends, she relents slightly, just enough to give him hope for more adventure and romance. However irrational his actions, he deeply craves direct experience. The title story, "The Night in Question," similarly heightens suspense in order to depict a complex emotional state with devastating power. Frank and Frances grew up under a violently abusive father. As adults, they seem familiar literary types: Frank has been the wild youth who now has gotten religion; Frances is the long-suffering, practical big sister. In the story, Frank repeats to Frances a sermon he has heard about a man who must choose between saving his beloved son and a passenger train. Frances will have none of the story's pat message about choice and trust in the heavenly Father. It becomes ever clearer as she listens that she is spiritually alive only when she is protecting her brother. In fact, as their names suggest—Frank (Francis) and Frances—their earthly father's violence has welded them into a single spiritual being. The story makes the psychological concept of codependency potently eerie.

Like Wolff's earlier collections, *The Night in Question* portrays the predicaments of human intercourse vividly and conveys their psychological or philosophical consequence by suggestion. Wolff rarely sermonizes. If he comments at all, he usually comments indirectly, through symbolism or his patented ending. Above all, Wolff is a lover of good stories and is content to tell them and let them stand on their own.

OTHER MAJOR WORKS

LONG FICTION: *The Barracks Thief*, 1984.

NONFICTION: *This Boy's Life: A Memoir*, 1989; *In Pharaoh's Army: Memories of the Lost War*, 1994.

EDITED TEXTS: *Matters of Life and Death: New American Stories*, 1983; *The Vintage Book of Contemporary American Short Stories* (1994); *The Best American Short Stories 1994*, 1994; *Writers Harvest 3*, (2000).

BIBLIOGRAPHY

Challener, Daniel D. *Stories of Resilience in Childhood: The Narratives of Maya Angelou, Maxine Hong Kingston, Richard Rodrigues, John Edgar Wideman, and Tobias Wolff*. New York: Garland, 1997. Compares the poverty-stricken childhoods of several notable writers, analyzing what led them to overcome early hardship and go on to literary greatness. Includes a bibliography and index.

Hannah, James. *Tobias Wolff: A Study of the Short Fiction*. Twayne's Studies in Short Fiction 64. New York: Twayne, 1996. A good critical study of the short fiction of Tobias Wolff.

Kelly, Colm L. "Affirming the Indeterminable: Deconstruction, Sociology, and Tobias Wolff's 'Say Yes.'" *Mosaic* 32 (March, 1999): 149-166. In response to sociological approaches to literature, argues that stories like Wolff's are polysemous and therefore not reducible to any single interpretation; provides a deconstructive reading of the story, setting it off against three possible readings derived from current sociological theory, in order to show how the story deconstructs the theories that attempt to explain it.

Peters, Joanne M., and Jean W. Ross. "Tobias Wolff (Jonathan Ansell)." In *Contemporary Authors*, edited by Hal May. Vol. 117. Detroit: Gale Research, 1986. Peters gives a brief overview of Wolff's work, but more important is the interview by Ross. In the interview, Wolff talks about his reasons for writing short stories, the writers who have influenced him, his working methods and sources of inspiration, his own reading, and his teaching of creative writing.

Prose, Francine. "The Brothers Wolff." *The New York Times Magazine*, February 5, 1989, 22. Prose's fine article, which is also collected in *The New York Times Biographical Service* (February, 1989), introduces the writing of the Wolff brothers, Geoffrey and Tobias. Traces how they grew up apart but became inseparable, even bearing striking resemblances to each other. The article also provides background on their parents, particularly their father.

Wolff, Tobias. "A Forgotten Master: Rescuing the Works of Paul Bowles." *Esquire* 103 (May, 1986): 221-223. Wolff's article not only helps rescue a forgotten master but also provides an index of what Wolff values in writing. He praises Bowles for the mythic quality of his stories, the clarity of his language, his ability to shift moods at will, and his ability to depict a wide range of international characters. He feels that Bowles's pessimism might have contributed to his lack of popularity.

_____. Interview by Nicholas A. Basbanes. *Publishers Weekly* 241 (October 24, 1994): 45-46. A brief biographical sketch and survey of Wolff's career; Wolff discusses his writing habits and his works.

_____. "An Interview with Tobias Wolff." *Contemporary Literature* 31 (Spring, 1990): 1-16. Wolff discusses lying in his story "The Liar" and the nature of "winging it" in his story "In the Garden of the North American Martyrs." Wolff also talks about the fable aspect of his story "The Rich Brother," as well as his fiction about the Vietnam War.

Harold Branam

VIRGINIA WOOLF

Born: London, England; January 25, 1882
Died: Rodmell, Sussex, England; March 28, 1941

PRINCIPAL SHORT FICTION

Two Stories, 1917 (one by Leonard Woolf)
Kew Gardens, 1919
The Mark on the Wall, 1919
Monday or Tuesday, 1921
A Haunted House and Other Short Stories, 1943
Mrs. Dalloway's Party, 1973 (Stella McNichol, editor)
The Complete Shorter Fiction of Virginia Woolf, 1985

OTHER LITERARY FORMS

Besides authoring short stories, Virginia Woolf was an acute and detailed diarist (her diary entries occupy five volumes in the authoritative collected edition); a prolific letter writer (six volumes in the authoritative collected edition); a biographer; a perceptive, original, and argumentative essayist and reviewer (her collected essays fill six volumes in the authoritative edition); and a pioneer of the modern novel in her ten works of long prose fiction, which include the acknowledged classics *Mrs. Dalloway* (1925), *To the Lighthouse* (1927), and *The Waves* (1931).

ACHIEVEMENTS

A distinguished and distinctive prose stylist, Virginia Woolf excelled in fiction, nonfiction, and her own unique hybrid of these genres in her two whimsical books *Orlando: A Biography* (1928) and *Flush: A Biography* (1933), which are variously categorized as fiction, nonfiction, or "other" by critics of her work. In nonfiction, essays such as "The Death of the Moth," "How Should One Read a Book?" and "Shakespeare's Sister" have been widely anthologized, and in their vividness, imagery, and keen analysis of daily life, literature, society, and women's concerns assure Woolf a place in the history of the essay.

In fiction, Woolf's classic novels, sharing much in style and theme with the nonfiction, have overshadowed the short stories. Reacting against the realistic and naturalistic fiction of her time, Woolf often emphasized lyricism, stream of consciousness, and the irresolute slice of life in both her novels and her stories, though she wrote more conventional fiction as well. Whether the conventional "well-made" or the experimental stream-of-consciousness variety, many of her approximately fifty short stories are accomplished works of art. Because of their precise and musical prose style, irony, ingenious spiral form (with narrative refrains), reversal or revelatory structure, and exploration of human nature and social life, they deserve to be better known and to be studied for themselves and not just for what they may reveal about the novels.

BIOGRAPHY

Virginia Woolf was born as Adeline Virginia Stephen and grew up in the household of her father, Leslie Stephen, a Victorian and Edwardian literary lion who was visited by many prominent writers of the time. The importance of books in her life is reflected in many of the short stories, such as "Memoirs of a Novelist," "The Evening Party," and "A Haunted House"; her father's extensive personal library provided much of her education, along with some private tutoring (especially in Greek). Despite Katherine Stephen, niece of Leslie Stephen, being the principal of Newnham College at the University of Cambridge (reflected in the story "A Woman's College from Outside"), Virginia was denied a formal college education because of persistent ill health (emotional and physical), as well as her father's male bias in this matter, all of which is echoed with mild irony in "Phyllis and Rosamond" (about two sisters who resemble Virginia and Vanessa Stephen, lacking a college education) and "A Society" (in which the character Poll, lacking a college education, receives her father's inheritance on condition that she read all the books in the London Library).

The early death of Woolf's mother, Julia, in 1895, the repeated sexual molestation by her half brother George Duckworth, her father's transformation of

Virginia Woolf (Courtesy D. C. Public Library)

Virginia's sisters Stella and Vanessa into surrogate mothers after Julia's death, and her own attachments to women such as Violet Dickinson and, later, Vita Sackville-West culminated in Virginia's cool and ambivalent sexuality, reflected by the general absence of sexual passion in many of the short stories as well as by what Woolf herself described as the "Sapphism" of "Moments of Being: 'Slater's Pins Have No Points.'" The more regular element of her adolescence and generally happy life with Leonard Woolf, whom she married in 1912, was the social round of upper-middle-class life, including horticultural outings in London (reflected in "Kew Gardens"), parties, private concerts, and theater-going (as in "The Evening Party," "The String Quartet," the Mrs. Dalloway party cycle of stories, "Uncle Vanya," and "The Searchlight"), and excursions to the country (as in "In the Orchard"), seashore (as in "Solid Objects" and "The Watering Place"), or foreign resorts (as in "A Dialogue upon Mount Pentelicus" and "The Symbol").

Clustering around Virginia and her sister Vanessa, when they moved to a house in the Bloomsbury district after Leslie Stephen's death in 1904, was a group of talented writers, artists, and intellectuals who came to be known as the Bloomsbury Group and were generally among the avant-garde in arts and letters. (This period is portrayed in "Phyllis and Rosamond.") Many intellectuals from the group continued to associate with Virginia and Leonard Woolf after their marriage, and some, such as T. S. Eliot, had books published by the Hogarth Press, which was set up by the Woolfs in 1917. Indeed, all Virginia Woolf's short stories in book form have been published in England by this press.

In 1919, the Woolfs, for weekend and recreational use, took a country cottage called Monks House, whose reputation for being haunted evoked "A Haunted House" and whose vicinity, Rodmell (as well as Leonard Woolf, by name), is jocularly referred to in "The Window and the Parrot: A True Story." Because of numerous family deaths as well as, later, the strain and letdown of completing her novels and the anxiety from World Wars I and II (referred to in many of the stories, and responsible in 1940 for the destruction of the Woolfs' London house), Woolf had been and continued to be subject to mental breakdowns. The motifs of liquid's destructiveness and death by drowning in several of the stories ("Solid Objects," "A Woman's College from Outside," "The Widow and the Parrot," "The New Dress," "The Introduction," "A Simple Melody," "The Fascination of the Pool") were actualized when, in early 1941, Woolf, at the onset of another breakdown, drowned herself in the Ouse River, near Rodmell and Monks House.

ANALYSIS

Perhaps related to her mental condition is Virginia Woolf's interest in perception and perspective, as well as their relationship to imagination, in many stories. In two short avant-garde pieces—"Monday or Tuesday" (six paragraphs) and "Blue and Green" (two paragraphs, one for each color)—Woolf attempts to convey the reality of the urban and natural worlds through discrete, apparently disconnected associative impressions.

"MONDAY OR TUESDAY" AND "BLUE AND GREEN"

In "Monday or Tuesday," a series of contrasts between up and down, spatially free timelessness (a lazily flying heron) and restrictive timeliness (a clock striking), day and night, inside and outside, present experience and later recollection of it conveys the ordinary cycle of life suggested by the title and helps capture its experiential reality, the concern expressed by the refrain question that closes the second, fourth, and fifth paragraphs: "and truth?"

Similar contrasts inform the two paragraphs describing the blue and green aspects of reality and the feelings associated with them in "Blue and Green." These two colors are dominant and symbolic throughout Woolf's short stories. Differing perspectives, which are almost cinematic or painterly, also structure "In the Orchard," as each of the story's three sections, dealing with a woman named Miranda sleeping in an orchard, focuses on, in order, the sleeping Miranda in relation to her physical surroundings, the effect of the physical surroundings on Miranda's dreaming (and thus the interconnection between imagination and external world), and finally a return to the physical environment, with a shift in focus to the orchard's apple trees and birds. The simultaneity and differing angle of the three perspectives are suggested by the narrative refrain that closes each section, a sentence referring to Miranda jumping upright and exclaiming that she will be late for tea.

The ability of the imagination, a key repeated word in Woolf's short stories, to perceive accurately the surrounding world is an issue in many of the stories. In "The Mark on the Wall," a narrator is led into associative musings from speculating about the mark, only to discover, with deflating irony, that the source of the imaginative ramblings is in reality a lowly snail (with the further concluding ironic reversal being an unexpected reference to World War I, whose seriousness undercuts the narrator's previous whimsical free associations). Even more difficult is the imagination's perception of people (who and what individuals really are) in the surrounding world. This is the chief problem of the biographer, a task at which Woolf herself was successful, though not the self-centered and somewhat dishonest novelist's biographer who narrates "Memoirs of a Novelist." In the four stories "An Unwritten Novel," "Moments of Being: 'Slater's Pins Have No Points,'" "The Lady in the Looking Glass: A Reflection," and "The Shooting Party," a major character or the narrator is led through small details into imaginative flights about the life and personality of an individual—only, in the story's concluding reversal, to be proved incorrect or be left very doubtful about the picture or account created. Likewise showing a connection between the literary artist's problem of depicting the truth and the imagination's problem in probing reality is the story "The Three Pictures," in which the first picture, of a sailor's homecoming to a welcoming wife, leads the narrator to imagine further happy events, undercut by the second and third pictures revealing the sailor's death from a fever contracted overseas and the despair of his wife.

The problem of "and truth?" (as phrased in "Monday or Tuesday") can be comically superficial, as in the narrator's wasted sympathetic imaginings in "Sympathy" in response to a newspaper account of Humphrey Hammond's death, only to discover in the story's conclusion that the article referred to the elderly father rather than the son (with ironic undercutting of the genuineness of the narrator's sympathy because of her chagrin about the "deception" and "waste"). In contrast, in "The Fascination of the Pool," the deeply evocative imagery and symbolism of never-ending layers of stories absorbed by a pool over time, and always going inexhaustibly deeper, have a meditative and melancholic solemnity.

"KEW GARDENS"

Related to imagination and art (which may or may not bridge the gap between human beings), as well as to social criticism and feminist issues (whether roles and identities unite or divide, fulfill or thwart people), is the motif of isolation and alienation in many of the stories. In "Kew Gardens," the first paragraph's twice-repeated detail of the heart-and-tongue shape of the colorful plants symbolizes the potential of love and communication to effect communion, while the colors projected by the flowers from sunlight on various things (mentioned in the first and last paragraphs)

symbolize the various couples' imaginations projected on the environs. In the social context of the park, however, the four sets of strollers are isolated from one another, as is the other major "character" described, the snail; each is solipsistically involved in its own affairs. Only in the fourth set, a romantic young couple, do love and communication seem to promise, though not guarantee, the hope of communion.

"SOLID OBJECTS"

In "Solid Objects," the first paragraph's emphasis on a changing perspective (a black dot on the horizon becomes four-legged and then two men) symbolizes how the protagonist's, John's, perspective changes from imaginative engagements with people, politics, and ideas, to engagements with small things or concrete objects, beginning with his discovery at the beach of a smooth, irregular fragment of glass. While Charles, John's friend, at the beach casts flat slate stones into the water, aware of objects only as a means of allowing physical action and release, John becomes attached to them with the child's and artist's fascination, which lures him away from the practical and pragmatic adult world of action and politics, in which he had a bright future. John thus becomes alienated from all those around him, including Charles. Symbolically during their last encounter, both end up conversing at cross purposes, neither person understanding the other.

"A HAUNTED HOUSE" AND "LAPPIN AND LAPINOVA"

"A Haunted House" and "Lappin and Lapinova" show, respectively, success and failure in human communion. The former story uses the convention of the ghost story and gothic fiction, almost satirically or ironically, to suggest the broader theme of the mystery of the human heart. Implicitly two kinds of mystery are contrasted: the mystery of ghosts, haunted houses, secret treasures, and so on, and the real, important mystery of what is most worthwhile in the universe—the ghostly couple's lesson at the story's close that the house's hidden treasure is love, "the light in the heart." The implicitly living couple presumably have love, paralleling the ghostly couple's bond. The cyclical repetitions in the story help convey, stylistically, the pulsation or beating of the human heart, the seat of this love. In contrast, the married couple in "Lappin and Lapinova" become alienated because the husband cannot genuinely share in the wife's imaginative fantasy of the two of them as rabbit and hare, reverting to his pragmatic and stolid family heritage and an arrogant masculine impatience.

MRS. DALLOWAY PARTY CYCLE

Most of the nine stories constituting the Mrs. Dalloway party cycle ("Mrs. Dalloway in Bond Street," "The New Dress," "Happiness," "Ancestors," "The Introduction," "Together and Apart," "The Man Who Loved His Kind," "A Simple Melody," "A Summing Up") naturally deal, by their focus on a social occasion, with communion or alienation, as suggested by the title "Together and Apart." In "Mrs. Dalloway in Bond Street," the title character remains isolated or insulated from the surrounding world, symbolized by the gloves that she is going to buy (perhaps for the party), by her general disregard of traffic and other phenomena while she muses about the death of a recent acquaintance, and by her disregard of a literal explosion that ends the story (though paradoxically she communes with an acquaintance by remembering and uttering the name while ignoring the explosion). At the party itself, Mabel Waring, the protagonist of "The New Dress," is alienated because her new dress, owing to her limited means, seems a failure and source of embarrassment; Stuart Elton, protagonist of "Happiness," remains withdrawn in himself to preserve an egocentric equilibrium that is his happiness; Mrs. Vallance, protagonist of "Ancestors," is alienated by the superficial and undignified talk and values of the young around her, in contrast to her past. Woolf's feminist concerns about the unjust subordination and oppression of women (prominent in "Phyllis and Rosamond," "The Mysterious Case of Miss V.," "The Journal of Mistress Joan Martyn," "A Society," "A Woman's College from Outside," and "The Legacy") are suggested by the isolation and alienation of Lily Everit, who feels inadequate when introduced to Bob Brinsley, symbol of thoughtless male power and conceit. Despite Everit's esteemed essay writing (paralleling Woolf's),

Brinsley negligently assumes that she must as a women write poetry, as his initial question shows. Everit feels crushed, stifled, and silenced by the weight of masculine accomplishment in the arts and sciences.

Two impromptu pairings in the Dalloway party cycle—Roderick Serle and Ruth Anning of "Together and Apart," and Prickett Ellis and Miss O'Keefe of "The Man Who Loved His Kind"—achieve temporary communion: Serle and Anning when they imaginatively attune to each other, sharing profound emotions about experiences in Canterbury; Ellis and O'Keefe when the latter concurs with the former's concern about the poor excluded from affairs such as Mrs. Dalloway's party. These couples, however, driven apart at story's end by the evening's experience—Serle and Anning when the former is mockingly accosted by a female acquaintance, and Ellis and O'Keefe when the former fails, with some self-centered posturing, to appreciate the latter's understanding of the need for beauty and imagination in the life lived at all social levels. Only the protagonists of the last two stories of the cycle, George Carslake in "A Simple Melody" and Sasha Latham in "A Summing Up," achieve a transcendence over isolation and alienation. Carslake melds all the partygoers and himself through a blend of imagination, art, and nature by meditating on a beautiful painting of a heath in the Dalloways' house and imagining the various partygoers on a walk there that reduces them all to fundamentally decent human beings coalesced in a common enterprise. Like Carslake, Latham achieves wisdom by fixing on inanimate objects, the Dalloways' beautiful Queen Anne house (art) and a tree in the garden (nature), and meditating on them; like Carslake, Latham sees people admirably united in motion—in her reverie, adventures and survivors sailing on the sea.

OTHER MAJOR WORKS

LONG FICTION: *The Voyage Out*, 1915; *Night and Day*, 1919; *Jacob's Room*, 1922; *Mrs. Dalloway*, 1925; *To the Lighthouse*, 1927; *Orlando: A Biography*, 1928; *The Waves*, 1931; *Flush: A Biography*, 1933; *The Years*, 1937; *Between the Acts*, 1941.

NONFICTION: *The Common Reader: First Series*, 1925; *A Room of One's Own*, 1929; *The Common Reader: Second Series*, 1932; *Three Guineas*, 1938; *Roger Fry: A Biography*, 1940; *The Death of the Moth and Other Essays*, 1942; *The Moment and Other Essays*, 1947; *The Captain's Death Bed and Other Essays*, 1950; *A Writer's Diary*, 1953; *Letters: Virginia Woolf and Lytton Strachey*, 1956; *Granite and Rainbow*, 1958; *Contemporary Writers*, 1965; *Collected Essays, Volumes 1-2*, 1966; *Collected Essays, Volumes 3-4*, 1967; *The London Scene: Five Essays*, 1975; *The Flight of the Mind: The Letters of Virginia Woolf, Vol. I, 1888-1912*, 1975 (pb. in the U.S. as *The Letters of Virginia Woolf, Vol. I: 1888-1912*, 1975; Nigel Nicolson, editor); *The Question of Things Happening: The Letters of Virginia Woolf, Vol. II, 1912-1922*, 1976; (pb. in the U.S. as *The Letters of Virginia Woolf, Vol. II: 1912-1922*, 1976; Nigel Nicolson, editor); *Moments of Being*, 1976 (Jeanne Schulkind, editor); *Books and Portraits*, 1977; *The Diary of Virginia Woolf*, 1977-1984 (Anne Olivier Bell, editor, 5 volumes); *A Change of Perspective: The Letters of Virginia Woolf, Vol. III, 1923-1928*, 1977 (pb. in the U.S. as *The Letters of Virginia Woolf, Vol. III: 1923-1928*, 1978; Nigel Nicolson, editor); *A Reflection of the Other Person: The Letters of Virginia Woolf, Vol. IV, 1929-1931*, 1978 (pb. in the U.S. as *The Letters of Virginia Woolf, Vol. IV: 1929-1931*, 1979; Nigel Nicolson, editor); *The Sickle Side of the Moon: The Letters of Virginia Woolf, Vol. V, 1932-1935*, 1979 (pb. in the U.S. as *The Letters of Virginia Woolf, Vol. V: 1932-1935*, 1979; Nigel Nicolson, editor); *Leave the Letters Till We're Dead: The Letters of Virginia Woolf, Vol. VI, 1936-1941*, 1980 (Nigel Nicolson, editor); *The Essays of Virginia Woolf*, 1987-1994 (4 volumes; Andrew McNeillie, editor).

BIBLIOGRAPHY

Banks, Joanne Trautmann. "Virginia Woolf and Katherine Mansfield." In *The English Short Story, 1880-1945: A Critical History*, edited by Joseph M. Flora. Boston, Mass.: Twayne, 1985. In about twelve pages, the philosophical themes of several stories (imagination, perception) are briefly ex- plored, plus the affinities of the two writers, deriving from feminist concerns and admiration of Anton Chekhov's short fiction.

Barrett, Eileen, and Patricia Cramer, eds. *Virginia Woolf: Lesbian Readings*. New York: New York University Press, 1997. This collection of conference papers features two essays on Woolf's stories: one on Katherine Mansfield's presence in Woolf's story "Moments of Being," and one that compares lesbian modernism in the stories of Woolf with lesbian modernism in the stories of Gertrude Stein.

Bleishman, Avrom. "Forms of the Woolfian Short Story." In *Virginia Woolf: Revaluation and Continuity*, edited by Ralph Freedman. Berkeley: University of California Press, 1980. In twenty-six pages, abstract theoretical issues concerning genre are discussed; then several stories are divided into the two categories of linear (for example, "The New Dress" and "Kew Gardens") and circular (for example, "The Duchess" and "Lappin and Lapinova") in form.

Daiches, David. *Virginia Woolf*. Norfolk, Conn.: New Directions, 1942. Brief comments are offered on "A Haunted House," "The Mark on the Wall," "Monday or Tuesday," "A Society," "The String Quartet," and "An Unwritten Novel."

Dick, Susan, ed. Introduction to *The Complete Shorter Fiction of Virginia Woolf*. 2d ed. San Diego: Harcourt Brace Jovanovich, 1989. Along with classification of stories into traditional ones and fictional reveries, with affinities in works of nineteenth century writers such as Thomas De Quincey and Anton Chekhov, invaluable notes are given on historical, literary, and cultural allusions, as well as textual problems, for every story.

Guiget, Jean. "Stories and Sketches." In *Virginia Woolf and Her Works*. Translated by Jean Stewart. London: Hogarth Press, 1965. In fourteen pages, the stories are divided into several groups by style (such as the impressionistic ones) or theme (such as the observer studying another person), with perceptive comments on specific symbols.

Head, Dominic. "Experiments in Genre." In *The Modernist Short Story: A Study in Theory and*

Practice. Cambridge, England: Cambridge University Press, 1992. Head discusses Woolf's search for a narrative texture that would adequately portray her notion of life as amorphous.

King, James. *Virginia Woolf*. New York: W. W. Norton, 1995. A literary biography that relates Woolf's life to her work. Shows how the chief sources of her writing were her life, her family, and her friends.

Lee, Hermione. *Virginia Woolf*. New York: Alfred A. Knopf, 1997. A detailed biography of Woolf, her complex family relationships, her lifelong battle with mental illness, and her relationship to the Bloomsbury group.

Meyerowitz, Selma. "What Is to Console Us? The Politics of Deception in Woolf's Short Stories." In *New Feminist Essays on Virginia Woolf*, edited by Jane Marcus. Lincoln: University of Nebraska Press, 1981. In fourteen pages, in contrast to formal aspects or general philosophical themes such as the quest for reality, the political and social content of several stories is stressed, particularly feminist issues of subordination and powerlessness, alienation, negative male traits, class conflict, and oppressive social institutions.

Reid, Panthea. *Art and Affection: A Life of Virginia Woolf*. New York: Oxford University Press, 1996. A biography based on new materials and facts about Woolf's life and thought; focuses on the relationship of her letters and other writings to her relatives and circle of friends.

Norman Prinsky

RICHARD WRIGHT

Born: Natchez, Mississippi; September 4, 1908
Died: Paris, France; November 28, 1960

PRINCIPAL SHORT FICTION
Uncle Tom's Children: Four Novellas, 1938
Uncle Tom's Children: Five Long Stories, 1938
Eight Men, 1961

OTHER LITERARY FORMS

Although Richard Wright is best known for his novel *Native Son* (1940), his nonfiction works, such as the two volumes of his autobiography *Black Boy: A Record of Childhood and Youth* (1945) and *American Hunger* (1977) along with books such as *Twelve Million Black Voices* (1941) and *White Man, Listen!* (1957), have proven to be of lasting interest. He developed a Marxist ideology while writing for the Communist *Daily Worker*, which was very influential on his early fiction, notably *Native Son* and *Uncle Tom's Children*, but which culminated in an article, "I Tried to Be a Communist," first published by the *Atlantic Monthly* in 1944. Although he abandoned Marxist ideology, he never abandoned the idea that protest is and should be at the heart of great literature.

ACHIEVEMENTS

Richard Wright is often cited as being the father of the post-World War II African American novel. The works of James Baldwin and Ralph Ellison owe a direct debt to the work of Wright, and his role in inspiring the Black Arts movement of the 1960's is incalculable. Further, he was one of the first African American novelists of the first half of the twentieth century to capture a truly international audience. Among his many honors were a Guggenheim Fellowship in 1939 and the Spingarn Award from the National Association for the Advancement of Colored People (NAACP) in 1941 for his novel, *Native Son*. This novel, which James Baldwin said was "unquestionably" the "most powerful and celebrated statement we have had yet of what it means to be a Negro in America," along with the first volume of his autobiography and the stories in *Uncle Tom's Children*, constitute Wright's most important lasting contributions to literature. His plots usually deal with how the harrowing experience of racial inequality transforms a person into a rebel—usually violent, and usually randomly so. The more subtle achievement of his fiction, however, is the psychological insight it provides into the experience of oppression and rebellion.

BIOGRAPHY

The poverty, racial hatred, and violence that Richard Nathaniel Wright dramatizes in fiction come directly from his own experience as the child of an illiterate Mississippi sharecropper. Richard was six years old when his father was driven off the land and the family moved to a two-room slum tenement in Memphis, Tennessee. The father deserted the family there. Richard's mother, Ella Wright, got a job as a cook, leaving Richard and his younger brother Alan alone in the apartment. When his mother became ill, the brothers were put in an orphanage. An invitation for Ella and the boys to stay with a more prosperous relative in Arkansas ended in panic and flight when white men shot Uncle Hoskins, who had offered the Wrights a home. The family lived for some time with Richard's grandparents, stern Seventh-day Adventists. In this grim, repressive atmosphere, Richard became increasingly violent and rebellious.

Although he completed his formal education in the ninth grade, the young Richard read widely, especially Stephen Crane, Fyodor Dostoevski, Marcel Proust, T. S. Eliot, and Gertrude Stein. The family eventually migrated to Chicago. Wright joined the Communist Party in 1933, and, in 1937 in New York City, became editor of the *Daily Worker*. The publication of *Uncle Tom's Children*, *Native Son*, and *Black Boy* brought Wright fame both in the United States and in Europe. In 1945, at the invitation of the French government, Wright went to France and became friends with Jean-Paul Sartre, Simone de Beauvoir, and other existentialists. His next novel, *The Outsider* (1953), has been called the first existential novel by an American writer. Wright traveled widely, lectured in several countries, and wrote journalistic accounts of his experiences in Africa and Spain. He died unexpectedly in Paris of amoebic dysentery, probably contracted in Africa or Indonesia under conditions his

Richard Wright (Library of Congress)

friend and biographer Margaret Walker, in *Richard Wright: Daemonic Genius* (1988), believes indicate at least medically questionable decisions, or, possibly, homicide.

ANALYSIS

"Fire and Cloud" in *Uncle Tom's Children* is perhaps the best representative of Richard Wright's early short fiction. It won first prize in the 1938 *Story* magazine contest which had more than four hundred entries, marking Wright's first triumph with American publishers. Charles K. O'Neill made a radio adaptation of the story after it appeared in *American Scenes*.

"FIRE AND CLOUD"

Unlike the later works concerning black ghetto experience, "Fire and Cloud" has a pastoral quality, recognizing the strong bond of the southern black to the soil and the support he has drawn from religion. Wright reproduces faithfully the southern black dialect in both conversation and internal meditations.

This use of dialect emphasizes the relative lack of sophistication of rural blacks. His protagonist, Reverend Taylor, is representative of the "old Negro," who has withstood centuries of oppression, sustained by hard work on the land and humble faith in a merciful God.

Wright's attitude toward religion, however, is ambivalent. Although he recognizes it as contributing to the quiet nobility of the hero, it also prevents Taylor from taking effective social action when his people are literally starving. The final triumph of Reverend Taylor is that he puts aside the conciliatory attitude which was part of his religious training and becomes a social activist. Instead of turning the other cheek after being humiliated and beaten by white men, he embraces the methods of his Marxist supporters, meeting oppression with mass demonstration. Strength of numbers proves more effective and appropriate for getting relief from the bigoted white establishment than all his piety and loving kindness. Early in the story Taylor exclaims "The good Lawds gonna clean up this ol worl some day! Hes gonna make a new Heaven n a new Earth!" His last words, however, are "Freedom belongs t the strong!"

The situation of the story no doubt reflects Wright's early experience when his sharecropper father was driven off the plantation. Taylor's people are starving because the white people, who own all the land, have prohibited the blacks from raising food on it. No matter how Taylor pleads for relief, the local white officials tell him to wait and see if federal aid may be forthcoming. When two Communist agitators begin pushing Taylor to lead a mass demonstration against the local government, white officials have Taylor kidnapped and beaten, along with several deacons of his church. Instead of intimidating them, this suffering converts them to open confrontation. As the Communists promised, the poor whites join the blacks in the march, which forces the white authorities to release food to those facing starvation.

The story's strength lies in revealing through three dialogues the psychological dilemma of the protagonist as opposing groups demand his support. He resists the Communists initially because their methods employ threat of open war on the whites—"N tha ain

Gawds way!" The agitators say he will be responsible if their demonstration fails through lack of numbers and participants are slaughtered. On the other hand, the mayor and chief of police threaten Taylor that they will hold him personally responsible if any of his church members join the march. After a humiliating and futile exchange with these men, Taylor faces his own church deacons, who are themselves divided and look to him for leadership. He knows that one of their number, who is just waiting for a chance to oust him from his church, will run to the mayor and police with any evidence of Taylor's insubordination. In a pathetic attempt to shift the burden of responsibility that threatens to destroy him no matter what he does, he reiterates the stubborn stand he has maintained with all three groups: He will not order the demonstration, but he will march with his people if they choose to demonstrate. The brutal horse-whipping that Taylor endures as a result of this moderate stand convinces him of the futility of trying to placate everybody. The Uncle Tom becomes a rebel.

Critics sometimes deplore the episodes of raw brutality described in graphic detail in Wright's fiction, but violence is the clue here to his message. Behind the white man's paternalistic talk is the persuasion of whip and gun. Only superior force can cope with such an antagonist.

"THE MAN WHO LIVED UNDERGROUND"

Wright's best piece of short fiction is "The Man Who Lived Underground." Although undoubtedly influenced by Dostoevski's underground man and by Franz Kafka's "K," the situation was based on a prisoner's story from *True Detective* magazine. The first version appeared in 1942 in *Accent* magazine under the subtitle "Two Excerpts from a Novel." This version began with a description of the life of a black servant, but Wright later discarded this opening in favor of the dramatic scene in which an unnamed fugitive hides from the police by descending into a sewer. This approach allowed the story to assume a more universal, symbolic quality. Although racist issues are still significant, the protagonist represents that larger class of all those alienated from their society. Eventually the fugitive's name is revealed as Fred Daniels, but so completely is he absorbed into his

Everyman role that he cannot remember his name when he returns to the upper world. His progress through sewers and basements becomes a quest for the meaning of life, parodying classic descents into the underworld and ironically reversing Plato's allegory of the cave.

Although Plato's philosopher attains wisdom by climbing out of the cave where men respond to shadows on the cave wall, Wright's protagonist gains enlightenment because of his underground perspective. What he sees there speaks not to his rational understanding, however, but to his emotions. He moves among symbolic visions which arouse terror and pity—a dead baby floating on the slimy water whose "mouth gaped black in a soundless cry." In a black church service spied on through a crevice in the wall, the devout are singing "Jesus, take me to your home above." He is overwhelmed by a sense of guilt and intuits that there is something obscene about their "singing with the air of the sewer blowing in on them." In a meat locker with carcasses hanging from the ceiling, a butcher is hacking off a piece of meat with a bloody cleaver. When the store proprietor goes home, Fred emerges from the locker and gorges on fresh fruit, but he takes back with him into the sewer the bloody cleaver—why he does not know.

When Fred breaks through a wall into the basement of a movie house, the analogy to Plato's myth of the cave becomes explicit. He comes up a back stair and sees jerking shadows of a silver screen. The Platonic urge to enlighten the people in the theater, who are bound to a shadow world, merges with messianic images. In a dream he walks on water and saves a baby held up by a drowning woman, but the dream ends in terror and doubt as he loses the baby and his ability to emulate Christ. All is lost and he himself begins to drown.

Terror and pity are not the only emotions that enlarge his sensibilities in this underground odyssey. As he learns the peculiar advantages of his invisibility, he realizes that he can help himself to all kinds of gadgets valued by that shadow world above ground. He collects them like toys or symbols of an absurd world. He acquires a radio, a light bulb with an extension cord, a typewriter, a gun, and finally, through a chance observation of a safe being opened by combination, rolls of hundred dollar bills, containers of diamonds, watches, and rings. His motivation for stealing these articles is not greed but sheer hilarious fun at acquiring objects so long denied to persons of his class.

In one of the most striking, surrealist scenes in modern literature, Fred delightedly decorates his cave walls and floor with these tokens of a society which has rejected him. "They were the serious toys of the men who lived in the dead world of sunshine and rain he had left, the world that had condemned him, branded him guilty." He glues hundred dollar bills on his walls. He winds up all the watches but disdains to set them (for he is beyond time, freed from its tyranny). The watches hang on nails along with the diamond rings. He hangs up the bloody cleaver, too, and the gun. The loose diamonds he dumps in a glittering pile on the muddy floor. Then as he gaily tramps around, he accidentally/on purpose, stomps on the pile, scattering the pretty baubles over the floor. Here, indeed, is society's cave of shadows, and only he realizes how absurd it all is.

When the euphoria of these games begins to pall, Fred becomes more philosophical, perceiving the nihilistic implications of his experience. "Maybe *any*thing's right, he mumbled. Yes, if the world as men had made it was right, then anything else was right, any act a man took to satisfy himself, murder, theft, torture." In his unlettered, blundering way, he is groping toward Ivan Karamazov's dark meditation: "If there is no God, then all things are permissible." Fred becomes convinced of the reality of human guilt, however, when he witnesses the suicide of the jewelry store's night watchman, who has been blamed for the theft he himself committed. At first, the scene in which police torture the bewildered man to force a confession strikes Fred as hilariously funny, duplicating his own experience. When the wretched man shoots himself before Fred can offer him a means of escape, however, Fred is shocked into a realization of his own guilt.

The protagonist ultimately transcends his nihilism, and like Plato's philosopher who returns to the cave out of compassion for those trapped there, Fred returns to the "dead world of sunshine and rain" to bear witness to the Truth. Like the philosopher who is blinded coming out of the light into cave darkness, Fred seems confused and stupid in the social world above ground. When he is thrown out of the black church, he tries inarticulately to explain his revelation at the police station where he had been tortured and condemned. The police think he is crazy, but because they now know they accused him unjustly, they find his return embarrassing. Fred euphorically insists that they accompany him into the sewer so that they too can experience the visions that enlightened him. When he shows them his entrance to the world underground, one of the policemen calmly shoots him and the murky waters of the sewer sweep him away.

This ironic story of symbolic death and resurrection is unparalleled in its unique treatment of existential themes. Guilt and alienation lead paradoxically to a tragic sense of human brotherhood, which seems unintelligible to "normal" people. The man who kills Fred Daniels is perhaps the only person who perceives even dimly what Daniels wants to do. "You've got to shoot this kind," he says. "They'd wreck things."

OTHER MAJOR WORKS

LONG FICTION: *Native Son*, 1940; *The Outsider*, 1953; *Savage Holiday*, 1954; *The Long Dream*, 1958; *Lawd Today*, 1963.

PLAYS: *Native Son: The Biography of a Young American*, pr. 1941 (with Paul Green).

NONFICTION: *Twelve Million Black Voices: A Folk History of the Negro in the United States*, 1941; *Black Boy: A Record of Childhood and Youth*, 1945; *Black Power: A Record of Reactions in a Land of Pathos*, 1954; *The Color Curtain*, 1956; *Pagan Spain*, 1957; *White Man, Listen!*, 1957; *American Hunger*, 1977; *Richard Wright Reader*, 1978 (Ellen Wright and Michel Fabre, editors).

BIBLIOGRAPHY

Fabre, Michel. *The Unfinished Quest of Richard Wright*. New York: William Morrow, 1973. Although this volume is one of the most important and authoritative biographies available on Wright, readers interested in Wright's life should consult Margaret Walker's biography as well (see below).

_____. *The World of Richard Wright*. Jackson: University Press of Mississippi, 1985. A collection of Fabre's essays on Wright. A valuable resource, though not a sustained, full-length study. It contains two chapters on individual short stories by Wright, including the short story "Superstition." Supplemented by an appendix.

Felgar, Robert. *Richard Wright*. Boston: Twayne, 1980. A general biographical and critical source, this work devotes two chapters to the short fiction of Wright.

Hakutani, Yoshinobu. *Richard Wright and Racial Discourse*. Columbia: University of Missouri Press, 1996. This study of Wright's fiction as racial discourse and the product of diverse cultures devotes one chapter to Wright's *Uncle Tom's Children*, focusing primarily on racial and cultural contexts of "Big Boy Leaves Home."

Kinnamon, Kenneth. *The Emergence of Richard Wright*. Urbana: University of Illinois Press, 1972. A study of Wright's background and development as a writer, up until the publication of *Native Son*.

_____, ed. *Critical Essays on Richard Wright's "Native Son."* New York: Twayne, 1997. Divided into sections of reviews, reprinted essays, and new essays. Includes discussions of Wright's handling of race, voice, tone, novelistic structure, the city, and literary influences. Index but no bibliography.

_____, ed. *A Richard Wright Bibliography: Fifty Years of Criticism and Commentary: 1933-1982*. Westport, Conn.: Greenwood Press, 1988. A mammoth annotated bibliography (one of the largest annotated bibliographies ever assembled on an American writer), which traces the history of Wright criticism. This bibliography is invaluable as a research tool.

Rand, William E. "The Structure of the Outsider in the Short Fiction of Richard Wright and F. Scott Fitzgerald." *CLA Journal* 40 (December, 1996): 230-245. Compares theme, imagery, and form of Fitzgerald's "The Diamond as Big as the Ritz" with Wright's "The Man Who Lived Underground" in terms of the treatment of the outsider.

Argues that both Fitzgerald and Wright saw themselves as outsiders—Wright because of race and Fitzgerald because of economic class.

Walker, Margaret. *Richard Wright: Daemonic Genius*. New York: Warner Publishing, 1988. A critically acclaimed study of Wright's life and work written by a friend and fellow novelist. Not a replacement for Michel Fabre's biography but written with the benefit of several more years of scholarship on issues that include the medical controversy over Wright's death. Walker is especially insightful on Wright's early life, and her comments on Wright's short fiction are short but pithy. Includes a useful bibliographic essay at the end.

Katherine Snipes, updated by Thomas J. Cassidy

Y

WILLIAM BUTLER YEATS

Born: Sandymount, near Dublin, Ireland; June 13, 1865

Died: Cap Martin, France; January 28, 1939

PRINCIPAL SHORT FICTION

John Sherman and Dhoya, 1891, 1969

The Celtic Twilight, 1893

The Secret Rose, 1897

The Tables of Law. The Adoration of the Magi, 1897

Stories of Red Hanrahan, 1904

Mythologies, 1959

OTHER LITERARY FORMS

William Butler Yeats, a prolific writer, composed hundreds of lyrical, narrative, and dramatic poems. It was not unusual to find characters from his short stories appearing in his poems; *Michael Robartes and the Dancer*, a collection of poems published in 1920, is one example. In addition to writing poetry, he contributed to the Irish dramatic movement, which culminated in the establishment of the Abbey Theatre in Dublin. His *Cathleen ni Houlihan* (1902) and *Deirdre* (1906) are typical plays of that early period. Yeats was a prolific and accomplished essayist and also produced various works of autobiography (collected in one volume entitled *Autobiographies*, 1926, 1955) as well as an ambitious philosophical treatise entitled *A Vision* (1925, 1937), which details his cosmology.

ACHIEVEMENTS

William Butler Yeats's reputation as one of the major poets of the twentieth century is unassailable, and his influence, particularly on the course of American verse, as practiced most notably by Robert Lowell, is equally well attested. His adaptation of native Irish materials for poetic ends, his mythic projection in verse of his life and times, and his conception of art as an antidote to history have exerted a powerful imaginative influence on poets succeeding him. In a more narrowly Irish context, his ideological pronouncements and cultural commitments—the latter culminating in the establishment of the Abbey Theatre—have constituted an overwhelmingly important instance of the relationship of the artist to society.

Yeats received honorary degrees from Queen's University (Belfast) and Trinity College (Dublin) in 1922. Receipt of the Nobel Prize in Literature followed in 1923, as well as honorary degrees from the University of Oxford in 1931 and the University of Cambridge in 1933.

BIOGRAPHY

Born in Dublin to the painter John Butler Yeats and Susan Pollexfen of Sligo, William Butler Yeats was of Irish Protestant background. His childhood was spent in London, Dublin, and Sligo. He was educated at the Godolphin School, Hammersmith, Dublin High School, and the Metropolitan School of Art, where he fell under the spell of George Russell (Æ) and other Dublin mystics. John O'Leary, the Fenian leader, and Maud Gonne, the passionate actress and patriot, were two Irish friends, while Arthur Symons and Lionel Johnson of the Rhymers' Club were London friends. When Maud Gonne and later her daughter Iseult rejected his marriage proposals, Yeats married Georgie Hyde-Lees, an Englishwoman, in 1917. They had one son and one daughter. After the Irish Civil War, he served as Senator for the Irish Free State, 1923-1928. Yeats traveled extensively, including lecture tours to the United States. In 1899, Yeats with Lady Gregory, Edward Martyn, and George Moore established an Irish theater, which led to the Abbey Theatre. With George Bernard Shaw and

George Russell (Æ), Yeats founded the Irish Academy of Letters in 1932. His complex life experiences were literary source material for his works. Acutely aware of the religious and philosophical conflict facing the world, he believed that a viable literature was an alternative resolution until religion and philosophy offered another solution.

ANALYSIS

With the exception of "John Sherman," William Butler Yeats's short stories mirror his attraction to the spirit world and reflect his fascination with good and evil. Since they were written during the *fin de siècle* period when literary and graphic artists, epitomized by the French symbolists, were expressing a world-weariness and pessimism that celebrated the triumph of evil, it is understandable that Yeats's tales articulate that prevailing mood. These early fictional works also identify the themes which were to occupy Yeats's poetic genius for the remainder of his life.

An integral part of the Irish literary movement, the tales have a dual purpose: to revitalize ancient Irish myths for modern Ireland and to serve as a model for artists attempting to write in Irish about Irish subjects. In the stories, Yeats celebrates the exploits of fairies and pagan Irish heroes which he discovered in the oral and written literary traditions; his tales thus become source material for other storytellers. Yeats's *The Celtic Twilight*, a collection of folklore gathered from local storytellers, became important material for Yeats's later work. In recording the fantastic behavior of the various spirits and their relationships to the country people, Yeats stored information which he used later to dramatize his belief in communication between the material and the immaterial worlds. "Dhoya" is an excellent example of a revitalized myth, and "The Twisting of the Rope" illustrates Yeats's role as a mentor for others.

"DHOYA"

In "Dhoya," Yeats writes about a local Sligo legend. He had recently edited *Fairy and Folk Tales of the Irish Peasantry* (1888), and his imagination was stimulated by the living nature of these expressions of the conflict between the natural and preternatural worlds. "Dhoya" honors an ancient Celt who lived

William Butler Yeats (Library of Congress)

before the time of the Pharaohs, Buddha, and Thor. In predating the time of known heroes, Dhoya, the Celt, exists before recorded history. It follows then that Yeats's native Sligo has indeed an ancient history, for Dhoya is deserted at the Bay of Ballah, the fictional name of Sligo Bay. The Formorians, an ancient Irish tribe, abandon Dhoya, a giant of tremendous strength, because he cannot control the violent rages which come over him. While enraged, he kills those around him and destroys whatever he can touch. He is believed to be possessed by demons, and a plan is concocted to exile him to the Bay of Ballah.

Dhoya, living alone in the forests and along the beaches, experiences more frequent attacks, but they are directed against his shadow or the halcyon, the beautiful and peaceful legendary bird. Years pass, and a quality of timelessness adds to the mystical nature of the tale, for Dhoya is hundreds of years old. One day he kills a great bull, and the herd chases him until he eludes it by running into the deepest part of the bay, a spot called Pool Dhoya. To this day, and in Yeats's day, the deepest part of Sligo Bay is known as Pool Dhoya, a fact which Yeats incorporates into the story to create a living legend.

Yeats also introduces legendary characters. Dhoya ranges over the mountains where Diarmuid and Grania, pagan lovers from the written Irish literature of pre-Christian Ireland, traveled. In time, Dhoya also experiences a love like Diarmuid. It comes to Dhoya as a gentle breeze upon his forehead, nothing more; but he longs for that touch, which remains only a touch for an untold number of years. Eventually, he develops a depression which he plans to shake off by building a huge bonfire at the rising of the moon. The unhappy lover prays to the moon and makes all kinds of sacrifices—strawberries, an owl, a badger, deer, swine, birds, and whatever else he can find to appease the moon. Soon thereafter, a voice calls "Dhoya, my beloved." Trembling, Dhoya looks into the forest, sees a white form which becomes a flowering plant as he touches it. Dazed, the giant returns to his cave where he finds a beautiful woman cleaning and rearranging the spears and skins.

She throws her arms about his neck, telling him that she yearns for his love. Having left her happy people from under the lake where age, sorrow, and pain are unknown, she desires love in the changing world, a mortal love which her people cannot experience. Dhoya loves her with a mad passion which is not matched by the beautiful fairy, unnamed by Yeats. Then a man from under the sea appears to reclaim the lady. Holding a spear tipped with metal, he challenges Dhoya, whose rage returns as he fights to keep his love. He wins that battle only to lose to the fairy who reappears and challenges him to a game of chess. Before she leaves Dhoya, the fairy sings a strange love song which was part of "The Wandering of Oisin" (1889):

> My love hath many evil mood
> Ill words for all things soft and fair
> I hold him dearer than the good
> My fingers feel his amber hair.

This stanza is central to "Dhoya" and to the great poems which follow. The happy spirit is unhappy and seeks human love which is neither perfect nor perpetual—a paradox which haunts Yeats.

"John Sherman"

"John Sherman," a realistic story which Yeats called a short romance and wanted to be judged as an Irish novel, is a variation of the Dhoya theme. Although the story lacks the cultural unity of the Irish novels of William Carleton, John Banim, and Gerald Griffin, it does demonstrate the great influence upon Yeats of William Blake, whose poetical works Yeats had recently edited.

The story takes place in Ballah and London, two contrary locations representing the virtuous countryside and the villainous city. There is also a set of contrary characters who, even if they were merged, would not represent the ideal character. John Sherman of Ballah and William Howard of London have different views on almost everything, yet they become engaged to the same woman. Mary Carton of Ballah and Margaret Leland of London are different, but both remain confused about their love for John Sherman. Sherman's mother and Margaret's mother really represent the country mother and the city mother; neither has a life beyond motherhood. Such artificial characterizations doom the plot of "John Sherman," which—although intended as a love story—with a little revision could have become a comedy or farce. Certainly, it is the lightest piece of work that Yeats produced; however, unlike other Irish writers, Yeats lacked a comic sense.

"Proud Costello, MacDermot's Daughter, and the Bitter Tongue"

"Proud Costello, MacDermot's Daughter, and the Bitter Tongue," from *The Secret Rose*, is a love story which exhibits the intensity of Dhoya's love for the fairy, but the lovers are mortals of the sixteenth century. Costello loves Una, daughter of MacDermot, who is promised by her father to MacNamara. Una loves Costello and sends a message to him by Duallach, the wandering piper. Costello must appear at her nuptial feast, at which she will drink to the man she loves. At the betrothal drink, to the amazement of all, she drinks to Costello; he is then attacked by the members of the wedding party and barely escapes with his life. Una dies without seeing Costello again, but at her funeral procession he sees the coffin and is considered her murderer. Loving her still, Costello swims to the island where Una is buried, mourning over her grave for three days and nights. Confused, he tries to swim back to the mainland but drowns in the attempt. His body is brought to the island and buried beside his beloved; two ash trees are planted over their grave site. They grow tall and the branches, like lover's arms, entwine themselves, symbolic of the undying love between Costello and Una. This motif, common in folklore, appealed to Yeats's sensibility because of the implied relationship between the natural world and the affairs of mortals.

"THE TWISTING OF THE ROPE"

From another perspective, Yeats writes again about that relationship in "The Twisting of the Rope." This story is one of the six connected stories grouped as the *Stories of Red Hanrahan* which tell of the plight of Hanrahan, a hedge schoolmaster enchanted by a spirit on Samhain Eve, the night (the equivalent of Halloween) on which the Celts believed spirits roamed the earth searching for mortals. Since his enchantment, Hanrahan has become a traveling poet of the Gael who sings of the past heroic age when the ancient Irish kings and queens ruled Ireland. The people, although they welcome Hanrahan into their cottages, fear him because he is of the other world and is able to charm others, especially young and impressionable women.

One night Hanrahan is observed casting his spell over Oona, an attentive listener to his tales; but her mother and a neighbor woman, watching Oona drift into the spirit world, plan to thwart Hanrahan's influence. They cannot order the poet out of the house because he might cast a spell over their animals and fields, destroying cattle and corn, so they devise a scheme whereby Hanrahan is asked to twist a rope from the bundles of hay which the women bring to him. Feeding him more and more rope and praising him for the fine job of rope-making, they eventually get Hanrahan to the door and out of the cottage. Realizing that he had been tricked, he composes a song, "The Twisting of the Rope." Douglas Hyde, who wrote the first Irish play for the new Irish dramatic movement (*Casad-an-Sugan*, 1901), selected Yeats's short tale for production. His success in revitalizing Irish myth and encouraging the continuation of the written Irish literary tradition assures Yeats a prominent place in Irish letters.

Another aspect of Yeats's personality was his fascination with the occult, an attraction which led him to explore Christian, Jewish, and Asian mysticism in his writings. As John O'Leary made Yeats conscious of the past political Irish culture, George Russell (Æ), to whom *The Secret Rose* was dedicated, indoctrinated Yeats into the Dublin Theosophist Circle, which was occupied with the study of Rosicrucianism. It was a subject about which Yeats could never learn enough, and in "Rosa Alchemica" he approaches the topic through the story of the life of Michael Robartes. Yeats says in an explanatory note to the collection of poems known as *Michael Robartes and the Dancer* (1920) that Robartes had returned to Dublin from Mesopotamia where he "partly found and partly thought out much philosophy."

This knowledge, which Robartes wants to share with his old friend, is revolutionary. It consists of an understanding that modern alchemy is not concerned with simply converting base metal to gold. On the contrary, the new science seeks to transform all things to the divine form; in other words, experiential life is transmuted to art. The process involves rituals through which novices are initiated gradually into the sect. Robartes brings his friend into a temple, but in order to proceed, he must first learn a series of intricate dance steps; then he is dressed in a costume of Greek and Egyptian origin for the mad dance. At this point the friend, fearing for his sanity, flees from the phantasmagoria.

"THE TABLES OF THE LAW" AND "THE ADORATION OF THE MAGI"

"The Tables of the Law" and "The Adoration of the Magi" are two other short stories that deal with religious mysteries. In "The Tables of the Law," Owen Aherne, like Michael Robartes, returns to Dublin after studying mysticism and alchemy. He hates life and cherishes a medieval book with its secrets of the spirit. Jonathan Swift, Aherne thinks, created a soul for Dublin gentlemen by hating his neighbor as himself. A decade later, the narrator sees Aherne again at a Dublin bookstore; his face is a lifeless mask, drained of the energy to sin and repent as God planned for mortal man. God's law tablets make mankind commit sin, which is abhorrent to Aherne.

Michael Robartes, appearing again in "The Adoration of the Magi," promises the return of the Celtic heroes. Three men in the tale, perhaps demons, watch the death of the Wise Woman. Civilization has not progressed; Christianity has not fulfilled its mission. The hope of nations lies in the reestablishment of the aristocratic order of the Celtic civilization. To a greater degree, Yeats develops this theme in later verse, essays, and plays with a blurring of the character of Cuchulain, the pagan Irish hero, with Christ and Saint Patrick.

Yeats's reputation as a poet and a dramatist overshadows his renown as a storyteller. His tales have intrinsic worth nevertheless, and can be read as a prelude to his later great works.

OTHER MAJOR WORKS

PLAYS: *The Countess Cathleen*, pb. 1892; *The Land of Heart's Desire*, pr., pb. 1894; *Cathleen ni Houlihan*, pr., pb. 1902; *The Pot of Broth*, pr. 1902 (with Lady Augusta Gregory); *The Hour-Glass*, pr. 1903; *The King's Threshold*, pr., pb. 1903 (with Lady Gregory); *On Baile's Strand*, pr. 1904; *Deirdre*, pr. 1906 (with Lady Gregory); *The Shadowy Waters*, pr. 1906; *The Unicorn from the Stars*, pr. 1907 (with Lady Gregory); *The Golden Helmet*, pr., pb. 1908; *The Green Helmet*, pr., pb. 1910; *At the Hawk's Well*, pr. 1916; *The Player Queen*, pr. 1919; *The Only Jealousy of Emer*, pb. 1919; *The Dreaming of the Bones*, pb. 1919; *Calvary*, pb. 1921; *Four Plays for Dancers*, pb. 1921 (includes *Calvary, At the Hawk's Well, The Dreaming of the Bones, The Only Jealousy of Emer*); *The Cat and the Moon*, pb. 1924; *The Resurrection*, pb. 1927; *The Words upon the Window-Pane*, pr. 1930; *The Collected Plays of W. B. Yeats*, pb. 1934, 1952; *The King of the Great Clock Tower*, pr., pb. 1934; *A Full Moon in March*, pr. 1934; *The Herne's Egg*, pb. 1938; *Purgatory*, pr. 1938; *The Death of Cuchulain*, pb. 1939; *Variorum Edition of the Plays of W. B. Yeats*, pb. 1966 (Russell K. Alspach, editor).

POETRY: *Mosada: A Dramatic Poem*, 1886; *Crossways*, 1889; *The Wanderings of Oisin and Other Poems*, 1889; *The Countess Kathleen and Various Legends and Lyrics*, 1892; *The Rose*, 1893; *The Wind Among the Reeds*, 1899; *In the Seven Woods*, 1903;

The Poetical Works of William B. Yeats, 1906, 1907 (2 volumes); *The Green Helmet and Other Poems*, 1910; *Responsibilities*, 1914; *Responsibilities and Other Poems*, 1916; *The Wild Swans at Coole*, 1917, 1919; *Michael Robartes and the Dancer*, 1920; *The Tower*, 1928; *Words for Music Perhaps and Other Poems*, 1932; *The Winding Stair and Other Poems*, 1933; *The Collected Poems of W. B. Yeats*, 1933, 1950; *The King of the Great Clock Tower*, 1934; *A Full Moon in March*, 1935; *Last Poems and Plays*, 1940; *The Poems of W. B. Yeats*, 1949 (2 volumes); *The Collected Poems of W. B. Yeats*, 1956; *The Variorum Edition of the Poems of W. B. Yeats*, 1957 (P. Allt and R. K. Alspach, editors); *The Poems*, 1983; *The Poems: A New Edition*, 1984.

NONFICTION: *Ideas of Good and Evil*, 1903; *The Cutting of an Agate*, 1912; *Per Amica Silentia Lunae*, 1918; *Essays*, 1924; *A Vision*, 1925, 1937; *Autobiographies*, 1926, 1955; *A Packet for Ezra Pound*, 1929; *The Autobiography of William Butler Yeats*, 1938; *Essays, 1931-1936*, 1937; *On the Boiler*, 1939; *If I Were Four and Twenty*, 1940; *The Letters of W. B. Yeats*, 1954; *The Senate Speeches of W. B. Yeats*, 1960 (Donald R. Pearce, editor); *Essays and Introductions*, 1961; *Explorations*, 1962; *Ah, Sweet Dancer: W. B. Yeats, Margot Ruddock—A Correspondence*, 1970 (Roger McHugh, editor); *Uncollected Prose by W. B. Yeats*, 1970, 1976 (2 volumes); *Memoirs*, 1972; *The Collected Letters of William Butler Yeats: Volume I, 1865-1895*, 1986.

MISCELLANEOUS: *The Collected Works in Verse and Prose of William Butler Yeats*, 1908.

BIBLIOGRAPHY

Aldritt, Keith. *W. B. Yeats: The Man and the Milieu*. New York: Clarkson Potter, 1997. Discusses Yeats's life and times.

Bloom, Harold. *Yeats*. New York: Oxford University Press, 1970. An influential work by a leading contemporary critic. The emphasis is on Yeats's Romanticism. The poet is seen as the English Romantic poetry's heir. The prosodic, aesthetic, and imaginative implications of the inheritance are the subject of much intense and sophisticated discussion.

Donoghue, Denis. *Yeats*. London: Fontana, 1971. The best brief survey of the subject. Yeats's life, works, and thoughts are clearly presented in their many complex interrelations. The study's unifying argument is the author's conception of Yeats's understanding of, and identification with, power. Contains a useful chronology and succinct bibliography.

Ellmann, Richard. *W. B. Yeats: The Man and the Masks*. New York: Macmillan, 1948. The first biography to avail itself of unrestricted access to Yeats's posthumous papers. The poet's doctrine of the mask is adopted as a biographical trope. Life and work are perceived as being mutually reinforcing. In many ways, the most satisfactory biographical treatment of Yeats.

Fleming, Deborah. *"A Man Who Does not Exist": The Irish Peasant in the Work of W. B. Yeats and J. M. Synge*. Ann Arbor: University of Michigan Press, 1995. Discusses Yeats's transforming Irish folklore into art and thus helping establish a new sense of cultural identity in Ireland. Examines Yeats as a postcolonial writer and his belief that peasant culture was a repository of ancient wisdom.

Foster, R. F. *W. B. Yeats: A Life*. New York: Oxford University Press, 1997. An excellent guide to Yeats and his work.

Jeffares, A. N. *A New Commentary on the Poems of W. B. Yeats*. London: Macmillan, 1984. This commentary was published in order to be in alignment with the 1983 edition of Yeats's poems. Otherwise the approach is the same as in the previous edition. The contents of Yeats's *The Collected Poems* are comprehensively annotated. Dates of composition are supplied, difficult allusions clarified, links to other works by Yeats made. An indispensable students' guide.

_____. *W. B. Yeats*. London: Hutchinson University Library, 1988. To some extent a redaction of the same author's *W. B. Yeats: Man and Poet* (1949). The earlier work made more extensive use of Yeats's papers than the Ellmann work cited above. Here the author adds more information from the same source. The overall effect, however, is one of narrative deftness.

McCormack, W. J. *Ascendancy and Tradition in Anglo-Irish Literary History from 1789 to 1939*. Oxford, England: Clarendon Press, 1985. A study that lives up to the broad range of its title. Contains a crucial culminating section on Yeats, conceived of as poet and playwright, and more importantly, as ideologue. Essential for an appreciation of Yeats in his Irish context. An important example of the realignment of Yeats's achievement and significance.

Torchiana, Donald. *Yeats and Georgian Ireland*. Evanston, Ill.: Northwestern University Press, 1966. One of the major ways in which Yeats derived myth from history was through his reading of the works of major Irish writers of the eighteenth century. This study analyzes Yeats's knowledge of Jonathan Swift, Bishop George Berkeley, Oliver Goldsmith, and Edmund Burke. The influence of these thinkers on Yeats's poetry and prose is then assessed. An illuminating study of the impact of the Irish context particularly on the poet's later work.

Tratner, Michael. *Modernism and Mass Politics: Joyce, Woolf, Eliot, Yeats*. Stanford, Calif.: Stanford University Press, 1995. Discusses the political context of Yeats's modernism. Reviews Yeats's poetics of violence. Although the chapter on Yeats is primarily concerned with his poetry, it is helpful for an understanding of Yeats's literary efforts to create a national mind.

Eileen A. Sullivan, updated by
George O'Brien

Z

YEVGENY ZAMYATIN

Born: Lebedyan, Russia; February 1, 1884
Died: Paris, France; March 10, 1937

PRINCIPAL SHORT FICTION

Uezdnoe, 1913 (novella; *A Provincial Tale*, 1966)
Na kulichkakh, 1914 (novella; *A Godforsaken Hole*, 1988)
Ostrovityane, 1918 (novella; *The Islanders*, 1972)
Povesti i rasskazy, 1963
The Dragon: Fifteen Stories, 1966

OTHER LITERARY FORMS

Yevgeny Zamyatin's most important piece of fiction was his novel *My* (1952; *We*, 1924), which was written in 1920-1921. A satirical examination of a future utopian state, the novel affirms the timeless value of individual liberty and free will in a world which places a premium on conformity and reason. This work exerted a significant influence on George Orwell's *Nineteen Eighty-Four* (1949). Zamyatin also wrote plays, adaptations, and film scenarios. His early dramatic works are historical plays—*Ogni svyatogo Dominika* (1922; *The Fires of Saint Dominic*, 1971) and *Attila* (1950; English translation, 1971)—while a later work, *Afrikanskiy gost* (1963; *The African Guest*, 1971), provides a comic look at philistine attempts to cope with Soviet reality. The author's most successful adaptation for the screen was a version of Maxim Gorky's *Na dne* (1902; *The Lower Depths*, 1912), which Zamyatin transformed into a screenplay for Jean Renoir's film *Les Bas-fonds* (1936; *The Lower Depths*, 1937).

ACHIEVEMENTS

Although Yevgeny Zamyatin is best known in the West for his novel *We*, it has been his short fiction that has been most influential in the Soviet Union, since *We* was not published there until 1987. In his short fiction, Zamyatin developed an original prose style that is distinguished by its bold imagery and charged narrative pacing. This style, along with Zamyatin's writings and teachings about literature in the immediate postrevolutionary period, had a decisive impact on the first generation of Soviet writers, which includes such figures as Lev Luntz, Nikolay Nikitin, Venyamin Kaverin, and Mikhail Zoshchenko. In addition, Zamyatin's unswerving defense of the principle of artistic and individual freedom remains a vivid element of his literary legacy.

BIOGRAPHY

Yevgeny Ivanovich Zamyatin was born on February 1, 1884, in Lebedyan, a small town in the Russian heartland. The writer would later point out with pride that the town was famous for its cardsharps, Gypsies, and distinctive Russian speech, and he would utilize this spicy material in his mature fiction. His childhood, however, was a lonely one, and as the son of a village teacher, he spent more time with books than with other children.

After completing four years at the local school in 1896, Zamyatin went on to the *Gymnasium* in Voronezh, where he remained for six years. Immediately after he was graduated, Zamyatin moved to St. Petersburg to study naval engineering at the Petersburg Polytechnic Institute. Over the next few years, Zamyatin became interested in politics and joined the Bolshevik Party. This political involvement led to his arrest late in 1905, when the student was picked up by the authorities who were trying to cope with the turbulent political agitation that swept the capital that year. Zamyatin spent several months in solitary confinement, and he used the time to write poetry and study English. Released in the spring of 1906,

Zamyatin was exiled to Lebedyan. He soon returned to St. Petersburg, however, and lived there illegally until he was discovered and exiled again in 1911.

By this time he had been graduated from the Institute and had been appointed a lecturer there. He also had made his debut as a writer: in 1908, he published the story "Odin" ("Alone"), which chronicles the fate of an imprisoned revolutionary student who kills himself over frustrated love, and in 1910, he published "Devushka," another tale of tragic love. Although neither work is entirely successful, they both demonstrate Zamyatin's early interest in innovative narrative technique. A more polished work of his was *Uezdnoe* (1913; *A Provincial Tale*, 1966), which Zamyatin wrote during the months of renewed exile in 1911 and 1912. Zamyatin's penetrating treatment of ignorance and brutality in the Russian countryside was greeted with warm approval by the critics. On the other hand, his next major work, *Na kulichkakh* (1914; at the end of the world), provided such a sharp portrait of cruelty in the military that the publication in which the story appeared was confiscated by the authorities.

In 1916, Zamyatin departed Russia for Great Britain, where he was to work on seagoing icebreakers. His experience abroad provided the impetus for two satires on the British middle class–*Ostrovityane* (1918; *The Islanders*, 1972) and "Lovets chelovekov" ("The Fisher of Men"). Zamyatin returned to Russia after the abdication of Czar Nicholas in 1917 and embarked upon a busy course of literary endeavors. The period from 1917 to 1921 was a time of remarkable fecundity for the writer: He wrote fourteen stories, the novel *We*, a dozen fables, and a play. This body of work evinces an impressive diversity of artistic inspiration. Zamyatin's subjects range from the intense passions found in rural Russia ("Sever," "The North") to the dire conditions afflicting the urban centers during the postrevolutionary period ("Peshchera," or "The Cave"; "Mamay"; and "Drakon," or "Dragon") to ribald parodies of saints' lives ("O tom, kak istselen byl inok Erazm," or "How the Monk Erasmus Was Healed").

In addition to his own literary creation, Zamyatin dedicated himself to encouraging the literary careers of others. He regularly lectured on the craft of writing to young writers in the House of Arts in Petrograd, and he took part in numerous editorial and publishing activities. Among those whose works he helped to edit were Anton Chekhov and H. G. Wells. For many of these editions, he also wrote critical or biographical introductions, and such writers as Wells, Jack London, O. Henry, and George Bernard Shaw received Zamyatin's critical attention. As a result of this editorial work and his involvement in such literary organizations as the All-Russian Union of Writers, which he helped to found, Zamyatin's own productivity began to decline after 1921, particularly his prose.

At the same time, Zamyatin found himself in the awkward position of having to defend himself against those who perceived something dangerous or threatening in the ideas his work espoused. In his prose fiction and in numerous essays, Zamyatin consistently articulated a belief in the value of continual change, innovation, and renewal. Seizing upon the thermodynamic theory of entropy—the concept that all energy in the universe tends toward stasis or passivity—Zamyatin warned against the dangers of stagnation in intellectual and artistic spheres. Exhorting writers to be rebels and heretics, he argued that one should never be content with the status quo, for satisfaction with any victory can easily degenerate into stifling philistinism. By the same token, Zamyatin denounced conformist tendencies in literary creation and decried efforts to subordinate individual inspiration to predetermined ideological programs.

Given the fact that one of the ideological underpinnings of the new Soviet state was a belief in the primacy of the collective over the interests of the individual, Zamyatin's fervent defense of individual freedom could not help but draw the attention of the emerging establishment. The writer was arrested in 1922 along with 160 other intellectuals and became subject to an order for deportation. Yet without his knowledge, and perhaps against his will, a group of friends interceded for him and managed to have the order withdrawn. After Zamyatin's release in 1923, he applied for permission to emigrate, but his request was rebuffed.

During the latter half of the 1920's, the political climate in the Soviet Union became more restrictive, and Zamyatin was among a number of talented writers who were singled out for public denunciation and criticism. He found that the doors to publishing houses were now closed to him and that permission to stage his plays was impossible to obtain. Zamyatin did not buckle before the increasingly vituperative attacks directed toward him. Indeed, he had once written that "a stubborn, unyielding enemy is far more deserving of respect than a sudden convert to communism." Consequently, he did not succumb to pressure and make a public confession of his "errors," as some of his fellow writers were forced to do. On the contrary, he stood up to this campaign of abuse until 1931, when he sent Joseph Stalin an audacious request for permission to leave the Soviet Union with the right to return "as soon as it becomes possible in our country to serve great ideas in literature without cringing before little men."

With Gorky's help, Zamyatin's petition was granted, and he left the Soviet Union with his wife in November, 1931. Settling in Paris, he continued to work on a variety of literary projects, including translations, screenplays, and a novel entitled *Bich bozhy* (1939; the scourge of God). Because of his interest in film, he envisioned a trip to Hollywood, but these plans never materialized. He died on March 10, 1937.

ANALYSIS

Perhaps the most distinctive feature of Yevgeny Zamyatin's short fiction is its charged, expressive narrative style. The writer characterized the style of his generation of writers in a lecture entitled "Contemporary Russian Literature," delivered in 1918. Calling the artistic method of his generation Neorealism, he outlined the differences between Neorealist fiction and that of the preceding Realist movement. He states:

> By the time the Neorealists appeared, life had become more complex, faster, more feverish. . . . In response to this way of life, the Neorealists have learned to write more compactly, briefly, tersely than the Realists. They have learned to say in ten lines what used to be said in a whole page.

During the first part of his career, Zamyatin consciously developed and honed his own unique form of Neorealist writing. Although his initial experimentation in this direction is evident in his early prose works (and especially in the long story *A Provincial Tale*), this tendency did not reach its expressive potential until the late 1910's, when it blossomed both in his satires on British life and in the stories devoted to Russian themes. The stories *The Islanders* and "The Fisher of Men" provide a mordant examination of the stifling philistinism permeating the British middle class. The former work in particular displays the tenor and thrust of Zamyatin's satiric style. The first character introduced into the tale is a minister named Vicar Dooley, who has written a *Testament of Contemporary Salvation*, in which he declares that "life must become a harmonious machine and with mechanical inevitability lead us to the desired goal." Such a vision raises the specter of death and stasis, not energy and life, and Zamyatin marshals his innovative narrative skills to expose the dangers that this vision poses for society.

THE ISLANDERS

One salient feature of Zamyatin's style is the identification of a character with a specific physical trait, animal, or object that seems to capture the essence of the character being depicted. Through this technique, the writer can both evoke the presence of the character by mentioning the associated image and underscore that character's fundamental personality type. What is more, once Zamyatin has established such an identification, he can suggest significant shifts in his characters' moods or situations by working changes on the associated images themselves. In *The Islanders*, this technique plays a vital role in the narrative exposition, and at times the associated images actually replace a given character in action. Thus, one character's lips are compared at the outset of the story to thin worms, and the women who attend Dooley's church are described as being pink and blue. Later, a tense interaction between the two is conveyed in striking terms: "Mrs. Campbell's worms twisted and sizzled on a slow fire. The blues and pinks feasted their eyes." Similarly, the central protagonist is compared to a tractor, and when his stolid reserve is shattered by feelings of love, Zamyatin writes that the tractor's "steering wheel was broken." Through this felicitous image Zamyatin not only evokes his hero's ponderous bulk but also suggests the unpredictable consequences which follow the release of suppressed emotion.

As striking as his satires on British conservatism are, however, it is in the stories that he wrote on Russian subjects that Zamyatin attained the apex of his vibrant expressionistic style. In his lecture on contemporary Russian literature, he spoke of his desire to find fresh subjects for literary treatment. Contrasting urban and rural settings, he declared: "The life of big cities is like the life of factories. It robs people of individuality, makes them the same, machinelike." In the countryside, Zamyatin concludes, "the Neorealists find not only genre, not only a way of life, but also a way of life concentrated, condensed by centuries to a strong essence, ninety-proof."

"THE NORTH"

As if to illustrate this premise, in 1918 he wrote the long tale entitled "The North." This story celebrates the primal forces of nature: In a swift succession of scenes, Zamyatin depicts a passionate yet short-lived affair between a true child of the forest—a young woman named Pelka—and a simple fisherman named Marey. Pelka is perhaps the closest embodiment of the ideally "natural" character in all of Zamyatin's works. She talks with the forest creatures, keeps a deer for a pet, and loves with a profound passion that cannot understand or tolerate the constraints imposed by civilized man. Sadly, her brief interlude of love with Marey is threatened by his foolish obsession with constructing a huge lantern "like those in Petersburg." Marey's desire to ape the fashions of the city destroys his romantic idyll with Pelka. After she vainly tries to stir Marey's emotions by having a short fling with a smug, callous shopkeeper named Kortoma, Pelka engineers a fatal encounter between herself, Marey, and a wild bear: The two lovers die at the hands of the natural world.

To illuminate this spectacle of extraordinary desire and suffering, Zamyatin utilizes all the tools of his Neorealist narrative manner. Striving to show rather than describe, Zamyatin avoids the use of such connectors as "it seemed" or "as if" in making comparisons; instead, the metaphorical image becomes the illustrated object or action itself. Especially noteworthy in "The North" is Zamyatin's use of charged color imagery. By associating particular characters with symbolic visual leitmotifs, the writer enhances his character portrayals. Thus, he underscores Pelka's naturalism by linking her to a combination of the colors red (as of flesh and blood) and green (as of the vegetation in the forest). Zamyatin compared his method to Impressionism: The juxtaposition of a few basic colors is intended to project the essence of a scene. At times, Zamyatin allows the symbolic associations of certain colors to replace narrative description entirely. Depicting the rising frenzy of a Midsummer Night's celebration, Zamyatin alludes to the surging flow of raw passion itself when he writes: "All that you could see was that . . . something red was happening."

Zamyatin's attention to visual detail in "The North" is matched by his concern with auditory effects. He thought that literary prose and poetry were one and the same; accordingly, the reader finds many examples of alliteration, assonance, and instrumentation in his work. He also gave careful consideration to the rhythmic pattern of his prose, revealing a debt to the Russian Symbolist writers who emphasized the crucial role of sound in prose. Seeking to communicate his perceptions as expressively and concisely as possible, he tried to emulate the fluidity and dynamism of oral speech. One notes many elliptical and unfinished sentences in Zamyatin's prose at this time, and his narratives resemble a series of sharp but fragmentary images or vignettes, which his readers must connect and fill in themselves. Zamyatin explained: "Today's reader and viewer will know how to complete the picture, fill in the words—and what he fills in will be etched far more vividly within him, will much more firmly become an organic part of him."

"IN OLD RUSSIA"

Zamyatin's other works on the deep recesses of the Russian countryside reflect his calculated attempt to evoke deep emotions and passionate lives in elliptical, allusive ways. The story "Rus" ("In Old Russia"), for example, is narrated in a warm colloquial tone in which the neutral language of an impersonal narrator is replaced by language that relies heavily on the intonations and lexicon of spoken Russian. This technique, called *skaz* in Russian, was popularized by writers such as Nikolay Leskov and Alexey Remizov, and Zamyatin uses it to good effect in this tale. His narrator's account of the amorous activities of a young married woman named Darya is accented with notes of sly understanding and tolerance. As the narrator describes her, Darya cannot help but give in to the impulses of her flesh. At the very outset, she is compared to an apple tree filling up with sap; when spring arrives, she unconsciously feels the sap rising in her just as it is in the apple and lilac trees around her. Her "fall," then, is completely natural, and so, too, is the ensuing death of her husband only a few days later. Again, Zamyatin's narrator conveys the news of the husband's death and the gossip that attended it in tones of warm indulgence. In the deep backwaters of Russia, he indicates, life flows on; such events have no more lasting impact than a stone which is dropped into a pond and causes a few passing ripples.

"THE CAVE" AND "MAMAY"

While Zamyatin was drawn to rural Russian subjects, he did not ignore urban themes: Two of his most striking works of 1920—"The Cave" and "Mamay"—exhibit his predilection for expressive imagery and his nuanced appreciation of human psychology. In "The Cave," Zamyatin depicts the Petrograd landscape in the winters following the Russian Revolution as a primordial, prehistoric wasteland. This image dominates the story, illustrating the writer's own admission that if he firmly believes in an image, "it will spread its roots through paragraphs and pages."

Yet while the overarching image of Petrograd's citizens as cave dwellers creates a palpable atmosphere of grimness and despair in "The Cave," the images with which Zamyatin enlivens "Mamay" are more humorous. This story continues a long tradition in Russian literature of depicting the life of petty clerks in the city of St. Petersburg. The protagonist here is a meek individual who bears the incongruous name of Mamay, one of the Tatar conquerors of Rus-

sia. Mamay's wife is a stolid woman so domineering that every spoonful of soup eaten by Mamay is likened to an offering to an imperious Buddha. The sole pleasure in little Mamay's life is book collecting, and it is this mild passion that finally stirs the character into uncharacteristic action. He had been gathering and hiding a large sum of money with which to buy books, and at the end of the story he discovers with dismay that his stockpile has been destroyed by an enemy. Enraged, he is driven to murder. This contemporary Mamay, however, is only a pale shadow of his famous namesake: The intruder proves to be a mouse, and Mamay kills it with a letter opener.

"A STORY ABOUT THE MOST IMPORTANT THING"

Zamyatin's pursuit of a charged, expressive narrative manner reached a peak in the early 1920's, and in at least one work, "Rasskaz o samom glavnom" ("A Story About the Most Important Thing"), the writer's ambition resulted in a work in which stylistic and structural manipulation overwhelms semantic content. Zamyatin creates a complex narrative structure in which he shifts back and forth among three plot lines involving the life of an insect, revolutionaries in Russia, and beings on a star about to collide with the Earth. The tale forcefully conveys the writer's sense of the power of the urge to live and procreate in the face of imminent death, but in certain passages, his penchant for hyperbole and intensity of feeling detracts from the effectiveness of the work as a whole.

"THE FLOOD"

Later in the decade, however, Zamyatin began to simplify his narrative techniques; the result can be seen in the moving story "Navodnenie" ("The Flood"), perhaps the finest short story of this late period. Written in 1928, "The Flood" reveals how Zamyatin managed to tone down some of his more exaggerated descriptive devices, while retaining the power and intensity of his central artistic vision. One finds few of his characteristic recurring metaphors in the story, but the few that are present carry considerable import. The work's central image is that of flooding, both as a literal phenomenon (the repeated flooding of the Neva River) and as a metaphorical element (the ebb and flow of emotions in the protagonist's soul). The plot of the story concerns a childless woman's resentment toward an orphaned girl named Ganka, who lives in her house and has an affair with her husband. Sofya's rising malice toward Ganka culminates on a day when the river floods. As the river rises and a cannon booms its flood warning, Sofya feels her anger surging too: It "whipped across her heart, flooded all of her." Striking Ganka with an ax, she then feels a corresponding outflow, a release of tension. Similar images of flooding and flowing accompany Sofya's childbirth, the feeding of her child, and the rising sensation of guilt in her heart. In the final scene of the story, the river again begins to flood, and now Sofya feels an irrepressible urge to give birth to her confession. As she begins to reveal her murderous secret, "Huge waves swept out of her and washed over . . . everyone." After she concludes her tale, "everything was good, blissful . . . all of her had poured out."

The recurring water images link all the major events in "The Flood," and Zamyatin achieves further cohesiveness through additional associations such as birth and death, conception and destruction. The tight austerity of his later fiction endows that body of work with understated force. The writer himself commented on the conscious effort he made to achieve this kind of effective simplicity: "All the complexities I had passed through had been only a road to simplicity. . . . Simplicity of form is legitimate for our epoch, but the right to simplicity must be earned."

The oeuvre that Zamyatin left behind provides an eloquent testament both to the man's skill as a literary craftsman and to the integrity and power of his respect for human potential. His innovations in narrative exposition exerted a palpable influence on his contemporaries, and his defense of individual liberty in the face of relentless repression holds timeless appeal for his readers.

OTHER MAJOR WORKS

LONG FICTION: *Bich bozhy*, 1939; *My*, 1952 (*We*, 1924).

PLAYS: *Ogni svyatogo Dominika*, pb. 1922 (*The Fires of Saint Dominic*, 1971); *Attila*, pb. 1950 (English translation, 1971); *Afrikanskiy gost*, pb. 1963 (*The African Guest*, 1971); *Five Plays*, pb. 1971.

SCREENPLAY: *Les Bas-fonds*, 1936 (*The Lower Depths*, 1937; adaptation of Maxim Gorky's novel *Na dne*).

NONFICTION: *Litsa*, 1955 (*A Soviet Heretic*, 1970).

MISCELLANEOUS: *Sobranie sochinenii*, 1929; *Sochineniia*, 1970-1972.

BIBLIOGRAPHY

Billington, Rachel. "Two Russians." *Financial Times*, January 5, 1985, p. I8. Discussion of Zamyatin's *Islanders*; notes that the anti-British story helped to make Zamyatin's name in Russia.

Brown, Edward J. "Zamjatin and English Literature." In *American Contributions to the Fifth International Congress of Slavists*. Vol. 2. The Hague: Mouton, 1965. Within general comments on Zamyatin, Brown discusses his interest in, and debt to, English literature stemming from his two-year stay in England before and during World War I.

Collins, Christopher. *Evgenij Zamjatin: An Interpretive Study*. The Hague: Mouton, 1973. In this ambitious study, Collins advances a rather complex interpretation of Zamyatin, mostly of *We*, on the basis of Carl Gustav Jung's idea of the conscious, unconscious, and individualism.

Kern, Gary, ed. *Zamyatin's "We": A Collection of Critical Essays*. Ann Arbor, Mich.: Ardis, 1988. A collection of essays on Zamyatin's magnum opus, *We*, covering the Soviet view, mythic criticism, aesthetics, and influences and comparisons. It includes one of the best essays on the subject, Edward J. Brown's "*Brave New World, 1984*, and *We*: An Essay on Anti-Utopia."

Mihailovich, Vasa D. "Critics on Evgeny Zamyatin." *Papers on Language and Literature* 10 (1974): 317-334. A useful survey of all facets of criticism of Zamyatin's opus, in all languages, through 1973. Good for gaining the introductory knowledge of Zamyatin.

Quinn-Judge, Paul. "Moscow's Brave New World: Novelist Zamyatin Revisited." *The Christian Science Monitor*, April 4, 1988, p. 8. A brief biographical background to accompany a story about the publication of Zamyatin's antitotalitarian novel *We* in Moscow.

Richard, D. J. *Zamyatin: A Soviet Heretic*. London: Hillary House, 1962. A brief overview of the main stages and issues in Zamyatin's life and works, paying some attention to his short fiction. An excellent, though truncated, presentation of a very complex writer.

Shane, Alex M. *The Life and Works of Evgenij Zamjatin*. Berkeley: University of California Press, 1968. The most comprehensive work on Zamyatin in English, covering, exhaustively but pertinently, his life and the most important features of his works, including short fiction. Using secondary sources extensively, Shane analyzes chronologically Zamyatin's works, in a scholarly but not dry fashion and reaches his own conclusions. Supplemented by an extensive bibliography of works by and about Zamyatin.

"Soviets to Publish *We*." *The New York Times*, June 25, 1987, p. C25. An article on the Soviet decision to publish *We*, the long-banned antitotalitarian novel.

Julian W. Connolly, updated by
Vasa D. Mihailovich

ZHANG JIE

Born: Beijing, China; April 27, 1937

PRINCIPAL SHORT FICTION

Ai, shi buneng wangj de, 1980 (*Love Must Not Be Forgotten*, 1986; includes the two novellas "Emerald" and "The Ark," as well as other stories)
Zai nei lu cao dishang, 1983
Fangzhou, 1983
Zum lu, 1985
Zhang Jie chi, 1986
As Long as Nothing Happens, Nothing Will, 1988
Yige zhongguo nuren zai Ouzhou, 1989
You Are a Friend of My Soul, 1990
Shi jie shang zui teng wo de na ge ren qu le, 1994

OTHER LITERARY FORMS

Besides her short stories, Zhang Jie has written novels, poetry, screenplays, and literary criticism. She has also published her experience abroad in a book entitled *Zai nei lu cao dishang* (1983; on a green lawn). Although no major collections of her poetry and critical essays have been published, her novels *Chenzhong de chibang* (1981; *Heavy Wings*) and *Zhi you yi ge taiyang* (1988; only one sun) have been quite successful.

ACHIEVEMENTS

Although Zhang Jie started writing fiction in her early forties, she has become one of the best-known Chinese women writers in the modern world. Her first novel *Heavy Wings* won the Maodun National Award for novels in 1985 (an award granted once every three years), and it has been translated and published in a dozen countries: Germany, France, Sweden, Finland, Norway, Denmark, Holland, Great Britain, the United States, Spain, Brazil, and the Soviet Union. Her second novel, *Zhi you yi ge taiyang*, was translated and published in Holland in 1988. Zhang, however, is better known as a short-story writer. In 1978, she began publishing numerous stories and subsequently won various prizes. Two collections of her stories, *Love Must Not Be Forgotten* and *As Long as Nothing Happens, Nothing Will*, are widely studied in European and American college classrooms. *As Long as Nothing Happens, Nothing*

Will won the Malaparte Literary Prize (Italy), a prize that has been won by famous writers such as Anthony Burgess and Saul Bellow.

Zhang's work has received considerable critical attention both in China and abroad. A feminist writer, she has forged a distinctive style that blends well her utopian idealism with social reality in her exploration of women's problems concerning love, marriage, and career. A social critic, she exposes China's hidden corruption and stubborn bureaucracy and vehemently champions the causes of democracy and reform through her literary forms. For her integrated concern for women and society, Zhang can be compared with Western writers such as Doris Lessing, Marge Piercy, and Ursula K. Le Guin. Her sentimental idealism and militant tone, however, have sometimes irritated critics and readers.

In her biographical note, "My Boat," Zhang made a modest statement: "A life still unfinished, ideals demanding to be realized. Beautiful, despondent, joyful, tragic. . . . All manner of social phenomena weave themselves into one story after another in my mind. . . . Like an artless tailor, I cut my cloth unskillfully according to old measurements and turn out garment factory clothes sold in department stores in only five standard sizes and styles." Although her statement applies to most of her stories, a few, with skillful innovations, cannot be judged by any "old measurements."

BIOGRAPHY

Zhang Jie was born in Beijing, China, on April 27, 1937. During the War of Resistance against Japan, her father left, and her mother, a teacher, brought her up in a village in the province of Liaoning. From childhood, she showed a strong interest in music and literature, but she was encouraged to study economics in order to be of greater use to the new China. After she was graduated from the People's University of Beijing in 1960, she was assigned to one of the industrial ministries. Her novel *Heavy Wings* and the short story "Today's Agenda" definitely benefit from her acquaintance with industrial management and bureaucracy. Later, Zhang transferred to the Beijing Film Studio, where she wrote the screenplays *The Search* and *We Are Still Young*. She started to write fiction at the age of forty, which coincided with the end of the Cultural Revolution. In 1978, her story "The Music of the Forest" won a prize as one of the best short stories of the year. In 1979, she won the Chinese national short-story award again for "Who Lives a Better Life." Meanwhile, her story "Love Must Not Be Forgotten" became widely read and controversial. With the success of her stories, Zhang became a full-time fiction writer. In 1985, she reached the climax of her literary career by winning the Maodun National Award for *Heavy Wings* and the National Novella Award for "Emerald." Zhang, who actively participates in international creative activities, has traveled to West Germany and the United States and was a visiting professor at Wesleyan University from 1989 to 1990. She has been a council member of the Chinese Writers' Association and the vice chair of the Beijing Association of Writers.

Zhang is known as a determined woman and a political activist. She took part in many political movements and joined the Chinese Communist Party at an early age. Although she mercilessly dissects the cause of China's backwardness and attributes it to feudal ideology as well as to the corruption of the Communist Party, she firmly defends the socialist system as that best suited to China. In spite of her support for socialism and genuine Marxism, however, she is often criticized inside China for her liberal tendencies. She proudly admits that she loves to read Western novels, particularly those of the eighteenth and nineteenth centuries. Like Dai Houying, Wang Anyi, and other contemporary Chinese writers, she believes that the humanism in classical Western literature is something that Chinese people should learn and promote. She was influenced by Western Romanticism as well as social critical realism. She stresses love and sacrifice, conscience and responsibility in all of her writings.

Zhang Jie is a pioneering feminist writer. She has one daughter and was divorced twice because she could not tolerate men who attempted to dominate women. From her bitter experience of social discrimination against women, especially those who are divorced or unmarried, Zhang attacks male supremacy and patriarchal ideology in Chinese social structure as well as in the consciousness or subconsciousness of every man, villain or hero. She staunchly insists on a woman's right to remain single and not to be discriminated against. Like early feminist writers in the West, however, she denies a woman's sexuality in order to achieve female autonomy.

Zhang Jie is fully aware that fiction writing in China is never separated from political reality. Partly because of her age and frail health and partly because of political risk, she envisages herself as an old, tattered boat sailing in the raging sea:

> . . . I renovate my boat, patch it up and repaint it, so that it will last a little longer: I set sail again. People, houses, trees on shore become smaller and smaller and I am reluctant to leave them. But my boat cannot stay beached for ever. What use is a boat without the sea?
>
> In the distance I see waves rolling toward me. Rolling continuously. I know that one day I will be smashed to bits by those waves, but this is the fate of all boats—what other sort of end could they meet?

ANALYSIS

Zhang Jie writes on a variety of themes and subjects, ranging from the national political and economic reform to an individual's daily problem (such as Professor Meng's obsession with finding a bathroom abroad), from an unmarried girl's idealistic pursuit to a divorced woman's alienation and hard struggle, and from doctors' housing problems to intellectuals' vicissitudes. Her short fiction, written in a vigorous, fresh, romantic style, can be divided into three groups: feminist stories, social stories, and fabulous animal stories.

LOVE MUST NOT BE FORGOTTEN

"Ai, shi buneng wangj de" ("Love Must Not Be Forgotten") and the novellas "Zum lu" ("Emerald") and "Fangzhou" ("The Ark") represent the best in the first group. "Love Must Not Be Forgotten" portrays a thirty-year-old woman who wonders whether she should accept a marriage proposal. Like Ding Ling's Sofia, in her "The Diary of Miss Sophia," the protagonist finds her tall, handsome suitor to be a philistine who lacks spiritual substance and intelligence. Encouraged by the example of her mother, a widow who

has lived all of her life in platonic love with an ideal man who has married another woman out of moral responsibility, she decides to remain single rather than waste her life in a loveless marriage. Although Zhang emphasizes love above all else in the story, she has said that "it is not a love story, but one that investigates a sociological problem." In the light of Chinese society by the end of the 1970's, the story obviously protests discrimination against "old women"—that is, either women from the countryside who return there "educated" or professional women who fail to find men whom they can admire. To Zhang, love is actually the spiritual and creative pursuit of the self. By insisting on love, she strongly rejects the increasing commercialism and demoralization of Chinese society. As a feminist story, "Love Must Not Be Forgotten" explores the female tradition through the mother-daughter relationship and advocates female autonomy by setting women free from marriage-bound traditional life. Zhang is brave enough to declare in the story that "a solitary existence" may manifest a "progress in different aspects of social life such as culture, education and taste."

"Emerald" further creates the image of a strong single woman. The story involves two women's sacrifices for one incompetent man named Zuowei. When Linger is in college, she falls in love with Zuowei. She nurses him when he suffers tuberculosis, helps him catch up in his studies, rescues him from a whirlpool, and serves as his scapegoat in his political crisis. When Linger is labeled a rightist and is sent to reform in a remote area, however, Zuowei abandons her and marries Beihe. Linger has an illegitimate son by Zuowei, and, in spite of humiliation and ostracism, she bravely brings him up in the role of father-mother. Although Beihe has a so-called happy marriage, her husband weighs upon her like a burden. The story begins with Beihe's scheming to make use of Linger, a brilliant mathematician, to support her husband as a newly promoted head of a computer research group; it ends with Linger's agreement to join the group, not as a sacrificial act for any man, but for the needs of society as well as for her own self-fulfillment. As a result of being abandoned twenty-five years earlier, Linger remains active and intellectually keen, whereas Beihe is dragged down by a dull married life. In spite of Beihe's realization of the slave/master relationship between man and woman, husband and wife, there seems to be no escape for her. Through the characterization of Linger, Zhang further stresses the correlation between female self-fulfillment and liberation from marital bondage.

"The Ark" exposes prejudices against women at all levels of leadership, especially man-created obstacles such as political discrimination against, and sexual harassment of, single women. The story portrays a community of spinsters and divorcées who struggle desperately for equality with men in work, human respect, and professional advancement. Not even one man appears to be free from patriarchal influence. The only hope is pinned on a little boy who lives in the community of women and shares their feelings and language.

Although Zhang wrote these three stories separately, they become particularly significant when viewed together. Through her use of an eccentric, idealistic mother who passes the message of life to her daughter, Zhang shows how an individual woman can achieve autonomy by flouting social codes. By using two boats to embody women running on opposite life tracks, Zhang breaks through the traditional jealous relationship between two women in love with one man to achieve a mutual understanding and a new female consciousness. By employing the image of the ark to represent the women's community, she demonstrates how female collective power, drawn from women's shared suffering, is needed to confront the combined patriarchal forces and transform the existing society.

"WHAT'S WRONG WITH HIM?"

"What's Wrong with Him?," "The Other World," and "Today's Agenda" are Zhang stories on social subjects. The title of the first story should have been "What's Wrong with Her?," "What's Wrong with Them?," "What's Wrong with Me?," and ultimately "What's Wrong with the Society?" Unlike her earlier stories, Zhang here discards the conventions of narrative strategies. The story contains no unifying plot, chronological order, or psychological details. What links all characters and phenomena together are the

theme of madness and the space of a mental hospital. The pervasiveness of madness reminds the reader of Lu Xun's "K'uang-jên jih-chi" ("The Diary of a Madman"). Unlike Lu Xun's madness, however, which is Kafkaesque paranoia caused by fear of persecution, Zhang's madness is schizophrenia, developed from repression of perversion or violence. Repressing his rage at the authority's corruption, Grandpa Ding turns to burning a tract of cotton that he has grown and becomes a Peeping Tom. Driven by insomnia and political discrimination, Doctor Hou Yufeng engages himself in a bloody fight with his roommate, a young carpenter, and finds his freedom only in becoming a madman. In order to get a decent room for receiving his foreign friends, a doctor in an eight-square-meter cell dreams day and night of a larger room. Finally, he finds three big rooms in his imagination and goes to the leadership to offer his two imaginary rooms for those in extreme want of housing.

This world of madness is patriarchal. Though women are not Zhang's sole concern, the exposure of sexual discrimination pervades the story. She perceives that men want to marry not women but vaginal membranes and that men call any woman of independent thought "neurotic." A sexually objectified woman is passed like a ball from an ex-convict to a thief, to a rogue, then to a nameless ugly man. The specter of the victim leads her mad daughter to rape the father.

To heighten the madness, Zhang adopts violent verbal expressions, weird imagination, and stylistic fragmentation. For all these features, her self-image of a "witch" is recognized by Chinese critics. Xu Wenyu actually pictures her as a witch spitting incantations and says that "there must be something wrong with her." The author is indeed mad; her madness lies in her unscrupulous power to snap off the evil of socialist China and penetrate into its dark consciousness.

"THE OTHER WORLD"

"The Other World" is a humorous satire reminiscent of Mark Twain's *The Prince and the Pauper* (1881), only more savage and absurd. The protagonist, Rong Changlan, is an unknown painter. When his talent is discovered by a foreigner and he is invited to go abroad, he is showered with overwhelming attention from politicians, writers, painters, reporters, and women. Because of Yi Yang, a conventional painter, Rong's authorization to go abroad is revoked, and he suddenly becomes a nobody again. Upon returning to the country, he finds countless lice and their eggs in the seams and throughout the fibers of his clothes, which obviously stand for corruption, nepotism, and hypocrisy at large in Chinese society.

When reading "The Other World," one is completely unaware of its narrator. In the absence of a narrator, irony functions as the most effective weapon. Yi Yang appears as the most ardent supporter of young artists such as Rong Changlan. Knowing that Rong cannot drink, Yi Yang offers him one drink after another until Rong gets drunk, barking at the dinner table like a dog. Consequently, Mrs. Hassen revokes her invitation to Rong because of his deceptive (Rong had told her that he does not drink) and barbarous behavior. Comrade Ke, the Party authority of the International Cultural Exchange who first insisted on accompanying Rong abroad, now imposes on Mrs. Hassen a delegation of three—Ke, Ke's son, and Yi Yang.

Another melodramatic device in the story is Zhang's use of comic-strip characters. Through this device, Zhang lashes out most fiercely at conventional women. Unlike her other stories, "The Other World" contains not even one positive image of women throughout the whole farce. Women writers and reporters, in order to go abroad by marrying Rong, fight bloodily. More absurd, a woman who calls herself Yu Ping comes to the hotel to force Rong to admit that he is the father of her illegitimate child. When the woman is challenged, she suffers an epileptic seizure.

The title of the story "The Other World" is particularly significant. The city, full of corruption and absurdity, is the other world to Rong Changlan. He is fooled by this world and finds his freedom again upon his abandonment by the city. In Zhang's view, Rong Changlan is an artist with a soul. His painting *A Ruined Pagoda* reminds the reader of T.S. Eliot's vision of the wasteland. Europe, which could have been the other world of artistic inspiration for artists such as Rong Changlan, is abused as the other world that only spurs Chinese selfishness and political corruption. To some extent, the story is also a caricature of the demoralized China, following its open-door policy.

"TODAY'S AGENDA"

"Today's Agenda" is a satirical story against bureaucracy. Jia Yunshan, the bureau chief, cannot have breakfast because of the irresponsibility of the Water Bureau. When he drops dead at his routine meeting, readers learn that the day's agenda concerned the building of a new block of flats for high-ranking intellectuals and the tracing of a robbery case that took place during the Cultural Revolution. After tedious trivial arguments over Jia's funeral expense and fighting for the position left by the dead man, the new cabinet continues to dwell on the old questions. The old agenda of the *bereau* remains forever today's agenda. In this story, Zhang uses a repetitive narrative structure to echo its thematic monotony and tediousness. Although it is a good story, probing problems in the process of China's industrial reform, for a more artistic and insightful treatment of the subject one must read her novel *Heavy Wings*.

"NOBBY'S RUN OF LUCK" AND "SOMETHING ELSE"

Among Zhang Jie's fabulous tales, "Nobby's Run of Luck" and "Something Else" are the most significant. The former portrays the life of Nobby, a prodigious circus dog. Nobby not only can do arithmetic, algebra, geometry, and trigonometry but also has all the noble qualities: He remains a bachelor in order to devote all of his energy to the circus show, he is never arrogant and domineering, and he shares any extra food with his colleagues. Yet when Nobby loses his mathematical brilliance as a result of constant political slandering, he is kicked around. He suffers from insomnia and eventually finds consolation in the majestic scene of the sea and the waves. The story ends with Nobby swimming into the ocean, in spite of the calling of love from Feiffer, a female dog. The reader is left to ponder whether Nobby drowns himself or commits a symbolic action to submerge into the world of nature and imagination.

"Something Else" is the story of a cat and his master, a bully. The cat is fed the heads and tails of fish eaten by the master and is beaten and kicked at the master's will. Even so, the cat thinks that he should stay with the master and be content, because the neighbor is rumored to eat cats and because the grass is not always greener on the other side.

These two well-written fables are also political satires. Nobby's luck can be everybody's fate, particularly that of an intellectual in China, while the cat's philosophy reveals an enslaved psychology and a conservatism that hold back the nation from rebelling against its tyranny and catching up with the Western world.

OTHER MAJOR WORKS

LONG FICTION: *Chenzhong de chibang*, 1981 (*Leaden Wings*, 1987; better known as *Heavy Wings*, 1989); *Zhi you yi ge taiyang*, 1988.

NONFICTION: *Fang mei sanji*, 1982; *Zongshi nanwang*, 1990.

BIBLIOGRAPHY

Bailey, Alison. "Travelling Together: Narrative Technique in Zhang Jie's *The Ark*." In *Modern Chinese Women Writers: Critical Appraisals*, edited by Michael S. Duke. Armonk, N.Y.: M. E. Sharpe, 1989. Bailey analyzes Zhang Jie's narrative technique according to Western theories and compares her "narrated monologue" with European writers of the nineteenth century. Bailey believes that Zhang's effacement of the narrator ensures the reader's identification with, and sympathy for, the three unconventional single women in the story.

Dillard, Annie. *Encounters with Chinese Writers*. Middletown, Conn.: Wesleyan University Press, 1984. Dillard, in her chapter on Zhang Jie, vividly presents her, to Chinese and Americans, as a woman and a writer, through different images of the author. Dillard believes that Zhang always retains her trim bearing, while in China she is considered a nonconformist in dressing; Dillard also observes Zhang's conservative reactions to political issues as well as to sexual allusions, while in China she is actually a most controversial, out-

spoken writer in both the matter of love and the question of political reform. The gap between the two images of Zhang points to the cultural and political distance between the United States and China.

Elder, Richard. "Chinese Lessons: *Heavy Wings*." *Los Angeles Times Book Review*, December 10, 1989, p. 3. A review of *Heavy Wings*; notes that the book is a panorama of small plots, vignettes, and sketches; claims that it is propagandistic, much of it reading like a fictionalized pamphlet.

Feldman, Gayle. "Zhang Jie: A Chinese Novelist Speaks." *Publishers Weekly* 230 (August 8, 1986): 27-28. Discusses the limitations of Zhang's writing in China before 1978; notes Zhang is a controversial figure, both for her subject matter—women's status in China—and for her use of "Western" writing techniques.

Hsu, Vivian Ling. "Contemporary Chinese Women's Lives as Reflected in Recent Literature." *Journal of the Chinese Teachers' Association* 23, no. 3 (1988): 1-47. Hsu analyzes several of Zhang Jie's stories about women. She particularly notes the two women's realization of their enslaved status in relation to the man whom they love in "Emerald."

Kenney, Michael. "Stories from China Make Sense of the Nonsensical." *The Boston Globe*, August 9, 1991, p. 47. A review of *As Long as Nothing Happens, Nothing Will*; argues that the value of the stories in the collection is that they reveal the nonsensical that lies behind the apparent orderliness in China; asserts that the compression of the short-story form here is heightened by the concreteness of the Chinese language.

Louie, Kam. *Between Fact and Fiction*. Sydney, Australia: Wild Peony, 1989. In chapter 5, "Love Stories: The Meaning of Love and Marriage in China, 1978-1981," Louie treats Zhang's story "Love Must Not Be Forgotten" as a social commentary against the background of China's present problems concerning love and marriage. He points out that the story aims at China's problem of "old maids" and that Zhang's shouting at the end of the story is truly significant because her heroine remains single, "in defiance of aspersions inevitably cast upon her desirability." Louie also discusses love stories by other Chinese writers published in the early 1980's. Includes an excellent bibliography.

Zhang, Jie. "My Boat." *Chinese Literature*, Summer, 1985, 51-54. Zhang Jie provides autobiographical information as well as her views on literature in relation to life, society, and the self. She believes that it is quite tragic for Chinese writers that the Chinese cannot separate fiction from real politics, thus persecuting writers endlessly.

Qingyun Wu

ÉMILE ZOLA

Born: Paris, France; April 2, 1840
Died: Paris, France; September 28, 1902

PRINCIPAL SHORT FICTION

Contes à Ninon, 1864 (*Stories for Ninon*, 1895)
Esquisses parisiennes, 1866
Nouveaux Contes à Ninon, 1874
Les Soirées de Médan, 1880 (a contributor)
Le Capitaine Burle, 1882 (*A Soldier's Honor and Other Stories*, 1888)
Naïs Micoulin, 1884
Contes et nouvelles, 1928
Madame Sourdis, 1929

OTHER LITERARY FORMS

Émile Zola is principally remembered as a novelist and also as the flamboyant journalist who took up the defense of Captain Alfred Dreyfus during the celebrated trial of the young Jewish officer which transfixed French society at the end of the nineteenth century. In addition to novels and journalistic essays, he is the author of numerous plays, essays, literary and artistic criticism, and an early youthful attempt at poetry.

ACHIEVEMENTS

Émile Zola will always be associated with the school of naturalism in France. He became the most widely read author at the beginning of the twentieth century, in part because of the sensationalism of his subjects, in part because of his early training as a public relations clerk. Because of his immense success, his aesthetic ideas were widely circulated, and a group of disciples was formed at Zola's country home outside Paris at Médan. Inspired by the medical advances made possible by scrupulous observation combined with precise analytical techniques, Zola proposed literature as a means of experimenting on humans. He specifically was interested in determining what happens when their environment is changed or their heredity tampered with; what would be the result of humans' gradual addiction to certain chemical compounds? When the literary subject matter was the lower class, envisioned is the unhealthy and the immoral side by side. One of his best known novels, *L'Assommoir* (1877; English translation, 1879), attempts to examine the effects of alcohol on the working class. Other works examine prostitution, political power, industrial power (the locomotive), and capitalism.

BIOGRAPHY

The son of an Italian engineer, Émile Zola grew up in Aix-en-Provence with a friend who was to become equally famous in the world of art, Paul Cézanne. Both came from modest families, and Zola learned early to resent the ordered and comfortable life of the bourgeoisie around him. The early death of his father prompted the family move to Paris, where his mother could find work, and where Zola attended the *lycée*. Failing to pass his *baccalauréat*, Zola gave up his studies and took a position in the civil service, then another with the distinguished Hachette publishing house, where he rose through the ranks to become head of public relations. During this time he made various attempts to write poetry and to penetrate the world of journalism, and he succeeded in establishing himself as an author with his collection of short stories *Contes à Ninon*. The following year, his novel *La Confession de Claude* (1865; *Claude's Confession*, 1882), attracted so much attention because of its sordid details that it aroused police interest. The unhappy management of Hachette ordered Zola to choose between publishing and writing, and the young author, already in the public eye, set out to earn his livelihood with his pen.

With his flair for publicity Zola was able to exploit both his public and his art with great success. Even his ideas of naturalism were tempered by what he realized the public wanted to hear. Inspired by Honoré de Balzac, he determined to develop a *comédie humaine* on his own terms; this time he determined not only to make the cycle of novels a coherent whole but also to ensure that the cycle would be complete and accurate in every detail, with no contradictions. His early exposure to his father's scientific career prepared him for a lifelong fascination with science and its theoreticians, and his humble origins made him especially sympathetic to the lofty position accorded the *savant*. As a result, the organizing principle for his series of novels became the aesthetic of naturalism, which he carefully defined in a series of essays inspired by scientific and particularly medical treatises. Adopting the realists' idea of a "slice of life," Zola sketched out a family tree, and then proceeded to write a novel about the major members of that family, whose name would form the title of the twenty-volume series: *Les Rougon-Macquart* (1871-1893; *The Rougon-Macquart Novels*, 1885-1907). The first volume, *La Fortune des Rougon* (1871; *The Fortune of the Rougons*, 1886), was a good novel, but it did not spark popular imagination. Five other volumes appeared in the next five years, but it was the appearance of *L'Assommoir*, an epic about alcohol's effect on the worker, that notoriety—and hence financial success—came to Zola. From that point on he became the most talked-about and widely read author in

Émile Zola (Library of Congress)

France. It was not that he could do no wrong: Ten years later, the appearance of *La Terre* (1887; *Earth*, 1954) so outraged the critics that Zola's then-disciples publicly repudiated him, declaring that his penchant for the sordid and the gruesome had betrayed the aesthetic of naturalism. The newspapers, however, eagerly printed the work, and the public eagerly bought it.

Zola attempted to soften this criticism of his work by writing novels and stories that erred in the other extreme: They were highly idealistic. Not only were some of *The Rougon-Macquart Novels* written in this more positive vein, but also, at the conclusion of the series, Zola embarked on two new series of novels, the romance *Les Trois Villes* (1894-1898; *The Three Cities*, 1894-1898) and what he called *Les Quatre Évangiles* (1899-1903; English translation, 1900-1903), the gospels of population, work, truth, and justice (which at his death were incomplete and published posthumously). This idealistic bent heightened Zola's outrage when he became increasingly convinced that the Dreyfus affair was, in fact, a vast conspiracy by the established government and military to denigrate a talented young Jewish officer. With his usual lack of tact, Zola published his findings on the front page of the newspaper *L'Aurore* in a public letter whose first words were "J'accuse." Promptly prosecuted for libel, Zola fled to England and worked there until he learned that public opinion favored his position and that a retrial was imminent. His vindication helped to establish Zola as the leading author of France at the beginning of the twentieth century; nevertheless, his reputation as a pornographer in fact prevented him from achieving his cherished goal: election to the Académie Française. He died of asphyxiation from a defective fireplace flue (some seriously consider that there may have been an assassination plot involved), on September 29, 1902, and was accorded a hero's public funeral, at which Captain Dreyfus was present.

ANALYSIS

Émile Zola's talent as a short-story writer is evident from the first sentence of "La Mort d'Olivier Bécaille" ("The Death of Olivier Bécaille"), included in the volume *Naïs Micoulin* of 1884. In this work the reader's curiosity is immediately piqued over the question of how a first-person narrator can deal with his own death. At first, the reader feels that Zola is perhaps presenting us with an example of a fleeting moment of consciousness after the physical body has died, as though he were presenting a distinction between body and soul, which, for a naturalist, would be an intriguing concept. As the narrative unfolds, however, the reader understands that Zola is instead exploring one of the most traditional of literary themes: the return from the dead. At age thirty-nine Zola is developing a theme that Guy de Maupassant would exploit in his story "En Famille" ("A Family Affair"). In contrast to Maupassant's objective narrative used for comic effect, Zola's first-person narrative not only captures interest but also develops it to a different effect: The reader understands, comes to sympathize with the narrator, and shares with him his experience of death.

"THE DEATH OF OLIVIER BÉCAILLE"

At the moment of death which begins the story, the narrator thinks back over his life and over the life-long obsession that death has held for him. The story gives a rapid flashback of his youth, marriage, and move to Paris, then returns to the present moment in a seedy hotel, where the narrator is taken ill and dies. The reader shares the narrator's outburst of affection for his young wife and the aroused interest of the neighbors and especially their children. As he did so successfully in *L'Assommoir*, Zola excels in capturing the atmosphere of the crowd. His pictures of unhealthy children are particularly moving; as aware as adults, their observations are all the more startling because they are true. Thus, when the first child cries out, "Il est mort, oh! maman, il est mort," her unsophisticated breach of social etiquette adds a moment of poignancy and accentuates the verisimilitude of the plot.

At first the reader wonders if the narrator is not simply dreaming, and Zola has the narrator ask himself the same question to heighten the tension. When a neighbor refers to the imminent arrival of the coroner, however, the question is answered. The cursory examination revolts the narrator, for he is conscious of being alive, in spite of the coroner's judgment; yet, like the condemned poets in Dante's *Inferno* (c. 1320), there is no outlet by which these frustrations can be expressed. Agonizing at his inability to summon help or attention, the narrator witnesses his own body being prepared for the funeral, observes the mourning of his wife, sees himself being enclosed in his own coffin, and hears the lid being nailed down. He experiences the funeral ceremony, the horror of being buried alive, and the climactic silence of an abandoned cemetery.

In spite of a perhaps unnecessary touch of scientific determinism, the story accelerates to its dramatic conclusion. Through superhuman effort the narrator manages to pry open his coffin, claw his way out of the ground, and stumble about on the street at night, before being overcome by exhaustion and emotion and injuring his head as he falls unconscious. When he regains his senses weeks later, he quickly realizes what has happened, that he has still not been able to make contact with his young wife in order to let her know that he is in fact alive. He escapes from his benefactors to rejoin his wife, only to find that she already has settled into a new life with a new man. Zola presents this absorbing tale with the control and economy required of an effective short story. The ordinary details of one's mundane existence take on a new proportion when viewed from beyond the tomb, and Zola does not hesitate to use imagery and symbolism to enhance the primitive and religious qualities of his story.

"THE ATTACK ON THE MILL"

Perhaps the best known of Zola's short stories is "L'Attaque du Moulin" ("The Attack on the Mill"). It is the lead story in the collection *Les Soirées de Médan*, and along with Maupassant's "Boule de Suif," is largely responsible for the success of the collection, which satirizes the Franco-Prussian War of 1870. Zola's contribution is a powerful account of humans' inhumanity to other humans, as war interrupts a pastoral romance and prompts its protagonists to actions of heroism and patriotism, only to leave them bloodied, nature devastated, and the windmill—a symbol rich in associations—laid waste. Humans' hubris ravishes both nature and humanity in this pacifist tale in which Zola demonstrates his characteristic poetic quality, which he retained despite his obsession with science. Like the Parnassian poets, his inability to follow rigorously his own aesthetic saved Zola and made possible his greatest writing. A visionary Romantic in the tradition of Victor Hugo, Zola, with his ability to evoke vast tableaux, both of human beings and of nature, and his lyrical vision of people lends epic proportions to his work.

OTHER MAJOR WORKS

LONG FICTION: *La Confession de Claude*, 1865 (*Claude's Confession*, 1882); *Le Vœu d'une morte*, 1866 (*A Dead Woman's Wish*, 1902); *Les Mystères de Marseille*, 1867 (*The Flower Girls of Marseilles*, 1888; also as *The Mysteries of Marseilles*, 1895); *Thérèse Raquin*, 1867 (English translation, 1881); *Madeleine Férat*, 1868 (English translation, 1880); *Les Rougon-Macquart*, 1871-1893 (*The Rougon-Macquart Novels*, 1885-1907; includes *La Fortune des Rougon*, 1871 [*The Rougon-Macquart Family*, 1879; also as *The Fortune of the Rougons*, 1886]; *La Curée*, 1872 [*The Rush for the Spoil*, 1886; also as *The Kill*, 1895]; *Le Ventre de Paris*, 1873 [*The Mar-* kets of Paris*, 1879; also as *Savage Paris*, 1955]; *La Conquête de Plassans*, 1874 [*The Conquest of Plassans*, 1887; also as *A Priest in the House*, 1957]; *La Faute de l'abbé Mouret*, 1875 [*Albine: Or, The Abbé's Temptation*, 1882; also as *Abbé Mouret's Transgression*, 1886]; *Son Excellence Eugène Rougon*, 1876 [*Clorinda: Or, The Rise and Reign of His Excellency Eugène Rougon*, 1880; also as *His Excellency*, 1897]; *L'Assommoir*, 1877 [English translation, 1879; also as *The Dram-Shop*, 1897]; *Une Page d'amour*, 1878 [*Hélène: A Love Episode*, 1878; also as *A Love Affair*, 1957]; *Nana*, 1880 [English translation, 1880]; *Pot-Bouille*, 1882 [*Piping Hot*, 1924]; *Au bonheur des dames*, 1883 [*The Bonheur des Dames*, 1883; also as *The Ladies' Paradise*, 1883]; *La Joie de vivre*, 1884 [*Life's Joys*, 1884; also as *Zest for Life*, 1955]; *Germinal*, 1885 [English translation, 1885]; *L'Œuvre*, 1886 [*His Masterpiece*, 1886; also as *The Masterpiece*, 1946]; *La Terre*, 1887 [*The Soil*, 1888; also as *Earth*, 1954]; *Le Rêve*, 1888 [*The Dream*, 1888]; *La Bête humaine*, 1890 [*Human Brutes*, 1890; also as *The Human Beast*, 1890]; *L'Argent*, 1891 [*Money*, 1891]; *La Débâcle*, 1892 [*The Downfall*, 1892]; *Le Docteur Pascal*, 1893 [*Doctor Pascal*, 1893]); *Les Trois Villes*, 1894-1898 (*The Three Cities*, 1894-1898; includes *Lourdes*, 1894 [English translation, 1894]; *Rome*, 1896 [English translation, 1896]; *Paris*, 1898 [English translation, 1898]); *Les Quatre Évangiles*, 1899-1903 (English translation, 1900-1903; includes *Fécondité*, 1899 [*Fruitfulness*, 1900]; *Travail*, 1901 [*Work*, 1901]; *Vérité*, 1903 [*Truth*, 1903]).

PLAYS: *Madeleine*, wr. 1865., pb. 1878; *Thérèse Raquin*, pr., pb. 1873 (adaptation of his novel; English translation, 1947); *Les Héritiers Rabourdin*, pr., pb. 1874 (*The Rabourdin Heirs*, 1893); *Le Bouton de rose*, pr., pb. 1878; *Théâtre*, pb. 1878; *Renée*, pr., pb. 1887 (adaptation of his novel *La Curée*); *Lazare*, wr. 1893, pb. 1921 (libretto, music by Bruneau); *Violaine la chevelue*, wr. 1897, pb. 1921; *L'Ouragan*, pr., pb. 1901 (libretto, music by Alfred Bruneau); *Sylvanire: Ou, Paris en amour*, wr. 1902, pb. 1921 (libretto, music by Robert Le Grand); *L'Enfant-Roi*, pr. 1905 (libretto, music by Bruneau); *Poèmes lyriques*, pb. 1921.

NONFICTION: *Mes haines*, 1866 (*My Hates*, 1893); *Le Roman expérimental*, 1880 (*The Experimental Novel*, 1893); *Les Romanciers naturalistes*, 1881 (*The Naturalist Novel*, 1964); *Documents littéraires*, 1881; *Le Naturalisme au théâtre*, 1881 (*Naturalism on the Stage*, 1894, best known as *Naturalism in the Theater*, 1968); *Nos auteurs dramatiques*, 1881; *Une Campagne*, 1882; *The Experimental Novel and Other Essays*, 1893 (includes *The Experimental Novel* and *Naturalism on the Stage*, better known as *Naturalism in the Theater*); *Nouvelle Campagne*, 1897; *La Vérité en marche*, 1901.

MISCELLANEOUS: *Œuvres complètes*, 1966-1968 (15 volumes).

BIBLIOGRAPHY

Baguley, David, ed. *Critical Essays on Émile Zola*. Boston: G. K. Hall, 1986. A collection of essays by noted scholars on Zola, including Philip D. Walker. Covers a wide variety of topics, including biographical and critical essays and articles. "The Experimental Novel" and "Zola's Ideology: The Road to Utopia" are two valuable entries from this collection. Contains a select bibliography of works on Zola for readers of English.

Berg, William J., and Laurey K. Martin. *Émile Zola Revisited*. New York: Twayne, 1992. Focusing on *The Rougon-Macquart Family*, this book employs textual analysis rather than biography to analyze each of the twenty volumes in Zola's most widely known series. Berg and Martin also use Zola's own literary-scientific principles to organize their study.

Brown, Frederick. *Zola: A Life*. New York: Farrar, Straus and Giroux, 1995. A detailed and extensive biography of Zola that discusses his fiction and the intellectual life of France of which he was an important part; examines Zola's relationship with Ivan Turgenev, Alphonse Daudet, Gustave Flaubert, and others. Shows how Zola's naturalism was developed out of the intellectual and political ferment of his time; argues that Zola's naturalism was a highly studied and artificial approach to reality.

Johnson, Roger, Jr. "Looking and Screening in Zola's *Vierge au cirage*." *Studies in Short Fiction* 29 (Winter, 1992): 19-25. Discusses the device of the beholder in Zola's tale; explains that the tale incorporates and illustrates Zola's definition of the fictional world of the art work as "seen." Asserts that in the story "looking" is both a central narrative event and a recurring motif.

Lethbridge, Robert, F. W. J. Hemmings, and Terry Keefe, eds. *Zola and the Craft of Fiction*. Leicester, England: Leicester University Press, 1990. A collection of essays published in honor of F. W. J. Hemmings. Six of the ten essays are written in English by notable Zola scholars such as David Baguley, Philip D. Walker, and Joy Newton.

Nelson, Brian. *Zola and the Bourgeoisie*. New York: Macmillan, 1983. Illuminates the specific aspects of Zola's writing that demonstrate the nineteenth century's class structure and the results of the burgeoning bourgeoisie that had replaced the aristocracy and had come to hold the bulk of the country's wealth. Explores how the bourgeoisie vilified the artist who uncovered the base side of that class's nature through his social vision.

Newton, Ruth, and Naomi Lebowitz. *The Impossible Romance: Dickens, Manzoni, Zola, and James*. Columbia: University of Missouri Press, 1990. Discusses the impact of religious sensibility on literary form and ideology in Zola's fiction.

Schom, Alan. *Émile Zola*. London: Queen Anne Press, 1987. This eleven-year research effort considers Zola the journalist, the novelist, and the man himself and his values. Places Zola in the context of the artist as crusader against nineteenth century France and its societal ills. This modern look at the whole man includes photographs, illustrations, and a select bibliography.

Walker, Philip D. *Zola*. London: Routledge & Kegan Paul, 1985. A biography drawn from this professor of French literature's own studies, as well as those of many other critics, historians, and biographers. With a select bibliography.

Robert W. Artinian, updated by Leslie A. Pearl

MIKHAIL ZOSHCHENKO

Born: Poltava, Russia; August 10, 1895
Died: Leningrad, U.S.S.R.; July 22, 1958

PRINCIPAL SHORT FICTION

Rasskazy Nazara Ilicha, gospodina Sinebryukhova,
   1922
Uvazhaemye grazhdane, 1926
Nervnye lyudi, 1927
O chem pel solovei: Sentimentalnye povesti, 1927
Siren' tsvetet, 1929
Lichnaya zhizn', 1933
Golubaya kniga, 1935
Russia Laughs, 1935
The Woman Who Could Not Read and Other Tales,
   1940, 1973
The Wonderful Dog and Other Tales, 1942, 1973
*Scenes from the Bathhouse, and Other Stories of
   Communist Russia*, 1961
Nervous People and Other Satires, 1963
A Man Is Not a Flea: Stories, 1989

OTHER LITERARY FORMS

Although the fame of Mikhail Zoshchenko rests
almost entirely on his short stories, he produced a few
works in other genres that are often discussed as
important facets of his opus, most notably longer
stories (*povesti*), which are almost invariably treated
as short novels outside Russia. Two of these, *Vozrash-
chennaya molodost'* (1933; *Youth Restored*, 1935)
and *Pered voskhodom solntsa* (1943, 1972; *Before
Sunrise*, 1974), show a different Zoshchenko from
that seen in his short stories—an author who is attempting to rise above the everyday reality of his stories. The first of these novels is a variation on an age-
old theme—a desire to regain lost youth, with a humorous twist in that the old professor renounces his
restored youth after failing to keep up with his young
wife. In *Before Sunrise*, Zoshchenko probed deeper
into his own psyche, trying to discover his origins,
going back even to the prenatal time. In order to
achieve this, he employed the psychoanalytical methods of Sigmund Freud and Ivan Pavlov, which were

and still are a novelty in Russian literature. His other
longer stories (a few occasional pieces written at the
behest of Soviet authorities in order to conform to the
political trends of the time) and playwriting attempts
do not enhance his stature; on the contrary, they de-
tract from his reputation so much that they are generally ignored by critics and readers alike.

ACHIEVEMENTS

Mikhail Zoshchenko was fortunate to enter literature in the 1920's, when Russian writers were relatively free to choose their subject matter and to express themselves. His kind of writing—humorous
stories and satire—seems to have been possible only
in that decade. One of Zoshchenko's most significant
achievements is making his brand of humor and satire
unmistakably his, not an easy task in a nation known
for its exquisite sense of humor. With an ear to the
ground, he demonstrated an infallible understanding
of human habits and foibles. He was able to see humor in almost every situation, although his humor is
often suffused with sadness deriving from the realization that life is not as funny as it often seems. He frequently spoke for the Soviet people when they were
not permitted to speak freely, yet he did it in such a
way that it was very difficult to pin on him a political
bias or hidden intentions until very late in his career.
Just as important was his ability to reproduce the language of his characters, a curious concoction of the
language of the lower classes and the bureaucratese
of political parvenus trying to sound politically sophisticated or conformist. As a consequence, his several hundred short stories serve as a gold mine for the
multifaceted study of the Soviet people in the first decades after the revolution. In this respect, Zoshchenko's writings resemble those of Damon
Runyon, Edward Lear, and perhaps Art Buchwald.
That he was able to achieve all this without sinking to
the level of a social or political commentator of the
period reveals his artistic acumen, which has not been
equaled before or after him.

BIOGRAPHY

Mikhail Mikhailovich Zoshchenko was born on August 10, 1895, in Poltava, Russia, to a lower-gentry, landowning family. His father was a painter of Ukrainian origin, and his mother was a Russian actress. Zoshchenko was graduated in 1913 from a high school in St. Petersburg, the city where he spent most of his life; one of the worst grades he received was in Russian composition. Later, he studied law at the University of Petersburg. World War I interrupted his studies, and he volunteered for service in the czarist army, became an officer, and was injured and gassed in 1916. In 1917, he volunteered again, this time for the Red Army, although his military duties were limited because of his former injuries. After the revolution, Zoshchenko settled in St. Petersburg (later Leningrad), trying several professions and not settling on any of them until he decided to be a freelance writer. For short periods of time he was a railroad ticket agent, a border-guard telephone operator, an instructor in rabbit and poultry raising, a militiaman, a census taker, a detective, a carpenter, a shoemaker, a clerk-typist, and a professional gambler, among other professions. This plethora of jobs served Zoshchenko later as a source of material for his stories; it also explains the authenticity of his fiction as well as his deep understanding of human nature. In 1921, he joined the famous literary group of writers calling themselves the Serapion Brothers, who gathered periodically to discuss their own works. His affiliation with this group would have far-reaching effects on him, lasting long after the group had ceased to exist. Being apolitical and having as its main goal the purely artistic improvement of its members, the society contributed significantly to the development of Russian literature at that time; it also left a stigma on its members, however, that would especially haunt Zoshchenko two decades later.

Zoshchenko wrote his first story in 1907 but did not publish anything until 1921. His first book, a collection of short stories, was published in 1922. He immediately became one of the most popular Soviet writers, publishing several additional collections and hundreds of stories. He continued as a freelance writer in the 1930's, his output unabated and his rep-

utation high. Yet the new political and cultural climate, manifested especially in the demand on the writers to follow the dictates of Socialist Realism, forced him to alter his style. His fiction from that time consequently suffered in quality. He tried his pen in new genres, such as psychological and documentary fiction, with varying success. During World War II, he was active during the siege of Leningrad and was decorated for his performance. Later, he was evacuated to Alma-Ata, where he spent the rest of the war, mainly writing *Before Sunrise*. In 1946, the enmity between Zoshchenko and the regime, which had been simmering below the surface throughout his writing career, burst into the open when the party cultural czar, Andrei Zhdanov, viciously attacked him, together with the poet Anna Akhmatova, for their "antisocial" and "dangerous" writings. The attack meant removal from the literary scene—a punishment from which Zoshchenko never fully recovered. He disappeared until Joseph Stalin's death in 1953, and even then he was able to publish only a few anemic stories, from which the old spark and power were gone. He died in Leningrad on July 22, 1958. Since then, his reputation has been restored, and his stories are republished regularly. His works, though somewhat dated, are still held in high esteem, especially among literary critics.

ANALYSIS

A typical Mikhail Zoshchenko story is a four- to six-page sketch about a seemingly unimportant event in the lives of ordinary Soviet citizens. Most of his stories take place in Leningrad, and most of his characters come from the lower-middle class—managers, clerks, workers, artists—and the intelligentsia of both sexes, although peasants often appear as well. The episodes usually involve an exaggerated conflict in which the characters reveal their thoughts and attitudes about everyday reality. This dramatic conflict is presented in humorous tones that endear the characters to the reader; its resolution makes the reader chuckle, sometimes laugh aloud, but it seldom leaves him bitter, angry, or demanding decisive action.

This outward innocence, however, quickly dissipates after a closer look at the characters and their vexing problems. The reader realizes that the author does not always mean what he says and does not say what he means, and that much more lurks beneath the surface. In the story "Spi skorei" ("Get on with the Sleeping"), for example, a traveler has difficulties finding a suitable room in which to sleep, and when he does, his problems begin to unfold: A window is broken and a cat jumps in because it mistakes the room for a rubbish dump, a pool of water lies in the middle of the floor, there is no light ("you're not thinking of painting pictures in it?" he is asked both innocently and sarcastically by the innkeeper), the traveler has to use a tablecloth for a blanket and slides down the bed as if it were an iceberg, and, finally, the room is infested with bedbugs and fleas. At the end of the story, a woman's passport is returned to him by mistake. This comedy of errors, neglect, and incompetence is mitigated by the traveler's last words that the passport's owner "proved to be a nice woman, and we got to know each other rather well. So that my stay at the hotel had some pleasant consequences after all."

THE HUMORIST

The inconveniences portrayed in Zoshchenko's tale are not tragic but rather amusing, and the author's habit of soothing conclusions—whatever their motives—tends to smooth over the rough edges. In "Melkii sluchai iz lichnoi zhizni" ("A Personal Episode"), the protagonist, after realizing that women no longer notice him, tries everything to become attractive again, only to discover that he has grown old. It is all lies and Western nonsense, anyway, he consoles himself. "Semeinyi kuporos" ("The Marriage Bond") shows a young wife who leaves her husband following a fight; after failing to find a suitable place to live, she returns to him. The author again moralizes, "There is no doubt, though, that this question of living accommodation strengthens and stabilizes our family life. . . . The marriage bond is rather strong nowadays. In fact very strong."

The husband in the story "Rasskaz o tom, kak zhena ne razreshila muzhu umeret'" ("Hen-Pecked") falls ill and is about to die, but his wife will not let him die, as they have no money for a funeral. He goes out and begs for money and, after several outings, re-

gains his health. "Perhaps, as he went outside the first time, he got so heated from excitement and exertion, that all his disease came out through perspiration." In another story, "Bogataia zhizn'" ("The Lucky Draw"), a married couple win a huge sum in a lottery but become very unhappy because they have nothing to do afterward. In "Administrativnyi vostorg" ("Power-Drunk"), an assistant chief of the local police is so overzealous in his off-duty efforts to punish a poor woman who allowed her pig to roam the streets that he arrests his own wife because she interceded for the woman.

In story after story Zoshchenko makes seemingly insignificant events so important to his characters that they find in them the moving force of their lives. The reader, however—usually a person who has been exposed to such chicanery at one time or another—cannot help but understand that there is something basically wrong with one's life when such trivial events, against which one feels so helpless, are often repeated in various forms, that such occurrences are not really trifles, and that the primary aim of Zoshchenko's satire is not only to amuse or to exercise social criticism but also to point, rather subtly, at the philosophical meaning of existence.

SOCIAL SATIRIST

Zoshchenko's reputation primarily as a social satirist is still perpetuated by both the connoisseurs of his stories and the Soviet authorities who condemn him, the former saying that Zoshchenko's criticism of the Soviet reality is justified and the latter that it is too harsh and ideologically motivated, even if sugarcoated with humor. There is no doubt that such an interpretation of his approach to reality is possible. Bureaucrats in particular are singled out for scorn. In "Koshka i liudi" ("The Stove"), a committee in charge of maintenance for an apartment building refuses to repair a fuming stove, pretending that nothing is wrong, even though one of them falls unconscious from the fumes. In "Bania" ("The Bathhouse"), checks for clothing are issued after the clothes are taken away, wrong clothes are returned, and there are not enough buckets. In the story "Butylka" ("Bottle"), a bottle lies broken on the street and nobody picks it up. When a janitor sweeps it aside, he is told by the militiaman to remove it altogether. "And, you know," the author chimes in, "the most remarkable thing is the fact that the militiaman ordered the glass to be swept up."

In perhaps Zoshchenko's harshest criticism of bureaucracy, "Kamennoe serdtse" ("A Heart of Stone"), a director demands of his business manager a truck for his personal needs. When the manager tells him that no truck is available, the director threatens to fire him, but the manager retorts, "Now, if you were a product of the old order, an attitude like that toward your subordinate would be understandable, but you are a man of the proletarian batch, and where you got a general's tone like that I simply can't understand." Nevertheless, the director succeeds in getting rid of the stubborn manager. The not-so-subtle implication here is that the revolution has changed little and that vulgarity (*poshlost'*) is as strong as ever. In all such stories, the bureaucrats, who seem to run the country, are satirized for their unjustified domination and mistreatment of their fellow men.

Seen through such a prism, Zoshchenko's attitude toward social problems in his country two decades after the revolution can be seen as direct criticism. In fact, Zhdanov used exactly such an interpretation to attack Zoshchenko in 1946 for his alleged anti-Soviet writings. Singling out one of the stories written for children, "Prikliucheniia obeziany" ("The Adventures of a Monkey"), Zhdanov excoriated the author for writing that a monkey, after escaping from a zoo in Leningrad during the war and experiencing many troubles with human beings, decides to return to the zoo because it is easier for him to live there. The question of whether Zoshchenko wrote this story simply to amuse children or as an allegory of the inhumane (or perhaps too human) conditions in the Soviet society remains unanswered. It is quite possible that the author meant to say the latter. Yet he refused to admit political ulterior motives or an ideological slant in his writings:

> Tell me, how can I have 'a precise ideology' when not a single party among them all appeals to me? . . . I don't hate anybody—there is *my* precise ideology. . . . In their general swing the Bolsheviks are closer to me

than anybody else. And so I'm willing to bolshevik around with them. . . . But I am not a Communist (or rather not a Marxist), and I think I never shall be.

If one is to believe his words, one must assume that the political or ideological criticism was not foremost on his mind. As for social criticism, he saw no crime in it; on the contrary, he believed that it was his duty to try to remedy ills and shortcomings by poking fun at them, as all satirists have done throughout history.

Immorality

It is more likely that Zoshchenko was primarily interested in criticizing the morals of his compatriots, and in this respect he is no better or worse than any other moralist. He himself said that for the most part he wrote about the petty bourgeoisie, despite the official claims that it no longer exists as a separate class: "For the most part I create a synthetic type. In all of us there are certain traits of the petty bourgeois, the property owner, the money grubber. I write about the petty bourgeoisie, and I suppose I have enough material to last me the rest of my life." When some of the stories containing such criticism are examined, it is hard to disagree with Zoshchenko and even harder to see them as simply political criticism of the new regime. It is the moral behavior of his characters rather than what the government tells them to do that fascinated Zoshchenko.

As a natural satirist, he was attracted mostly to the negative traits in human nature. Foremost among these traits is marital morality or, rather, the lack thereof. Infidelity seems to be rampant among Zoshchenko's marriage partners and, what is even more interesting, they have few qualms about it. In one example of a marital merry-go-around, "Zabavnoe prikliuchenie" ("An Amusing Adventure"), three couples are interwined through their infidelity, somewhat incredibly, to be sure, but in a way symptomatic of the loosening of moral fiber within Soviet society. Dishonesty and cheating also seem to be rampant. In "Ne nado spekulirovat" ("The Greedy Milkwoman"), a young milkmaid, eager to pocket a large reward, recommends her husband to a widow seeking a new husband, mistakenly believing that after the marriage ceremony things will return to normal. The husband, however, likes the new arrangement and refuses to return to his lawful wife. Hypocrisy is revealed by workers who praise a deceased fellow worker even though they had not said a kind word about him when he was alive in "Posledniaia nepriiatnost'" ("A Final Unpleasantness"). Bribery is still abundant despite the official disclaimers, and thievery seems to be as common as winter snow. In two stories, "Telefon" ("The Telephone") and "Dobrorozhelatel'," the occupants of an apartment building are called away on urgent business only to find upon their return that their apartments have been robbed and ransacked. In "Akter" ("The Actor"), a reluctant actor is robbed right on the stage by fellow performers who pretend that their crime is part of the play.

Zoshchenko hints at an explanation for such behavior in the persistent discrepancy between the ideal and the real, between official facade and reality, and between appearance and substance. Another explanation can be found in the perpetual clash between an individual and the collective. In a charming one-page sketch, "Karusel'" ("The Merry-Go-Round"), the author destroys the myth that everything can be free in a society by having a young fellow ride a wooden horse, simply because it is free, until he almost dies.

Another likely explanation can be found when untenable living conditions require several people to share not an apartment but a single room: Those who live in the room are packed like sardines; all the tenants rush to the scene whenever even the smallest incident happens, and the room's occupants have completely lost any sense of privacy. How, it is implied, can a person preserve his own dignity and respect for others when he is given a bathroom for an apartment, in which his wife, a small child, and a mother-in-law struggle to live while thirty-two other tenants use the same bathroom ("Krizis"; "The Crisis")? Or when the tenants collectively pay the electricity bill until they almost come to blows because some use more and some use less electricity ("Letniaia peredyshka"; "Electricity in Common")? Similarly humiliating struggles are presented in "Istoriia bolezni" ("History of an Illness"), in which a person prefers to be ill at home rather than in a hospital because there he is thrust in the same bathtub with an old, deranged

woman and contracts whooping cough while eating from the same plate that the sick children next door have used. Regardless of whether the Soviet citizens will ever learn to adjust to this omnipresent communal life, they are paying a terrible price in overwrought nerves and general misanthropy.

Perhaps the best explanation for the immorality portrayed in Zoshchenko's stories, however, is simply the imperfection of human nature. Many of Zoshchenko's characters display the same weaknesses found in all ages and societies, which a political system can only exacerbate. His characters are egotistical and selfish to the core, as in the story "Liubov'" ("Love"), in which a young man declares his undying love for a girl on a night stroll, but when they are attacked by a robber he protests when the girl is not robbed at all.

Zoshchenko's characters are also often insensitive toward one another: A man on a train mistreats his woman companion; when people protest, he is surprised, saying that it is only his mother. Other characters are greedy, taking advantage of others; an innocent man is arrested by the secret police, and his relatives sell all of his possessions, even his apartment allotment; he returns, however, in a few hours. In another story, "Vodianaia feeriia" ("A Water Ballet"), when a man comes to a city, all of his acquaintances pay him a visit mainly to take a bath in his hotel. The characters are jealous (an illiterate woman finally agrees to learn how to read only after she stumbled upon a fragrant letter her husband had received from a teacher urging him to arrange for his wife's reading classes), and they are vain (a woman defends her moonshining husband before the judge but balks when the husband reveals that she is older than he). All these traits demonstrate that Zoshchenko's characters are normal human beings sharing weaknesses and problems with people everywhere.

One can read into these traits the corroding impact of a repressive governmental system, but more likely, these characters would behave the same way regardless of the system under which they lived. Nor does Zoshchenko believe them to be beyond salvation. In one of his best stories, "Ognibol'shogo goroda" ("Big-City-Lights"), a peasant father visits his son in

Leningrad with the intention of staying there permanently. When everyone makes fun of his peasant ways, however, the old man becomes irritated and starts to cause problems for everyone, until one day he is treated with deep respect by a militiaman. This causes the old man to change his ways, and he returns happily to his village. In the words of an intellectual in the story, "I've always been of the opinion that respect for individuals, praise and esteem, produce exceptional results. Many personalities unfold because of this, just like roses at daybreak." Whether Zoshchenko is revealing his naïveté here or is adding a didactic touch to mollify the ever-present censors is immaterial; in these few words he diagnoses one of the gravest ills of any totalitarian society.

THE ABSURD AND GROTESQUE

There is another strain in Zoshchenko's storytelling that, again, sets him apart from other humorists and satirists: his penchant for the absurd and grotesque. Many of his characters and situations lead to a conclusion that in essence life is absurd more often than one thinks. As a result, some of his stories are paragons of an absurd set of circumstances that no one can fathom or untangle. In "Ruka blishnego" ("My Brother's Hand"), for example, a nice person, wishing to shake hands with all people, finds out belatedly that one person who was extremely reluctant to shake hands is a leper. The best story depicting this absurdity shows a shipwrecked man during the war unknowingly holding on to a floating mine, happy about his salvation and making plans about his future ("Rogul'ka"; "The Buoy"). The pessimism and pervasive sadness of Zoshchenko's fiction break through in stories such as these despite the humor, proving the old adage that often there is only one step between laughter and tears.

There are other facets of Zoshchenko's short-story repertoire that are less significant, stories that are simply humorous without any pretense or deeper meaning, parodies of other famous literary pieces, stories showing the Russians' veneration of everything foreign, and others. They contribute to a multicolored mosaic of a life rich in human idiosyncrasies, in emotions and weaknesses, in lessons for those who need or seek them, which offers plain enjoyment to connoisseurs of good literature. In this respect, Zoshchenko made a significant contribution to the wealth of both Russian and world literature, ranking among those first-rate humorists and satirists— Nikolai Gogol, Nikolay Leskov, and Anton Chekhov—who influenced him.

OTHER MAJOR WORKS

LONG FICTION: *Vozvrashchennaya molodost'*, 1933 (*Youth Restored*, 1935); *Pered voskhodom solntsa*, 1943, 1972 (*Before Sunrise*, 1974).

BIBLIOGRAPHY

Carleton, Gregory. *The Politics of Reception: Critical Constructions of Mikhail Zoshchenko*. Evanston, Ill.: Northwestern University Press, 1998. An in-depth look at Zoshchenko's work.

Domar, Rebecca A. "The Tragedy of a Soviet Satirist: Or, The Case of Zoshchenko." In *Through the Glass of Soviet Literature*, edited by E. J. Simmons. New York: Columbia University Press, 1953. Domar begins her essay with Zoshchenko's excommunication from literary life by the political powers in 1946, then proceeds with the analysis of his stories and other works. Her conclusion is that conflict was inevitable given the nature of Zoshchenko's satire, and that satire cannot survive in a totalitarian atmosphere such as that ruling Soviet literature. Domar considers the breaking of Zoshchenko's spirit a heavy loss for Russian literature.

McLean, Hugh. Introduction to *Nervous People and Other Satires*. New York: Random House, 1965. McLean attributes Zoshchenko's popularity with the readers to his making their hard life easier to bear through laughter. Life has not changed at all in the Soviet society, and Zoshchenko capitalized on that in his stories.

May, Rachel. "Superego as Literary Subtext: Story and Structure in Mikhail Zoshchenko's *Before Sunrise*." *Slavic Review* 55 (Spring, 1996): 106-124. This psychoanalytic reading of Zoshchenko's *Before Sunrise* argues that the book, which explores the author's alleged cure for the debilitating melancholy of his youth in an idiosyncratic blend of personal narratives and psychological discussion, illustrates the parallel between psychological and literary boundaries at different levels of consciousness and with different degrees of seriousness.

Mihailovich, Vasa D. "Zoshchenko's 'Adventures of a Monkey' as an Allegory." *Satire Newsletter* 4, no. 2 (1967): 84-89. Mihailovich's contention is that this seemingly innocuous story published in 1946 is anything but that. It is basically anti-Soviet and the authorities' alarm was justified, from their point of view, leading directly to Zoshchenko's ostracism and to the end of his career.

Monas, Sidney. Introduction to *Scenes from the Bathhouse, and Other Stories of Communist Russia*. Ann Arbor: University of Michigan Press, 1961. An informative introduction to the stories. Monas makes some interesting remarks, such as those about Zoshchenko's lack of development as a writer.

Scatton, Linda H. *Mikhail Zoshchenko: Evolution of a Writer*. Cambridge, England: Cambridge University Press, 1993. An excellent look at Zoshchenko's life and career.

Titunik, Irwin R. "Mikhail Zoshchenko and the Problem of *Skaz*." *California Slavic Studies* 6 (1971): 83-96. Titunik examines the *skaz* technique as individualized speech and how Zoshchenko practiced it differently from other writers, leading to a conclusion that there are no safe assumptions about *skaz* and that it will continue to be evaluated by critics.

Von Wiren-Garczynski, Vera. "Zoshchenko's Psychological Interests." *Slavic and East European Journal* 11 (1967): 3-22. Zoshchenko's interest in psychological problems was brought on by his own neurasthenia and by his desire to understand the domain of the subconscious. Von Wiren traces the results of his exploration in *Youth Restored, Before Sunrise*, and some short stories. She believes that Zoshchenko would have developed into a much deeper writer than the one he is usually seen as, had his career not been cut short.

Zholkovskii, A. K. "'What Is the Author Trying to Say with His Artistic Work?': Rereading Zoshchenko's Oeuvre." *Slavic and East European Journal* 40 (Fall, 1996): 458-474. Examines the thematic unity of Zoshchenko's serious and comical texts, discussing the central theme of fear; claims that Zoshchenko's anxieties focus on the violation of the social being's personal boundaries.

Vasa D. Mihailovich

CRITICAL SURVEY
OF
SHORT FICTION

GEOGRAPHICAL INDEX

GEOGRAPHICAL INDEX

CATEGORY INDEX

CATEGORY INDEX

REGIONAL STORIES. *See also* LOCAL COLOR

RELIGIOUS STORIES

ROMANCE

ROMANTICISM

RUSSIAN CULTURE

SATIRE. *See also* MANNERS, FICTION OF, SOCIAL SATIRE

SOCIAL SATIRE. *See also*
MANNERS, FICTION OF,
SOCIAL REALISM

SOUTH AFRICAN CULTURE

**SOUTHERN UNITED
STATES**

**SOUTHWESTERN UNITED
STATES**

SPANISH CULTURE

SUPERNATURAL STORIES.
See also **GHOST, GOTHIC,
GROTESQUE STORIES,
HORROR, MAGICAL
REALISM, OCCULT,
SUSPENSE**